Kraus' Recreation and Leisure in Modern Society

NINTH EDITION

Daniel D. McLean, PhD
University of Nevada, Las Vegas

Amy R. Hurd, PhD, CPRP
Illinois State University

JONES & BARTLETT
LEARNING

World Headquarters
Jones & Bartlett Learning
40 Tall Pine Drive
Sudbury, MA 01776
978-443-5000
info@jblearning.com
www.jblearning.com

Jones & Bartlett Learning
Canada
6339 Ormindale Way
Mississauga, Ontario L5V 1J2
Canada

Jones & Bartlett Learning
International
Barb House, Barb Mews
London W6 7PA
United Kingdom

Jones & Bartlett Learning books and products are available through most bookstores and online booksellers. To contact Jones & Bartlett Learning directly, call 800-832-0034, fax 978-443-8000, or visit our website, www.jblearning.com.

Substantial discounts on bulk quantities of Jones & Bartlett Learning publications are available to corporations, professional associations, and other qualified organizations. For details and specific discount information, contact the special sales department at Jones & Bartlett Learning via the above contact information or send an email to specialsales@jblearning.com.

Production Credits
Publisher, Higher Education: Cathleen Sether
Senior Acquisitions Editor: Shoshanna Goldberg
Senior Associate Editor: Amy L. Bloom
Editorial Assistant: Prima Bartlett
Production Manager: Julie Champagne Bolduc
Production Editor: Jessica Steele Newfell
Associate Marketing Manager: Jody Sullivan
VP, Manufacturing and Inventory Control: Therese Connell
Composition: Cape Cod Compositors, Inc.
Cover Design: Kristin E. Parker
Associate Photo Researcher: Sarah Cebulski
Cover and Title Page Images: (top) © Steinar Figved/Dreamstime.com; (bottom) © Rob Vomund/Dreamstime.com
Printing and Binding: Malloy, Inc.
Cover Printing: Malloy, Inc.

Library of Congress Cataloging-in-Publication Data
McLean, Daniel D.
Kraus' recreation and leisure in modern society / Daniel D. McLean, Amy R. Hurd.—9th ed.
p. cm.
Includes bibliographical references and index.
ISBN 978-0-7637-8159-0 (pbk. : alk. paper)
1. Recreation—North America—History. 2. Leisure—Social aspects—North America. 3. Play—North America—Psychological aspects. 4. Recreation—Vocational guidance—North America.
I. Hurd, Amy R. II. Title.
GV51.K7 2012
790.097—dc22

2010046754

6048
Printed in the United States of America
15 14 13 12 11 10 9 8 7 6 5 4 3 2 1

BRIEF CONTENTS

CONTENTS

PREFACE

Recreation and leisure touch the lives of all people in one way or another, whether through participating in sports and games, attending a theater production, visiting an art museum, traveling to another country, or simply enjoying a local park. A world without recreation and leisure is unfathomable—no parks, no open space, no swimming, no lounging on beaches, and no traveling to other parts of the world just for fun. We often take these things for granted. The purpose of *Kraus' Recreation and Leisure in Modern Society, Ninth Edition* is for students to gain an understanding and appreciation of the value of the leisure-service industry from many perspectives. This text provides a comprehensive look at the field, detailing its foundation and potential development. The industry is viewed from the standpoints of age, race, gender, and ethnicity as well as societal and personal benefits. Furthermore, recreation and leisure is a viable career that employs hundreds of thousands of people in North America, so a career overview includes the latest information in sport, tourism, nonprofits, therapeutic recreation, and more.

Recreation and Leisure in Modern Society is the ninth edition of a text that has been used by hundreds of college and university departments of recreation, parks, and leisure studies throughout the United States. It is designed for use in courses covering the history and philosophy of recreation and leisure on the world scene and, more specifically, the role of organized leisure services today in American communities. This text is revised to reflect recent societal changes and the challenges that face leisure-service managers in the twenty-first century. It also provides an in-depth analysis of the basic concepts of recreation and leisure, the motivations and values of participants, and trends in the overall field of organized community services. Throughout the text, several important themes and emerging issues are emphasized, including:

- The changing nature of the political, economic, and social environment has forced park and recreation agencies to reevaluate traditional approaches to delivering public parks and recreation. Many communities are utilizing the human services approach by serving all segments of the populations and by building super-sized recreation centers with membership fees and programs catering to upscale populations. The economic climate is forcing agencies to reduce services and, in some cases, eliminate services.
- Recreation and leisure increasingly are tied to the maturing fields of tourism and sport. Understanding these relationships is important for the success of leisure service managers.
- Wellness will continue to be a major issue in the field, but obesity is the most immediate issue facing public parks and recreation agencies. Major efforts are being made to provide health and wellness opportunities, control obesity, and preserve cardiovascular health through parks and recreation. *Well-being* has become an inclusive term, looking beyond traditional wellness indicators.
- Tourism is the world's largest economy. Many communities are presenting themselves as a tourist destination in order to increase resources available to community members through jobs, attractions, and revenue generation.

- The baby boomers are beginning to retire and impact the parks and recreation profession. They have more discretionary income than ever before and are willing to spend it on experiences through travel and tourism, participation in programs, health and fitness, and adventure recreation.
- Sport is increasing its influence and importance in the local, national, and international arena. Youth sport is taking on the forms and actions of professional sport, frequently to the detriment of the participants. The Fan Cost Index depicts the actual cost of attending a professional sporting event. Sport and tourism have become major community partners emphasizing economic community development.
- There is a loss of an environmental ethic in the United States. Open space is shrinking due to community development of subdivisions, business, and more. Americans are using more than their share of natural resources: they comprise only 5% of the world's population but use 25% of all natural resources.
- The growth of the nearby nature and nature deficit disorder movements recognize the negative impacts of not having contact with nature.
- Globalization has impacted leisure through the ability to share models, lessons learned, adaptation to local settings, and the greater awareness a global perspective brings to the profession.
- Socioeconomic status impacts leisure through available opportunities, activity choices, and ways in which leisure is experienced. Often urban communities provide expanding services at increasing consumer costs while inner-city urban areas continue to struggle to provide basic leisure services to residents.

The *Ninth Edition* represents the addition of case studies. Society is changing so rapidly it is a challenge to capture the diversity and depth of change. The latest research, trends, and issues in the field are included in this new edition. No discourse of change is complete without an intensified treatment of the impact of technology in our lives. There is an enhanced focus on social capital. As we find more competition for our time, the pace of American life in contemporary times and the impact on our definition of leisure is reviewed. The Hull House and its women have been revisited and expanded. The dramatic changes and historical accounts of leisure and recreation in the 1990s and early twenty-first century are strengthened.

Recreation therapy, as well as recreation's role in health and wellness, has taken on a great importance in the text and in daily life. As the Boomers move through the early stages of retirement, or what is called the "new retirement," the impact on generations and the meanings of leisure, wealth, and the future are addressed. The nature of work in the leisure profession has changed, and it is acknowledged and shared. Leisure originally focused on public agencies. This is no longer the case. Leisure involves nonprofits, sport, and tourism agencies. This discussion has been expanded throughout the text, and sport and tourism are now separate chapters. There are new real-world examples and updated research throughout. This text concludes with a discussion of the state of the profession and careers in the field.

In addition, online resources for instructors include an Instructor's Manual, PowerPoint Presentations, and a TestBank, and Web Links and Practice Quizzes for students are available on a student companion website at http://health.jbpub.com/recreation/9e.

Recreation and Leisure in Modern Society is meant to make readers think about the field and how it impacts their lives on a daily basis. Its aim is to make the reader appreciate the recreational opportunities that are available in North America and to educate each reader on what it means to be a parks and recreation professional.

ACKNOWLEDGMENTS

There is little more valuable to the completion of this book than the stories, examples, brochures, reports, photos, and information provided by the numerous public, private, nonprofit, commercial, and other organizations that have given material to us. Although it is difficult to thank everyone who has supported this edition, we truly appreciate the support of the University of Nevada (Las Vegas) and Illinois State University as well as our families who understand the sacrifices needed to complete this project. In addition, thank you to the Discovery Museum of McLean County, the YMCA of Greater Des Moines (Iowa), the National Recreation and Park Association, the National Institute for Child Centered Coaching, and the American Alliance for Health, Physical Education, Recreation and Dance for providing examples of their services.

In addition to these sources, we also wish to acknowledge the important contributions made by a number of leading recreation and leisure-studies educators whose writings—both in textbooks and scholarly articles—influenced our thinking. While it is not possible to name all of these individuals, they include the following: Lawrence Allen, Maria Allison, John Crompton, Dan Dustin, Geoffrey Godbey, Tom Goodall, Karla Henderson, Debra Jordan, John Kelly, Leo McAvoy, James Murphy, Ruth Russell, Wayne Stormann, and Charles Sylvester.

We would like to thank the reviewers of the *Ninth Edition*, whose comments and suggestions have truly made this a better text: Don Rockey, PhD, Coastal Carolina University; David A. Brown, PhD, Scottsdale Community College; Jan Louise Jones, PhD, Southern Connecticut State University; Lance P. Kaltenbaugh, EdD, CTRS, Ashland University; and Donald Peterson, PhD, NPSI, San Diego State University.

This book could not have been published without the efforts of the staff at Jones & Bartlett Learning: Shoshanna Goldberg, Senior Acquisitions Editor; Amy Bloom, Senior Associate Editor; Megan Turner, Senior Associate Editor; Jess Newfell, Production Editor; Sarah Cebulski, Associate Photo Researcher; and Jody Sullivan, Associate Marketing Manager.

We are particularly indebted to the late Dr. Richard Kraus, who has left a tremendous gap in the parks and recreation field. To carry on his work is both important and critical. His efforts for more than 40 years as a writer, practitioner, and educator helped to shape this profession. This textbook has become a standard, and, as future editions are prepared, we hope to stay close to the roots that Dr. Kraus nurtured while remaining current with the changes in the profession.

CHAPTER 1

RECREATION AND LEISURE

An Introduction

◆ ◆ ◆

A phone call is how the excitement all started. We made the decision to attend the NASCAR race in Las Vegas for the sixth year in a row. What is it that keeps drawing us back to this fun-packed weekend? Maybe it is the thrill of being involved in such an awesome event that truly puts the pedal to the metal. Preparing to get to a NASCAR race is just as exciting as being at the race. We go to dinner with the friends who are going with us at least once a month prior to the weekend of the race. The discussions we have about what we are going to do and how we are going to get there keep the excitement alive. As the weekend gets closer and closer, our anticipation grows. The weekend before the race, we go to dinner one more time and finalize all of the weekend's plans. When we get to the race weekend, our anticipation is overwhelming. The behind-the-scenes action at the race is incredible. There is a carnival atmosphere behind the scenes that fans get to experience only when attending a race. You walk through the souvenir area and see all sorts of crazy items. In addition, there are more than 20 NASCAR sponsors promoting their products from oil, to power tools, to home improvement stores. You walk through this carnival-like atmosphere and get caught up in the excitement because there are so many promotions and free goodies to take home. If you are lucky enough to get into the pits, this brings a whole different level of understanding and emotions. Going through the pits gets you close to the action of the race. It's amazing to see these pit crews make a simple adjustment on the race car simply to get it to go one-tenth of a second faster. You get caught up in their excitement and determination to win the race. In this sport, the drivers are incredible people; they truly believe that the fans are important to their success. When you walk through the pits and see your favorite driver, your emotions run high and you are on a natural high.

When you attend a NASCAR race and you have never been to one before, you get the real sense of the camaraderie among the fans. People from all walks of life are there and have come together to watch this great sport. Your driver may not win the race, but the competition among the fans during the race keeps your level of adrenaline high. (One year we sat by a Jeff Gordon fan at a race. This fan was hilarious to watch as he showed so much emotion in his body language as Gordon was doing well—and then crashed.) It's fun to watch people interact as they talk about their favorite drivers. A local race track does not have the level of excitement as a NASCAR race does. It's exciting to meet people from all over the world. We are all there for one reason: to see a great race and experience the fun.

◆ ◆ ◆

INTRODUCTION

Recreation and leisure have multiple meanings based on individual perceptions. Recreation, from an individual perspective, involves, as an example, watching television, attending an opera, base jumping, mowing the lawn, taking your children to the zoo, playing checkers, downloading music, writing a book, an evening on the town, or whatever one chooses to make it. Theorists even struggle to agree on what to call these types of experiences. Is it recreation, leisure, free time, available time, creativity, selfishness, or hedonism? One's own perceptions are so important in the defining of leisure and recreation that researchers continue to argue their meaning to society, individuals, and culture. However, as this book will show, recreation, parks, and leisure services have become an important part of government operations and a vital program element of nonprofit, commercial, private-membership, therapeutic, and other types of agencies. Today, recreation and leisure constitute major forces in our national and local economies and are responsible for millions of jobs in such varied fields as government, travel and tourism, popular entertainment and the arts, health and fitness programs, hobbies, participatory and spectator sports, and travel and tourism. Beyond its value as a form of sociability, recreation also provides major personal benefits in terms of meeting physical, emotional, philosophical, and other important health-related needs of participants. In a broad sense, the leisure life of a nation reflects its fundamental values and character. The very games and sports, entertainment media, and group affiliations that people enjoy in their leisure help to shape the character and well-being of families, communities, and society at large.

For these reasons, it is the purpose of this text to present a comprehensive picture of the role of recreation and leisure in modern society, including (1) the field's conceptual base, (2) the varied leisure pursuits people engage in, (3) their social and psychological implications, (4) both positive and negative outcomes of play, (5) the network of community organizations that provide recreational programs and related social services, and (6) the development of recreation as a rich, diversified field of professional practice.

VARIED VIEWS OF RECREATION AND LEISURE

For some, recreation means the network of public agencies that provide such facilities as parks, playgrounds, aquatic centers, sports fields, and community centers in thousands of cities, towns, counties, and park districts today. They may view these facilities as an outlet for the young or a means of achieving family togetherness or pursuing interesting hobbies, sports, or social activities or as a place for growth and development for all ages.

For others, recreation may be found in a senior center or golden age club, a sheltered workshop for people with cognitive disabilities, or a treatment center for physical rehabilitation. For some, traveling, whether it be by trailer, motorcoach, airplane, train, or cruise ship, is the preferred mode of recreation. The expansion of the travel and tourism industry has been staggering. Travel clubs have become increasingly popular, with several airlines built around short trips through extended travel. Disney has initiated a line of cruise ships that focuses on family and has extended the idea of travel and tourism yet again. Resort destinations from Vail, Colorado, to Orlando, Florida, to Las Vegas, Nevada, have developed travel and tourism with new levels of services and lodging, including a dramatic growth in timeshares.

Recreation occurs in many forms with group involvement highly desirable for some individuals.

For a growing generation of young people, recreation and leisure have taken on new meanings of adventure, risk, excitement, and fulfillment as they seek to meld technology and recreation. The idea of recreation participation may not include any physical activity but focus instead on Internet-based games, social networking, sharing music, instant messaging, and new ventures yet to emerge. The activity may be as dissimilar as sitting in front of a computer to being involved in extreme activities such as skateboarding on a Bob Burnquist–designed and built 360-foot skateboard ramp with a 70-foot gap that must be negotiated to safely complete the experience. It may involve participation in ESPN's X-Games as a participant, spectator, or video game. ESPN has defined extreme sports through sponsorship and promotion sponsorship. The X-Games include activities such as inline skating, BMX racing, snow sports including snowboards and free-style skiing, surfing, streetball, and motorcycles.

Environmentalists may be chiefly concerned about the impact of outdoor forms of traditional and emerging play on our natural surroundings—the forests, mountains, rivers, and lakes that are the national heritage of all Americans. More frequently, the environmental movement includes a growing awareness and global perspective.

Without question, recreation and leisure are all of these things. They represent a potentially rewarding and important form of human experience and constitute a major aspect of economic development and government responsibility today. It is important to recognize that this is not a new development. Recreation and leisure are concepts that have fascinated humankind since before the golden age of ancient Athens. Varied forms of play have been condemned and suppressed in some societies and highly valued and encouraged in others.

Today, for the first time, there is almost universal acceptance of the value of play, recreation, and leisure. As a consequence, government at every level in the United States has accepted responsibility for providing or assisting leisure opportunities through extensive recreation and park systems, tourism support systems, and sport facilities and complexes.

Diversity in Participation

Often we tend to think of recreation primarily as participation in sports and games or in social activities and ignore other forms of play. However, recreation includes an extremely broad range of leisure pursuits, including travel and tourism, cultural entertainment or participation in the arts, hobbies, membership in social clubs or interest groups, nature-related activities such as camping or hunting and fishing, attendance at parties or other special events, and fitness activities.

Recreation can occur any place and includes a variety of activities.

Recreation may be enjoyed along with thousands of other participants or spectators or may be an intensely solitary experience. It may be highly strenuous and physically demanding or may be primarily a cerebral activity. It may represent a lifetime of interest and involvement or may consist of a single, isolated experience.

As discussed later in this text, the diversity and depth of participation are similar to looking inside a three-dimensional box (**Figure 1.1**) and seeing on the vertical plane the diversity represented by the different kinds of activities and experiences one might engage in as part of recreation and along the horizontal plane the depth or intensity of participation. On the third plane, which gives the box dimension, the aspect becomes more complex because

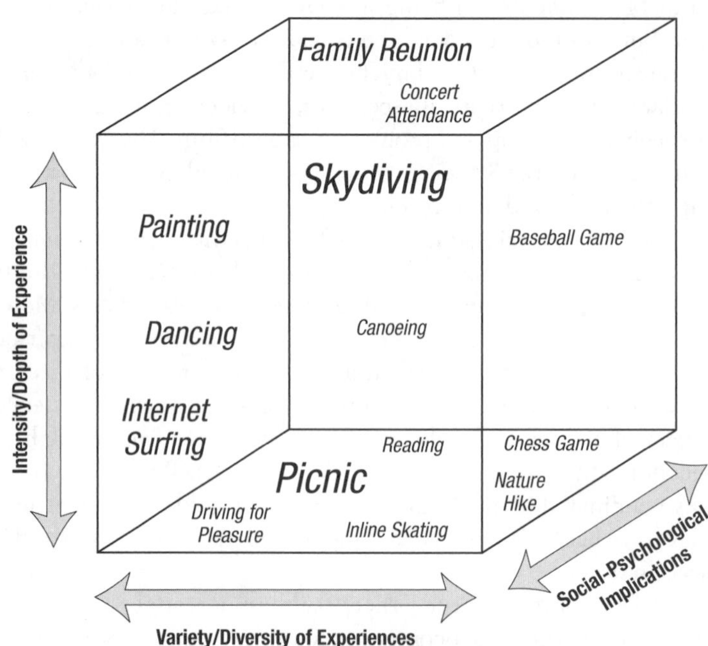

FIGURE 1.1 Simplistic Representation of the Complexity of the Recreation and Leisure Experiences

An Analysis of the NASCAR Weekend

The introduction to this chapter provides an excellent opportunity to analyze a leisure experience.

- Attendance at the NASCAR event did not begin with the decision but rather with the anticipation, based on previous experiences. Note how the author describes the introduction to the opportunity: "A phone call is how the excitement all started." From that phone call the decision was initiated, but what aided in the final decision, among many competing factors, was the previous six experiences in Las Vegas.
- The author asks, "What is it that keeps drawing us back to this fun-packed weekend?" and then goes on to explain that part of it is anticipation, part is preparation and the recognition that the preparation is part of the experience, and part is all of the on-site experiences surrounding this event.
- One might ask, Is it leisure or recreation if you are just a spectator? But in this case, being a spectator is only part of the event. Engaging in the related activities, such as eating with friends, shopping, visiting the pits and garages, being in the crowd, and finalizing all of the details, are all part of being at the race.
- In regard to Figure 1.1, there is an intensity related to this experience. It may primarily be emotional, but feelings resulting from the experience are real and sometimes intense. These feelings and experiences contribute to the social-psychological aspects of leisure and affect the intensity and diversity of the experience.
- Upon arrival, the intensity of the engagement becomes even more pronounced as "our anticipation is overwhelming. The behind-the-scenes action at the race is incredible. There is a carnival atmosphere behind the scenes that fans get to experience only when attending a race."

Watching a pit crew is part of the experience for NASCAR fans.

Looking at an experience through the eyes of a participant enhances one's understanding of the leisure experience. It helps the leisure researcher and practitioner to understand why people participate in activities, what they want to gain from involvement, and the potential outcomes and benefits. As valuable as studying and experience are, for the novice, involvement and reflection may provide the best way to describe the experience.

one has to take into account why people participate (psychological aspects) as well as with whom they participate (social aspects), the time (free time versus obligated time) spent in the activity, and the costs associated with involvement or away from other activities (economic). Figure 1.1 shows in a very simple way the challenges faced when exploring a leisure activity. Researchers have invested years and written thousands of articles attempting to explain the leisure experience. Figure 1.1 depicts that challenge and fails to take into account individual perceptions of the experience, which are all important. This text explores each of these aspects in detail. By the conclusion, readers will have gained an understanding of the diversity and complexity of the leisure environment, services, involvement, and participation.

Motivations for Recreational Participation

In addition to the varied forms that recreation may take, it also meets a wide range of individual needs and interests. Although later chapters in this text describe play motivations and outcomes in fuller detail, they can be summarized as follows. Many participants take part in recreation as a form of relaxation and release from work pressures or other tensions. They may be passive spectators of entertainment provided by television, movies, or other forms of electronic amusement. Other significant leisure motivations are based on the need to express creativity, develop hidden talents, enhance physical skills, or pursue excellence in varied forms of personal expression.

For some participants, active, competitive recreation may offer a channel for releasing frustration and aggression or for struggling against others or the environment in adventurous, high-risk pursuits. Others enjoy recreation that is highly social and provides opportunities for making new friends or cooperating with others in group settings.

Other individuals take part in leisure activities that involve community service or that permit them to provide leadership in fraternal or religious organizations. Still others take part in activities that promote health and physical fitness as a primary goal. A steadily growing number of participants enjoy participation in the expanding world of computer-based entertainment and communication, including CD-ROMs, Internet games, video games, smart phones with applications, iPods, the Internet, and much more. Others are deeply involved in forms of culture such as music, drama, dance, literature, and other forms of fine arts. Exploring new environments through travel and tourism or seeking self-discovery or personality enrichment through continuing education or various educational activities represents other important leisure drives.

WHY WE STUDY RECREATION AND LEISURE

This text is intended to provide comprehensive information that will be helpful to its readers in developing sound personal philosophies and gaining a broad awareness of the leisure-service field and in answering questions not with learned-by-rote solutions, but rather through intelligent analysis, critical thinking, and problem solving.

Leisure-service professionals should have in-depth understanding of the full range of recreational needs and motivations and agency programs and outcomes. This understanding should be based on a solid foundation with respect to the behavioral and social principles underlying recreation and leisure in contemporary society.

To have a sound philosophy of the goals and values of recreation and leisure in modern life, it is essential to understand recreation's history and to be aware of its social, economic, and psychological characteristics in today's society. Should recreation be regarded chiefly as an amenity or should it be supported as a form of social therapy? What are the recreation needs of such populations as girls and women, those who are aging, those who are disadvantaged, ethnic and racial minorities, persons with disabilities, or others who have not been served fully in the past?

Leisure-service professionals must understand the basics of recreation and leisure and be able to work with other professionals.

What environmental priorities should recreation and park professionals fight to support, and how can outdoor forms of play be designed to avoid destructive ecological outcomes? How can leisure-service practitioners strike a balance between entrepreneurial management approaches, which emphasize fiscal self-sufficiency, and human service programming that responds to individual and community needs?

Throughout this text, contemporary issues are discussed in detail. Case studies provide in-depth exploration of a topic relevant to the chapter. Through a vivid depiction of the field's conceptual base, history, and current status; through an examination of existing agencies and programs; and through a comprehensive summary of research studies and recent reports, the reader should gain a full, in-depth understanding of the role of recreation and leisure in modern society.

This text promotes no single philosophical position; its purpose is to clarify the values promoted by recreation and leisure in modern society. Ultimately, these values are responsible for the field's ability to flourish as a significant form of governmental or voluntary-agency service or as a commercial enterprise.

In the following chapters, this book focuses on multiple aspects of leisure and recreation. The content provides the reader with an in-depth discussion of recreation, leisure, sports, tourism, and parks as present in the American culture. The intended outcome is for the reader to gain an enhanced appreciation and understanding of how leisure affects individuals, groups, and society and the roles that leisure plays in people's lives and in our society. This book looks at the roles of leisure in everyday life; the impacts of leisure on our culture; and how leisure influences individual choice, society mores, social engagements, the economy, and individual and community quality of life.

The text makes liberal use of sidebars, highlighting more detailed information on related and narrower topics. Case studies, new to this edition, allow in-depth discussions on topics relevant to the text. Readers will find these helpful in clarifying and illuminating principles presented in the text. At the conclusion of each case study are review questions designed to provoke further discussion and exploration.

Chapter 2 introduces the reader to theories of play and leisure, focusing on their origins, influences, and importance to earlier and contemporary society. Six views of leisure provide students with insights into how theorists, practitioners, and participants view leisure today. The foundation provided in this chapter prepares the student to understand how leisure fits into our society, is influenced by societal change, and influences society and individuals. The terms *leisure*, *play*, and *recreation* and their various interpretations also are discussed in this chapter, providing the reader with insights into their use by researchers, practitioners, and participants.

Chapters 3 and 4 narrate the history of recreation and leisure from early civilizations to the end of World War II in 1945. Chapter 3 is influenced by a European and North American perspective but increasingly recognizes the influences from cultures emerging in local and national society. The discussions of leisure are American, focusing on the influences of religion, colonization, and societal organization, and traces how different historical periods have acted on our perceptions of leisure and recreation. Chapter 4 focuses on the dramatic changes that have occurred since World War II, recognizes the growing influence of globalization, and introduces the impact of technology on how people play and recreate.

Chapter 5 is an introduction to motivations for participating in leisure and recreation. It includes an in-depth discussion of physical, social, and psychological motivation as it relates to recreation participation. The chapter also examines motivation from the perspective of taboo recreation and serious leisure.

Chapter 6 recognizes the growing influence cultural and social factors have on leisure. Included in this chapter are discussions of gender, sexual orientation, race and ethnicity, and socioeconomic status. Understanding how these factors have traditionally affected leisure is as important as understanding how the factors are changing the perceptions of leisure and recreation in the twenty-first century.

Leisure and recreation traditionally have been represented from a community perspective and as a community resource. In Chapter 7, the 10 social functions of leisure are discussed. Social functions of leisure influence public policy, public commitment to organized leisure and recreation, and community development, all of which are critical in the twenty-first century. The chapter ends by suggesting the importance of a coherent philosophy of service for community leisure-service organizations.

Children engage in play and social interaction, enhancing their ability to function in group settings.

Chapter 8 presents the types of leisure-service organizations. The three organizational types include government, nonprofit, and commercial. This chapter identifies the three types of organizations, expands on them to address subtypes, compares and contrasts them, discusses their purposes, and identifies generally who is served, types of programming, types of services and areas, and intended outcomes.

Specialized leisure service organizations and areas are discussed in Chapter 9. Included are therapeutic recreation services for people with disabilities, armed forces recreation for military personnel and their dependents, employee services recreation for corporate employees, campus recreation for university students, and private-membership recreation for private club members. This chapter concludes with a comparison of the different types of organizations.

Chapters 10 and 11 address travel and tourism first and then sport. Both of these industries have grown independent of leisure and recreation in recent years, yet their roots remain firmly within the leisure field. Chapter 10 provides an overview of the travel and tourism aspect of the hospitality and leisure industries. The approach allows the reader to better understand how travel, tourism, and leisure complement each other. Sport, as discussed in Chapter 11, has grown into a major commercial enterprise over the last 30 years and is increasingly seen as an economic engine versus a leisure experience. However, much of sport remains strongly fixed in the leisure sector. This chapter explores the growth of sport as a worldwide phenomenon, its place in the business sector, its roots in the leisure context, and the role of participation and spectating. Finally, it looks at sport from a business perspective.

CASE STUDY: Writing as Leisure: Why I Like to Write

The following is a first-person account of a recreation/leisure activity. As you read the account, think about your recreation activities. Ask yourself how you see this as leisure and how you don't see it as leisure. Compare it to what you do for recreation. One of the discoveries you will make in this book is that leisure is varied and its value or worth is frequently determined by the individual participant.

One thing that motivates me to write is the feeling of growth and accomplishment I get from finishing something I have enjoyed doing. I love to see results that I feel good about. I write mostly for that feeling, and not very often for other people. My writing is very personal to me. I don't write for praise or recognition or to be published. Right now, I'm unsure how much of that is my fear of rejection and criticism or just not being interested in other people reading what I write.

I consider all of my writing to be autobiographical in some way. I am my own most compelling subject, both because I know myself better than I know anything else and also because I still have so much to discover about myself. The most enjoyable writing for me is the writing I do in my journal because I am able to go through the process of formulating my thoughts and emotions onto the page without censorship. I am constantly amazed by the growth and self-discovery I gain through this process. For many of the same reasons, I also enjoy the genre of personal essay and am very interested in memoir as well. It is a lifelong dream of mine to someday write a memoir.

Leaving the world of prose, I often find that I am able to express something in poetry that I had struggled with using other genres. The conciseness of verse is very freeing for me. Poetry works best for me when it is able to flow freely from within, such as in a free write, where I let myself go and let the unconscious speak. I struggle to write when forced into a structure or topic. It is always best when I let my inner self speak, often voicing things about myself that were unknown even to me.

For the present, writing is all the things I talked about. It is an emotional release and self-discovery. It is also something I am able to work on and find self-worth through the progress and growth I can make. However, it still remains to be seen if writing will ever become more than something I do in my free time for personal reasons. I believe one of the reasons I am reluctant to become published is that I am afraid of something I love to do so much becoming more work than pleasure.

Questions to Consider

1. Respond to the following statement: "I write mostly for that feeling, and not very often for other people." How is the process of engaging in activities for yourself different than engaging in actiities for others?
2. Select a recreation activity you enjoy and write about it. Write about why you do it, how it feels to be involved in the activity, and what you expect to achieve because you participated in the activity.

Recreation centers provide opportunities for community members to engage in planned and spontaneous recreation experiences individually and as part of a group.

Chapter 12 considers at the leisure industry and addresses opportunities as well as how it has changed. Finally, Chapter 13 addresses the future of leisure and recreation and specifically looks at trends, influences, economic impacts, societal impacts, and predictions for the future. The chapter presents the influence of technology; how demographics and the growth of minorities are changing the way leisure is perceived and delivered; the impact of youth and a youth culture on society and especially as it contrasts with the baby boomer culture; global climate change issues, local environmental concerns, and how they relate; and, finally, globalization and its influence on leisure and recreation.

SUMMARY

This chapter provides an introduction to the study of recreation, park, and leisure services, seen as vital ingredients in the lives of Americans and as growing areas of career opportunity and professional responsibility. It outlines several of the unique characteristics of leisure involvement, such as the diverse forms of recreational involvement and motivations shared by persons of all ages and backgrounds.

The chapter includes a brief description of the recreation, park, and leisure-service profession and emphasizes the need for specialized educational preparation for those holding responsible positions in this field. It suggests reasons for studying recreation and leisure and ends with a synopsis of the remaining chapters.

QUESTIONS FOR CLASS DISCUSSION OR ESSAY EXAMINATION

1. Read the case study, and then explain what leisure means to you.
2. If motivations are important in the study of leisure, explore some of the reasons you participate in recreation activities and be prepared to discuss why and how you are motivated.
3. Review Figure 1.1 and explain the variables that influence decisions about participation in recreation activities.

CHAPTER 2

BASIC CONCEPTS

Philosophical Analysis of Play, Recreation, and Leisure

◆ ◆ ◆

A Call for Action from the U.S. Play Coalition

We believe that play is a basic human need and the foundation of strong intellectual, physical, and emotional development. We believe play is essential to a person reaching his or her full potential. Unfortunately, we also believe that an erosion of the value of play has occurred in modern society and we are beginning to see the negative impacts of this devaluation among our citizens, manifest in greater incidences of obesity, attention deficit disorder, and limited creativity, to name but a few. We therefore call for the establishment of an initiative to promote the value of play in our society. We believe that a culture that encourages playfulness in daily life is healthier in mind and body. We believe that playful experiences, whether physical or cognitive in nature, enable people to adjust and adapt to political, economic, and social change and make these institutions stronger. We believe that equal access to all forms and types of play opportunities for people of all ages and abilities in our communities is essential to enhancing the quality of life for all and building stronger communities.[1]

◆ ◆ ◆

INTRODUCTION

Any consideration of the broad field of recreation and leisure should include a clarification of terms and concepts. The words *play*, *leisure*, and *recreation* are frequently used interchangeably, as if they meant the same thing. However, although related, they have distinctly different meanings and it is important for both students and practitioners in this field to understand their varied implications and the differences among them.

The rationale for stressing such conceptual understanding is clear. Just as a doctor must know chemistry, anatomy, kinesiology, and other underlying sciences to practice medicine effectively, so too the recreation and park professional must understand the meaning of leisure and its motivations and satisfactions if he or she is to provide effective recreation programs and services. Such conceptual understandings are critical to the development of a sound philosophy of recreation service and to interpreting leisure-service goals and outcomes to the public at large.

THE MEANING OF PLAY

The word *play* is derived from the Anglo-Saxon *plega,* meaning a game or sport, skirmish, fight, or battle. This is related to the Latin *plaga,* meaning a blow, stroke, or thrust. It is illustrated in the idea of striking or stroking an instrument or playing a game by striking a ball. Other languages have words derived from a common root (such as the German *spielen* and the Dutch *spelen*) whose meanings include the playing of games, sports, and musical instruments. Although play is traditionally considered a child's activity, it is often recognized that people of all ages take part in play.

It is difficult to arrive at a single definition of play because it takes so many forms and appears in so many contexts. However, a general definition would describe play as a form of human or animal activity or behavioral style that is self-motivated and carried on for intrinsic, rather than external, purposes. It is generally pleasurable and often is marked by elements of competition, humor, creative exploration and problem solving, and mimicry or role playing. It appears most frequently in leisure activities, but may be part of work. It is typically marked by freedom and lack of structure, but may involve rules and prescribed actions, as in sport and games.

Historical Perspectives

In ancient Greece, play was assigned a valuable role in the lives of children, based on the writings of Plato and Aristotle. The Athenians placed great value on developing qualities of honor, loyalty, and beauty and other elements of productive citizenship in children. For them, play was an integral element of education and was considered a means of positive character development and teaching the values of Greek society.

Later, as the Catholic Church gained dominance among the developing nations of western Europe, play came to be regarded as a social threat. The body was thought to detract from more spiritual or work-oriented values, and every effort was made to curb the pleasurable forms of play that had been popular in the Greek and Roman eras.

Gradually, however, educators and philosophers such as Froebel, Rousseau, and Schiller came to the defense of play as an important aspect of childhood education. For example, Froebel wrote of play as the highest expression of human development in childhood:

> Play is the purest, most spiritual activity of man at this stage. . . . A child that plays thoroughly with self-active determination, perseveringly until physical fatigue forbids, will surely be a thorough, determined man, capable of self-sacrifice for the promotion of the welfare of himself and others.[2]

EARLY THEORIES OF PLAY

In the nineteenth and early twentieth centuries, a number of influential scholars evolved comprehensive theories of play that explained its development and its role in human society and personal development.

Surplus-Energy Theory

The English philosopher Herbert Spencer, in his mid-nineteenth-century work *Principles of Psychology*, advanced the view that play was primarily motivated by the need to burn excess energy. This theory asserts that running, playing soccer, or jumping rope on the playground are done so because people have excess energy to use. A criticism of this theory is that play also occurs in people with little energy and does not account for nonphysical play.

Relaxation Theory

An early explanation of play that was regarded as the converse of surplus energy was relaxation theory. Rather than to burn excess energy, play was done to restore it. Play was seen as a means to energize a person who was exhausted from work, school, or the stresses of daily life. It was believed that when a person is either mentally or physically tired, play can restore energy. So, exercising after a long day at work can serve to help an individual relax and restore. Spending time on Facebook during a study break or playing after school are both examples of relaxation theory.

Preparation Theory

Preparation theory suggests that play is a means for children to practice adult life. Children who play house, doctor, or school are preparing to experience these things as older children or adults. Preparation theory also suggests that people learn teamwork and role playing in their play. A weakness of this theory is that it does not account for adult play.

Catharsis Theory

The catharsis theory is based on the view that play—particularly competitive, active play—serves as a safety valve for the expression of bottled-up emotions. Among the ancient Greeks, Aristotle saw drama as a means of purging oneself of hostile or aggressive emotions; by vicarious sharing in the staged experience, onlookers purified themselves of harmful feelings. Biking a long distance after a hard day at work, playing a musical instrument after an argument with a friend, and hitting a bucket of golf balls to blow off steam after a nonproductive meeting are all examples of the catharsis theory of play.

Coupled with the surplus-energy theory, the catharsis theory suggests a vital necessity for active play to help children and adults burn excess energy and provide a socially acceptable channel for aggressive or hostile emotions and drives.

TWENTIETH-CENTURY CONCEPTS OF PLAY

During the first three decades of the twentieth century, a number of psychologists and educators examined play, particularly as a developmental and learning experience for children.

Self-Expression Theory

Two leading physical educators, Elmer Mitchell and Bernard Mason, saw play primarily as a result of the need for self-expression. Humans were regarded as active, dynamic beings with the need to find outlets for their energies, use their abilities, and express their personalities. The specific types of activity that an individual engaged in were, according to Mitchell and Mason, influenced by such factors as physiological and anatomic structure, physical fitness level, environment, and family and social background.[3]

Play as a Social Necessity

During the late nineteenth century, leaders of the public recreation movement called for the provision of organized recreation for all children. Joseph Lee, who is widely regarded as the father of the play movement in America and who promoted the establishment of numerous playgrounds and recreation centers, was instrumental in the public acceptance of play as an important force in child development and community life. Jane Addams, founder of the Hull House Settlement in Chicago and a Nobel Peace Prize winner, advocated the need for organized play opportunities that served as an alternative to the difficult life children living in poverty faced on the streets. These values continue to be embraced by contemporary communities, as is evidenced by public and private support of parks and recreation departments, community recreation programs, after-school programs, and other play-based activities.

Typologies of Play Activity

In the twentieth century, more and more social and behavioral scientists began to examine play empirically. One such investigator, the French sociologist Roger Caillois, examined the play experience itself by classifying the games and play activities that were characteristic of various cultures and identifying their apparent functions and values. Caillois established four major types of play and game activity: agon, alea, mimicry, and ilinx.

Agon refers to activities that are competitive and in which the equality of the participants' chances of winning is artificially created. Winners are determined through such

Joseph Lee's Thoughts on Play

Joseph Lee believed that play contributed to the wholesome development of personal character because it involved lessons of discipline, sacrifice, and morality. He saw it as more than a mere pleasurable pastime, but rather as a serious element in the lives of children and—along with his contemporary pioneer, Luther Halsey Gulick—as a vital element in community life. This view extended itself to a literal application of play as a means of preparing children for the adult work world.

qualities as speed, endurance, strength, memory, skills, and ingenuity. Agonistic games may be played by individuals or teams; they presuppose sustained attention, training and discipline, perseverance, limits, and rules. Clearly, most modern games and sports, including many card and table games involving skill, are examples of agon.

Alea includes games of chance—those games or contests over whose outcome the contestant has no control; winning is the result of fate rather than the skill of the player. Games of dice, roulette, and baccarat, as well as lotteries, are examples of alea.

Mimicry is based on the acceptance of illusions or imaginary universes. Children engage in mimicry through pretend play. This category includes games in which players make believe, or make others believe, that they are other than themselves. For children, Caillois writes:

> The aim is to imitate adults. . . . This explains the success of the toy weapons and miniatures which copy the tools, engines, arms and machines used by adults. The little girl plays her mother's role as cook, laundress and ironer. The boy makes believe he is a soldier, musketeer, policeman, pirate, cowboy, Martian, etc.[4]

Ilinx consists of play activities based on the pursuit of vertigo or dizziness. Historically, ilinx was found in primitive religious dances or other rituals that induced the trancelike state necessary for worship. Today it may be seen in children's games that lead to dizziness by whirling rapidly and in the use of swings and spring riders. Among adults, ilinx may be achieved through amusement park rides such as roller coasters and a variety of adventure activities, including skydiving and bungee jumping.

Contrasting Styles of Play

Caillois also suggested two extremes of play behavior. The first of these, *paidia,* involves exuberance, freedom, and uncontrolled and spontaneous gaiety. The second, *ludus*, is characterized by rules and conventions and represents calculated and contrived activity. Each of the four forms of play may be conducted at either extreme of paidia or ludus or at some point on a continuum between the two.

The Play Element in Culture

Probably the most far-reaching and influential theory of play as a cultural phenomenon was advanced by the Dutch social historian Johan Huizinga in his provocative work *Homo Ludens* (*Man the Player*). Huizinga presented the thesis that play pervades all of life. He saw it as having certain characteristics: It is a voluntary activity, marked by freedom and never imposed by physical necessity or moral duty. It stands outside the realm of satisfying physiological needs and appetites. It is separate from ordinary life both in its location and its duration, being "played out" within special time periods and in such special places as the arena, the card table, the stage, and the tennis court. Play is controlled, said Huizinga, by special sets of rules, and it demands absolute order. It is also marked by uncertainty and tension. Finally, it is not concerned with good or evil, although it has its own ethical value in that its rules must be obeyed.

In Huizinga's view, play reveals itself chiefly in two kinds of activity: contests for something and representations of something. He regarded it as an important civilizing influence in human society and cited as an example the society of ancient Greece, which was permeated with play forms. He traced historically the origins of many social institutions as ritualized forms of play activity. For example, the element of play was initially dominant in the

CASE STUDY: Recess Coaches

The *New York Times* ran an article explaining the role of recess coaches on the playground.[a] Here is what they had to say.

Recess coaches have been hired by schools to facilitate organized playground activities during recess. They plan activities that involve all children and encourage those who are not active during recess or are excluded from playing to fully participate. No longer is recess unstructured and up to the child to determine how to spend the break from the classroom. The coaches plan weekly activities that teach cooperation, teamwork, and basic sport skills and enhance fitness levels. Here are a few of the positive outcomes of recess coaches that were outlined in the article:

- Discipline problems have decreased because the activities are more structured and groups of children are not being exiled or bullied by classmates on the playground.
- Children are learning how to have fun without their iPod or computer.
- Recess contributed to refreshing the children, which carried over to the classroom.
- Playground injuries decreased.

Dr. Romina M. Barros, who is known for her work on the benefits of recess, argues that children benefit most when they are allowed to play freely, use their imagination, and do as they choose during recess. A structured recess is simply an extension of the classroom rather than a true break.

Playworks, a nonprofit organization dedicated to advancing play in all children, has provided the recess coaches for many schools through a grant from the Robert Wood Johnson Foundation. Here is what Playworks has to say about those against recess coaches:

> There is some debate about the importance of structured vs. unstructured play. Our experience is that diminishing opportunities for unsupervised play in our society have left kids with a very thin understanding of how to manage their own play and that it is important to have grown-ups introduce some basic rules to make play work. We build the culture of play at a school so that kids feel safe and included. This structure is designed to encourage kids themselves to take ever-increasing responsibility for the quality of play and for each other. Ultimately our unique brand of play fosters greater independence and leadership among children.
>
> We also believe that there is value in having grown-ups play alongside of children. A grown-up standing on the sidelines barking instructions only serves to perpetuate the less-than-playful status quo. Grown-ups playing introduces an important element of silliness and shared humanity, making the play more accessible, and helping children feel safer and more connected.[b]

Questions to Consider

1. What are the pros and cons of having recess coaches in schools?
2. Select a side of this issue and debate it with your classmates.

Sources

a. Winnie Hu, "Forget Goofing Around: Recess Has a New Boss," *New York Times*, March 14, 2010, http://www.nytimes.com/2010/03/15/education/15recess.html?pagewanted=1.
b. Playworks, "Playworks' Philosophy," http://www.playworksusa.org/about/philosophy.

evolution of judicial processes. Law consisted of a pure contest between competing individuals or groups. It was not a matter of being right or wrong; instead, trials were conducted through the use of oracles, contests of chance that determined one's fate, trials of strength or resistance to torture, and verbal contests. Huizinga suggested that the same principle applied to many other cultural institutions:

> In myth and ritual the great instinctive forces of civilized life have their origin: law and order, commerce and profit, craft and art, poetry, wisdom, and science. All are rooted in the primeval soil of play.[5]

PSYCHOLOGICAL ANALYSIS OF PLAY

Over the past several decades, numerous authorities in the fields of psychology and psychoanalysis have examined play and its role in personality development, learning theory, mental health, and related areas.

Play in Personality Development

The theoretical foundations of play have a long history with little consensus on one overall theory of play. Over the past 40 years, much research has been done on the benefits of play. The psychological aspects have been prominent. Personality is shaped by play in many different ways. Play prompts enjoyment, freedom, and fun. It prompts self-expression, creativity, imagination, and self-confidence. Play allows children to learn to interact with others through cooperative, sharing, and conflict-resolution activities. All of these experiences affect an individual's personality and contribute to the type of person the individual will become.

Psychoanalytical Perspectives on Play

Sigmund Freud, the father of modern psychoanalysis, had a number of distinctive views regarding the meaning and purpose of play. Freud saw play as a medium through which children are able to gain control and competence and to resolve conflicts that occur in their lives. He believed that children are frequently overwhelmed by their life circumstances, which may be confusing, complex, and unpleasant. Through play, they are able to reexperience threatening events and thus to control and master them. In this sense, play and dreams serve a therapeutic function for children. In general, Freud thought that play represented the child's way of dealing with reality—in effect, by playing with it, making it more acceptable, and exerting mastery over it.

Play can be viewed from developmental, psychological, anthropological, creative, and cultural perspectives.

CASE STUDY: Urban versus Suburban Play

University of Michigan produced a video titled *Where Do the Children Play?*[a] It looks at how play and nature have disappeared from the lives of children. Play is much different than it was a generation ago. Then, parents were more hands-off and let children create their own play. There was no perception of the city being dangerous, and the outdoors was much more appealing to children than indoor play was. Today, organized activities such as t-ball and dance are seen as more important than free play. The video compares city kids and suburban kids. It suggests that suburban kids are loaded into minivans (with DVD players) and taken to play spaces or organized activities. They do not have blocks or neighborhoods with parks and play spaces. Suburban kids live in isolation and lack imagination because they spend so much time in front of a computer (they average 4–6 hours). For city kids not living in poverty, cities are considered better places for kids to grow up because they are more multicultural, kids still play in the parks, and they walk to school rather than being driven.

A study was done through Carnegie Mellon University that examined how children understand their surroundings. Kids were given a 20-foot by 40-foot base on which to build their community using cardboard. There were stark differences in how the suburban and city kids each viewed their communities. Here are the findings:

- Suburban kids all worked alone except when they built the mall.
- The city kids worked in groups throughout the entire activity.
- Suburban kids did not put any people or amenities in their buildings.
- City kids had people in all of their buildings, had doors that opened, and even put furniture in places like schools and hospitals.
- Suburban kids put no public spaces in their communities and there were no pedestrians. The community was nothing but buildings.
- The city kids built public spaces, had flowerpots in front of buildings, and had public transportation. The people were the essence of the community, not the buildings.

A major concern of many parents today in allowing their children free play time focuses on the safety of children. Research disputes all of these concerns by showing that crime against children has decreased; kidnapping and sex offenses against children are 10 times more likely to be committed by a parent, friend, or acquaintance; children are 10 times less likely to be harmed at school than in the home; and 64% of crimes against children happen in the home.

Questions to Consider

1. Is this an accurate depiction of the differences between suburban children and city children?
2. Why do children not have more free play in their lives?
3. Is free play less or more valuable than are organized activities?
4. What can be done to suburbs to make them more conducive to outdoor play?
5. What can be done in cities to make them more conducive to outdoor play?

Source

a. *Where Do the Children Play?* produced and directed by Chris Cook (Ann Arbor, MI: Metrocom International, 2007). Copyright Michigan Television.

> Might we not say that every child at play behaves like a creative writer, in that he creates a world of his own, or, rather, rearranges the things of his world in a new way which pleases him? It would be wrong to think he does not take his play seriously; on the contrary he takes his play very seriously and he expends large amounts of emotion on it. The opposite of play is not what is serious but what is real.[6]

A number of Freud's other theories, such as the "pleasure principle" and the "death wish," have also been seen as having strong implications for the analysis of play. The Freudian view of play influenced many psychotherapists and educators in their approach to childhood education and treatment programs. Bruno Bettelheim, Erik Erikson, and Anna Freud, Freud's daughter, all experimented with the use of play in treating children with mental and emotional issues.

Play as Creative Exploration

Other contemporary theories of play emphasize its role in creative exploration and problem solving. Studies of arousal, excitement, and curiosity led to two related theories of play: the stimulus-arousal and competence-effectance theories.

Stimulus-Arousal Theory This approach is based on the observation that both humans and animals constantly seek stimuli of various kinds, both to gain knowledge and to satisfy a need for excitement, risk, surprise, and pleasure. Often this is connected with the idea of fun, expressed as light amusement, joking, and laughter.

However, the expectation that play is always light, enjoyable, pleasant, or humorous can be misleading. Often, play activities can be frustrating, boring, unpleasant, or even physically painful—particularly when they lead to addiction (as in the case of drug, alcohol, or gambling abuse) and subsequent ill health or economic losses.

Competence-Effectance Theory A closely related theory holds that much play is motivated by the need of the player to test the environment, solve problems, and gain a sense of mastery and accomplishment. Typically, it involves experimentation or information-seeking behavior, in which the player—whether human or animal—observes the environment, tests or manipulates it, and observes the outcome. Beyond this, the player seeks to develop competence, defined as the ability to interact effectively with the environment. Often this is achieved through repetition of the same action even when it has been mastered. The term *effectance* refers to the player's need to be able to master the environment and, even when uncertainty about it has been resolved, to produce desired effects in it.

Cziksentmihalyi's "Flow" Principle Related to the competence-effectance theory is Mihaly Cziksentmihalyi's view of play as a process in which ideally the player's skills are pitched at the challenge level of the tasks. If the task is too simple, it may become boring and lacking in appeal. If it is too difficult, it may produce anxiety and frustration, and the player may discontinue the activity or change the approach to it so that it becomes more satisfying. Beyond this idea, Cziksentmihalyi suggests that there is a unique

If the slopes match the skier's ability, downhill skiing is an optimal activity in which an individual might experience flow.

element in true play, which he identifies as a sense of flow. This is the sensation players feel when they are totally involved with the activity. It includes a feeling of harmony and full immersion in play; at a peak level, players might tend to lose their sense of time and their surroundings and experience an altered state of being. Such flow, he argues, could be found in some work situations, but it is much more commonly experienced in play such as games or sport.[7]

With the obesity epidemic at record levels, a new focus has been put on the value of play. Organizations such as the U.S. Play Coalition, Voice of Play, and many others are providing resources and information on the value of play to parents, community leaders, and parks and recreation professionals. This overview of play theories and the role of play provides a foundation for the value of play that should be instilled in recreational professionals.

THE MEANING OF LEISURE: SIX VIEWS

What exactly is leisure? The concept of leisure as a unique, desirable component of the human experience was first articulated by ancient Greeks. In more recent centuries, scholars attempted to define leisure in terms of both its role in society and impact on the individual. For the Athenians particularly, leisure was the highest value of life, and work the lowest. Because the upper classes were not required to work, they were free to engage in intellectual, cultural, and artistic activity. Leisure represented an ideal state of freedom and the opportunity for spiritual and intellectual enlightenment. Within modern philosophies of leisure that have descended from this classical Athenian view, leisure is still seen as occurring mostly in time that is not devoted to work. However, it is considered far more than just a temporary release from work used to restore one for more work. Etymologically, the English word *leisure* seems to be derived from the Latin *licere*, meaning "to be permitted" or "to be free." From *licere* came the French *loisir*, meaning "free time," and such English words as *license* (originally meaning immunity from public obligation) and *liberty*. These words are all related; they suggest free choice and the absence of compulsion.

The early Greek word *scole* or *skole* meant "leisure." It led to the Latin *scola* and the English *school* or *scholar*—thus implying a close connection between leisure and education. The word *scole* also referred to places where scholarly discussions were held. One such place was a grove next to the temple of Apollo Lykos, which became known as the *lyceum*. From this came the French *lycée*, meaning "school"—again implying a bond between leisure and education.

The Classical View of Leisure

Aristotle regarded leisure as "a state of being in which activity is performed for its own sake." It was sharply contrasted with work or purposeful action, involving instead such pursuits as art, political debate, philosophical discussion, and learning in general. The Athenians saw work as ignoble; to them it was boring and monotonous. A common Greek word for work is *ascholia*, meaning the absence of leisure—whereas we do the opposite, defining leisure as the absence of work.

How meaningful is this classical view of leisure today? Although the Greek view of leisure as a necessary and integral piece of a holistic life has merit, this view has two flaws. First, it is linked to the idea of an aristocratic class structure based on the availability of a substantial underclass and slave labor. When Aristotle wrote in his *Treatise on Politics* that "it is of course generally understood that in a well-ordered state, the citizens should have leisure and not have to provide for their daily needs," he meant that leisure was given to a comparatively few patricians and made possible through the strenuous labor of the many.

In modern society, leisure cannot be a privilege reserved for the few; instead, it must be widely available to all. It must exist side by side with work that is respected in our society, and it should have a meaningful relationship to work. The implication is that leisure should be calm, quiet, contemplative, and unhurried, as implied by the word *leisurely*. Obviously, this concept would not apply to those uses of leisure today that are dynamic, active, and demanding or that may have a degree of extrinsic purpose about them.

Leisure as a Symbol of Social Class

The view of leisure as closely related to social class stemmed from the work of Thorstein Veblen, a leading American sociologist of the late nineteenth century. Veblen showed how, throughout history, ruling classes emerged that identified themselves sharply through the possession and use of leisure. In his major work, *The Theory of the Leisure Class*, he points out that in Europe during the feudal and Renaissance periods and finally during the industrial age, the possession and visible use of leisure became the hallmark of the upper class. Veblen attacks the "idle rich"; he sees leisure as a complete way of life for the privileged class, regarding them as exploiters who lived on the toil of others. He coined the phrase "conspicuous consumption" to describe their way of life throughout history. This theory is dated because of the rise of greater working-class leisure and because many members of extremely wealthy families work actively in business, politics, or other demanding professions.

To some degree, however, Veblen's analysis is still relevant. The wealthy or privileged class in modern society continues to engage in a wide variety of expensive, prestigious, and sometimes decadent leisure activities even though its members may not have an immense amount of free time. They tend to travel widely, entertain, patronize the arts, and engage in exclusive and high-status pastimes. Recent scholars have characterized contemporary leisure in Western cultures as consumerist and motivated by the pursuit of diversionary experiences that can be purchased. Ramsey expresses the following critique of consumerist leisure:

> So the nasty face of consumerist leisure expresses acquisitiveness, possessiveness, what the ancient Greeks called *plenoxia*: the desire for more than one's appropriate share. . . . The paradox around obligation-free leisure time is the drive quality, the compulsions

> and obsessions around purchase and use, to which many people are vulnerable due to the sheer vastness and success and ease of consumerism.[8]

Leisure as Unobligated Time

The most common approach to leisure is to regard it as unobligated or discretionary time. Discretionary time is time that is not used for work obligations and personal maintenance. This view of leisure sees it essentially as time that is free from work or from such work-related responsibilities as travel, study, or social involvements based on work. It also excludes time devoted to essential life-maintenance activities, such as sleep, eating, and personal care. Its most important characteristic is that it lacks a sense of obligation or compulsion. This approach to defining leisure is most popular among economists or sociologists who are particularly concerned with trends in the economic and industrial life of the nation. Other scholars, including feminists, have found this definition useful in the study of time constraints faced by working adults in contemporary society.

Although this definition appears to be convenient and largely a matter of arithmetic (subtracting work and other obligated tasks from the 24 hours that are available each day and coming out with a block of time that can be called leisure), it has some built-in complexities. For example, is it possible to say that any time is totally free of obligation or compulsion or that any form of leisure activity is totally without some extrinsic purpose? Is it also possible to say that all unobligated time is intrinsically rewarding and possesses the positive qualities typically associated with leisure? For example, some uses of free time that are not clearly work or paid for as work may contribute to success at work. A person may read books or articles related to work, attend evening classes that contribute to work competence, invite guests to a party because of work associations, or join a country club because of its value in establishing business contacts or promoting sales. Within community life, those nonwork occupations that have a degree of obligation about them—such as serving on a school board or as an unpaid member of a town council—may also be viewed as part of a person's civic responsibility.

The strict view of leisure as time that lacks any obligation or compulsion is suspect. If one chooses to raise dogs as a hobby or to play an instrument in an orchestra, one begins to assume a system of routines, schedules, and commitments to others. Stebbins discusses the concept of obligation as an aspect of leisure experience, pointing out that so-called "semi-leisure" may degenerate into "anti-leisure," defined by Godbey as

> activity which is undertaken compulsively, as a means to an end, for a perception of necessity, with a high degree of externally imposed constraints, with considerable anxiety, and with a minimum of personal autonomy.[9]

Leisure as Activity

A fourth common understanding of leisure is that it is activity in which people engage during their free time. Obviously, this concept of leisure is closely linked to the idea of recreation (as you will see in the section on recreation) because it involves the way in which free time is used for activity purposes. Early writers on recreation stressed the importance of activity; for example, Jay B. Nash urged that the procreative act be thought of as an active, "doing" experience. Recuperation through play, he wrote, isn't wholly relegated to inertia—doing nothing—but is gained through action.

For many individuals, Nash's view of leisure would be too confining. They would view relatively passive activities, such as reading a book, going to a museum, watching a film, or even dozing in a hammock or daydreaming, to be appropriate leisure pursuits, along with forms of active play.

Feminist scholars have criticized conceptualizations of leisure as activity as irrelevant for many women whose everyday life experiences cannot be easily categorized into a work/leisure dichotomy. Furthermore, definitions of leisure as activity do not accommodate individual perceptions about particular activities. Some individuals may view preparing a meal as a pleasurable activity of self-expression, whereas others view the activity as a monotonous, domestic obligation. In response to this criticism, contemporary scholars who study leisure as activity are primarily concerned with the outcomes of a particular activity rather than the activity itself.

Leisure as a State of Being Marked by Freedom

The fifth concept of leisure places the emphasis on the perceived freedom of the activity and on the role of leisure involvement in helping the individual achieve personal fulfillment and self-enrichment. Neulinger writes:

> To leisure means to be engaged in an activity performed for its own sake, to do something which gives one pleasure and satisfaction, which involves one to the very core of one's being. To leisure means to be oneself, to express one's talents, one's capacities, one's potentials.[10]

This concept of leisure implies a lifestyle that is holistic, in the sense that one's view of life is not sharply fragmented into a number of spheres such as family activities, religion, work, and free time. Instead, all such involvements are seen as part of a whole in which the individual explores his or her capabilities, develops enriching experiences with others, and seeks "self-actualization" in the sense of being creative, involved, expressive, and fully alive. The idea of leisure as a state of being places great emphasis on the need for perceived freedom. Recognizing the fact that some constraints always exist, Godbey defines leisure in the following way:

> Leisure is living in relative freedom from the external compulsive forces of one's culture and physical environment so as to be able to act from internal compulsion in ways which are personally pleasing and intuitively worthwhile.[11]

Such contemporary leisure theorists stress the need for the true leisure experience to yield a sense of total freedom and absence from compulsion of any kind. Realistically, however, there are many situations in which individuals are pressured to participate or in which the activity's structure diminishes his or her sense of freedom and intrinsic motivation.

Leisure as Spiritual Expression

A sixth way of conceptualizing leisure today sees it in terms of its contribution to spiritual expression or religious values. Newly founded faith-based social welfare organizations in the late nineteenth century were a driving force behind the growth of public and philanthropic leisure services during that time. During the early decades of the twentieth century, play and recreation were often referred to as uplifting or holy kinds of human experiences.

Volunteering, such as in local parks, is an excellent leisure activity that promotes the public good and builds social capital.

A more modern approach to spirituality moved beyond religion to an inner peace, understanding of the values that drive a person, and the meaning people assign to their lives. Leisure's connection to spirituality may not seem immediately obvious. However, leisure plays a major role in spirituality. The most common spiritual leisure pursuits are outdoor and nature activities. Walking through the woods, sitting on the bank of a creek, or paddling a canoe across a calm lake are means to spirituality for some. Others may prefer meditation, yoga, or other relaxation and contemplative exercises.

Leisure Defined

Recognizing that each of the six concepts of leisure just presented stems from a different perspective, a general definition that embraces several of the key points follows.

Leisure is that portion of an individual's time that is not directly devoted to work or work-connected responsibilities or to other obligated forms of maintenance or self-care. Leisure implies freedom and choice and is customarily used in a variety of ways, including to meet one's personal needs for reflection, self-enrichment, relaxation, pleasure, and affiliation. Although it usually involves some form of participation in a voluntarily chosen activity, it may also be regarded as a holistic state of being or even a spiritual experience.

THE MEANING OF RECREATION

In a sense, recreation represents a fusion between play and leisure and is therefore presented as the third of the important concepts that provide the framework for this overall field of study. The term itself stems from the Latin word *recreatio*, meaning that which refreshes or restores. Historically, recreation was often regarded as a period of light and restful activity, voluntarily chosen, that permits one to regain energy after heavy work and to return to work renewed.

This point of view lacks acceptability today for two reasons. First, as most work in modern society becomes less physically demanding, many people are becoming more fully engaged, both physically and mentally, in their recreation than in their work. Thus, the notion that recreation should be light and relaxing is far too limiting. Second, the definition of recreation as primarily intended to restore one for work does not cover the case of persons who have no work, including the growing retiree population, but who certainly need recreation to make their lives meaningful.

In contrast to work, which is often thought of as tedious, unpleasant, and obligatory, recreation has traditionally been thought of as light, pleasant, and revitalizing. However, this contrast too should be reconsidered. A modern, holistic view of work and recreation would be that both have the potential for being pleasant, rewarding, and creative and that both may represent serious forms of personal involvement and deep commitment.

CONTEMPORARY DEFINITIONS OF RECREATION

Most modern definitions of recreation fit into one of three categories: (1) Recreation has been seen as an activity carried on under certain conditions or with certain motivations; (2) recreation has been viewed as a process or state of being—something that happens within the person while engaging in certain kinds of activity, with a given set of expectations; and (3) recreation has been perceived as a social institution, a body of knowledge, or a professional field.

Typically, definitions of recreation found in the professional literature have included the following elements:

1. Recreation is widely regarded as activity (including physical, mental, social, or emotional involvement), as contrasted with sheer idleness or complete rest.
2. Recreation may include an extremely wide range of activities, such as sport, games, crafts, performing arts, fine arts, music, dramatics, travel, hobbies, and social activities. These activities may be engaged in by individuals or by groups and may involve single or episodic participation or sustained and frequent involvement throughout one's lifetime.
3. The choice of activity or involvement is voluntary, free of compulsion or obligation.
4. Recreation is prompted by internal motivation and the desire to achieve personal satisfaction, rather than by extrinsic goals or rewards.
5. Recreation is dependent on a state of mind or attitude; it is not so much what one does as the reason for doing it, and the way the individual feels about the activity, that makes it recreation.
6. Although the primary motivation for taking part in recreation is usually pleasure seeking, it may also be meeting intellectual, physical, or social needs. In some cases, rather than providing "fun" of a light or trivial nature, recreation may involve a serious degree of commitment and self-discipline and may yield frustration or even pain.

Within this framework, many kinds of leisure experiences may be viewed as recreation. They may range from the most physically challenging pursuits to those with much milder demands. Watching television, listening to a symphony orchestra, reading a book, or playing chess are all forms of recreation.

Voluntary Participation

Although it is generally accepted that recreation participation should be voluntary and carried out without any degree of pressure or compulsion, often this is not the case. We tend to be influenced by others, as in the case of the child whose parents urge him to join a Little League team, or the gymnast or figure skater who is encouraged in the thought that he or she might become a professional performer. Although ideally recreation is thought of as being free of compulsion or obligation, once one has entered into an activity—such as joining a company bowling league or playing with a chamber music group—one accepts a set of obligations to the other members of the team or group. Thus, recreation cannot be entirely free and spontaneous and, in fact, assumes some of the characteristics of work in the sense of having schedules, commitments, and responsibilities.

Motives for Participation

Definitions of recreation generally have stressed that it should be conducted for personal enjoyment or pleasure—ideally of an immediate nature. However, many worthwhile activities take time to master before they yield the fullest degree of satisfaction. Some complex activities may cause frustration and even mental anguish—as in the case of the golf addict who is desperately unhappy because of poor putting or driving. In such cases, it is not so much that the participant receives immediate pleasure as that he or she is absorbed and challenged by the activity; pleasure will probably grow as the individual's skill improves.

What about the view that recreation must be carried on for its own sake and without extrinsic goals or purposes? It is essential to recognize that human beings are usually goal-oriented, purposeful creatures. James Murphy and his coauthors have identified different recreational behaviors that suggest the kinds of motives people may have when they engage in activity:

- *Socializing behaviors:* Activities such as dancing, dating, going to parties, or visiting friends, in which people relate to one another in informal and unstereotyped ways.
- *Associative behaviors:* Activities in which people group together because of common interests, such as car clubs; stamp-, coin-, or gem-collecting groups; or similar hobbies.
- *Competitive behaviors:* Activities including all of the popular sport and games, but also competition in the performing arts or in outdoor activities in which individuals compete against the environment or even against their own limitations.
- *Risk-taking behaviors:* An increasingly popular form of participation in which the stakes are often physical injury or possible death.
- *Exploratory behaviors:* In a sense, all recreation involves some degree of exploration; in this context, it refers to such activities as travel and sightseeing, hiking, scuba diving, spelunking, and other pursuits that open up new environments to the participant.[12]

To these may be added the following motives: *vicarious experience*, such as watching movies or sports events; *sensory stimulation*, which might include drug use, sexual involvement, or listening to rock music; and *physical involvement for its own sake*, as opposed to competitive games. Creative arts, intellectual pursuits, or community volunteerism might also be considered important categories of recreational experience.

Recreation as an Outcome

Recognizing that different people may have many different motives for taking part in recreation, Gray and Greben suggest that it should not be considered simply as a form of activity. Instead, they argue that recreation should be perceived as the outcome of participation—a "peak experience in self-satisfaction" that comes from successful participation in any sort of enterprise.

> Recreation is an emotional condition within an individual human being that flows from a feeling of well-being and self-satisfaction. It is characterized by feelings of mastery, achievement, exhilaration, acceptance, success, personal worth, and pleasure. It reinforces a positive self-image. Recreation is a response to aesthetic experience, achievement of personal goals, or positive feedback from others. It is independent of activity, leisure, or social acceptance.[13]

Historically, leisure researchers have focused on the social-psychological outcomes of recreation. More recently, significant attention has been given to physical outcomes. Researchers and practitioners are particularly interested in the relationship between recreation participation and physical health outcomes, including reduction of obesity and other chronic health conditions.

People are motivated to engage in high-adventure activities because of the risk involved.

Commitment to Sport

The degree to which many individuals become deeply committed emotionally to their recreational interests may be illustrated within the realms of sports and popular entertainment. So fervently do many Americans root for popular sports teams and stars that sport has increasingly been referred to as a form of religion. The glorification of leading athletes as folk idols and the national preoccupation with such major events as the Stanley Cup, the World Series, or the Super Bowl demonstrate the degree to which sports—as a popular form of recreation—capture the emotional commitment of millions of Americans today.

CASE STUDY: Social Acceptability of Recreation

Another question arises with respect to defining recreation. Should activity that is often widely disapproved, such as drug use or vandalism, be regarded as a form of recreation? One school of thought maintains that *any* form of voluntarily chosen, pleasurable, leisure-time activity should be regarded as recreation. This view is expressed in the commonly used terms *recreational sex* and *recreational drug use*.

Other writers take the opposite view—that recreation must be wholesome for the individual and for society and must serve to re-create the participant physically, psychologically, spiritually, or mentally. Some even argue that recreation should be clearly distinguished from mere amusement, time-filling, or negative forms of play.

There is no argument that when activities are provided as a form of community-based service, supported by taxes or voluntary contributions, they must be attuned to prevailing social values and must be aimed at achieving desirable and constructive results.

Questions to Consider

1. Which school of thought is correct in terms of socially acceptable activities?
2. Are drug use, gambling, graffiti, and vandalism considered recreational activities? Are there different levels of these activities that may make them recreational activities?

Recreation as a Social Institution

Recreation is identified as a significant institution in the modern community, involving a form of collective behavior carried on within specific social structures. It has numerous traditions, values, channels of communication, formal relationships, and other institutional aspects.

Gardening is an example of a recreation activity that is freely chosen and has elements of intrinsic and extrinsic motivation.

Once chiefly the responsibility of the family, the church, or other local social bodies, recreation in contemporary society is the responsibility of a number of major agencies in today's society. These may include public, nonprofit, or commercial organizations that operate parks, beaches, zoos, aquariums, stadiums, or sports facilities. Recreational activities may also be provided by organizations such as hospitals, schools, correctional institutions, and branches of the armed forces. Clearly, recreation emerged in the twentieth century as a significant social institution, complete with its own national and international organizations and an extensive network of programs of professional preparation in colleges and universities.

Beyond this development, over the past century, there has been general acceptance of the view that community recreation, in which citizens take responsibility for supporting organized leisure services to meet social needs, contributes significantly to democratic citizenship. Community recreation is offered through city or county park and recreation departments. The role of leisure in the community is discussed further in Chapter 7.

CASE STUDY: Closed for Business: What Park Closures Mean for Our Cities, Neighborhoods, and Children

The *Huffington Post* ran an article titled "Closed for Business: What Park Closures Mean for Our Cities, Neighborhoods, and Children." The beginning of the article follows:[a]

> Our parks are in crisis. As cities and states across the country face record-breaking budget deficits, Parks and Recreation Departments are being forced to reduce hours, lay off staff, trim back maintenance efforts, and close some parks altogether.
>
> The situation is so severe that America's state parks are number one on the National Trust for Historic Preservation's 11 Most Endangered Historic Places list. According to a recent survey, as many as 400 state parks are in danger of closure. Here are some other depressing numbers:
>
> - 150 parks in California have seen reduced services and part-time closures.
> - New Jersey's state park budget has been slashed from $11.6 million to $3.4 million.
> - More than 120 state park jobs have been eliminated in Missouri and the state's backlog of deferred maintenance totals $200 million.
> - New York plans to close 41 state parks and 14 historic sites.

On the city level, the outlook is equally grim:

- Sacramento, California, is proposing to slash about $8.3 million and 145 positions from its Department of Parks and Recreation.
- Further south, Los Angeles recently eliminated 125 jobs in its Department of Recreation and Parks.
- Dallas, Texas is looking at a budget reduction from $75 million to $45 million between this year and next.

It may even be worse for smaller towns, many of which have frozen their capital budgets. Montvale, New Jersey, which has a population of about 7500, is cutting its Parks and Recreation budget by 53%, the largest of all its budget cuts. Like any living thing, parks need care and attention to thrive. Back in January, the *Denver Post* outlined the heartbreaking situation in Colorado Springs:

"The parks department removed trash cans last week, replacing them with signs urging users to pack out their own litter. . . . Neighbors are encouraged to bring their own lawn mowers to local green spaces, because parks workers will mow them only once every two weeks. . . . Water cutbacks mean most parks will be dead, brown turf by July."

A closed or ill-maintained park becomes vulnerable to vandalism and crime. A playground covered in graffiti invites more graffiti; a field scattered with trash invites more trash. A single park closure can launch a vicious cycle that changes the entire character of a neighborhood. It can also lower property values and deter tourists.

In fact, as parks writer Anne Schwartz points out in *Gotham Gazette*, "When parks are well-maintained, attractive and accessible, the economic boost they provide—in increased real estate values, tourism dollars, jobs and tax revenues—far outweighs the cost of upkeep."

Questions to Consider

1. What do budget deficits mean for recreation, play, and leisure?
2. What can cities and states do to combat this problem?
3. How can a city justify keeping parks open when it must cut police, fire, libraries, and other city services?

Source

a. Darrell Hammond, "Closed for Business: What Park Closures Mean for Our Cities, Neighborhoods, and Children." *Huffington Post*, June 22, 2010. Available at: http://www.huffingtonpost.com/darell-hammond/closed-for-business-what_b_620765.html accessed August 24, 2010.

Recreation Defined

Acknowledging these contrasting views of the meaning of recreation, the following definition of the term is offered. Recreation consists of human activities or experiences that occur in leisure time. Usually, they are voluntarily chosen for intrinsic purposes and are pleasurable, although they may involve a degree of compulsion, extrinsic purpose, and discomfort, or even pain or danger. Recreation may also be regarded as the emotional state resulting from participation or as a social institution, a professional career field, or a business. When provided as part of organized community or voluntary-agency programs, recreation should be socially constructive and morally acceptable in terms of prevailing community standards and values.

RELATIONSHIPS AMONG PLAY, LEISURE, AND RECREATION

Obviously, the three terms discussed in this chapter are closely interrelated. Leisure, for example, provides an opportunity to carry on both play and recreation. Much of our free time in modern society is taken up by recreation, although leisure may also include such activities as continuing education, religious practice, or community service, which are not usually thought of as forms of recreation. In turn, it should be understood that although play and recreation tend to overlap, they are not identical. Play is not so much an activity as a form of behavior, marked stylistically by teasing, competition, exploration, or make-believe. Play can occur during work or leisure, whereas recreation takes place only during leisure.

Recreation obviously includes many forms of play, but it also may involve distinctly nonplay-like activities such as traveling, reading, going to museums, and pursuing other cultural or intellectual activities. As a social institution, recreation has broader applications than play or leisure in two ways: Recreation is often provided by institutions that do not have leisure as a primary concern, such as the armed forces or business concerns; and recreation agencies often provide other social or environmental services and may in fact become an important linkage between municipal governments and the people they serve.

Leisure is a subject of scholarly study for many economists and sociologists; it also has come increasingly under the scrutiny of psychologists and social psychologists. However, to the public at large, leisure tends to be a somewhat abstract or remote concept. Although many academic departments and some community agencies use the term *leisure* in their titles, it lacks a sense of urgency or strong appeal as a public issue or focus of government action.

Of the three terms, *recreation* is at once the most understandable and significant for many people. It is easily recognizable as an area of personal activity and social responsibility, and its values are readily apparent for all age groups and special populations as well. For these reasons, it is given primary emphasis in the chapters that follow, particularly in terms of program sponsorship and professional identity.

Role of Recreation and Leisure in Professional Education Curricula

Both recreation and leisure are the focus of higher education curricula for individuals planning to enter the overall leisure-service field. Mannell and Kleiber point out that they demand different teaching emphases. Leisure studies scholars, they write, draw on the knowledge and approaches of both the social and management sciences, with their findings reported in various national and international journals and conferences dealing with leisure studies. They continue:

> Most college and university recreation and leisure studies programs encourage their students to integrate and understand the interplay between "people," "resource" and "policy" issues.
>
> In other words, leisure studies curricula require students to study individual and group leisure behavior as a function of social and cultural factors, the planning and management of natural and built resources for free time use, and policy/management issues associated with the provision of public and private leisure services.[14]

The themes that have just been introduced are explored more fully throughout this text, as the historical development of recreation and play and the evolution of the present-day

CASE STUDY: Is It Leisure?

Determine whether each of the following activities is considered leisure, recreation, or both. If it is leisure or recreation, by which definition (such as spiritual expression, time, activity)? Determine whether the activity contradicts any of the definitions of leisure or recreation.

Activity	Definition Supporting Activity as Leisure, Recreation, or Both	Definition Contradicting Activity as Leisure or Recreation
1. Mom spending the day watching her daughter's soccer matches		
2. Sleeping		
3. Relaxing in a lawn chair under a tree		
4. Reading a book for fun		
5. Planting a vegetable garden		
6. Reading a book related to your job		
7. Playing in a golf outing with acquaintances to build a network within the community		
8. Going to a mandatory softball practice prior to the start of league play		
9. Attending a church service		

leisure-service system are described. Throughout, issues related to the social implications of recreation and leisure and to the role of recreation and park professionals are fully discussed, along with the challenges that face practitioners in this field in the twenty-first century.

SUMMARY

Play, recreation, and leisure represent important basic concepts that are essential aspects of the overall field of organized leisure services. They have been explored by philosophers, psychologists, historians, educators, and sociologists from ancient Greek civilizations to the present.

Play may best be understood as a form of activity or behavior that is generally nonpurposeful in terms of having serious intended outcomes, but that is an important element in the healthy growth of children and in other societal functions. The chapter presents various theories of play, ranging from the classical views of Herbert Spencer to more contemporary concepts that link play to Freudian theory or to exploratory drives of human personality.

Six concepts of leisure are presented that depict it as the possession of the upper classes or aristocrats throughout history, as free time or activity, as a state of being, and as a form of spiritual expression. Recreation is also explored from different perspectives, with a key issue being whether it must be morally constructive or socially approved to be considered recreation. The role of recreation as an important contemporary social institution and force in economic life is also discussed.

QUESTIONS FOR CLASS DISCUSSION OR ESSAY EXAMINATION

1. This chapter presents several perspectives on play, including a review of traditional definitions of play, its role as a social ritual in community life, and its contribution to personality development. Which of these do you find most interesting and useful? Why?
2. Recreation has been simply defined as socially desirable activity carried on voluntarily in free time for purposes of fun or pleasure. Critically analyze this definition. For example, must activity always be considered socially desirable to be regarded as recreation? Is recreation always pleasurable? Is it always carried on voluntarily? What elements would you add to this definition to make it more meaningful?
3. The chapter presents two contrasting views of leisure—one as the slow-paced, relaxed, or contemplative use of free time and the other as active participation in a wide range of often challenging or demanding activities. Which of these do you believe is the more accurate picture of leisure today?
4. Discuss the contrasting meanings of *play*, *leisure*, and *recreation*, and show how they overlap and differ from each other in their separate meanings. Which of the three do you feel is the more useful term as far as public understanding of this field is concerned?
5. How does the amount of free time change as we age (for example, for young children, teens, college students, parents, at retirement)?

6. List three activities that you enjoy that fall distinctly within the category of play, recreation, and leisure. What definition influenced your decision on which category to place the activity?

ENDNOTES

1. U.S. Play Coalition, "A Call for Action," http://usplaycoalition.clemson.edu.
2. Friedrich Froebel, cited in George Torkildsen, *Leisure and Recreation Management* (London: E. and F. N. Spon, 1992): 48–49.
3. The original source of this theory was W. P. Bowen and Elmer D. Mitchell, *The Theory of Organized Play* (New York: A. S. Barnes, 1923).
4. Roger Caillois, *Man, Play, and Games* (London: Thames and Hudson, 1961): 21.
5. Johan Huizinga, *Homo Ludens: A Study of the Play Element in Culture* (Boston: Beacon Press, 1944; 1960): 5.
6. Sigmund Freud, quoted in M. J. Ellis, *Why People Play* (Englewood Cliffs, NJ: Prentice Hall, 1973): 60.
7. M. Csikszentmihalyi, *Flow: The Psychology of Optimal Experience (P.S.)* (New York: HarperCollins Publishers, 2007).
8. Hayden Ramsey, *Reclaiming Leisure: Art, Sport and Philosophy* (New York: Palgrave Macmillan, 2005).
9. Robert Stebbins, "Obligation as an Aspect of Leisure Experience," *Journal of Leisure Research* (Vol. 32, No. 1, 2000): 153.
10. John Neulinger, *The Psychology of Leisure* (Springfield, IL: Charles C. Thomas, 1974): xi.
11. Geoffrey Godbey, *Leisure in Your Life: An Exploration* (Philadelphia: W. B. Saunders, 1981): 10.
12. James Murphy et al., *Leisure Service Delivery Systems: A Modern Perspective* (Philadelphia: Lea and Febiger, 1973): 73–76.
13. David Gray and Seymour Greben, "Future Perspectives," *Parks and Recreation* (July 1974): 49.
14. Roger Mannell and Douglas Kleiber, *A Social Psychology of Leisure* (State College, PA: Venture Publishing, 1997): 11.

CHAPTER 3

EARLY HISTORY OF RECREATION AND LEISURE

◆ ◆ ◆

In the year A.D. *80, the Roman Colosseum opened with what must stand as quite the longest and most disgusting mass binge in history. . . . Various sorts of large-scale slaughter, both of animals and men, were appreciatively watched by the Emperor Titus and a packed audience for 100 days. . . . Titus was quite happy footing the enormous bill just as he and his father, the imperial Vespasian, had already footed the bill for building this vast arena. Such payments were the privilege of power.*[1]

In the long run, industrialization brought the reduction of work time. The hours per year committed to work have declined in the industrial West in a range from 3000–3600 to 1800–2000 from 1840 to the present. . . . This redistribution of time has been accompanied by a drastic "repackaging" of leisure hours making possible new forms of leisure time, including the typically modern notions of free evenings, the weekend, paid summer vacations, as well as a lengthy childhood and retirement.[2]

◆ ◆ ◆

INTRODUCTION

To provide a meaningful background for the study of recreation and leisure in modern society, it is helpful to have a clear understanding of its role in the past. We can trace the origins of many of our contemporary views of leisure and related cultural customs to the traditions and practices of ancient cultures. The history of recreation and leisure is a rich tapestry of people, places, events, and social forces, showing the role of religion, education, and government and the customs and values of different cultures, their arts, sport, and pastimes. By becoming familiar with the evolution of our recreation and leisure, we are better able to understand and deal effectively with the present.

Tribal View of Work and Leisure

Tribal people do not make the same sharp distinction between work and leisure that more technologically advanced societies do. Whereas the latter set aside different periods of time for work and relaxation, a tribal, pretechnological society has no such precise separations. Instead, work is customarily done when it is available or necessary, and it is often infused with rites and customs that lend it variety and pleasure. In such tribal societies, work tends to be varied and creative, rather than being a narrow, specialized task demanding a sharply defined skill, as in modern industry. Work is often accompanied by ritual that is regarded as essential to the success of the planting or harvesting or to the building or hunting expedition. The ritual may involve prayer, sacrifice, dance, or feasting, which thus becomes part of the world of work.

THE PLAY OF EARLY SOCIETIES

One would expect a chronological study to begin by examining the play of prehistoric peoples during the Paleolithic and Neolithic epochs. However, relatively little is known about the nature of leisure and play in these early periods. Archaeologists have uncovered artifacts that provide some first-hand evidence of the creative, athletic, and recreation activities of primitive peoples from around the world. We also have extrapolated from the accounts of "primitive" societies written by missionaries and anthropologists in the nineteenth and early twentieth centuries.

Origins of Games and Sport

In primitive societies, play may have had many sources. Popular games were often vestiges of warfare, practiced as a form of sport. Musical instruments were likely created for use in religious rituals. Pottery, painting, drawings, and other early art provided a record of both daily life and cultural mythology. Beads and other types of jewelry were created as external symbols of individual status and group affiliations. When an activity was no longer useful in its original form (such as archery for hunting or warfare), it became a form of sport offering individuals and groups the opportunity to prove physical skill and strategy. Often, the origin was a religious ritual, in which games were played to symbolize a continuing struggle between good and evil or life and death.

The game of *tlachtli*, widely practiced in Central America centuries ago, is an example of such a contest. Tlachtli courts were about 200 feet long and 30 feet wide and were situated near temples. A stone ring was fixed about halfway up a wall at either end. The players struck a rubber ball with their knees or hips, the purpose being to drive it through one of the hoops. Blank writes:

> The rubber ball used in the ancient game symbolized the sun, and by making it carom across the court, players hoped to perpetuate the daily arc of the heavenly sphere. . . . Mesoamerican ball was no schoolyard shoot-around: Win or lose, the athletes played for keeps. . . . [I]n pre-Columbian games, members of the losing team were commonly offered up for ritual sacrifice, their hearts cut out with blades of razor sharp obsidian. That's one way to shorten the post-game interviews.[3]

Other Play Functions

On the North American continent, play had similar functions among Native American tribes, helping to equip the young for adult life. Boys practiced warriors' skills and were taught to survive unarmed and unclothed in the wilderness. Girls were taught the household crafts expected of mature women. Through dancing, singing, and storytelling, both sexes learned the history and religion of their cultures. Among such southwestern Native American tribes as the Navajo, Zuni, or Hopi, shamans or medicine men practiced healing rites that made use of chanting, storytelling, dancing, sacred *kachina* dolls, and elaborate, multicolored sand paintings.

Early Chinese societies developed highly organized cultural events.

Archeologists Uncover Ancient Flutes Used in Cultural Celebration

In a period ranging from May 1986 to June 1987, archaeologists at the early Neolithic site of Jiahu in Henan Province, China, uncovered 25 flutes between 7000 and 9000 years old. Most of the flutes were found at grave sites. Six of the instruments were intact and are now believed to be the earliest, playable multinote instruments. The flutes, which were made of bone, contain seven holes that correspond to a scale similar to the Western eight-note scale. This tone scale indicates that musicians living in 7000 B.C. could compose and play music. Archaeologists cannot be certain of why so many flutes were located in this part of China. Some believe that the flutes were part of religious rituals; others believe that music was simply a part of community life. In any case, the discovery of these flutes helps us recognize the very old tradition of using music as a means of personal expression and cultural celebration.[4]

RECREATION AND LEISURE IN ANCIENT CIVILIZATIONS

As prehistoric societies advanced, they developed specialization of functions. Humans learned to domesticate plants and animals, which permitted them to shift from a nomadic existence based on hunting and food gathering to a largely stationary way of life based on grazing animals and planting crops. Ultimately, ruling classes developed, along with soldiers, craftsmen, peasants, and slaves. As villages and cities evolved and large estates (often with complex water storage and irrigation systems) were tilled and harvested by lower-class workers, the upper classes gained power, wealth, and leisure. Thus, in the aristocracy of the first civilizations that developed in the Middle East during the five millennia before the Christian era, we find for the first time in history a leisure class.

Ancient Egypt

The Egyptian culture was a rich and diversified one; it achieved an advanced knowledge of astronomy, architecture, engineering, agriculture, and construction. The Egyptians had a varied class structure, with a powerful nobility, priesthood, and military class and lesser classes of workers, artisans, peasants, and slaves. This civilization, which lasted from about 5000 B.C. well into the Roman era, was richly recorded in paintings, statuary, and hieroglyphic records.

The highest form of leisure usually occurred among the elite in ancient societies.

The ancient Egyptians led a colorful and pleasant life; it is said that their energies were directed to the arts of living and the arts of dying. They engaged in many sports as part of education and recreation, including wrestling, gymnastic exercises, lifting and swinging weights, and ball games. Bullfighting was a popular spectacle and, at least at its inception, was religiously motivated. Music, drama, and dance were forms of religious worship as well as social entertainment. The Egyptians had complex orchestras that included various stringed and percussive instruments. Groups of female performers were attached to temples, and the royal houses had troupes of entertainers who performed on sacred or social occasions.

Ancient Assyria and Babylonia

The land known as the "fertile crescent" between two great rivers, the Tigris and the Euphrates, was ruled by two powerful empires, Assyria in the north and Babylon in the south. These kingdoms were in power for approximately 26 centuries, from about 2900 B.C. until the invasion by Alexander the Great in 330 B.C. Like the ancient Egyptians, the Assyrians and Babylonians had many popular recreation activities, such as boxing, wrestling, archery, and a variety of table games.

In addition to watching dancing, listening to music, and giving banquets, Assyrians were also devoted to hunting; the nobles of Assyria went lion hunting in chariots and on foot, using spears. The chase was a daily occupation, recorded for history in numerous reliefs, sculptures, and inscriptions. As early as the ninth century B.C., parks were established as sites for royal hunting parties. They also provided settings for feasts, assemblies, and royal gatherings. On the estates of other monarchs during the ninth and tenth centuries B.C. were vineyards, fishponds, and the famed hanging gardens of Babylon.

Ancient Israel

Among the ancient Israelites, music and dancing were performed for ritual purposes as well as for social activities and celebrations. The early Hebrews distinguished dances of a sacred or holy character from those that resembled pagan ceremonies. Although there are no wall reliefs or paintings to tell of dance as performed by the ancient Hebrews, there are abundant references to this practice in the Old Testament. Dance was highly respected and was particularly used on occasions of celebration and triumph.

Like other ancient societies, the ancient Hebrews also engaged in hunting, fishing, wrestling, and the use of such weapons as the sword and javelin for both recreational and defensive purposes. As for leisure itself, their major contribution was to set aside the seventh day—the Sabbath—as a time for people to rest from work and to worship.

Ancient Greece

In the city-states of ancient Greece, particularly in Athens during the so-called Golden Age of Pericles from about 500 to 400 B.C., humankind reached a new peak of philosophical and cultural development. The Athenians took great interest in the arts, in learning, and in athletics. These pursuits were generally restricted to wellborn, aristocratic noblemen, who had full rights of citizenship, including voting and participation in affairs of state. Craftsmen, farmers, and tradespeople were also citizens but had limited rights and less prestige. Labor was performed by slaves and foreigners, who outnumbered citizens by as much as two or three to one.

The amenities of life were generally restricted to the most wealthy and powerful citizens, who represented the Athenian ideal of the balanced man—a combined soldier, athlete, artist, statesman, and philosopher. This ideal was furthered through education and the various religious festivals, which occupied about 70 days of the year. The arts of music, poetry, theater, gymnastics, and athletic competition were combined in these sacred competitions.

Sport appears to have been part of daily life and to have occurred mainly when there were mass gatherings of people, such as the assembly of an army for war or the wedding or funeral of some great personage. There were also bardic or musical events, offering contests on the harp and flute, poetry, and theatrical presentations. Physical prowess was celebrated in sculpture and poetry, and strength and beauty were seen as gifts of the gods.

From earliest childhood, Athenian citizens engaged in varied athletic and cultural activities. Young children enjoyed toys, dolls, carts, skip ropes, kites, and seesaws. When boys reached the age of seven, they were enrolled in schools in which gymnastics and music were primary elements. They were intensively instructed in running and leaping, wrestling, throwing the javelin and discus, dancing (taught as a form of military drill), boxing, swimming, and ball games.

Greek Philosophy of Recreation and Leisure The Athenian philosophers believed strongly in the unity of mind and body and in the strong relationship of all forms of human qualities and skills. They felt that play activity was essential to the healthy physical and social growth of children.

Plato believed that education should be compulsory and that it should provide natural modes of amusement for children:

> Education should begin with the right direction of children's sports. The plays of childhood have a great deal to do with the maintenance or nonmaintenance of laws.[5]

Changes in the Greek Approach to Leisure The ancient Greeks developed the art of town planning and customarily made extensive provisions for parks and gardens, open-air theaters and gymnasiums, baths, exercise grounds, and stadiums. During the time of Plato, the gymnasium and the park were closely connected in beautiful natural settings, often including indoor halls, gardens, and buildings for musical performances. Early

Athens had many public baths and some public parks, which later gave way to privately owned estates.

Women in Ancient Greece

Women did not enjoy the leisurely pursuits of men in ancient Greece, although there are some historical accounts of women receiving modest education, and young girls participated in some athletic competitions. Citizens were, by definition, men.

A gradual transition occurred in the Greek approach to leisure and play. At first, all citizens were expected to participate in sports and games, and the Olympic games were restricted to free-born Greeks only. Gradually, however, the religious and cultural functions of the Olympic games and other festivals were weakened by athletic specialization, corruption, and commercialism. In time, sport and other forms of activity such as drama, singing, and dance were performed only by highly skilled specialists (drawn from the lower classes or even slaves) who trained or perfected their skills throughout the year to appear before huge crowds of admiring spectators.

Ancient Rome

Like the Greek city-states, the Roman republic during its early development was a vigorous and nationalistic state. The Roman citizen, although he belonged to a privileged class, was required to defend his society and fight in its wars. Citizens participated in sport and gymnastics, intended to keep the body strong and spirit courageous. Numerous games held in connection with the worship of various Roman gods later developed into annual festivals. Such games were carefully supervised by the priesthood and were supported by public funds, frequently at great cost. The most important of the Roman games were those that celebrated military triumphs, which were usually held in honor of the god Jupiter, the head of the Roman pantheon.

Like the early Greeks, young Roman children had toy carts, houses, dolls, hobbyhorses, stilts, and tops and engaged in many sport and games. Young boys were taught various sport and exercises such as running and jumping, sword and spear play, wrestling, swimming, and horseback riding. The Romans, however, had a different concept of leisure than the Greeks. Although the Latin words for "leisure" and "business" are *otium* and *negotium*, suggesting the same view of leisure as a positive value (with work defined negatively as a lack of leisure), the Romans supported play for utilitarian rather than aesthetic or spiritual reasons. The Romans were much less interested than the Athenians in varied forms of cultural activity. Although they had many performing companies, usually composed of Greek and southern Italian slaves, the Romans themselves did not actively participate in the theater.

Even more than the Greeks, the Romans were systematic planners and builders. Their towns generally included provisions for baths, open-air theaters, amphitheaters, forums for public assemblies, stadiums, and sometimes parks and gardens. They developed buildings for gymnastic sport, modeled after the Greek *palaestra* and including wrestling rooms, conversation areas for philosophers, and colonnades where games might be held in win-

The Roman Colosseum is considered one of the greatest architectural achievements of antiquity. Built almost 2000 years ago, the Colosseum is a monument to the achievements and culture of ancient Rome.

ter despite bad weather. Wealthier Romans often had private villas, many with large gardens and hunting preserves.

As the empire grew more powerful, the simple agricultural democracy of the early years, in which all male Romans were citizens and free men, shifted to an urban life with sharply divided classes. There were four social levels: the *senators*, who were the richest, holding most of the land and power; the *curiae*, who owned more than 25 acres of land and were officeholders or tax collectors; the *plebs*, or free common people, who owned small properties or were tradesmen or artisans; and the *coloni*, who were lower-class tenants of the land.

The society became marked by the wealth and profiteering of businessmen and speculators, with the cooperation of the rulers and governing officials. In time, a huge urban population of plebs lived in semi-idleness because most of the work was done by *coloni* and slaves brought to Rome. Gradually, it became necessary for the Roman emperors and senate to amuse and entertain the *plebs*; they did so with doles of grain and with public games—in other words, "bread and circuses."

As early as the reign of the Emperor Claudius in the first century A.D., there were 159 public holidays during the year, 93 of which were devoted to games at public expense, including many new festivals in honor of national heroes and foreign victories. By A.D. 354, there were 200 public holidays each year, including 175 days of games. Even on working days, the labor began at daybreak and ended shortly after noon during much of the year.

As leisure increased and the necessity for military service and other forms of physical effort declined for the Roman citizen, entertainment became the central life activity of many citizens. The normal practice was for the citizen to be entertained or to follow a daily routine of exercise, bathing, and eating. Men were no longer as active in sport as they once had been. They now sought to be amused and to entertain their guests with paid acrobats, musicians, dancers, and other artists. Athletes now performed as members of a specialized profession with unions, coaches, and training schools and with conditions of service accepted and approved by the emperor himself.

Corruption of Entertainment Gradually, the focus on the traditional sports of running, throwing, and jumping gave way to an emphasis on human combat—first boxing and wrestling and then displays of cruelty in which gladiators fought to the death for the entertainment of mass audiences. By the time of Emperor Tiberius (A.D. 14–37), competitive sport in the Roman Empire had become completely commercialized. To maintain political popularity and placate the bored masses, the emperors and the senate provided great parades, circuses, and feasts.

The Roman games featured contests that were fought to the death between gladiators using various weapons, on foot, on horseback, or in chariots. Even sea battles were fought in artificially constructed lakes in the Roman arenas. Imported wild beasts, such as tigers and elephants, were pitted against each other or against human antagonists. Christians, in particular, were slaughtered in such games. Tacitus wrote that many

> were dressed in the skins of wild beasts, and exposed to be torn to pieces by dogs in the public games, were crucified, or condemned to be burnt; and at nightfall serve in place of lamps to light the darkness, Nero's own gardens being used for the purpose.[6]

Both animals and humans were maimed and butchered in cruel and horrible ways. Spectacles were often lewd and obscene, leading to mass debauchery, corruption, and perversion that profoundly weakened the Roman state.

EARLY CHRISTIAN ERA: DARK AND MIDDLE AGES

Under attack by successive waves of northern European tribes, the Roman Empire finally collapsed. For a period of several centuries, Europe was overrun with warring tribes and shifting alliances. The organized power of Rome, which had built roads, extended commerce, and provided civil order, was at an end. Gradually, the Catholic Church emerged to provide a form of universal citizenship within Europe. Having suffered under the brutal persecutions of the Romans, the early Christians condemned all that their pagan oppressors had stood for—especially their hedonistic way of life. Indeed, the early church fathers believed in a fanatical asceticism, which in the Byzantine, or Eastern, Empire was marked by the Anchorite movement, with its idea of salvation through masochistic self-deprivation.

Change Comes to the Roman Life in the Dark and Middle Ages

Many aspects of Roman life were forbidden during the Dark and Middle Ages. The stadiums, amphitheaters, and baths that had characterized Roman life were destroyed. The Council of Elvira ruled that the rite of baptism could not be extended to those connected with the stage, and in A.D. 398 the Council of Carthage excommunicated those who attended the theater on holy days. The great spectacles and organized shows of imperial Rome were at an end. The Roman emphasis on leisure was replaced by a Christian emphasis on work. The influential Benedictine order in particular insisted on the dignity of labor. Their rule read, "Idleness is the great enemy of the soul. Therefore, monks should always be occupied either in manual labor or in sacred readings."

It would be a mistake, however, to assume that the Catholic Church eliminated all forms of play. Many early Catholic religious practices were based on the rituals of earlier faiths. Priests built churches on existing shrines or temple sites, set Christian holy days according to the dates of pagan festivals, and used such elements of pagan worship as bells, candles, incense, singing, and dancing.

Pastimes in the Middle Ages

Despite disapproval from the church, many forms of play continued during the Middle Ages: Medieval society was marked by rigid class stratification; below the nobility and clergy were the peasants, who were divided into such ranks as freemen, villeins, serfs, and slaves.

Life in the Middle Ages, even for the feudal nobility, was crude and harsh. Manors and castles were little more than stone fortresses—crowded, dark, and damp. Knights were responsible for fighting in the service of their rulers; between wars, their favorite pastimes were hunting and hawking. Hunting skill was considered a virtue of medieval rulers and noblemen. The sport was thought to be helpful in keeping hunters from the sin of idleness. (A vigorous and tiring sport, it was also believed to prevent sensual temptation.) Hunting also served as a useful preparation for war. In a later era, the Italian Machiavelli pointed out that since the main concern of the prince must be war, he must never cease thinking of it. In times of peace, thoughts of war should be directed to the sport of hunting.

Other pastimes during the Middle Ages were various types of games and gambling, music and dance, sport, and jousting. The games played in castles and medieval manors included early forms of chess, checkers, backgammon, and dice. Gambling was popular, although forbidden by both ecclesiastical and royal authority.

As the chaos of the Dark Ages yielded to greater order and regularity, life became more stable. Travel in reasonable safety became possible, and by the eleventh century, commerce was widespread. The custom of jousting emerged within the medieval courts, stemming from the tradition that only the nobility fought on horseback; common men fought on foot. Thus, the term *chivalry* (from the French *cheval,* meaning horse) came into being. By the dawn of the twelfth century, the code of chivalry was developed, having originated in the profession of arms among feudal courtiers. (The tournament was a contest between teams, and the joust was a trial of skill between two individual knights.) An elaborate code of laws and regulations was drawn up for the combat, and no one below the rank of esquire was permitted to engage in tournaments or jousting.

Games of the Common People Meanwhile, what of the life of the peasantry during the Middle Ages? Edward Hulme suggests that life was not all work for the lower classes. There were village feasts and sport, practical joking, throwing weights, cockfighting, bull baiting, and other lively games. "Ball games and wrestling, in which men of one village were pitted against men of another, sometimes resulted in bloodshed."[7]

There was sometimes dancing on the green, and, on holidays, there were miracle and morality plays (forms of popular religious drama and pageantry). However, peasants usually went to bed at dark, reading was a rare accomplishment, and there was much drinking and crude brawling. For peasants, hunting was more a means of obtaining food than a sport. Although the nobility usually rode through the hedges and trampled the fields of the peasantry, peasants were not allowed to defend their crops against such forays or even against wild animals. If peasants were caught poaching, they were often maimed or hanged as punishment.

Typically, certain games were classified as rich men's sport and others as poor men's sport; sometimes a distinction was also made between urban and rural sport. As life in the Middle Ages became somewhat easier, a number of pastimes emerged. Many modern sport were developed at this time in rudimentary form.

The people of the Middle Ages had an insatiable love of sightseeing and would travel great distances to see entertainments. There was no religious event, parish fair, municipal

The "Fight Between Carnival and Lent," painted in 1559 by Pieter Bruegel, presents the contrast between two sides of contemporary life, as shown by the inn on the left side (for recreation) and the church on the right side (for religious intolerance).

feast, or military parade that did not bring great crowds of people. When the kings of France assembled their principal retainers once or twice a year, they distributed food and liquor among the common people and provided military displays, court ceremonies, and entertainment by jugglers, tumblers, and minstrels.

An illustration of the extent to which popular recreation expanded during the Middle Ages is found in the famous painting of children's games by the Flemish artist Pieter Breughel. This painting depicts more than 90 forms of children's play, including marbles, stilts, sledding, bowling, skating, blind man's bluff, piggyback, leapfrog, follow-the-leader, archery, tug-of-war, doll play, and dozens of others, many of which have lasted to the present day.

THE RENAISSANCE

Historians generally view the first half of the Middle Ages in Europe (roughly from A.D. 400 to 1000) as the Dark Ages, and the next 400 to 500 years as *le haut Moyen* Age, or High Middle Age. The Renaissance is said to have begun in Italy about A.D. 1350, in France about 1450, and in England about 1500. It marked a transition between the medieval world and the modern age. The term *renaissance* means rebirth and describes the revived interest in the scholarship, philosophy, and arts of ancient Greece and Rome that developed at this time. More broadly, it also represented a new freedom of thought and expression, a more rational and scientific view of life, and the expansion of commerce and travel in European life.

As the major European nations stabilized during this period under solidly established monarchies, power shifted from the church to the kings and their noblemen. In Italy and France, particularly, the nobility became patrons of great painters, sculptors, musicians, dancers, and dramatists. These artists were no longer dominated by the ideals and values of the Catholic Church, but were free to serve secular goals. A great wave of music and literature swept through the courts of Europe, aided by the development of printing. Dance and theater became more complex and elaborate, and increasingly lavish entertainments and spectacles were presented in the courts of Italy and France.

Play as Education

Varied forms of play became part of the education of the youth of the nobility at this time. The French essayist Michel de Montaigne, in discussing the education of children, wrote:

> Our very exercises and recreations, running, wrestling, music, dancing, hunting, riding, and fencing will prove to be a good part of our study. . . . It is not a soul, it is not a body, that we are training up; it is a man, and we ought not to divide him into two parts.[8]

The Athenian philosophy that had supported play as an important form of education was given fuller emphasis during the Renaissance by such educators and writers as François Rabelais, John Locke, and Jean Jacques Rousseau. In early sixteenth-century France, Rabelais advanced a number of revolutionary theories on education, emphasizing the need for physical exercises and games as well as singing, dancing, modeling and painting, nature study, and manual training. His account of the education of Gargantuan describes play as an exercise for mind and body. Locke, an Englishman who lived from 1632 to 1704, was also concerned with play as a medium of learning. He recommended that children make their own playthings and felt that games could contribute significantly to character development if they were properly supervised and directed. "All the plays and diversions of children," he wrote, "should be directed toward good and useful habits." Locke distinguished between the play of children and recreation for older youth and adults. "Recreation," he said, "is not being idle . . . but easing the wearied part by change of business."

INFLUENCE OF THE PROTESTANT REFORMATION

The Reformation was a religious movement of the 1500s that resulted in the establishment of a number of Protestant sects whose leaders broke away from Roman Catholicism. It was part of a broader stream that included economic, social, and political currents. In part it represented the influence of the growing middle classes, who allied with the nobility in the emerging nations of Europe to challenge the power of the church.

Throughout Europe, there was an aura of grim dedication to work and a determination to enforce old codes against play and idleness. The "Protestant work ethic" that emerged during the Reformation led to periods of strict limitations on leisure and recreation throughout the history of many Christian cultures, including societies in North America. This same ethic has heavily influenced our contemporary Western views of the relative value of work and leisure.

The Protestant Puritanism

The new Protestant sects tended to be more solemn and austere than the Catholic Church. Calvin established an autocratic system of government in Geneva in 1541 that was directed by a group of Presbyters, morally upright men who controlled the social and cultural life of the community to the smallest detail. They ruthlessly suppressed heretics and burned dissenters at the stake. Miller and Robinson describe the unbending Puritanism in Geneva:

> "Purity of conduct" was insisted upon, which meant the forbidding of gambling, card playing, dancing, wearing of finery, singing of gay songs, feasting, drinking and the like. There were to be no more festivals, no more theaters, no more ribaldry, no more light and disrespectful poetry or display. Works of art and musical instruments were removed from the churches.[9]

Puritanism in England

The English Puritans waged a constant battle to limit or condemn sport and other forms of entertainment during the period from the sixteenth to the eighteenth century. Maintaining strict observation of the Sabbath was a particular issue. Anglican clergy during the Elizabethan period bitterly attacked stage plays, church festival gatherings, dancing, gambling, bowling, and other "devilish pastimes" such as hawking and hunting, holding fairs and markets, and reading "lascivious and wanton books."

James I, however, recognized that the prohibition of harmless amusements such as dancing, archery, and the decorating of maypoles caused public anger. In 1618, he issued a Declaration on Lawful Sports, in which he asked, "When shall the common people have leave to exercise, if not upon the Sundayes and holy daies, seeing they must apply their labour and win their living in all working daies?" James stressed the military value of sport and the danger of an increase in drinking and other vices as substitute activities if sport were denied to people.

DEVELOPMENT OF PARKS AND RECREATION AREAS

During the Middle Ages, the need to enclose cities within protective walls necessitated building within a compact area that left little space for public gardens or sports areas. As the walled city became more difficult to defend after the invention of gunpowder and cannon, residents began to move out of the central city. Satellite communities developed around the city, but usually with little definite planning.

As the Renaissance period began, European town planning was characterized by wide avenues, long approaches, handsome buildings, and similar monumental features. The nobility decorated their estates with elaborate gardens, some of which were open to public use, as in Italy at the end of the thirteenth century. There were walks and public squares, often decorated with statuary. In some cases, religious brotherhoods built clubhouses, gardens, and shooting stands for archery practice that were used by townspeople for recreation and amusement.

Types of Major Parks

Three major types of large parks came into existence during the late Renaissance. In almost every instance they were derived from private estates of nobles or the elite. The first were royal hunting preserves or parks, some of which have become famous public parks today, such as the 4000-acre Prater in Vienna and the Tiergarten in Berlin. Second were the ornate and formal garden parks designed according to the so-called French style of landscape architecture. Third were the English garden parks, which strove to produce naturalistic landscape effects. These three types of parks became the prevailing style in most European cities. The French style and English garden parks competed as the most popular design approach.

In England, efforts at city planning began during the eighteenth century. Business and residential streets were paved and street names posted. Because it was believed that overcrowding led to disease (in the seventeenth century, London had suffered from recurrent attacks of the plague), an effort was made to convert open squares into gardens and to create more small parks. Deaths from contagious disease declined during each successive decade of the eighteenth century, and this improvement was believed to have been the result of increased cleanliness and ventilation within the city.

Use of Private Estates

From 1500 to the latter part of the eighteenth century, the European nobility developed increasingly lavish private grounds. These often included topiary work (trees and shrubbery clipped in fantastic shapes), aviaries, fishponds, summer houses, water displays, outdoor theaters, hunting grounds and menageries, and facilities for outdoor games. During this period, such famed gardens as the Tuileries and the Luxembourg in Paris, as well as the estate of Versailles, were established by the French royalty; similar gardens and private estates were found all over Europe. Following the early Italian example, it became the custom to open these private parks and gardens to the public—at first occasionally and then as a regular practice.

Popular Diversions in England

Great outdoor gardens were established in England to provide entertainment and relaxation. Vauxhall, a pleasure resort founded during the reign of Charles II, was a densely wooded area with walks and bowers, lighting displays, water mills, fireworks, artificial caves and grottoes, entertainment, eating places, and tea gardens. The park was supported by the growing class of merchants and tradesmen, and its admission charge and distance from London helped to "exclude the rabble."

Following the Restoration period in England, Hyde Park and St. James Park became fashionable centers for promenading by the upper classes during the early afternoon. Varied amusements were provided in the parks: wrestling matches, races, military displays, fireworks, and illuminations on special occasions. Aristocrats, merchants, and tradesmen all rode, drove carriages, and strolled in the parks. Horse racing, lotteries, and other forms of gambling became the vogue.

The English natural park school of thought emphasized using nature as the primary tool of creating a park rather than adding nonnative species of plants to a park.

Among the lower classes, tastes in entertainment varied according to whether one lived in the country or city. Countrymen continued to engage vigorously in such sport as football, cricket, wrestling, or "cudgel playing," and to enjoy traditional country or Morris dancing and the singing of old folk songs.

Concerns About Leisure: Class Differences

Gradually, concerns about the growing number of holidays and the effect of leisure activities on the working classes began to be voiced. In France, for example, in the eighteenth century, wealthy individuals had the opportunity for amusement all week long—paying social visits, dining, and passing evenings at gaming, at the theater, ballet, opera, or clubs. In contrast, the working classes had only Sundays and fête days, or holidays, for their amusements. La Croix points out, however, that these represented a third of the whole year. In addition to those holidays decreed by the state, many other special celebrations had been either authorized or tolerated by the Catholic Church. Many economists and men of affairs argued that the ecclesiastic authorities should be called upon to reduce the number. Voltaire wrote in 1756:

> Twenty fête days too many in the country condemn to inactivity and expose to dissipation twenty times a year ten millions of workingmen, each of whom would earn five pence a day, and this gives a total of 180 million livres . . . lost to the state in the course of a twelve-month. This painful fact is beyond all doubt.[10]

In the larger cities in France, many places of commercial amusement sprang up. Cafés provided meeting places to chat, read newspapers, and play dominoes, chess, checkers, or billiards.

RECREATION IN AMERICA: THE COLONIAL PERIOD

We now cross the Atlantic to examine the development of recreation and leisure in the early American colonies. First, it needs to be recognized that when English and other European settlers came to the New World, they did not entirely divorce themselves from the customs and values of the countries they had left. Commerce was ongoing; governors and military personnel traveled back and forth; and newspapers, magazines, and books were exchanged regularly. Thus, there was a constant interchange of ideas and social trends; one historian has summed it up by saying that an Atlantic civilization existed that embraced both sides of the great ocean. Michael Kraus writes:

> What came from the New World . . . was embedded . . . in the pattern of European life. The revolutions of the sixteenth and seventeenth centuries—political, scientific, religious, and commercial—make for a remarkable fertility of speculation and social reorientation. . . . The era of democratization was thus well begun, and this, truly, was in large measure the creation of the Atlantic civilization.[11]

Despite this linkage, the North American settlements represented a unique and harsh environment for most Europeans who arrived during the period of early colonization. The first need of seventeenth-century colonists was for survival. They had to plant crops, clear forests, build shelters, and in some cases defend themselves against attack by hostile Native American tribes. More than half of the colonists who arrived on the *Mayflower* did not survive the first harsh winter near Plymouth. In such a setting, work was all-important; there was little time, money, or energy to support amusements or public entertainment. Without a nobility possessing the wealth, leisure, and inclination to patronize the arts, there was little opportunity for music, theater, or dance to flourish—but the most important hindrance to the development of recreation was the religious attitude.

Restrictions in New England

The Puritan settlers of New England came to the New World to establish a society based on a strict Calvinist interpretation of the Bible. Although the work ethic had not originated with the Puritans, they adopted it enthusiastically. Idleness was detested as the "devil's workshop," and a number of colonies passed laws binding "any rougs, vagabonds, sturdy beggards, masterless men or other notorious offenders" over to compulsory work or imprisonment.

Puritan magistrates attempted to maintain curbs on amusements long after the practical reasons for such prohibitions had disappeared. Early court records show many cases of young people being fined, confined to the stocks, or publicly whipped for such "violations" as drunkenness, idleness, gambling, dancing, or participating in other forms of "lascivious" behavior. However, despite these restrictions, many forms of play continued. Football was played by boys in Boston's streets and lanes, and although playing cards (the "devil's picture-books") were hated by the Puritans, they were freely imported from England and openly on sale.

Other ordinances banned gambling, drama, and nonreligious music, with dancing—particularly between men and women—also condemned. There was vigorous enforcement of the Sabbath laws: Sunday work, travel, and recreation, even "unnecessary and unseasonable walking in the streets and fields," were prohibited. Merrymaking on religious holidays such as Christmas or Easter was banned.

Leisure in the Southern Colonies

A number of the southern colonies had similar restrictions during the early years of settlement. The laws of Virginia, for example, forbade Sunday amusements and made imprisonment the penalty for failure to attend church services. Sabbath-day dancing, fiddling, hunting, fishing, and card playing were strictly banned. Gradually, however, these stern restrictions declined in the southern colonies. There, the upper classes had both wealth and leisure from their large estates and plantations, on which the labor was performed by indentured servants and slaves. Many of them had ties with the landed gentry in England and shared their tastes for aristocratic amusements. As southern settlers of this social class became established, plantation life for the upper class became marked by lavish entertainment and hospitality.

The lifestyles of slaves in the colonies were a stark contrast to the lavish lifestyles of their owners. The majority of slaves in the colonies were of West African ancestry. They were able to bring nothing with them to the colonies other than language and customs, both of which they were compelled to disregard upon arrival. The customs that thrived in the harsh life of the colonies included music, folktales and storytelling, and dance. Music and dance were an integral piece of the culture of most West African societies. Dance was associated with religious and cultural celebrations, as well as secular recreation. Storytelling was an important instrument for passing history from one generation to the next. In the colonies, and later in the southern

The U.S. Southern economy was built on the labor of slaves—who had little time for recreation—which allowed slave owners to create a life of leisure and luxury.

states, slaves had very few opportunities for leisure. Most worked 14 hours a day or more, six days a week. Free time that was available was highly cherished and spent in the company of fellow slaves. Slave masters used free time as a "reward" to improve morale and often enforced strict rules about what could happen during that free time. Owners were especially interested in assimilating slaves into Western culture and, as a consequence, limited expression of African culture through music and dance and required practice of European customs, including Christian worship.[12]

Decline of Religious Controls

Despite the stern sermons of New England ministers and the severe penalties for infractions of the established moral code, it was clear that play became gradually tolerated in the colonies. The lottery was introduced during the early 1700s and quickly gained the sanction and participation of the most esteemed citizens. Towns and states used lotteries to increase their revenues and to build canals, turnpikes, and bridges. This "acceptable" form of gambling helped to endow leading colleges and academies, and even Congregational, Baptist, and Episcopal churches had lotteries "for promoting public worship and the advancement of religion."

Even in the area of drinking, the climate began to change despite the very strong opposition of the Puritan magistrates in New England. Under Puritan law, drunkards were subject to fines and imprisonment in the stocks, and sellers were forbidden to provide them with any liquor thereafter. A frequent drunkard was punished by having a large *D* made of "Redd Cloth" hung around his neck or sewn on his clothing, and he lost the right to vote. Yet, by the early part of the eighteenth century, taverns were widely established throughout New England, providing places where gentlemen might "enjoy their bowl and bottle with satisfaction" and engage in billiards, cards, skittles, and other games.

Play Attached to Work Gains Acceptance

Gradually, restrictions against play were relaxed in New England and elsewhere. Recreation became more acceptable when amusements could be attached to work, and thus country fairs and market days became occasions for merrymaking. Social gatherings with music, games, and dancing were held in conjunction with such work projects as house raisings, sheep shearing, logrolling, or cornhusking bees. Many social pastimes were linked to other civic occasions such as elections or training days for local militia. On training days in Boston, more than a thousand men would gather on the Boston Common to drill and practice marksmanship, after which they celebrated at nearby taverns.

By the mid-1700s, the stern necessity of hard work for survival had lessened, and religious antagonism toward amusements had also declined. However, the Sunday laws continued in many settlements, and there was still a strong undercurrent of disapproval of play.

Parks and Conservation in the Colonial Era

Compared with the nations of Europe, the early American colonies showed little concern for developing parks in cities and towns. With land so plentiful around the isolated settlements along the eastern seaboard, there seemed to be little need for such planning. The earliest planned outdoor spaces were "commons" or "greens," found in many New England communities and used chiefly for pasturing cattle and sheep but also for military drills, market days, and fairs. Similar open areas were established in towns settled by the Spanish in the South and Southwest, in the form of plazas and large squares in the center of towns or adjacent to principal churches.

Beautiful village greens established during the colonial period still exist throughout Massachusetts, Connecticut, Vermont, and New Hampshire. In the design of new cities, the colonists began to give attention to the need for preserving or establishing parks and open spaces. Among the first cities in which such plans were made were Philadelphia, Savannah, and Washington, D.C.

The Boston Common, often credited as the first community park in the United States because of its 1634 creation, continues to provide opportunities for recreation and park experiences.

Early Conservation Efforts

Almost from the earliest days of settlement, there was concern for the conservation of forests and open land in the New England countryside. As early as 1626 in the Plymouth Colony, the cutting of trees without official consent was prohibited by law. The Massachusetts Bay Colony passed the Great Ponds Act in 1641, which set aside 2000 bodies of water, each more than 10 acres in size, for such public uses as "fishing and fowling." The courts supported this conservation of land for recreational use. Pennsylvania law in 1681 required that for every 5 acres of forest land that were cleared, 1 was to be left untouched. Other laws prohibiting setting woods on fire or cutting certain types of trees were enacted long before the Revolution.

As early as the late seventeenth century, Massachusetts and Connecticut defined hunting seasons and established rules for hunting certain types of game. Although originally a means of obtaining food, hunting rapidly became a sport in the colonies. What appeared to be an inexhaustible supply of wildlife began to disappear with the advance of settlements and the destruction of the forests. Wildfowl in particular were ruthlessly hunted, especially in New England, and so unlicensed had the destruction of the heath hen become in New York that in 1708 the province determined to protect its game by providing for a closed season. Thus, before the Revolution, the colonists had shown a concern for the establishment of parks and urban open spaces and for the conservation of forests and wildlife.

NINETEENTH-CENTURY CHANGES: IMPACT OF THE INDUSTRIAL REVOLUTION

During the nineteenth century, great changes took place in both Europe and the United States. It was a time of growing democratization, advancement of scientific knowledge and technology, and huge waves of immigration from Europe to the New World. More than any other factor, the Industrial Revolution changed the way people lived, and it also had a major effect on popular patterns of recreation and leisure. By the early decades of the twentieth century, leisure was more freely available to all, and a widespread recreation movement had begun in the United States.

The Industrial Revolution extended from the late eighteenth through the twentieth century. Science and capital combined to increase production, as businessmen invested in the industrial expansion made possible by newly invented machines. Industry moved from homes and small workshops to new mills and factories with mechanical power. The invention of such devices as the spinning jenny, the water frame, the weaving machine, and the steam engine (all during the 1760s) drastically altered production methods and increased output.

Urbanization

Throughout the Western world, there was a steady shift of the population from rural areas to urban centers. Because factory wages were usually higher than those in domestic industry or agriculture, great numbers of people moved from rural areas to the cities to work. Millions of European peasant families immigrated because of crop failures, expulsion from their land, religious or social discrimination, or political unrest. During the latter part of the nineteenth century, tens of thousands of African Americans, disillusioned by the failed reconstruction, emigrated to northern cities in search of a better quality of life.

The American population increased rapidly during this period. When Andrew Jackson became president in 1829, about 12.5 million people lived in the United States. By 1850 the total had reached 23 million, and a decade later America's population was 31 million. In the large cities, the proportion of foreign-born inhabitants was quite high: 45% of New York City's population in 1850 was foreign born, mostly Irish and German. About 85% of the population in 1850 was still rural, living in areas with populations of less than 2500. However, as more and more people moved into factory towns and large cities along the eastern seaboard or around the Great Lakes, the United States became an urban civilization.

Rural townspeople and foreign immigrants moved into the congested tenement areas of growing cities, living in quarters that were inadequate for decent family life. Often a family lived crowded in a single room under unsanitary and unsafe conditions. The new urban slums were marked by congestion and disease. Their residents were oppressed by low wages and recurrent unemployment and by monotonous and prolonged labor, including the use of young children in mills, mines, and factories and at piecework tasks at home.

Reduction in Work Hours

Throughout this period, there was steady pressure to reduce the workweek, both through industry-labor negotiation and legislation. Benjamin Hunnicutt points out that the effort to obtain shorter work hours was a critical issue in reform politics in the United States throughout the nineteenth century and up until the period of the Great Depression:

> It was an issue for the idealistic antebellum [pre–Civil War] reformers. It had a prominent place in the Populists' Omaha platform and the Bull Moose platform, and appeared in both the Democratic and Republican platforms as late as 1932.[13]

The eight-hour day had been a union objective for many years in the United States, paralleling efforts to reduce the workweek in other countries. In 1868, Congress established the eight-hour day by law for mechanics and laborers employed by or under contracts with the federal government. Following the 1868 law, labor unions made a concerted effort to obtain the eight-hour day in other areas, and in 1890 began to achieve success.

The Changing Workweek

Overall, the average workweek declined from 69.7 hours per week for all industries (including agriculture) in 1860 to 61.7 hours in 1890, and to 54.9 hours in 1910. (See **Figure 3.1**.) As a consequence, during the last half of the nineteenth century, concerns about increases in free time began to appear—including fears about the dangers of certain forms of play and the broader question of what the potential role of leisure might be in the coming century.

Religious Revivalism and Recreation

Fueled by a religious revival before the Civil War, there was a strong emphasis on the importance of "honest toil," during the middle and latter parts of the nineteenth century. Many Americans believed, and continue to believe, that hard work alone is sufficient for an individual to improve his or her social and economic status. Clergy, policymakers, civic leaders, and scholars were particularly concerned that new immigrants and the urban poor develop appropriate social values through hard work and appropriate, disciplined use of leisure time.

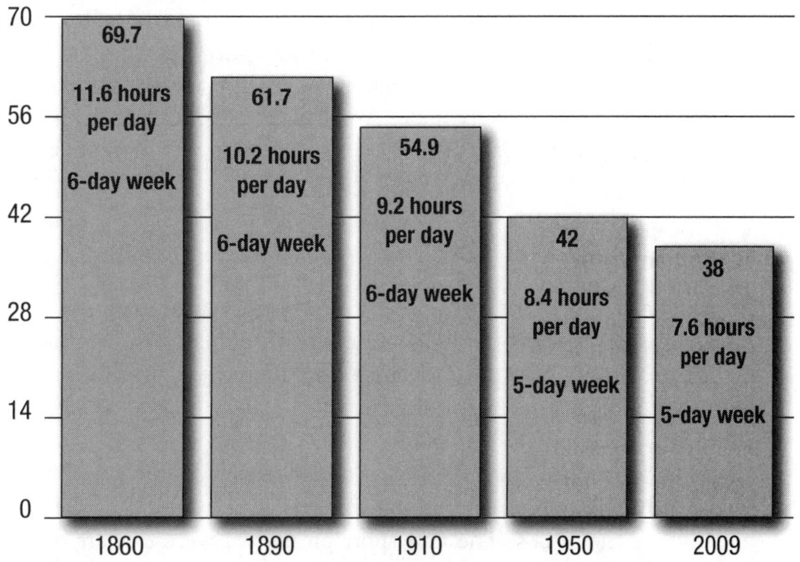

FIGURE 3.1 How the Average Workweek Has Changed (in hours)
Data from the Bureau of Labor Statistics. 2009. Available at: http://www.bls.gov. Accessed November 10, 2010.

Churches Attack Leisure

Work was considered the source of social and moral values, and therefore the proper concern of churches, which renewed their attack upon most forms of play. The churches condemned many commercial amusements as "the door to all the sins of iniquity." As late as 1844, Henry Ward Beecher, a leading minister, savagely attacked the stage, the concert hall, and the circus, charging that anyone who pandered to the public taste for commercial entertainment was a moral assassin.

GROWTH OF POPULAR PARTICIPATION IN AMERICA

Despite such antiamusement efforts, the first half of the nineteenth century saw a gradual expansion of popular amusements in the United States. The theater, which had been banned during the American Revolution, gradually gained popularity in cities along the eastern seaboard and in the South. Large theaters were built to accommodate audiences of as many as 4000 people. Performances were usually by touring players who joined local stock companies throughout the country in presenting serious drama as well as lighthearted entertainment, which later became burlesque and vaudeville. By the 1830s, about 30 traveling shows were regularly touring the country with menageries and bands of acrobats and jugglers. Ultimately, the latter added riding and tumbling acts and developed into circuses.

Drinking also remained a popular pastime. At this time, the majority of American men were taverngoers. Printed street directories of American cities listed tavern keepers in staggering numbers. J. Larkin writes that as the nation's most popular centers of male sociability,

> taverns were often the scene of excited gaming and vicious fights and always of hard drinking, heavy smoking, and an enormous amount of alcohol-stimulated talk. . . . Taverns accommodated women as travelers, but their barroom clienteles were almost exclusively male. Apart from the dockside dives frequented by prostitutes, or the liquor-selling groceries of poor city neighborhoods, women rarely drank in public.[14]

Growing Interest in Sport

A number of sport gained their first strong impetus during the early nineteenth century. Americans enjoyed watching amateur wrestling matches, foot races, shooting events, and horse races during colonial days and along the frontier. In the early 1800s, professional promotion of sport events began as well.

Professionalism in Sport Crowds as large as 50,000 drawn from all ranks of society attended highly publicized boating regattas, and 5- and 10-mile races of professional runners during the 1820s. The first sport promoters were owners of resorts or of commercial transportation facilities such as stagecoach lines, ferries, and, later, trolleys and railroads. These new sport impresarios initially made their profits from transportation fares and accommodations for spectators; later, they erected grandstands and charged admission.

Sailing regattas were a popular form of recreation and as a popular spectator sport in the early 1800s.

Horse racing flourished; both running and trotting races attracted crowds as large as 100,000 spectators. Prize fighting also gained popularity as a professional contest. It began as a brutal, bare-knuckled sport that was often prohibited by legal authorities; by the time of the Civil War, however, gloves were used and rules established, and boxing exhibitions were becoming accepted. Baseball was enjoyed as a casual diversion in the towns of New England through the early decades of the nineteenth century (in the form of "rounders" or "townball"), and amateur teams, often organized by occupation (merchants and clerks or shipwrights and mechanics), were playing on the commons of large eastern cities by the mid-1850s.

Social Class Impacts Sport

Social class differences had a strong influence on sport involvement and attendance. George Will points out that professional baseball initially appealed to the brawling urban working classes:

> The sport was so tangled up with gambling and drinking that its first task was to attract a better class of fans. This it did by raising ticket prices, banning beer, not playing on Sundays, and giving free tickets to the clergy. Most important, baseball replaced wooden ball parks with permanent structures of concrete and steel [with impressive lobbies and other architectural features].[15]

CHANGING ATTITUDES TOWARD PLAY

During the last half of the nineteenth century, the Industrial Revolution was flourishing, with factories, expansion of urban areas, and railroads criss-crossing the country. Free public education had become a reality in most regions of the country, and health care and life expectancy were improving. As the industrial labor force began to organize into craft unions, working conditions improved, levels of pay increased, and the hours of work were cut back. Children, who had worked long, hard hours in factories, mines, and big-city sweatshops, were freed of this burden through child labor legislation.

Gradually, the climate grew more receptive toward play and leisure. Although the work ethic was still widely accepted and there was almost no public provision for recreation, leisure was about to expand sharply. The strong disapproval of play that had characterized the colonial period began to disappear.

By the 1880s and 1890s, church leaders recognized that religion could no longer arbitrarily condemn all play and offered "sanctified amusement and recreation" as alternatives to undesirable play. Many churches made provisions for libraries, gymnasiums, and assembly rooms.

The growth of popular amusements, such as music, vaudeville, theater, and dance, that characterized the first half of the century became even more pronounced. Popular hobbies such as photography caught on and were frequently linked to new outdoor recreation pursuits. Sport was probably the largest single area of expanded leisure participation, with increasing interest being shown in tennis, archery, bowling, skating, bicycling, and team games such as baseball, basketball, and football.

Rise of Sport

As the country neared the end of the nineteenth century, a series of athletic crazes swept through the eastern states.

> Baseball developed from its humble beginnings in the days before the Civil War to its recognized status as America's national game. The rapid spread of croquet caused the startled editors of *The Nation* to describe it as "the swiftest and most infectious epidemic the country had ever experienced. Lawn tennis was introduced to polite society by enthusiasts,"and "archery was revived as still another fashionable lawn game. Roller-skating attained a popularity which extended to all parts of the country."[16]

Athletic and outdoor pastimes steadily became more socially acceptable. Skating became a vogue in the 1850s, and rowing and sailing also grew popular, especially for the upper social classes. The Muscular Christianity movement—so named because of the support given to it by leading church figures and because sport and physical activity were thought to build morality and good character—had its greatest influence in schools and colleges, which began to initiate programs of physical education and athletic competition. In addition, the newly founded Young Men's Christian Association (YMCA) based its program on active physical recreation.

College Sport

In the United States, colleges initiated their first competitive sports programs. In colonial New England, youthful students had engaged in many pastimes, with some tolerated by college authorities and others prohibited. The first college clubs had been founded as early as 1717, and social clubs were in full swing by the 1780s and 1790s. By the early nineteenth century, most U.S. colleges had more or less officially recognized clubs and their social activities. The founding of social fraternities in the 1840s and the building of college gymnasiums in the 1860s added to the social life and physical recreation of students.

Intercollegiate sport competition in rowing, baseball, track, and football was organized. The first known intercollegiate football game was between Princeton and Rutgers in 1869; interest spread rapidly, and by the late 1880s college football games were attracting as many as 40,000 spectators.

Amateur Sport

Track and field events were widely promoted by amateur athletic clubs, some of which, like the New York Athletic Club, had many influential members who formed the Amateur Athletic Union and developed rules to govern amateur sport competition. Gymnastic instruction and games were sponsored by the German *turnvereins*, the Czech *sokols*, and the YMCA, which had established some 260 large gymnasiums around the country by the 1880s and was a leader in sport activities.

Other Activities

Other popular pastimes included croquet, archery, lawn tennis, and roller-skating, which became so popular that skating rinks were built to accommodate thousands of skaters and spectators. Women began to participate in recreational pastimes, enjoying gymnastics, dance, and other athletics in school and college physical education programs. Bicycling was introduced in the 1870s, and within a few years hundreds of thousands of people had become enthusiasts. During the last decades of the nineteenth century, there was a growing vogue for outdoor activities. Americans began to enjoy hiking and mountain climbing, fishing and hunting, camping in national forests and state parks, and nature photography.

During the late 1800s, a number of economic factors also combined to promote sport interest. With rising wages and a shorter workweek, many workers began to take part in organized sport on newly developed sports fields in city parks. Cheap train service carried players and fans to games, and newspapers publicized major sporting events to build circulation.

GROWTH OF COMMERCIAL AMUSEMENTS

Particularly in larger cities, new forms of commercial amusement sprang up or expanded during the nineteenth century. The theater, in its various forms, was more popular than ever. Dime museums, dance halls, shooting galleries, bowling alleys, billiard parlors, beer gardens, and saloons provided a new world of entertainment for pay. In addition to these, many cities had "red light districts" where houses of prostitution flourished. Drinking, gambling, and commercial vice gradually became serious social problems, particularly when protected by a tacit alliance between criminal figures and big-city political machines.

Amusement parks grew on the outskirts of cities and towns, often established by new rapid transit companies offering reduced-fare rides to the parks in gaily decorated trolley cars. Amusement parks featured such varied attractions as parachute jumps, open-air theaters, band concerts, professional bicycle races, freak shows, games of chance, and shooting galleries. Roller coasters, fun houses, and midget-car tracks also became popular.

Concerns About Leisure

Intellectual and political leaders raised searching questions about the growing amusement industry. The English author Lord Lytton commented, "The social civilization of a people is always and infallibly indicated by the intellectual character of its amusements." In 1876, Horace Greeley, a leading American journalist, observed that although there were teachers for every art, science, and "elegy," there were no "professors of play." He asked, "Who will teach us incessant workers how to achieve leisure and enjoy it?" And, in 1880, President

Amusement Parks

Wideopenness was how a *New York Times* 1899 editorial headlined the presence of "public amusements" in the city. "The world of 'public' amusements, was in its 'publicity,' its accessibility, its 'wide-openness,' a world like no other, situated in a magical corner of the city, where the city's peoples came together to have a good time in public."[17] New York City was but a single example of the new craze for excitement and freedom in leisure. A host of amusement parks sprang up close to many large and middle-sized cities. These public amusements encompassed a wide range of popular attractions, including bathing facilities, band pavilions, dance halls, vaudeville theaters, sideshows, circus attractions, freak displays, food and drink counters, and daredevil rides of every imaginable description.

James Garfield declared in a speech at Lake Chautauqua, "We may divide the whole struggle of the human race into two chapters: first, the fight to get leisure; and then the second fight of civilization—what shall we do with our leisure when we get it."

This new concern was an inevitable consequence of the Industrial Revolution. Americans now lived in greater numbers in large cities, where the traditional social activities of the past and the opportunity for casual play were no longer available.

THE BEGINNING RECREATION MOVEMENT

The period extending from the mid-nineteenth through the early twentieth century is referred to by recreation scholars as the *public recreation movement*. The period was characterized by the widespread development of organized recreation activities and facilities by government and voluntary agencies with the intent of achieving desirable social outcomes. There were four major streams of development during the public recreation movement: the adult education movement; the development of national, state, and municipal parks; the establishment of voluntary organizations; and the playground movement.

The Adult Education Movement

During the early nineteenth century, there was considerable civic concern for improving intellectual cultivation and providing continuing education for adults. Again, this was found in other nations as well; in France, workers' societies were determined to gain shorter workdays and more leisure time for adult study and cultural activities, and they pressed vigorously for the development of popular lectures, adult education courses, and municipal libraries.

In the United States, there was a growing conviction that leisure, properly used, could contribute to the idealistic liberal values that were part of the American intellectual heritage. As early as the founding of the republic, such leaders as Thomas Jefferson and John Adams envisioned the growth of a rich democratic culture. Adams wrote of his children's and America's future as follows:

> I must study Politicks and War that my sons may have liberty to study Mathematicks and Philosophy. My sons ought to study Mathematicks and Philosophy, Geography,

> Natural History, Naval Architecture, Navigation, Commerce and Agriculture, in order to give their Children a right to study Painting, Poetry, Musick, Architecture, Statuary, Tapestry and Porcelaine.[18]

One of the means of achieving this dream took the form of the Lyceum movement, a national organization with more than 900 local chapters. Its program consisted chiefly of lectures, readings, and other educational events, reflecting the view that all citizens should be educated to participate knowledgeably in affairs of government.

The Lyceum movement was widely promoted by such organizations as Chautauqua, which sponsored both a lecture circuit and a leading summer camp program in upstate New York for adults and families, with varied cultural activities, sport, lectures, and other educational features. Whereas the professed purpose of Chautauqua was education, it actually provided substantial entertainment and amusement to its audiences as well. By the twentieth century, circuit Chautauquas were formed, in a fusion of the Lyceum movement and independent Chautauquas, to provide educational programs, culture, and entertainment.

A closely related development was the expansion of reading as a recreational experience, which was furthered by the widespread growth of free public libraries. This development was linked to the adoption of compulsory universal education and to the increasing need for better-educated workers in the nation's industrial system. As an example of the growing interest in cultural activity, the arts and crafts movement found its largest following in the United States in the beginning of the twentieth century. Between 1896 and 1915, thousands of organized groups were established throughout the country to bring artists and patrons together, sponsor exhibits and publications, and promote the teaching of art in the schools.

The Development of National, State, and Municipal Parks

Concern for preservation of the natural heritage of the United States in an era of increasing industrialization and despoilment of natural resources began in the nineteenth century. The first conservation action was in 1864, when Congress set aside an extensive area of wilderness primarily for public recreational use, consisting of the Yosemite Valley and the Mariposa Grove of Big Trees in California. This later became a national park. The first designated national park was Yellowstone, founded in 1872. In 1892, the Sierra Club was founded by John Muir, a leading Scottish-born conservationist who, along with Theodore Roosevelt, encouraged national interest in the outdoors and ultimately the establishment of the National Park Service.

Old Faithful and the geysers of Yellowstone have made this first national park a popular destination since 1872.

All such developments did not lend themselves immediately to an emphasis on recreation. The primary purpose of the national parks at the outset was to preserve the nation's natural heritage and wildlife. This contrasted sharply with the Canadian approach to wilderness, which saw it as primitive and untamed.

John Muir

In 1901, John Muir wrote a book titled *Our National Parks* to make the general public more aware of the beauty and diversity of the existing parks. Writing about the national parks as a whole, and Yellowstone National Park in particular, Muir said the following:

> "The National Parks are not only withdrawn from sale and entry like the forest reservations but are efficiently managed and guarded by small troops in United States Calvary, directed by the Secretary of the Interior. Under this care, the forests are flourishing, protected from both action fire; and so, of course, are the shaggy beds of underbrush and herbaceous vegetation. The so-called curiosities also are preserved, and furred and feathered tribes, many of which in danger of extinction a short time ago, are now increasing in numbers—a refreshing thing to see amid the blind, ruthless destruction that is going on in the adjacent regions. In pleasing contrast to the noisy, ever-changing management, or mismanagement, of blundering, plundering, money-making vote-sellers who receive their places from boss politicians as purchased goods, the soldiers do their duty so quietly that the traveler is scarce aware of their presence."[19]

Parks, as in Great Britain and Europe, were seen as landscaped gardens, and intensive development for recreation and tourism guided early Canadian policy. Indeed, Banff National Park was initially a health spa, and early provincial parks were designed to be health resorts.[20]

State Parks As federal park development gained momentum in the United States, state governments also became concerned with the preservation of their forest areas and wildlife. As early as 1867, Michigan and Wisconsin established fact-finding committees to explore the problem of forest conservation; their example was followed shortly by Maine and other eastern states. Within two decades, several states had established forestry commissions. Between 1864 and 1900, the first state parks were established, as were a number of state forest preserves and historic parks.

Municipal Parks Until the nineteenth century, North America lagged far behind Europe in the development of municipal parks, partly because this continent had no aristocracy with large cultivated estates, hunting grounds, and elaborate gardens that could be turned over to the public. The first major park to be developed in an American city was Central Park in New York; its design and the philosophy on which it was based strongly influenced other large cities during the latter half of the nineteenth century.

There long had been a need for open space in New York City. During the first 30 years of the nineteenth century, plans were made for several open squares to total about 450 acres, but these were not carried out completely. By the early 1850s, the entire amount of public open space in Manhattan totaled only 117 acres. Pressure mounted among the citizens of the city for a major park that would provide relief from stone and concrete. The poet William Cullen Bryant wrote:

> Commerce is devouring inch by inch the coast of the island, and if we would rescue any part of it for health and recreation it must be done now. All large cities have their extensive public grounds and gardens, Madrid and Mexico [City] their Alamedas, London its Regent's Park, Paris its Champs Elysées, and Vienna its Prater.[21]

When the public will could no longer be denied, legislation was passed in 1856 to establish a park in New York City. Construction of the 843-acre site began in 1857. Central Park, designed by landscape architects Frederick Law Olmsted and Calvert Vaux, was completely man-made: "Every foot of the park's surface, every tree and bush, as well as every arch, roadway and walk has been fixed where it is with a purpose." The dominant need was to provide, within the densely populated heart of an immense metropolis, "refreshment of the mind and the nerves" for citydwellers through the provision of greenery and scenic vistas. The park was to be heavily wooded and to have the appearance of rural scenery, with roadways screened from the eyes of park users wherever possible. Recreational pursuits permitted in the park included walking, pleasure driving, ice skating in the winter, and boating—but not organized or structured sport. It also was designed to provide needed social controls to prevent misuse of the park environment or destructive behavior by the "lower" classes.

Central Park was America's first large urban park and was the prototype for other large city parks across the nation for the next 50 years.

CASE STUDY: Types and Uses of Urban Parks, 1850–1965

Early urban parks in the United States were places seen as an antidote to the problems of cities, which were perceived as dangerous, dirty, and unhealthy places. Parks formed an important component of the urban environment, and cities embraced them. Those same parks today provide a type of precursor to the emerging sustainable park of the twenty-first century. Cranz and Boland define three periods of park development beginning in 1850 and continuing through 1965. The three periods include the following:

- Pleasure ground (1850–1900)
- Reform park (1900–1930)
- Recreation facility (1930–1965)

Each of the park types is described in terms of social goal, activities, size, relation to city, elements, promoters, and beneficiaries.

The importance of understanding the different park movements from 1850 to the mid-1960s is to gain a greater appreciation of how citizens, politicians, and social and environmental movements affected park design and use. The first wave saw the large urban parks created all across the country, including such places as Central Park in New York City, Golden Gate Park in San Francisco, and Grant Park in Chicago. These large urban parks became major components of large urban areas, most becoming the core of larger and more diverse park and recreation systems.

The three park systems described in **Table 3.1** show how the movements shifted as did the population. In most cases, the park movement followed, rather than led, public needs and desires. As social reform advanced, the pleasure ground gave way to a more active and focused reform park, many of which still boast the same services and benefits today, although they have been changed several times. The recreation facility, a continuing popular model, was an expression of efforts to move from the city core to the suburbs.

Questions to Consider

1. Discuss how the three park movements mirrored society in the United States.
2. What were the actual benefits to the beneficiaries of the different types of parks?
3. How many of these types of parks have you visited? How have they changed?

TABLE 3.1

TYPOLOGY OF URBAN PARKS, 1850–1965

	Pleasure Ground (1850–1900)	Reform Park (1900–1930)	Recreation Facility (1930–1965)
Social goal	Public health and social reform	Social reform, children's play, assimilation	Recreation service
Activities	Strolling, carriage racking, bike riding, picnics, rowing, classical music, nondidactic education	Supervised play, gymnastics, crafts, Americanization classes, dancing, plays, and pageants	Active recreation, basketball, tennis, team sports, spectator sports, swimming
Size	Very large, 1000+ acres	Small, city blocks	Small to medium, follow formula
Relation to city	Set in contrast	Accepts urban patterns	Suburban
Elements	Woodlands and meadow, curving paths, placid water bodies, rustic structures, limited floral displays	Sandlots, playgrounds, rectilinear paths, swimming pools, fieldhouses	Asphalt or grass play area, pools, rectilinear paths, standard play equipment
Promoters	Health reformers, transcendentalists, real estate interests	Social reformers, social workers, recreation workers	Politicians, bureaucrats, planners
Beneficiaries	All citydwellers (intended), upper-middle class (reality)	Children, immigrants, working class	Suburban families

Adapted from Galen Cranz and Michael Boland. "Defining the Sustainable Park: A Fifth Model for Urban Parks." *Landscape Journal*, (Vol. 23, No. 2, 2004): 102–140.

County Park Systems Planning for what was to become the nation's first county park system began in Essex County, New Jersey. Bordering the crowded industrial city of Newark, it was outlined in a comprehensive proposal in 1894 that promised that the entire cost of the park project would be realized through tax revenues from increased property values. Set in motion in the following year, the Essex County park system proved to be a great success and set a model to be followed by hundreds of other county and special district park agencies throughout the United States in the early 1900s.

CASE STUDY: The YMCA as the Prototype of the Social Movement of the Late 1800s

The Young Men's Christian Association was founded in London, England, in 1844 and migrated to the United States in 1851. George Williams was the founder of the YMCA, working with friends to find a way to get people off of London's streets. "The YMCA idea, which began among evangelicals, was unusual because it crossed the rigid lines that separated all the different churches and social classes in England in those days. This openness was a trait that would lead eventually to including in YMCAs all men, women and children, regardless of race, religion or nationality. Also, its target of meeting social need in the community was dear from the start."[a]

> The movement grew rapidly. Within several years, YMCAs were started in Boston and other American cities. Initially, only those converted to evangelical churches could become members. Soon, however, young men were allowed to join even if not converted, although the management of the association was reserved to members of evangelical churches. . . .
>
> Although the causes of the association's expansion are not clear, certain factors stand out. First, the definite Christian orientation of the movement tied it into the religious revivals of the time. The YMCA participated in organizing tent revivals as well as sponsoring prayer meetings, Bible readings, and lecture series. Thus the YMCA movement had definite goals and programs that focused its members' energies. Second, the movement spread by a diffusion process based on local enthusiasm rather than by a process of centralized direction and allocation of personnel. Visitors to the London YMCA or to the early YMCA in Boston became enthusiastic about the idea and took it back to their own communities. This method of expansion depended on strong local support, ensuring a continuing base in each community. Finally, each local YMCA usually had a reading room, a list of job openings, a coffee shop, and a list of wholesome boarding homes. These gave the association a material base in the community and also allowed it to minister to some of the basic needs of the young, single male."[b]

It became obvious to the leaders that if the YMCA was going to grow and serve a broader population it needed to adapt, so "the basic goal of the organization changed from evangelism to the broader and more secularized one of developing the 'whole man'; membership criteria were successively broadened to include all religions, ages, and both sexes; and control was extended to followers of any religion." Also, "program emphasis shifted away from the overtly religious to the development of the mental, physical, and social capacities of members. The inclusion of activities for physical training created more conflict than did programs for mental or intellectual development, because it challenged conservative religious views of the proper forms of recreation."[c]

One of the other factors that has made the YMCA successful was efforts to avoid politics. YMCA services have focused on prevention rather than rehabilitation. The YMCA "has generally implemented its goals by serving clientele rather than by attempting to change the environment."[d]

Questions to Consider

1. Explain the importance of the YMCA changing from an evangelical type of organization to a social organization.
2. It is suggested that the YMCAs grew "by a diffusion process based on local enthusiasm." Discuss how this is similar to movements created via social networks today. How do you think this diffusion process occurred in the late nineteenth century?
3. Discuss the differences between a preventive- and rehabilitative-focused organization.

Sources

a. YMCA, "About Us." Available at: http://www.ymca.net/about_the_ymca/history_of_the_ymca.html.
b. M. N. Zald and P. Denton, "From Evangelism to General Service: The Transformation of the YMCA." *Administrative Science Quarterly,* (Vol. 8, No. 2, 1963):216.
c. Ibid., 217–218.
d. Ibid., 221.

Establishment of Voluntary Organizations

During the nineteenth century, a number of voluntary (privately sponsored, nonprofit) organizations were founded that played an important role in providing recreation services, chiefly for children and youth. In many cases, voluntary organizations were the outgrowth of their founders' desires to put religious principles into action through direct service to the unprivileged. The widespread establishment of voluntary organizations in the nineteenth and early twentieth centuries should be viewed as both a religious and a social movement. One such body was the Young Men's Christian Association, founded in Boston in 1851 and followed by the Young Women's Christian Association (YWCA) 15 years later. At first, the Y's provided fellowship between youth and adults for religious purposes. They gradually enlarged their programs, however, to include gymnastics, sport, and other recreational and social activities.

Another type of voluntary agency that offered significant leisure programs was the settlement house—neighborhood centers established in the slum sections of the East and Midwest. Among the first were University Settlement, founded in New York City in 1886, and Hull House, founded in Chicago in 1889. Their staffs sought to help poor people, particularly immigrants, adjust to modern urban life by providing services concerned with education, family life, and community improvement.

The Playground Movement

To understand the need for playgrounds in cities and towns, it is necessary to know the living conditions of poor people during the latter decades of the nineteenth century.

The wave of urbanization that had begun earlier now reached its peak. The urban population more than doubled—from 14 to 30 million—between 1880 and 1900 alone. By the century's end, there were 28 cities with more than 100,000 residents because of the recent waves of migration. A leading example was New York, where nearly five of every six of the city's 1.5 million residents lived in tenements in 1891. Social reformers of the period described these buildings as crowded, with dark hallways, filthy cellars, and inadequate cooking and bathroom facilities. In neighborhoods populated by poor immigrants, there was a tremendous amount of crime, gambling, gang violence, and prostitution.

Boston Sand Garden: A Beginning Within poor working-class neighborhoods, there were few safe places where children might play. The first such facility—and the one that is generally regarded as a landmark in the development of the recreation movement in the United States—was the Boston Sand Garden. The city of Boston has been the arena for many important developments in the park and recreation movement in the United States. The Boston Common, established in 1634, generally is regarded as the first municipal park; a 48-acre area of green, rolling hills and shade trees, it is located in the heart of the city. Boston was also the site of the first public garden with the establishment of an outstanding botanic garden in 1838.

The famous Boston Sand Garden was the first playground in the country designed specifically for children. A group of public-spirited citizens had a pile of sand placed behind the Parmenter Street Chapel in a working-class district. Young children in the neighborhood came to play in the sand with wooden shovels. Supervision was voluntary at first, but by 1887 when 10 such centers were opened, women were employed to supervise the children. Two years later, the city of Boston began to contribute funds to support the sand gardens. So it was that citizens, on a voluntary basis, began to provide play opportunities for young children.

New York's First Playgrounds In the nation's largest city, Walter Vrooman, founder of the New York Society for Parks and Playgrounds, directed the public's attention to the fact that in 1890 there were 350,000 children without a single public playground of their own. Although the city now had almost 6000 acres of parkland, none of this land was set aside specifically for children. Civic leaders pointed out that children of working parents lacked supervision and were permitted to grow up subject to various temptations. Vrooman wrote that such children

> are driven from their crowded homes in the morning . . . are chased from the streets by the police when they attempt to play, and beaten with the broom handle of the janitor's wife when found in the hallway, or on the stairs. No wonder they learn to chew and smoke tobacco before they can read, and take a fiendish delight in breaking windows, in petty thievery, and in gambling their pennies.[22]

Gradually, the pressure mounted. Two small model playgrounds were established in poor areas of the city in 1889 and 1891 by the newly formed New York Society for Parks and Playgrounds, with support from private donors. Gradually, the city assumed financial and legal responsibility as many additional playgrounds were built in the years that followed, often attached to schools.

The period between 1880 and 1900 was of critical importance to the development of urban recreation and park programs. More than 80 cities initiated park systems; a lesser number established sand gardens, and, shortly after, playgrounds. Illinois passed a law permitting the establishment of local park districts in which two or more municipalities might join together to operate park systems.

EFFECTS OF RACIAL AND ETHNIC DISCRIMINATION

Throughout this period, public and nonprofit youth-serving organizations often discriminated against members of racial or ethnic minorities. As late as the 1930s and 1940s, prejudice against those perceived as lower-class "undesirables" or those from less-favored

European nations was evidenced in many organizations. Such practices reflected widespread attitudes of snobbery, as well as the nativist political agitation of the nineteenth century that opposed the flow of immigration from Europe, preached hatred against Catholics and Jews, and barred citizens of color from mainstream American life.

Prejudice Against Minorities

Generally, the most severe discrimination was leveled against African Americans, who, though no longer slaves, were kept in a position of economic servitude through the practice of sharecropping and were without civil, political, or judicial rights in the southern and border states. However, there was an extreme degree of prejudice against Mexican Americans and other Hispanics of mixed racial origins. For example, Anglo settlers in Texas regarded Mexicans as savage "heathens" who historically practiced human sacrifice and saw them as a decadent and inferior people. Most prejudice was expressed in racial terms.

A popular journal, the *Southern Review,* expressed the dominant feeling of many white Americans at this time with respect to *mongrelism*, the term often applied to mixing among different racial groups. In time, intermarriage between whites and blacks or Native Americans was defined as *miscegenation* and forbidden by law throughout much of the country.

There was also widespread prejudice expressed against Asian Americans, mostly Chinese nationals who began to arrive in California in the mid-1800s and who worked on the transcontinental railroad. As the number of Asians grew, so did xenophobia. Americans viewed them as heathens who could not readily be assimilated within the nation's essentially Anglo-Saxon framework and condemned them as unsanitary, immoral, and criminal. Based on such prejudice, Chinese were often the victims of mob violence, particularly at times of national depression, and were barred from entry into the United States by the Oriental Exclusion Acts of 1882 and 1902.

Similar views were frequently expressed against Americans of African origin, who were increasingly barred from social contact, economic opportunity, or recreational involvement with whites by a wave of state legislation and local ordinances in the late nineteenth and early twentieth centuries.

RECREATION AND PARKS: EARLY TWENTIETH CENTURY

For the majority of Americans, however, the beginning of the twentieth century was an exciting period marked by growing economic and recreational opportunity. By 1900, 14 cities had made provisions for supervised play facilities. Among the leading cities were Boston, Providence, Philadelphia, Pittsburgh, Baltimore, Chicago, Milwaukee, Cleveland, Denver, and Minneapolis.

At the same time, municipal parks became well established throughout the United States. In addition to the urban parks mentioned earlier, the first metropolitan park system was established by Boston in 1892. In the West, San Francisco and Sacramento in California as well as Salt Lake City, Utah, were among the first to incorporate large open spaces in town planning before 1900. The New England Association of Park Superintendents, the predecessor of the American Institute of Park Executives, was established in 1898 to bring together park superintendents and promote their professional concerns.

Growth of Public Recreation and Park Agencies

Gradually, the concept that city governments should provide recreation facilities, programs, and services became widely accepted. By 1906, 41 cities were sponsoring public recreation programs, and by 1920, the number was 465. More and more states passed laws authorizing local governments to operate recreation programs, and between 1925 and 1935 the number of municipal recreation buildings quadrupled.

Playgrounds became more popular in the early decades of the 20th century in large urban areas.

Municipalities were also discovering new ways to add parks. Many acquired areas outside their city limits, while others required that new real estate subdivision plans include the dedication of space for recreation. Some cities acquired major park properties through gifts. The pattern that began to develop was one of placing a network of small, intensively used playgrounds throughout the cities, particularly in neighborhoods of working-class families, and placing larger parks in outlying areas.

Federal Park Expansion

As president, Theodore Roosevelt, a dedicated outdoorsman, encouraged the acquisition of numerous new areas for the federal park system, including many new forest preserves, historic and scientific sites, and wildlife refuges. Thanks in part to his assistance and support, the Reclamation Act of 1902, which authorized reservoir-building irrigation systems in the West, was passed, along with the Antiquities Act of 1906, which designated the first national monuments. Establishment of the U.S. Forest Service in 1905 and of the National Park Service 11 years later helped place many of the scattered forests, parks, and other sites under more clearly defined policies for acquisition, development, and use. (See **Figure 3.2**.)

EMERGENCE OF THE RECREATION MOVEMENT: THREE PIONEERS

As the recreation field developed during the first three decades of the twentieth century, several men and women emerged as influential advocates of play and recreation. Three of the most effective were Joseph Lee, Luther Halsey Gulick, and Jane Addams.

Joseph Lee

Regarded as the "father" of the playground movement, Joseph Lee was a lawyer and philanthropist who came from a wealthy New England family. Born in 1862, he took part in a survey of play opportunities conducted by the Family Welfare Society of Boston in 1882. Shocked to see boys arrested for playing in the streets, he organized a playground for them in

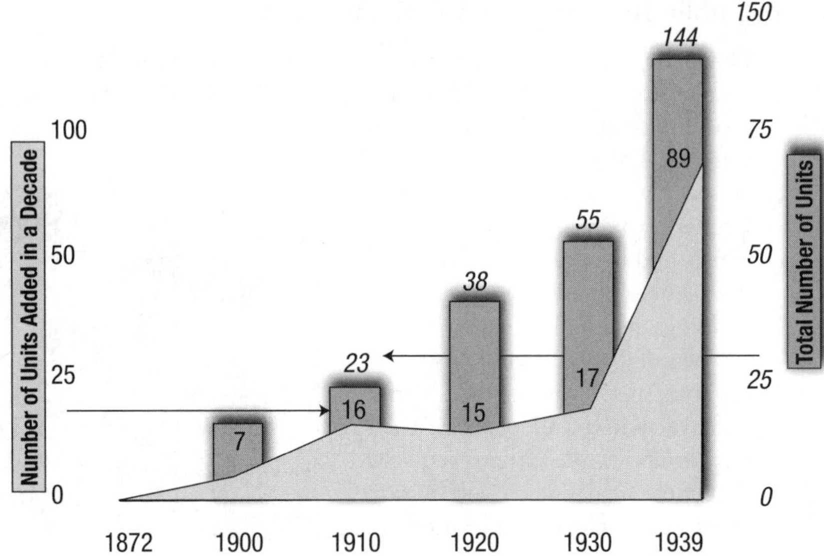

FIGURE 3.2 Growth of the National Park System 1900–1939
Data from National Park System. "National Park System Areas Listed in Chronological Order of Date Authorized Under DOI." Available at: http://www.nps.gov/applications/budget2/documents.chronop.pdf. Accessed October 7, 2010.

an open lot, which he helped supervise. In 1898, Lee helped create a model playground on Columbus Avenue in Boston that included a play area for small children, a boys' section, a sport field, and individual gardens. Lee's influence soon expanded; he was in great demand as a speaker and writer on playgrounds and served as vice president for public recreation of the American Civic Association. President of the Playground Association of America for 27 years, he was also the president and leading lecturer of the National Recreation School, a one-year program for carefully selected college graduates.

Lee's view of play is idealistic and purposeful. In *Play in Education*, he outlines a set of major play instincts that he believed all children shared and that governed the specific nature of play activities. He believed that play forms had to be taught and that this process required capable leadership. Lee did not make a sharp distinction between work and play, but saw them as closely related expressions of the impulses to achieve, to explore, to excel, and to master.

Luther Halsey Gulick

Another leading figure in the early recreation movement was Luther Halsey Gulick. A physician by training, he developed a special interest in physical education and recreation. He also had a strong religious orientation, as did many of the early play leaders. Beginning in 1887, Dr. Gulick headed the first summer school of "special training for gymnasium instructors" at the School for Christian Workers (now Springfield College) in Massachusetts. He was active in the YMCAs in Canada and the United States, was the first president of the Camp Fire Girls, and was instrumental in the establishment of the Playground Association of America in 1906. Gulick lectured extensively on the significance of play and recreation and taught a course in the psychology of play as early as 1899. He also vigorously promoted expanded recreation programs for girls and women.

Gulick distinguished play from recreation. He defines play as "doing that which we want to do, without reference primarily to any ulterior end, but simply for the joy of the process." But, he goes on to say, play is not less serious than work:

> The boy who is playing football with intensity needs recreation as much as does the inventor who is working intensely at his invention. Play can be more exhausting than work, because one can play much harder than one can work. No one would dream of pushing a boy in school as hard as he pushes himself in a football game. If there is any difference of intensity between play and work, the difference is in favor of play. Play is the result of desire; for that reason it is often carried on with more vigor than work.[23]

The Radical Women of Hull House

Jane Addams and Ellen Gates Starr were among the first college-educated women in the United States to dedicate their lives to public service. Addams and Starr opened the Hull House Settlement in 1889. Although Addams, Starr, and their colleagues were sometimes viewed as radical and dangerous, their work is a testament to the ability of women to collectively improve social conditions. The women of Hull House were directly involved in the establishment of the following social programs and movements of the Industrial Revolution:

- Immigrant aid and protection
- Public school nursing
- Labor reform
- Development of public playgrounds and kindergarten
- Industrial medicine
- Establishment of the juvenile court system
- Birth control
- Consumer advocacy
- Antialcohol and drug legislation
- Pure food and drug laws
- Public sanitation
- Elimination of child labor
- Infant and maternity health care
- Child day care
- Visiting nurses
- Public school lunches
- Industrial health and safety
- Peace initiatives
- Suffrage

Jane Addams

Jane Addams was a social work pioneer who established Hull House in Chicago. Her interest in the needs of children and youth, and in the lives of immigrant families and the poor in America's great cities, led her to develop outstanding programs of educational, social, and recreational activities. Beyond this, she was a leading feminist pioneer and so active a reformer that she was known as "the most dangerous woman in America."

Mary Duncan points out that Jane Addams, along with a number of other recreation and park leaders in the late nineteenth and early twentieth centuries, was part of a wider radical reform movement in America's cities. Joining with muckraking editors, writers, ministers, and other social activists, they continually fought city hall, organized labor strikes, marched in the street, gave public speeches, and wrote award-winning articles deploring the living conditions of the poor. The issues and problems they faced were well defined: slavery, the aftermath of the Civil War, thousands of new immigrants, slums, child labor, disease, the suffrage movement, World War I, and a rapidly industrializing nation.[24]

Contrasting Roles of Recreation Pioneers

Although Lee, Gulick, and Addams were described as muckraking radicals, it is clear that they also were individuals who worked through the major societal institutions of government and voluntary agencies. Addams, for example, helped to found the Playground Association of America, encouraged the Chicago School Board's involvement in playground and recreational sport programs, and supported the early development of the Chicago Park District. Indeed, these early recreation pioneers often walked a tightrope between their desire on the one hand to promote individuality, to give youth the opportunity for creative development, and to overcome old barriers of prejudice and class distinction and the need on the other hand to maintain order and control and to indoctrinate youth with traditional social goals.

While these three fought to help the downtrodden and illiterate immigrant families living in crowded urban slums, they were also using recreation to maintain the status quo and enforce traditional values. Play was seen as a means of "Americanizing" foreigners and perpetuating and protecting the traditional small-town, moralistic, white Anglo-Saxon heritage that had dominated national culture over the past century. Recreation would be used as a way of repressing the "overwhelming temptation of illicit and soul-destroying pleasures."[24]

EMERGING NEW LIFESTYLES

Such views of recreation, play, and leisure were not shared by the entire population. The early twentieth century was a time when the traditional Victorian mentality that had been taught and enforced by the home, school, and church was being challenged. For the first time, many young women took jobs in business and industry in cities throughout the country. With relative freedom from disapproving, stern parental authority, and with money to spend, they frequented commercial dance halls, boat rides, drinking saloons, social clubs, and other sources of popular entertainment. Kathy Peiss describes the new freedom for working-class youth in general:

> They fled the tenements for the streets, dance halls, and theaters, generally bypassing their fathers' saloons and lodges. Adolescents formed social clubs, organized entertainments, and patronized new commercial amusements, shaping, in effect, a working-class youth culture expressed through leisure activity.[25]

Part of what appealed to young people were the playgrounds, parks, public beaches, and picnic grounds. However, often these were considered too tame and unexciting, and more and more young people became attracted to commercial forms of entertainment involving liquor, dancing, and sex that were viewed by the establishment as immoral and dangerous. Increasingly, organized recreation programs were promoted by churches, law enforcement agencies, and civic associations in an attempt to resist the new, hedonistic forms of play. They sought to promote traditional, idealistic activities, such as youth sport, music, games, crafts, and dramatic activities, as a way to repress the urge for more "sinful" behavior.

PUBLIC CONCERNS ABOUT THE USE OF LEISURE

To some degree, the support for public recreation was based on the fear that without public programs and facilities, adult leisure would be used unwisely. Many industrial leaders and civic officials believed that the growth of leisure for the working classes represented a dangerous trend; when unemployment increased, they expressed concern about what idle men would do with their time. Similarly, when the eight-hour workday laws first came under discussion, temperance societies prepared for increased drunkenness, and social reformers held international conferences on the worker's spare time and ways to use it constructively.

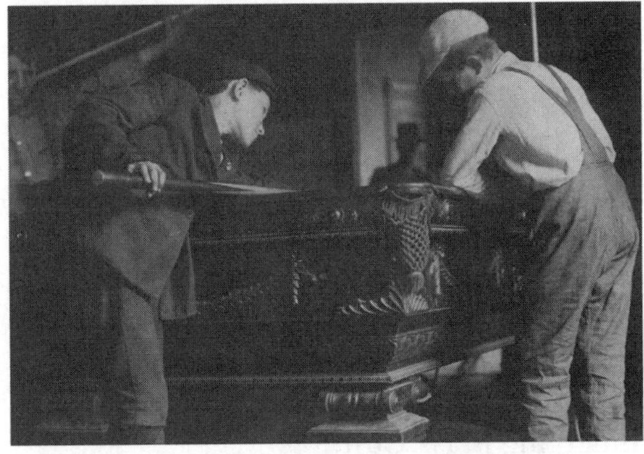

Billiard parlors, also known as pool halls, were often frequented by youths and adults alike as a form of entertainment.

The major concern, however, was for children and youth in the large cities and their need for healthful and safe places to play. Indeed, much "juvenile delinquency" arose from children being arrested for playing on city streets. Authorities during this period reported reduced rates of juvenile delinquency in slum areas where playgrounds had been established. A probation officer of the juvenile court in Milwaukee described "a very noticeable dropping off of boys coming before the court" and a disappearance of "dangerous gangs," concluding that playgrounds and social centers were "saviors" for American youth. Typically, the judge of the juvenile department of the Orange County Court in Anaheim, California, noted that after the opening of supervised playgrounds in the public park in the summer of 1924, juvenile delinquency decreased. During the first six months of 1925, it was 70% less than for the same period in 1924.[26]

Concern About Commercial Amusements

At this time, there was also fear that unregulated and unsupervised places of commercial amusement posed a serious threat to children and youth. Commercially sponsored forms of entertainment and recreation had grown rapidly during the early twentieth century, with many new pool and billiard parlors, dance halls, vaudeville shows and burlesque, and other amusement attractions. In major cities such as Milwaukee, Detroit, Kansas City, and San Francisco, extensive recreation surveys scrutinized the nature of commercial amusements, the extent and kind of their patronage, and their character. There was much concern about movies and stage performances, with frequent charges that they were immoral and led to the sexual corruption of youth.

A high percentage of privately operated dance halls had attached saloons that were freely patronized by young girls. Dancing seemed to be only a secondary consideration. Pick-ups occurred regularly, often of young girls who had come to cities from the nation's farms and small towns with a presumed degree of innocence; so-called white slavers, who trapped or recruited girls and women into prostitution, appeared to ply their trade with little interference. Dance halls were often attached to disreputable rooming houses, and girls in their early and middle teens were easily recruited into prostitution.

The same studies that examined commercial amusements also surveyed the socially approved forms of recreation. They found that in many cities the schools were closed in the evening and throughout the summer, that libraries closed at night and on weekends, that churches closed for the summer, and that publicly provided forms of recreation were at a minimum. Jane Addams concluded that the city had "turned over the provision for public recreation to the most evil-minded and the most unscrupulous members of the community." Gradually, pressure mounted for more effective control of places of public amusement. In city after city, permits were required for operating dance halls, pool parlors, and bowling alleys, and for the sale of liquor.

There was also a fear that Americans were moving away from the traditional active ways of using their leisure to pursuits in which they were passive spectators. Some critics commented that instead of believing in the wholesome love of play, Americans now had a love of being "played upon." It had become wholly outdated to make one's own fun.

Emerging Mass Culture

Such complaints and fears were the inevitable reactions of civic leaders to what they perceived to be a threat to traditional morality and values. The reality is that the United States in the early decades of the twentieth century was undergoing massive changes in response to changing economic and social conditions. These included the emergence of new middle-class and working-class people who had the time and money to spend on leisure, as well as a steady infusion of varied ethnic peoples who contributed new ideas and values to American society. Part of the change involved a growing rejection of authoritarian family structures and church-dominated social values, as well as a readiness to accept new kinds of roles for young people and women. All of these influences resulted in a new mass culture that emerged during the new century. John Kasson writes:

> At the turn of the century this culture was still in the process of formation and not fully incorporated into the life of society as a whole. Its purest expression at this time lay in the realm of commercial amusements, which were creating symbols of the new cultural order.[27]

Kasson goes on to point out that nineteenth-century America was governed by a coherent set of values—highly Victorian in nature and directed by a self-conscious elite group of ministers, educators, and reformers drawn chiefly from the Protestant middle class of the urban Northeast. These apostles of culture preached the values of character, moral integrity, self-control, sobriety, and industriousness. They believed that leisure should be spent in ways that were edifying and that had moral and social utility. They founded museums, art galleries, libraries, and symphony orchestras, and they lent moral sanction to the recreation and park movement. However, they were unable to exert a significant influence on the growing masses of urban working classes and new immigrant groups.

The Challenges of Defining Popular/Mass Culture

Popular culture (or pop culture) is the totality of ideas, perspectives, attitudes, memes, images, and other phenomena that are deemed preferred per an informal consensus within the mainstream of a given culture. Popular culture is heavily influenced by mass media, and becomes ingrained in everyday life.[28]

Defining *popular* and *culture* is complicated with multiple competing definitions. The preceding definition represents mainstream perceptions of popular culture. However, among many there is a strong undercurrent that popular culture is not so easily defined. For example, John Storey, in *Cultural Theory and Popular Culture*, discusses six definitions:[29]

1. The quantitative definition of culture tries to qualify and measure culture but has the problem that much "high culture" (e.g., television dramatizations of Jane Austen) is widely favored. *High culture* is often defined as "the set of cultural products, mainly in the arts, held in the highest esteem by a culture."[29]
2. *Pop culture* is also defined as the culture that is left over when we have decided what high culture is. However, many works straddle or cross the boundaries, such as Shakespeare and Charles Dickens.
3. A third definition equates pop culture with mass culture. This is seen as a commercial culture, mass produced for mass consumption. From a Western European perspective, this may be compared to American culture.
4. Alternatively, *pop culture* can be defined as an authentic culture of the people, but this can be problematic because there are many ways of defining the *people*.
5. Storey argues that there is a political dimension to popular culture that sees popular culture as a struggle between the resistance of subordinate groups in society and the forces of incorporation operating in the interests of dominant groups in society.
6. A postmodernism approach to popular culture would no longer recognize the distinction between high and popular culture.

Popular culture changes constantly and occurs uniquely in place and time. Items of popular culture most typically appeal to a broad spectrum of the public.

MAJOR FORCES PROMOTING ORGANIZED RECREATION SERVICES

At the same time that mass culture was providing new kinds of pastimes that challenged traditional community values and standards, the forces that sought to guide the American public in what they regarded as constructive uses of leisure were becoming active.

Development of the Amusement Park

As a single example of the new craze for excitement and freedom in leisure, a host of amusement parks were developed close to various cities around the country. Typically, they put together a mélange of popular attractions, including bathing facilities, band pavilions, dance halls, vaudeville theaters, sideshows, circus attractions, freak displays, food and drink counters, and daredevil rides of every description.

Growth of Voluntary Organizations

In the opening decades of the twentieth century, a number of important youth-serving, nonprofit organizations were formed, either on a local basis or through nationally organized movements or federations. The National Association of Boys' Clubs was founded in 1906, the Boy Scouts and the Camp Fire Girls in 1910, and the Girl Scouts in 1912. Major civic clubs and community service groups such as the Rotary Club, Kiwanis Club, and the Lions Club were also founded between 1910 and 1917.

The Boy Scouts have provided outdoor recreation experiences for youths since 1910.

By the end of the 1920s, these organizations had become widely established in American life and were serving substantial numbers of young people. One of every seven boys in the appropriate age group in the United States was a Scout. The YMCA and YWCA had more than 1.5 million members in 1926. In contemporary society, voluntary organizations are a significant provider of community recreation services that are utilized by tens of millions of children and adults.

CASE STUDY: The Creation of the National Park Service

The creation of new federal agencies is a complicated and highly political process. Even though the need is apparent to those most concerned, there is always the need to convince key leaders in the executive and legislative branches of government. Typically, a proposal for a new agency moves forward from the executive branch to the legislative branch. Although not always the case, the presence of a growing number of national parks administered by the Department of the Interior—but without a direct governing body—resulted in inconsistent administration of the national parks. "There military engineers and cavalrymen developed park roads and buildings, enforced regulations against hunting, grazing, timber cutting, and vandalism, and did their best to serve the visiting public. Civilian appointees superintended the other parks, while the monuments received minimal custody. In the absence of an effective central administration, those in charge operated without coordinated supervision or policy guidance."[a]

The National Park Service was created by act of Congress in 1916, 44 years after the establishment of the world's first national park—Yellowstone National Park. A number of national parks were created between 1872 and the early 1900s. By 1916, the Department of the Interior was responsible for a number of national parks and national monuments and, yet, had no organizational structure to manage the growing number of areas dedicated to preservation and recreation. In the absence of a formal structure and, in many cases, guidelines, the areas set aside by Congress were vulnerable to competing interests. Matters seemed to have come to a head when in 1913 Congress authorized the creation of a dam in Hetch Hetchy Valley of Yosemite National Park.

"When San Francisco sought to dam Yosemite's Hetch Hetchy Valley for a reservoir after the turn of the century, the utilitarian and preservationist wings of the conservation movement came to blows. Over the passionate opposition of John Muir and other park supporters, Congress in 1913 permitted the dam."[a] In 1915, Stephen T. Mather, a well-connected and wealthy Chicago businessman, complained to Secretary of the Interior Franklin K. Lane about the mismanagement of the parks. Lane responded by inviting Mather to serve as his assistant for park matters, and Mather accepted. Serving as Mather's aide and guiding the legislation through Congress, Horace M. Albright, working hand in hand with his superior, crusaded "for a National Parks Bureau" and the two of them "effectively blurred the distinction between utilitarian conservation and preservation by emphasizing the economic value of parks as tourist meccas."[a]

Not relying wholly on their contacts within Congress, the two men initiated a public relations campaign that resulted in articles in the *Saturday Evening Post*, *National Geographic*, and other popular magazines. Mather "hired his own publicist and obtain funds from 17 western railroads to produce the National Parks Portfolio, a lavishly illustrated publication sent to Congressmen and other influential citizens." On August 25, 1916, Congress approved the creation of the National Park Service (NPS), and President Woodrow Wilson signed the legislation. The legislation specifically required the NPS "to conserve the scenery and the natural and historic objects in the wild life therein and to provide for the enjoyment of the same in such manner and by such means as leave them unimpaired for the enjoyment of future generations."[a]

Questions to Consider

1. Prepare a series of arguments in favor of creating a National Park Bureau/Service.
2. Prepare a series of arguments opposing the creation of a National Park Bureau/Service.
3. How do you think the National Park system would be different today if it did not have an agency to manage it?

Source

a. Barry Mackintosh, "The National Park Service: A Brief History," ParkNet, http://www.nps.gov/history/history/hisnps/NPSHistory/npshisto.htm.

Playground Association of America

In the early 1900s, leading recreation directors called for a conference to promote public awareness of and effective practices in the field of leisure services. Under the leadership of Luther Halsey Gulick, representatives of park, recreation, and school boards throughout the United States met in Washington, D.C., in April 1906. Unanimously agreeing upon the need for a national organization, the conference members drew up a constitution and selected Gulick as the first president of the Playground Association of America. The organization had President Theodore Roosevelt's strong support.

A basic purpose of the Playground Association was to develop informational and promotional services to assist people of all ages in using leisure time constructively. Field workers traveled from city to city, meeting with public officials and citizens' groups and helping in the development of playgrounds and recreation programs. To promote professional training, the association developed *The Normal Course in Play*, a curriculum plan of courses on play leadership on several levels.

In keeping with its broadening emphasis, the organization changed its name in 1911 to the Playground and Recreation Association of America, and in 1926 to the National Recreation Association. It sought to provide the public with a broader concept of recreation and leisure and to promote recreation as an area of government responsibility.

Recreation Programs in World War I

The nation's rapid mobilization during World War I revealed that communities adjacent to army and navy stations and training camps needed more adequate programs of recreation. The Council of National Defense and the War Department Commission on Training Camp Activities asked the Playground and Recreation Association to assist in the creation of a national organization to provide wartime community recreation programs. The association established the War Camp Community Service (WCCS), which utilized the recreation resources of several hundred communities near military camps to provide wholesome recreation activities for both military personnel and civilians.

At its peak, WCCS employed a national staff of approximately 3000 paid workers who organized programs in 755 cities with the help of more than 500,000 volunteers. At other military bases in the United States and Europe, organizations such as the Young Men's Christian Association sponsored canteens and other morale-boosting services.

Role of the Schools

As indicated earlier, a number of urban school boards initiated after-school and vacation play programs as early as the 1890s. This trend continued in the twentieth century. Playground programs were begun in Rochester, New York, in 1907; in Milwaukee, Wisconsin, in 1911; and in Los Angeles, California, in 1914. These pioneering efforts were strongly supported by the National Education Association, which recommended that public school buildings be used for community recreation and social activities.

With such support, public opinion encouraged the expansion of organized playground and public recreation programs in American communities. Between 1910 and 1930, thousands of school systems established extensive programs of extracurricular activities, particularly in sport, publications, hobbies, and social- and academic-related fields. In 1919, the first college curriculum in recreation was established at Virginia Commonwealth University.

In addition to playgrounds, other facilities of the schools that could be useful for recreational purposes were assembly rooms and gymnasiums, swimming pools, music and arts rooms, and outdoor areas for sport and gardening. Education for the "worthy use of leisure" was vigorously supported as an important goal for secondary schools throughout the United States.

Outdoor Recreation Developments

The role of the federal and state governments in promoting outdoor recreation was enlarged by the establishment of the National Park Service in 1916 and an accelerated pattern of acquisition and development of outdoor areas by the U.S. Forest Service. In 1921, Stephen Mather, director of the National Park Service, called for a national conference on state parks. This meeting made it clear that the Park Service was primarily to acquire and administer areas of national significance; it led to the recommendation that state governments take more responsibility for acquiring sites of lesser interest or value.

Park administrators began to give active recreation a higher priority in park design and operation. The founding of the American Association of Zoological Parks and Aquariums in 1924 was an indication that specialized recreational uses of parks were becoming widespread in American communities.

The End of Shorter Hours

At the same time that the recreation movement continued to gain impetus, a reverse trend took place as the movement to shorten the workweek and provide workers with more free time gradually slackened. Benjamin Hunnicutt points out that the most dramatic increase in free time occurred in the period between 1901 and 1921, when the average workweek dropped from 58.4 hours to 48.4 hours, a decline never before or since equaled.[30]

Since the mid-nineteenth century, shorter hours and higher wages had been a campaign issue for progressive politicians. Union pressure, legislation, and court decisions achieved the eight-hour day in jobs under federal contracts, sections of the railroad industry, and certain hazardous occupations. The policy was supported by the findings of scientific management experts such as Frederick Taylor, who argued that workers' efficiency declined significantly after eight hours. It also responded to a trend in other industrialized nations, such as France, Germany, Italy, and Belgium, to approve legal restriction of working time, based on the eight-hour day or 48-hour workweek.

New problems began to arise in the American economy, though, as overproduction and "economic maturity" left the nation with an excess of goods and services. Many leading businessmen and economists began to promote a "New Gospel of Consumption" during the 1920s. They argued that the way to stimulate the economy was not to provide more leisure, but to increase productivity and public spending on a broad range of consumer goods.

IMPACT OF THE GREAT DEPRESSION

Following the flourishing 1920s, the Great Depression of the 1930s mired the United States—and much of the industrial world—in a period of almost total despair. The Depression resulted in mass unemployment and involuntary idleness for American workers. By the end of 1932, an estimated 15 million people, nearly one-third of the labor force, were unemployed. Individuals who were employed also experienced greater free time as the average workweek declined. During this period, scholars and public officials became concerned that leisure had become too commercial and passive and would contribute to the decline of American culture. Furthermore, there was widespread concern that excessive free time was linked to crime.

In response to these concerns and in conjunction with a broad plan to combat the effects of the Depression, the federal government soon instituted a number of emergency work programs related to recreation. The Federal Emergency Relief Administration, established early in 1933, financed construction of recreation facilities such as parks and swimming pools and hired recreation leaders from the relief rolls. A second agency, the Civil Works Administration, was given the task of finding jobs for four million people in 30

Civilian Conservation Corps (CCC) camps were located throughout the United States during the Depression.

days! Among other tasks, this agency built or improved 3500 playgrounds and athletic fields in a few months.[31]

Both the National Youth Administration and the Civilian Conservation Corps carried out numerous work projects involving the construction of recreational facilities. During the five years from 1932 to 1937, the federal government spent an estimated $1.5 billion developing camps, buildings, picnic grounds, trails, swimming pools, and other facilities. The Civilian Conservation Corps helped to establish state park systems in a number of states that had no organized park programs before 1933. The Works Progress Administration allocated $11 billion or 30% of their budget to recreation-related projects that spanned the nation and included 12,700 playgrounds, 8500 gymnasiums or recreation buildings, 750 swimming pools, 1000 ice skating rinks, and 64 ski jumps.[32] These programs initiated under President Franklin D. Roosevelt's New Deal had a beneficial effect on the development of the recreation and park movement throughout the United States: They made it clear that leisure was an important responsibility of government.

CASE STUDY: President Franklin D. Roosevelt's Legacy for Parks and Recreation

During the Great Depression of the 1930s, President Franklin D. Roosevelt created a legacy that has had enduring and significant influence on parks and recreation. It can be argued that Roosevelt's New Deal was a tool that initiated a growth of public parks and recreation areas, state parks, national parks, conservations, and wildlife areas.

The New Deal was a product of one of the most difficult periods in American history. Roosevelt was elected after the 1929 stock market crash and came to office in 1933. He saw the need to put Americans to work. The term "New Deal" was introduced during Franklin Roosevelt's 1932 Democratic presidential nomination acceptance speech, when he said, "I pledge you, I pledge myself, to a new deal for the American people."[a] Roosevelt summarized the New Deal as a "use of the authority of government as an organized form of self-help for all classes and groups and sections of our country."[a]

The New Deal represented a major shift in government involvement in everyone's lives. Its main purpose was to put people back to work and improve the economy. It is important to remember that during this period unemployment hovered at 30% nationwide. Among the important initiatives created, two significantly influenced parks and recreation. They were the Civilian Conservation Corps (CCC) and the Works Progress Administration (WPA).

The Civilian Conservation Corps initially targeted putting three million young men, between the ages of 18 and 25 years, to work. The CCC was involved in road building, forest maintenance and restoration, and flood control. The West saw the heavy use of CCC and the Works Progress Administration's workers in national forests, national parks, on Indian reservations, and in municipal and state parks for work on natural resource–related projects.[b] During the existence of the CCC, members planted nearly three billion trees to help reforest America and constructed more than 800 parks nationwide that would become the start of many state parks.[c]

At the height of the program, 47 of 48 states participated in CCC programs, and in 1935 there were 475 CCC camps on state park lands. By the end of the CCC program, 405 state parks directly benefited from the program. In some cases, whole state parks were turned over to appreciative states. Georgia, as an example of a benefiting state, in 2010 identified 11 state parks that still had CCC-constructed facilities. The structures include a bathhouse, casino, dam, pumphouse, residences, comfort stations and picnic shelters, springhouse, bridge and walkways, museum building, blacksmith shop, and group shelters, to name a few. Georgia's legacy of the CCC is similar to many states that point to the WPA and CCC as an unexpected boon.[d]

The Works Progress Administration, established in 1935 and renamed in 1939 as the Work Projects Administration, similarly focused on creating jobs for the unemployed. It became the largest of the New Deal programs carrying out public works projects that involved the construction of public buildings and roads, and it operated large arts, drama, media, and literacy projects. It fed children and redistributed food, clothing, and housing. Almost every community in the United States had a park, bridge, or school constructed by the agency. The WPA spent billions of dollars on reforestation, flood control, construction of facilities and parks and recreation areas, and many other conservation and community projects. From a municipal and state perspective, the WPA had a significant impact on communities and their ability to provide park and recreation resources and services. For example, the WPA hired artists, actors, and musicians to provide programming, create art, and hold concerts for local communities. In some cases, the construction of park shelters, restrooms, picnic shelters, swimming pools, and other facilities remain today.

An example WPA project from New York City is in McCarren Pool, located in Brooklyn. McCarren Pool was the eighth of 11 giant pools built by the Works Progress Administration, opening during the summer of 1936. With a capacity of 6800 swimmers, the pool served as the summertime social hub. The pool was closed in 1984, but in 2006 the abandoned pool was the site of a series of Sunday afternoon concerts. The mayor of New York announced in 2007 that major renovations would be undertaken to reopen the pool.[e]

The National Park Service has done the most effective job of chronicling the CCC and WPA involvement with their areas. The NPS budget was $10.8 million in 1933, and yet, NPS took advantage of the New Deal, receiving $218 million for emergency conservation projects between 1933 and 1939. The NPS said, "Almost all federal conservation activities after 1933, including those in the national parks and monuments, were designed in part as pump-priming operations that would not only protect our national resources but also indirectly stimulate the economy."[f]

The work of New Deal organizations from 1933 to 1942 provided a foundation that would be expanded upon throughout the remainder of the twentieth century.

Questions to Consider

1. How do you think recreation areas, national parks, and wildlife areas would be different today without the New Deal?
2. Prepare a series of justifications for implementation of a New Deal program today.
3. Go on the Internet and find a state or community that is still using CCC- or WPA-constructed facilities and report on how they are used, how they were changed, and the legacy it has left upon the community or state? (Hint: do a search for "New Deal" facilities.)

Sources

a. Works of Franklin D. Roosevelt, Roosevelt's Nomination Address, Chicago, IL. July 2, 1932. http://newdeal.feri.org/speeches/1932bhtm.

b. The National Archives, "The Great Depression and the New Deal," http://www.archives.gov/pacific-alaska/picturing-the-century/great-depression.html.

c. Harlan Unraw and G. F Williss, *Expansion of the National Park Service in the 1930s: Administrative History* (Washington, DC: National Park Service, 1982), http://www.nps.gov/history/history/online_books/unrau-williss/adhi3.htm.

d. Georgia Department of Natural Resources, http://www.georgiastateparks.org.

e. New York City Department of Parks and Recreation, "McCarren Park," http://www.nycgovparks.org/parks/mccarrenpark.

f. Ibid., c.

Sharpened Awareness of Leisure Needs

The Depression helped to stimulate national concern about problems of leisure and recreational opportunity. For example, a number of studies in the 1930s revealed a serious lack of structured recreation programs for young people, especially African Americans, girls, and rural youth. In the early 1930s, the National Education Association carried out a major study of leisure education in the nation's school systems and issued a report, *The New Leisure Challenges the Schools*, that urged the educational establishment to take more responsibility for this function and advocated enlarging the school's role in community recreation.

Recreation during the Depression came in many forms and frequently was family-oriented.

Shortly thereafter, the National Recreation Association examined the public recreation and park programs in a number of major European nations with nationalized recreation programs and published a detailed report that included implications for American policymakers. The American Association for the Study of Group Work studied the overall problem and in 1939 published an important report, *Leisure: A National Issue*. Written by Eduard Lindeman, a leading social work administrator who had played a key role in government during the Depression, the report stated that the "leisure of the American people constitutes a central and crucial problem of social policy."[33]

Lindeman argued that in the American democracy, recreation should meet the true needs of the people. Pointing out that American workers were gaining a vast national reservoir of leisure estimated at 390 billion hours per year, he suggested that the new leisure should be characterized by free choice and a minimum of restraint. He urged, however, that if leisure were not to become "idleness, waste, or opportunity for sheer mischief," a national plan for leisure had to be developed, including the widespread preparation of professionally trained recreation leaders.

A NATION AT WAR

World War II, in which the United States became fully involved on December 7, 1941, compelled the immediate mobilization of every aspect of national life: peoplepower, education, industry, and a variety of social services and programs. The Special Services Division of the U.S. Army provided recreation facilities and programs on military bases throughout the world, making use of approximately 12,000 officers, even more enlisted personnel, and many volunteers. About 1500 officers were involved in the Welfare and Recreation Section of the Bureau of Naval Personnel, and expanded programs were offered by the Recreation Service of the Marine Corps. These departments were assisted by the United Service Organizations (USO), which was formed in 1941 and consisted of the joint effort of six agencies: the Jewish Welfare Board, the Salvation Army, Catholic Community Services, the YMCA, the YWCA, and the National Travelers Aid. The USO functioned in the continental United States and outside of military camps and in clubs, hostels, and lounges throughout the Western Hemisphere. The American National Red Cross established approximately 750 clubs in wartime theaters of operations throughout the world and about 250 mobile entertainment units, staffed by more than 4000 leaders. Its military hospitals overseas and in the United States involved more than 1500 recreation workers as well.

Many municipal directors extended their facilities and services to local war plants and changed their schedules to provide programs around the clock. Because of the rapid increase in industrial recreation programs, the National Industrial Recreation Association (later known as the National Employee Services and Recreation Association) was formed in 1941 to assist in such efforts. Also, the Federal Security Agency's Office of Community War Services established a new recreation division to assist programs on the community level. This division helped set up 300 new community programs throughout the country, including numerous child-care and recreation centers, many of which continued after the war as tax-supported community recreation programs. The Women's Bureau of the U.S. Department of Labor developed guidelines for recreation and housing for women war workers, based on their needs in moving from their home environments into suddenly expanded or greatly congested areas.

By the end of World War II, great numbers of servicemen and servicewomen had participated in varied recreation programs and services and thus had gained a new appreciation for this field. Many people had been trained in recreation leadership (more than 40,000 people were in the Special Services Division of the U.S. Army alone) and were ready to return to civilian life as professionals in this field.

SUMMARY

This chapter shows the long history of recreation, play, and leisure by discussing their roles in the ancient civilizations of Assyria, Babylonia, and Egypt; then in the Greek and Roman eras; during the Middle Ages and the Renaissance in Europe; and from the pre-Revolutionary period in the North American colonies to the mid-twentieth century.

Religion and social class were major factors that influenced recreational involvement in terms of either prohibiting certain forms of activity or assigning them to one class or another. Leisure, seen as an aristocratic devotion to knowledge, the arts, athletics, philosophy, and contemplation in ancient Athens, took a different form in Rome, where it became a political instrument devoted to perpetuating the rule of the Roman emperors by entertaining and placating the common people.

During the Dark and Middle Ages, the Catholic Church placed a strong value on work and worship and sought to prohibit forms of play that had descended from pagan sources. However, such activities as sport and games, music, dance, the theater, and gambling persisted, even under the stern condemnation of the new Protestant sects that gained influence during the period of the Reformation. At this time, class distinctions in terms of appropriate forms of play became clearly evident in England, France, and other European nations. However, the value of play as a form of childhood education was championed in the writings of numerous educators and philosophers of that era.

In the pre-Revolutionary American colonies, New England Puritans were very strict in their condemnation of most recreational pursuits. After an initial conservative period, however, play and varied social pursuits flourished in the plantations of the southern colonies, which had been settled by members of the English gentry who used slaves and indentured servants to make their own leisure possible.

The chapter traces the influence of the Industrial Revolution, which brought millions of immigrants from Europe to America, where they lived in crowded tenements in large cities or in factory towns. It also led to increased attempts to impose the stern strictures of the Protestant work ethic on the nation's population.

By the middle of the nineteenth century, however, religious opposition to varied types of play and entertainment began to decline. Sport became more popular and accepted and, after reaching a high point at mid-century, work hours began to decline. Four major roots of what was ultimately to become the recreation and park movement appeared: (1) the establishment of city parks, beginning with New York City's Central Park, and the later growth of county, state, and national parks; (2) the growing interest in adult education and cultural development; (3) the appearance of playgrounds for children, sponsored first as charitable efforts and shortly after by city governments and the public schools; and (4) the development of a number of nonprofit, youth-serving organizations that spread throughout the country.

Popular culture gained momentum during the Jazz Age of the 1920s, with college and professional sport, motion pictures and radio, new forms of dance and music, and a host of other crazes capturing the public's interest. Although the Great Depression of the 1930s had a tragic impact on many families, the efforts of the federal government to build recreation facilities and leisure services to provide jobs and a morale boost for the public at large meant that the Depression was a powerful positive force for the recreation movement in general.

By the early 1940s, organized recreation service was firmly established in American life, and both government officials and social critics began to raise searching questions about its future role in postwar society.

QUESTIONS FOR CLASS DISCUSSION OR ESSAY EXAMINATION

1. Contrast the attitudes toward sport and other uses of leisure that were found in ancient Greece with those found in the Roman Empire. How did their philosophies differ, and how did the Roman philosophy lead to a weakening of that powerful nation? Could you draw a parallel between the approach to leisure and entertainment in ancient Rome and that in the present-day United States?

2. Trace the development of religious attitudes and policies regarding leisure and play from the Dark and Middle Ages, through the Renaissance and Reformation periods, to the colonial era in seventeenth- and eighteenth-century North America. What differences were there in the approach to recreation between the northern and southern colonies at this time?
3. In the second half of the nineteenth century, the roots of what was to become the modern recreation and park movement appeared. What were these roots (e.g., the adult education or Lyceum movement), and how did they relate to the broad social needs of Americans?
4. Three important pioneers of the early recreation movement in the United States were Lee, Gulick, and Addams. Summarize some of the key points of their philosophies and their contributions to the playground and recreation developments of the pre–World War I era. Describe the conflict between the traditional Victorian values and code of morality and the emerging popular culture, especially during the 1920s.
5. Trace the expanding role of government in terms of sponsoring recreation and park programs during the first half of the twentieth century, with emphasis on federal policies in wartime and during the Depression of the 1930s. What were some of the growing concerns about leisure during this period?

ENDNOTES

1. John Pearson, *Arena: The Story of the Colosseum* (New York: McGraw-Hill, 1973): 7.
2. Gary Cross, *A Social History of Leisure Since 1600* (State College, PA: Venture Publishing, 1990): 73.
3. Jonah Blank, "Playing for Keeps," *U.S. News and World Report* (28 June 1999): 64.
4. Zhang Juzhong and Lee Yun Kuen, "The Magic Flutes," *Natural History* (Vol. 114, No. 7, 2005): 43.
5. Plato, *The Laws*, translated by R. G. Bury (Cambridge, MA: Harvard University Press, 1926, 1961): 23.
6. Cited in Lincoln Kirstein, *Dance: A Short History of Classical Theatrical Dancing* (New York: G. P. Putnam, 1935): 57.
7. Edward Maslin Hulme, *The Middle Ages* (New York: Holt, 1938): 604.
8. Cited in Fred Leonard, *A Guide to the History of Physical Education* (Philadelphia: Lea and Febiger, 1928): 55.
9. Norman P. Miller and Duane M. Robinson, *The Leisure Age* (Belmont, CA: Wadsworth, 1963): 66.
10. Cited in Paul La Croix, *France in the Middle Ages* (New York: Frederick Ungar, 1963): 346.
11. Michael Kraus, *The Atlantic Civilization: 18th Century Origins* (Ithaca, NY: Cornell University Press, 1949): 3.
12. Jearold Winston Holland, *Black Recreation: A Historical Perspective* (Chicago: Burnam, 2002).
13. Benjamin Hunnicutt, "The End of Shorter Hours," *Labor Review* (Vol. 3, 1984): 373–374.
14. J. Larkin, "The Secret Life of a Developing Country (Ours)," *American Heritage* (September–October 1988): 60.
15. George Will, review of G. Edward White, "Creating the National Pastime," *New York Times Book Review* (7 April 1996): 11.
16. Foster Rhea Dulles, *A History of Recreation: America Learns to Play* (New York: Appleton-Century-Crofts, 1965): 182.

17. David Nasaw, *Going Out: The Rise and Fall of Public Amusements*, (New York: Basic Books, 1993): 2.

18. Reprinted by permission of the publishers from *The Adams Papers:Adams Family Correspondence, Volume* 3, April 1778–September 1780, edited by L. H. Butterfield and Marc Friedlander, p. 342, Cambridge, Mass: Harvard University Press, Copyright © 1973 by the Massachusetts Historical Society.

19. John Muir, (original 1901). *Our National Parks* (Madison: University of Wisconsin Press, 1981): 40.

20. Paul Heintzman, "Wilderness and the Canadian Mind: Impact upon Recreation Development in Canadian Parks" (NRPA Research Symposium, 1997): 75.

21. Cited in Henry H. Reed and Sophia Duckworth, *Central Park: A History and a Guide* (New York: Clarkson N. Potter, 1967): 3.

22. Walter Vrooman, "Playgrounds for Children," *The Arena* (July 1894): 286.

23. Luther H. Gulick, *A Philosophy of Play* (New York: Scribner, 1920): 125.

24. Mary Duncan, "Back to Our Radical Roots," in Thomas Goodale and Peter Witt, eds., *Recreation and Leisure: Issues in an Era of Change* (State College, PA: Venture Publishing, 1980): 287–295.

25. Kathy Peiss, *Cheap Amusements: Working Women and Leisure in Turn-of-the-Century New York* (Philadelphia: Temple University Press, 1986): 57.

26. James Rogers, "The Child and Play," *Report on White House Conference on Child Health and Protection* (New York: The Century Co., 1932): 27.

27. John Kasson, *Amusing the Millions: Coney Island at the Turn of the Century* (New York: Hill and Wang, 1978): 3–4.

28. Art and Popular Culture, "Popular Culture." http://www.artandpopularculture.com/Popular_Culture.

29. John Storey, *Cultural Theory and Popular Culture* (Atlanta: University of Georgia Press, 1998).

30. Benjamin Hunnicutt, "Historical Attitudes Toward the Increase of Free Time in the Twentieth Century: Time for Leisure, for Work, for Unemployment," *Loisir et Societe* (Vol. 3, 1980): 196.

31. Richard Knapp, "Play for America: The New Deal and the NRA," *Parks and Recreation* (July 1973): 23.

32. Susan Currell, *The March of Spare Time: The Problem and Promise of Leisure in the Great Depression* (Philadelphia: University of Pennsylvania Press, 2005): 51.

33. Eduard Lindeman, *Leisure: A National Issue* (New York: American Association for the Study of Group Work, 1939): 32.

CHAPTER 4

RECREATION AND LEISURE IN THE MODERN ERA

◆ ◆ ◆

During the 1950s and 1960s, organized recreation had a marked impact on community life. The growing movement was advanced by an increasing concern for physical fitness; programs for the ill, aged, and disabled; an upsurge in outdoor recreation and park development; involvement in the arts; professional education; unification of the parks and recreation professional organization; and the impact of civil unrest and youth dissent. . . . During this time, recreation and leisure services . . . came to be seen as an opportunity system to improve the quality of life, reduce social pathology, build constructive values in citizens, and generally make communities better places to live.[1]

◆ ◆ ◆

INTRODUCTION

From the end of World War II to the turn of the twenty-first century, recreation, park, and leisure services evolved from a relatively minor area of government responsibility and nonprofit agency or business function to an enormous, complex enterprise. This chapter chronicles the expansion and diversification of the recreation movement, seen against the broader background of social and economic change in the United States. In addition to describing these elements, the chapter presents a number of trends in leisure involvement and professional services that were influenced by environmental, demographic, social, and economic trends in the postwar era.

These trends included (1) growing concern about the natural environment, global climate change, and government's role in protecting them; (2) stronger emphasis on recreation's role in combating poverty and racial tensions; (3) programs designed to serve girls and women more fully, along with people with disabilities and older adults; (4) the emergence of a number of specialized disciplines and professional groups serving the military, business, private-membership groups, and other interests; (5) a period of economic austerity during the 1980s and early 1990s, followed by a dramatic upsurge in the nation's economy during the last years of the twentieth century; and (6) then, the longest and deepest economic decline since the Depression as the United States entered the first years of the twenty-first century.

How Earlier Authors Presented the Importance of Leisure and Recreation

There has rarely been a dispute among leisure researchers about the importance of leisure. The discussions, however, come from clarifying and defining how and why leisure and recreation are important. Like many movements, researchers respond to new research as well as social norms. As a result, authors vary in their perceptions of how they view the importance of leisure. Textbooks from three different decades have precented a view of the importance of leisure and recreation. Some have been more eloquent than others; some are written in greater detail; and some are brief. All wrote considerably more than can be shared here, but their comments are representative of the period of the dilemma of identifying the importance of leisure and recreation.

> *1963:* "Recreation is as old as the human race; only in recent years, however, has its importance been appreciated. Today it stands, along with education, work, and religion as a necessary part of a balanced life. All recreation is based on the satisfaction of certain urges or desires. Among these are the desire for security, for social contact, for recognition, for new experiences, for giving service, for belonging, for enjoying the beautiful, for learning, and creating. For many people, satisfaction of these urges and desires exists in one or more of the wide variety of recreation activities."[2]
>
> *1975:* "In leisure may lie the final test of our civilization. The nature of our society is determined . . . by the quality of our leisure. This leisure provides the means either for improving the quality of our living or for destroying our civilization."[3]
>
> *1992:* "Leisure is the opportunity you have to maximize the delights of life, to impart meaning to your life far beyond the mere struggle to survive and prosper."[4]

POST–WORLD WAR II EXPECTATIONS

Immediately after World War II, expectations for the growth of leisure in the United States were high. In the 1950s and 1960s, it was predicted that leisure—usually defined as non-work or discretionary time—would expand dramatically and have an increasing influence on the lives of Americans in the years ahead.

Think tanks such as the Rand Corporation and the Hudson Institute and special planning bodies such as the National Commission on Technology envisioned futurist scenarios with such alternatives as lowering the retirement age to 38, reducing the workweek to 22 hours a week, or extending paid vacations to as many as 25 weeks a year. Other authorities predicted that the three-day or four-day workweek, which some companies had been experimenting with, would soon be widespread.

It was also assumed that leisure would become an increasingly important source of personal values and life satisfaction for many Americans. There was widespread agreement that the work ethic was declining sharply, with work in the industrial era having become more and more specialized, routine, and unfulfilling. Leisure was seen as having immense potential, and writers and educators such as David Gray and Seymour Greben suggested that it offered new possibilities for confronting such social problems as human misery and suffering, health and fitness concerns, environmental and energy problems, and worker dissatisfaction.

Birdwatching is an example of an expanding outdoor recreation sport.

In the early and mid-1990s and again on a much broader scale in 2008 and beyond, widespread company downsizing and other business trends led to the firing of millions of employees and an atmosphere of economic pessimism. There was a strong business recovery in the late 1990s, unemployment declined sharply, prosperity was widespread, and government budgets began to show surpluses on every level. By early 2009, however, there was a new decline with more far-reaching impact on personal income and government budgets, layoffs and unemployment at levels not seen since the Great Depression, loss of homes, and closing of businesses nationwide and a general sense of hopelessness among many.

EXPANSION OF RECREATION AND LEISURE

Over the last 60 years, recreation and leisure witnessed an immense growth in participation. There was a steady increase in sport, the arts, hobbies, outdoor recreation, and fitness programs, along with a parallel expansion of home-based entertainment through the use of computer, television, media players, handheld devices, and other electronic equipment.

Influence of National Affluence

An important factor in the growth of recreational participation was the national affluence of the postwar years. The gross national product rose from $211 billion in 1945 to more than a trillion dollars annually in 1971. In the late 1950s, it was reported that Americans were spending $30 billion a year on leisure—a sum that seemed huge then but that is dwarfed by the $841 billion spent in 2007.[5]

Recreation participation continues to grow rapidly around the world. This three-tiered driving range, popular in Japan, demonstrates the popularity of golf as well as a creative use of limited urban space to accommodate large numbers of users.

> Involvement in varied forms of recreation exploded during this period. Visits to national forests increased by 474 percent between 1947 and 1963, and to national parks by 302 percent during the same period. Overseas pleasure travel increased by 440 percent, and attendance at sports and cultural events also grew rapidly. Sales of golf equipment increased by 188 percent, of tennis equipment by 148 percent, and use of bowling lanes by 258 percent. Hunting and fishing, horse-racing attendance, and copies of paperback books sold all gained dramatically and—most strikingly—the number of families with television sets grew by 3,500 percent over this 16-year period.[6]

Government recreation and park agencies dramatically expanded their budgets, personnel, facilities, and programs until the mid-1970s. Then, many federal, state, and local agencies were forced by funding cuts to cut back or freeze budgets. At the same time, the recreation and park profession continued to grow in numbers and public visibility. Preprofessional curricula were established in many colleges and universities during the 1960s and 1970s, and several national organizations, including the National Recreation Association, the American Recreation Society, and the American Institute of Park Executives, merged to form the National Recreation and Park Association—a stronger and more unified voice for the park and recreation field overall.

Effect of Demographic Changes: Suburbanization and Urban Crises

In the years immediately after World War II, which had disrupted the lives of millions of servicemen and -women, great numbers of young couples married. Within a few years, many of these new families with young children moved from the central cities to new homes in surrounding suburban areas. In these suburban communities, recreation for growing families became an important concern. Most suburbs were quick to establish new recreation and park departments, hire personnel, and develop programs and facilities to serve all age groups—often in concert with local school districts.

At the same time, the population within the inner cities changed dramatically. With the rapid mechanization of agriculture in the South and the abandonment of the sharecropper system, millions of African Americans moved from the South to the cities and industrialized areas of the Northeast, the Midwest, and the West in search of jobs and better opportunities. Growing numbers of Hispanic immigrants surged into the cities from the Caribbean islands and Central America. Generally, these new residents faced economic hardships, including limited employment opportunities, that resulted in health, housing, and welfare concerns for cities.

TRENDS IN PROGRAM SPONSORSHIP

As a result of such population shifts and changes in lifestyle, a number of trends in recreation program functions and in the role to be played by government emerged. These included (1) programs aimed at improving physical fitness, (2) emphasis on environmental concerns, (3) activities and services designed to meet specific age group needs, (4) recreation for persons with disabilities, (5) increasing programming in the arts, (6) services for people living in poverty, and (7) programs concerned with the needs of racial and ethnic minorities.

The Impact of Economic Declines on Spending for Leisure and Recreation

Over the course of the last quarter of the twentieth century and the first decade of the twenty-first century, the U.S. economy has experienced periodic economic declines. The declines are called recessions and take place when the economy contracts, or gets smaller. Recessions are characterized by high unemployment, stagnant wages, and falls in retail sales. Most recent recessions have been short-lived and their impact on public parks and recreation is documented elsewhere in this chapter. The impact on personal and public spending for recreation has broader implications. Not only does it affect public parks and recreation, but nonprofits providing recreation programs, the arts, and commercial recreation enterprises. The major recessions of the last 30 years occurred in 1981 (14 months), 1990 (8 months), 2001 (8 months), and 2007 (19 months). It was generally assumed that personal spending declines during a recession. However, spending data do not support that assumption. Between 1981 and 2009, there was only one quarter showing a decline in personal spending, and that occurred in 1991, during the dot-com bust. Through the early part of the twenty-first century, personal spending continued to increase in every quarter. That ended with the 2009 recession. This is the most broad-based recession since 1929, and almost everyone has been touched in some way. Some economists suggest that as a result of the 2009 recession personal spending will decline by 2% to 3%, which translates into $200 billion to $300 billion annually. Spread over several years, such spending declines have a major impact on public and nonprofit organizations. In 2010, evidence suggests people are continuing to find ways to cut expenses and reduce personal spending. The Internet, which was a nonfactor in previous recessions, is a source individuals are turning to for ways to reduce costs. Consumers bargain shop, look for coupons and special offers, do research on products, and so forth, all in an effort to reduce their spending.

Prior to the recession of 2009, conventional wisdom suggested that some spending reluctance would occur but would be short term and have minimal impact on personal spending. The widespread impact of the 2009 recession, although the recession has been declared officially over, continues in many states and is not expected to see a recovery before 2012. For leisure and recreation, the impact can be felt in a variety of ways. From a positive perspective, public agencies are experiencing high levels of enrollment from families and individuals replacing more costly commercial enterprises they used to patronize. Commercial enterprises are finding they have to be more cost effective and efficient, market more effectively, and ensure that their products and experiences are perceived as a value.

Simultaneous with the increase in demand, public and nonprofit-based parks and recreation agencies are facing the most significant funding crisis since the tax revolt of the early 1970s. Agencies are laying off staff, closing recreation centers, raising fees for programs, and looking for partnerships to survive.

Emphasis on Physical Fitness

Beginning in the 1950s, there was a strong emphasis on the need to develop and maintain the physical fitness of youth. In both world wars, a disappointingly high percentage of male draftees and enlistees had been rejected by the armed forces for physical reasons. Then,

The President's Council on Physical Fitness and Sport was created by President Eisenhower in 1956 and continues into the twenty-first century.

after World War II, comparative studies such as the Kraus-Weber tests showed that American youth were less fit than the youth of several other nations. Vice President Richard Nixon convened the President's Conference on the Fitness of American Youth at the United States Naval Academy in Annapolis, Maryland, in 1956. The recommendations from the conference included increasing public awareness, increasing public funding of community recreation, supporting nonprofit youth-serving agencies through private and public funds, increasing and improving community recreation facilities, improving fitness opportunities for girls, and improving leadership for physical activity. In 1956, President Dwight Eisenhower also established the President's Council on Youth Fitness to serve as a catalyst for motivating communities and individuals to adopt active lifestyles. In response to the conference, schools strengthened their programs of physical fitness, and many public recreation departments expanded their leisure activities to include fitness classes, conditioning, jogging, and sports for all ages.

Environmental Concerns

A key concern of the recreation field has been the environment. In the postwar period, it became evident that there was a critical need to preserve and rehabilitate the nation's land, water, and wildlife resources. U.S. citizens permitted the country's great rivers and lakes to be polluted by waste, forests to be ruthlessly razed by lumbering interests, and wildlife to be ravaged by overhunting, lack of adequate breeding areas, chemical poisons, and invasion of their environments. Greater and greater demands had been placed on the natural resource bank, with open space shrinking at an unprecedented rate.

In the late 1950s, President Dwight Eisenhower and the Congress formed the Outdoor Recreation Resources Review Commission to investigate this problem. The result was a landmark, heavily documented report in 1962 that helped to promote a wave of environmental efforts by federal, state, and municipal governments. The Federal Water Pollution Control Administration divided the nation into 20 major river basins and promoted regional sewage treatment programs in those areas. The Water Quality Act of 1965, the Clean Water Restoration Act of 1966, the Solid Waste Disposal Act of 1965, the Highway Beautification Act of 1965, and the Mining Reclamation Act of 1968 all committed the United States to a sustained program of conservation and protection of its natural resources. Another major piece of legislation was the Wilderness Act of 1964, which gave Congress the authority to declare certain unspoiled lands permanently off-limits to human occupation and development.

Many states and cities embarked on new programs of land acquisition and beautification and developed environmental plans designed to reduce air and water pollution. Nonprofit organizations such as the American Land Trust, the Nature Conservancy, and the Trust for Public Lands took over properties encompassing hundreds of thousands of acres—many of them donated by large corporations—for preservation or transfer to public agencies

A Short History of the Land and Water Conservation Fund

The legislation creating the Land and Water Conservation Fund (LWCF) was passed by Congress in 1964 and became law in 1965. The LWCF became the primary source of revenue for park and recreation agencies at the federal, state, and local levels and continues to play an important role. The LWCF initially had three sources of revenue: proceeds from sales of federal properties, motorboat fuel taxes, and user fees for recreation use of federal lands. This raised $100 million annually, but it quickly became evident the level of funding was inadequate to meet the goals of the program. In 1968, the funding level was raised to $200 million per year for five years, and an additional funding source, revenues from leasing of the Outer Continental Shelf oil and gas resources, was added. Congress gradually raised the funding level to $900 million annually.

Currently, approximately $900 million is annually accumulated into the fund. Through 2006, the fund accumulated $29 billion with 62% of the allocation going to federal land acquisition, 28% to state grant programs, and 10% to other programs. The major roadblock preventing greater success of the fund is that the allocation is not automatic but must be authorized annually by Congress. The president recommends a level of spending of the LWCF and in some years has recommended low levels of spending. Congress can override this recommendation and sometimes has. However, there have been more years when the fund has been spent below authorized levels than at authorized levels.

Appropriations from the fund have been made for three general purposes: (1) federal acquisition of land and waters and interests therein; (2) grants to states for recreational planning; acquiring recreational lands, waters, or related interests and developing outdoor recreation facilities; and (3) other federal purposes.

One of the key provisions of the fund is a requirement that every state create a "state comprehensive outdoor recreation plan" to be eligible to receive monies from the fund. Another important aspect of the program requires that all grants made to states be matched by state or local dollars. At the state level, funding is administered through a state organization, with some money going to state parks, wildlife, and other outdoor recreation managers. The remainder of the funding is provided to cities and counties on a competitive basis. Between 1965 and 2008, 41,000 grants were made to states. "This figure includes 10,600 grants for acquisition; 26,420 grants for developing recreation facilities; 2760 grants for redeveloping older recreational facilities; and 641 state planning grants for studies of recreation potential, need, opportunity, and policy."[7] From these funds the National Park Service reported, "2.6 million acres of state and local parkland through direct acquisition, and many times that number of acres is statutorily protected through development projects which protect lands acquired and developed from non-outdoor recreations uses in perpetuity."[8]

Results at the federal level have been equally impressive as the four recipient federal agencies (National Park Service, Forest Service, Fish and Wildlife Service, and Bureau of Land Management) have protected more than 4.5 million acres.

Outdoor recreation and nature areas have benefitted from the environmental efforts that began with Yellowstone National Park and continue today.

for recreational use. Such programs were accompanied by efforts within federal agencies such as the National Park Service, the Forest Service, the Fish and Wildlife Service, and the Bureau of Land Management to meet public needs for outdoor recreation.

In the early 1980s, federal expenditures for parks and environmental programs were sharply reduced, the rate of land acquisition was cut back, and government policies regulating the use of wild lands for mining, timber cutting, grazing, oil drilling, and similar commercial activities were dramatically relaxed.

Although national outdoor recreation planning ended in 1981, a number of major studies continued to assess the nation's natural resources and environmental concerns through the decades that followed.[9]

Meeting Age-Group Needs

In addition to the demographic trends cited earlier, three important changes in the nation's population that gathered force in the postwar decades were (1) the dramatic rise in the birth rate, with millions of children and youth flooding the schools and community recreation centers; (2) the lengthening of the population's life span, resulting in a growing proportion of older adults in society; and (3) the increasing pressures on families with children due to growing numbers of single-parent households and the entrance of millions of women into the workforce.

In response to these trends, thousands of governmental and nonprofit organizations expanded their programs for children and youth, and numerous youth sport leagues such as Little League, Biddy Basketball, and American Legion Football recruited millions of participants. At the other end of the age range, public and nonprofit organizations, including many municipal park and recreation agencies, developed golden age clubs or senior centers, often with funding from the federal government through the Administration on Aging.

Changing family households confirmed the need for recreation programs to provide day care services for children of working parents and to meet other leisure-related needs. Religious organizations in particular are stressing family-oriented programming today in an effort to strengthen marital bonds and improve parent–child relationships.

Special Recreation for Persons with Disabilities

An area of increased emphasis in the postwar era was the provision of supportive services for persons with physical and mental disabilities. As in the environmental field, this trend was strengthened by federal legislation. Various government agencies concerned with rehabilitation were expanded to meet the needs of individuals with physical disabilities, especially the large numbers of returning veterans who sought to be integrated into community life.

To better serve people with developmental disabilities, the federal government sharply increased its aid to special education. In recreation, assistance was given to programs serving children, youth, and adults with developmental disabilities. Beginning in the mid-1960s, there was an increased emphasis on developing social and recreational programs for aging persons in both institutional and community settings. Overall, the specialized field of what came to be known as therapeutic recreation service expanded steadily in this period. With the establishment of the National Therapeutic Recreation Society in the mid-1960s and the American Therapeutic Recreation Association in the 1980s, professionalization in therapeutic recreation service developed rapidly. The establishment of curriculum guidelines for courses in professional preparation, the setting of program standards, and the development of registration and certification plans all served to make this field a significant specialized area within the broad leisure-service field.

People with disabilities engage in a variety of sport and recreation activities today, including street hockey, tennis, and snow skiing.

Increased Interest in the Arts

Following World War II, the United States embarked on an expansion of cultural centers, museums, and art centers. In part, this represented a natural follow-up to the stimulus that had been given to art, theater, music, and dance by emergency federal programs during the Great Depression. Another element, however, was that Americans now had come to respect and enjoy the arts as both spectators and participants. Through the 1970s and early 1980s,

The Special Olympics

In 1968, Eunice Kennedy Shriver (1921–2009) organized the first International Special Olympic Games in Chicago, Illinois. The Special Olympics were an outgrowth of a day-camp program started in 1962 by Shriver for people with developmental disabilities. During the first international games, 1000 athletes from the United States and Canada competed. In 1977, the first winter games were held in Steamboat Springs, Colorado, and included 500 athletes. Today, 3.18 million athletes from 180 countries compete in local, state, national, and international Special Olympics events. The Special Olympics movement and the tireless work of Shriver have had an extraordinary impact on the public's understanding of people with developmental disabilities and creation of supportive public policy. Her comments at the 1987 Special Olympics have become a rallying cry for the rights of individuals with disabilities:

> "The right to play on any playing field?
> You have earned it.
>
> The right to study in any school?
> You have earned it.
>
> The right to hold a job?
> You have earned it.
>
> The right to be anyone's neighbor?
> You have earned it."[10]

community arts activities continued to flourish, with the assistance of federal funding through the National Endowment for the Arts, which helped to support state arts units, choreographers and composers, and individual performers and companies.

In the mid- and late 1980s, some decline in attendance at music, drama, and dance events was noted, possibly a result of declining federal support, increased ticket prices, and to the increasing public interest in home-based video entertainment. To meet this challenge, many cultural organizations in the fine and performing arts, as well as many museums, libraries, and similar institutions, developed new methods of fundraising by diversifying their offerings and marketing them to a broader community audience. As an example, art, natural history, and science museums today offer lectures, tours, classes, films, innovative displays, special fundraising dinners, and other events designed to attract a wide spectrum of patrons. As a result of these creative programming efforts, attendence at community theaters has grown steadily over the past 15 years.

Recreation's Antipoverty Role

An important development of the 1960s was the expanded role given to recreation as an element in President Lyndon Johnson's "war on poverty." Initially, the nation's concern about the economically and socially disadvantaged had been aroused by a widely read book on poverty in America by Michael Harrington, published in 1962 at a time of great prosperity for most citizens.

Candlestick Point State Recreation Area in California, which is surrounded by San Francisco's historically underserved Hunter's Point neighborhood, is described by the California State Parks division as "the first California State Park unit developed to bring state park values into the urban setting." Occupying 34 acres—much of which has suffered years of abuse as landfill and dumping grounds—the project involves the restoration of natural wetlands and subsequent habitat diversity that will benefit the Bay Area as well as the entire state.

During the 1930s and 1940s, a number of federal housing programs provided funding to support small parks, playgrounds, or centers in public housing projects. Now, a new wave of legislation, such as the Economic Opportunity Act of 1964, the Housing and Urban Development Act of 1964, and the Model Cities program approved in 1967, provided assistance for locally directed recreation programs to be conducted by disadvantaged citizens themselves in depressed urban neighborhoods. Other federal programs, such as the Job Corps, VISTA (Volunteers in Service to America), and the Neighborhood Youth Corps, also included recreation-related components.

Segregation and Integration in Recreation

The public recreation movement of the late nineteenth and early twentieth centuries did not equally benefit all Americans. Throughout most of the United States, separate recreation facilities had been built for African and Caucasian Americans. As with public education, the result of this segregation was highly disparate opportunities. The first widespread attempts at racial integration were in the late 1950s and early 1960s following the Supreme Court's landmark *Brown v. the Board of Education* decision.

Unfortunately, it was not until the late 1960s, following escalated racial tensions in many cities, that the federal government dedicated serious financial resources to serving African Americans, particularly those living in impoverished urban centers. Hundreds of millions of dollars were granted each year to local governments and to organizations of local residents to provide enriched recreation services aimed particularly at youth. These included sports and social activities, cultural pursuits, job-training and tutorial programs, and trips and similar recreation activities. On a national scale, the Job Corps, VISTA, Neighborhood Youth Corps, and an aggregate of special projects known as Community Action Programs continued into the 1970s but were gradually terminated in the years that followed.

COUNTERCULTURE: YOUTH IN REBELLION

During the late 1960s, what came to be known as the counterculture made its appearance in America. The term *counterculture*, as John Kelly points out, is generally applied to a movement that develops in opposition to an established and dominant culture—often in political, religious, or lifestyle terms—and that manifests itself in language, symbols, and behavior.

Rejection of the Work Ethic

A significant aspect of the counterculture movement was its rejection of work as the be-all and end-all of one's life and of the widely accepted goal of "making it" in the business or professional world. As Chapter 3 showed, a deep-rooted belief in the value of hard work, which was linked to an essentially conservative, industrious, and moralistic view of life, had long been a fundamental tenet of American society.

However, since World War II, there had been a retreat from the stern precepts of the Protestant work ethic. As establishment values and monetary success were undermined in the thinking of young people during the counterculture period, leisure satisfactions assumed new importance. Writers urged new, holistic approaches to the use of free time that would integrate varied aspects of human personality and lead to the self-actualization spoken of by Maslow and other psychologists.

The counterculture movement in the United States during the 1960s was part of a larger youth movement that challenged the political, economic, and educational establishments in a number of other nations around the world. Here, it symbolized the rebellion of young people against parental authority and the curricular and social controls of schools and colleges. Much of it stemmed from mass protests against the Vietnam War as students initiated strikes and takeovers of administrative offices in a number of universities. Rock music and lyrics that challenged traditional values became popular, and some young people joined "hippie" communes or fled to neighborhoods like Haight-Ashbury in San Francisco or the East Village in New York City, where they experimented with drugs and a variety of alternative lifestyles.

Protestant Work Ethic Rejected

The rejection of the Protestant work ethic was widely expressed in the music, art, and literature of the 1960s. The historical record of the baby boomers of the 1960s, however, indicates that the demise of Americans' obsession with work is more myth than reality. A study published by the Families and Work Institute in 2006 indicates that baby boomers are more likely to live work-centric lifestyles than the generations that preceded and follow them. A 2004 study by the same institute indicates that baby boomers work longer hours and are more likely to feel overworked than employees of other generations.

DRIVES FOR EQUALITY BY DISADVANTAGED GROUPS

Another important aspect of the counterculture movement was that it provided a climate within which various populations in American society that had historically been disadvantaged were encouraged to press vigorously for fuller social and economic rights.

Racial and Ethnic Minorities

For racial and ethnic minorities, there was a strong thrust during the 1960s and 1970s toward demanding fuller recreational service in terms of facilities and organized programs. In response, many public recreation and park departments not only upgraded these traditional elements, but also began to provide mobile recreation units that would enter affected neighborhoods to offer cultural, social, and other special services. Building on projects that had been initiated during the war on poverty and in response to escalating racial tensions in cities, many departments initiated classes, workshops, festivals, and holiday celebrations designed to promote ethnic pride and intercultural appreciation.

Rock concerts began in earnest in the 1960s and continue today.

Through legislation, Supreme Court decisions, other judicial orders, and voluntary compliance, public, nonprofit, and commercial facilities were gradually desegregated through the 1970s and 1980s. Major youth and adult social membership organizations such as the Girl Scouts and the YMCA, which had tended either to maintain segregated units for racial minorities or not to serve them at all, opened up their memberships and in some cases identified racial justice as a high-priority mission for the years ahead. In terms of the broader culture, greater numbers of racial and ethnic minorities began to achieve great success in such leisure-related areas as college and professional sports and popular entertainment such as music, television, and motion pictures.

CASE STUDY: Designing for Ethnic Minorities

One of the key concerns of outdoor recreation resource managers is the low number of racial and ethnic minorities visiting and participating in programs at outdoor recreation areas. Although not a new issue, land management agencies continue to struggle to find ways to engage these groups, especially as their population increases as a percentage of the total U.S. population. In a report prepared by the National Park Service (NPS) in 2008, five research hypotheses were reported that attempt to explain the lack of involvement in outdoor recreation. The hypotheses are marginality, subculture/ethnicity, discrimination, opportunity, and acculturation.

The *marginality* hypothesis suggests the differences in racial/ethnic minority representation are a result of socioeconomic factors caused by historical discrimination and include barriers such as limited financial resources, lower levels of education, and limited employment opportunities. The *subculture/ethnicity* hypothesis recognizes the influence of marginality on leisure and recreation patterns but argues the differences in park visitation, at least partially, are a result of cultural norms, value systems, social organizations, and socialization practices. Examples of cultural values or norms can include size of recreational groups, preferred activities (e.g., hiking, biking, swimming, picnicking), and development level of sites (e.g., bathrooms, pavilions, visitor centers).[a]

> The *discrimination* hypothesis places importance on contemporary, post civil rights discrimination that occurs from interpersonal contact with other visitors or park personnel or through institutional policies. The *opportunity* hypothesis examines the relationship between the residential location of minority populations, recreational sites, and recreation preferences. The *acculturation* hypothesis examines the relationship between cultural assimilation into the majority culture and recreational choices. According to this hypothesis, as a minority culture assimilates into the majority culture, they begin to take on the recreational patterns of the majority culture.[a]

Understanding the hypotheses is important, and moving from hypotheses to action is much more challenging. It frequently requires agencies to rethink how they do business, charge organizational culture, recognize the organization is not representative of the population it is designated to serve, and finally, strive to overcome bureaucratic inertia that promotes preservation of the norm over change. Each outdoor management agency deals with the challenge in its own way, and often in multiple ways. Federal agencies initiate plans and actions at the director, regional, and local levels. Much of the actual work falls to the local level because, at this level, the situation is direct and immediate. For example, in the mid-1990s, the Pacific regional director for the NPS determined that the public relations programs were focusing only on traditional media resources such as major newspapers, television, and radio stations. He organized a taskforce charged with identifying alternative media outlets in the San Francisco Bay area. In a short period of time, they identified more than 300 media outlets focusing on specific racial and ethnic minority groups, as well as women, gays and lesbians, and people with disabilities.

The U.S. Army Corps of Engineers approached the development and renovation of recreation sites with a focus on providing facilities, amenities, and programs designed to meet the expressed needs of racial and ethnic minorities. In 2002, the Army Corps of Engineers published a report titled *Managing for Ethnic Diversity: Recreation Facility and Service Modifications for Ethnic Minorities* in which the premise was that ethnically universal designs can meet the needs of a progressively more diverse population. Ethnically universal design focuses on creation of programs and facilities that are more inclusive of ethnic cultural diversity. Specifically, the report suggests moving away from the traditional design model, called an ethnically neutral design, which focuses wholly on white middle-class nuclear families with the assumption that other ethnic groups would adapt to the design model. The new approach moves toward a model of embracing cultural pluralism. Further, the report argues that the development of day-use facilities are essential to the success of this model.[b]

The report suggests a variety of facilities and services that appeal to Hispanics, Asians, and African Americans. These services include the following:

- Group shelters to provide shade and protection from inclement weather
- Larger tables, or modular movable tables, to accommodate large family groups
- Larger and easier-to-maintain grills and cookers for recreational cooking for large groups
- Shade trees in picnic sites
- Playgrounds (kids' zones) near picnic areas
- Open grassy play areas for sports that can accommodate a wide variety of activities
- Facilities for communities events (e.g., large group shelter, gazebo, amphitheaters)
- Use of universal symbols on signs
- Interpretive signs on walking trails in Spanish and other dominant languages of the region
- Mass transportation facilities (bus loading areas) at the most popular areas
- Improved security through increased ranger patrols, bilingual rangers, and improved gatehouses at park entrances[b]

Questions to Consider

1. How has the move away from ethnically neutral design intended to improve attendance at outdoor areas?
2. Why is it important to understand the reasons why ethnic populations may not see the outdoors as a special place?
3. Put yourself in the role of a resource manager and determine how you would increase participation by racial and ethnic minorities.

Sources

a. R. S. McCowan and D. N. Laven, *Evaluation Research to Support National Park Service 21st Century Relevance Initiatives*, (Washington, DC: National Park Service, 2008): 3.

b. R. A. Dunn, *Managing for Ethnic Diversity: Recreation Facility and Service Modifications for Ethnic Minorities*, ERDC/EL TR-02-14, (Vicksburg, MS: U.S. Army Research and Development Center, 2002).

CASE STUDY: African Americans Blog About the Outdoors

Much has been written about the absence of racial and ethnic minorities in the outdoors: whether it be recreation participation or involvement in the environmental movement. In recent years, however, this has begun to change and the Internet is providing a forum for those who choose to write about their involvement. Not only do they write blogs about outdoor involvement, they engage other individuals and are building a community of individuals who have the same interests and concerns.

Rooted in the Earth: Reclaiming the African American Environmental Heritage

Rooted in the Earth is a blog written by Dianne Glave, an African American history professor. In her introductory blog, she writes:

> As an African American woman, it has been a long lonely difficult journey sharing the stories of African Americans and the environment. It has also been one of my greatest joys. My goal in my inaugural May 2010 blog carnival is for diversity/environmental bloggers to share their successes along with their trials and tribulations. We have been doing the good but difficult work of getting the word out about diversity and the environment. I invite and challenge you to come join with me to connect with people and find support in one another. Some are connected and others are not. For those who are connected, continue with me creating community. For those who are not, please do join in."[a]

In an earlier blog, she talks about how she became involved:

> When I began doing the work on African American environment there were no definitions. Even today, if you google African American environmental history, a definition does not pop up. That's so unlike Google. One of my early efforts in working towards defining African American environmental history was an article on African American women and gardening.
>
> In my personal and professional struggle, I have been an academic for many years. There were few people of color I could count on, and that I knew of who work in various areas concerning diversity and the environment. So my cohorts and primary audience were mainstream academics. I was frustrated and alone. . . .
>
> I still teach. I still think like a historian. In many ways, I still write like a historian. What's different though is I have more people to connect with now that I'm writing for a broader audience with the upcoming book and my ongoing blog."[b]

OutdoorAfro.com

The author of *Outdoor Afro* has a tagline on her blog stating, "Where black people and nature meet." Rue Map has a broader purpose for the blog: "Outdoor Afro is a community that reconnects African Americans with natural spaces and one another through recreational activities such as camping, hiking, biking, fishing, gardening, skiing—and more! Outdoor Afro uses social media to create interest communities, events, and to partner with regional and national organizations that support diverse participation in the Great Outdoors."[c] The blog focuses on her individual and family experiences in outdoor places, the experiences of other individuals, the reasons they seek the outdoors, and of special events, places to visit, and how to connect. A recent blog entry was about a field trip as part of an Audubon Birdathon:

> Yesterday a group of Outdoor Afro fans from the San Francisco Bay area convened at Martin Luther King, Jr. Shoreline. The occasion was the Golden Gate Audubon (GGA) Birdathon, but the trip ended up as a leisurely education on birds and their habitat led by veteran birder and GGA docent Judith Dunham. This was a relatively unknown part of East Oakland for some of the participants, many of whom have lived in the area for many years.
>
> We started at the Arrowhead Marsh parking lot and walked along the path to the boardwalk, then returned and enjoyed lunch (that included some home made cornbread muffins) on the dock near the channel. Over lunch, Rue read from Camile Dungy's book, *Black Nature*, a favorite poem The Hummingbird, by Cyrus Cassells.
>
> Next, we drove to Damon Slough and looked at birds in the bay and the seasonal pond. We saw a wonderful variety of birds. Some, like the herons and egrets, live here year-round. Others, like the Long-Billed Dowitchers and Black-Bellied Plovers, will soon migrate north to the places where they breed. As an extra bonus, we saw American Coots with young and Mallards with ducklings. Thanks to everyone for making this such a rewarding trip![d]

Questions to Consider

1. Why is it important for African Americans to write about the outdoors?
2. Identify the values of using a blog to tell about the outdoors.
3. How can public land managers use this information to assist them in their responsibilities?

Sources

a. Dianne Glave, "Inaugural Blog Carnival," *Rooted in the Earth*, http://dianneglave.wordpress.com/2010/05/24/inaugural-blog-carnival-challenges-of-doing-diversity-and-environment/.
b. Dianne Glave, "How I Got into African American Environmental History," *Rooted in the Earth*, http://dianneglave.wordpress.com/2010/05/22/how-i-got-into-african-american-environmental-history/.
c. Rue Map, "So What Is Outdoor Afro?" *Outdoor Afro*, http://outdoorafro.com/about.
d. Rue Map, "Outdoor Afro Birders," *Outdoor Afro*, http://outdoorafro.com/2010/05/outdoor-afro-birders.html.

Progress for Women

In the 1960s and 1970s, feminist groups mobilized to attack two major areas of gender-based discrimination in recreation and leisure: employment practices and program involvement. A number of studies showed that women tended to secure fewer high-level administrative positions and were paid lower salaries than men in recreation and park departments throughout the United States.

In response to equal opportunity laws and other pressures, governmental recreation and park departments and other agencies began to hire women in greater numbers than in the past. Several states hired their first women park rangers, naturalists, and park superintendents; in a number of cities women were appointed as directors of the recreation and park departments.

A fundamental principle in community recreation has been that all persons should be given an equal opportunity, regardless of sex, religion, race, or other personal factors. However, in the postwar decades, it became evident that this principle had not been applied to participation of girls and women in public recreation programs in the United States.

In 1972, growing pressure from women's groups led to the approval of groundbreaking legislation, Title IX of the Education Amendments Act. Title IX was the first legislation to prohibit sex discrimination in educational institutions. Although Title IX prevents discrimination in all aspects of public education, including recruitment, admission, and employment, the primary focus of public discourse over the past 40 years has been equality in athletics.

During the 1970s and 1980s, community recreation organizations joined the nationwide effort to offer equal opportunities for girls and women. A significant development at this time was the merger of formerly sex-separated organizations into organizations serving both sexes, such as the Boys and Girls Club of America. As a result of these changes, girls and women today have a far greater range of sport and physical recreation opportunities than they did in the past.

Women's World Cup Soccer

From an international perspective, the Olympic Games were among the first true competitive events for women. Yet, it was Women's World Cup Soccer that captured the imagination of the world and firmly placed women as equals on the international sport stage. The International Federation of Association Football (FIFA) is the governing body for international football (soccer) and has been responsible for the men's World Cup since 1930. FIFA initiated the first Women's World Cup in 1991, and the event was held in China with 12 teams participating. Although it had an inauspicious start, the FIFA Women's World Cup has become an icon for women's equality in sport. The 1995 World Cup, held in Sweden, had a total attendance of 112,213 with one match only drawing 250 spectators. The 1999 World Cup, held in the United States, was the breakout World Cup with more than 1.1 million spectators and more than 1 billion television viewers. (See **Table 4.1**.) The Women's World Cup provided the American team's first international success, with championships in 1991 and 1999 and players such as Mia Hamm and Brandi Chastain becoming overnight household names. The success of the United States women's national soccer team, which resulted in two World Cups and three Olympic tournaments from 1990 to 2008, has helped earn soccer a place in the hearts of American society. Beyond that, it has opened women's sport on an international basis in areas where it might not otherwise have flourished.

TABLE 4.1

HISTORY OF THE WOMEN'S WORLD CUP: TEAMS IN FINALS AND TOTAL ATTENDANCE

Year	Location	No. of Teams	Champion	Attendance
1991	China	12	United States	510,000
1995	Sweden	12	Norway	112,213
1999	United States	16	United States	1,194,221
2003	United States	16	Germany	679,664
2007	China	16	Germany	997,433
2011	Germany			

Data from FIFA. Available at: http://www.fifa.com/womensworldcup/index.html. Accessed October 26, 2010.

Gays and Lesbians

Gay, lesbian, and bisexual individuals compose a third group who traditionally have been disadvantaged in American society. During the counterculture era, gay activists began to mobilize as an economic and political force. In the 1960s and 1970s, many gay and lesbian groups began to organize and promote their recreational and social activities openly on college campuses and in community life. In a number of cities, they had to fight through the courts for the right to take part in community celebrations, parades, and other civic events.

In other cases, when homosexual groups sought to participate in big-city St. Patrick's Day parades, or when they held a huge gay festival at Florida's Walt Disney World, a number of conservative Christian organizations protested vigorously. In retaliation, when rural Cobb County, Georgia, passed a resolution condemning the gay lifestyle as incompatible with its values, gay groups and their allies pressured the International Olympic Committee to withdraw some of its featured events from the county after they had already been scheduled to take place there as part of the 1996 Olympics.

Older Adults in Community Life

Although the counterculture was primarily a youth movement in the United States and abroad, it also prompted many middle-aged and older persons to examine their value systems and their status in community life.

Older adults at this time represented a fourth group of disadvantaged persons in the sense that they were generally regarded and treated as powerless individuals who were both physically and economically vulnerable. However, under the leadership of such growing organizations as the American Association of Retired Persons and the much smaller Gray Panthers, older adults began to mobilize and exert political clout to obtain improved benefits. With support from various federal programs, including the Administration on Aging, senior citizens' groups and golden age clubs around the United States began to offer diversified programs of health care, social services, nutrition, housing and transportation assistance, and recreation.

Programming for Persons with Disabilities

Although significant progress had been made following World War II, both treatment-centered and community-based programming for persons with disabilities received a major impetus during the counterculture period. Like other disadvantaged groups that had essentially been powerless, persons with disabilities began to act as their own advocates, demanding their rights and opportunities. People with disabilities began to mobilize politically to promote positive legislation and increased community services for those with physical, mental, or social disabilities.

At the same time that therapeutic recreation specialists began to include a broader range of disabilities within their scope of service, numerous organizations went one step further and promoted such innovative programming as theater arts for people with physical disabilities, skiing for individuals with visual impairments, and a full range of sports and track-and-field events for the people with mobility impairments.

AUSTERITY AND FISCAL CUTBACKS: 1970S AND 1990S

Despite this general picture of positive progress, the recreation, parks, and leisure-service field faced a serious threat in the 1970s and 1980s as mounting costs of government led to tax protests and funding cutbacks in states and cities across the United States. As early as the mid-1970s, a number of older industrial cities in the nation's Rust Belt, an area of the Midwest where iron and steel are produced and manufactured, began to suffer from increased energy costs, welfare and crime problems, and expenses linked to rising infrastructure maintenance problems. Along with some suburban school districts confronted by skyrocketing enrollments and limited tax bases, such communities experienced budget deficits and the need to freeze expenditures.

In periods of austerity and fiscal cut backs, states sometimes close state parks as a cost-saving measure.

In 1976, a tax limitation law was passed in New Jersey, and in 1978 California's much more radical Proposition 13 sharply reduced local property tax rates and assessment increases. A "tax revolt" soon spread rapidly across the United States. By the end of 1979, statutory provisions had been approved in 36 states that either reduced property, income, or sales taxes or put other types of spending limits in place. Austerity budgets had to be adopted in many communities, counties, and other governmental units. Typically, Proposition 13 resulted in major funding cutbacks for parks, libraries, recreation, social services, and street sweeping and maintenance, while police and fire departments tended to be protected against cuts.[11]

Expanding Use of Revenue Sources

Many local recreation and park agencies adopted the policy of instituting or raising fees and charges for participation in programs, for use of the facilities, for rental of equipment, and for other types of involvement in a wide range of leisure activities and services. In the past, it generally had been the practice to provide all basic play opportunities, particularly for children and youth, without charge and to impose fees only for classes with special expenses or for admission to facilities such as skating rinks, swimming pools, golf courses, or tennis courts—often with arrangements made for annual permits at modest cost.

Acceptance of Marketing Orientation Directly linked to this trend was the widespread acceptance of an entrepreneurial, marketing-oriented approach to recreation and park programming and administration. It was argued by both educators and practitioners that it was necessary to be aggressive in seeking out new program opportunities and creative in responding to fiscal challenges rather than relying on past, and often outmoded, formulas or policies.

References were being made to recreation as an "industry" in both the popular and the professional literature. Typically, in 1986, the *American Association for Leisure and Recreation Reporter* described the recreation field as a mosaic of thousands of businesses woven directly or subtly into the American economy.

In other professional publications, it was argued that managers of recreation and park programs, directors of nonprofit youth organizations, and operators of commercial play facilities were all essentially in the same "business"—that of meeting the public's leisure needs and interests.

Trends, published by the National Recreation and Park Association and the National Park Service, agreed:

> Managed recreation is a profession that provides services to consumers of all demographic stripes and shades. Under this designation, a public park superintendent is in the same business as a resort owner . . . a theme park operator and the fitness directors of a YMCA.[5]

It was often argued that to compete effectively public recreation agencies had to adopt the philosophy and businesslike methods of successful companies. This meant that at every stage of agency operations—from assessing potential target populations and planning programs to pricing, publicizing, and distributing services—sophisticated methods of analysis and businesslike approaches to attracting and satisfying "customers" were to be used.

Prominence of Fees and Charges for Activities

Even when recreation programs are provided by public local or nonprofit agencies, price tags are placed today on almost every kind of sponsored recreational opportunity. Typically, the annual or seasonal program brochures of public recreation and park agencies list various classes, aquatic or sport facilities, camps, tournaments, or special events—invariably with attached fees and charges that may run into several hundreds of dollars.

Privatization of Recreation and Park Operations

As a second type of response to the era of austerity that began in the 1980s, many recreation, park, and leisure-service agencies resorted to privatization—subcontracting or developing concession arrangements with private organizations—to carry out functions that they could not themselves fulfill as economically or efficiently.

Privatization has become a major thrust in American life as the role of government has been challenged. Many cities now rely on private businesses to construct or maintain facilities, provide food and health services, or manage a variety of other formerly public functions. In a number of cases, prisons and correctional institutions are managed by for-profit companies under contract with public authorities, and several cities have experimented with assigning private organizations the responsibility for running all or part of their school systems.

As for recreation and parks, numerous public departments have contracted with private businesses to operate golf courses, tennis complexes, marinas, and other facilities under agreements that govern the standards they must meet and the rates they may impose. Particularly in the construction of massive new facilities such as sports stadiums and arenas, similar arrangements have been made with commercial developers or businesses for private funding of all or part of construction expenses, with long-term leases being granted to owners of major sports teams.[12]

Impact of Funding Cuts

In 1978, the National Urban Recreation Study reported that hiring freezes and staff cutbacks had taken place in a majority of urban park and recreation departments during the preceding five years. Two years later, a study of U.S. cities having more than 150,000 in population found that a majority of the responding recreation and park departments experienced major cutbacks that necessitated personnel freezes and staff discharges, program eliminations, rejection of bond issues, and reduced facility maintenance.

Some reports suggested that many municipal and county recreation and park agencies weathered the financial crisis that followed the tax revolt and reached a point of relative stability. A study of small-town public recreation departments in several Western and Midwestern states by Ellen Weissinger and William Murphy found that although these departments experienced somewhat similar cutbacks to those reported in larger cities, they generally avoided drastic reductions in staff and programs.[13]

However, the reality is that in many larger cities, which have the greatest number of poor families and are marked by high welfare statistics, school dropouts, drug and alcohol abuse, youth gangs, and random violence, recreation and park programs today offer only the most minimal opportunities. The facilities that are provided are often vandalized and covered with graffiti, staff members are threatened, and overall agency operations are extremely limited.

Beyond this, Jack Foley and Veda Ward point out that in the early 1990s the most severely disadvantaged communities, such as South Los Angeles, nonprofit sports groups like Little League, Pony League, AAU swimming, and gymnastic and track clubs (which use public facilities but rely on volunteer leaders and membership fees) do not exist. There is also no commercial recreation in the form of movie theaters, malls, skating rinks, or bowling alleys. They continue:

> Boys and Girls Clubs, YMCAs and YWCAs, Scouts, and so forth, which rely on business and community support, are under-represented and financed in poor communities. A market equity policy (one gets all the recreation one can buy) [has] created a separate, unequal, and regressive City of Los Angeles recreation system. Many city parks [in wealthier neighborhoods] raise from $50,000 to $250,000 annually from user fees and donations for state-of-the-art services, while recreation centers in South Los Angeles exist on small city subsidies and what money they can squeeze out of the parents of poor children.[14]

EXPANSION OF OTHER RECREATION PROGRAMS

In sharp contrast with this negative picture, other forms of recreation services have flourished over the past three decades. Today, the largest single component of leisure services is the diversified field of commercial recreation businesses. Travel and tourism; fitness spas; professional sport and sport equipment; the manufacture and sale of hobbies, toys, and games; and varied forms of popular entertainment represent only part of this major sector of leisure involvement.

Similarly, most of the other areas of specialized recreation programming, such as therapeutic recreation, employee services, campus recreation, and private-membership and residential leisure services, have expanded steadily. In each case, these fields have sharpened their own identities and public images by developing professional societies or business associations, sponsoring national and regional conferences, publishing newsletters and magazines, and in some cases establishing continuing education and certification programs.

The Importance of Individual Donors to Nonprofits

Nonprofit organizations are dependent upon the goodwill of individuals and organizations to provide financial donations. This is especially true when the nonprofit desires to renovate existing buildings or to construct new buildings. The annual operating budget of a nonprofit is highly dependent upon individual donations. Many organizations gain a share of their operating budget from the United Way, but this is rarely sufficient to maintain day-to-day operations, and for an organization to improve its physical facilities it is wholly dependent upon contributions and grants. Physical facilities can be as simple as furniture for a meeting room and a softball complex for girls and women or can be major structures, such as multisport facilities, community centers, hospitals, and the like. The Salvation Army was recipient to such a goodwill gift in 1998 and the gift has allowed it to change the way it delivers community services in some communities.

The Kroc Centers, operated by the Salvation Army, are major community centers that provide multiple services, including recreation.

In 1998, Mrs. Joan Kroc, widow of McDonald's founder Ray Kroc, donated $90 million to the Salvation Army to build a comprehensive community center in San Diego, California. Her goal was to create a center, supported in part by the community, where children and families would be exposed to different people, activities and arts that would otherwise be beyond their reach. Completed in 2001, the center sits on 12 acres and offers an ice arena, gymnasium, three pools, rock climbing walls, a performing arts theatre, an Internet-based library, computer lab, and a school of visual and performing arts.

When Mrs. Kroc passed away in October 2003, she left $1.5 billion—much of her estate—to the Salvation Army, by far the largest charitable gift ever given to the Army, and the largest single gift given to any single charity at one time. The initial disbursements of this bequest began in January 2005. The gift had by then grown to $1.8 billion and was split evenly among the four Army Territories—Central, East, South, and West. The money was designated to build a series of state-of-the-art Salvation Army Ray and Joan Kroc Corps Community Centers nationwide patterned after the San Diego center. From the very beginning, the Salvation Army envisioned this as a long-term project, which could take up to 10 or 15 years to have all of the centers open and operational. No other U.S. charity—faith-based or otherwise—has ever undertaken such a sweeping fundraising or construction effort with the potential to impact millions of people.[15]

By the end of 2010, 10 such centers will be open with an additional 15 centers scheduled to open in following years until 25 centers are in place. They are located throughout the United States in cities such as San Francisco, California; Atlanta, Georgia; Ashland, Ohio; Coeur d'Alene, Idaho; Omaha, Nebraska; Salem, Oregon; Dayton, Ohio; Grand Rapids, Michigan; Kerrville, Texas; Puerto Rico; and Phoenix, Arizona.

An example of the success of the Kroc Centers comes from Coeur d'Alene, Idaho, which saw its own center completed in 2009.

The Kroc turns 1 today—and what a year it has been. Before it opened, it shot for around 2000 members, keeping its fingers crossed for 5000 at the one year mark. Today, it has 20,500 members, and has entertained around 630,000 visitors since May 11, 2009—while staff has increased to 272 employees compared to around 70 when it opened. And, a dozen cities, including Philadelphia, Chicago, Honolulu, and now Quincy, have toured the most populated Kroc Center in the West as a guide for their future hometown facilities.[16]

TRENDS IN THE 1990s AND EARLY TWENTY-FIRST CENTURY

This section describes several important demographic, social, economic, and technological trends beginning in the 1990s that influenced the provision of recreation and leisure services in the years immediately before and after the turn of the century. Chapter 13 deals with these and more trends in greater detail.

Economic Stratification: Income Gaps and "Luxury Fever"

Historically, the United States was viewed as a land of opportunity, in which every individual might climb the socioeconomic ladder and in which the middle class represented the backbone of society. During the 1990s and into the twenty-first century, these assumptions were sharply reversed. Several new studies on the growing concentration of U.S. wealth and income challenged the nation's cherished self-image. Bradsher writes:

> They show that rather than being an egalitarian society, the United States has become the most economically stratified of industrial nations. . . . Indeed the drive [under the so-called Contract with America] to reduce federal welfare programs and cut taxes is expected to widen disparities between rich and poor.[17]

In part, this development stemmed from the emergence of a winner-take-all mentality in American business and public life, as more and more Americans competed for ever fewer and bigger prizes, encouraging "economic waste, income inequality, and an impoverished cultural life."[18]

The growth of the number of wealthy families in the United States in the 1990s was not accompanied by reduction of families living in poverty. In 1993, the nation's poverty rate rose to a 10-year high of 15.1%. In 2008, 13.2% of U.S. citizens, or 39.1 million people, lived in poverty. Although the poverty rate fluctuates a few percentage points across each decade, there has been very little change since the mid-1960s when a number of antipoverty social programs were implemented. (See **Figure 4.1**.)

Starting in the 1990s, there were growing concerns about the ability of the middle class to make ends meet. Meanwhile, the middle class was declining, both in terms of numbers, income, and morale. In 1995, Labor Secretary Robert Reich concluded:

> Today's middle class is split into three groups. An underclass largely trapped in center cities, increasingly isolated from the core economy; an overclass of those who are positioned to profitably ride the waves of change; and in between, the largest group,

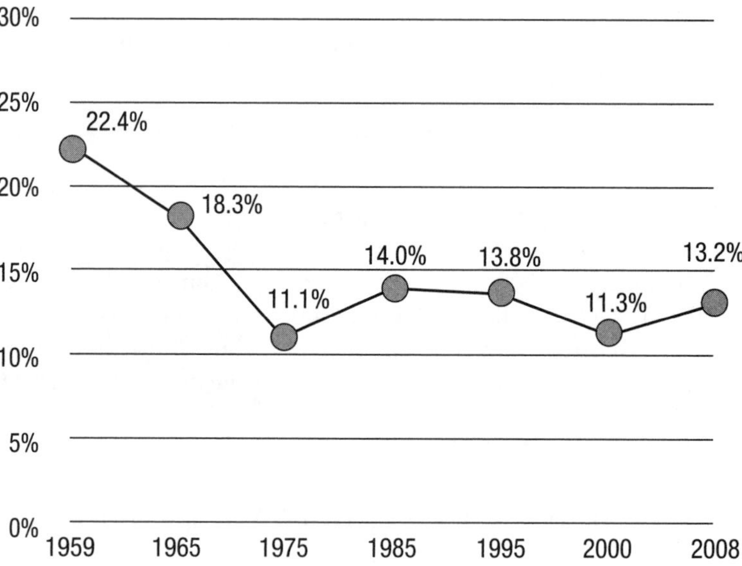

FIGURE 4.1 Poverty Level in the United States, 1959–2008
Data from U.S. Census Bureau. *Alternative Poverty Estimates in the United States: 2003* (Washington, DC: U.S. Census Bureau, 2005); and U.S. Census Bureau. *Poverty: 2007 and 2008 American Community Surveys* (Washington, DC: U.S. Census Bureau, 2009).

> an anxious class, most of whom hold jobs but who are justifiably . . . uneasy about their own standing and fearful for their children's futures.[19]

Stratification of Salaries and the Middle Class

Much has been written about the stratification of salaries, including in this chapter. Less has been written about the impact on the middle class. Robert Frank's book *Falling Behind* is among several books addressing the effects of salary stratification on middle-class Americans.[20] A key premise of the book looks at the income gains at the highest level. Frank suggests that although the rich have gotten richer, the middle class has not kept up with income increases. There is no accepted definition of the middle class, so when annual income is considered as a measure, and individuals are asked if they are part of the middle class, people with annual incomes ranging from $40,000 to $250,000 say yes, they are middle class. These respondents typically say that they are stretched to make ends meet. They have not seen their salaries grow at a pace with the rich, yet they are purchasing more expensive homes, engaging in more expensive activities, and appear to be enjoying it less. Frank addresses the "rising cost of adequate" and uses homes as an example. When the rich build new homes or mansions, those at the top of the middle class begin to build larger homes sometimes stretching what they can afford. There is a trickle-down effect to other levels of middle class as families see the community expectation for middle class rise. It is what Frank calls a cascading effect, where what top income earners spend their money on influences the spending patterns of the group directly below them, and on down until the effect reaches individuals at the bottom of the middle-class spectrum.

Implications for Leisure What does this growing separation of U.S. society into rich and poor mean for recreation and leisure? First, a growing number of individuals became immensely wealthy. In 1999, it was reported that 4.1 million of the nation's 102 million households had a net worth of $1 million or more.

In what seemed to be a vivid replay of Thorstein Veblen's view of "conspicuous consumption," these individuals were caught up in what Cornell economist Robert Frank described as *luxury fever*—a rage to spend wildly on vehicles, clothing, toys and hobbies, and a host of other possessions.

> Multimillion-dollar megamansions were being built throughout the country, often on relatively small lots. Many of the newly rich were paying huge sums to build elaborate swimming pools or buy luxury yachts or giant motor homes for vacation travel. One billionaire's ex-wife demanded $4400 a day to raise their daughter after divorce, and parents began paying sports coaches $70 an hour—sometimes more—to coach their youngsters in Little League baseball skills.[21]

The absence of recreation and park services in some urban areas force youth to use streets and vacant lots for recreation.

Meanwhile, children in less-affluent neighborhoods or school districts often attended schools that lacked even the most minimal resources for play, as well as spaces and equipment for classes. Throughout the nation at the century's end, the growing gap between rich and poor evidenced itself in jarring contrasts in terms of recreation, parks, and leisure opportunities.

Growing Conservatism in Social Policy

Accompanying the nation's division into rich and poor social classes, there was a pronounced shift in the late 1980s and the twenty-first century toward more conservative social and economic policies. This trend took many forms, including a sharp withdrawal of assistance for welfare and for inner-city programs serving the economically disadvantaged. Particularly in the mid-1990s (and again in the early twenty-first century), there were renewed efforts to open the nation's parks and forests to economic exploitation and to reduce support for environmental education programs.

The election of President Barak Obama and the initiation of the 2009 great recession for a short time loosened the growing social conservatism. However, once the initial crisis was over, Congress and the public became gridlocked in ideological discussions. There were continuing assaults on federal support for the National Endowment for the Arts and other cultural programs. Funding for the National Endowment for the Arts was cut from $162 million in 1995 to $99 million in 1996. The arts turned more and more to private funding.

Throughout the past three decades, newspaper headlines illustrated the impact of conservative political thrusts on American life in such areas as mandates for child welfare, nursing home beds for the elderly, health care, environmental protection enforcement, legal help for the urban poor, and youth programs. The widespread decline in support for needed public services and the harsh resistance to government policies benefiting minorities and the poor inevitably posed a severe challenge to many public and nonprofit leisure-service organizations.

Commodification and Privatization of Leisure Services

There is a continued blurring of functions among different types of organizations in American society: governmental, nonprofit, private, and commercial. Instead of having clearly marked areas of responsibility and program operations in the leisure-service field, these separate kinds of organizations overlap each other through partnerships or cosponsorship arrangements; privatization by expanding their missions and undertaking new, innovative ventures; by adopting new fiscal policies, and by turning their operations over to the private sector. This overall trend had two related components: commodification and privatization.

The New Realities: New, Revisited, or Just Pessimism?

A consistent theme appearing in the literature of public and nonprofit recreation and leisure publications is that the recession of 2009–2010 has changed funding models forever. It is true that the recession diminished funding for public and nonprofit organizations. These organizations are almost always negatively affected by a recession, even when for-profit enterprises appear to be less affected.

One of the dilemmas faced by public and nonprofit organizations when the economy is in recession is an increasingly greater need for public services. People turn to public agencies for basic and recreational needs. Unfortunately, as demand increases, public agencies are facing similar financial challenges, frequently resulting in budget cuts and reduction of services. What is particularly challenging in the 2009 recession is the loss of revenue from multiple funding sources. Cities count on property, income, and sales taxes for the bulk of their operating revenues. Each source is somewhat volatile, but for the last 30 years property taxes have steadily increased until 2010, when property values dropped across major portions of the country. The new realities for recreation agencies may be that funding has changed forever. It did in the early 1970s when the tax revolt affected many states and communities. However, it is easy to assume things will not get better. That is a wrong-thinking attitude. Government funding sources, although traditionally stable, have not always been so, and to approach change from a negative perspective guarantees that opportunities will be missed.

It is important that public organizations and nonprofits maintain quality and focus on the future. In Las Vegas, Nevada, where more than 150 park and recreation employees were laid off and five community centers were closed, the director stated, "We will be a smaller, more efficient, and more responsive organization in the future." The new realities are that in the short term public and nonprofit organizations will rethink, reorganize, and reprioritize their services and programs. Simultaneously, however, they need to plan for and aggressively act on the future.

Commodification Simply defined, *commodification* describes the process of taking any product or service and commercializing it by designing and marketing it to yield the greatest degree of financial return or profit. Political scientist Sebastian de Grazia described the fuller meaning of this trend:

> Commodification of leisure is understood as a necessary element in the subordination of the entire social system to the reproduction of capitalism and its institutional structure. The consequence to the worker is surrendering to forms of leisure which turn away from self-defining, creative experience and, instead, consume vast quantities of market-produced goods and services.[22]

On the national scene, as part of the effort to gain fuller financial support in an increasingly consumer-oriented society, art museums, libraries, and theater, orchestra, and ballet companies all have become centers of popular entertainment, offering chartered trips abroad, film series and lecture programs, social events, and jazz concerts.

Privatization As described earlier in this chapter, *privatization* refers to the growing practice of having private corporations take on responsibility for providing services, maintaining facilities, or performing other functions formerly carried out by government agencies.

During the 1990s, privatization grew increasingly widespread in such areas as the so-called prison industry, in which growing numbers of commercial businesses gained contracts for managing prisons or correctional centers, and such civic functions as trash removal, building maintenance, or the operation of utility or water-supply systems. In terms of public recreation and park privatization, the most striking event was the 1998 contract for a private group, the Central Park Conservancy, to operate New York City's famous and historic Central Park, with joint public and private funding. A more common approach to privatization is to contract with a nonprofit to provide recreation services. This has been a frequent model in smaller communities where a nonprofit exists and no public recreation agency exists. The same model is present in large cities where existing recreation and park agencies cannot provide the level of service requested. A major recreation center is built, at public expense, and then leased to a nonprofit for day-to-day operation. In many cases, the nonprofit continues to require a membership fee and may exclude some lower-income users.

Maturation of Organized Leisure-Services Field

The nature of municipal, state, and federal governments has changed dramatically in the almost 140 years of organized recreation in the United States. Today's city government is markedly different from that of our forebears. Government is more dependent on alternative income sources and less reliant on taxes. Public park and recreation agencies have, of necessity, become entrepreneurial. Where few fees once existed, now public agencies depend on fees and charges to make up as much as 90% of their operating budget. Parks and recreation agencies are hard pressed to serve all of those who either desire or have a need for services. Nonprofit and commercial agencies fill the gap in many instances. In today's environment of rapidly changing demand for different types of leisure activities, public, commercial, and nonprofit organizations strive to respond, but often public agencies and nonprofits do not have the resources, financial capital, or ability to respond effectively. Commercial enterprises typically respond more quickly to what initially may appear to be fringe activities such as paintball, skateboarding, laser tag, and the like.

Maturation does not suggest the organized leisure-services field is not changing, but rather that growth in the public and nonprofit sector is constrained by available funds, politics, public interest, and the perceived opportunity for growth. Public and nonprofit agencies have developed an infrastructure of parks, recreation centers, sports fields, cultural centers, and others that become a burden to agencies' ability to rapidly respond to change. The traditional programming of public and nonprofit agencies remains in place, although there is less of it and more of the emerging programs, but change is coming slowly. Where communities once built a 50-meter swimming pool, today they build a small to medium waterpark—except when politicians or other influential groups intervene and demand a traditional or old-fashioned approach. The leadership is changing and new; younger leaders are emerging. Values are being reassessed, commitments rethought, demands evaluated, and expectations challenged.

New Environmental Initiatives

As this chapter has shown, the nation's support for environmental protection and the recovery of polluted lakes and streams, as well as the continuing acquisition and preservation of wilderness areas, faced a sharp challenge through the end of the twentieth century.

Several decades of neglect and overcrowding left the nation's park system and forests in a precarious state. In 1997, *Time* cited Yellowstone as a leading example:

> There is little doubt that the preservationists are losing ground. The ills that beset the nation's first and still most magnificent park affect the park system as a whole: underfunding and overcrowding, pollution, encroaching commercial development, invasion of exotic species, and the decline of natural, historical, and cultural treasures.[23]

Commercial recreation is present in or near national parks as evidenced by the new glass walkway over the Grand Canyon—it exists on Native American land.

With national concern mounting, park authorities and Congress moved ahead in the years that followed. In a number of the major parks, they instituted new fees to gather additional revenue and restricted automobile traffic into interior sections. Increasingly, corporate sponsors were recruited to assist in park maintenance, and major environmental organizations such as the National Park Trust provided support for the acquisition of new parks and wildlands.

Although public concerns focused chiefly on the ecological recovery of parks and wilderness areas, they also were directed to problems of clean air and water that affected major metropolitan areas. At the same time, major efforts were made in such older cities as Baltimore and Boston to revive waterfront and disused industrial areas. In such settings, cities developed new harbor facilities such as aquariums, museums, sport stadiums, marinas, theme parks, and other cultural and entertainment attractions—both to improve their image and attract tourists and to serve their own residents with appealing leisure programs.

Technological Impacts on Leisure

Beyond the effects of technological innovation described, a number of other scientifically based advances had a major impact on American leisure in the final decades of the twentieth century. Many of these had to do with forms of travel. Apart from the use of computers in tourism planning and reservations, Global Positioning System (GPS) services became able to direct an automobile trip through every turn until reaching the desired destination. Electronic navigation simulators created by companies such as Maptech, Inc., provided piloting assistance for boating enthusiasts. For the vacationing family, movies and video games replaced license-plate Bingo, as cars became entertainment centers with the latest audio and video technology that was being displayed at consumer electronic shows.

Home environments became increasingly "smart," with "Nanny cams" to watch over sleeping babies or "intelligent" wallpaper that turned the wall of a room into a television screen, virtual aquarium, or other visual feature. Home theater systems can control lighting; digital, CD, and MP3 systems; window shades; satellite service; and BlueRay players, while other lines wirelessly accommodate the family's telephones, fax machines, and computers—all at a distance.

Television, video games, and children's toys represent impressive examples of technology's impact on family leisure. As of the late 1990s, almost 80% of homes had cable or satellite television, and many studies reported that about 40% of Americans' free time was spent watching the home screen.

Into the twenty-first century, television watching has continued to be the most popular form of viewing media; however, it is receiving stiff competition from Internet-based sources used by computers and handheld devices. Nielsen's quarterly analysis of viewing shows that in the first quarter of 2009 people watched an average of 153 hours of television every month. This is an all-time high, but what is even more noteworthy is the impact the Internet has on viewing. In the past, almost all viewing was on the television. Now television viewing is shared with watching television or videos on the Internet. The availability of handheld video devices means that individuals no longer need to be at home to watch videos. They can download them and watch them while traveling, or they can watch live feeds at work, while on vacation, or in a variety of settings. The most current figures suggest people watch 3.5 hours of video each month on their mobile phone.[24]

RECREATION AND WELLNESS REVISITED

Public health officials have recognized that the sedentary lifestyles led by a large percentage of adults and children in the United States are directly contributing to a prevalence of obesity in the population that approaches epidemic levels. Childhood obesity also is of significant concern. As with adults, excessive caloric intake and inadequate physical activity are the primary contributors to obesity.[25,26] Unfortunately, the rise in childhood obesity has coincided with a decline in student time spent in physical education classes, recess, and outdoors.

Today, recreation and leisure-service providers and the federal government recognize the role of community recreation in encouraging physical activity. Federally funded initiatives include the establishment of community trail systems and support of after-school

Maryland Finds Success in Promoting Physical Activity

County and municipal parks and recreation facilities across Maryland are promoting good health through a wide array of supportive policies, such as not using food as a reward in youth sports programs, designing trails to be accessible to wheelchairs, and promoting safety for pedestrians and bicyclists.

A recently released survey of the state's parks and recreation programs found that such policies are helping state residents get active and eat better. The survey is, in part, a response to the Maryland Department of Health and Mental Hygiene's Nutrition and Physical Activity Plan, which asks each state agency to help address Maryland's almost 60% rate of overweight and obesity among adults.

The survey found that sports teams and classes are widely offered, as are out-of-school programs and trips, fitness programs for all ages, and therapeutic recreation programs. The survey documents more than 17,000 core physical activity programs serving more than 360,000 Marylanders. About 70% of the state's recreation programs responded to the survey. For example, the Montgomery Village Association offers a lunchtime walking program called "Walking for Health," aimed at stay-at-home moms, seniors, and other adults. The Tie Rockville Department of Recreation and Parks works with three elementary schools to promote International Walk to School Day.

Fitness challenges in the state often mix physical activity with nutrition education to encourage kids and adults to improve their overall fitness levels. The Get Active Howard County program aims to encourage those living or working in the county who don't already exercise regularly to become acquainted with the area's trails, health clubs, athletic fields, and gyms and to work out regularly over a 10-week period. More than 1200 people participated in the effort. The Family Fitness Challenge in Annapolis urges city employees and community members to eat more fruits and vegetables and get physically active. The survey also details a number of health fairs that seek to expose community members to recreation activities and healthier eating habits. Sponsored sporting events include running races; a youth biathlon as well as a triathlon; a punt, pass, and kick contest; and a walk designed especially for toddlers and kindergarten-age children.

A report on the survey includes a summary of policies that help support the state's efforts to cut down on obesity. For example, in Ocean City, the police department holds semiannual bike safety seminars and bike checks, and the city sponsors a "Walk Safe" campaign. In Worcester County, pathways accessible to people with disabilities were recently installed in all county parks with athletic fields to give universal access to fields and playgrounds as required by the Americans with Disabilities Act. A project under way in St. Mary's County will transform a 28-mile county-owned railroad right of way into a trail for walking, running, bicycling, and horseback riding.

Ron Schroers, president of the Maryland Recreation and Parks Association and director of recreation and parks for the city of Westminster, says the report helped those in the recreation field share ideas and make plans for future programs.[27]

programs. The Surgeon General's Office recommended the development of public policy that addresses community access to safe physical activity. A growing number of nonprofits focusing on childhood obesity, lack of fitness orientations and programs, and the decline in children's contact with the outdoors and nature have emerged and are providing leadership. More discussion on obesity and the role of recreation can be found in Chapter 5.

Changing Demographics

The face of the United States began to change in the 1990s and will continue to change over the next several decades. As a result, the population served by recreation and leisure organizations in the twenty-first century will differ substantially from that served in the twentieth century. Some of the primary changes include the following:

- The number of adults 65 years and older grew from 25 million in 1980 to more than 36 million in 2005. By 2050, the 65-and-over population is projected to grow to more than 70 million.
- The composition of households in the United States will become increasingly diverse, as the number of households without children and single-parent households continue to grow.
- The growth of the Hispanic population in the United States will continue throughout the next few decades as Hispanic Americans become the largest ethnic minority group in the United States. This growth will occur throughout the country, including regions, such as the rural Midwest, that historically have had homogeneous populations.

A changing population requires new approaches to delivery of leisure services. Agencies are challenged to serve an older population that will include several cohorts with different values and views of aging. Traditional recreation programs for older adults may not appeal to baby boomers, who highly value independence and resist aging stereotypes. The range and number of programs targeted at older adults will have to increase to meet the demands of this growing population.

The changing ethnic composition of U.S. society will require leisure-service providers to examine the cultural framework that underlies programs and services. Agencies in certain geographic areas and some urban areas currently are responding to the need for truly multicultural programming. In other areas, particularly those with little history of ethnic diversity, significant work remains to be accomplished.

SUMMARY

The years following World War II represented a period of immense change in the lives of Americans. From 1945 to the early 1970s, it was a time of prosperity and optimism for most families. As great numbers of young people—generally white and working- or middle-class—moved into suburban areas, recreation and park programs flourished, and leisure was seen as part of the good life.

Recognizing that a substantial part of the population continued to live in urban slums, with limited economic and social opportunities, the federal government launched a "war on poverty," in which recreation played a significant role. Under pressure from the civil rights movement, many recreation and park agencies began to give a higher level of priority to serving minorities. With the inner-city riots of the mid- and late 1960s, this effort was expanded throughout the country. At the same time, the counterculture movement, which saw young people rebelling against traditional authority and establishment values, transformed society with its resistance to the work ethic and its acceptance of drugs.

The late 1960s and 1970s were also a time when minority groups—including women, older adults, persons with disabilities, and those who are gay, lesbian, bisexual, or transgender—began to demand greater social, economic, political, and leisure opportunities. For them, recreation represented a means of gaining independence and achieving their fullest potential.

Beginning in the 1970s and intensifying during the decade that followed, recessions, inflation, rising costs of welfare and crime, and declining tax bases created an era of austerity that affected many government agencies. With sharp cutbacks in their budgets, many recreation and park agencies imposed severe staffing and maintenance cuts and relied more markedly on fees and privatization to maintain their programs. The entrepreneurial marketing strategy that prevailed widely at this time meant that many public departments were forced to give less emphasis to socially oriented programming.

At the same time, political conservatism in areas related to race relations, the criminal justice system, services for the poor, and environmental programs gained support. Studies in the 1980s and 1990s indicate that many Americans were working longer hours because of changes in family patterns and technological influences on business. At the end of the 1990s, with economic prosperity and more positive social and environmental concerns gaining acceptance, the place of recreation and leisure in contemporary life appeared to be more secure than ever.

Parks and recreation agencies face new challenges and opportunities in the twenty-first century. The population has started to change dramatically, requiring parks and recreation professionals to develop appropriate programs and services. Growing health concerns have provided an opportunity for agencies to play a greater role as public health advocates. The rapidly growing older population has time and resources for leisure, but may reject traditional senior programs for more youthful and diverse opportunities. Changing household composition, including an increase in the number of singles, has challenged agencies that have historically focused on providing programs for families with children. Increasing ethnic diversity provides an opportunity for agencies to increase multicultural programming. In addition to changing demographics, parks and recreation agencies have experienced growing pressure to provide evidence of financial accountability through outcomes assessment. In the early twenty-first century, the place of recreation and leisure as a cultural and social institution seems secure.

QUESTIONS FOR CLASS DISCUSSION OR ESSAY EXAMINATION

1. The federal government has progressively pushed for stronger regulation of the environment since the mid-1950s. Explain how these efforts have affected, in positive and negative ways, the nation's perceptions and commitment to the environment and parks and recreation.
2. Explain the role that recreation and leisure had in helping to bridge the challenges of racial unrest and the counterculture movement of the 1960s and 1970s, and describe the influence recreation and leisure has on today's issues.
3. Explain why free time has not met expectations. Take a position in favor of or against increased free time and defend your position.
4. Discuss the impact of the fluctuating economy on parks and recreation over the past 20 years.
5. Explain counterculture. How has the counterculture impacted parks and recreation?

ENDNOTES

1. J. Murphy, E. W. Niepoth, L. Jamieson, and J. Williams, *Leisure Systems: Critical Concepts and Applications* (Champaign, IL: Sagamore Publishers, 1991): 94.
2. R. E. Carlson, T. R. Deppe, and J. R. MacLean, *Recreation in American Life* (Belmont, CA: Wadsworth Publishing, 1963): 14.
3. R. E. Carlson, T. R. Deppe, and J. R. MacLean, *Recreation in American Life*. 2nd ed. (Belmont, CA: Wadsworth Publishing, 1975): 3.
4. G. Bammel and L. L. Bammel, *Leisure and Human Behavior*. 2nd ed. (Dubuque, IA: Wm. C. Brown Publishers, 1992): 380.
5. U.S. Census Bureau, "2010 Statistical Abstract," http://www.census.gov/compendia/statab/.
6. Richard Kraus, *Leisure in a Changing America: Multicultural Perspectives* (New York: Macmillan College Publishing, 1994): 61.
7. Carol Hardy Vincent, *Land and Water Conservation Fund: Overview, Funding History, and Current Issues* (Washington, DC: Congressional Research Service, 2006): 3, http://nationalaglawcenter.org/assets/crs/RL33531.pdf.
8. M. Walls, *Federal Funding for Conservation and Recreation: The Land and Water Conservation Fund* (Washington, DC: Resources for the Future, 2009): 5.
9. Jack Zenger, "Leadership: Management's Better Half," *Training* (Vol. 22, No. 12, 1985): 44–53.
10. Eunice Kennedy Shriver, home page, http://www.eunicekennedyshriver.org.
11. Kevin O'Leary, "The Legacy of Proposition 13," *Time* (June 27, 2009).
12. Richard Kraus, *New Directions in Urban Parks and Recreation: A Trends Analysis Report* (Philadelphia: Temple University and Heritage Conservation and Recreation Service, 1980): 6.
13. Ellen Weissinger and William Murphy, "A Survey of Fiscal Conditions in Small-Town Public Recreation Departments from 1987 to 1991," *Journal of Park and Recreation Administration* (Vol. 11, No. 3, 1993): 61–71.
14. Jack Foley and Veda Ward, "Recreation, the Riots and a Healthy L.A.," *Parks and Recreation* (March 1993): 68.
15. Salvation Army, "Salvation Army Ray and Joan Kroc Corps Community Centers," http://www.salvationarmyusa.org/usn/www_usn_2.nsf/vw-dynamic-arrays/E9D8660ADDBB36C7802573F500587F26?openDocument&charset=utf-8.
16. Ray and Joan Kroc Center, "Croc Center Celebrates One Year." http://www.kroccda.org/main.php?page=63&newsitem=27
17. Keith Bradsher, "Gap in Wealth in U.S. Called Widest in West," *New York Times* (April 17, 1995): 1.
18. Robert Frank and Philip Cook, *The Winner Take All Society* (New York: Free Press, 1995).
19. Robert Reich, cited in "A New Profile of Middle Class," *Employee Services Management* (May/June 1995): 4.
20. Robert H. Frank, *Falling Behind: How Rising Inequality Harms the Middle Class* (Berkeley: University of California Press, 2007).
21. Robert Frank, *Luxury Fever: Why Money Fails to Satisfy in an Era of Excess* (New York: Free Press, 1999).
22. Sebastian de Grazia, cited in J. S. Shivers and L. J. DeLisle, *The Story of Leisure: Context, Concepts, and Current Controversy* (Champaign, IL: Human Kinetics, 1996): 173.
23. Michael Satchell, "Parks in Peril," *U.S. News and World Report* (June 21, 1997): 24.
24. NielsenWire, "Americans Watching More TV Than Ever; Web and Mobile Video Up Too," 20 May 2009, http://blog.nielsen.com/nielsenwire/online_mobile/americans-watching-more-tv-than-ever/.

25. C. L. Ogden, M. D. Carroll, L. R. Curtin, M. A. McDowell, C. J. Tabak, and K. M. Flegal, "Prevalence of Overweight and Obesity in the United States, 1999–2004," *Journal of the American Medical Association* (Vol. 295, No. 13, 2006): 1549–1555.

26. U.S. Department of Health and Human Services, *The Surgeon General's Call to Action to Prevent and Decrease Overweight and Obesity* (Rockville, MD: U.S. Department of Health and Human Services, Public Health Service, Office of the Surgeon General, 2001).

27. "Maryland Finds Success in Promoting Physical Activity," *Nation's Health* (October 1, 2007): 8.

CHAPTER 5

LEISURE MOTIVATION

◆ ◆ ◆

On May 25, 2001, Erik Weihenmayer became the only blind man in history to reach the summit of the world's highest peak—Mount Everest. On August 20, 2008, when he stood on top of Carstenz Pyramid, the tallest peak in Australasia, Weihenmayer completed his quest to climb the Seven Summits, the highest mountains on each of the seven continents. Erik is joined by fewer than 100 mountaineers who have accomplished this feat. Additionally, he has scaled El Capitan, a 3300-foot overhanging granite monolith in Yosemite; Lhosar, a 3000-foot ice waterfall in the Himalayas; and a difficult and rarely climbed rock face on 17,000-foot Mount Kenya.

In September 2003, Erik joined 320 stellar athletes from 17 countries to compete in the Primal Quest, the richest and toughest multisport adventure race in the world: 457 miles through the Sierra Nevadas, nine days, 60,000 feet of elevation gain, and no time-outs. Averaging only two hours of sleep a night, Erik and his team surged past the finish line on Lake Tahoe, becoming one of the 42 teams to cross the finish line out of the 80 teams that began.[1]

◆ ◆ ◆

INTRODUCTION

Having reviewed the history of leisure on the world scene and over the past three decades in the United States, we now examine it from personal and societal perspectives. This chapter outlines the varied motivations that impel individuals to take part in a wide range of recreational activities. These motivations are examined from the perspective of positive leisure experience, recreation activities that involve extreme risks, and those activities that are considered to be taboo, such as illegal drug use and gambling.

MOTIVATION: WHAT IS IT?

Why do people choose to watch television for hours on end, play competitive sports, or conquer Mount Everest? The reasons are as varied as people are. Recreation enthusiasts derive different qualities from their activities, and these qualities are what drive them to participate. These driving factors are called *motivators*. Motivation can be defined as an internal or external element that moves people toward a behavior. A recreation-related motivator could be the desire to develop soccer skills or to learn about the visual arts.

When discussing motivation at the theoretical level, the names Edward L. Deci and Richard M. Ryan always emerge. They have studied motivation for many years and developed Self-Determination Theory (SDT). SDT is a general psychological theory that "examines the psychological processes that occur within the social context and how these influence one's reasons or motivation to act or behave"[2]

Ryan and Deci outline six different types of motivation on a self-determination continuum that spans from no control over a situation to complete autonomy:

1. *Amotivation:* Performance done without any intention of doing so. For example, amotivation is present when a parent takes a child to see a baseball game when the child has no desire or interest in seeing it. The child goes along because he has no choice and it is beyond his control.
2. *Extrinsic motivation:* Performance of an activity because of an external force or reward. For example, a professional athlete receives compensation for playing for his or her team. This compensation is an external reward and is most likely one of the driving factors behind the athlete's participation. Another example of an extrinsic motivator is that of the golfer who plays with a regular foursome and bets $5 per hole with her friends. If she plays because of the money involved, this is an extrinsic motivator.
3. *Introjected motivation:* Performance of an activity to alleviate guilt and anxiety or to enhance ego. Participation occurs in an activity because others desire that participation and the individual would feel guilty or anxious about letting people down. In terms of enhancing the ego, some participate in activities simply because they can demonstrate their skills to others. A professional athlete may continue playing the sport because of the admiration from the fans when in reality the athlete does not really enjoy playing.
4. *Identified motivation:* Performance is done because the individual sees the value in the activity and gets something out of it. This could be building skills or increasing physical fitness. For example, if a person is running to enhance her fitness level and increase weight loss and not for the pure love of running, she is experiencing identified motivation.
5. *Integrated motivation:* Performance of an activity matches the individual's values and desires, yet there are external reasons too. For example, the individual who runs for fitness and weight loss understands the need for physical health and has chosen running as an activity to achieve it.
6. *Intrinsic motivation:* Performance of an activity for the behavior itself and the feelings that result from the activity. For example, completing a half-marathon for the first time could lead to a sense of accomplishment and pride in the fact that a goal was reached. These feelings are intrinsic motivators. The half-marathon was done because of the benefits of the activity and not because an external reward was dictating or influencing the person's behavior. The rewards are internal to the person, and the activity is done for its own sake.[3]

In leisure services, intrinsic motivation is most desired. Ryan and Deci summarize the importance of intrinsic motivation by saying, "Perhaps no single phenomenon reflects the positive potential of human nature as much as intrinsic motivation, the inherent tendency to seek out novelty and challenges, to extend and exercise one's capacities, to explore, and to learn."[4] Intrinsic motivation is enhanced and more likely to occur when there is a sense of autonomy, competence, and relatedness. Autonomy is the freedom to determine your own behavior, to guide your own actions, and to be in control of the situation. Competence occurs when an individual feels capable, skilled, and able to meet an acceptable level of challenge. Feelings of competence result from effective and positive feedback from performance. Last, relatedness is a sense of belonging, security, and connection with others. These three things enhance the likelihood of intrinsic motivation. The following sections look at motivation from a variety of perspectives.

Although there is a plethora of ways to look at motivation, including by activity type, age, and gender, it is important to look at broad motivating factors that relate to leisure preferences. In describing the major areas of human development, behavioral scientists use such terms as *cognitive* (referring to mental or intellectual development), *affective* (relating to emotional or feeling states), and *psychomotor* (meaning the broad area of motor learning and performance). Because these terms are somewhat narrow in their application, this chapter instead uses the following more familiar terms: (1) *physical*, (2) *social*, (3) *psychological*, and (4) *emotional*. Most, if not all, motivators of leisure participation can fit into one or more of these four categories.

PHYSICAL MOTIVATORS

Active recreational pursuits such as sport and games, dance, and even such moderate forms of exercise as walking or gardening have significant positive effects on physical development and health. The value of such activities obviously will vary according to the age and developmental needs of the participants. For children and youth, the major need is to promote healthy structural growth, fitness, endurance, and the acquisition of physical qualities and skills. It is essential that children learn the importance of fitness and develop habits of participation in physical recreation that will serve them in later life. This is particularly important in an era of electronic games, labor-saving devices, and readily available transportation, all of which save time and physical effort but encourage a sedentary way of life.

Youth baseball serves as a physical motivator where health, wellness, and other physical qualities are gained.

Physical motivators can best be summarized as control of obesity and preserving cardiovascular health. Although each is discussed separately, they are intertwined. Most of what drives people who are motivated by the physical aspects of leisure is achieving wellness. A means to wellness is cardiovascular health and reduced obesity.

Society is changing and starting to realize how important an active lifestyle is, and parks and recreation play an active role in this.

Control of Obesity

Scientists agree that physical activity plays a major role in weight control. Obesity among American adults has grown steadily and is now a serious health problem in this country. Nearly 73% of the U.S. population is overweight and of those 34.5% are considered obese. Children are not exempt from this weight problem because 17.0% of children ages 6–11, 17.6% of teens ages 12–19, and 12.4% of all preschoolers are overweight.[5]

Not only is there a difference in obesity rates based on age, race and geography also show differences. Non-Hispanic blacks were 51% more likely to be obese, and Hispanics showed a 21% greater prevalence of obesity when compared with non-Hispanic whites.[6] The states with the highest population of overweight and obese people include South Carolina, Tennessee, West Virginia, Alabama, and Oklahoma while the healthiest state by far is Colorado (18.5%).[7]

The main reason for these obesity rates is inactivity. It is evident that inactivity is not just a youth or an adult problem. It stretches to all ages, races, genders, and income levels. In 2003, only 36.8% of adults ages 18–44 got regular physical activity, which is up from 33.5% in 1998, and this activity rate decreases as people age. Of those 45–64 years old, only 31.3% and only 23.3% of those 65 and older got regular physical activity. Overall, men (35.4%) get more physical activity than women (30.6%). With respect to race, Caucasians (33.9%) and biracial adults (32.6%) get the most regular physical activity followed by Asians (33.1%), African Americans (25.5%), and Hispanics/Latino Mexicans (24.4%). Education is also an indicator of regular physical activity levels. People without a high school diploma (18.1%) are least likely to get regular physical activity followed by those with a high school diploma (27.0%) and those with some college education (38.2%).[8]

The American Heart Association and the American College of Sports Medicine recommend that people over the age of two get regular physical activity. They suggest that families do this together and that a gym is not necessary to meet the activity level requirements that are outlined on page 125. The benefits for both children and adults are decreased obesity, decreased incidences of coronary disease, diabetes, high blood pressure, and stroke. Although many of these diseases do not occur in children, obese children are more likely to become obese adults.

Because of these statistics, public, nonprofit, and commercial agencies have come together to offer programs and education to help people become more active. For example, Healthy People 2020 is an organization through the U.S. Department of Health and Human Services dedicated to helping people live longer and have a better quality of life. It includes 10 indicators as to what makes a person healthy, and physical activity is at the top of the list.[9]

Preserving Cardiovascular Health

Of all the fitness-related aspects of active recreation, maintaining cardiovascular health may represent the highest priority. Cardiovascular diseases include such things as high blood pressure, heart failure, stroke, and coronary heart disease. More than 80 million people (36.3%) in the United States have cardiovascular diseases, and they are the leading cause of death in Hispanics and Latinos. It was also an underlying or contributing factor in 56% of all deaths in 2005.[10]

CASE STUDY: The Obesity Epidemic in the United States

Travel internationally to places such as Europe and Asia and it is easy to see that people in these countries are much more physically fit than are Americans. The United States ranks first in obesity rates followed distantly by Mexico, England, Slovakia, and Greece.[a] The terms *overweight* and *obese* both mean that a person's weight is greater than what is considered healthy. A person who is overweight weighs more than normal for someone of the same age, height, and build.[b] Obesity is a condition where too much fat is stored on the body. The amount of fat stored on the body is measured by body mass index (BMI). BMI is the ratio of weight to height of a person. Someone who is overweight has a BMI of 25–29.9, whereas an obese person has a BMI of 30+. You can test your own BMI at www.nhlbisupport.com/bmi/.[c]

The statistics in this chapter show the impact of obesity on the physical child. Several other issues are associated with obesity as well. Here are a few examples:

- Kids younger than 6 years spend an average of two hours a day in front of the television.[d]
- Older children spend 5.5 hours a day in front of a screen—television, DVDs, computers, and so forth.[e]
- A television in the bedroom increases the likelihood of obesity for children.[f]
- A child's risk of obesity increases if one or both parents are obese because they have similar eating habits and attitudes toward being overweight.
- Women who are obese by the age of 18 are more likely to be infertile.[g]
- Common mental health issues such as anxiety and depression may increase a person's risk of being obese.[h]
- Studies on people with disabilities and excess weight are limited. However, a recent study shows that people with mental disabilities were no more likely to be overweight or obese than were people without mental disabilities.[i]

So, what is being done about this? A quick search of the Web can uncover hundreds of different programs and a plethora of advice for helping children and adults be healthier. One such program comes from the Leadership for Healthy Communities, a nonprofit organization dedicated to advancing policies to support healthy eating and active living.[j] This group works with agencies such as the American Association of School Administrators; Council of State Governments; and National League of Cities Institute for Youth, Education, and Families to develop an action plan to make communities healthier. Note that omitted from this list is the National Recreation and Park Association or any other recreation-related entity, even though many areas for improvement suggested by the group are recreation-related. Some suggestions to build healthy communities include the following:

1. Expand trails, bicycle lanes, and connections. Cities with trails, sidewalks, and walkways see an increase in physical activity in their communities. Furthermore, people are more likely to walk or ride their bikes to locations when they have a safe route to do so. A study found that in highly walkable neighborhoods people took twice as many walking trips as those in less walkable communities.[k]
2. Increase access to recreation facilities and open spaces, including parks and community gardens. People who have access to these amenities are more physically active than those who do not. It was found that people with greater access to a facility were 43% more likely to exercise regularly than those without good access to facilities.[l] In a study of low-income areas (where obesity is higher than in the general population), people who lived within 1 mile of a park were 38% more likely to exercise regularly than those who lived farther away.[m]

3. Support farmers markets. Farmers markets provide fresh, and oftentimes organic, produce at reasonable prices.
4. Support community gardens. Community gardens can provide a space for people to grow their own fruits and vegetables, and they are also a way to improve vacant lots.

Questions to Consider

1. Why is the United States the most overweight and obese country in the world?
2. Select two nearby communities. Compare and contrast their health-related programs and facilities to assess how well they provide and promote opportunities for physical activity.

Sources

a. Nation Master, "Health Statistics. Obesity by Country," http://www.nationmaster.com/graph/hea_obe-health-obesity.
b. Medline Plus, "Medical Dictionary: Overweight," http://www2.merriam-webster.com/cgi-bin/mwmednlm?book=Medical&va=overweight.
c. National Heart Lung and Blood Institute, "Calculate Your Body Mass Index," http://www.nhlbisupport.com/bmi/.
d. Kids Health, "Overweight and Obesity," http://kidshealth.org/parent/general/body/overweight_obesity.html#.
e. Ibid.
f. Ibid.
g. Tina Hesman Saey, "Study Clarifies Obesity-Infertility Link," *Science News*, http://www.usnews.com/science/articles/2010/09/08/study-clarifies-obesity-infertility-link.html.
h. Robert Preidt, "Troubled Mind Can Mean Wider Waistlines: Repeat Episodes of Anxiety, Depression Tied to Weight Gain, Study Finds," http://health.msn.com/health-topics/anxiety/articlepage.aspx?cp-dcumentid=100246182.
i. NLM Gateway, "Impact of Health Education on Weight in People with Disabilities," http://gateway.nlm.nih.gov/MeetingAbstracts/ma?f=103622756.html.
j. Leadership for Healthy Communities, *Action Strategies Toolkit: A Guide for Local and State Leaders Working to Create Healthy Communities and Prevent Childhood Obesity,* (Washington, DC: Robert Wood Johnson Foundation, 2009), http://www.leadershipforhealthycommunities.org/content/view/352/154/.
k. B. Saelens, J. Salis, and L. Frank, "Environmental Correlates of Walking and Cycling: Findings from the Transportation, Urban Design, and Planning Literatures," *Annals of Behavioral Medicine*, (Vol. 25, No. 2, Spring 2003): 80–91.
l. B. Giles-Corti R. and Donovan, "The Relative Influence of Individual, Social, and Physical Environment Determinants of Physical Activity," *Social Science and Medicine*, (Vol. 54, No. 12, June 2002): 1793–1812.
m. D. Cohen, T. McKenzie, A. Sehgai, et al., "Contribution of Public Parks to Physical Activity," *American Journal of Public Health*, (Vol. 97, No. 3, January 2007): 509–514.

Even with these known statistics, physical inactivity is the main culprit with a sedentary lifestyle being every bit as bad for one's heart as smoking, high cholesterol, or high blood pressure. The American College of Sports Medicine and the American Heart Association updated their physical activity guidelines. Adults 18–65 years of age need 30 minutes of moderate-intensity aerobic activity five days per week or vigorous-intensity aerobic physical activity for 20 minutes three days per week. Moderate-intensity aerobic activity increases a person's heart rate and can be accomplished by participating in activities that increase the heart rate in episodes of at least 10 minutes. As such, a person could walk briskly or ride a bike three times a day for 10 minutes each time to achieve the standard. Vigorous-intensity activity causes rapid breathing and a substantial increase in heart rate such as would be experienced from activities such as running or riding a bicycle at an accelerated speed. It is also recommended that adults select activities that will increase muscle strength and endurance at least twice per week.[11] Children younger than age 18 years should get at least one hour a day of physical activity. Three days per week a child should do activities that are muscle strengthening and another three days should include activities that are bone strengthening. Muscle-strengthening activities work the major muscle groups such as legs, arms, and chest. These can include rope climbing, tree climbing, swinging, climbing walls, or cross-country skiing. Bone-strengthening activities put a force on the bones and help them grow and strengthen through impact with the ground. Bone-strengthening activities include such things as hopping, skipping, jumping, running, volleyball, and gymnastics.[12]

However, recent research involving thousands of men and women indicates that even moderate forms of exercise, including such activities as walking, stair climbing, gardening, and housework, have a beneficial long-term effect on one's health. Although high-intensity, pulse-pounding workouts yield the most dramatic benefits, more modest forms of exercise do yield significant benefits. Beyond these findings, other research demonstrates that regular exercise reduces the incidence of other diseases such as diabetes, colon cancer among men and breast and uterine cancer among women, stress, osteoporosis, and other serious illnesses.

Although there is a plethora of reasons why people should be physically active and the implications of not being active are widely known, the obesity rate is still quite high. A line of research on the constraints to physical activities demonstrates some of the reasons why. Constraints are things that keep people from participating in leisure activities or participating as much as they would like or that compromise the quality of participation. A few findings that researchers uncovered about physical activity suggest the following:

- The healthier a person is, the less likely that person will find reasons not to participate in physical activity.[13]
- The more people see the benefits of being physically active, the more likely they are to choose these types of activities.[14]
- Time, family obligations, and lack of energy are main reasons people give for not participating in physical activity.[15]
- Enjoyment of an activity is a major predictor of selecting an activity, including sedentary activities.[16]
- Cost, work obligations, time, and other priorities diminished the likelihood of participating in physical activity.[17]
- An increased preference for sedentary activities has been found among children who are overweight or obese.[18]

Given all of this, the most effective forms of physical activity are those that are most enjoyable to different people. The challenge comes with those who prefer sedentary over physical activities.

If people are motivated to participate in park and recreation activities based on physical motivators, then there are plenty of opportunities to be found. More and more employers have fitness facilities, offer discounted memberships at local clubs, or give paid time off for employees to participate in fitness activities. Organizations such as YMCAs, YWCAs, local parks and recreation agencies, and hospitals all provide activities to get people moving. Even the travel industry is trying to help. Seeing the value of health and fitness, the travel industry is taking action by making health easier for guests. Many hotels offer more healthy options on room service menus, but more important, they are catering to the health conscious. For example, Omni Hotels brings a workout kit to the guest's hotel room. The Get Fit Kit arrives in a canvas bag and includes a mini radio headset, floor mat, dumbbells, exercise bands, and a workout booklet. Omni Hotels has expanded this program to include a mini-bar with healthy drinks and snacks and a treadmill for a small additional cost.[19]

SOCIAL MOTIVATORS

The need to be part of a social group and to have friends who provide companionship, support, and intimacy is at the heart of much recreational involvement. It helps to explain why people join sororities, fraternities, or other social clubs, senior citizen centers, tour groups, or other settings where new acquaintances and potential friends may be met. It is an underlying element in sport in terms of the friendships and bonds that are formed among team members. There are a number of specific social motivators that must be mentioned, including being with others, reducing loneliness, and developing social norms among people.

Being with Others and Reducing Loneliness

Many adults today find their primary social contacts and interpersonal relationships not in their work lives, but in voluntary group associations during leisure hours. Even in the relatively free environment of outdoor recreation, where people hike, camp, or explore the wilderness in ways of their own choosing, interaction among participants is a key element in the experience. Only 2% of all leisure activities are done alone. This indicates that people like to participate in activities with others.

Two college friends take time away from their senior internships to walk the beach in Garrapata State Park in California.

Social contact, friendship, or intimacy with others is key to avoiding loneliness. Loneliness is a widespread phenomenon among all ages. Typically, as many as three-quarters of all college students report being lonely during their first term away from home. As adults age, they begin to experience increased loneliness as significant others and friends begin to pass away and children leave home. Loneliness can have unpleasant and even life-threatening consequences and often is directly linked to depression, obesity, high blood pressure, and heart problems.[20]

Involvement in recreation activities with others can alleviate feelings of loneliness. People can join the YMCA, YWCA, their local recreation center, or take classes at their local parks and recreation department where they can learn new skills or exercise while also meeting others who enjoy these same activities. Keep in mind there is a difference between loneliness and solitude. Russell suggests that time spent alone is an important part of our lives and can be a much desired state. People participate in certain activities to reduce loneliness, but they also do things to escape or focus totally on themselves such as the case with solitude.[21]

Social Norms

Clearly, different types of recreation groups and programs impose different sets of social norms, roles, and relationships that participants must learn to accept and that contribute to their own social development. For children, play groups offer a realistic training ground for developing cooperative, competitive, and social skills. Through group participation, children learn to interact with others to accept group rules and wishes, and, when necessary, to subordinate their own views or desires to those of the group. They learn to give and take, to assume leadership or follow the leadership of others, and to work effectively as part of a team.

The Relationship Between Happiness and Socializing

In a survey of 140,000 Americans, it was found that people are happiest when they spend six to seven hours per day socializing. People who are alone all day are least happy and experience higher levels of stress than those who are more social. Furthermore, there is a weekend effect where people experience more happiness and less stress than during the week.[22]

As children age, their social groups increase in importance in their lives. Social peer groups for teens are a major sense of support and help them form their social identity. Into adulthood, social groups reflect our social status and position in society whether it is playing golf at the country club or camping with family and friends. As people reach senior adulthood (65+), social connections increase in importance as the social group starts to decrease in numbers due to life changes and death. It also is in our older years where loneliness and isolation become more prevalent as our social networks diminish. Although social connections change throughout our lives, they always remain a significant part of our leisure lives.[23]

The social aspect of leisure is a significant motivator for many people. It may be a terrific opportunity to participate in activities with a friend or significant other or to participate in a setting to increase the possibility of meeting people for friendship or more.

PSYCHOLOGICAL MOTIVATORS

Often, recreational activities are seen as a means of providing excitement and challenge, as a means of relaxation and escape, as a way to relieve stress, or as a way to balance work and play. These are psychological motivators that contribute to our mental health.

Sense of Adventure, Excitement, and Challenge

A great deal of recreational involvement today is based on the need for excitement and challenge, particularly in such outdoor recreation activities as skiing, mountain climbing, or hang gliding, or in active, highly competitive individual or team sports. These activities are a part of adventure recreation, also called risk recreation. Adventure recreation is activity in the natural environment that has challenge, personal risk, uncertainty, and a reasonable chance for success.[24] People choose some of these leisure activities because they have an inherent risk associated with them. Participants thrive on the adrenalin rush, the challenges they are taking, and the thrill they get from completing the activity. As people participate in these types of activities, their perception of risk decreases and perception of skill increases.[25] In other words, people become less afraid while doing such things as backcountry backpacking or rock climbing, while they also feel their skills are increasing. Adventure recreation activities have also shown to enhance psychological well-being for people.

In addition to outdoor recreation, there has been tremendous growth in adventure sports because of the need for adventure, excitement, and challenge. For example, the 2009 Summer X Games in Los Angeles featured BMX Freestyle, Moto X, Skateboard, and Rally Car Racing. The Winter X Games, to be held in Aspen, Colorado, through 2012, include curling, dog sledding, hunting, ice climbing, ice fishing, ice hockey, ice skating, skiing, and snowboarding. For those who are less skilled but who still crave that rush from adventure recreation, tourism companies are capitalizing on this motivational aspect. Some companies specialize in white-water rafting, sea kayaking, off-road vehicle trips, snowmobiling, and mountain trekking.

Sisters engage in an exciting and challenging activity together.

For many people, the urge for adventure, excitement, and challenge is met through spectatorship—by watching action-oriented movies or television shows—or in the form of video games based on high-speed chase or conflict. For others, ballooning, skydiving, parasailing, amateur stock car racing, or scuba diving satisfy risk-related motivations. Although varied forms of deviant social behavior, such as gang fighting, vandalism, or other types of juvenile crime, are not commonly considered as leisure pursuits, the reality is that they often are prompted by the same need for thrills, excitement, and challenge that other, more respectable recreation pursuits satisfy. This is discussed later in the chapter.

Stress Management

A closely related value of recreation is its usefulness in stress reduction. A leading authority on stress, Dr. Hans Selye, defines *stress* as the overall response of the body to any extreme demand made upon it, which might include threats, physical illness, job pressures, and environmental extremes—or even such life changes as marriage, divorce, vacations, or taking a new job. Increasing amounts of stress in modern life have resulted in many individuals suffering from pain, heart disease, sleep deprivation, excessive tiredness, and depression.

Once it was thought that the best approach to stress was rest and avoidance of all pressures, but today there is an awareness that some degree of stress is desirable and healthy. Today, researchers point out that physical activity can play a significant role in stress reduction. Typically, people work off anger, frustration, and indignation by taking long walks or engaging in some kind of physical activity such as exercise. All of the body's systems—the working muscles, heart, hormones, metabolic reactions, and the responsiveness of the central nervous system—are strengthened through stimulation. Following periods of extended exertion, the body systems slow, bringing on a feeling of deep relaxation. Attaining this relaxed state is essential to lessening the stress reaction.

Relaxation and Escape

When you consider the positive side of leisure and why people choose the activities they do, often relaxation and escape are mentioned as key benefits to leisure. Escaping from work, home, or the everyday pressures of life can be done by taking a bike ride, going for a hike, or becoming absorbed in a creative activity through art or drama.

Relaxation allows people to forget the stresses they face. They can temporarily forget about upcoming deadlines, the need to find a job, or pressure to select a good graduate school. Choosing relaxing activities allows individuals to forget about these issues and become absorbed in the activity itself. Relaxation and escape can come from activities or doing nothing at all. Sitting in the backyard, laying on the beach, and taking a nap in the middle of the day are means for relaxation and escape resulting from use of leisure time. Relaxation experts often suggest deep breathing, meditation, exercise, sex, music, and yoga as a way to relax from stress.[26]

Healthy Balance of Work and Play

The role of work and leisure in our lives has changed dramatically from the thinking of the Greeks and Romans to whom leisure was the root of happiness and something enjoyed by those who did not have to work. Today, society sees leisure as something for all, and for most people, emotional well-being is greatly strengthened if they are able to maintain a healthy balance of work and recreation in their lives. Today, we recognize that there can be too much commitment to work, resulting in the exclusion of other interests and personal involvements that help to maintain mental health.

The emphasis on work and leisure is shifting in the United States. Much has been said in the news about the different generations and how the baby boomers (born 1940–1960) are affecting our lives. The baby boomers are today's upper management. They live to work and view themselves as having a strong work ethic. A strong work ethic is characterized by this group as working long hours and weekends to meet customer demands. This group likes recognition for a job well done and sees working long hours as a way of getting this reward. It was with this group that the divorce rates and stress levels skyrocketed and the number of latchkey kids increased.[27]

The tendency to place excessive emphasis on work, at the expense of other avenues of expression, has been popularly termed *workaholism*. For some people, work is an obsession and they are unable to find other kinds of pleasurable release. For those who find their work a deep source of personal satisfaction and commitment, this may not be an altogether undesirable phenomenon.

CASE STUDY: Funemployed

In the past couple of years, the United States has seen a decline in the economy and an increase in unemployment. These two issues have been detrimental to leisure services in that people are traveling less, eating out fewer times per week, taking day trips rather than extended vacations, and buying less recreation equipment. It is easy to see how the economy has affected the profession. Peter Jamison in his article on *funemployment* takes a different perspective on employment.[a]

Funemployment is a period of time when a person does not have a job but enjoys the time off. People who are laid off receive unemployment benefits for up to 79 weeks, and the unemployment check can be upward of $450. The younger generations, those in their twenties and thirties, who are usually single and are most taking advantage of funemployment. This group does not identify as heavily with their jobs, and neither do they feel their jobs define who they are. As such, the funemployed are taking full advantage of their leisure time as they seek new employment or simply take time off to experience things they would otherwise be missing. The funemployed have used severance pay and/or unemployment checks to take extended ski vacations, train for a 129-mile bike ride through the Sierras, volunteer for social service organizations, investigate returning to school for a graduate degree, or learn to travel cheaply.

Some may look unfavorably upon the attitude that unemployment can be a positive thing, while others suggest it has allowed them to discover new things about themselves. Either way, unemployment and funemployment have affected leisure in a multitude of ways.

Questions to Consider

1. How would your parents react to suddenly becoming unemployed? Would they see it as a positive or a negative?
2. Assume you have had a full-time job for three years in your chosen field. How do you think you would react to unemployment?
3. Given the limited size of the unemployment check, list 20 things that you would want to do that would be considered funemployed activities.

Source

a. P. Jamison, "Funemployment: Jobless Young San Franciscans Are Welcoming the Worst Recession of Their Lives with Open Arms. Too Bad the Party Can't Last Forever," *SF Weekly* (3 June 2009), http://www.sfweekly.com/content/printVersion/1544761.

The idea of workaholism will always be prevalent in society, but Generation X (born 1965–1980) and the Millennial generation (born 1981–1997) will most likely decrease this phenomenon. Generation Xers prefer a balance of work and play. They are today's middle and upper managers who were the latchkey kids coming home to find their parents still at work. They feel work productivity is important but not at the cost of what is most important to them—their leisure, family, and friends. The Millennial generation works to live. They have a job so that they can make money to do the things they really want to do. They have been involved in a number of leisure activities their whole lives, from soccer to piano lessons, and they enjoy these things. This group sees the value of leisure and plans to take advantage of it rather than work excessive hours.[28]

Leading authorities on business management and personnel practices now stress the need for business executives to find outside pleasures that open up, diversify, and enrich their lives. The guilt that successful people too often have about play must be assuaged, and they must be helped to realize that, with a more balanced style of life, they are likely to be more productive in the long run—and much happier in the present. Generation X and the Millennial generation already know this and are probably better than their older supervisors and coworkers in taking advantage of the services offered by recreation professionals.[29]

CASE STUDY: Balance Between Work and Leisure

Cooper, Becket, Terrance, and Ty are friends from college. They graduated with their bachelor's degrees 10 years ago, and none of them have started families yet. Here is an overview of their lives since college.

Cooper is the coordinator of outdoor programs at a local university. She spends an average of 10 hours a day at work, often six or seven days a week. Cooper loves what she does because she gets to interact with students interested in outdoor activities and she plans and leads outdoor recreation-oriented trips all over the country. When Cooper is not at work, she is most likely outside camping with friends, hiking, bike riding, or kayaking. It is difficult to tell when Cooper is working and when she is at play.

Becket is in middle management in an accounting firm. She finds accounting to be good in that it pays the bills quite well, but the job itself offers few challenges and little excitement. The upside is that Becket has a nine-to-five job and can leave the workplace behind when she goes home. There is some level of stress associated with her job, but it is her mission to forget about the job at the end of the day. After work Becket is active, enjoying staying physically fit, playing golf, and running. Becket's friends are varied. Her two closest friends also work with her. She regularly sees three other people who she met through golf. This entire group is quite close and enjoys many of the same activities.

Terrance is a professor at the same university where Cooper works. He enjoys his job but looks forward to having time off during the semester break and summers, even though he spends a lot of time in the office on these breaks getting things done that he ignored during the semester. Terrance's social life revolves around other faculty. This group of friends often is seen dining out, going to theater performances, and enjoying other cultural experiences. This group has a tendency to talk a lot about work when they are out relaxing.

Ty was always the fun guy in the group. He barely got through college because of his lack of focus on his education, but he was the life of the party. Ty helped the other three be more outgoing, take more risks, and try new things. Each of them believes Ty made them better people and helped them see things from a different perspective. Currently, Ty works part-time at a hardware store. He works about 30 hours a week and loves the job. At the end of the day, he is out the door looking for his next big adventure. He plans to buy a used RV and travel across the country, stopping whenever he runs out of money to get a job to increase his bank account, and then move on. Ty's goal is to visit as many national parks as possible.

We can look at leisure and work from many different perspectives. As previously discussed, people can spend too much time at work, thus leading to workaholism. They can spend too little time at work, creating a financial strain in their lives, or they can find a healthy balance between work and leisure. However, identifying what is a healthy balance between these two is quite subjective. Scott Young, in his blog *Get More Out of Life*, suggests the following strategies to help people figure out how to get the maximum amount of work done and take full advantage of free time:

1. Get rid of time wasters that we do not really enjoy. Why watch a television show if we are not really interested? Find something that is interesting.
2. Finding time for activities is not always enough. It takes energy to do work and recreate. Reduce mentally draining activities at work, eat a proper diet, and exercise.
3. Take breaks from mentally draining activities at work. A break does not mean checking e-mail or focusing on a different problem. It means a clean break from work. Walk around the building or grounds or sit outside and enjoy the sunshine.
4. Do not sacrifice leisure for work. A time consuming project can easily eat into leisure time when that time is important for our physical and mental well being. Set specific time aside for leisure activities and adhere to this schedule.[a]

Questions to Consider

1. What are the positives and negatives of achieving a balance between work and leisure?
2. Which of these four people do you think you will most identify with when you are 30+ years old? Why?
3. How well does each of these people balance work and leisure? Who does the best job and who does the worst job of balancing both?
4. Consider Young's suggestions. What advice would you give each of these people to achieve more balance in their lives?

Source

a. S. H. Young, "Balancing Work and Leisure," *Get More From Life*, http://www.scotthyoung.com/blog/2006/03/18/balancing-work-and-leisure/.

EMOTIONAL MOTIVATORS

Emotional health is typified by positive self-esteem, a positive self-concept, ability to deal with stress, and a person's ability to control emotions and behaviors. Emotionally healthy people handle the daily stresses of life, build healthy relationships, and lead productive lives. Leisure is a major contributor to emotional well-being.

Leisure activity can provide strong feelings of pleasure and satisfaction and can serve as an outlet for discharging certain emotional drives that, if repressed, might produce emotional distress or even mental illness. The role of pleasure is increasingly recognized as a vital factor in emotional well-being. Some researchers have begun to analyze the simple concept of fun, defined as intense pleasure and enjoyment and an important dimension of social interactional leisure.

In leisure, people predominantly seek fun in their free time. Why do a leisure activity if it is not fun? Fun is the reason we play, enjoy the outdoors, and socialize with others. Associated with fun is laughter. There are a number of benefits of laughter, including binding people together, enhancing intimacy, providing stress relief, and because it simply feels good. Fun and laughter can enhance emotional well-being and can be experienced through such activities as going to a comedy show, trying a brand-new activity with friends, or having a game night with family.[30]

In addition to fun and laughter, self-actualization has been linked to emotional well-being. Self actualization is a term that became popular in the 1970s chiefly through the writings of Abraham Maslow, who stressed the need for individuals to achieve their fullest degree of creative potential. Maslow developed a convincing theory of human motivation in which he identified a number of important human needs, arranging them in a hierarchy. As each of the basic needs is met in turn, a person is able to move ahead to meet more advanced needs and drives. Maslow's theory includes the following ascending levels of need:

- *Physiological needs:* Needed for human survival, physiological needs include food, rest, shelter, sleep, and other basic survival needs.
- *Safety needs:* Safety needs encompass self-protection needs such as health and well-being and physical safety from danger and threats.
- *Social needs:* Sometimes labeled as love/belonging, these needs include association with others, friendship, intimacy, and connection with family.
- *Esteem needs:* People have a need for self-esteem, confidence, recognition, achievement, attention, and the respect of and for others.
- *Self-actualization:* The highest level of the hierarchy is the need for being creative and for realizing one's maximum potential in a variety of life spheres, and the need for spontaneity.

The lower-level needs—physiological, safety, social, and esteem needs—are considered deficiency needs and come from a lack of something in our lives. Unless something in these three areas is missing, these needs are considered met and are rarely acknowledged. When they do not exist, people experience unpleasant feelings. The higher-level need, self-actualization, is a growth need and results in a drive to grow and develop as individuals, to master something, and to reach our full potential.

CASE STUDY: The Fun Theory

In Europe, Volkswagen has embarked on a new initiative called Fun Theory.[a] Fun Theory posits that the easiest way to get people to change their behavior is by making things fun. Volkswagen gives out awards for fun initiatives that work. Here are a couple of examples:

> In an Odeplam, Stockholm, train station the stairs have been replaced with what looks and acts like piano keys. As people step onto the stairs, different notes play. As a result, 66% more people use the stairs than the escalators.
>
> A bottle arcade has flashing lights and makes arcade-like sounds when bottles are deposited for recycling. The bottle bank arcade was constantly used throughout the day compared to two uses of the nearby conventional machine.
>
> A combination pinball machine and exercise step machine was placed at a bus stop. The peddles on the step machine controlled the flippers on the pinball machine. This fun and physically active game is played in locations where people typically stand and wait for a bus rather than be physically active.

Questions to Consider

1. What are the positive and negative aspects of Fun Theory? Do you think these inventions will last over time, or are they a novelty?
2. Brainstorm ideas for products or activities that will change people's behaviors in fun ways.

Source

a. Volkswagen, Thefuntheory.com, http://www.thefuntheory.com.

A group of backpackers seek to achieve social, ego, and self-actualization needs through a backpacking trip on the Appalachian Trail.

Obviously, play and recreation can be important elements in satisfying at least the last three levels of need in Maslow's hierarchy. Much discussion has already been attributed to social needs. Esteem needs can be met from participating in team sports, enhancing fitness levels, or building skills in an activity such as skiing, soccer, or diving. Self-actualization can be realized in both work and leisure. In leisure, creativity can come from art, theater, or drama. Continued participation can continually build self-esteem to the point of self-actualization or continued participation and drive can help people become self-actualized by reaching a self-imposed goal of completing a marathon or climbing Mount McKinley.

A discussion of the emotional and psychological implications of leisure must also include the work of Mihaly Csikszentmihalyi, who developed flow theory.[32] Csikszentmihalyi posited that people are most happy and content when they reach a state of flow. Flow is a state of mind that occurs when the challenge and skill in an activity are in synch with each other. In other words, the person has the skill to meet the challenges presented in participating in the activity. When these two are out of balance a range of emotions occurs. For example, when there is a low skill and low challenge required, a person will experience apathy and boredom. Whereas low skill and high challenge can result in worry and anxiety because the individual is anxious about his or her ability to meet the challenge ahead. Activities that trigger flow in a person vary. It may be a night kayak, creating an oil painting, or playing the guitar that leads a person to experience flow. Notice that flow encompasses several motivational issues already discussed, including intrinsic motivation. However, one of the major benefits is escape because of the total absorption in the activity itself.

The Benefits of Laughter

Laughter provides physical, mental, and social benefits:[31]

Physical Health Benefits	Mental Health Benefits	Social Benefits
• Boosts immunity	• Adds joy and zest to life	• Strengthens relationships
• Lowers stress hormones	• Eases anxiety and fear	• Attracts others to us
• Decreases pain	• Relieves stress	• Enhances teamwork
• Relaxes muscles	• Improves mood	• Helps diffuse conflict
• Prevents heart disease	• Enhances resilience	• Promotes group bonding

Happiness and Well-Being

In general, people want to be happy. Happiness is "frequent positive affect, high life satisfaction, and infrequent negative affect."[33] Lyumbomirsky and colleagues analyzed many studies on the subject and learned that happiness generates many positive rewards including obtaining a positive state of mind, higher marriage success rates, having more friends and social connections, superior work outcomes, increased mental health, more activity and energy, and experiencing flow more often. They also found that happiness is determined from three sources. First, 50% of happiness is established by our genetics and is set with little chance of changing it. Another 10% is established by the circumstances we find ourselves in. This could be the part of the world we live in, our personal demographics, life events that we experience, and circumstantial factors such as marital status, job, and income levels. The last piece of happiness, which makes up 40%, is determined by intentional activity. Based on this model, 40% of happiness is determined by the actions we purposefully do. Recreation can play a major role in these intentional activities. The activities in which we participate in general are likely to contribute to happiness.

In addition to happiness, well-being is a major motivator in leisure. Well-being is "a state of successful, satisfying, and productive engagement with one's life and the realization of one's full physical, cognitive, and social-emotional potential."[34] In essence, happiness is central to well-being. When people experience well-being, they also experience happiness and are satisfied with most aspects of their lives.[35] Carruthers suggests that leisure plays several roles in well-being and happiness including the following:

- Positive emotion can result from leisure.
- Leisure serves as a mechanism for individuals to cultivate their personal strengths, and personal strengths enhance happiness.
- Leisure can help individuals attain their full potential by building their competence, sense of purpose, and ability to take risks.[36]

This insight into happiness and well-being demonstrates that leisure plays a major role in people's ability to be happy and feel good emotionally. Because intentional activities influence 40% of individuals' happiness and happiness enhances well-being, choosing leisure activities that fit well for individuals is an important motivator.

Intellectual Outcomes

Of all the personal benefits of play and recreation, probably the least widely recognized are those involving intellectual or cognitive development. Play is typically considered physical activity rather than mental and has by definition been considered a nonserious form of involvement. How then could it contribute to intellectual growth? Researchers have slowly come to realize that physical recreation tends to improve personal motivation and make mental and cognitive performance more effective. Numerous studies, for example, have documented the effects of specific types of physical exercise or play on the development of young children. Other research studies show a strong relationship between physical fitness and academic performance. Although a number of these studies focus on formal instructional programs, others use less-structured experimental elements. Several studies show that playfulness as a personal quality is closely linked to creative and inventive thinking among children.

In the past, play was viewed as a frivolous activity, and children were discouraged from playing to devote fuller effort to serious learning activities. Today, we recognize that play contributes to cognitive growth and, indeed, may provide a uniquely effective way of learning. How does this happen?

The leading psychologist in the field of child development over the past several decades was Jean Piaget, once a professor at the University of Geneva and director of the Institut Rousseau. Piaget suggested that there are two basic processes to all mental development: assimilation and accommodation. *Assimilation* is the process of taking in, as in the case of receiving information in the form of visual or auditory stimuli. *Accommodation* is the process of adjusting to external circumstances and stimuli. In Piaget's theory, play is specially related to assimilation, the process of mentally digesting new and different situations and experiences. Anything important that has happened is reproduced in play, which is a means of assimilating and consolidating the child's emotional experiences.

Games also have been used to help children learn simple scientific, mathematical, and linguistic concepts. Games like Payday and Head Full of Numbers focus on math. Children and adults learn about geography from games such as Sequence—States & Capitals; logic and strategy from Clue, Sudoku, and Battleship; vocabulary from Scrabble and Boggle; and general knowledge from games such as Cranium or the vast array of Trivial Pursuit games on the market.

In the early age of games in North America, the sole purpose of playing was for intellectual stimulation. Although the focus has moved away from learning to that of a means of having fun, many games still have an intellectual aspect. For example, Monopoly was first developed so that people could begin to understand economic principles, and Snakes and Ladders (later renamed Chutes and Ladders) taught about morality and ethical behavior.

CASE STUDY: Video Games

The National Institute on Media and the Family came out with a fact sheet on the impact of video game playing on children. The following statistics help illustrate the breadth of video game playing:

- 83% of kids, 8 to 18 years, have at least one video game player in their home, 56% have 2+ video game players, and 49% have video game systems in their bedrooms.[a]
- 97% of all teens ages 12–17 years play video games regularly.[b]
- The average video game player spent approximately $38 per month on video games and associated products.[c]
- 11.9% of video game players fulfill diagnostic criteria of addiction concerning their gaming behavior.[d]

The institute also listed some pros and cons of video game playing:

Pros

- Video game playing introduces children to computer and information technology.
- Games can give practice in following directions.
- Some games provide practice in problem solving and logic.
- Games can provide practice in use of fine-motor and spatial skills.
- Games can provide occasions for parent and child to play together.
- Some games have therapeutic applications with patients.
- Games are entertaining and fun.

Cons

- Overdependence on video games could foster social isolation because games are often played alone.
- Women are often portrayed as weaker characters that are helpless or sexually provocative.

- Game environments are often based on plots of violence, aggression, and gender bias.
- Practicing violent acts may contribute more to aggressive behavior than passive television watching. Studies do find a relationship between violent television watching and behavior.
- Many games do not offer action that requires independent thought or creativity.
- In many violent games, players must become more violent to win. In "first-person" violent video games, the player may be more affected because he or she controls the game and experiences the action through the eyes of his or her character.[e]

Questions to Consider

1. What can you add to these lists of pros and cons? Do you agree with the lists as presented? Why or why not?
2. Do video games deserve the negative image they receive? Why or why not?
3. How would you justify allowing your five-year-old child to play video games? Your 12-year-old? Your 16-year-old?

Sources

a. V. Rideout, D. F. Roberts, and U. G. Foehr, "Generation M: Media in the Lives of 8–18 Year Olds," Kaiser Family Foundation, http://www.kff.org/entmedia/upload/Executive-Summary-Generation-M-Media-in-the-Lives-of-8-18-Year-olds.pdf.

b. Pew Internet and American Life, "Teens, Video Games, and Civics," National Writing Project, http://www.nwp.org/cs/public/print/resource/2777.

c. NPD Group Inc., "More Americans Play Video Games Than Go Out to the Movies," http://www.npd.com/press/releases/press_090520.html.

d. S. M. Grusser, R. Thalemann, and M. D. Griffiths, "Excessive Computer Game Playing: Evidence for Addiction and Aggression? *CyberPsychology & Behavior* (Vol. 10, 2007): 290–292, http://www.liebertonline.com/doi/abs/10.1089/cpb.2006.9956.

e. National Institute on Media and the Family, "Effects of Video Game Playing on Children," http://www.mediafamily.org/facts/facts_effect.shtml.

On another level, a reporter for *Forbes* magazine points out that business executives frequently enjoy high-level competitive play in games such as contract bridge, chess, or backgammon, and that they value competence in these pastimes in the people they employ. Investment advisors in particular recognize the risk-taking elements involved in such games and the need for strategic flair in taking calculated risks. Whether the game is poker, gin rummy, bridge, backgammon, or chess, the skills involved are all equally important in business.[37]

Spiritual Values and Outcomes

A final area in which recreation and leisure make a vital contribution to the healthy growth and well-being of human beings is within the spiritual realm. The term *spiritual* is commonly taken to be synonymous with *religion*, but here it means a capacity for exhibiting humanity's higher nature—a sense of moral values, compassion, and respect for other humans and for the earth itself. It is linked to the development of one's inner feelings, a sense of order and purpose in life, and a commitment to care for others and to behave responsibly in all aspects of one's existence.

How does recreation contribute in this respect? Josef Pieper, in his 1963 book *Leisure: The Basics of Culture*, and others suggest that in their leisure hours, humans are able to express their fullest and best selves. Leisure can be a time for contemplation, for consideration of ultimate values, for disinterested activity. This means that people can come together simply as people, sharing interests and exploring pleasure, commitment, personal growth, beauty, nature, and other such aspects of life.

In part, the use of outdoor settings for organized recreation experiences is based on the view of the natural world as "God's great temple," which has often been expressed in literature on the outdoors. Such settings often provide places for wilderness retreats, Bible study, or other religiously oriented programs. The Zen Buddhist view that sees God in every aspect of nature and in the relationships of human beings with the natural world underlies this concept. For men and women who accept the challenge of being alone in the natural world, even in perilous circumstances, the experience may often be a highly religious one.

Thus far, this chapter has examined the important personal values of recreation and leisure involvement from three different perspectives: physical; social; and psychological. It is essential to recognize that these are not distinctly separate components of motivation, but are instead closely interrelated from a holistic perspective. Furthermore, it must be understood that leisure means different things to different people. The motivators behind one person bicycling may be completely different from what another gets out of it. The same is true for the outcomes from participation. The first individual may feel great after biking because of the exercise element, whereas the second person may not think about the exercise portion but the feeling of joy he or she gets from contributing to a healthy environment by biking to work rather than driving. Leisure motivators are as unique as the participants themselves.

SERIOUS LEISURE

Much of the discussion so far on leisure motivation focuses on the average person who enjoys leisure time for a multitude of reason, from physical and social to intellectual and spiritual. A different perspective on leisure is serious leisure. Serious leisure is "the systematic pursuit of an amateur, hobbyist, or volunteer activity sufficiently substantial and interesting for the participant to find a career there in the acquisition and expression of a combination of its special skills, knowledge, and experience."[38] People who undertake a leisure activity to the point it extensively extends into their everyday lives could consider that activity to be serious leisure. On the other hand, most people participate in what is labeled as casual leisure. Casual leisure is an "immediately, intrinsically rewarding, relatively short-lived pleasurable activity requiring little or no special training to enjoy it."[39] The difference for most between casual and serious leisure is time, money, and effort dedicated to the activity. For example, a musician who plays with friends a couple of times a month in someone's garage would be a casual participant. If that same person practiced every night, arranged for gigs every weekend, and invested many hours in music each week, that could be considered serious leisure.

Serious leisure has six defining qualities:

- *Perseverance:* Serious leisure is defined by the need to persistently persevere through adverse conditions over time. This may mean a runner must work through pain, fatigue, or poor weather conditions. A performer must deal with stage fright or embarrassment. People are willing to overcome what some would see as negative situations because of the positive feelings they ultimately get from the activity.

- *Leisure career:* Although the individual is most likely not paid for participation, serious leisure emulates a career in that it has stages of achievement. Individuals exhibit a career-like commitment to the leisure activity, where they work to improve and achieve set goals.
- *Significant effort:* Serious leisure is characterized by people developing special knowledge, skills, or abilities. This requires considerable effort that is beyond the ordinary skill development of casual leisure.
- *Durable outcomes:* Serious leisure pursuits are steeped in outcomes including enrichment, self-actualization, self-expression, enhanced self-image, self-gratification, re-creation, and sometimes financial returns. Although these attributes can be found in casual leisure, it is the depth that distinguishes serious leisure. These activities may not be fun at times, but the skills people are developing are used and these durable outcomes emerge and make the activity more positive for the individual.
- *Unique ethos:* A unique ethos is a subculture among those who participate in serious leisure. These people share similar ideals, values, norms, and beliefs that pertain to the activity. Social relationships and networks emerge that focus on the leisure pursuit.

CASE STUDY: Serious Leisure

When Mike's 15-year-old daughter started talking about getting her license and a car, Mike started to worry about the dangers of driving and the possibility of an accident. Mike decided to buy his daughter a car that was 20 years old, very large, and made of sturdy materials. He also brought this car home on a trailer with many parts in boxes because the car would not run and had not been driven in years. It was Mike's idea to fix this car so his daughter could drive it, and, if she crashed it, the chances of getting hurt were diminished. Mike became absorbed in rebuilding this car in the family garage. Each night after work, Mike worked on this car. It took many months, but Mike finished the car by his daughter's 16th birthday. What Mike did not anticipate was that the car turned out so beautifully that it could be entered into classic car shows.

Now that the one car is done, Mike bought others to rebuild, renting a large garage to hold these cars as he rebuilt them. Mike continued building these cars during the week and spent his weekends at car shows. At the car shows, Mike would eventually sell his cars so that he could purchase others to work on. Mike retired at age 50 so he could spend more time working on these cars in his garage. This garage became a social stop for many guys in town. They would drop by the garage to see what Mike was working on, and others who worked on classic cars just came by to talk about their latest projects.

As Mike becomes older, the physical work becomes more difficult. He still works on cars, but he buys cars that are in better shape so they require less work. He keeps three to five cars in his garage at once and still travels to car shows to sell the completed cars. He also ventures out to buying and selling cars on eBay. The buying and selling aspect of cars requires Mike to spend hours researching the value of cars and locating specific cars.

Questions to Consider

1. Take the six defining qualities of leisure and determine what attributes of each Mike is displaying.
2. Do you know anyone who participates in serious leisure? Discuss their behaviors based on these six defining qualities.
3. Is there a leisure activity that you could see yourself becoming serious about? Why or why not?

- *Identification with the pursuit:* The individual strongly identifies with the leisure activity. These people talk excitedly about their activity, are proud of the activity, and are quite committed to it.[40]

Given these six distinguishable characteristics, you can see that the commitment and motivation for serious leisure are far more intense than for casual leisure.

TABOO RECREATION

So far, this chapter has examined leisure motivation from the physical, social, psychological, and emotional perspectives. All of these motives have been positive, yet there is a negative side of leisure that requires some discussion. Russell suggests that leisure is not always done for the person's well-being, and these types of activities are considered taboo recreation.[41] Taboo recreation is leisure behavior that is restricted by society's norms. Because societal norms are subjective and change from group to group, it is difficult to decide what falls under taboo recreation and what are simply fringe activities. For example, some sects of the Catholic Church and some Scottish politicians have claimed that the Hokey Pokey was written to mock the actions and language of priests leading the Latin mass.[42] Other religious groups denounce dancing as evil. Because of the disagreement on a clear delineation of what constitutes taboo recreation, two common pursuits are discussed as examples.

Gambling Statistics

- There are more casinos in the United States than in any other country in the world.
- Forty-seven states have legal gambling facilities (casinos and parimutuel facilities) with 1511 legal gambling facilities available.
- Nevada has more casinos than any other state, with 327 casino operators.
- The largest casino in the United States is Mohegan Sun, which is located in Uncasville, Connecticut. Mohegan Sun has 302 table games and 13,600 casino slot machines/video poker games.

Gambling

Gambling is wagering money or something of value on a preselected outcome. Examples of gambling include betting on horse races, buying lottery tickets, and entering a National Collegiate Athletic Association (NCAA) Final Four Tournament pool. Gambling has a storied past and actually began during colonial times when lotteries were implemented to generate revenues. Lotteries were also used to fund some of the most prestigious universities in the United States, including Harvard, Yale, and Princeton.[43] It did not take long for gambling to become illegal and an underground activity. Gambling made a resurgence during the Great

Depression because it was seen as a way to stimulate the economy.[43] Also at this time Nevada legalized most forms of gambling. In these early years, gambling was infiltrated with organized crime. In the 1950s, the federal government cleaned up gambling and organized crime got out of the business. The prevalence of gambling has increased exponentially in the past 30 years. What started out as a few casinos has expanded to include parimutuel betting, Internet gambling, and riverboat casinos.

Because the focus of this chapter is not on gambling, per se, but motivation, the question arises as to why people gamble. Research shows a wide variety of reasons including fun, risk, excitement, challenge, adrenalin rush, and relaxation—all motivators that were previously discussed. If it stops at this, there would be no reason to discuss gambling separately from any other activity. However, gambling is taboo when it becomes a problem. Gamblers Anonymous defines someone with a gambling addiction as a compulsive gambler (**Table 5.1**). Compulsive gambling is an illness that progressively worsens, can never be cured, but that can be stopped.[44] The motivation to gamble at this point in a person's life is where it becomes taboo recreation.

CASE STUDY: Gambling

Some religious groups feel that gambling is morally wrong. It has been argued that people should work for their money, money should come from something of benefit, and gambling undermines the work ethic and leads people to profit from the loss of others.[a] On the other side of this argument, revenues from lotteries are used to fund parks and recreation. For example, money from the lottery in Alberta, Canada, funds recreation and sports facilities, the arts, major special events, and fairs and exhibitions. Fifteen percent of the proceeds from the lottery in Oregon go to the parks and natural resources fund[b]—and, there are many other examples of this across the country. Raffles, drawings, and bingo also are revenue generators for recreation. While gambling can be a lucrative source of revenue, should our moral obligation outweigh the financial gains?

Questions to Consider

1. Develop the pros and cons of gambling as leisure.
2. Should recreation agencies benefit from gambling proceeds?
3. Should churches benefit from gambling proceeds, such as bingo nights?
4. John Doe won $100,000 playing blackjack in Las Vegas. John decided to donate $75,000 of his winnings to local charities. It was offered to the YMCA, the parks and recreation department, and John's church. Should each of these groups accept the money? Why or why not?

Sources

a. The Gospel Way, "Is Gambling Moral or Immoral?," http://gospelway.com/morality/gambling.php.
b. Oregon State Legislature, "Lottery Revenue," http://www.leg.state.or.us/comm/commsrvs/background_briefs2008/briefs/BudgetRevenue/LotteryRevenue.pdf.

TABLE 5.1

PROBLEM GAMBLING QUIZ

Gamblers Anonymous developed a 20-question quiz to ascertain if gambling is a problem for an individual.

1. Did you ever lose time from work or school due to gambling?
2. Has gambling ever made your home life unhappy?
3. Did gambling affect your reputation?
4. Have you ever felt remorse after gambling?
5. Did you ever gamble to get money with which to pay debts or otherwise solve financial difficulties?
6. Did gambling cause a decrease in your ambition or efficiency?
7. After losing did you feel you must return as soon as possible and win back your losses?
8. After a win did you have a strong urge to return and win more?
9. Did you often gamble until your last dollar was gone?
10. Did you ever borrow to finance your gambling?
11. Have you ever sold anything to finance gambling?
12. Were you reluctant to use "gambling money" for normal expenditures?
13. Did gambling make you careless of the welfare of yourself or your family?
14. Did you ever gamble longer than you had planned?
15. Have you ever gambled to escape worry, trouble, boredom, or loneliness?
16. Have you ever committed, or considered committing, an illegal act to finance gambling?
17. Did gambling cause you to have difficulty in sleeping?
18. Do arguments, disappointments, or frustrations create within you an urge to gamble?
19. Did you ever have an urge to celebrate any good fortune by a few hours of gambling?
20. Have you ever considered self-destruction or suicide as a result of your gambling?

Most compulsive gamblers will answer "yes" to at least seven of these questions.

Courtesy of Gamblers Anonymous. Available at: http://www.gamblersanonymous.org/20questions.html. Accessed December 21, 2010.

Substance Abuse

Russell defines substance abuse as "over indulging in and depending on a drug, alcohol, or other chemical, to the detriment of physical and mental health."[41] Substance abuse can exist with illegal drugs such as cocaine and marijuana, or with legal drugs such as alcohol and prescription narcotics. Alcohol and drug use changes as people age (**Table 5.2**). In addition to this data, 50% of the adult population are considered regular drinkers, consuming 12+ drinks per year, and another 14% are infrequent drinkers having fewer than 12 drinks per year.[45]

For those using illegal drugs or consuming alcohol underage, the taboo recreation label fits this behavior. Social drinking, on the other hand, is not considered taboo recreation until it becomes a problem. Just like gambling, alcohol and drug use have signs that indicate when this activity becomes problematic. Also like gambling, there are motives for engaging in this activity. It could be for escape, relaxation, to fit in with a group, to socialize, to take risks, or to be more outgoing.

Social drinking is a major subculture in North America. A few examples are as follows:

- Young adults go to clubs and drink socially around their friends and to meet people.
- Wine tasting and beer making are leisure activities and social events.

TABLE 5.2

DRUG USE

	High School Seniors	18–25 Years	26+ Years
Alcohol use in last 30 days	44.4%	—	—
Alcohol use in last 12 months	66.4%	—	—
Marijuana use in last 30 days	18.8%	16.3%	4.2%
Marijuana use in last 12 months	31.7%	28.0%	6.8%
Cocaine use in last 30 days	2.0%	2.2%	0.8%
Cocaine use in last 12 months	5.2%	6.9%	1.8%

Data from Bureau of Justice Statistics. Drug and Crime Facts. Available at: http://bjs.ojp.usdoj.gov/content/dcf/contents.cfm. Accessed November 10, 2010.

- Tourism capitalizes on trips to wineries.
- Beermakers and restaurants are partnering to present beer and dinner events.
- Wine glass making is an art form.

There are far more examples of potential taboo recreation pursuits that could be discussed here. For example, viewing pornography, adult entertainment and erotica, vandalism, dog fighting, or excessive Internet use can be deemed as taboo by some portions of our society. To many people gambling, the use of legal drugs and limited use of alcohol are no different than any other leisure activity. For those who see these activities as morally wrong or abuse any of them, the taboo recreation label emerges. Regardless of whether an individual sees these activities as acceptable and at what level they are acceptable, the motivation to participate varies for each person but focuses strongly on the social and psychological motivations for leisure.

SUMMARY

Beyond the familiar motivations of seeking fun, pleasure, or relaxation, people engage in leisure pursuits for a host of different reasons. Recreational motivations include personal goals such as the need for companionship, escape from stress or the boredom of daily routines, and the search for challenge.

The outcomes of recreational involvement may be classified under four major headings: physical, social, psychological, and emotional.

Physical motivators have never been as important as they are in today's society. The obesity rates of both children and adults continue to grow. Recreational activities help people control weight, fight against obesity, and improve cardiovascular health. The social motivation for leisure results in reduced loneliness, strengthens relationships, and promotes social bonding. The psychological motivations for leisure are quite extensive. People seek adventure, relaxation, escape, stress reduction, and overall well-being and happiness. The emotional motivators involve fun, happiness, intellectual outcomes, and spiritual values. Leisure can bring all of these rewards to a person.

Serious leisure requires a person to be highly motivated to participate in their chosen activity. Those engaged in serious leisure have their leisure activities consume a major part of their lives and are quite committed to participation.

Although all of these motives are viewed as having positive outcomes, there is a part of leisure that not everyone sees as positive. Taboo recreation, or leisure that is seen as negative based on societal standards, can include such activities as gambling, illegal drug use, and excessive use of alcohol. Society's views vary and some see any involvement in these activities as taboo while others base judgment on the frequency and extent to which participation occurs.

This chapter focused on why people choose the activities that they do and what outcomes they receive from participation. These motives are subjective and vary from person to person. No one activity provides the same outcomes for everyone. Because of this people must assess their own needs and choose activities that meet these needs.

QUESTIONS FOR CLASS DISCUSSION OR ESSAY EXAMINATION

1. The physical benefits of exercise have been well documented. Vigorous use of exercise machines and treadmills, running, swimming, and bicycling all contribute greatly to cardiovascular health. Why is it desirable to approach such activities as recreation rather than as prescribed exercise carried on for fitness purposes alone? In addition to cardiovascular benefits, what other important health outcomes have been identified?
2. The chapter describes some of the specific contributions of recreation to emotional or mental health. What are they? On the basis of your own experience, can you describe some of the positive emotional outcomes resulting from recreational involvement?
3. Recreation centers are increasingly adding fitness equipment designed for children. This equipment includes such tools as smaller treadmills and stationary bicycles. Do you think this is a good use of money and will stimulate physical activity in children? Why or why not? What other activities could recreation centers implement to help fight childhood obesity? What role do parents play in this problem?
4. Define *taboo recreation*. What motives do people have for participating in these types of activities? Give examples of other taboo activities that were not discussed in this text.
5. A number of psychological motivators were discussed. What are they? How do they relate to your choices for leisure activities?
6. Think of an activity that you could see yourself engaging in to the point of it being serious leisure. Describe your participation level and what would make that activity serious leisure.
7. Select your five favorite recreational activities and then answer the following question: Why do you participate in these activities (motives)? Predict how this list will change in the next 10, 20, 30, and 50 years.

ENDNOTES

1. About Erik Weihenmayer, http://www.touchthetop.com/about.htm.
2. A. Gillard, C. E. Watts, and P. A. Witt, "Camp Supports for Motivation and Interest: A Mixed-Methods Study," *Journal of Park and Recreation Administration*,(Vol. 27, No. 2, 2009): 74–96.
3. R. M. Ryan and E. L. Deci, "Self-Determination Theory and the Facilitation of Intrinsic Motivation, Social Development, and Well-Being," *American Psychologist*, (Vol. 55, No. 1, 2000): 68–78.
4. Ibid., 70.

5. Centers for Disease Control and Prevention, *NHANES Surveys (1976–1980 and 2003–2006)*, Division of Nutrition, Physical Activity and Obesity, National Center for Chronic Disease Prevention and Health Promotion, http://www.cdc.gov/nchs/data/hestat/overweight/overweight_adult.htm.

6. "Differences in Prevalence of Obesity Among Black, White, and Hispanic Adults—United States, 2006–2008," *Morbidity and Mortality Weekly Report* (17 July 2009), Department of Health and Human Services, Centers for Disease Control and Prevention, http://www.cdc.gov/mmwr/preview/mmwrhtml/mm5827a2.htm.

7. Centers for Disease Control and Prevention, "U.S. Obesity Trends: Trends by State 1985–2008," Division of Nutrition, Physical Activity and Obesity, National Center for Chronic Disease Prevention and Health Promotion, http://www.cdc.gov/obesity/data/trends.html#Race.

8. National Center for Health Statistics, *Health, United States, 2005, with Chartbook on Trends in the Health of Americans* (Hyattsville, MD: 2005).

9. Healthy People 2010. http://www.healthypeople.gov/About/goals.htm.

10. American Heart Association, "Heart Disease and Stroke Statistics: 2009 Update-at-a-Glance," American Heart Association, http://www.americanheart.org/downloadable/heart/123783441267009Heart%20and%20Stroke%20Update.pdf.

11. W. L. Haskell, I. Lee, R. R. Pate, K. E. Powell, S. N. Blair, B. A. Franklin, C. A. Macera, G. W. Heath, P. D. Thompson, and A. Bauman, "Physical Activity and Public Health: Updated Recommendation for Adults from the American College of Sports Medicine and the American Heart Association," American Heart Association (1 August 2007), http://circ.ahajournals.org/cgi/reprint/CIRCULATIONAHA.107.185649v1.

12. Centers for Disease Control and Prevention, *2008 Physical Activity Guidelines for Americans: Fact Sheet for Health Professionals on Physical Activity Guidelines for Children and Adolescents*. Department of Health and Human Services, Center for Disease Control and Prevention, http://www.cdc.gov/nccdphp/dnpa/physical/pdf/PA_Fact_Sheet_Children.pdf.

13. J. S. Son, D. L. Kerstetter, and A. J. Mowen, "Illuminating Identity and Health in the Constraint Negotiation of Leisure-Time Physical Activity in Mid to Late Life," *Journal of Park and Recreation Administration* (Vol. 27, No. 3, 2009): 96–115.

14. Ibid.

15. S. A. Wilhelm Stanis, I. E. Schneider, D. J. Chavez, and K. J. Shinew, "Visitor Constraints to Physical Activity in Park and Recreation Areas: Differences by Race and Ethnicity," *Journal of Park and Recreation Administration* (Vol. 27, No. 3, 2009): 78–95.

16. J. Salmon, N. Owen, D. Crawford, A. Bauman, and J. F. Sallis, "Physical Activity and Sedentary Behavior: A Population-Based Study of Barriers, Enjoyment, and Preference," *Health Psychology* (Vol. 22, No. 2, 2003): 178–188.

17. Ibid.

18. J. Wardle, C. Guthrie, S. Sanderson, L. Birch, and R. Plomin, "Food and Activity Preferences in Children of Lean and Obese Parents," *International Journal of Obesity and Related Metabolic Disorders* (Vol. 25, 2001): 971–977.

19. Andrew Cohen, "Real Room Services," *Athletic Business* (2002 June).

20. E. Scott, "Top 10 Stress Relievers: The Best Ways to Feel Better," http://stress.about.com/od/generaltechniques/tp/toptensionacts.htm.

21. R. Russell, *Pastimes: The Context of Contemporary Leisure*, 4th ed. (Champaign, IL: Sagamore Publishing, 2009).

22. J. Harter and R. Arora, "Social Time Crucial to Daily Emotional Well-Being in U.S.," http://www.gallup.com/poll/107692/social-time-crucial-daily-emotional-wellbeing.aspx.

23. D. J. Jordan, *Leadership in Leisure Services: Making a Difference*, 3rd ed. (State College, PA: Venture Publishing, 2007).

24. C. R. Jensen and S. P. Guthrie, *Outdoor Recreation in America*, (Champaign, IL: Human Kinetics, 2006).

25. S. Priest and G. Carpenter, "Changes in Perceived Risk and Competence During Adventurous Leisure Experiences," *Journal of Applied Recreation Research* (Vol. 18, No. 1, 1993): 51–71.

26. WebMD, "Stress Management: Ways to Relieve Stress," http://www.webmd.com/balance/stress-management/stress-management-relieving-stress.

27. C. Raines, *Connecting Generations* (Menlo, CA: Crisp Publications, 2003).

28. Ibid.

29. Ibid.

30. Helpguide.org, "Laughter Is the Best Medicine: The Health Benefits of Humor and Laughter," http://helpguide.org/life/humor_laughter_health.htm.

31. Ibid.

32. M. Csikszentmihalyi, *Finding Flow: The Psychology of Engagement With Everyday Life* (New York: Basic Books, 1997).

33. S. Lyubomirsky, K. M. Sheldon, and D. Schkade, "Pursuing Happiness: The Architecture of Sustainable Change," *Review of General Psychology* (Vol. 9, 2005): 111–131.

34. C. Carruthers and C. D. Hood, "Building a Life of Meaning Through Therapeutic Recreation: The Leisure and Well-Being Model, Part I," *Therapeutic Recreation Journal* (Vol. 41, No. 4, 2007): 276–298.

35. C. Carruthers and C. Hood, *Beyond Coping: Adversity as a Catalyst for Personal Transformation*. Educational session presented at the American Therapeutic Recreation Association Annual Conference, Kansas City, MO, 2004.

36. C. Carruthers, *The Power of the Positive: Leisure and the Good Life*. Educational session presented at the Nevada recreation and Park Society Annual Conference, 2009.

37. A. Hurd, "Board Games," in G. Cross, ed., *Encyclopedia of Recreation and Leisure in America* (New York: Charles Scribner's Sons, 2004).

38. R. A. Stebbins, *Amateurs, Professionals, and Serious Leisure* (Montreal: McGill-Queen's University Press, 1992).

39. R. A. Stebbins, "Casual Leisure: A Conceptual Statement," *Leisure Studies* (Vol. 16, 1997): 17–25.

40. J. Gould, D. Moore, F. McGuire, and R. Stebbins, "Development of the Serious Leisure Inventory and Measure," *Journal of Leisure Research* (Vol. 40, No. 1, 2008): 47–69.

41. R. V. Russell, *Pastimes: The Context of Contemporary Leisure*. 4th ed. (Champaign, IL: Sagamore Publishing, 2009: 196).

42. A. Cramb, "Doing the Hokey Cokey 'Could Be Hate Crime'," http://www.telegraph.co.uk/news/newstopics/howaboutthat/3883838/Doing-the-Hokey-Cokey-could-be-hate-crime.html.

43. History of Gambling in the United States, http://www.library.ca.gov/crb/97/03/chapt2.html.

44. Gambler's Anonymous, http://www.gamblersanonymous.org/qna.html.

45. Centers for Disease Control and Prevention, "Alcohol Use," http://www.cdc.gov/nchs/fastats/alcohol.htm.

CHAPTER 6

SOCIOCULTURAL FACTORS AFFECTING LEISURE

◆ ◆ ◆

Calvin Coolidge Senior High School in Washington, DC, hired Natalie Randolph, an African American woman, to coach the high school football team. Randolph had served two seasons as assistant coach for the varsity football team at H.D. Woodson High School in Washington, DC. In addition, Natalie played five seasons for the D.C. Divas in the Independent Women's Football League.[1]

"I think it's wonderful," said Shawn Ladda, president of the NAGWS. "I applaud Natalie, and I applaud the school administration for hiring her. But it's also a clear indication that we have a long way to go that it's such an anomaly to hire a woman to coach a boys' high school football team."

◆ ◆ ◆

INTRODUCTION

This chapter deals with sociocultural factors that affect personal leisure values and involvement today: age, gender, sexual orientation, racial and ethnic identity, and socioeconomic status.

It is easy to see the major changes that children experience as they grow. The same thing holds true for adults. Albeit, we change at a much slower pace, but differences exist based on age. Our leisure preferences evolve. We try new activities. Some of them remain activities for a lifetime and others stay with us until we reach a certain point in our lives. Interests may influence these changes as well as physical abilities, family status, education, or work, among others. Progress in this field has been striking with respect to expanded recreational opportunities for girls and women in sport and outdoor recreation. Although the chief concern has been about females and leisure, the role of boys and men in contemporary leisure has also been an issue.

Sexual orientation affects leisure pursuits in a number of ways. Focus is changing from ignoring this group to seeing them as a viable market as the numbers of identified lesbian, gay, bisexual, and transgendered people increase.

Racial and ethnic identity also has limited many individuals from full participation in organized recreation in the past and continues to influence the leisure involvement not only of African Americans, but also of the growing number of Hispanics and those of Asian background. With continuing waves of immigration from other parts of the world, religion linked to ethnic identity will pose new policy questions as Muslims, as well as other people who are neither Christian nor Jewish, become part of the national landscape.

Socioeconomic status limits leisure participation as well as where people participate in leisure activities. Those who are in poor or working classes have fewer opportunities and get most of their services from the nonprofit and public sector, whereas the upper class has relatively unlimited access to services and utilizes commercial services almost exclusively. This is only the beginning of the vast differences among classes.

AGE FACTORS INFLUENCING LEISURE

The influence of one's age on recreational values, motivators, and patterns of participation have been analyzed in numerous recreation and leisure-service programming textbooks. There are key states of the life span as well as growth processes and development tasks to be accomplished at each stage. Apart from differences in individual personalities within each age bracket, there is also the reality that developments in modern technology, economic and social trends, and shifts in family relationships have been responsible for major changes in age-related norms of human behavior. Our patterns of birth and parenthood have been radically altered by innovative technology in medical practice. We now have the potential for mothers to give birth to their own daughter's babies through the surgical implantation of fertilized ova. Similarly, men can now father babies for many years after their own deaths.

We have seen dramatic shifts in life experiences. Today, children are exposed to the realities of life and mature physically at a much earlier point than in the past. At the same time, paradoxically, they have a longer period of adolescence and schooling before entering the adult workforce. Adults now tend to marry later and have fewer children, and many adults are choosing not to marry at all. Older people have a much longer period of retirement, and a significantly greater number of older persons live more active and adventurous leisure lives today than in the past.

To fully understand the impact of societal trends on public involvement in recreation, park, and leisure-service programs, it is helpful to examine each major age group in turn. Rather than discuss the development stages of each age group, an overview of some important issues is presented.

Recreation in the Lives of Children

Childhood is the age group that includes children from early infancy through the preteen years. Throughout this period, play satisfies important developmental needs in children—often helping to establish values and behavior patterns that will continue throughout a lifetime. Psychologists have examined the role of play at each stage of life, beginning with infancy and moving through the preschool period, middle and late childhood, and adolescence.

Children typically move through several stages: (1) solitary play, carried on without others nearby; (2) parallel play, in which children play side by side without meaningful interplay; (3) associative play, in which children share a common game or group enterprise but concentrate on their own individual efforts rather than group activity; and (4) cooperative play, beginning at about age 3, in which children actually join together in games, informal dramatics, or constructive projects. By the age of 6 or 7, children tend to be involved in loosely organized play groups, leading to much more tightly structured and organized groups in the so-called gang age between 8 and 12.[2]

Children develop physically, emotionally, and socially through play and recreation.

Typically, we tend to think of childhood as a happy time, picturing it in literature or other forms of entertainment as a period of innocence, marked by a warm nostalgic glow. Television shows of the 1950s, for example, generally idealized the American family in terms of love, support, and security. Within this context, family play was presented as an experience that all could share, one with elements of companionship, humor, and self-discovery. Over the past three decades, however, a number of major changes have taken place that have radically changed the lives of children in terms of their family and neighborhood environments, the community services provided to meet their needs, and the commercial forces that entertain them and shape their personal values and view of the world.

Change of the Family Structure No longer is there a typical family structure with two parents raising their children together. The number of single-parent households has remained steady since 1994 at about 9% (12.9 million). Of these, there are 10.4 million single mothers and 2.5 million single fathers. Eight percent (5.7 million) of today's youth live in a household with at least one of their grandparents. In addition, the number of stay-at-home parents is declining. In 2007, there were an estimated 5.8 million stay-at-home parents—5.6 million being mothers and another 200,000 being fathers. This change in family structure means an increased need for recreation services for working families. This includes such things as after-school and before-school programming, child and grandchild activities, and mentoring programs for children with single parents.

Overscheduled Children The overscheduling of children is becoming a problem in today's culture. For example, there are increasing opportunities for youth to participate in sport clinics, camps, and leagues for children as young as 4. Many go on to be a part of traveling sport teams that go to different communities on the weekends to play in tournaments. Couple this with the demands of household responsibilities, school assignments, and any number of other recreation activities, classes, and clubs and the result is dwindling free time for today's youth.

Although art and music lessons as well as sport and other educational activities may be beneficial to the child, there comes a point when the child has too many things going on in her life. This can result in damage to a child's self-esteem because she sees that her parents are always trying to improve her and she is not good enough the way she is. This overscheduling can add unnecessary stress to a child's life and quite possibly lead to escalated incidences of depression and substance abuse in the teen years.[3]

Overparenting Each generation seems to increase its role of parenting and obsession with protecting their children. The recently coined terms "helicopter parenting" and "snowplow parenting" are becoming more common in our language. Helicopter parents are very involved in their child's education, experiences, and issues. They have a tendency to hover and are never far away from their children. Helicopter parents try to solve problems for their children, and, as a result, the children become reliant on their parents to do this for them. The snowplow parents are ones who plow right through any obstacles that stand in their child's way. Both helicopter and snowplow parents are raising children to believe they have few faults and will always be successful. These same parents are the first to confront a teacher or coach about unfair treatment of their child.

CASE STUDY: Helicopter Parents

Jason is the internship coordinator in Parks and Recreation for State University. He has asked an agency to take Joe Smith for his senior internship. Joe's potential supervisor, Alex, calls Jason to discuss a recent conversation she had with Joe's father and her past history with Joe's family.

Alex: Jason, I saw that you wanted to assign Joe to our agency for his senior internship. Before I could even review his resume, Joe's father called me and said that I should take Joe as an intern and that he needs to learn some skills such as human resources management and budgeting that will make him more marketable in the job search in the fall. Joe's father is concerned about some of the things that Joe learned, or didn't learn, in the classroom. He also indicated that when he sent Joe to State University and completed Joe's entire application for him, that he wanted Joe to get the best job possible when he graduated.

Jason: Alex, we do not advocate parents calling prospective internship sites. For that we do apologize. We also stress that the student is to work with the agency to establish the internship. It is up to you if you take Joe as an intern.

Alex: That isn't all. We have a history with Joe and his family. Both of his parents were extremely involved in the parks and recreation department when Joe was growing up. Or I should say—in Joe's activities. They called more than one instructor and coach to complain about the instruction Joe got and the playing time he received. He worked for us part time one summer and his mother called his potential supervisor to set up his interview. Against her better judgment she hired Joe. It wasn't long before Joe's mother was calling other staff to cover some of Joe's shifts for him because he had places to go and other things he wanted to do.

Jason: If you decide not to accept Joe, I think it would be very beneficial if you explained all of these things to him. He needs to understand how this is affecting his future. Although I am not at liberty to discuss Joe's academic record with you, I will say that I am not surprised by anything you are telling me.

Questions to Consider

1. Should Alex take Joe as an intern? Why or why not?
2. How should Alex handle this entire situation?
3. What are the positives and negatives of Joe's parents' actions?
4. Should Jason have any conversations with Joe's parents?
5. Should Alex have any conversations with Joe's parents?

Helicopter parenting inhibits children's ability to make decisions for themselves—and not just young children but also young adults.[4] These children sometimes are also unable to accept responsibility for their actions because their parents bail them out of problems and issues they have gotten into.[5] Although helicopter parenting is often portrayed as a negative thing, and most parents deny they are helicopter parents, there are positives to this. A close relationship with a child and one where the parent helps a child make good decisions is beneficial to the child becoming a self-sufficient adult.

The recession is slowly changing some of this overparenting behavior. A CBS News poll found that parents have cut back some of their children's extracurricular activities and simplified their childrens' schedules because they have had to financially. A poll done by *Time* found that four times as many parents indicated that their relationship with their children had actually improved because of recession-induced changes.[6]

Influence of Commercial Media: Violence and Sex Another important influence on the lives of children today stems from the overwhelming barrage of violence and sexual content contained in the movies, television shows, video games, and music that saturate their environment.

Because children spend more time watching television than any other activity and 54% of all children have televisions in their bedrooms, it is not surprising that the shows affect their behavior. Two-thirds of all television shows contain sexual activity and/or violence. It is estimated that children are exposed to 14,000 sexual messages each year and by the age of 18, they will have seen 16,000 simulated murders and 200,000 acts of violence.[7] For the past 30 years, the American Psychological Association has posited that media increases aggressive behavior in children. Additionally, limiting violence seen on television can reduce aggressive behaviors in children toward their peers.[8]

Lack of Outdoor Play Children are staying inside and spending more and more time with their computers, video games, and televisions rather than being outside experiencing all that nature has to offer. Richard Louv authored a book in which he explains how children do not have the same outdoor experiences previous generations had.[9] Parents keep a closer watch over children and limit where they can play and explore. They prefer the structured, supervised activities to free play in the outdoors. The radius that children are allowed to roam outside of their home is one-ninth of what it was 20 years ago. Much of this is because of safety concerns when in actuality child safety has steadily improved during the past decade, and they are far safer than they were 30 years ago.[10]

Outdoor and nature activities can improve emotional and physical health for children and adolescents.

Louv reviewed research on the positive effects of children being close to nature. It

CASE STUDY: Children, Play, and Nature

The study of play is experiencing a resurgence in a society where children are being regimented and overscheduled; where computer time exceeds outdoor time considerably; and where parents are afraid to let their children outdoors. Cities are not planned and managed for the benefit of children's play. According to Churchman,

> [Cities] do not provide many or sufficient places that adequately and appropriately meet the developmental needs of children. They do not facilitate and encourage the independent use of the city by children. . . . They do not welcome children in all areas of the city with open arms, or project a message that says this is for you too.[a]

Children seek out natural play environments, and the younger they are, the more important such environments are to their development. Whether it be the backyard, neighborhood park, a natural area, or state park, these areas appear to provide important opportunities for experiences that can have positive developmental outcomes for children of all ages. One of those important outcomes is the opportunity to develop imagination using items found in the environment, such as rocks, twigs, flowers, and so forth. One researcher suggests that such opportunities to develop imagination results in high social and cognitive benefits.[b] In another study conducted with children in poor urban environments, when the family was relocated to areas with more nearby nature the children had higher levels of cognitive ability.[c]

The terms *natural play* and *natural play environments* have different connotations. Natural play environments are outdoor settings, or settings that primarily have not been manicured or prepared by individuals into a more formal park setting. Natural play, by contrast, is the process of children playing without intervention from adults, support devices such as playground equipment, and other external influences. Natural play is also called child-directed play. The importance of natural play, regardless of the setting, is its recognized contributions to social, emotional, cognitive, and physical well-being of children and youth.[d]

Questions to Consider

1. When you were a child, how often did you play outdoors? What are your best memories of play as a child?
2. How has play outdoors changed for children today?
3. Ask your parents or an older adult how they played outdoors as children. What did they say? How is that different from your play?
4. Do children engage in natural play today? Why or why not?
5. Think about the community you grew up in. What elements of that community inhibit children from playing in natural environments? What elements foster this same sort of play?

Sources

a. A. Churchman, "Is There a Place for Children in the City?" *Journal of Urban Design* (Vol. 8, No. 2, 2003): 101.
b. J. H. Heerwagen and G. H. Orians, "The Ecological World of Children," In *Children and Nature: Psychological, Sociocultural, and Evolutionary Investigations*, P. H. Kahn and S. R. Keller (eds.) (Cambridge, MA: MIT Press, 2002).
c. N. M. Wells, "At Home with Nature: Effects of 'Greenness' on Children's Cognitive Functioning," *Environment & Behavior* (Vol. 32, No. 6, 2000): 775–795.
d. K. R. Ginsburg, "The Importance of Play in Promoting Healthy Child Development and Maintaining Strong Parent–Child Bonds," *Pediatrics* (Vol. 119, No. 1, 2007): 182–191.

was determined that nature can improve a child's emotional health. Furthermore, nature helps relieve everyday stress that leads to depression, and children with nature near their home had fewer problems with behavior disorders, anxiety, and depression.[11] Nature also is seen as an intellectual enhancer. Moore and Hong suggest that natural settings will stimulate a child's senses and bring together informal play with formal learning and that these sensory experiences help a child grow intellectually.[12]

Attention Deficit Hyperactivity Disorder (ADHD) is a growing phenomenon among today's youth. More and more children are taking prescription drugs to curb the symptoms of ADHD that include a difficulty in paying attention, focusing, listening, and following directions. Researchers have claimed that being in nature can boost a child's attention span and relieve symptoms of ADHD.[13] Something as simple as taking a walk in the woods, playing in an open space such as a park, or spending time in the backyard can have tremendous rewards, yet these types of activities are on the decline.

Recreation in the Lives of Adolescents

The teenage population, which began to climb in the early 1990s following years of decline, is expected to keep growing until at least 2045, according to U.S. Census Bureau projections. By then, it is projected there will be more than 51 million Americans between the ages of 10 and 19.

This group of young people matures faster, is quite technologically savvy, and knows what they want from their leisure. The group is proving to be quite challenging for parks and recreation professionals for many different reasons, some of which are discussed here.

Teen Employment The teen employment rate is declining. Part of this is because of the economy and unemployment rate of the general population. One-time teen-dependent jobs such as fast food restaurants are now being taken by those who have lost their jobs as a result of the economy and need to make ends meet for their families. Another reason is helicopter parents who are choosing to have their children focus on their education and extracurricular activities rather than working after school. The largest impact on leisure services this will have is the need for more programs for this age group and a decreased ability to fill summer jobs such as lifeguards and day camp counselors.

Trends in Negative Adolescent Leisure Pursuits Negative leisure pursuits by teens include such things as drug and alcohol use, gambling, and sexuality, among others. Participation rates are changing with each one. For example, the National Institute on Drug Abuse saw a decline in marijuana use from the 1990s until recently, when it has seemed to level off. Cigarette smoking by teens is at the lowest levels ever; and stimulant, amphetamine, and alcohol use are also declining. The United States is seeing an increase in the use of prescription drugs by teens for nonmedical purposes. These drugs include Vicodin (hydrocodone) and Oxycontin (oxycodone).[14]

Alcohol is also a major problem with adolescents. The problem is not so much social drinking as it is binge drinking. Binge drinking is consuming a large amount of alcohol over a short period of time. This means that at least twice within the past 2 weeks males have consumed five drinks in a row and females four.[15] Binge drinking continues to decline from 41.2% of the population in 1980 to 25.4% in 2006.[16] The results or consequences of binge drinking are fighting, aggressiveness, blackouts, increased sexuality, and memory loss.

Teen gambling is also on the rise. It is estimated that 60–80% of all teens have gambled at least once in the last year. That may include buying lottery tickets, small bets with friends, online gambling, or participating in an NCAA basketball tournament pool. If gambling becomes a problem among adolescents, suicide attempts escalate, and depression increases, as do petty crimes and delinquent activities.[17] Online gambling may be a major player in teen gambling behaviors because tens of thousands of Web sites are available to them as well as advertisements running on television. There is never a lack of exposure to gambling opportunities for this age group.

In 2009, the Planned Parenthood Federation reported that the United States had the highest rate of teen pregnancies among Western developed nations. However, teen pregnancy rates are declining.[18] By the time they are seniors, 66.2% of females and 62.8% of males have had sexual intercourse. Fourteen percent of these adolescents have had four or more sexual partners. Sexual activity is strongly influenced by alcohol use in that one-quarter of those sexually active used alcohol or drugs during their most recent encounter, and 51% felt that alcohol and drugs increased their chances of "doing more" sexually than they had originally planned.[19]

Influence of Mass Media As is the case with younger children, there is widespread concern about the influence of movies, television, mass media, and music on the values and behavior of teenagers. First, there is the conviction that excessive television watching may have serious outcomes. The thousands of hours that children and youth spend in passive contemplation of the screen during their formative years are hours stolen from the time needed to learn to relate to others and gain usable and enjoyable skills of active participation. It is believed that intensive exposure to television stifles creative imagination and encourages a passive outlook toward life.

As previously discussed, there is mounting evidence that television actually encourages violent, criminal, and sexual youth behavior. As early as 1969, the National Commission on the Causes and Prevention of Violence concluded that violence on television had to be reduced because it encouraged imitation and strengthened "a distorted, pathological view of society." Studies repeatedly have documented lowered inhibitions of aggressive behavior after exposure to violence on television, and there have been numerous examples of crimes committed shortly after similar crimes were shown on television. Research shows that teens ages 12–17 years who watched more television with sexual content were more likely to engage in sexual behaviors earlier and these behaviors would escalate.[20]

Boredom and the Need for Excitement Since the last decades of the nineteenth century, the perceived need to provide positive recreation programs and facilities for children and youth has been based on the belief that constructive free-time alternatives not only keep youngsters off the street but also help prevent the kinds of delinquent play that otherwise might result from boredom. Again and again, adolescents apprehended for criminal activity use the excuse that they were bored, that there was nothing else to do, or that their delinquent actions were a form of fun. Often, however, such forms of thrill-seeking play end in tragic episodes of violence, drug- and alcohol-fueled accidents, or other self-destructive experiences.

Changing Teen Experiences Adolescence is a challenging time for the teens, their friends, and their families. They are struggling with self-identity issues, moodiness, puberty, greater reliance on friends, and a greater need for privacy and independence.[21] They are overly concerned with being popular; they challenge the status quo; they are concerned with their appearance; and they are strongly influenced by their peers.[22] Although parents feel this is a difficult time for them, it also is difficult for the adolescent.

Recreation in the Lives of Adults

The adult population in modern society, defined as those in their late teens to their early or mid-sixties, may logically be subdivided into several age brackets, lifestyle patterns, or generations. Although many life experiences occur in this broad age range, it is important to look at an overall picture of how people progress through these years.

Generations

Generations are groups of people who share similar formative years by experiencing history, fads, and events. One way to divide the generations is as follows:

Silent generation: Born between 1937 and 1945, they experienced the Depression, World War II, Amelia Earhart's solo flight across the Atlantic, and the passage of the Social Security Act.

Baby boomer generation: Born between 1946 and 1964, this group saw Woodstock, the Korean War, Jackie Robinson break into Major League Baseball, and the assassinations of Bobby and President John Kennedy and Martin Luther King.

Generation X, or Gen X: Born between 1965 and 1976, they experienced Watergate, the peak of Michael Jackson, break dancing, and Madonna.

Generation Y, or Millennial generation: Born between 1977 and 1990, this group experienced the technology boom with MP3 players, cell phones, and handheld computers.[23]

Young Adults The population of young adults, extending from late teens to early or mid-30s, includes Gen X and a few of the older Millennial generation. For them, the single population has exploded. People are marrying later, if at all. In the past, the word *single* usually meant a lonely person, or a "loser" whose solitary status was a temporary sidetrack on the way to happy matrimony. However, in the decade of the "Me Generation," with its emphasis on narcissistic pleasure and self-fulfillment, singlehood came to be regarded as a happy ending in itself—or at least an enjoyable prolonged phase of postadolescence. When this trend became obvious, a vast number of singles-only institutions sprang up to meet the needs of this newly recognized population that had an estimated $40 billion of annual spending power. Singles apartment complexes, bars, weekends at resort hotels, social groups at local churches, cruises, and a variety of other leisure programs or services emerged—including computer-dating services and speed dating.

As a subgroup of the young adult population, college students are usually strongly influenced in their choice of leisure activities by their status as students. Students living at home are likely to have relatively little free time, often holding jobs and traveling back and forth to school, and they often find much of their recreation with friends in their neighborhoods. Students living on college campuses generally take part in social or religious clubs, athletic events, fraternity or sorority functions, and college union programs, entertainment, or cultural activities. Many young college students regard their first experience in living away from home for a sustained period of time as an opportunity to engage in hedonistic forms of play without parental supervision. In part, this appears to be a response to the stress that challenges many first-year college students. Both male and female freshmen suffered from higher levels of anxiety than in past generations, with almost twice as many women as men reporting severe levels of stress.[24]

Despite the problems attached to alcohol and drug abuse previously discussed, the majority of young single adults are able to use their leisure time in positive and constructive ways. Particularly for those who have finished school and are financially independent, travel, participation in sport or fitness clubs, social clubs, or forms of popular entertainment and involvement in hobbies and creative activities enrich their lives, both in colleges and in community settings.

Although millions of men and women have joined the trend toward a continuing single lifestyle, a majority of young adults today choose marriage and family life. Leisure behavior is markedly affected when people marry and have children. Social activities tend to center around the neighborhood in which the couple lives, and the home itself becomes a recreation center for parent and child activities. The family takes part in social programs sponsored by religious agencies, civic and neighborhood associations, or PTAs. As children move into organized community programs, parents begin to use their leisure time for volunteer service as adult leaders for Scout groups, teachers in cooperative nursery schools, coaches and managers of sport teams, or in similar positions.

Leisure for young adults often encompasses both family and friends.

The group in this age bracket that is most deprived of leisure consists of single parents who often must work, raise a family under difficult economic and emotional circumstances, and try at the same time to find needed social outlets and recreational opportunities for themselves.

Middle Adults The current middle adult age group is considered the baby boomers. They are approximately 45–65 years old and make up the largest section of the population.

Baby boomers have immense diversity in their lifestyles as well. Some are devoted to their families; others remain unattached. Some boomers are sport minded or wilderness oriented, whereas others are committed to the arts, hobbies, or literary pursuits. Growing numbers of this age group have begun to place a high value on the creative satisfaction found in work or to devote a fuller portion of their time to family and personal involvements.

Boomers Are Boosting the RV Market

Fifty percent of recreational vehicle (RV) owners are part of the baby boomer generation. This $20 billion a year industry is seeing record numbers of people buying popup campers, travel trailers, and motor homes. The increasingly high gas prices have not deterred this group from spending an average of 26.5 nights per year in campgrounds and RV parks around the country.[25] RVing is not just for retired couples. RVing Women is a recreation, support, and information network for women who enjoy RVing.[26]

For parents in the middle adult years, patterns of leisure involvement begin to change as children become more independent and even establish their own families. Many non-working parents, who have devoted much time and energy to the family's needs, begin to find these demands less pressing. They have more available time, as well as a need to find a different meaning and fulfillment in life through new interests and challenges.

Many leisure-service providers are realizing the impact of the baby boomers and what it means for their agencies. As more of this age group moves into retirement, they are going to be looking for activities to keep themselves busy. This group is going to retire with money to spend, and they are healthier than retirees of the past. Furthermore, baby boomers are not afraid to try new things and go to new places. They refuse to retire and go quietly to a senior citizens center to play passive games, because they do not see themselves as seniors. They plan to stay active to show that they are not old and will need recreation and tourism services to do it.

CASE STUDY: The Boomer Impact

There are more than 76 million people who are considered baby boomers. These boomers are changing the shape of leisure services in a drastic way. Boomers have always been hard working, they like to have experiences in life, and they are willing to spend money to get these experiences. This group is beginning to retire, and they expect their lives to continue to be experience filled. Here are a few boomer bits:

- Boomers work hard, play hard, and spend hard.
- Boomers say they feel 10 years younger than their actual age.
- Retirement is viewed as midlife and they plan to continue working part time, starting a new business, or doing something completely different.
- They are dedicated to health and fitness, which has resulted in the rise of fitness centers over the last two decades.
- Boomers value education and will want to continue to learn through such organizations as community colleges or parks and recreation programs.
- They enjoy nostalgia, especially in terms of music. They will continue to go to concerts by artists such as Mick Jagger, Bob Dylan, and Paul McCartney.
- They like upscale locations such as Club Med and country clubs.
- Boomers will disassociate themselves with anything that makes them feel old, including senior centers and activities for the older population.
- Swimming pools are for health and wellness more so than for relaxing and splashing.
- Boomers will remain busy even after retirement, so long-term programs (such as 8 weeks) and a full round of golf need to be adapted to a short workshop and nine holes of golf.[a]

Questions to Consider

1. Think about your parents or grandparents who are baby boomers. How do they use their leisure time? Which of the boomer bits describe your parents or grandparents?
2. How will leisure services change to meet the needs of the baby boomers?

Source

a. J. Ziegler, "Recreating Retirement: How Will Baby Boomers Reshape Leisure in Their 60s?" *Parks and Recreation*. http://findarticles.com/p/articles/mi_m1145/is_10_37/ai_93611647.

Recreation in the Lives of Older Adults

Older adults are defined here as people in their mid-60s and older, or the current Silent generation. Given the increase in life expectancy, this group is quite large and diverse. They pass through several stages, much like those in the adult category do.

Active Older Adults Recreation and leisure assume a high priority in the lives of most older adults, particularly for those in their late 60s and beyond who have retired from full-time jobs. Without work to fill their time and often with the loss of partners or friends, such persons find it necessary to develop new interests and often to establish new relationships.

Older adults are choosing a variety of nontraditional activities in which to participate.

It is now popular to assert that older adults are far more active, vigorous, economically secure, and happier than had been assumed in the past. With improved financial support and pension plans, a much higher percentage of older persons are relatively well-to-do and able to enjoy a far longer period of retirement. Research has shown that many older adults continue to enjoy sexual relations and to maintain active and creative lives well into their 70s and 80s.

The lives of older adults have changed dramatically over the past three or four decades. Not only can they expect to live much longer, but their living circumstances are likely to be radically different from those of past generations in terms of familial roles, social activities, economic factors, and other important conditions.

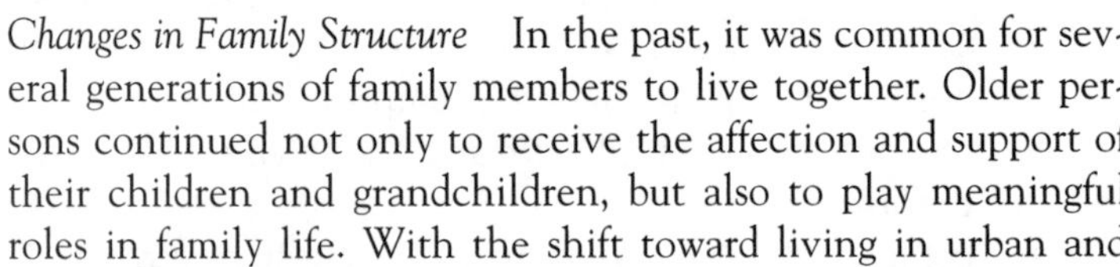

Changes in Family Structure In the past, it was common for several generations of family members to live together. Older persons continued not only to receive the affection and support of their children and grandchildren, but also to play meaningful roles in family life. With the shift toward living in urban and suburban apartments and small one-family homes, increasing numbers of older adults must now live separately. Although many do not want to live in a nursing home, there is still need for some additional care as people age. The number of senior living communities, retirement communities, and assisted-living environments is growing. Depending on the level of care needed (from no care at all to full-time nursing care), these types of living situations can meet the needs of people as they age. These communities provide nursing care, daily living assistance, socialization, and recreation opportunities for the residents. Many see this as a better alternative than living with grown children and their families. Some retirement facilities have graduated living quarters where the level of care increases based on what the individual needs. An older adult may enter the

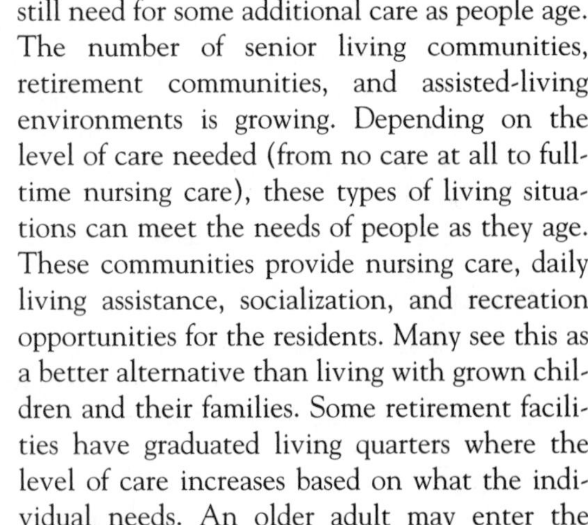

Older adults are breaking away from stereotypical leisure pursuits and engaging in a variety of activities.

facility being totally self-sufficient and, as health declines, can be moved to other areas within the same facility. This living arrangement lends itself to continuity and familiarity to the individual.

A second shift in the family structure is found in the growing number of cases where grandparents are forced to take responsibility for young children because their own children—the parents—are unable to maintain a stable household. Approximately 6 million children are being raised by their grandparents in the United States.[27] This number increased as military personnel are deployed to Iraq and Afghanistan.

House-Swapping Becomes a Popular Vacation Option

Older adults are increasingly engaging is house swapping. *House swapping* is when people offer their home to someone in another geographic location, often another country, in exchange for use of that person's home. So, a couple in Florida allows a couple in Spain to use their home for a 2-week vacation in exchange for the Florida couple using the home in Spain at the same time. The most popular home-swapping destinations include the United States, France, and Australia.[28]

Positive Changes Even though these negative trends must be acknowledged, the reality still is that most older people are living longer, happier, and healthier lives than in the past. Indeed, there is striking new evidence that the very old are enjoying remarkably good health in comparison with other age groups. The average annual Medicare bill for people who live to their late 80s and 90s is significantly lower than that for those who die sooner. Part of the reason is that older adults tend to be relatively robust. Cancer and heart disease, the two chief killers of retired persons in the younger age brackets, tend not to affect the very old, and Alzheimer's disease also attacks slightly younger men and women. Today, there are more and more centenarians—people who have made it to their 100th birthday—there is an estimated 30,000 to 50,000, according to demographers, which is a sharp increase from the 1980 estimate of 15,000.

With improved medical care, people are not just living longer, healthier lives—they are living them differently. Particularly in the so-called retirement states of New Mexico, Arizona, Nevada, and Florida, which have fast-growing populations of older men and women, they are engaging in active sports, volunteering, going back to school, and developing new networks of friends and relationships.

Specific Contributions of Recreation and Leisure Research confirms that recreational involvement meets a number of important physical, emotional, and social needs of older adults. Numerous studies have shown that regular physical exercise has immense health-related value for older persons, with a range of specific benefits that include preventing heart disease, stroke, cancer, osteoporosis, and diabetes; assisting in weight reduction; improving immunity against common infections; reducing arthritic symptoms; countering depression; and even helping to improve memory and the quality of the older individual's sleep.

In terms of social benefits, one of the key problems affecting older adults is that they tend to become isolated and lose a sense of playing a significant role in family life or in the community at large. Therefore, community service and volunteerism are useful leisure activities for older adults. In fact, volunteerism is frequently conceptualized as a satisfactory substitute for paid work for older persons. Older adults gain an important sense of recognition and self-worth through volunteerism. It provides structure in their lives in terms of regular time commitments and offers social contacts that often lead to friendship and other group involvement.

Art Towns Attract Retirees

Best retirement towns for the arts:

- Architecture—Columbus, Indiana
- Music—Athens, Georgia
- Fine arts—Santa Fe, New Mexico
- Best outdoor art—Madison, Connecticut[29]

Best adventure towns—Boise, Idaho; Durango, Colorado; Portland, Maine; and Spokane, Washington[30]

Another important leisure pursuit for older adults consists of continuing education—either on a fairly casual basis with classes or workshops and community center programs or on a more formal basis in noncredit courses taken through Road Scholar (previously known as Elderhostel) or other college-sponsored programs.

A growing number of older persons also are traveling the "information superhighway," learning computer skills and exploring the Internet. Still others break new ground by entering a new period of creative development in the arts, writing, social service, or other unknown kinds of personal involvement. Much of today's increased life expectancy has been added, it seems, not to the end but to the middle of our lives—extending the opportunity for "late bloomers" to realize their dreams.

GENDER FACTORS INFLUENCING LEISURE

Beyond the issue of one's age group, a second factor that plays an important role in leisure has to do with sexual or gender identity and values.

A distinction should be made between the two terms *sex* and *gender*. Although they are often used interchangeably, social scientists generally accept the principle that the term *sex* should be used to identify biological or physical classification in terms of the structure and functions that are possessed by one sex or the other. In contrast, the word *gender* is used to describe a broad range of characteristics, roles, or behaviors that society usually attaches to males and females. Stated simply, the words *male* and *female* apply to one's sex, whereas the words *masculine* and *feminine* are descriptive adjectives applying to gender traits.

Throughout history, distinctions between males and females have been made that extend beyond the procreative functions. These distinctions encompass family or marital roles, educational status, career opportunities, political influences, and all other aspects of daily life.

Among younger children, play has served to reinforce gender-related stereotypes. Little boys were given toy guns or cowboy outfits and encouraged to playact in stereotypically masculine roles such as doctors, fire fighters, or airline pilots. Girls were given dolls or play equipment designed to encourage stereotypically feminine roles such as caring for babies, cooking and sewing, or playing as nurses or flight attendants. Only after the resurgence of the feminist movement following World War II did society begin to question these roles and assumptions and challenge such sexist uses of play in childhood.

Women and Leisure

During the early decades of the twentieth century, leadership roles and activities assigned to girls and women, as well as the expectations regarding their ability to work well in groups, reflected past perceptions of women as weak and inferior in skills and lacking drive, confidence, and the ability to compete. Victorian prudery and misconceptions about physical capability and health needs also limited programming for girls and women.[31] Physical activity was seen as detracting from womanliness, having a negative effect on motherhood, and being detrimental to women's mental health.[32]

Impact of the Feminist Movement Although times have changed since the Victorian age, there are still differences in experiences, attitudes, and expectations of women's participation in sport and recreation versus that of men. A major influential factor in the changes toward equality was the feminist movement.

Leisure for girls and women has changed and improved from the impact of the feminist movement.

Feminism is defined as political, social, and economical equality among men and women. This equality first came to light politically with women wanting the right to vote just as men could. With the passage of the Nineteenth Amendment in 1920 giving women this right, feminism virtually disappeared until women entered the workforce in large numbers starting in the 1950s. As women entered the workforce, they wanted equal pay as well as access to jobs that were stereotypically a "man's job." Political and economic aspects of feminism still exist today, but it is the social aspect of feminism that is most affected by leisure.

What did this mean for leisure? Feminism gave women an understanding that they had freedom in their choices of activities and participation. Limits and stereotypes could be removed. Furthermore, it gave women the same opportunities as men in terms of leisure.

Title IX

Title IX of the Education Amendments of 1972 states that "No person in the United States shall, on the basis of sex, be excluded from participation in, be denied the benefits of or be subjected to discrimination under any education program or activity receiving Federal financial assistance." Although many associate Title IX with athletics, it also covers education (including career and vocational programs), admissions and employment policies, standardized testing, and treatment of pregnant and parenting teens.

Title IX has been instrumental in improving opportunities for female athletes at both the high school and collegiate levels. Those opposed to Title IX often argue that it decreases athletic opportunities for men. However, this is not an accurate assessment. Here are the numbers of athletes from 1972–2001[33]:

	1972	2001
Men (college)	170,384	208,866
Women (college)	31,852	150,916
High school girls	Fewer than 300,000	2.78 million

Implications for Women's Leisure Women's leisure has been a prominent topic in research for more than 20 years. By examining what scholars have learned, Russell identifies several conclusions regarding women's leisure.

1. Women experience inequity in leisure when compared with men. Even in households with two working adults, women do a disproportionate amount of the housework, and this leaves less time for leisure than men typically have.[34] In addition to time, women still have fewer choices in leisure activities. For example, outdoor recreation and sport have seen unequal participation from men and women. With sport in particular, women increasingly have become engaged in a wide range of individual and team sport, achieving a higher participation rate in secondary school and college competitive programs. As professional athletes or international competitors in such sports as tennis, golf, gymnastics, and skiing, they have been successful. Beyond this, many highly skilled women have achieved success as race car drivers, horse racing jockeys, dogsled racers, and triathletes. These changes have occurred not only in schools and colleges and at

Golf Sometimes Excludes Female Members

Some golf courses in the United States have been resistant to accepting female members. A $1.9 million lawsuit was filed because female members were denied full memberships and equal access to prime playing times at Haverhill Golf and Country Club in Massachusetts.[35] Although this was more than a decade ago, Augusta National Golf Club, home of the Master's tournament, still has no female members.[35] Few of the PGA players have come out against this discriminatory practice.

CASE STUDY: Title IX

Title IX was signed into law in 1972 and was designed to give equitable treatment to men and women in terms of education and athletics. In terms of intercollegiate athletics, there are three areas of concern for athletics departments to be in compliance:

1. *Athletic financial assistance:* Financial assistance must be awarded based on the number of male and female athletes and must be proportionate to the ratio of male to female athletes.
2. *Accommodation of athletic interests and abilities:* The opportunities for male and female athletes must be in proportion to the enrollments of each at the university.
3. *Other program areas:* Benefits, opportunities, and treatments of the athletes are to be equivalent, but do not have to be identical. This includes such factors as equipment, scheduling of games and practice times, travel and per diem allowance, facilities, support services, and recruitment, among others.[a]

Julie Foudy, captain of the 1991 and 1999 winning World Cup teams, two-time Olympic Gold Medalist, and four-time All-American at Stanford, says, "We were Title IX babies," which she says is the reason that she is a professional athlete today: "I think it all trails back to Title IX, for sure."[b] Although Title IX has been good for women's sports, some argue that men have suffered. To add women's sports, some universities have chosen to cut men's sports. Wrestling, gymnastics, and track and field were affected hardest by cuts. Nancy Hogshead-Makar, an Olympic gold medalist in swimming and currently a professor in the Florida Coastal School of Law, argues, "When they do cut a men's team, I want them to be honest and straight with why they're cutting that team. And they're not cutting that team because of Title IX. They're cutting that team because it is a budget decision that they make." She goes on to explain, "To say that you can't afford men's minor sports is ridiculous," she says. "There are three genders—men, women, and football."[c] (*Note:* There are approximately 125 players on a football roster).

Arizona State University recently built new women's soccer and softball complexes and worked diligently to add female athletes. Even with these improvements, the university is still not in compliance with Title IX because 54% of their student body is female compared to only 40% of their athletes. The university has considered adding women's rowing to aid in compliance—in a desert state.

Universities have chosen to deal with Title IX compliance in a number of ways. Some have cut men's sports, some have absorbed the additional costs of women's sports, and others have cut costs while maintaining the sports needed for compliance.

Questions to Consider

1. Is Title IX an example of reverse discrimination? Why or why not?
2. Is it discrimination when men's sports are cut and women's sports are added?
3. How could athletics be made fairer to both men and women?

Sources

a. Mary Curtis and Christine H. B. Grant, "About Title IX," http://bailiwick.lib.uiowa.edu/ge/aboutRE.html.

b. Rebecca Leung, "The Battle over Title IX," CBS Worldwide www.cbsnews.com/stories/2003/06/27/60minutes/main560723.shtml.

c. Ibid.

professional levels of sport participation, but also in many community-based programs. On another level, growing numbers of girls and women have been taking part in such formerly male pursuits as rugby, ice hockey, boxing, and even tackle football. With the emergence of women's professional basketball and softball leagues, the breakdown of gender-based barriers gathered momentum in recent years, yet there is still much inequality between men and women in terms of leisure.

2. Combining role obligations with leisure is a common focus for many women. Often, the family and a woman's role as wife and mother define her leisure. Women are more likely to set their leisure around their family and household responsibilities whereas men do not do this.[36] Women, particularly mothers, feel the need to put others' needs before their own and forgo their own leisure because it is perceived as more important to go to their child's soccer game than to spend time doing something that they truly enjoy as a leisure activity because of their role as the mother. Others feel that the family should take first priority. Family defines leisure for women. Women sometimes feel guilty participating in leisure because it takes time away from the family,[37] so a woman's leisure should be part of the family and not her own.
3. Women's leisure is more likely to occur in the home, to be unstructured, and to be fragmented. With household and family obligations filling the lives of many women, leisure time outside the house is limited. Many women claim to find leisure at home with such activities as reading and gardening. Also because of these household obligations, leisure activities must fit into small windows of opportunities rather than require major blocks of time. This results in unstructured activities that can be "squeezed in" whenever a few free moments occur.
4. Many women do not feel entitled to leisure. This may be more prevalent with homemakers. Because they do not have a job outside the home, they perceive that they do not directly contribute financially to the household. Without this financial contribution, many women feel they have not "earned" the right to have leisure. Women also feel the pressure of the "second shift"; after the remainder of the family comes home from work, they have that second shift at night that consists of fixing dinner, getting the children ready for bed, and other household tasks. This second shift prohibits much time spent on their own leisure because this has to be their priority, and they feel they are not entitled to their own leisure because of these other obligations.

These issues make women's leisure quite complex. Their lives mean assuming several different roles over time that affect leisure choices.

Men and Leisure

Although most of the professional literature and research studies dealing with gender in recreation and leisure focuses on past discrimination against girls and women and the efforts made to strengthen their opportunities today, it is essential to examine the changing role of males in this area as well. Generally, men have been portrayed as the dominant sex within most areas of community life and have been seen as responsible for denying women access to a full range of leisure pursuits and professional advancement. However, it would be misleading to assume that men's lives are invariably richer and more satisfying than those of women.

Shifting Masculine Identities Parents, family, friends, and teachers all play a major role in helping a child define what it means to be masculine. The media portrays males as being in control of themselves and situations around them, aggressive, physically desirable, heroic, and sometimes violent. Male-oriented magazines show men with muscular bodies, well dressed, and successful. Although these images encourage men to behave in certain ways, not all men buy into this image. Increasingly, men are breaking free of these rigid stereotypes and behaving as they want, regardless of the associated stereotypes.[38]

Metrosexuals Increase in Numbers

The term *metrosexual* has become more prevalent and one that shows some of the blurring of gender stereotypes. *Metrosexual* is a merging of the terms *metropolitan* and *heterosexual*. Here are a few descriptors of metrosexuals:

- Modern, usually single man in touch with himself and his feminine side.
- Well-groomed, fashionably dressed, both for work and play.
- Has discretionary income and stays up-to-date on the latest styles and trends.
- Confuses some regarding his sexuality.
- Considered successful with women by other guys.
- Women enjoy the metrosexual's appreciation for art and literature, flair for cooking, and ability to choose good wine and music.
- Those considered metrosexuals include David Beckham, Brad Pitt, and Hugh Jackman.[39]

The Role of Fatherhood A man's role as father has changed drastically over the past two decades. With more women entering the workforce, fathers are taking more responsibilities for raising children and contributing to the household responsibilities. Some studies show that more men are beginning to take on child-care responsibilities, for reasons ranging from rising day-care costs to the growth in the number of working women. In addition, the stay-at-home dad is not quite so rare as he once was. There are 200,000 stay-at-home dads in the United States. As women's salaries are rivaling men's, many families are finding it just as beneficial if the father stays home to raise the children.

In addition to fathers who are living in the same household as their children, there are fathers who are living elsewhere or who started another family. There is an increased expectation that fathers will be more involved in their children's lives,[40] more emotionally connected to their children, and more egalitarian in terms of gender role expectations.[41] No longer is it a given that in a divorce the mother is automatically granted custody. The quality of parenting is a bigger dictator than gender is in most states.

Men, and fathers in particular, are using leisure as a means to build social relationships. For men in general, similar interests such as poker, hunting, fishing, or watching football on Sunday afternoons are used as social outlets. Fathers are participating in leisure activities to share experiences with their children. They may coach their child's soccer team, go to their piano lesson, or take their little girl to the Daddy–Daughter Dance at the local recreation center. Like mothers, these fathers are sometimes constrained in the fact that they choose leisure activities not because they particularly want to participate, but because their child wants to participate or the father understands the value of participating with the child.

Constraints to Leisure It is evident that both men and women have issues that affect their leisure participation. These issues have been labeled as constraints to leisure. An entire body of research examines these constraints and their impact. Constraints to leisure occur when an individual is unable to participate in a leisure activity, unable to participate as much as the individual would like, or when the quality of the experience is diminished for some reason. Constraints are categorized as interpersonal, intrapersonal, and structural.

Interpersonal constraints are associated with the individual's relationship with others. The constraint occurs because of this relationship with friends, family, or even co-workers. An example of an interpersonal constraint would be lacking another person to participate with or participating in an activity because of the desires of others rather than an actual desire to do so. If a person goes along with friends to see a baseball game but really has no interest in the game, this is considered an interpersonal constraint.

Intrapersonal constraints are factors that affect an individual's preference for, or interest in, an activity. For example, a person may not feel he or she is skilled at an activity and as a result will choose not to participate. Another example is having feelings of self-consciousness. Women in particular sometimes feel self-conscious about their bodies. If this self-consciousness leads to a woman not joining a gym, she is experiencing an intrapersonal constraint. Likewise, if a man has interest in improving his cardiovascular fitness, he will most likely avoid an aerobics class because it is seen as an activity for women, even though he is interested in taking an aerobics class.

Finally, *structural constraints* are factors that intervene between the desire to participate and actual participation in an activity. The most common structural constraint is a lack of time. Other examples include lack of transportation, money, or opportunity.

While women face constraints to leisure, so do their male counterparts. A major constraint that men face more than women is the lack of companions with which to participate. Women are much more likely to find a friend for such things as taking a class or attending a cultural event than men are. Furthermore, men are more likely to feel the constraints of gendered activities than women. Traditionally female activities such as ballet or aerobics are often seen as prohibitive for male participants because of the fear of being perceived as less than masculine.

Implications for Men's Leisure What are the implications of these trends in masculine identity and lifestyle values for recreation and leisure? First, many boys and men who formerly felt pressured to be involved heavily in sports, both as participants and as spectators, may now feel free not to conform to this traditional masculine image. Further, growing numbers of males are increasingly likely to take part in domestic functions or hobbies, the creative arts, or other leisure pursuits that in the past might have raised questions about their degree of "maleness." This new freedom to engage in leisure pursuits once considered inappropriate for men also extends to attitudes toward women. Increasingly, many parents are becoming sensitive to the way they permit their sons to behave toward girls.

With respect to both sexes, it is important to note that many of the barriers that separated males and females in the past have been broken down in recent years. For example, a number of leading youth organizations that formerly were separate in terms of membership have now joined forces, as in the case of Boys and Girls Clubs of America. In other cases, national organizations such as the Young Men's Christian Association not only have substantial numbers of members who are girls and women, but also in some communities are directed by women executives and division heads.

SEXUAL ORIENTATION FACTORS INFLUENCING LEISURE

Leisure is affected by sexual orientation as well as by gender. Although everyone has a sexual orientation, whether it is heterosexual, homosexual, or bisexual, the focus here is on those who identify themselves as lesbian, gay, bisexual, or transgendered (LGBT). This group of people faces additional situations, challenges, and obstacles in their leisure and their life as a whole.

Members of this group have had a difficult past in terms of acceptance by the mainstream population. In the 1930s and 1940s, a backlash developed against gay forms of entertainment, with state assemblies barring the performance of plays dealing with sexual "degeneracy" and Hollywood agreeing not to depict homosexuality in movies. State liquor authorities closed many bars that catered to gay and lesbian clientele, and in the 1950s, homosexual government employees lost their jobs because it was assumed that they could be easily blackmailed into spying for other countries on the basis of their hidden identities.

In the 1960s and 1970s, the effect of the Stonewall Riot in New York City (a mass protest against police persecution of gays and lesbians), the impact of the counterculture movement with its emphasis on sexual freedom, and the activism of leaders such as Harvey Milk, a San Francisco city supervisor who was assassinated in 1978, all converged to help homosexuals gain a greater measure of public acceptance.

Although today there are more identified LGBT people than ever before—an estimated 29 million—some must continue to hide their sexual orientation. In the last 20 years, tremendous strides toward acceptance have been made, including the following:

- Universities are increasingly hiring LGBT faculty members to institute courses and curricula in gay, lesbian, and bisexual studies and are approving student organizations that sponsor publications, events, and other programs for LGBT students.
- Gay and lesbian community centers are being established in a number of cities to promote LGBT issues and concerns.
- School curricula and textbooks are being adopted that provide information about homosexuality, gay and lesbian families, and related issues of prejudice and discrimination.
- Schools are allowing and encouraging students to establish Gay/Straight Alliances to show support for LGBT students. Increasingly, same-sex couples are being accepted at school proms and other functions.
- Gay and lesbian issues began to appear more positively in popular culture, with LGBT-related themes seen in books, theater, dance, fine arts events, and prime time television. Logo is a cable television channel dedicated solely to programming for LGBT people.
- Sirius Satellite Radio has OUTQ Radio.
- Canada has allowed gay marriage since 2005. Same-sex couples are legally recognized in Connecticut; Washington, DC; Iowa; New Hampshire; Massachusetts; and Vermont. New York recognizes same-sex marriages and civil unions performed in other states but does not perform them.
- More and more companies are extending domestic partner health benefits to their employees and their partners.

Implications for Leisure

There are several issues to consider with this group in terms of recreation. First, LGBT people have been labeled a gold mine for recreation companies and agencies. This group is more highly educated and has a higher income level than the national average. It is estimated that they have $500 billion per year in buying power and spend $54.1 billion per year on travel.[42] Second, on a more negative note, teens who identify as LGBT have a higher-than-average suicide rate among their peers. They often feel isolated and rejected by family or friends and have very few outlets for social and recreational opportunities where they feel comfortable. Third, LGBT people are increasingly becoming parents through past marriages, adoptions, or other means. All of these factors affect their leisure in a number of ways.

The following are a few examples of how these issues have sparked leisure-service providers to welcome and support LGBT people:

- Golf clubs and fitness centers are recognizing the abundant LGBT dollars and granting equal membership and benefits to same-sex couples as are granted to heterosexual couples.
- In Boulder, Colorado, a play group has been established for young children of gay and lesbian couples.
- Olivia Cruise Lines focuses solely on cruises for gays and lesbians.[43] R Family Vacations offers family cruises for gays and lesbians with children.[44]
- The Monroe County Tourist Development Council in Key West, Florida, specifically targets gay and lesbian tourists by promoting the city as a tourism destination and providing information on gay/lesbian-friendly hotels, resorts, restaurants, and recreational opportunities.[45]
- The Lavender Youth Recreation and Information Center (LYRIC) is a recreation center for youth aged 23 and younger. It was opened in 1988 and offers social and recreational programs and services for LGBT youth. The center provides community, education, and recreation programs and events.[46]
- In New York City, there is a nonprofit group called Services and Advocacy for LGBT Elders (SAGE). SAGE started in 1977 for adults, serving as a drop-in center and offering discussion groups and various recreational activities such as arts, exercise, dances, and trips.[47]
- Fort Lauderdale, Florida opened a federally funded day-care center for older gays and lesbians. Although the center is open to all adults, gays and lesbians are the primary target audience because of the special needs of this group in terms of family structure. The center is located on the church grounds of Fort Lauderdale's Sunshine Cathedral, a predominantly gay and lesbian church. A wide variety of recreational activities is planned for participants.[48]

Given the growing numbers of LGBT people, the economic impact of this group, and the special issues faced by them, it is pertinent that recreation and leisure-service agencies understand the need to offer programs, activities, and events for LGBT youths to adults.

RACE AND ETHNICITY FACTORS INFLUENCING LEISURE

A fourth major sociocultural factor is of key importance in determining leisure values and behaviors. A succession of past research studies shows that recreational involvement is heavily influenced by one's racial or ethnic identity. The provision of public, nonprofit, and other forms of recreation facilities and programs is also affected by these demographic factors, and the broader fields of popular culture—including the sport and entertainment worlds—continue to reflect their impact.

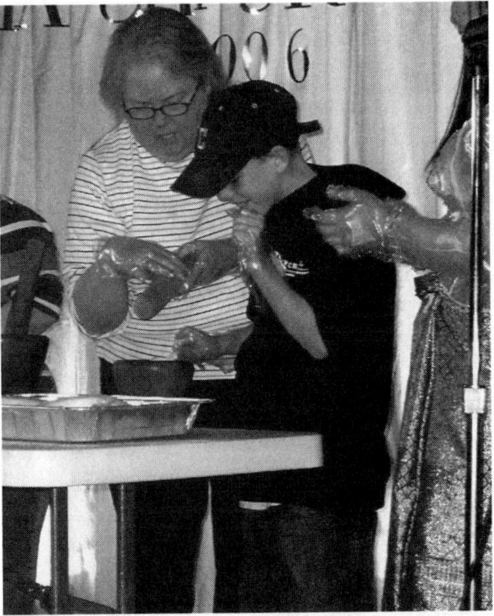

Participants at the Thai Culture Night learn about traditions from Thailand through food demonstrations.

Meaning of Race and Ethnicity

Before examining the actual influence of race and ethnicity on recreation and leisure, it is helpful to clarify the meaning of the two terms. Although they are often used interchangeably, social scientists distinguish between them. *Race* refers to the genetic makeup of a person. The genetic makeup often results in biological characteristics that are exhibited among various groups. These characteristics include such things as the shape of one's eyes, texture of one's hair, and the color of one's skin.

In contrast, *ethnicity* involves having a unique social and cultural heritage that is passed on from one generation to another. Ethnic groups are often identified by patterns of language, family life, religion, recreation, and other customs or traits that distinguish them from other groups.

Classifying Race in the Census

The U.S. Census Bureau is confounded by the difficulty of classifying race for people in the United States. In 1990, people could choose from the following categories: white, black, Asian and Pacific Islanders, and American Indian or Alaska Native. In 2000, the census expanded to include 18 races including a category for "other" and the ability to select more than one race. In 2010, there were 15 racial categories with space to insert any specific races omitted.[49]

Implications for Recreation and Leisure

Despite the limitations of racial or ethnicity-based identification and its meaning in scientific terms, the reality is that the public continues to accept the concept of race and to apply it in terms of popular stereotypes about one group or the other. This is particularly significant for recreation and leisure because our traditional patterns of facility development and program planning were essentially based on the assumption that the public being served was predominantly a white, middle-class population familiar with the literature, traditions, and customs that came to North America from the British Isles.

Now, we are seeing the rapid growth of non-European populations in the United States as a consequence of recent immigration and birthrate trends. In a number of major cities throughout the country, nonwhites now outnumber those of European background, with the percentage of African American, Hispanic American, and Asian American children in the schools representing sizable majorities in some cases. States such as California are seeing nonwhite Hispanics become a majority group, and major cities across the country are not showing any majority groups.

Maypole Dancing is a featured activity at this festival reflecting Scandinavian culture.

This population trend has seen Hispanics become the largest minority group in the United States; it is estimated that by 2050 they will represent 25% of the U.S. population. Similarly, the number of Asian Americans has grown from 3.5 million in 1980 to more than 10.2 million in 2000 and is expected to climb steadily in the decades ahead.[50]

Another striking trend has evolved in the growing number of Muslims and Buddhists in the United States. The American Religious Identification Survey (ARIS) claims that there are 1,104,000 Muslims in the United States, which is a 109% growth since 1990. The number of Buddhists has grown 170% in that same time period, and that religion has 1,082,000 followers in the United States.[51]

The racial and ethnic composition in the United States is rapidly changing. Beyond the sheer numbers, it is evident that growing minority populations are also exerting powerful influences on the nation's cultural scene and recreational life. No longer is it acceptable to offer programs from a predominantly white, middle-class perspective and interest level. Leisure services need to be more inclusive than that. Programs can be offered from a "melting pot" perspective or a "mosaic" perspective. The melting pot perspective gives leisure-service providers the opportunity to merge groups to allow people to learn about different races, cultures, and ethnicities together, whereas the mosaic perspective allows programmers to offer activities, programs, and events tailored to the unique wants, values, attitudes, and beliefs of a particular group.

Focus on Race- and Ethnicity-Related Differences and Constraints

Research in leisure behavior has increased its focus on racial and ethnic groups in terms of their leisure participation and use patterns. There is no one explanation for similarities and differences among and between racial and ethnic groups. However, there are several issues to consider.

First, the marginality hypothesis suggests that some groups are denied access or have limited access to some recreation opportunities because of such issues as lack of money, transportation, and program availability. Floyde, Shinew, McGuire, and Noe explain the marginality model in terms of the limited economic resources of and historical patterns of discrimination against African Americans. Stated differently, they write:

NCAA Race and Gender Data

Every 2 years, the National Collegiate Athletic Association (NCAA) collects race and gender data from its member institutions. Minority groups are underrepresented in many jobs within these institutions. For example:

- Men make up 81.8% of all athletic directors, a decrease of 3% from 1995–1996.
- Seven percent of all athletic directors are African American men and 1.5% are African American women. The percentage of African American men has stayed consistent, but the number of women has increased almost 1%.
- The head coaches for women's teams are predominantly white men (51.2%), followed by white women (34.9%), African American men (5.8%), and African American women (3.4%). Male head coaches have increased slightly from 1995–1996.[52]

> [B]y occupying a subordinate class position, minorities have had limited access to society's major institutions which negatively affects life-chances and lifestyles, and which is reflected in reduced participation in certain types of activities.[53]

The second idea, the ethnicity hypothesis, essentially says that different racial groups are influenced in their leisure choices by different norms, values, and socialization processes. This hypothesis suggests that if people are not socialized or do not have the opportunity to experience certain activities and places, then they do not participate as readily as someone who has had these experiences. An example of values and norms as related to leisure participation is the size of groups in which Hispanics and Asians participate. These two racial groups tend to participate in outdoor recreation in large groups. One explanation for these participation patterns is the cultural beliefs and value placed on participating with their extended families.[54]

Third, acculturation may contribute to leisure behavior differences. Acculturation is "the process whereby diverse groups retain their own cultural norms while adopting aspects of the dominant culture." Acculturation does not imply that individuals totally assimilate or take on the entire dominant culture. It is more likely that they may select some recreational activities of the dominant culture, while also maintaining some aspects of their own culture.[55]

In general, all three factors may serve as partial explanations of the distinctive behaviors of racial and ethnic minority populations—combined with continuing factors of social exclusion and self-segregation. A number of examples of race-based exclusion have continued to the present day. Well into the 1990s, a major chain of commercial health and fitness clubs covertly sought to exclude or discourage African American members, believing that their presence would have a negative effect on white club members. Private-membership golf clubs systematically excluded African American or other minority group members until forced to accept them by public pressures relating to the sponsorship of major tournaments. An understanding of the influence of each can be helpful in understanding how to make leisure available to everyone. This does

CASE STUDY: Racial Differences in Basketball Participation

David Ogden and Michael Hilt looked at the increased participation of African Americans in basketball over the participation rates in baseball.[a] Only 3% of all NCAA Division 1 baseball players are African American. Less than 5% of the spectators at Major League Baseball games and 10% of the players are African American.[b] Yet 80% of the players in the National Basketball Association (NBA) are African American and a large proportion of NCAA Division 1 basketball players are black. At one time in our history, baseball was a prominent sport for African Americans. This was the case at the time of the Negro National League (1920–1931; 1933–1948). The league inspired players and fans to love the sport. In 1947, Jackie Robinson's first year in the major leagues, the Negro League all-star game drew more than 48,000 spectators. Many were there to see future major leaguers.[c] It was suggested that the decline of baseball was the result of the demise of the Negro League and the movement of the best players from the Negro League to the major league. A second reason for the decline may be the lack of African American youth who are playing on travel baseball (select) teams. Only 9% of these players are African American, and these teams are a major source of talent for college teams. Last, athletics facilities such as baseball are limited to select neighborhoods and are not as prominent in inner-city parks.

The rise in basketball and its dominance within the African American community can be attributed to four factors. First, youth are encouraged by authority figures to pursue basketball. This encouragement helps facilitate playing the game. Youth are encouraged by parents, teachers, and coaches to play. Second, basketball portrays empowerment and is a form of expression. Basketball is seen as a status symbol. Third, there is an abundance of black role models in basketball—80% of all NBA players are African American. The top performers and role models in basketball are also African American. Last, basketball has an influence on social mobility. Youth see basketball as a means to a high income and a way out of their current situation.

Questions to Consider

1. Are there other reasons that baseball participation has declined among African Americans?
2. Are there other reasons that basketball is so popular among African Americans?
3. What can communities do to increase baseball participation among African American youth?
4. Are there other sports that are dominated by one or more racial and ethnic groups? How can participation in these sports be evened among other racial and ethnic groups?

Sources

a. D. C. Ogden and M. L. Hilt, "Collective Identity and Basketball: An Explanation for the Decreasing Number of African-Americans on America's Baseball Diamonds," *Journal of Leisure Research* (Vol. 35, No. 2, 2003): 213–227.

b. "MLB Sees Rise in Black Players," *Washington Post* (16 April 2009). www.washingtonpost.com/wp-dyn/content/article/2009/04/15/AR2009041503372.html.

c. R. Peterson, *Only the Ball Was White*. (Englewood Cliffs, NJ: Prentice Hall, 1970).

not mean making traditional "white" activities available and hoping for participation. A much better approach is to determine the needs of the population and provide those activities and services.

Muslim Recreation Participation

Islam is a worldwide religion with more than 1 billion followers. Leisure is closely connected with religious activities for Muslims because free time is allotted to be spent with family and on religious activities and festivals.[56] Activity and sport are encouraged in Islamic countries for the purpose of a healthy body and mind. Livengood and Stoldolska found that Muslim Americans participate in the same mainstream leisure activities that the rest of Americans do, but their leisure style, location of leisure, and the individuals with whom they participate were different.[57] Lack of participation by Muslims in leisure has been attributed to such issues as disapproval from family, concern over contact with the opposite sex, which is discouraged, unacceptable facilities, immodest sport clothes, agency dress codes for participation that go against religious beliefs about what parts of the body should be covered, lack of experience in an activity, and obligations to family.

Including Racial and Ethnic Groups

Chavez suggests a three-pronged approach to ensuring that all groups feel welcome to participate in leisure services. She posits that groups must be (1) invited, (2) included, and (3) involved.[58] The first step is to invite racial and ethnic groups to participate in programs, activities, and events and to use available facilities. This may mean printing brochures in languages reflecting the makeup of the community as well as showing pictures of people from the different racial and ethnic groups, among other things. Second, include members of different groups in planning activities for their group or neighborhood. The Skokie, Illinois, Park District does this by inviting representatives from more than 24 different racial and ethnic groups residing in the community to serve on the planning committee for the Skokie Festival of Cultures. Each group is represented and plans its facet of the event, including food, art, entertainment, and activities. Third, involve people in the organization as a whole, from the board to full-time staff members at all levels.

A Muslim family plays cricket in London's Kensington Gardens.

Obviously, racial and ethnicity issues go beyond what recreation and park professionals are expected to deal with. However, within the total field of intergroup relations, it is essential that leisure-service managers plan programs that will contribute to intergroup understanding and favorable relations. This may be done through community

CASE STUDY: Racial and Ethnic Constraints

A recent study examined what constraints racial and ethnic groups faced in terms of physical activity in recreation and park areas. The study was done because of the differences in obesity rates based on race (see Chapter 5). Many park and recreation areas are available to everyone at a low cost and are often found within the neighborhood, thus increasing access. However, different racial groups face different constraints in terms of using these areas. Here is what the study found:

- Hispanics/Latinos are most constrained and whites are least constrained.
- Hispanics were fearful of physical assault and not enough lighting.
- Blacks and Hispanics/Latinos are more constrained than whites, stating that they did not have enough energy; they fear racial conflict; they feel unwelcome; and the location of the park area is not close enough to home.
- Asian and Hispanics/Latinos were more fearful of sexual assault than white respondents.
- Black and Hispanics/Latinos were more concerned about the location not offering the activities that they want than Asians or whites.[a]

Questions to Consider

1. Why do you think there are differences in the constraints the various racial and ethnic groups face?
2. What can be done at these park areas to make them more inviting to all racial and ethnic groups?

Source

a. S. A. Wilhelm Stanis, I. E. Schneider, D. J. Chavez, and K. J. Shinew, "Visitor Constraints to Physical Activity in Park and Recreation Areas: Differences by Race and Ethnicity," *Journal of Park and Recreation Administration* (Vol. 27, No. 3, 2009): 78–95.

celebrations, holidays, ethnic and folk festivals, friendly sport competition, and a host of other activities. It is also essential that leisure-service managers continue to strive to overcome the long-standing patterns of prejudice and racial discord that linger in many communities today.

SOCIOECONOMIC STATUS

Socioeconomic status (SES), or *social class*, is a means of classifying people based on their income, education, occupation, and wealth. Although sociologists have developed several labels for the different social classes, there are five common ones: poor, working class, middle class, upper middle class, and upper class. Most people have no difficulty determining what class they are in.[59] People within a class have similar attitudes, values, and interests, and these factors affect leisure activity choices.[60]

Social class affects leisure in a number of ways. The amount of education and/or the amount of money a person has dictates the amount of free time and discretionary income available for leisure. Traditionally, lower classes are underrepresented in recreation activity participation. It was seen in the previous chapter that this was particularly true for health and fitness programs. On the other hand, those in higher classes usually have more education and money and look for more refined and prestigious leisure.[61]

In the United States, the poor, the working class, and the middle class have been the dominant users of public and nonprofit services. Depending on the agency, these sectors provide programs for all income levels but target the lower and middle classes in particular. Logically, as income increases, so does the ability to pay more for services; thus, the upper class will use commercial services almost exclusively. This could be for a number of reasons. For example, it may be an attitude of "you get what you pay for" where the commercial sector is seen as higher quality. Arguably, this is not an accurate assessment at all because many public and nonprofit agencies offer recreation services that rival commercial agencies. Another reason for using commercial services over the other two sectors may be a prestige or status issue. Status is assigned to such things as exclusive club memberships or exotic travel destinations booked through a travel agency.

Implications for Recreation and Leisure

Although there are several activities that transcend all social classes such as watching television, reading, or socializing, many others could be placed within each social class almost exclusively. For example, yachting, attending the symphony, or having a second home in the Hamptons would most likely be assigned to the upper class, whereas a trip to Disney World, golfing at a public course, or a camping trip would more likely be activity choices of the middle classes.

Sometimes there are activities that are popular among all classes, but the way in which they are enjoyed differs. Travel is a common activity to all classes. However, the poor and lower class may take short day or overnight trips and stay with family and friends; the middle class may vacation in a popular tourism destination in the United States and stay at a Holiday Inn; whereas the upper class may take an extended cruise, travel abroad, or stay in a luxury hotel where a night's stay is equal to a month's rent for people in the lower classes.

In ancient Greece, leisure and upper classes were supported by the poor, slaves, and women. In some ways, this has not changed in modern society. The leisure of the middle and upper classes is also supported by the poor and working classes. Take tourism, for example. The economically stable classes travel to destinations and enjoy activities where the workers are making minimum wage. In today's economy, minimum wage is below the poverty level. In addition, when an area is tourism dependent, there is a tendency to drive up the cost of living including housing and food. This makes it difficult for the workers to live in these communities that provide leisure for the middle and upper classes.[62]

Gender, race, and socioeconomic status all have some impact on leisure activity choices, and it is the responsibility of leisure professionals to understand these impacts and provide services that meet the needs of the community. Because it is not feasible for all agencies to provide services to all people, the different segments and agencies must find their niche and work to understand the needs, leisure patterns, and preferences of their intended population so that no group is underrepresented or denied leisure opportunities.

PROGRESS IN THE NEW MILLENNIUM

Although this chapter deals in detail with many of the past limitations that have affected the ages, genders, people of different sexual orientation, racial and ethnic minorities, and people with different socioeconomic status with respect to recreation and leisure, it must also be stressed that immense progress has been made over the past several decades. Both women and members of sexual minorities are treated today with far greater respect and have achieved impressive levels of public support and access to a wide range of recreational opportunities that were not accessible to them in the past. Furthermore, women and men alike have been more accepted in activities that are stereotypical for the opposite sex.

In terms of race, similar gains have been achieved—particularly for African Americans—even though injustices and forms of discrimination continue. In many cities, particularly in such states as Florida, Texas, and California, large Hispanic American populations have begun to achieve economic success and a degree of political power.

Racist Remarks Still Plague Sports

Racist remarks in sports have led to several firings and suspensions of media personalities. In 2007, Don Imus made inexcusable racist remarks about the Rutgers women's basketball team after their loss to Tennessee in the NCAA Championship game. In 2008, in a discussion about how to stop Tiger Woods's dominance in golf, broadcaster Kelly Tilghman said, "Lynch him in the back alley." In 2009, Bob Griese said of Juan Pablo Montoya being a top five race car driver, "Montoya isn't in that top five because he's out having a taco."[63]

Although the majority of Native American tribes still suffer from extreme levels of poverty, unemployment, and other social ills, many Native Americans have experienced an unexpected wave of prosperity stemming from such ventures as tourism and successful tribal casinos. Gambling revenues have helped a number of Native American tribes establish successful new businesses and in some cases give all tribal members generous annual allowances. In a striking illustration of such casino-based wealth, the Florida Seminoles, who pioneered the Native American gambling business in the late 1970s, earned about $1.9 billion in 2008 from gambling.[64]

Ability to pay for leisure services by individuals and the ability of agencies to fund free programs for low-income people are issues. With the economy the way it is today, many agencies have to generate income to stay in business, even nonprofit and public entities. So, "pay to play" becomes the norm and, in turn, eliminates the poor and working classes. However, great strides have been made by nonprofit and public agencies to offer services to those who cannot afford them. Many agencies offer program scholarships, programs that are free to the public and supported by sponsors or tax dollars, or they seek local, state, and federal grants to pay for much-needed programs. Although access to leisure is not equal, and probably never will be, much improvement is being made.

SUMMARY

Major influences on recreation and leisure in contemporary society are the sociocultural factors of age, gender, sexual orientation, race and ethnicity, and socioeconomic status. This chapter defines these terms and shows how they have affected recreational participation in the past and continue to do so today.

As people age, their leisure preferences and patterns change. Children experience a tremendous amount of growth and try different leisure activities. As people enter and move through adulthood, family has a major influence on leisure participation. In an individual's latter years, physical abilities and social elements are key factors in leisure.

As the chapter notes, women and girls have historically been denied many of the leisure opportunities open to men and boys. However, the feminist movement has succeeded in urging colleges, school systems, and community recreation agencies to provide more support to female participants in a wide range of sports and physical activities. This helps women to develop positive self-images and feelings of empowerment. In addition, many women have overcome barriers to professional advancement in various types of agencies in the leisure-service field. Women are also being admitted to business and social groups that had excluded females in the past.

The status of males with respect to recreation and leisure is also discussed. In the past, many men were pressured to adopt stereotypical "macho" roles in leisure activities. Today, they are being encouraged to play a more open, sensitive, and creative role in their recreational pursuits, as well as in domestic life and their relationships.

The issue of sexual orientation is dealt with as well. LGBT people have developed a wide range of recreational groups and are beginning to be courted as patrons by different sectors of the commercial recreation field.

There is rapid change going on in the United States in relation to race and ethnicity. Given that not all forms of discrimination have been erased, it is essential that organized recreation service contribute to positive intergroup relations in community life. This can be done through inviting, including, and involving all racial and ethnic groups.

Socioeconomic status plays a powerful role in what leisure opportunities are available to people. There is a major difference in the leisure lives of the poor versus the leisure lives of the upper class; as with most other things in society, the upper class has more access than the poor. However, the public and nonprofit sectors understand their responsibility in providing services to a group of people who have a great need for quality recreation near their homes and at a price they can afford.

QUESTIONS FOR CLASS DISCUSSION OR ESSAY EXAMINATION

1. Select one of the following age groups: children, teens, young adults, middle adults, or older adults. What are this group's special needs for recreation in modern society, and what barriers or problems does it face in the appropriate choice of satisfying leisure activity?
2. Older adults make up a rapidly growing segment of the population. How has society traditionally considered the aging process and the role of older persons in community life? What new views have developed in recent years? What are the implications of these changes for recreation practitioners working with older persons?

3. How have women's roles with respect to recreation and leisure differed from those of men, in terms of societal attitudes and constraints, throughout history? How have they changed from the past? As a class, have male and female students analyze and compare their gender-related patterns of leisure interests and involvement.
4. Although there is still some resistance to considering LGBT people as a minority population, there has been major progress in terms of their legal standing and status in community life. What issues do you perceive as critical in terms of involving gays and lesbians as identifiable groups in community recreation programs? How has this group been targeted by tourism agencies?
5. In terms of the general cultural scene, members of different racial and ethnic minorities have gained prominence in recent years in film, television, and other artistic or literary areas. What images are generally presented?
6. How do you think race, ethnicity, and socioeconomic status interrelate? How is leisure affected by these sociocultural factors?
7. Although LGBT people are increasingly gaining acceptance in the United States, there are still a large number of people who disagree with alternative sexual orientations. Should public agencies, which are supported with public tax dollars, provide programs for LGBT people? Should these same agencies provide programs specifically targeted at specific ethnic or religious groups such as Muslims?
8. Define the three categories of leisure constraints. What constraints do LGBT people face? Men? Women?
9. Differentiate between *race* and *ethnicity*.
10. Define *ethnicity hypothesis*, *marginality hypothesis*, and *acculturation*.

ENDNOTES

1. *NAGWS Gazette*, National Association for Girls and Women in Sport (Summer 2010). http://www.aahperd.org/nagws/publications/gazette/upload/Summer-2010-Newsletter-FINAL_2.pdf.
2. G. V. Payne and L. D. Isaacs, *Human Motor Development: A Lifespan Approach* (Boston, MA: McGraw-Hill, 2008).
3. A. Rosenfeld and N. Wise, "The Overscheduled Child: Avoiding the Hyper-Parenting Trap," Spark Action (30 July 2001). http://www.connectforkids.org/node/296.
4. CNN, "How to Ground a 'Helicopter Parent,'" CNN.com. www.cnn.com/2008/LIVING/personal/08/13/helicopter.parents/index.html.
5. Ibid.
6. Time, "The Growing Backlash Against Overparenting," Time. www.time.com/time/nation/article/0,8599,1940395-1,00.html.
7. Parents Television Council, "Facts and TV Statistics," http://www.parentstv.org/PTC/facts/mediafacts.asp.
8. T. N. Robinson et al., "Effects of Reducing Children's Television and Video Game Use on Aggressive Behavior," *Archives of Pediatrics and Adolescent Medicine* (Vol. 155): 17–23.
9. R. Louv, *Last Child in the Woods: Saving Our Children from Nature-Deficit Disorder* (Chapel Hill, NC: Algonquin Books of Chapel Hill, 2005).
10. K. C. Land, *The Foundation for Child Development and Youth Well-Being Index (CWI), 1974–2004, with Projections for 2005* (Durham, NC: Duke University, 2006).
11. N. Wells and G. Evans, "Nearby Nature: Buffer of Life Stress Among Rural Children," *Environment and Behavior* (Vol. 35, 2003): 311–330.

12. R. C. Moore and H. H. Hong, *Natural Learning: Creating Environments for Rediscovering Nature's Way of Teaching* (Berkeley, CA: MIG Communications, 1997).

13. A. F. Taylor et al., "Coping with ADD: This Surprising Connection to Green Play Settings," *Environment Behavior* (Vol. 33, 2001): 54–77.

14. National Institute on Drug Abuse, "NIDA InfoFacts: High School and Youth Trends." www.nida.nih.gov/Infofacts/HSYouthtrends.html.

15. TeensHealth, "Binge Drinking." http://kidshealth.org/teen/drug_alcohol/alcohol/binge_drink.html.

16. Alcohol Problems and Solutions, "Binge Drinking." www2.potsdam.edu/hansondj/bingedrinking.html.

17. K. Hardoon et al., "Empirical vs. Perceived Measures of Gambling Severity: Why Adolescents Don't Present Themselves for Treatment," *Addictive Behaviors* (Vol. 28, 2003): 933–246.

18. *Teen Pregnancy Rates in the United States, 1990–2005*, National Campaign to Prevent Teen and Unplanned Pregnancy. www.thenationalcampaign.org/national-data/pdf/pregrate_Oct2006.pdf.

19. "U.S. Teen Sexual Activity," *Kaiser Family Foundation* (January 2005). www.kff.org/youthhivstds/upload/U-S-Teen-Sexual-Activity-Fact-Sheet.pdf.

20. R. L. Collins et al., "Watching Sex on Television Predicts Adolescent Initiation of Sexual Behavior," *Pediatrics* (Vol. 114, 2004): 280–289.

21. Diana S. DelCampo, *Understanding Teens, Bringing Science to Your Life* (Guide F-122). http://aces.nmsu.edu/pubs/_f/f-122.pdf.

22. Eileene Welker, "Understanding Teens: Opening the Door to a Better Relationship," News for Parents.org. www.newsforparents.org/expert_understanding_teens.html.

23. S. Jones and S. Fox, "Generations online in 2009," Pew Internet and American Life Project, Pew Research Center. http://pewinternet.org/Reports/2009/Generations-Online-in-2009.aspx.

24. Jodi Wilgoren, "Freshman Year as Stress Test," *New York Times* (30 January 2000): WK2.

25. National Association of RV Parks and Campgrounds, *National Association of RV Parks and Campgrounds Explores the Lives and Travels of Active Campers and RV Owners* (24 January 2006). http://www.funoutdoors.com/files/ARVCStudyOverview.pdf.

26. RVing Women. www.rvingwomen.org/.

27. S. Stritof and B. Stritof, "Raising Grandkids: A Growing Trend," About.com. http://marriage.about.com/cs/grandparenting/a/raisinggrandkid.htm.

28. C. Forestieri, "Swapping My House for Yours," AARP (Spring 2009). www.aarp.org/family/housing/articles/swapping_my_home_for_yours.html.

29. "Best Retirement Towns for the Arts," TopRetirements.com. www.topretirements.com/tips/Best_Communities/Best_Retirement_Towns_for_the_Arts.html.

30. "Your Kind of Town: Pittsburgh, Pennsylvania," National Geographic Adventure. www.nationalgeographic.com/adventure/relocating/pittsburgh-pennsylvania.html.

31. F. R. Dulles, *A History of Recreation: America Learns to Play* (New York: Appleton-Century-Crofts, 1965): 96.

32. K. A. Henderson et al., *Both Gains and Gaps: Feminist Perspectives on Women's Leisure* (State College, PA: Venture Publishing, 1996).

33. *AAHPERD Title IX Quick Facts*, American Alliance for Health, Physical Education, Recreation and Dance. www.aahperd.org/nagws/programs/titleix/upload/Quick-Facts-Title-IX.pdf.

34. R. Russell, *Pastimes: The Context of Contemporary Leisure*, 3rd ed. (Champaign, IL: Sagamore Publishing, 2005).

35. *Judith Burne and others v. Haverhill Golf and Country Club, Inc.*, 58 Mass. App. Ct. 306, December 19, 2002–June 13, 2003; and R. Cohen, "Is Golf Unethical?" *New York Times* (18 August 2009). http://ethicist.blogs.nytimes.com/2009/08/18/is-golf-unethical/?scp=2&sq=martha%20burk&st=cse.

36. T. Kay, "Having It All or Doing It All? The Construction of Women's Lifestyle in Time Crunched Households," *Society and Leisure/Loisir et Societe* (Vol. 21, 1998): 435–454.

37. S. Thompson, "Playing Around the Family: Domestic Labour and the Gendered Conditions of Participation in Sport," *ANZALS Leisure Research Series* (Vol. 2, 1995): 125–136.

38. Media Awareness Network, "How the Media Define Masculinity." www.media-awareness.ca/english/issues/stereotyping/men_and_masculinity/masculinity_defining.cfm.

39. J. Brennan, "Are You a Metrosexual?" AskMen.com. www.askmen.com/daily/austin_100/102_fashion_style.html.

40. R. J. Palkovitz, *Involved Fathering and Men's Adult Development: Provisional Balances* (Hillsdale, NJ: Lawrence Erlbaum, 2001).

41. D. J. Eggebeen and C. Knoester, "Does Fatherhood Matter for Men?" *Journal of Marriage and the Family* (Vol. 62, No. 2, 2001): 381–393.

42. Philadelphia Gay Tourism Caucus. http://philadelphiagaytourism.com/.

43. Olivia Cruises and Resorts. www.olivia.com.

44. R Family Vacations. www.rfamilyvacations.com.

45. Monroe County Tourist Development Council. www.fla-keys.com/gaykeywes.cfm.

46. Lavender Youth Recreation and Information Center. www.lyric.org.

47. SAGE. www.sageusa.org.

48. Deborah Sharp, "Florida Church Plans Gay Senior Center," *USA Today* (21 January 2002).

49. Population Reference Bureau, "The 2010 Census Questionnaire: Seven Questions for Everyone." www.prb.org/Articles/2009/questionnaire.aspx.

50. Elizabeth M. Grieco and Rachel C. Cassidy, "Overview of Race and Hispanic Origin," *Census 2000 Brief*. www.census.gov/prod/2001pubs/c2kbr01-1.pdf, March 2001.

51. Graduate Center, "American Religious Identification Survey." www.gc.cuny.edu/faculty/research_briefs/aris/key_findings.htm.

52. "NCAA Race and Gender Demographics." www.ncaapublications.com/P-4195-race-and-gender-demographics-2008-09-ncaa-member-institutions-personnel-report.aspx.

53. M. Floyd et al., "Race, Class, and Leisure Activity Preferences: Marginality and Ethnicity Revisited," *Journal of Leisure Research* (Vol. 26, No. 2, 1994): 159.

54. D. J. Chavez, "Invite, Include, and Involve! Racial Groups, Ethnic Groups, and Leisure," in M. T. Allison and I. E. Schneider, eds., *Diversity and the Recreation Profession: Organizational Perspectives* (State College, PA: Venture Publishing, 2000).

55. E. Gomez, "The Ethnicity and Public Recreation Participation Model," *Leisure Sciences* (Vol. 24, 2002): 123–142.

56. W. Martin and S. Mason, "Leisure in Three Middle Eastern Countries," *World Leisure* (Vol. 1, 2003): 37–46.

57. J. Livengood and M. Stodolska, "The Effects of Discrimination and Constraints Negotiation on Leisure Behavior of American Muslims in the Post–September 11 America," *Journal of Leisure Research* (Vol. 36, 2004): 183–208.

58. D. J. Chavez, "Invite, Include, Involve!"

59. M. R. Jackman, "The Subjective Meaning of Social Class Identification in the United States," *Public Opinion Quarterly* (Vol. 43, 1979): 443–462.

60. M. F. Floyd et al., "Race, Class, and Leisure Activity Preferences: Marginality and Ethnicity Revisited," *Journal of Leisure Research* (Vol. 26, 1994): 158–173.

61. K. van Eijck, "Leisure, Lifestyle, and the New Middle Class," *Leisure Sciences* (Vol. 26, 2004): 373–392.

62. J. R. Kelly and V. J. Freysinger, *21st Century Leisure Current Issues* (Boston: Allyn and Bacon, 2000).
63. "Bob Griese Makes Racists Joke About Juan Pablo Montoya," PoliticalArticles.net (26 October 2009). www.politicalarticles.net/blog/2009/10/26/bob-griese-makes-racist-joke-about-juan-pablo-montoya/.
64. J. Hafenback, "Seminole gambling revenues defy recession, jump in 2008," *Sun Sentinal* (December 10, 2009), http://weblogs.sun-sentinel.com/news/politics/broward/blog/2009/12/seminole_gambling_revenues_def.html.

CHAPTER 7

SOCIAL FUNCTIONS OF COMMUNITY RECREATION

◆ ◆ ◆

When a nation abandons a tradition that has served it well, adopts a course that ignores what its citizens value most, allows indifference to a cherished part of its heritage, and diminishes the ways we can make a difference in the lives of Americans—then it is time to act.

Urban parks enrich our lives. They educate, protect, and enrich America's young people. They provide places to play after school and during summer vacations, and give individuals and families countless hours of recreation and relaxation.

Parks produce clean air and protect cities from floodwaters. They help to increase property value, grow the local tax base, contribute to education, reduce crime, attract businesses, and create jobs.[1]

◆ ◆ ◆

INTRODUCTION

As Chapter 2 shows, earlier definitions of recreation suggested that it served to restore participants' energy for renewed work but did not seek to achieve other, extrinsic purposes. Today, it is quite clear that this is no longer the case. Contemporary recreation programs and services—whether sponsored by public, nonprofit, educational, therapeutic, or other types of agencies—are goal oriented and intended to achieve constructive outcomes for both participants and the community at large. These outcomes range from improving the quality of life for all community residents and reducing antisocial and destructive uses of leisure to promoting the arts, serving special populations, and protecting the environment. This chapter outlines the societal benefits of organized recreation service and provides a strong rationale for supporting recreation as an essential community function.

NEW EMPHASIS ON COMMUNITY BENEFITS

Thus far in this text, recreation and leisure have been described conceptually as important aspects of human experience. We now examine their contribution to community well-being on a broader scale. The term *community* is used here to mean a significant clustering of people who have a common bond, such as the residents of a city, town, or neighborhood. It may also refer to other aggregations of people, such as the employees of a company or those who live and work on an armed forces base.

Agencies like the YMCA of Greater Des Moines offer summer camps for youths that focus on setting values, building character, and enhancing creativity.

Until recently, there was little concerted effort to identify the values and outcomes of community recreation. However, beginning with the period of fiscal austerity that affected many units of government and nonprofit social agencies during the 1980s, after September 11th, 2001, and again beginning in 2007, it became necessary to document the positive benefits derived from organized recreation programs and services to secure support for them. While communities called for more police protection, park and recreation agencies had to show how they contribute to communities and how they can make their community a better place to live, work, and play.

A number of major reports have been issued that present the demonstrated outcomes of organized recreation. The Parks and Recreation Federation of Ontario, Canada, and several cooperating Canadian organizations concluded that the benefits of community recreation fell under four major headings: personal, social, economic, and environmental.[2] The National Recreation and Park Association (NRPA) undertook a similar charge and titled their benefits categories as individual, community, economic, and environmental. These benefits aided parks and recreation service providers in repositioning themselves from being the people who provided softball leagues, dance lessons, or resorts to organizations that provided outcomes that improved the quality of life for people.[3] The benefits movement helped agencies focus less on the activities offered and more on the experiences that people have.[4]

CASE STUDY: Benefits of Parks and Recreation

The NRPA explained the four benefits categories as follows:

Individual benefits are attributed to the person who is actually experiencing leisure activities. These benefits may include such things as increased self-esteem, improvement of physical and mental health, and relaxation and stress relief.

Community benefits affect both the community as a whole and clusters of people including our friends, family, and neighbors. Stronger families, social support for the aging population, reduced crime and delinquency, and increased cultural understanding are just a few of the community benefits resulting from recreation.

Economic benefits improve the lives of individuals and community members by being an investment in the future rather than an expenditure of resources. Parks and recreation generates revenue for communities and provides jobs, parks enhance land value, and healthcare costs are reduced when people are active.[a]

Environmental benefits result when beautification, conservation, and preservation are outcomes of leisure. For example, preserving green space, planting trees, and building ecologically sound parks and play areas result in cleaner air and water, enhanced property values, and serve as an attractive place for people to relocate.

Annually, NRPA awards the Gold Medal to the nation's top parks and recreation department in their given population category. The awards are based on planning, resources management, and the ability to meet the needs of the community.[b] In 2009, Milwaukee County Department of Parks, Recreation and Culture received this prestigious award. In partnership Milwaukee County Parks offers a program called Milwaukee's Conservation Leadership Corp. The program is described as crews of high school students who spend seven weeks during the summer completing vital conservation projects to preserve public lands and improve access to Milwaukee parks. During the program, members complete hands-on conservation projects, build job skills, develop a strong work ethic, and gain a personal sense of stewardship for the environment. Program accomplishments include building 6600 feet of new trail, restoring and maintaining more than 40,000 feet of existing trail, leading educational activities and peer mentoring for more than 500 elementary and middle school youth, and restoring habitat by removing invasive plant species and planting more than 10,000 native plants, shrubs, and trees.[c]

Questions to Consider

1. What benefits categories did Milwaukee County Department of Parks, Recreation and Culture use to describe their Conservation Leadership Corp program?
2. What specific benefits were mentioned?
3. What benefits could the department list for these programs they also offer:[d]
   a. Cool Fool Kite Festival, held on New Year's Day—the event features free admission, complimentary hot chocolate, ice sculpturing, horse and buggy rides, and kite flying for all ages.
   b. Free Ice-Fishing Clinics for Children 15 and Younger
   c. BrewCity Bruisers Roller Derby

Sources

a. E. L. O'Sullivan, *Setting a Course for Change—The Benefits Movement in Parks and Recreation* (Arlington, VA: National Recreation and Park Association, 1999).

b. National Recreation and Park Association, "Gold Medal Awards." www.nrpa.org/Content.aspx?id=650.

c. Milwaukee's Conservation Leadership Corps. www.county.milwaukee.gov/ImageLibrary/Groups/cntyParks/highlights/MCLC_fact_sheet3_yr_summary.pdf.

d. Milwaukee County Parks, "2010 Year-at-a-Glance calendar." www.county.milwaukee.gov/ImageLibrary/Groups/Everyone/ParksUpload/Calendars/2010_EventsCalendar.pdf.

In a detailed text in the early 1990s, Driver, Brown, and Peterson outlined the overall benefits of organized recreation services, with an emphasis on recreation and park functions.[5] Similarly, a major study supported by the National Institute on Disability and Rehabilitation Research of the U.S. Department of Education summarized hundreds of research reports showing the benefits of therapeutic recreation, chiefly in a medical or rehabilitative context.[6] Furthermore, the Trust for Public Land has a wide range of publications that address benefits of parks, including such things as economic value of parks, economic benefits of land conservation, and health benefits of open space.[7]

Given this understanding, we now examine 10 major areas of recreation's contribution to community life, drawing documentation from formal research studies and from anecdotal or qualitative evidence. In several cases, the benefits cited are similar to those presented in preceding chapters dealing with the personal values of recreation. However, here they apply to broader community needs and benefits.

FUNCTION 1: ENRICHING THE QUALITY OF LIFE

Purpose: To enrich the quality of life in the community setting by providing pleasurable and constructive leisure opportunities for residents of all ages, backgrounds, and socioeconomic classes.

Quality of life can be looked at as what makes living in a community good.[8] Assessing quality of life looks at very quantifiable items as well as a personal perspective of the community. In terms of the quantifiable aspects of quality of life, Mercer's Quality of Life Survey is released annually and rates cities across the world on their perceived livability based on such factors as safety, education, health care, and political and economic environments. It also looks at factors such as recreation, the natural environment, and sociocultural factors.[9] In addition, International Living rates the livability of countries. They use categories of cost of living (15%), culture and leisure (10%), economy (15%), environment (10%), freedom (10%), health (10%), infrastructure (10%), safety and risk (10%), and climate (10%).[10]

Parks, activities, and special events enhance the quality of life for community members of all ages and abilities.

As mentioned, some things contribute to quality of life that are not so quantifiable and are personal to the individual. In terms of recreation, these measure such things as available social opportunities, cultural activities, special events, parks, trails, lakes, restaurants, streetscaping, and facilities to enjoy ample recreation programs. Recreation's most obvious value is the opportunity that it provides for fun, relaxation, and pleasure through active participation in leisure involvements.

Parks provide a vivid illustration of the social value of leisure. During the warmer months of the year, they provide outdoor living spaces that are used by people of all ages and backgrounds. In swimming pools, zoos, playgrounds, nature centers, and sports facilities, community residents enjoy vigorous and sociable forms of group recreation. In community centers, children and adults can join clubs and special interest groups, take courses in a variety of enriching hobbies or self-development skills, and find both relaxation and challenge. The personal perspective of quality of life can be affected by family and friends, neighborhood, culture of the community, sense of well-being, love of a job, and overall life satisfaction. People place different values on these items and the indicators listed previously. Different people would view a 50-mile biking path, 5-minute access to a beach, and a premier theatrical venue quite differently, thus influencing their quality of life. In many ways, organized leisure service contributes significantly to the overall quality and enjoyment of community life.

CASE STUDY: Quality of Life

Charlottesville, Virginia, is a town of 40,000 residents in the foothills of the Blue Ridge Mountains. It has repeatedly been recognized as a top community in which to live in the United States. It uses the following bragging points to illustrate why it has a high quality of life:

- It is home to the University of Virginia, which is considered one of the top five universities in the country.
- Charlottesville is a reader's and writer's paradise and hosts the Virginia Festival of the Book.
- It has four full seasons and a mild climate averaging 24 inches of snow a year—enough for the several ski resorts nearby.
- Charlottesville is the cultural and entertainment capital of Central Virginia, complete with 26 neighborhood parks, extensive series of walking trails, a 4000-seat amphitheater, 1200-seat historic theater, and a 16,000-seat arena that has hosted such performers as Dave Mathews Band, Billy Joel, and Cirque du Soleil.
- It has 30 local vineyards in the area.
- Tourism is thriving, with 2 million visitors a year coming to experience Charlottesville's historic legacy.[a]

Questions to Consider

1. Are these good indicators of quality of life? Why or why not?
2. Based on the quality of life indicators discussed in this chapter, what other factors could be addressed to enhance the perceived quality of life?
3. Think about the community in which your university is located. What bragging points would you use to convey a positive quality of life to someone thinking about relocating to the community?
4. When looking for a job in another city, what things about the community will you want to know more about? Which ones will be important to your decision to move there?

Source

a. City of Charlottesville, "Better Quality of Life." www.charlottesville.org/Index.aspx?page=153.

FUNCTION 2: CONTRIBUTING TO PERSONAL DEVELOPMENT

Purpose: To contribute to a person's healthy physical, social, emotional, intellectual, and spiritual development, as well as to family cohesion and well-being.

The Children's Discovery Museum of Central Illinois promotes the benefits of recreation in a learning environment. It offers programs designed to strengthen families and communities, allows children to grow and develop, and stimulates imagination and wonder.

As earlier chapters in this text illustrate, recreation does far more than simply provide fun or pleasure for participants. It also makes an important contribution to their growth and development at each stage of life. Although we often tend to focus on such obvious goals as improving physical fitness or social adjustment, recreation participation also can help people to reach their full potential as integrated human beings. For example, psychologists point out that many individuals have vivid memories of sports experiences in their childhood. Such experiences often play a key role in developing positive self-concepts and, beyond this, help to strengthen the bonds between parents and their children. In addition to providing benefits for children, these experiences may also contribute to the parent's own sense of well-being and mental health.

Varied types of community-sponsored recreation programs provide a rich setting in which children and youth are able to explore and confirm their personal values, experience positive peer relationships, discover their talents, and achieve other important personal benefits.

Camp Fire USA, originally called the Campfire Girls of America, has expanded its services, mission, and goals from its inception in 1912. Today Camp Fire USA is committed to providing activities and services to all boys and girls and their families in the United States. The organization is dedicated to enhancing the lives of adults and children. It describes itself as follows:

> We are inclusive and open to every person in each community we serve. We work to realize the dignity and worth of every individual and to eliminate human barriers based on all assumptions that prejudge individuals. In addition, our program standards are

> designed and implemented to reduce sex-role, racial and cultural stereotypes and to foster positive intercultural relationships. With Camp Fire USA's variety of outcome-based programs, youth find a fun and inclusive place with caring adults committed to providing a positive youth development environment. It's a place where children form lasting relationships, develop a sense of belonging and are actively involved in their own learning.[11]

Similarly, the Girl Scouts of America strives to help young girls grow up in a healthy and positive way, able to face the stresses and challenges that threaten all children and youth today. Many of its programs and activities promote leadership, creative thinking and problem solving, feelings of self-worth, skills in relating to people, and other important areas of personal growth. The mission of Girl Scouts states that Girl Scouting builds girls of courage, confidence, and character, who make the world a better place.[12]

How effective are such programs? Although it is difficult to demonstrate their effectiveness through rigorous experimental research studies, there is a wealth of information regarding the positive benefits of membership in youth organizations. For example, a detailed study of the outcomes of youth involvement in a Boys and Girls Club in a large city in the Southwest showed that the club that was studied made important contributions within several core areas, including cultural enrichment, developing conflict resolution skills, developing citizenship and leadership skills, accepting positive adult role models, and resisting negative or antisocial forms of play.[13]

In other studies, youth participation in sports and other extracurricular activities results in increased self-image and decreased levels of emotional distress, alcohol consumption, marijuana use, and vandalism.[14] Furthermore, the Child Trends Data Bank summarized the effects of participation in the arts by youth to decrease negative social behaviors,[15] increase student participation and attendance, increase self-esteem and motivation,[16] and have higher cognitive skills.[17] All of these are considered individual benefits.

FUNCTION 3: MAKING THE COMMUNITY A MORE ATTRACTIVE PLACE TO LIVE AND VISIT

Purpose: To improve the physical environment and make the community a more attractive place to live and visit by providing a network of parks and open spaces, incorporating leisure attractions in the redesign and rehabilitation of run-down urban areas, and fostering positive environmental attitudes and policies.

The gardens at Temple Square in Salt Lake City, Utah, serve as an attraction for both residents and visitors.

In local governments, the recreation function is closely linked to the management of parks and other open spaces, historical sites, and cultural facilities. Together, they help to make cities and towns more physically appealing as places to live. Inner cities and other communities have areas that have deteriorated over time. Gradually, we have come to realize that we no longer can permit our urban centers to be congested by cars, poisoned by smog, cut off from natural vistas, and scarred by the random disposal of industrial debris, ugly signs, auto junkyards, decaying railroad yards, and burned-out slum tenements. It is essential to protect and grace rivers with trees, shaded walkways, boating facilities, and cafés; to eliminate auto traffic in selected areas by creating pedestrian shopping centers; and to provide increased numbers of malls, playgrounds, and sitting areas that furnish opportunities for both passive and active uses of leisure.

Over the past few decades, numerous cities throughout the world have adopted ambitious projects of promoting recreation and tourism through the revitalization of their waterfronts—both in the redevelopment of decayed harbor areas and in the recreational uses of formerly polluted rivers. In a number of American cities, once-abandoned freight yards, wharves, waterfront ports, or junk-filled streams winding through inner-city slums have been dramatically transformed into new, attractive open plazas and parklike settings. Frequently with the help of the business community, these eyesores have been rebuilt into condominium housing, offices, upscale shopping centers, marinas for boating or waterfront play, and outdoor amphitheaters for various forms of entertainment throughout the year. Run-down architectural masterpieces have been restored, and older ethnic neighborhoods preserved while adding restaurants, art galleries, and other cultural activities that appeal to tourists and residents.

Beyond recreation's role in helping to maintain and improve the environment in the central cities themselves, it also is a key player in helping to reclaim or protect natural areas within the larger framework of surrounding county or metropolitan regions. Environmental planners and park authorities are collaborating in many communities on remodeling abandoned railway corridors and establishing greenways to permit outdoor play or environmental education, provide hiking trails, or protect historic sites.

There are numerous examples of redeveloping land into usable space across North America. The Rio Salado Habitat Restoration Area managed by the City of Phoenix, Arizona, Parks, Recreation, and Library Department is a 5-mile stretch of land running along the Salt River. This space was once a deteriorated dumping site where hundreds of tons of old tires were removed and recycled as well as other debris. This area was transformed into a trail system that winds through various habitats including a wetland area, a mesquite Bosque habitat, and a waterfalls area.[18]

The city of Detroit, most known for its cars, has refurbished Campus Martius, its public square. Prior to this $25 million project, the downtown area was deserted. People are finally going back downtown for concerts, the 200+ annual special events held there, movies, ice skating that goes 125 days a year, a 365-day-a-year water fountain, and more. The space was designed to be the center of activity downtown. Because of this improved public square, $500 million of new investments has resulted, including office buildings, retail shops, and lofts.[19]

To foster environmental attitudes, University of California Irvine's new Anteater Recreation Center has earned Leadership in Energy and Environmental Design (LEED)

Times Square Becomes Pedestrian Mall

In spring 2009, New York City Mayor Michael Bloomberg closed a stretch of Broadway between 42nd and 47th and 33rd and 35th Streets to vehicle traffic to create a pedestrian mall. The area has chairs, benches, and café tables for people to sit in the area and enjoy Times Square from a different perspective than in the past. The move was done to make Manhattan more livable by reducing pollution, decreasing pedestrian accidents, and reducing traffic congestion because of the diagonal direction of Broadway that interrupts traffic flow.[20]

Gold Certification. LEED certification requires buildings to be constructed and operated according standards that are environmentally sustainable. The 115,000-square-foot facility achieved the following to receive the certification:

- Outperforming California's Energy Code (Title 24) by 25%
- Obtaining more than 70% of the center's electricity from renewable sources
- Using 43% less water (at least 96,000 gallons annually) than a conventional facility
- Diverting 75% of construction waste (more than 200 tons) from landfills[21]

FUNCTION 4: PROVIDE POSITIVE OPPORTUNITIES FOR YOUTH DEVELOPMENT

Purpose: To provide positive recreation opportunities and experiences for youth to help them overcome or avoid negative use of free time.

As Chapter 3 shows, one of the major objectives of the early recreation movement in the United States was to help prevent or reduce juvenile delinquency. Indeed, during the last decades of the nineteenth century and for much of the first half of the twentieth century, it was widely accepted that vigorous group activities were helpful in burning up the excess energy of youth, diverting their aggressive or antisocial drives, and "keeping them off the streets" and sheltered from exposure to criminal influences.

Keeping youths engaged in recreation activities can reduce incidences of delinquent behavior.

In the United States, there was widespread support for playgrounds, community centers, and other recreation programs for city youth by the police, juvenile court judges, and other youth authorities (see Chapter 3). A number of sociologists pointed out that much delinquent behavior on the part of younger children stemmed from the search for excitement, risk taking, and the need to impress their peers. It was argued that if other, more challenging, forms of constructive play could be offered to youngsters at this stage, it would be possible to divert them from more serious involvement in criminal activities. Other investigators pointed out that much juvenile crime was committed for "the heck of it"—apart from considerations of gain or profit.

This diversion concept has grown and changed over the past couple of decades. It was not until the mid-1980s that a strong focus on youth development and recreation emerged in the recreation research. Many terms have been used for the concept such as *youth at risk*. This term in particular had a tendency to be viewed as only minority youth, inner-city, and low-income. In actuality, all children can benefit from recreation programs and focus should not be limited to those traditionally labeled as "at-risk." Because of this broader and better perspective, the term *positive youth development* emerged and has been accepted in the profession. Peter Witt, a leading researcher in youth development, suggests that *youth development* is efforts made to "create organizations and communities that enable youth to move along the pathways to adulthood by supplying the support and opportunities necessary to develop beyond simple problem prevention."[22] The definition of youth development pushes recreation professionals beyond simply getting kids off the streets, as was the idea in the early recreation movement. Youth development challenges recreation professionals to provide programs with a purpose and goal in mind. The case study presented here focuses on the positive benefits of after-school programs. Youth sport also has a large amount of benefits despite some of the negatives seen in sport such as overly critical parents, adults fighting with officials, and crowds getting out of control. How sport programs are developed can lead to positive benefits for participants.[23] They should be designed so that specific outcomes occur. Developing sport programs with specific benefits in mind can lead to sport programs that have moral, physical, mental, and cognitive development outcomes;[24] reduced obesity and increased health;[25] and that build character.[26]

One model that has been used nationwide to develop youth is the Search Institute's 40 Development Assets for Adolescents. These assets are said to contribute to a healthy, caring and responsible young adults. The 40 assets are broken down into four age groups covering children 3–18 years of age.[27] Here are a few examples for 12- to 18-year-olds regarding what they should do as it relates to recreation:

> *Creative Activities*. Young person spends 3 or more hours per week in lessons or practice in music, theater, or other arts.
>
> *Youth Programs*. Young person spends 3 or more hours per week in sports, clubs, or organizations at school and/or in community organizations.
>
> *Time at Home*. Young person is out with friends "with nothing special to do" two or fewer nights per week.[27]

Here are a few examples of programs specifically designed to provide positive experiences for youth:

- Outward Bound is "a non-profit educational organization that serves people of all ages and backgrounds through active learning expeditions that inspire character development, self-discovery and service both in and out of the classroom. Outward Bound delivers programs using unfamiliar settings as a way for participants across the country to experience adventure and challenge in a way that helps students realize they can do more than they thought possible."[28]
- The Alex Fiore Thousand Oaks Teen Center is for seventh through twelfth graders and features a gymnasium, sound-proof music room, computer lab, classrooms, and a 1700-square-foot game room complete with three pool tables, two Ping-Pong tables, air hockey, foosball, assorted video games, and a 50-inch high-def plasma TV. Programs include sports leagues, surfing lessons, dance, fitness, music lessons, snowboarding, L.A. Lakers excursions, and a wide variety of special events.[29]
- Seattle (Washington) Parks and Recreation Department offers Late Night Recreation Programs for teens. The goal of the program is to create opportunities for success and to provide positive alternatives to drugs, gangs, and other negative behaviors. The Seattle Police Department asserted that crime reduced 30% in areas where the Late Night Teen Programs were held. Programs include tutoring, computers, teen parenting, cultural and ethnic dance, and sports.[30]

America's Promise Alliance

America's Promise Alliance, a nonprofit organization founded by Colin and Alma Powell, was created to ensure that youth received five promises:

1. *Caring adults*. Children need caring and supportive adults in their family and schools, and as coaches, neighbors, and mentors.
2. *Safe places*. Children need safe schools, homes, and communities. They also need a healthy balance between structured and unstructured activities. These places must be safe, but they also must engage them physically, emotionally, and intellectually.
3. *A healthy start*. To be healthy children need physical and emotional health. They need good health care, nutrition, and exercise and to develop good habits to continue these positive behaviors.
4. *An effective education*. Children need a good education and skills to motivate them to be lifelong learners. High school graduation is the number one predictor of whether or not a child is successful.
5. *Opportunities to help others*. Children need the opportunity to make a difference in the lives of their families, friends, and communities. Volunteering in the community instills a sense of responsibility and pride.[31]

CASE STUDY: Impact of After-School Programs

The nonprofit organization Fight Crime: Invest in Kids produced a report on the value of after-school programs. The following is excerpted from it:

The Prime Time for Juvenile Crime

When the school bell rings, turning millions of children and teens out on the street with neither constructive activities nor adult supervision, violent juvenile crime suddenly soars. On school days, the hours from 3–6 PM are the peak hours for teens to:

- Commit crimes
- Be victims of crime
- Be in or cause a car crash
- Smoke, drink, or use drugs

After-School Programs Cut Crime, Teach Skills, and Values

Quality youth development programs can cut crime immediately and transform this prime time for juvenile crime into hours of academic enrichment, wholesome fun, and community service. They protect both kids and adults from becoming victims of crime, and cut teen pregnancy, smoking, and drug use while they help youngsters develop the values and skills they need to become contributing citizens. For example:

- Randomly selected high school freshmen from welfare families were assigned to participate in the Quantum Opportunities four-year, after-school and graduation incentive program. Six years later, compared to those who received the program, boys left out averaged six times more criminal convictions, and girls and boys left out were nearly four times more likely to be without a high school degree. They were also 50% more likely to have had children during their high school years.

- In a study conducted in several U.S. cities, five housing projects without Boys and Girls Clubs were compared to five receiving new clubs. At the beginning, drug activity and vandalism were the same. But by the time the study ended, the projects without the programs had 50% more vandalism and scored 37% worse on drug activity.
- Young people who were randomly assigned to a Big Brothers/Big Sisters waiting list were almost twice as likely to begin illegal drug use and nearly three times more likely to hit someone compared to those who were given a mentor.
- The Bay View Safe Haven after-school program in San Francisco matched participants with similar nonparticipants. For the youths with prior histories of arrest, participants were half as likely as nonparticipants to be rearrested within 6 months of joining the program.
- A study of an after-school and summer program in a Canadian housing project showed that compared to the 2 years prior to the program, the number of juvenile arrests declined by 75%.[a]

Questions to Consider

1. How do after-school programs contribute to positive youth development?
2. Do you think these are typical results of all after-school programs? Why or why not?
3. Discuss your experience with after-school programs as a participant and an employee, if applicable.
4. What would make an after-school program successful?

Source

a. J. A. Fox, E. A. Flynn, S. Newman, and W. Christeson, *America's After-School Choice: Juvenile Crime or Safe Learning Time,* Fight Crime: Invest in Kids (15 October 2003). http://www.ctafterschool network.org/PDF%20Files/Americas_Afterschool_Choice_FightCrime.pdf.

FUNCTION 5: IMPROVING INTERGROUP AND INTERGENERATIONAL RELATIONS

Purpose: To help improve intergroup relations among community residents of different racial, ethnic, or religious backgrounds and among different generational groups, through shared recreational and cultural experiences.

Racial and ethnic identity plays an important role in shaping the leisure-related values and behavior patterns of community residents throughout the United States. Clearly, this presents a challenge to recreation and park professionals in terms of the need to provide program opportunities suited to the tastes and traditions of different racial and ethnic groups, while at the same time maintaining a core of shared values and interests.

As discussed in Chapter 6, Chavez suggests that if agencies want to make all groups feel welcome and want to participate in recreation activities, agencies need to (1) invite, (2) include, and (3) involve these groups.[32] Providing activities and events for different cultures serves as a means to educate the community about different cultures, races, and ethnicities.

Arab World Fest

Arab World Fest, held in Milwaukee, Wisconsin, showcases the histories, values, and cultures of more than 22 Arabian countries. Activities include Arab art, food, educational programs, dance, music, and other performers. The event is planned by Arabian Festivals, Inc. They describe the organization as "a non-political, non-religious, nonprofit organization dedicated to fostering a better understanding and appreciation of Arab people and their rich cultural heritage."[33]

Special events in particular represent a major area of opportunity for sharing cultural traditions and increasing the self-knowledge and pride of different racial and ethnic populations. These events are designed to celebrate culture because they are planned by people within the specific culture, but they are designed for everyone regardless of race or ethnicity. As an example, the Wisconsin Department of Tourism promotes 30+ ethnic festivals held in the state from May through November. They include such events as Syttende Mai, a Norwegian independence day festival; Fyr Bal Festival, a Scandinavia midsummer's eve celebration of heritage; an Irish Fest; and the African World Festival.[34] The Skokie, Illinois, Park District sponsors the Skokie Festival of Cultures, which features food, music, merchandise, and activities representing many of the 80 languages spoken in Skokie. Cultures represented at the festival include Armenian, Assyrian, Bangladeshi, Chinese, Cuban, Danish, Filipino, Finnish, Hellenic, Indian, Israeli, Japanese, Korean, Lebanese, Mexican, Pakistani, Scottish, Swedish, Thai, Turkish, West Indian, and more.

The National Recreation and Park Association promotes the social benefits of being active participants in parks and recreation through intergenerational activities.

The Franklin, Indiana, Parks and Recreation Department features several cultural special events such as the Ethos Art Show as well as ongoing programs. For example, the department offers a preschool program with the head of the program from Wales and an assistant instructor from Palestine. This attracts many different youth culturally because the ethnically diverse preschoolers include Russian, Latin American, Hispanic, German, Palestinian, Romanian, and others. These programs and events are promoted as learning experiences for the community, while also trying to make those members of the community who have culturally diverse backgrounds and heritage feel welcome in Franklin.

In some cases, leisure-service agencies and programs may focus on problems of intergroup hostility and prejudice through meetings, staff training programs, workshops, and similar efforts. Organizations such as the YWCA have focused on the elimination of prejudice and discrimination as a key program goal, and in some cases youth camping programs have been established to promote intercultural friendship and understanding. In one such camp, the Seeds of Peace camp in Wayne, Maine, teens from Egypt, Israel, Jordan, Palestine, and others are selected each year from their respective governments to participate in the camp that is based on academic achievement and leadership abilities. The youth come together to share cultural traditions and to begin to build respect, friendship, and leadership skills.[35]

CASE STUDY: Intergenerational Programming

Intergeneration programming involves people from different generations coming together to participate in the same activities and events. Sunnyside Community Services is a nonprofit organization established to provide social, health, education, and recreational services to people in Western Queens (New York). In addition to providing programs for all ages with a special emphasis on 60+ and 5 to 21-year-olds, Sunnyside Community Services offers intergenerational programs such as the following:

1. *Tutoring and mentoring.* During the school day, older adults help second graders at a local elementary school who need additional attention. Much of this need is because English is a second language for the child. In the afternoon, elementary children come to the senior center for help with homework.
2. *Pen Pals.* Children and older adults exchange letters and holiday cards throughout the year. At the end of the year, children serve lunch to their pen pal and they spend time together.
3. *Sharing.* Older adults and middle school and/or high school students plan and implement a community service project.[a]

The intergenerational programs are designed to bridge the differences in age, language, economic status, and national origin.

Questions to Consider

1. What benefits do the older adults get from intergenerational programs such as these?
2. What benefits do the youth get from intergenerational programs such as these?
3. The local YMCA has asked you to develop five intergenerational programs for it. What programs do you develop? Compare your programs to your classmates'. Select the 10 best programs.

Source

a. Sunnyside Community Services, "Intergenerational Programs." http://www.scsny.org/services/intergenerational/index.html.

FUNCTION 6: STRENGTHENING NEIGHBORHOOD AND COMMUNITY TIES

Purpose: To strengthen neighborhood and community life by involving residents in volunteer projects or service programs and events to enhance civic pride and morale.

An important tenet of the early recreation movement was that shared recreational experiences helped to strengthen neighborhood and community ties by giving residents of all backgrounds a sense of belonging and common purpose, helping them to maintain social traditions and cultural ties, and enabling them to join together in volunteer service roles. Recreation's role in strengthening neighborhood and community ties lies in the concepts of human and social capital. Human capital is the tools and training that can enhance an individual or collective productivity. When people give their time and talent to the workforce or the community, they are using human capital. Although human capital is important, using it with social capital enriches the lives of those in the community. Social capital is defined as "connections among individuals—social networks and the norms of reciprocity and trustworthiness that arise from them."[36] Communities are made up of networks of people through schools, employment, the neighborhoods we live in, and of course recreation. These networks of people form valuable relationships that bond them together. Recreation and parks provide a plethora of opportunities for the human and social capital to merge and strengthen the community. Here are a few examples of how recreation and parks strengthen and improve communities:

> Groups of people can make a difference in a community simply by building networks for a good cause. For example, a group called Save the Bay, located in Rhode Island, has as its main purpose to educate residents and visitors about acting in an environmentally responsible manner. Save the Bay's Narragansett Bay project helped the community establish an estuary protection program, involve citizens in bay-water quality testing, and educate and lobby local business owners to become more environmentally responsible.[37]
>
> The New York Restoration Project (NYRP), founded by actress Bette Midler, strives to reclaim, restore, and redevelop parks, open space, and community gardens in New York City primarily in economically disadvantaged neighborhoods.[38] For example, the Curtis "50 Cent" Jackson Community Garden is a 15,120-square-foot space (almost a half acre) located by an embankment and railroad tracks in the Jamaica section of Queens, New York. 50 Cent's Foundation partnered with the NYRP to fund the revitalization of this run-down lot. The garden now has a children's learning garden, vegetable plots, a patio area, shade trees, and a water harvesting system for the gardeners.[39]

More and more leisure-service providers are realizing the value of volunteers to the agency, the individual, and the community. For example, Champaign Park District in Illinois, which was one of the first public parks and recreation agencies to hire a volunteer coordinator, uses volunteers in all aspects of its operations, from recreation to maintenance. Each year, volunteers spend more than 23,000 hours working in day camps, at special events, planting flowerbeds, and coaching youth sports. In addition, the Champaign Park District has an adopt-a-park

Street rod owners form their own social community through a common hobby.

program in which neighborhoods take ownership of their area parks through such things as building flowersbeds, planting flowers, holding their own special events, raising money for playground equipment, and working with staff on park decisions. The adopt-a-park program allows the parks to be maintained at a higher level than ordinarily possible.

Community Builds Accessible Playground

Oconomowoc, Wisconsin, Community Built Playground is a project undertaken by the community to build a universally accessible playground for children with and without disabilities. The playground is environmentally friendly, designed with input from local children, and funded and built by the community.[40]

In many communities, recreational projects related to sports, the environment, the arts, people with disabilities, and similar concerns serve to promote civic pride and neighborhood cooperation. Many municipal recreation and park departments have mobilized community volunteers to provide emergency relief and survival assistance at times of disaster.[41] After Hurricane Katrina ravished Mississippi, a National Recreation and Park Association staff member and long-time Mississippi resident stated:

> One thing that I realized on my trip was just how much parks and recreation is a thread in every community. It's a common stabilizer and when people see it returning, they know their community is healing. The emotional impact we have on our communities is immeasurable. In this tragedy I believe that parks and recreation stood up quicker than anyone because we could. Parks and recreation is not about facilities and fields—we are about people and a sense of community.[42]

Unselfish involvement in civic-betterment activities is particularly important today, when many Americans see the signs of a spreading social and moral breakdown around them. At such a time, it is critical that every means be explored to develop a true sense of community, of sharing and mutual support in neighborhood life. Clearly, volunteerism and the kinds of projects just described help to promote such values and positive interactions among community residents.

FUNCTION 7: MEETING THE NEEDS OF SPECIAL POPULATIONS

Purpose: To serve special populations such as those with physical or mental disabilities, both through therapeutic recreation service in treatment settings and through community-based programs serving individuals with a broad range of disabilities.

All people need diversified recreational opportunity; those with disabilities are no different. It is estimated that one in five people in the United States has a disability, and as adults age, this number is likely to increase.[43] Add to these the number of men and women who are returning from serving in Iraq and Afghanistan with disabilities ranging from amputations and visual impairments to traumatic head injuries and posttraumatic stress syndrome. As such, it is important to focus special attention on providing leisure services to this group.

Recreation for people with disabilities is provided from three different standpoints. First, recreation can be used as a form of treatment and delivered in a hospital, a residential facility, or outpatient programs that focus on the purposeful intervention to achieve a healthy leisure lifestyle. This form of recreation is often referred to as *therapeutic recreation*. Therapeutic recreation programs have been used to assist clients to become self-sufficient, increase self-esteem, improve functional states, learn social skills, or learn to use leisure wisely. A second form of recreation for people with disabilities focuses on participation for the activity itself rather than as a means of therapy. This form of recreation is called *inclusive recreation*. Inclusive programs provide opportunities for people with and people without disabilities to interact together. The last form focuses on recreation programs designed for people with disabilities and is called *special recreation*. Opportunities for people with disabilities are as varied as the agencies that provide these services: Easter Seals, Special Olympics, and Disabled Sports USA.

Many of the opportunities for people with disabilities arose because of federal legislation. The Americans with Disabilities Act (ADA), passed in 1990, mandated that people not be denied opportunities, segregated, or discriminated against because of their disability. Recreation service providers had to ensure that equal opportunities were available for all constituents and that if some specialized services were available that people with disabilities had a choice of participating in the general or the special program. ADA also stipulates that facilities should be accessible and that programs be offered for all residents regardless of abilities. Furthermore, if a person has a disability, reasonable accommodations for participation must be made for that individual.

The Iraq and Afghanistan conflicts have contributed to an increased need for programs for people with disabilities. Many servicemen and -women return home injured in the line of duty. Often referred to as "wounded warriors," these people initially receive services through the military medical centers and hospitals. Once released, some servicemen and servicewomen participate in recreation programs through parks and recreation departments in their communities. In addition to these opportunities, special programs are being designed to accommodate wounded warriors. Here are two examples:

- U.S. Paralympics has expanded to include programs for the United States Army Warriors Transition Units (WTU). The sports and fitness programs were created to help these servicepeople by providing postrehabilitation support. These programs are also done in partnership with local parks and recreation, as is the case with the Fort Bragg WTU and Fayetteville-Cumberland Parks and Recreation Department.[44]
- Disabled Sports USA has the Wounded Warrior Disabled Sports Project. This program is designed to teach people how to use adapted equipment to participate in sport. Individualized instruction is given in hopes the individual will easily integrate back into the community, participate in sport, and possibly serve as a mentor for others in similar situations.[45]

FUNCTION 8: MAINTAINING ECONOMIC HEALTH AND COMMUNITY STABILITY

Purpose: To maintain the economic health and stability of communities by acting as a catalyst for business development and a source of community or regional income and employment and by keeping neighborhoods desirable places to live.

The Ice Rink at Rockefeller Center is an economic stimulant for the city of New York because of the large number of visitors throughout the winter holiday season.

Recreation has become a major focus of business investment and an essential element in the total national economy. It is estimated that leisure is a $400 billion industry annually; it is the nation's third largest retail industry, and the second largest employer behind the health industry. Communities with commercial, public, and nonprofit agencies have benefited economically from recreation. Such economic benefits may arise through taxes, such as bed taxes at hotels, or taxes from the lottery that go to support local parks and recreation. Furthermore, recreation increases property values, such as for homes on lakes, by parks, or on golf courses. For example, living on a golf course can increase property value from 5–19% although only 30–40% of the residents even play golf. This increase in property value may be attributed to the desire to live near green space and/or the natural beauty associated with many golf courses.[46]

Some cities have set out deliberately to transform themselves into centers of entertainment, culture, and sports. Indianapolis, Indiana, built nine major sports arenas between 1974 and 2008 to revitalize the city. This includes a 10,000-square-foot tennis facility, a 12,111-seat track and field facility, a natatorium, a minor league ballpark, Conseco Fieldhouse (home of the Indiana Pacers and Fever), and Lucas Oil Stadium (home of the Indianapolis Colts). In addition, the cultural and entertainment opportunities were expanded with the Indiana Theatre renovation and when the Circle Theatre (home of the Indianapolis Symphony) was reopened and the Indianapolis Zoo and Botanical Gardens was built. To expand the convention opportunities in Indianapolis, once the Colts moved from the RCA Dome to Lucas Oil Stadium, the Indiana Convention Center was renovated and expanded into the RCA Dome.[47] In other cases, cities depend on special events and attractions to stimulate economic activity.

Economic activity is better known as economic impact, or the measure of the amount of new dollars infused into the community by the agency. Economic impact is usually examined from the standpoints of direct and indirect. Direct economic impact is the amount of money that is directly generated by the event such as staff salaries, concessions, program fees, construction costs, and operating expenditures. Indirect impact is the money spent that results from the program or event. For example, the money spent by a staff person or money spent at a hotel or in restaurants when a team is playing at a local softball tournament.

Here are some examples of economic impact from leisure services:

- The St. Louis Zoo, which has free admission, generates $105 million for the local economy. This includes revenues from food, lodging, programs, and souvenir sales from its 2,956,741 annual visitors; its 300 full-time employees and 220 part-time employees; and its $45.3 million indirect revenue to local businesses.[48]

- The Portland, Oregon, Rose Festival attracts over 2 million people and generates an estimated $80 million annually for the local and state economies.[49]
- The Key Arena in Seattle, Washington, boasted an economic impact of more than $353 million for the city in 2005. This included 3252 jobs and more than $33 million in tax revenue. In addition, 4370 of all Key Arena visitors come from outside of Seattle, which means nonresidents are generating a large amount of tax money to sustain the city for its residents.[50]
- Americans for the Arts conducted a study on the economic impact of nonprofit arts and cultural organizations (for example, Broadway) and found they had a $166.2 billion economic impact on communities across the country: $63.1 billion was from spending by the organizations, and the remaining $103.1 billion by the audience for event-related purchases. This industry also supports 5.7 million full-time jobs.[51]
- The Tournament of Roses Parade had a direct economic impact of $208.1 million and $370.3 million in total economic impact to southern California. One million people attend the parade each year and another 68.5 million watch it on television.[52]
- The 2008 Super Bowl generated $500.6 million in direct and indirect spending for the Phoenix, Arizona area.[53]
- The Illinois Association of Park Districts commissioned a study to show the economic impact of park and forest preserve districts and parks and recreation departments. They found that it is a $3 million industry in Illinois; they employ 62,900 people each year (full and part time); spending on park and facility development supports about 4000 construction jobs each year with earnings of $185 million.[54]

In summary, evidence shows that public, private, and commercial leisure attractions and resources of cities are key elements in their economic health and stability, not only in bringing tourism revenues but also in the positive picture they present to potential residents and companies that are seeking to relocate.

FUNCTION 9: ENRICHING COMMUNITY CULTURAL LIFE

Purpose: To enrich cultural life by promoting fine and performing arts, special events, and cultural programs and by supporting historic sites, folk heritage customs, and community arts institutions.

It is generally recognized that the arts provide a vital ingredient in the culture of nations. Through the continued performance and appreciation of the great works of the past, in the areas of symphonic and choral music, opera, ballet, theater, painting, and sculpture, or through contemporary ventures in newer forms of expression, such as modern dance or experimental art forms, people of every age and background gain a sense of beauty and human creativity. Arts and culture manifest themselves in many different ways in communities. Art and culture can be found in the architecture of buildings, the design of parks, in museums, through educational programs, or by attending concerts. Enriching a community through art and culture does not require that one be an artist or have talent in the areas of drawing, painting, or music. A community benefits when art and cultural opportunities are available to be appreciated or to educate the community. In addition, art and culture are not just for the rich; opportunities should be available for all ages and income levels.

As such, it is imperative that community agencies, both public and nonprofit, play a strong role in presenting programs in the arts that improve the level of popular taste and provide an opportunity for direct personal expression through music, dance, theater, and arts and crafts. One such program is found in Austin, Texas, at the Dougherty Arts School. The Dougherty Arts School is operated through the city of Austin Parks and Recreation Department and is a community-based arts organization that offers classes in such subjects as photography, drawing, jewelry making, and computer graphics and animation for students ages 3 and older.[55] The center offers a creative arts programs for teens called Totally Cool, Totally Art (TCTA). TCTA is a free program that exposes teens to art that they ordinarily would not experience. Sessions include such topics as blacksmithing, computer animation, filmmaking, printmaking, installation, conceptual art, portraiture, and urban painting.[56]

Central Park Art

On February 12, 2005, artists Christo and Jeanne-Claude completed installation of their temporary work of art: *The Gates, Central Park, New York, 1979–2005*. The 7503 gates were 16 feet tall and anywhere from 5'6" to 18' wide. The saffron-colored gates stretched 23 miles through the sidewalks of New York's Central Park.[57] In 2008, New York unveiled Olafur Eliasson's $15 million Waterfalls public art project. Four waterfalls, ranging from 9 to 120 feet, were constructed at the foot of the Brooklyn Bridge. The Waterfalls are as tall as the Statue of Liberty and three-quarters as tall as Niagara Falls.[58] The exhibits served as a public art installation for New York City residents as well as a tourist attraction for people from all over the world.

This sculpture park in Skokie, Illinois, provides high-quality art free to the public.

In Kansas City, Missouri, visitors can stroll through the free 22-acre Kansas City Sculpture Park that was a collaboration between the Hall Family Foundation, the Kansas City Board of Parks and Recreation Commissioners, and the Nelson-Atkins Museum of Art. In addition to the 30+ sculptures located throughout the park, the impeccable landscape is carefully planned and maintained to reflect the art and culture of the entire park.[59]

Seattle, Washington, has the Olympic Sculpture Park that was opened in 2006. This 8.5-acre park on the waterfront contains classic, modern, and contemporary permanent sculptures, temporary art installations, art-related musical and theatrical performances, and year-round educational programming in the arts.[60] Without parks such as these, many people would never be exposed to art at this level.

The City of Lone Tree, Colorado's, Passport to Culture won the 2009 NRPA Dorothy Mullins Award recognizing outstanding arts programs. Passport to Culture is a series of workshops, performances, and events where children can receive hands-on experience to learn all forms of art, from theater and music to dance and food, from cultures around the world. Programs include Junkio Shigeta Japanese Strings and Culture Workshop; The Indulgers, an Irish Step

Dance group Workshop; African stores and dance; and World Music through Drums.[61]

Art is not just for the rich and cultured. It benefits the entire community. As shown in these examples, art does not have to be in a museum. Art can be found in the parks, as murals on buildings, in flower gardens, and even in the architecture of buildings. Art enhances the livability and beauty of the community as a whole.

The *Gates Installation* is one example of public art that can be enjoyed by all residents free of charge.

CASE STUDY: Youth Arts

Some communities have directly linked the arts to current social needs, such as serving youth who have a higher probability of experiencing negative risk factors such as low academic performance, problem behaviors, or family conflict. One such program, YouthARTS, began as a consortium between the Regional Arts and Culture Council in Portland, Oregon; Fulton County Arts Council in Atlanta; the City of San Antonio Department of Arts and Cultural Affairs; and Americans for the Arts. These agencies wanted to measure the impact they were having on youth in their communities. They collected data on these impacts and developed a model of best practices in youth art programming. The result was YouthARTS. This program can be implemented by any community by following the program plan established by these agencies.[a]

Research results indicate that successful programs have the following best practices:

- Successful programs recognize that art is a vehicle that can be used to engage youth in activities that can increase their self-esteem.
- The delivery of the program is a collaborative effort among the artist, social service provider, teacher, agency staff, youth, and family.
- Successful programs recognize and involve the community in which the youth live.
- Programs that involve the youths' families provide the opportunity for the greatest impact.
- Successful programs provide a safe haven for youth.
- Successful programs emphasize dynamic teaching tactics such as hands-on learning, apprentice relationships, and the use of technology.
- Successful programs culminate in a public performance or exhibition in an effort to build participants' self-esteem through public recognition.[b]

Questions to Consider

1. What type of arts programs could be established in your community? Create several different programs to meet the varied needs of youth.
2. Which agencies should collaborate to provide arts programs?
3. How can the best practices be implemented into the arts programs you develop?
4. Go to the following Web site and compare and contrast the three model programs that formed YouthARTS: http://www.americansforthearts.org/youtharts/about/sites.asp#publicart.

Sources

a. YouthARTS, "About YouthARTS." http://www.americansforthearts.org/youtharts/about/.

b. YouthARTS, "Best Practices." http://www.americansforthearts.org/youtharts/bestpractices.asp.

FUNCTION 10: PROMOTING HEALTH AND SAFETY

Purpose: To promote community health and safety by offering needed services and programs, including leadership training and certification courses and supervision or regulation of high-risk activities.

Parks offer unlimited opportunities for both children and adults to be physically active to improve their health.

A little-recognized but extremely important value of community recreation is its role in promoting public health and safety. As shown in Chapter 5, community recreation's most obvious value is the effect that its varied programs of sports and other physical activities have in promoting fitness. Many communities have developed programs such as fitness classes, dance programs, and sports leagues for all abilities to promote health and fitness. Although these programs most likely have a fee attached to them, these same communities also are promoting free opportunities for health through their parks and trails so that all residents can become physically active and healthier. Parks and trails allow for close-to-home, low-cost activities for people. With any community, the key is to get people to use the parks. It has been discovered that 70% of all park visitors are engaged in moderate to vigorous physical activity while they are in the park, demonstrating the relationship between health and use of local parks.[62] A National Recreation Foundation study found that people living near a park were twice as likely to use the park than those who do not live near one.[63]

In addition to parks, trails are also an important part of many cities. Walking and biking trails have been built through and around cities all over the United States. Trails have been built along rivers and streams, where railroads once stood, and on utility right of ways. These trails are used for fitness purposes as well as for transportation on foot, bike, or inline skates. A study done by the Eppley Institute for Parks and Public Lands found that 70–95% of people living near a trail actually use it.[64]

Whether it is playing tennis with a friend, participating in a sand volleyball league, playing with a child on the playground, or biking on a trail, people who are in parks are physically active. There are thousands of examples of what local parks and recreation agencies are able to do in their communities to make their residents healthier. Here are a few examples:

- Many cities boast of their extended bike/walking trails built for residents as well as visitors to communities. For example, what once was a railroad bed connecting Chicago and Milwaukee has now become a continuous 100-mile bike trail that is promoted as a healthy tourism destination.
- Carmel Clay Parks and Recreation Department in Indiana constructed a 150,000-square-foot facility that focuses on health and wellness programming including a space dedicated just to youth fitness programming. The room has youth-sized fitness equipment as well as state-of-the-art technology such as dance revolution to keep kids moving.

In addition to health factors, parks and recreation departments affect the safety of youth and adults. In terms of popular activities such as swimming, which remains a leading cause of accidents for children, hundreds of thousands of youngsters receive water safety and skills instruction each year.

Fittest and Fattest U. S. Cities

Each year *Men's Fitness Magazine* ranks the 50 largest cities in the United States from the fittest to the fattest. Rankings are determined by such indicators as the number of gyms and sporting goods stores, participation in exercise and sports, the number of parks, the amount of open space, and the number and types of recreation facilities available. In 2009, Salt Lake City, Utah, and Colorado Springs, Colorado, were at the top of the fittest list and Miami, Florida, and Oklahoma City, Oklahoma, topped the fattest cities list.[65]

In numerous other ways, public, private, and nonprofit agencies are working to reduce the injuries and deaths that frequently result from high-risk recreational activities. For example, many state commissions today regulate the use of boats—requiring that children or adults operating them have boating safety certificates—govern the use of jet skis, and maintain strict controls by prohibiting the use of alcohol while boating. Many states have skiing safety acts that define skiers' and ski area operators' responsibilities on the slopes. Commercial companies and business associations provide safety education and guidelines along with training programs in such areas as scuba diving, inline skating, skateboarding, and other popular forms of outdoor play. At the same time, it is necessary to recognize that many accepted, even traditional, activities contain a high-risk component. For example, it is estimated that 156,000 children annually are hurt and fatalities occur playing on playgrounds. This number would be a lot higher if it were not for NRPA's National Playground Safety Institute that is dedicated to training certified playground inspectors. These people inspect the playgrounds in their communities—often on a daily basis—to keep children safe.[66]

Park and recreational professions are instrumental in keeping children safe on playgrounds by adhering to national safety standards.

Although it is the goal of recreation agencies to provide a safe and enjoyable experience, not all activities can always be safe. Many people like an activity because of its real or perceived danger. Any outdoor recreation activity has an element of danger. Recreation service providers need to reduce as much risk as possible without changing the experience so much that it becomes a completely different experience. For example, whitewater rafting will always have an inherent danger to it. Rather than not offer this experience, rafting companies have found ways for people to still experience whitewater rafting while taking every precaution possible to make it safer. These safety precautions include such measures as requiring skilled and highly trained guides or ensuring that all participants wear safety helmets.

San Antonio Reduces Graffiti

San Antonio Parks and Recreation Department has a program called Place Light Upon Graffiti (PLUG). Graffiti decreases property values and makes neighborhood residents feel unsafe. The PLUG program helps eliminate graffiti by removing or painting over graffiti in public parks, encourages property owners to plant trees and ivy near walls where graffiti is common, and works with youth and adults to create murals on buildings to deter graffiti.[67]

Children learn proper kayaking skills from a qualified instructor at REI's flagship store prior to attempting the sport on their own.

In addition to providing a safe atmosphere for participation in activities, many community programs are focused on teaching safety skills through programs and events. These programs include such things as swim lessons, basic water safety programs, and boater and hunter safety programs. For example, the Appleton Parks, Parks and Recreation Department offers a program called Safety Town for children ages 4–6. The children learn about bike, car, and fire safety. The children have three-wheeled trikes, pedestrians, school buses, seat belts, and a miniature city complete with miniature buildings, street signs, power lines, and traffic signals.[68]

Although health, and particularly safety, is not always at the forefront on many people's minds as a function of community recreation, it is a major player. Community recreation is a vital part of keeping people healthy in their communities, providing safe and enjoyable experiences, as well as offering programs that teach people to live safe lives.

SUMMARY

Far from simply providing casual or superficial amusement, organized recreation services help to satisfy a number of significant community needs, including the following:

1. *Quality of life*. Constructive and enjoyable leisure for people of all ages and backgrounds contributes significantly to their quality of life and satisfaction with their communities.
2. *Personal development*. Organized recreation promotes healthy personal development in physical, emotional, social, intellectual, and spiritual terms, thus contributing to overall community well-being.

3. *Environmental attractiveness*. Recreation and park agencies maintain parks, nature reserves, riverfronts, and other natural areas and may assist in rehabilitating or sponsoring historic and cultural settings.
4. *Positive opportunities for youth development*. As an important element in the community's educational, social, and other services for youth, organized recreation assists in preventing or reducing delinquency and other deviant forms of play and giving youth positive alternatives to develop into health adults.
5. *Improving intergroup and intergenerational relations*. Recreation serves as a useful tool in promoting ethnic, racial, and intergroup understanding and cooperation.
6. *Strengthening community ties*. Volunteerism and taking part in neighborhood efforts to improve the community environment and similar involvements help to build civic togetherness.
7. *Needs of special populations*. In both treatment settings and in the community at large, therapeutic recreation service promotes inclusion and independence for persons with physical, mental, or social disabilities.
8. *Maintaining economic health*. As a growing form of business enterprise, recreation employs millions of people today. By helping to attract tourists, industries that are relocating, or new residents, it also provides income and promotes community stability.
9. *Enriching cultural life*. Many public and nonprofit leisure-service agencies today assist or sponsor programming in the various artistic and cultural fields, strengthening this important dimension of community life.
10. *Promoting health and safety*. Increasingly, recreation is recognized as a health-related discipline by helping individuals to maintain sound lifestyles and by helping to promote safety in outdoor recreation and other risk-related leisure pursuits.

QUESTIONS FOR CLASS DISCUSSION OR ESSAY EXAMINATION

1. This chapter presents 10 different areas in which recreation, parks, and leisure services contribute to community life. If you had to present a positive argument for establishing or expanding a community recreation and park department, which of these areas would you emphasize, and why?
2. Explain and discuss the importance of community recreation within one of the following areas: (1) economic contribution; (2) health-related benefits; (3) promoting the cultural arts; or (4) improving intergroup relations among residents of different socioeconomic, racial, or cultural backgrounds.
3. The four benefits of parks and recreation are discussed early in the chapter. Select your favorite recreation activities and identify the benefits associated with them.
4. Think about the community in which you live. Give examples of how the 10 functions of community recreation are demonstrated in that community. Which ones are missing?

ENDNOTES

1. Rachel Roberts, "Urban Legends," *Parks & Recreation* (Vol. 41, No. 7, 2006): 58.
2. Ontario, Canada, Parks and Recreation Federation, *The Benefits of Parks and Recreation*. See Programmers Information Network, *National Park and Recreation Association* (Vol. 4, No. 4, 1993): 1.
3. E. L. O'Sullivan, *Setting a Course for Change—The Benefits Movement in Parks and Recreation* (Arlington, VA: National Recreation and Park Association, 1999).

4. Ibid.
5. B. L. Driver, P. Brown, and G. Peterson, eds., *Benefits of Leisure* (State College, PA: Venture Publishing, 1991).
6. C. Coyle, W. W. Kinney, and J. Shank, *Effect of Therapeutic Recreation and Leisure Lifestyle on Rehabilitation Outcomes and on the Physical and Psychological Health of Individuals with Physical Disability* (Philadelphia: Temple University and U.S. Department of Education, Office of Special Education and Rehabilitative Services, 1993).
7. Trust for Public Land, "Benefits of Parks." www.tpl.org/tier2_cl.cfm?folder_id=725.
8. K. A. Henderson et al., "It Takes a Village to Promote Physical Activity: The Potential for Public Park and Recreation Departments," *Journal of Park and Recreation Administration* (Vol. 19, No. 1, 2001): 23–41.
9. Mercer, "Defining 'Quality of Living'." www.mercer.com/referencecontent.htm?idContent=1306640.
10. International Living, "2010 Quality of Life Index: 194 Countries Ranked and Rated to Reveal the Best Places to Live." www.internationalliving.com/Internal-Components/Further-Resources/quality-of-life-2010.
11. Camp Fire USA, "Frequently Asked Questions." www.campfireusa.org/FAQs.aspx.
12. Girl Scouts, "Facts." www.girlscouts.org/who_we_are/facts/.
13. C. Carruthers and J. Busser, "A Qualitative Outcome Study of Boys and Girls Club Program Leaders, Club Members and Parents," *Journal of Park and Recreation Administration* (Vol. 18, No. 1, 2000): 50–67.
14. Patricia A. Harrison and Gopalakrishnan Narayan, "Differences in Behavior, Psychological Factors, and Environmental Factors Associated with Participation in School Sports and Other Activities in Adolescence," *Journal of School Health* (Vol. 73, No. 3, 2003): 113–120. Abstract available at: http://www.ncbi.nlm.nih.gov/entrez/query.fcgi?cmd=Retrieve&db=PubMed&list_uids=12677730&dopt=Abstract.
15. E. Winner and L. Hetland, eds., "Arts and Academic Improvement: What the Research Shows," *Journal of Aesthetic Education* (Vol. 34, 2000): 3–4. Executive summary available online at: www.pz.harvard.edu/Research/REAP.htm.
16. Robin Rooney, *Arts Based Learning and Teaching. A Review of the Literature*. Literature prepared for VSA Arts, Washington, D.C. www.vsarts.org/documents/resources/research/VSAarts_Lit_Rev5-28.pdf, May 2004.
17. Francis H. Rauscher, *Can Music Instruction Affect Children's Cognitive Development?* Champaign, IL: ERIC Clearinghouse on Elementary and Early Childhood Education. Available at: www.ericdigests.org/2004-3/cognitive.html, 2003.
18. Rio Salado Restoration Project, http://phoenix.gov/RIOSALADO/index.html.
19. "Magic in the Motor City." www.pps.org/squares/info/campusmartius.
20. William Neuman and Michael Barbaro, "Mayor Plans to Close Parts of Broadway to Traffic," *New York Times* (25 February 2009). www.nytimes.com/2009/02/26/nyregion/26broadway.html.
21. UCIrvine Today, "Anteater Recreation Center Expansion Receives LEED Gold Certification," news release (16 September 2009). www.today.uci.edu/news/nr_leedgoldarc_090916.php.
22. P. A. Witt, "Youth Development: Going to the Next Level," *Parks & Recreation* (Vol. 37, No. 3, 2002): 52–59.
23. J. L. Fraser-Thomas, J. Cote, and J. Deakin, "Youth Sport Programs: An Avenue to Foster Positive Youth Development," *Physical Education and Sport Pedagogy* (Vol. 10, No. 1, 2005): 19–40.
24. P. David, "Children's Rights and Sports," *International Journal of Children's Rights* (Vol. 7, 1999): 53–81.

25. R. Hedstrom and D. Gould, *Research in Youth Sports: Critical Issues Status* (East Lansing, MI: Institute for the Study of Youth Sports, 2004).

26. J. Coakley, *Sports in Society: Issues and Controversies*, 8th ed. (New York: McGraw-Hill, 2004).

27. Search Institute, "40 Developmental Assets for Adolescents." www.search-institute.org/content/40-developmental-assets-adolescents-ages-12-18.

28. Outward Bound, "About Outward Bound." www.outwardbound.org/index.cfm/do/ind.about.

29. Thousand Oaks Teen Center. www.thousandoaksteencenter.com/.

30. Seattle.gov, "Late Night Recreation Program for Teens." www.seattle.gov/parks/teens/latenightrec.htm.

31. America's Promise Alliance. www.americaspromise.org/.

32. D. J. Chavez, "Invite, Include, and Involve! Racial Groups, Ethnic Groups, and Leisure," in M. T. Allison and I. E. Schneider, eds., *Diversity and the Recreation Profession: Organizational Perspectives* (State College, PA: Venture Publishing, 2000).

33. Arab World Fest, http://www.arabworldfest.com.

34. Travel Wisconsin.com, "Entertainment and Attractions, Fairs and Festivals." www.travelwisconsin.com/Fairs_and_Festivals_Events.aspx.

35. Seeds of Peace, www.seedsofpeace.org.

36. R. D. Putnam, *Bowling Alone: The Collapse and Revival of American Community* (New York: Simon & Schuster, 2000): 19.

37. Save the Bay. www.savebay.org.

38. New York Restoration Project. https://nyrp.org/about.htm.

39. New York Restoration Project, "Queens." www.nyrp.org/Parks_and_Gardens/Community_Gardens/Queens/Curtis_50_Cent_Jackson.

40. Friends of Imagination Station Universally Accessible Playground. www.oconomowocplayground.org/index.html.

41. Sheila Franklin, "Operation Recreation Relief," *Parks and Recreation* (October 1999): 78.

42. T. McAdory, "A Sad Journey Home," *Parks & Recreation* (Vol. 41, No. 2, 2006): 71.

43. ADA Ohio, "Census Data on People with Disabilities." www.ilru.org/healthwellness/html/census.html.

44. D. Vaira, "A Soldier's Story," *Parks & Recreation* (Vol. 44, No. 12, 2009): 32–36.

45. Disabled Sports USA, "Wounded Warrior Disabled Sports Project." www.dsusa.org/programs-wwdsp-about.html.

46. Sarah Nichols, "Measuring the Impact of Parks on Property Values," *Parks and Recreation* (Vol. 39, 2004): 24–32.

47. M. M. S. Rosentraub, *Major League Winners: Using Sports and Cultural Centers as Tools for Economic Development* (Boca Raton, FL: CRC Press, 2010).

48. Saint Louis Zoo, "Economic Impact." www.stlzoo.org/home/economicimpact.htm.

49. Portland Rose Festival. www.rosefestival.org/support/sponsorships.shtml.

50. W. B. Beyers, "Key Arena Economic Impact Assessment." www.seattlecenter.com/images/media/pdf/KeyArenaEconomicImpactAssessment.pdf.

51. Americans for the Arts, *Arts and Economic Prosperity III*. www.artsusa.org/pdf/information_services/research/services/economic_impact/aepiii/highlights.pdf.

52. Pasadena Tournament of Roses, "Rose Parade FAQs." www.tournamentofroses.com/roseparade/parade faqs.asp.

53. Knowledge@W.P. Carey, "Economic Impact Study: Phoenix Scores Big with Super Bowl XLII" (23 April 2008). http://knowledge.wpcarey.asu.edu/article.cfm?articleid=1597.

54. Illlinois Association of Park Districts, *Economic Impact of Parks, Districts, Forest Preserves, Conservation and Recreation Agencies in Illinois.* www.ilparks.org/resource/resmgr/files/position_paper_economic_impa.pdf.

55. Austin Parks and Recreation Department. http://www.ci.austin.tx.us/dougherty/programs.htm.

56. Austin Parks and Recreation Department, "Totally Cool, Totally Art." www.ci.austin.tx.us/tcta/.

57. Christo and Jeanne-Claude. http://christojeanneclaude.net/tg.shtml.

58. Sewell Chan, "Waiting for the Water to Fall," *New York Times* (16 June 2008). http://cityroom.blogs.nytimes.com/2008/06/16/waiting-for-the-water-to-fall/.

59. The Nelson-Atkins Museum of Art, "Kansas City Sculpture Park." www.nelson-atkins.org/art/KCSP/index.cfm.

60. Seattle Art Museum, "Olympic Sculpture Park." www.seattleartmuseum.org/visit/osp/.

61. City of Lone Tree, "Passport to Culture." www.cityoflonetree.com/index.aspx?NID=496.

62. G. Godbey et al., "Final Report on Health and Park Use Study for NRPA Board of Trustees," (Arlington, VA: NRPA).

63. R. C. Brownson et al., "Environmental and Policy Determinants of Physical Activity in the United States," *American Journal of Public Health* (Vol. 91, No. 12, 2003): 1995–2003.

64. Indiana University, School of Health, Physical Education and Recreation, *Summary Report Indiana Trails Study: A Study of Trails in 6 Indiana Cities* (Bloomington, IN: Eppley Institute for Parks and Public Lands, 2001).

65. Men's Fitness, "2009 Fittest/Fattest Cities." www.mensfitness.com/lifestyle/215.

66. National Recreation and Park Association, "Playground Safety Inspector Training." ww.nrpa.org/Content.aspx?id=593.

67. City of San Antonio, "Painting Community Murals." www.sanantonio.gov/graffiti/murals.asp.

68. Appleton Parks and Recreation Department. http://www.appleton.org/departments/page_3f5a00fb61c5/?department=6fbb3e4ba77d&sudepartment=b83dddbc7f49.

CHAPTER 8

THE LEISURE-SERVICE SYSTEM

Governmental, Nonprofit, and Commercial Recreation Agencies

◆ ◆ ◆

America is a land of majestic beauty, and we are blessed with immeasurable natural wealth. Americans are united in the belief that we must preserve this treasured heritage and conserve these natural resources for the benefit and enjoyment of the American people.

As a nation, we can be proud of our diverse parklands, ranging from the rugged wilderness of snow-capped mountains, thick forests, sweeping desert sands, and remote canyons to national symbols such as the Statue of Liberty and the Lincoln Memorial. Our National Park Service has a long and important history. In 1864, the Federal Government ensured a grand natural landscape for generations to come when it designated Yosemite Valley and the Mariposa Grove of giant sequoias to be "held for public use, resort, and recreation . . . inalienable for all time." Eight years later in 1872, Congress created the first national park in the Yellowstone region of the Territories of Montana and Wyoming. Finally, in 1916, the National Park Service was established to efficiently administer our growing number of parks, which today includes 388 national parks on more than 84 million acres of public lands. These lands continue to be cherished by all our citizens.[1]

◆ ◆ ◆

INTRODUCTION

We now turn to a detailed examination of the overall leisure-service system in the United States at the turn of the twenty-first century. This chapter deals with three major types of recreation providers that share a broad responsibility for sponsoring recreation, park, and related leisure facilities and programs for the public at large: governmental agencies, nonprofit community organizations, and commercial recreation enterprises. In each case, the background, mission, and chief program elements of sponsoring agencies are described, with numerous examples drawn from the field that illustrate recreation and leisure services today.

KEY ELEMENTS IN THE LEISURE-SERVICE SYSTEM

There are 10 different types of leisure-service organizations in modern society, as shown in **Table 8.1**. Of these, three of the major types that meet a broad range of public needs are described in this chapter, with the other seven in the two chapters that follow.

CASE STUDY: Understanding the 10 Major Elements in the Modern Leisure-Service Delivery System

Understanding the modern leisure-service delivery system is the essence of this chapter. **Table 8.1** provides a matrix of how leisure services are structured and delivered. The table is a simple representation of a complex process of relationships, interchanges, and decisions leading to outcomes in the form of benefits.

Across the top of the table are the five categories representing the major process and outcomes of delivery of a leisure program by an organization. Below, each of the major processes is subdivided into narrower and more specific descriptors. These in turn allow processes to be classified as the examples will show.

Each major process is described as follows:

- The *types of recreation-sponsoring organizations* are general categories or types of groups or organizations that offer recreation programs. The 10 areas are the major elements in a modern leisure-service delivery system. Most delivery types can be grouped within the list of 10 types of sponsors and in some cases a single agency is more than one sponsoring organization.
- The *partnered with support groups and services* is present when a sponsor is working with another sponsor(s) to deliver a program.
- The process to *provide leisure programs consisting of* types of delivery systems represents the traditional orientation of leisure services.
- The *to satisfy public needs for* category represents (1) types of program areas and (2) the variables that influence demand for leisure services and public needs and desires.
- The *yielding major benefits* category addresses the importance of leisure activities in providing measurable benefits to individuals, groups, organizations, and communities.

How to Use Table 8.1

Step 1: Beginning with column A, Types of Recreation-Sponsoring Organizations, select an agency that provides a program. For example, the municipal parks and recreation department provides a volleyball league. In column A, public agencies (1) is selected as the type of sponsoring organization.

Step 2: Are there any partnering organizations (column B)? In this case, the local high school has made its gymnasium available for the volleyball league. The high school is another civic agency (7) and the parks and recreation department's partner.

Step 3: The parks and recreation department is providing the volleyball league (column C), taking on the role of direct program leadership (1).

Step 4: The volleyball league satisfies the public need (column D) for games and sport as well as personal enjoyment. In this case, more than one spectrum of involvement is considered. The decision to offer the program was influenced by a number of factors such as age, gender, physical health, and so forth.

TABLE 8.1

THE 10 MAJOR ELEMENTS IN THE MODERN LEISURE-SERVICE DELIVERY SYSTEM

(A) Types of Recreation-Sponsoring Organizations →	(B) Partnered with Groups and Services →	(C) Provide Leisure Programs Consisting of →	(D) To Satisfy Individual and Public Needs for →	(E) Yielding Major Benefits
(1) Public agencies	(1) Trade associations	(1) Direct program leadership	(1) Full spectrum of involvement in: Games Sport Outdoor recreation Cultural activities The arts Hobbies Special events Club and other social groups Personal enjoyment Travel Electronic media Other social services	(1) Personal values (health, emotional wellness, mental development, well-being)
(2) Nonprofit organizations	(2) Professional associations	(2) Provision of facilities for undirected public use	(2) With needs influenced by: Age group Gender Socioeconomic status Educational background Racial/ethnic factors Residential and regional factors Physical and emotional health Ability/disability Family status	(2) Social and community-based outcomes
(3) Commercial recreation enterprises	(3) Special-interest groups	(3) Education for leisure		(3) Economic benefits, employment, taxes, and other fiscal returns
(4) Employee service and recreation programs	(4) Sponsors of special programs and events	(4) Information referral services		(4) Environmental values, both natural and urban settings
(5) Armed Forces morale, welfare, and recreation	(5) Professional preparation institutions	(5) Enabling facilitation		
(6) Private membership organizations	(6) Private groups that subcontract leisure functions	(6) Advocacy and leadership in special areas		
(7) Campus recreation programs	(7) Other civic agencies and citizen groups	(7) Jointly sponsored campaigns and events		
(8) Therapeutic recreation services	(8) Corporations	(8) Authentic leisure experiences		
(9) Sport management organizations	(9) Individuals	(9) Opportunities for well-being		
(10) Tourism and hospitality industry				

Step 5: Participation in the volleyball league should result in tangible and intangible benefits (column E) to the participant. This can include the personal values (1) and social outcomes (2).

Table 8.2 shows how the volleyball league program moved through Table 8.1. The table allows the reader to look at the variables influencing leisure-service delivery and track the relationships of those variables. It is not a neat and clean process but often is messy. What the table does is provide an improved understanding of the complexity of delivery of leisure-service programs and offerings.

A Complex Example

The initial example was relatively simple. In **Table 8.3**, the community orchestra is performing at the city's central park outdoor performance center. The city is cosponsoring with the orchestra. A local bank is providing funding and matching costs with the city and the community orchestra. The orchestra is a nonprofit organization. There will be food available for purchase that has been contracted with from a local restaurant and caterer. Finally, the event is being webcast live on the orchestra's Web site. The view depicted in Table 8.3 is from the perspective of the city's parks and recreation department.

The initiating organization was the community orchestra and the venue was managed by the parks and recreation department. These two organizations have a partnership relationship. The bank works directly with the community orchestra and has minimal, if any, relationship with the parks and recreation department. The food vendor is contracted by the parks and recreation department. The community orchestra may or may not have an involvement with the food vendor. Finally, the webcasting of the performance is handled through the community orchestra with the parks and recreation department working to determine what special needs the webcast may require. By diagramming the program process, it becomes easier to see the relationships and dependencies that are present. Knowing the type of agency, whether there is a partnership present, the kind of provision of services committed, why the program or service is offered, and the influencers allows the agency to predict benefits on a broad base.

Questions to Consider

1. Choose a leisure activity you participate in and work it through Table 8.1. Even if it appears to be an individual activity, you should still be able to track it through the process.
2. Is it possible to begin anywhere in Table 8.1 and work both ways to show the process of leisure program development?
3. What is the role of the nonprofit organization in (A2)?

TABLE 8.2

SIMPLE VERSION

(A) Types of Recreation-Sponsoring Organizations →	(B) Partnered with Groups and Services →	(C) Provide Leisure Programs Consisting of →	(D) To Satisfy Individual and Public Needs for →	(E) Yielding Major Benefits
(1) Public agencies	(1) Trade associations	(1) Direct program leadership	(1) Full spectrum of involvement in:	(1) Personal values (health, emotional wellness, mental development, well-being)
(2) Nonprofit organizations	(2) Professional associations	(2) Provision of facilities for undirected public use	Games and sport	(2) Social and community-based outcomes
(3) Commercial recreation enterprises	(3) Special-interest groups	(3) Education for leisure	Outdoor recreation	(3) Economic benefits, employment, taxes, and other fiscal returns
(4) Employee service and recreation programs	(4) Sponsors of special programs and events	(4) Information referral services	Cultural activities	(4) Environmental values, both natural and urban settings
(5) Armed Forces morale, welfare, and recreation	(5) Professional preparation institutions	(5) Enabling facilitation	The arts	
(6) Private membership organizations	(6) Private groups that subcontract leisure functions	(6) Advocacy and leadership in special areas	Hobbies	
(7) Campus recreation programs	(7) Other civic agencies and citizen groups	(7) Jointly sponsored campaigns and events	Special events	
(8) Therapeutic recreation services	(8) Corporations	(8) Authentic leisure experiences	Club and other social groups	
(9) Sport management organizations	(9) Individuals	(9) Opportunities for well-being	Personal enjoyment	
(10) Tourism and hospitality industry			Travel	
			Electronic media	
			Other social services	
			(2) With needs influenced by:	
			Age group	
			Gender	
			Socioeconomic status	
			Educational background	
			Racial/ethnic factors	
			Residential and regional factors	
			Physical and emotional health	
			Ability/disability	
			Family status	

TABLE 8.3

COMPLEX VERSION

Ⓐ Types of Recreation-Sponsoring Organizations →	Ⓑ Partnered with Groups and Services →	Ⓒ Provide Leisure Programs Consisting of →	Ⓓ To Satisfy Individual and Public Needs for →	Ⓔ Yielding Major Benefits
(1) Public agencies	(1) Trade associations	(1) Direct program leadership	(1) Full spectrum of involvement in: Games and sport Outdoor recreation Cultural activities The arts Hobbies Special events Club and other social groups Personal enjoyment Travel Electronic media Other social services	(1) Personal values (health, emotional wellness, mental development, well-being)
(2) Nonprofit organizations	(2) Professional associations	(2) Provision of facilities for undirected public use	(2) With needs influenced by: Age group Gender Socioeconomic status Educational background Racial/ethnic factors Residential and regional factors Physical and emotional health Ability/disability Family status	(2) Social and community-based outcomes
(3) Commercial recreation enterprises	(3) Special-interest groups	(3) Education for leisure		(3) Economic benefits, employment, taxes, and other fiscal returns
(4) Employee service and recreation programs	(4) Sponsors of special programs and events	(4) Information referral services		(4) Environmental values, both natural and urban settings
(5) Armed Forces morale, welfare, and recreation	(5) Professional preparation institutions	(5) Enabling facilitation		
(6) Private membership organizations	(6) Private groups that subcontract leisure functions	(6) Advocacy and leadership in special areas		
(7) Campus recreation programs	(7) Other civic agencies and citizen groups	(7) Jointly sponsored campaigns and events		
(8) Therapeutic recreation services	(8) Corporations	(8) Authentic leisure experiences		
(9) Sport management organizations	(9) Individuals	(9) Opportunities for well-being		
(10) Tourism and hospitality industry				

PUBLIC RECREATION, PARK, AND LEISURE SERVICES

Public, or government, leisure-service agencies have the following characteristics: (1) They were the first type of agency to be formally recognized as responsible for serving the public's recreation needs and, as such, have constituted the core of the recreation movement; (2) the primary means of support for most government recreation and park agencies traditionally has been tax funding, although in recent years other revenue sources have begun to be used more extensively; (3) government agencies have a major responsibility for the management of natural resources; and (4) they are obligated to serve the public at large with socially useful or constructive programs because of their tax-supported status.

ROLE OF THE FEDERAL GOVERNMENT

The federal government's responsibility for managing parks and recreation areas and providing or assisting other leisure services evolved gradually. The growth of the parks and recreation movement began with the early immigrants to New England, with Boston Common being an archetype of future park development across the United States. National and state parks grew differently from urban parks, and recreation evolved still differently—yet people talk of parks and recreation as if they were one. This is a U.S. institution ranging from Central Park in the late 1850s to the formation of the first national park in 1872. The growth of government and nonprofit involvement, beginning with experience such as the Boston Sand Gardens and expanding dramatically under Franklin Roosevelt's New Deal policies, solidified government's role in parks and recreation.

The federal government in the United States developed a great variety of programs related to recreation in dozens of different departments, bureaus, or other administrative units. Typically, recreation functions evolved in federal agencies as secondary responsibilities. For example, the initial purposes of the Tennessee Valley Authority lakes and reservoirs were to provide flood control and rural electrification; only over time did recreation uses become important. The following list examines the responsibilities and role of the federal government.

- *Direct management of outdoor recreation resources:* The federal government, through such agencies as the National Park Service, the National Forest Service, and the Bureau of Land Management, owns and operates a vast network of parks, forests, lakes, reservoirs, seashores, and other facilities used extensively for outdoor recreation.
- *Conservation and resource reclamation:* Closely related to the preceding function is the government's role in reclaiming natural resources that have been destroyed, damaged, or threatened and in promoting programs related to conservation, wildlife, and antipollution control.
- *Assistance to open space and park development programs:* Chiefly with funding authorized under the 1965 Land and Water Fund Conservation Act, the federal government has provided billions of dollars in matching grants to states and localities to promote open-space development. Also, through direct aid to municipalities carrying out housing and urban development projects, the federal government subsidized the development of local parks, playgrounds, and centers.
- *Direct programs of recreation participation:* The federal government operates a number of direct programs of recreation service in Veterans Administration hospitals and other federal institutions and in the armed forces on permanent and temporary bases throughout the world.

- *Advisory and financial assistance:* The federal government provides varied forms of assistance to states, localities, and other public or voluntary community agencies. For example, many community programs serving economically and socially disadvantaged populations have been assisted by the Departments of Health and Human Services, Housing and Urban Development, Labor, and others.
- *Aid to professional education:* Federal agencies concerned with education and the needs of special populations have provided training grants for professional education in colleges and universities throughout the United States.
- *Promotion of recreation as an economic function:* The federal government has been active in promoting tourism, providing aid to rural residents in developing recreation enterprises, 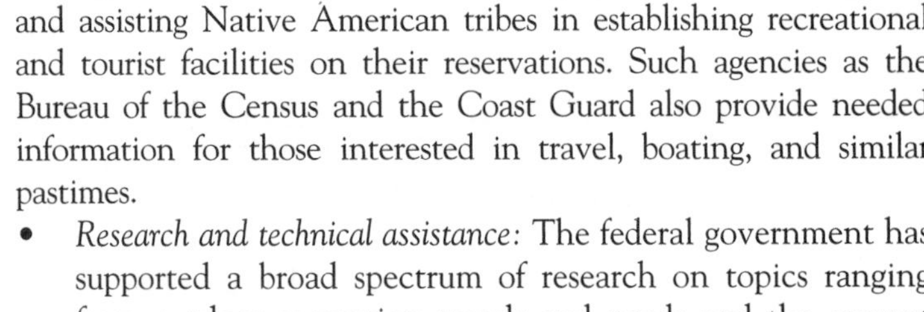 and assisting Native American tribes in establishing recreational and tourist facilities on their reservations. Such agencies as the Bureau of the Census and the Coast Guard also provide needed information for those interested in travel, boating, and similar pastimes.
- *Research and technical assistance:* The federal government has supported a broad spectrum of research on topics ranging from outdoor recreation trends and needs and the current status of urban recreation and parks to specific studies of wildlife conservation, forest recreation, or the needs of special populations.
- *Regulation and standards:* The federal government has developed regulatory policies with respect to pollution control, watershed production, and environmental quality. It has also established standards with respect to rehabilitative service for those who are ill or those with disabilities and architectural standards to guarantee access to facilities for people with disabilities.

Providing interpretive services to visitors is essential to individuals understanding park and natural settings.

The first two areas of responsibility (one, direct management and conseration, and two, resource reclamation) are carried out by seven major federal agencies that are either service units or bureaus in cabinet departments or separate authorities. They are the National Park Service, the U.S. Forest Service, the Bureau of Land Management, the Bureau of Reclamation, the U.S. Fish and Wildlife Service, the Tennessee Valley Authority, and the U.S. Army Corps of Engineers.

The National Park Service

The leading federal agency with respect to outdoor recreation is the National Park Service (NPS) (www.nps.gov), housed in the Department of the Interior. Its mission has been stated as follows:

> The National Park Service preserves unimpaired the natural and cultural resources and values of the national park system for the enjoyment, education, and inspiration of this and future generations. The Park Service cooperates with partners to extend the benefits of natural and cultural resource conservation and outdoor recreation throughout this country and the world.

Most of the property administered by the NPS in its early years was west of the Mississippi, and it has since added major seashore parks and other areas throughout the country and closer to urban centers. For example, East Coast sites now include the Fire Island National Seashore on Long Island, Acadia National Park in Maine, Assateague National Seashore on the Maryland coast, Cape Hatteras National Seashore in North Carolina, and Gateway East in the New York and New Jersey harbor area.

The Appalachian Trail is an example of a national trail used by tens of thousands of people annually for one-day to multi-day trips.

The national park system consists of almost 84 million acres (34 million hectares) of land, about 5% of which remains in private ownership. The system generates a huge volume of tourism, with appeal for both domestic travelers and foreign visitors that yields major benefits for the nation's economy and the balance of trade with other countries. In 2008, the national park system experienced 274.9 million visitors, spread across the 392-unit system. The level of usage in the national parks has created overcrowding at what are frequently called the "crown jewels."

NPS and National Geographic Partner for Biodiversity

The National Park Service has partnered with many organizations over its history. One of those organizations is the National Geographic Society, a nonprofit organization whose mission is "to explore the planet and sustain its extraordinary places, creatures, and cultures."[2]

Beginning in 2006, the two organizations initiated a *24-hour all-taxa BioBlitz*. It is a 10-year program of hosting a major biological survey of 10 selected national park units over a 24-hour period. The first 24-hour BioBlitz was in 2007, at Rock Creek Parkway in Washington, DC.

As the NPS reports, "the BioBlitzes [bring] the diverse capabilities of local natural historians, professional and amateur scientists, and students to the national parks en masse to explore, share findings, and educate the public about biodiversity."[3] In 2007, the Rock Creek Park found more than 660 species. The second BioBlitz, in the Santa Monica Mountains National Recreation Area, resulted 1716 species identified. These are not new species, but a cataloging of what is currently in the park. The 2009 event occurred at Indiana Dunes National Lakeshore, in northern Indiana near greater Chicago, and 1200 species were counted.

The NPS has expanded the BioBlitz into numbers of additional parks partnering with schools, universities, research institutes, and friends groups. Read about the BioBlitz at the National Geographic blog: http://blogs.nationalgeographic.com/blogs/bioblitz/.

The Forest Service

A second federal agency that administers extensive wilderness preserves for public recreation use is the U.S. Forest Service within the Department of Agriculture (USFS) (www.fs.fed.gov). The resource management responsibilities of the NPS and USFS have blurred in recent years, even though their management mandates have not. Both agencies had responsibilities for managing national monuments, recreation areas, trails, and wild and scenic rivers. The USFS is best known for its management of huge areas of forests and grasslands. The USFS was a predecessor to the National Park Service and had a very different

The U.S. Forest Service and Climate Change

The Strategic Framework for Responding to Climate Change is based on the U.S. Forest Service mission to sustain the health, diversity, and productivity of the nation's forests and grasslands to meet the needs of present and future generations.

Society relies on the ecosystem services provided by forests and grasslands such as clean water, clean air, biological diversity, wood products, and recreation. Global climate change is dramatically altering forests and grasslands and many of the most urgent forest and grassland management problems of the past 20 years—wildfires, changing water regimes, and expanding forest insect infestations—have been driven, in part, by changing climate.

The Strategic Framework has seven goals to address climate change. To achieve these goals, the Forest Service must work with a broad range of partners. The goals are the following:

Science: Advance our understanding of the environmental, economic, and social implications of climate change and related adaptation and mitigation activities on forests and grasslands.

Adaptation: Enhance the capacity of forests and grasslands to adapt to the environmental stresses of climate change and maintain ecosystem services.

Mitigation: Promote the management of forests and grasslands to reduce the buildup of greenhouse gases, while sustaining the multiple benefits and services of these ecosystems.

Policy: Integrate climate change, as appropriate, into Forest Service policies, program guidance, and communications and put in place effective mechanisms to coordinate across and within Deputy Areas.

Sustainable Operations: Reduce the environmental footprint of Forest Service operations and be a leading example of a green organization.

Education: Advance awareness and understanding regarding principles and methods for sustaining forests and grasslands, and sustainable resource consumption, in a changing climate.

Alliances: Establish, enhance, and retain strong alliances and partnerships with federal agencies, state and local governments, tribes, private landowners, nongovernmental organizations, and international partners to provide sustainable forests and grasslands for present and future generations.[4]

role. It adopted the multiple-use concept of federally owned land under its control; mining, grazing, lumbering, recreation, and hunting are all permitted in the national forests.

The recreation function of the USFS has continued to grow steadily. In 2009, it oversaw a total forest system of 192.9 million acres (78 million hectares), which included 35 million acres (14.2 million hectares) of wilderness as well as major elements of the National Scenic Byways and National Wild and Scenic Rivers Systems, national volcanic areas, wildlife and fish habitats, and numerous other special-use areas. In the same year, the USFS recorded 205 million visits on 14,077 recreation sites. Its major recreational uses in 2004 were for relaxation and viewing scenery; camping, picnicking, and swimming; hiking, horseback riding, and water travel; winter sports; and hunting and fishing.

Many threats are on forest service–administered lands. The USFS identified four main threats: fires and fuels, invasive species, loss of open space, and unmanaged recreation. Data suggest the loss of more than 3000 acres a day over a 6-year period, mostly to development, in lands near or adjacent to USFS areas. The loss of open space will place greater stress on forest service lands. Unmanaged recreation comes mostly in the form of off-highway vehicles (OHV). There were a reported 36 million OHV owners in 2000, a number that climbed until gas prices and the recession devastated the market. The use of OHVs in USFS lands has resulted in increased erosion, creation of new unplanned roads, and watershed and habitat degradation. The USFS has established action plans for each of the threats.

Other Federal Agencies

The Bureau of Land Management (BLM) (www.blm.gov) administers more than 256 million acres (105 million hectares), chiefly in the western states and Alaska. Its properties are used for a variety of resource-based outdoor recreation activities (including camping, biking, hunting and fishing, mountain climbing, and cycle racing), as well as mining, grazing, and lumbering activities that yield more than $800 million a year in revenues, much of it returned to state and local governments.

Pacific Remote Islands National Monument

The U.S. Fish and Wildlife Service administers the National Wildlife Refuge System. The Pacific Remote Islands Marine National Monument was created on January 6, 2009, by then-President George W. Bush.[5] The area falls within the Central Pacific Ocean, ranging from Wake Atoll in the northwest to Jarvis Island in the southeast. The seven atolls and islands included within the monument are farther from human population centers than any other U.S. area. They represent one of the last frontiers and havens for wildlife in the world, and they comprise the most widespread collection of coral reef, seabird, and shorebird protected areas on the planet under a single nation's jurisdiction.

The U.S. Fish and Wildlife Service (USFWS) (www.fws.gov) originally consisted of two federal bureaus, one dealing with commercial fisheries (which was transferred to the Department of Commerce) and the other dealing with sports fisheries and wildlife (which remained in the Department of the Interior). Its functions include restoring the nation's fisheries, enforcing laws, managing wildlife populations, conducting research, and operating the National Wildlife Refuge System. This system includes 550 units comprising

150 million acres (40.1 million hectares). In addition to meeting the ongoing needs of hunters and fishers, the USFWS particularly has been active in helping to ensure the survival of endangered species, conserving migratory birds, and administering federal aid programs that assist state wildlife programs and tribal lands programs.

The federal Bureau of Reclamation (BOR) (www.usbr.gov) is responsible for water resource development, primarily in the western states. Although its original function was to promote irrigation and electric power, it has accepted recreation as a responsibility since 1936. The policy of the Bureau of Reclamation is to transfer reservoir areas wherever possible to other federal agencies; often these become classified as National Recreation Areas and are assigned to the NPS for operation. The emphasis is on active recreational use such as boating, camping, hiking, hunting, and fishing rather than sightseeing. The National Park Service, Forest Service, Fish and Wildlife Service, and the Bureau of Reclamation have provided employment opportunities for thousands of young men and women through the Youth Conservation Corps (YCC), which has habilitated or built campgrounds and boating facilities at recreation areas throughout the West.

BLM's Contribution to American's Natural Heritage

The BLM manages more than 258 million acres (104.4 hectares), almost all of it in the western United States. The BLM's management program is called the National Landscape Conservation System and includes more than 850 units, dedicated to preserving natural resources.[6] The BLM-managed lands are home to approximately 30,000 free-roaming wild horses and burros; approximately 31,000 additional animals are cared for in short-term and long-term holding facilities. Managed areas include Wilderness and Wilderness Study Areas, Wild and Scenic Rivers, National Scenic and Historic Trails, National Monuments, and National Conservation Areas. (See **Table 8.4**.)

Additionally, the BLM manages 16,000 miles of multiple-use trails, including approximately 6000 miles of trails classified within the National Trails System; a vast array of geologic, historic, and archaeological sites, including 800 caves and 271,000 archaeological and historic recorded sites such as lighthouses, ghost towns, petroglyphs, pictographs, and cliff dwellings; and more than 117,000 miles of fisheries habitat and 4 million acres of reservoirs and lakes.[7]

The Tennessee Valley Authority (TVA) (www.tva.gov) operates extensive reservoirs in Kentucky, North Carolina, Tennessee, and other southern or border states. The TVA does not manage recreation facilities itself, but makes land available to other public agencies or private groups for development. Today the visitor-day total is reported to be approximately 14 million a year, but this includes those involved with the more than 20 universities and colleges that participate in resource management, environmental education, and campground operation through a consortium program at the Land Between the Lakes, an outstanding natural facility of more than 170,000 acres (68,796.6 hectares) located in west Kentucky and Tennessee.

The U.S. Army Corps of Engineers civilian side (usarmy.dod.gov) is responsible for the improvement and maintenance of rivers and other waterways to facilitate navigation and flood control. It constructs reservoirs, protects and improves beaches and harbors, and administers more than 12 million acres (4.9 million hectares) of federally owned land and water impoundments. This includes 460 reservoirs and lakes; the majority of these are managed by

TABLE 8.4

BLM'S NATIONAL LANDSCAPE CONSERVATION SYSTEM

Category	Areas	Number	BLM Acres	BLM Miles
Monuments and national conservation areas	National monuments	16	4,815,760	
	National conservation areas	16	4,112,798	
	Similar designations	5	435,829	
Wilderness	Wilderness areas	222	8,662,214	
	Wilderness study areas	545	12,790,291	
Wild and scenic rivers		67	1,164,014	2419
Trails	National historic trails	10		5342
	National scenic trails	5		664
Totals		**886**	**Approximately 27 million**	**8425**

Source: U.S. Department of the Interior, Bureau of Land Management, "National Landscape Conservation System Summary Tables." Available at: http://www.blm.gov/wo/st/en/prog/blm_special_areas/NLCS/summary_tables.html. Accessed September 30, 2010.

the corps, and the remainder are managed by state and local agencies under lease. Army Corps of Engineers recreation sites are heavily used by the public for boating, camping, hunting, and fishing.

Several other agencies in the Department of Agriculture have important recreation functions. The Farm Service Agency's (www.fsa.usda.gov) conservation programs focus on several areas, three of which are relevant to parks and recreation. The Conservation Reserve Enhancement Program (CREP) is a state and federal partnership allowing farmers "to receive incentive payments for installing specific conservation practices that help protect environmentally sensitive land, decrease erosion, and restore wildlife habitat." The Farmable Wetlands Program "reduces downstream flood damage, improves surface and groundwater quality, and recharges groundwater supplies by restoring wetlands." Finally, the Grassland Reserve Program "helps landowners restore and protect

Participation in outdoor recreation continues to hold steady. The variety of outdoor recreation activities demands diversity in the provision of natural recreation agencies.

grassland, and provides assistance for rehabilitating grasslands."[8] The Farmers Home Administration (www.rurdev.usda.gov) gives credit and management advice to rural organizations and farmers in developing recreation facilities. The Extension Service aids community recreation planning in rural areas and advises states on outdoor recreation development, working in many states through extension agents at land grant agricultural colleges.

The Bureau of Indian Affairs (www.bia.gov) exists primarily to provide service to Native American tribes in such areas as health, education, economic development, and land management. However, it also operates (under civilian control in the Department of the Interior) Native American–owned properties of about 56 million acres, with more than 5500 lakes that are used heavily for recreational purposes, including camping, museum visits, hunting, and fishing.

Programs in Health and Human Services, Education, and Housing

A number of federal agencies related to health and human services, education, and housing and urban development have provided funding, technical assistance, and other forms of aid to recreation programs designed to meet various social needs in U.S. communities. Within the federal Department of Health and Human Services (www.hhs.gov), such units as the Administration for Children and Families (www.acf.hhs.gov), and the Public Health Service have been active in this area. For example, the Administration on Aging, authorized by the Older Americans Act of 1965 and reauthorized in 2006, promotes comprehensive programs for older persons and supports training programs and demonstration projects intended to prepare professional personnel to work with older people. It also gathers information on new or expanded programs and services for the aging and supports research projects in this field.

The Rehabilitation Services Administration (www.ed.gov/about/offices/list/osers/rsa/index.html) administers the federal law authorizing vocational rehabilitation programs designed to help persons with physical or mental disabilities gain employment and lead fuller lives. It has oversight of formula and discretionary grant programs. Other federal legislation, such as Section 504 of the Rehabilitation Act of 1975 (often called the "nondiscrimination clause") and the Americans with Disabilities Act of 1990, has been instrumental in pressuring school systems, units of local government, and other agencies to provide equal opportunity for people with disabilities in a wide range of community opportunity fields.

The federal Department of Housing and Urban Development (HUD) (www.hud.gov) was established in 1965, with responsibility for a range of federally assisted programs, including urban renewal and planning, public housing, and open space. HUD's primary responsibility lies with urban development. Its mission is to increase homeownership, support community development, and increase access to affordable housing free from discrimination. Through its $39 billion budget, it administers a wide variety of programs focusing on community development. The Community Development Block Grant (CDBG), first authorized in 1974, is HUD's most valuable and effective community development program. Examples of use of CDBG funds include roads, sewers, and other infrastructure investments, or for community centers and parks. HUD also funds housing development and rehabilitation through CDBG, HOME, Youthbuild, and Lead Hazard Control grants.

Arts and Humanities Support

Another area of federal involvement in leisure pursuits in the United States has reflected public interest in the arts and a wide range of cultural activities. The National Foundation on the Arts and the Humanities Act of 1965 resulted in the creation of the National Endowment for the Arts (NEA) (www.nea.gov), which functions as an independent federal agency supporting and encouraging programs in the arts (including dance, music, drama, folk art, creative writing, and the visual media) and humanities (including literature, history, philosophy, and the study of language).

Although there was strong conservative resistance to some controversial programs in the 1990s, the NEA had its highest appropriation ever in 2002 and by 2009 administered a $155 million budget. Over its 40-year history, NEA has awarded more than 120,000 grants to com-

Attendance at cultural events is an important component of public services provided by leisure-service and cultural arts agencies.

Initiatives of the National Endowment for the Arts

The National Endowment for the Arts (NEA) has long been a sponsor of initiatives that bring art and culture to the public. Controversial at times, the NEA has several initiatives going at any given time, all attempting to reach different audiences. Some of those initiatives include the following.

Poetry Out Loud

The NEA and the Poetry Foundation have partnered with the State Arts Agencies of the United States to create Poetry Out Loud. This program encourages high school students to memorize and perform great poems. Poetry Out Loud invites the dynamic aspects of slam poetry, spoken word, and theater into the English class.[9]

Operation Homecoming: Writing the Wartime Experience

The NEA created Operation Homecoming in 2004 to help U.S. troops and their families write about their wartime experiences. Through this program, some of America's most distinguished writers have conducted workshops at military installations and contributed to educational resources to help the troops and their families share their stories. A related ongoing call for writing submissions has resulted in more than 1200 submissions and 12,000 pages of writings.[10]

The Big Read

The Big Read is an initiative of the National Endowment for the Arts designed to revitalize the role of literature in American popular culture and bring the transformative power of literature into the lives of its citizens. Created by the National Endowment for the Arts in partnership with the Institute of Museum and Library Services and Arts Midwest, the Big Read aims to bring the power of reading into the lives of Americans.[11] The program boasts its own Web page (www.neabigread.org) and blog (www.arts.gov/bigreadblog).

munities, arts groups, and artists. In 2002, the NEA initiated the National Initiative program and by 2009, eight initiatives were present. They include both short- and long-term initiatives lasting from a single year to many years. The initiatives include NEA arts journalism institutes, Operation Homecoming: Writing the Wartime Experience, American Masterpieces, Shakespeare in American Communities, NEA Jazz Masters, Great American Voices Military Tour, Poetry Out Loud, and the Big Read. All of the initiatives follow the NEA model of working with local communities and arts organizations.

Physical Fitness and Sports Promotion

Another recreation-related federal program has been the President's Council on Physical Fitness and Sports (www.fitness.gov). Created in 1956 to help upgrade the fitness of the nation's youth, and broadened in 1968 to include the promotion of sport participation, the Council has operated to encourage public awareness of fitness needs and to stimulate school and community-based sport and fitness programs. It has conducted nationwide promotional campaigns through the media and sponsored many regional physical fitness clinics. This effort continued through the 2000s, with a President's Challenge Physical Fitness Program providing for state and federal goals and guidelines, school championships, and participant fitness awards. Along with community school systems, many local recreation and park agencies and professional groups have assisted in such fitness programs.

RECREATION-RELATED FUNCTIONS OF STATE GOVERNMENTS

The role of state governments in recreation and parks generally has rested on the Tenth Amendment to the Constitution, which states, "The powers not delegated to the United States by the Constitution, nor prohibited by it to the States, are reserved to the States respectively, or to the people." This amendment, commonly referred to as the "states' rights amendment," is regarded as the source of state powers in such areas as public education, welfare, and health services.

Outdoor Recreation Resources and Programs

Each state government today operates a network of parks and other outdoor recreation resources. The National Association of State Park Directors (NASPD) (www.naspd.org) developed categories of facilities and areas:[12]

- *State parks areas:* Containing a number of coordinated programs for the preservation of natural and/or cultural resources and provisions of a variety of outdoor recreation activities supported by those resources.
- *State recreation areas:* Where a clear emphasis is placed on the provision of opportunities for primarily active recreation activities; this category includes recreational beaches, water theme parks, and so forth.
- *State natural areas:* Where a clear emphasis is placed on protection, management, and interpretation of natural resources of features; this category includes wilderness areas, nature preserves, natural landmarks, and sanctuaries.
- *State historic areas:* Where a clear emphasis is placed on protection, management, and interpretation of historical and/or archaeological resources or features; this category includes monuments, memorials, shrines, museums, and so forth dealing with historical and/or archaeological subjects, as well as areas that actually contain substantive remains

(e.g., forts, burial mounds) and areas where historic events took place (e.g., battles, discoveries, meetings).

- *State environmental education sites:* Used exclusively or primarily for conducting educational programs on environmental subjects, natural resources, and conservation; this category includes nature centers, environmental education centers, "outdoor classrooms," and so forth.
- *State scientific areas:* Set aside exclusively or primarily for scientific study, observation, and experimentation involving natural objects, processes, and interrelationships; any other allowable uses are secondary and incidental.
- *State trails:* Linear areas outside any other unit of the state park system that provide primarily for trail-type recreational activities (hiking, cycling, horseback riding, etc.); they normally do not contain any land areas large enough to support nontrail activities.

During the 1960s and early 1970s, most state governments expanded their recreation and park holdings, primarily with funding assistance from the Land and Water Conservation Fund but also through major bond issues totaling hundreds of millions of dollars in many cases. In the 1990s, many states again secured major bond issues for park renovation, new construction, and land acquisition. Open space and natural beauty were widely supported concepts, and the public enthusiastically supported programs of land acquisition and water cleanup. State parks are perceived as a close-to-home outdoor recreation experience available to most residents. Attendance at state parks exceeds all national agencies except the USFS. Attendance at state parks in 2007 was 730 million on 14.1 million acres (5.7 million hectares). State park acreage is only 18% of the size of the National Park system and yet state parks have 2.6 times as many visitors. State parks are essential to outdoor recreation activities of many citizens. (See **Table 8.5**.)

TABLE 8.5

AREAS, ACREAGE, AND VISITATION FOR SELECTED OUTDOOR RECREATION AGENCIES

Agency	Areas	Acreage[a]	Visitation[a]
National Park Service	392	84	274.9
U.S. Forest Service	1477[b]	193	205
U.S. Fish and Wildlife Service[c]	550	150	40
Bureau of Land Management	[d]	256	57
Army Corps of Engineers	460[e]	11	25
State Parks (all 50 states)	>6000	13.9	730.1

[a]number in millions—45 means 45 million
[b]recreation sites (may be more than one per area)
[c]National Wildlife Refuge System
[d]Measured in multiple ways, but total acreage is primary method
[e]reservoirs and lakes

Data from U.S. Census Bureau, "2010 Statistical Abstract: The National Data Book." Available at: http://www.census.gov/compendia/statab. Accessed November 5, 2010.

Other State Functions

An important function of state government is to assist and work with local governments in environmental efforts. Just as no single municipality can clean up a polluted stream that flows through a state, so in the broad field of urban planning, recreation resource development, and conservation, problems must be approached on a statewide or even a regional basis. In such planning, as in many other aspects of federal relationships with local communities, the state acts as a catalyst for action and as a vital link between the national and local governments.

Individuals with disabilities actively engage in sports, sometimes with individuals without disabilities.

Many state governments have offices or sponsor arts councils that distribute funds to nonprofit organizations and performing groups or institutions in various areas of creative and cultural activity. A unique aspect of state-sponsored or state-assisted recreation is the state fair. This term covers a wide variety of fairs and expositions held each year throughout the United States and includes carnivals and midways, displays and competitions of livestock and produce, farm equipment shows, and a host of special presentations by corporations of every type. The majority of such fairs are run by nonprofit organizations that are publicly owned and operated, including a number of bona fide state agencies. Attended by about 160 million persons each year, they promote civic and state boosterism, offer a showcase for agricultural and other regional industries or attractions, and provide varied forms of entertainment.

An important function of state governments is to promote all aspects of leisure involvement that support economic development. Many states assist or coordinate outdoor recreation ventures, tourism campaigns, regional recovery projects, and other efforts to attract visitors and revive local economies. Travel and tourism to urban and rural areas have become increasingly important to economies. States are providing leadership, assistance, and funding to local levels.

Therapeutic Recreation Service Each state government provides direct recreation services within the institutions or agencies it sponsors, such as mental hospitals or mental health centers, special schools for people who are mentally retarded, and penal or correctional facilities. Many of the largest networks of facilities that employ therapeutic recreation specialists are tax-supported state mental health systems or similar organizations, although their overall numbers have been reduced because of deinstitutionalization policies.

Promotion of Professional Advancement Although states promote effective leadership and administrative practices in recreation and parks by developing personnel standards and providing conferences and research support, their major contribution lies in the professional preparation of recreation practitioners in state colleges and universities. Of the colleges and universities in the United States with professional recreation and park curricula, a substantial majority are part of state university systems.

Many state agencies also assist professional development by conducting annual surveys of municipal and county recreation and parks departments and publishing their findings on facilities, fiscal practices, and personnel.

Development and Enforcement of Standards States also have the function of screening personnel by establishing standards and hiring procedures, or by requiring Civil Service examinations, certification, or personnel registration programs in recreation and parks.

Some also have developed standards relating to health and safety practices in camping and similar settings. State departments enforce safety codes, promote facilities standards, ensure that recreation resources can accommodate persons with disabilities, regulate or prohibit certain types of commercial attractions, and in some cases carry out regular inspections of camps, pools, or other facilities.

THE ROLE OF COUNTY AND LOCAL GOVERNMENTS

Although federal and state governments provide major forms of recreation service in the United States, the responsibility for meeting year-round day-to-day leisure needs belongs to agencies of local government. These range from counties, special park districts, and townships (which embrace larger geographical areas) to cities, villages, and other political subdivisions.

For recreation and parks in the United States, all powers that are not vested in the federal government belong to the states. In turn, local governments must get their authority through enabling laws passed by state legislatures or through other special charter or home rule arrangements. Of all branches of government, the local government is closest to the people and therefore most able to meet the widest range of recreation needs.

The Illinois Park District System

The Illinois Park District system is not unique in its organization but is among the largest collection of park districts in the United States. A *park district* is a geographically and politically bounded separate taxing district serving a distinct population with recreation, park and leisure services, and programs. The districts are created by state enabling legislation and voted into creation at the local level. Each district has an elected board that is responsible for the operations of the park district. Typically, they are policy-setting boards and hire an executive director and staff to run day-to-day operations. They are unique because most municipal park and recreation systems operate under a city government organization in which they compete for resources with other city agencies. A park district's independent status allows it to make investments and provide services with less conflict and competition than agencies that are part of city and county government. This does not remove the park districts from needing to create relationships with cities, counties, planning agencies, and the like. Park districts do not necessarily conform to traditional political boundaries such as cities and school districts. The Illinois Association of Park Districts (www.ilparks.org) has membership from 283 park districts, 9 forest preserve districts, 7 conservation districts, 22 special recreation associations, and 39 city park and recreation agencies.

County and Special Park District Programs

As an intermediate stage between state and incorporated local government agencies, county or special district park and recreation units provide large parks and other outdoor recreation resources as a primary function. They may also sponsor services for special populations; that is, programs for those aging or having a disability as well as services for all residents of the county, such as programs in the fine and performing arts.

During the early decades of the century, county governments had relatively limited functions. However, since World War II, the rapid growth of suburban populations around large cities has given many county governments new influence and power. Counties have become a base for coordinating and funneling numerous federal grants-in-aid programs. As a result, county park and recreation departments expanded rapidly.

Regional and Special Park Districts

Several states, including California, Illinois, Oregon, and North Dakota, have enabling legislation that permits the establishment of special park and recreation districts. Illinois has more than 300 such districts, including forest preserve and conservation districts. North Dakota has 225 park districts, California 118, and Ohio 26, while Oregon has 17 park and recreation districts.

Many special recreation and park districts are in heavily populated areas; in some cases, they may encompass a number of independent, separate counties and municipalities in a

County Park Agencies

Two similar examples of leading county park agencies are Miami–Dade County Park and Recreation Department in south Florida and the East Bay Regional Park District, comprising Alameda and Contra Costa on the eastern side of San Francisco Bay, California. Miami–Dade County Park and Recreation Department operates 12,000 acres of carefully planned and developed park and recreation facilities, serving 25 million plus visitors annually. The Crandon Zoo, Dade County Auditorium, and other facilities are important elements in this recreation-oriented metropolitan area, which depends heavily on its tourists. In addition, the Miami–Dade County department promotes numerous other privately owned or nonprofit attractions and leisure facilities, such as an impressive array of art museums, galleries, and collections in the metropolitan area that are sponsored by universities, individuals, and civic groups.

The East Bay Regional Park District's vision statement says "The East Bay Regional Park District will preserve a priceless heritage of natural and cultural resources open space, parks and trails for the future and will set aside park areas for enjoyment and healthful recreation for generations to come. An environmental ethic guides us in all that we do." The system started with three parks and two employees and now includes 98,000 acres (39,659 hectares) and operates an outstanding network of 65 regional parks, recreation areas, wilderness, shorelines, preserves and land bank areas, 29 regional interpark trails, 1150 miles of trails within parklands, 11 freshwater swimming areas, boating and/or stocked fishing lakes and lagoons, a disabled-accessible swimming pool, 40 fishing docks, 3 bay fishing piers, 235 family campsites, 42 youth camping areas, 2 golf courses, 9 interpretive and education centers, 18 children's play areas, and more than 600 employees. Consistent with the vision, 90% of the district's lands are protected and operated as natural parklands.

single structure. Frequently, special park districts and counties are able to carry out vigorous programs of land acquisition in a combined effort or to impose other means of protecting open space. Many counties enacted laws requiring home developers to set aside community recreation areas. One such example is Anne Arundel County, Maryland, which since 1957 has required all developers to allocate 5% of the land to be developed as park areas. Another common approach used by cities and counties to secure funds and lands is to require owners of new homes to pay an impact fee. The impact fee is based on the concept that current tax payers should not have to pay for new development; it should be the responsibility of the new owner to pay for community improvements to the neighborhood. Park and recreation departments have been recipients of these funds. Some county governments are establishing permanently protected green belts to halt or lessen the tide of construction. Strengthened zoning policies and more flexible building codes that permit cluster zoning of homes with larger and more concentrated open spaces are also helpful.

MUNICIPAL RECREATION AND PARK DEPARTMENTS

Municipal government is the term generally used to describe the local political unit of government, such as the village, town, or city, that is responsible for providing the bulk of direct community service such as street maintenance, police and fire protection, and education. Most areas depend on municipal government to provide many important recreation and park facilities and program opportunities, in addition to those provided by voluntary, private, and commercial agencies.

With the widespread recognition of this responsibility, municipal recreation and park agencies expanded rapidly in the United States during the period following World War II, with a steady increase in the number of departments, amount of acreage in park and recreation areas, number of full- and part-time or seasonal personnel, and total expenditures.

Functions and Structure of Municipal Agencies

The most common structure for delivery of services is a combined parks and recreation department. In some few cases, parks and recreation may include other social service organizations such as libraries, assistance agencies, and the like. Some remain separate parks and recreation departments.

Other municipal agencies may also sponsor special leisure services that are linked to their own missions. They may include (1) police departments, which often operate youth service centers or leagues; (2) welfare departments or social service agencies, which may operate day-care centers or senior centers; (3) youth boards, which tend to focus on out-of-school youth or teen gangs; (4) health and hospital agencies, which sometimes operate community mental health centers or similar services; (5) public housing departments, which sometimes have recreation centers in their projects; (6) cultural departments or boards, which frequently sponsor performing arts programs or civic celebrations; and (7) school systems and local community colleges.

Programs of Municipal Agencies

Municipal recreation and parks departments operate programs within several categories of activity: games and sports, aquatics, outdoor and nature-oriented programs, arts and crafts, performing arts, special services, social programs, hobby groups, and other playground and community center activities.

Playful City USA

Playful City USA is a national program honoring cities and towns that put children's well-being first by recognizing and harnessing the power of play. Sponsored by KaBOOM!, a national nonprofit focusing on places for children to play, the vision is to have "great places to play within walking distance of every child in America."[13] They work with communities to build playspaces and require active involvement by community members. Playful City USA is an extension of KaBOOM! and focuses on encouraging best practices and innovation in providing great playspaces. To qualify a community needs to do the following:

- Create a local play commission task force
- Design an annual action plan for play
- Conduct a playspace audit of all publicly accessible play areas
- Identify current spending on capital projects and maintenance of playspaces
- Proclaim and celebrate an annual "KaBOOM! Play Day"

KaBOOM! National Campaign for Play

Playful City USA honors cities and towns nationwide.

In Nevada, Henderson is the only community to receive this recognition. "It is an honor for us to be named a Playful City USA for the second year in a row," said Mayor Andy Hafen. "This recognizes our efforts to make play spaces safer and more accessible to Henderson children and validates our work to make diverse recreation opportunities available to all Henderson residents."

"One area we're particularly proud of is our commitment to installing shade shelters in our parks," said the director of the City of Henderson Parks and Recreation Department. "To date, we are about halfway toward our goal of adding a shade shelter at 67 play spaces throughout the city. Shade structures are now part of our park design standards, so they will be incorporated into any planned and future parks."

Henderson has designated September 24 as its official "Come Out and Play Day." During the day, more than 400 children at 37 different Henderson sites will celebrate the fun and importance of play with simultaneous activities in the afternoon. Activities include art contests, relays, swimming, jump rope, and more.[14]

In addition, public recreation and parks departments often sponsor large-scale special events such as holiday celebrations, festival programs, art and hobby shows, and sport tournaments. These departments also assist other community agencies to organize, publicize, and schedule activities. Frequently, sport programs for children and youth, such as Little League or American Legion baseball, are cosponsored by public departments and associations of interested parents who undertake much of the actual management of the activity, including coaching, fundraising, and scheduling. Similarly, many cultural programs, such as civic opera or little theater associations, are affiliated with and receive assistance from public recreation departments.

CASE STUDY: The Influence of Homeowner Associations on Community Park and Recreation Agencies

It's not what it seems at first glance: Parents lounge on lawn chairs in the warm Nevada sun, flipping through books and magazines while kids splash in the pool. The gentle thud of tennis balls echoes in the background as a group of teens test their skills on the nearby courts.

This summer scene could be set in many of Nevada's public parks, but instead takes place within a private community. A growing number of neighborhoods are providing amenities that duplicate those traditionally created and maintained by parks and recreation departments. So what does this mean for the public agencies and facilities?

Nevada's construction boom in the late 1990s and early 2000s brought not just new houses but developments that offered facilities and other extras. "This can include grassy areas, volleyball and basketball courts, tot lots, pools, dog parks, or water features," said Heather Herrod, director of marketing and public relations for RMI Management, LLC, a company that represents about 230 different community associations in and around Las Vegas. "Some communities even host special events for community members, including barbecues or festivals, at the expense of the homeowners association."

There are nearly 3000 neighborhoods with homeowners associations (HOAs) in and around Las Vegas and nearly 800,000 residents live in those communities. HOA fees vary, depending on the amenities and features of each community, along with how many homeowners live in the neighborhood.

In Somersett, a Reno-area master-planned golf community about a 10-minute drive west of downtown, the amenities include two recreational centers, a nine-hole golf course, two pools, tennis courts, hiking and biking trails, and a park.

Our residents like the community because everything is here," said Michele Attaway, chief operating officer of Somersett Development Company and president of the Somersett Owners Association. In communities such as Somersett, some of the neighborhood's facilities are open to the public and some of the taxes collected from builders are given over to the city or county to help fund a nearby public facility. A portion of the Somersett Owners Association fees—approximately $30,000 to $50,000 annually—is used to maintain the community's trails and parks, some of which are open to the public.[a]

Homeowner Associations

Homeowner association is a common term for residential private governments. Private government, in this instance, applies to associations created by private developers and that are later converted into nonprofit corporations governed by a board of directors elected from homeowners or dwellers. In 2008, there were 300,800 HOAs nationwide, representing a population of 59.5 million people in 24.5 million residences.[b] At least one source has suggested 20% of all Americans now live in community associations. This is the fastest growing form of privatization in the United States.

In many cases, HOAs are located within the boundaries of a municipality. Unlike cities who have limits and expectations prescribed by state government, HOAs have the authority to demand mandatory payments, regulate behavior, and impose penalties to enforce their rules.

Some 60,000 (19.9%) have professional managers, leaving a large percentage with either no manager or managed by one of 10,000 estimated association management companies. HOAs located within the corporate limits of a city are subject to all city regulations and requirements as well as those created by the HOA. There is a distinction between gated and ungated communities. Gated communities are perceived as more exclusive and nonresidents can only gain entrance through a resident. Nongated HOAs may offer similar services, but their facilities may be open to the general public.

One of the key issues associated with HOAs is the perceived competition they have with city governments. The term *competition* may appear to be too strong, but in some HOAs public parks and recreation minimally exist. In some instances, HOAs have created their own recreation centers, parks, and trails, while in other HOAs there has been either full or limited cooperation between local government and the HOA. The challenge has always been how public agencies can balance public need and services to those they tax and at the same time ensure equal access to provided facilities.

The problem occurs when the public-private partnership or wholly public service is located within a distinct, ungated HOA and other community residents feel they cannot use the facilities or parks. A second issue is present when partnerships between HOAs and government occur and residents in the HOA appear to receive preferential treatment because their partner facilities and services are better then those provided outside of the HOA. What other residents fail to realize is that HOAs frequently subsidize government maintenance operations within their boundaries to maintain property value and HOA resident expectations. The appearance of higher quality service is a result of the application of HOA fees that are more easily targeted than tax dollars.

As the number of HOAs continues to grow, community parks and recreation will have to find ways to work with them and integrate or partner in the provision of services and facilities.

Questions to Consider

1. Should HOAs be allowed to have their own parks?
2. What are the advantages to HOAs having their own parks? What are the advantages to the city they are located in? What are the disadvantages?
3. What restrictions or guidelines should cities place on homeowner association parks?

Sources

a. B. Schlossberg, "Park Agencis adjust to the Rise of Homeowners Associations," *Nevada Recreation & Park Society* (May 2009): 2–5.
b. Community Associations Institute, "Industry Data: National Statistics." http://www.caionline.org/info/research/Pages/default.aspx.

Varied Program Emphases

Cities tend to have common and unique emphases in their recreation and park operations. Omaha, Nebraska, for example, has an established department that operates a major auditorium and stadium complex, extensive boating facilities, and other unusual physical facilities, including an outstanding indoor tennis complex and a trap and skeet shooting facility. With revenues from these sources, it is able to support a substantial portion of its overall recreation operations.

Vancouver, British Columbia, has given high priority to developing and maintaining an extensive network of parks, beaches, pools, golf courses, conservatories, ice rinks, community centers, and an outstanding zoo in famed Stanley Park. This landmark, established more than 100 years ago, has a remarkable seawall promenade, a zoo, an aquarium, outstanding sports facilities, and other sites for leisure participation. A section of Stanley Park was named a Heritage Park Site in 1980, and its meadows and forests are carefully preserved as magnificent examples of relatively untouched natural environments.

CASE STUDY: What Makes an Excellent City Park System

The Trust for Public Lands (TPL) (www.tpl.org) is a national nonprofit organization that "conserves land for people to enjoy as parks, community gardens, historic sites, rural lands, and other natural places, ensuring livable communities for generations to come."[a] Their Parks for People initiative has published a variety of reports including *The Excellent City Park System*.[b] The report provides seven measures of an excellent city park system. They include (1) a clear expression of purpose; (2) an ongoing planning and community development process; (3) sufficient assets in land, staffing, and equipment to meet the systems goals; (4) equitable access; (5) user satisfaction; (6) safety from crime and physical hazards; and (7) benefits for the city beyond the boundaries of the parks.

A park system is an organized structure of parks connected and forming a complex whole *system*. A park system comprises a variety of different types of park units, ranging from large parks to small neighborhood parks including trails, special facilities, sport areas, cemeteries, natural and man-made areas, specialized areas such as zoos, gardens, and the like. When viewed as a total complex system, it includes a balance of different types of facilities that meet the needs of a community.

Following are criteria to judge whether a park is excellent:

A clear expression of purpose: A park system's expression of purpose includes a statement of why the park system exists, what benefits it provides, and how it will go about achieving its purpose. The purpose drives the decision making for the park system focusing on outcomes. For example, the Minneapolis Park and Recreation Board (MPRB) states its mission as: "The Minneapolis Park and Recreation Board shall permanently preserve, protect, maintain, improve, and enhance its natural resources, parkland, and recreational opportunities for current and future generations. The Minneapolis Park and Recreation Board exists to provide places and recreation opportunities for all people to gather, celebrate, contemplate, and engage in activities that promote health, well-being, community, and the environment."[c]

Ongoing planning and community development processes: These processes are present when the park system has a master plan. A master plan drives future intents of the park system and when followed facilitates good decisions. A master plan should include an inventory of natural, recreational, historical, and cultural resources; a needs analysis; an analysis of connectivity and gaps; an analysis of the agency's ability to carry out its mandate; an implementation strategy (with dates), including a description of other park and recreation providers' roles; a budget for both capital and operating expenses; a mechanism for annual evaluation of the plan.

The MPRB spent 2 years engaging the community in its comprehensive planning process. It visited with almost 4000 "residents, visitors, and elected officials contributed to the development of this plan, and more than 100 staff have been involved in one or more phases of the comprehensive planning process."[d]

Sufficient assets in land, staffing, and equipment to meet the systems goals: In today's economy, this requirement is the most significant challenge to park systems. Adding land, increasing staffing, and adding equipment all for the purpose of maintaining a park system at a level that meets the purpose of the system is a more difficult measure to assess. The Dallas Parks and Recreation Department (DPRD) benchmarked (measured against how others perform) with national averages and low-density cities. The Trust for Public Land (TPL) suggests multiple measures include acres in natural areas, acres in designed areas, acres in undeveloped areas, partnerships in land management, expenditures for operations and land acquisition, and so forth. There are few common measures across agencies. The TPL effort is one of several targeted at identifying common measures.

Equitable access: Equitable access refers to whether a system is accessible to everyone regardless of residence, physical abilities, or financial resources. Individuals have access from wherever they live.

The MPRB addresses accessibility as a standard for planning and for public entry into park areas. In addition, it has developed standards for activity delivery or opportunities within the park system. Popularity of an activity and the absence or presence of unique resources help determine the level of equitable access that can occur.

User satisfaction: This focuses on usage and measuring the usage of the parks. The higher the usage, the better the system. Focusing on measuring when, where, and how people use the parks and measuring this against demographics allows the park system to determine shortfalls, needs, and to estimate for the future. Most public agencies now have some type of system for gathering data about customer or user satisfaction. The DPRD uses a questionnaire focusing on a specific area or facility and asks questions about the purpose of the visit, quality of the staff, the quality and cleanliness of different areas at the facility, programs, and questions about how they got to the facility, how often they have come, size of the group, and overall service rating. When sufficient numbers are gathered, the data can be useful to the park system.

Safety from crime and physical hazards: Safety is a growing concern nationwide. The report suggests staff in uniforms reassure users and that youth programs have been proven to reduce delinquency.

The MPRB provides in its vision focus the following: "Safety, both real and perceived, is achieved through a combination of preventive and corrective measures. Delivering consistently safe parks also requires that they are well maintained and designed to prevent accidental injury. The plan calls for bolstering preventive measures that include developing ongoing relationships with park visitors, setting clear expectations of appropriate behavior in the park system, providing training to staff and visitors, and providing parks and park facilities that are safe by design."[e]

Benefits for the city beyond the boundaries of the parks: This is best described as follows:

> The excellent city park system is a form of natural infrastructure that provides many goods for the city as a whole; cleaner air, as trees and vegetation filter out pollutants by day and produce oxygen by night; cleaner water, as roots trap silt and contaminants before they flow

into streams, rivers and lakes; reduced health costs from sedentary syndromes such as obesity and diabetes, thanks to walking and running trails, sports fields, recreation centers, bikeways, golf courses, and other opportunities for physical fitness; improved learning opportunities from "outdoor classrooms" in forests, meadows, wetlands and even recovering brownfields and greyfields (previously used tracts); increased urban tourism based on attractive, successful parks, with resulting increased commerce and sales tax revenue; increased business vitality based on employer and employee attraction to quality parks; and natural beauty and respite from traffic and noise.[f]

Questions to Consider

1. How does your community measure up to the standards for an excellent park system?
2. Do you think it is good to measure whether park systems are excellent? What are the advantages? The disadvantages?
3. Can a park be excellent without the whole park system being excellent? How?

Sources

a. Trust for Public Land, "About TPL." (http://www.tpl.org/tier2_sa.cfm?folder_id=170).
b. P. Harnik, *The Excellent City Park System: What Makes It Great and How to Get There*, (Washington, DC: Trust for Public Lands, 2006).
c. Minneapolis Park and Recreation Board, *Comprehensive Plan. 2007–2020*. www.minneapolis parks.org/default.asp?PageID=933.
d. Ibid., 2.
e. Ibid., 3.
f. Harnik, *Excellent City Park*, 32.

Fitness Programming Many cities have undertaken special programs to promote health, fitness, and sport. This effort has been assisted by the Step Up to Health program, sponsored by the National Recreation and Park Assocation. The NFL Youth Football fund supported a series of summits to train communities on Step Up to Health in 2006. The program continues park and recreation department efforts to be in the forefront of the healthy lifestyle movement. Linked to this program emphasis is the recent trend by many city and county recreation departments to build outstanding new aquatic facilities that include extensive exercise and sport components. Littleton, Colorado, for example, completed in March 2005 a 53,000-square-foot (4924-square-meter) recreation center with separate community and recreation wings. The community wing includes classrooms, commercial kitchen, a child-care area, and the recreation wing including an aquatic center, fitness room, aerobics and

Exercise classes are frequently offered at local recreation centers.

dance studio, and gymnasium. The cost was $9.98 million. In Dickinson, North Dakota, a new 80,452-square-foot (7474-square-meter) recreation center was constructed to include a lounge, climbing wall, lap pool, leisure pool, child-care area, and fitness room.

Indianapolis Builds Sport and Cultural Facilities

Indianapolis, Indiana, is an excellent example of a city that has combined vigorous expansion of its sports and cultural facilities and programs with a sound public recreation and parks program to enhance its appeal to new businesses, residents, and tourists. Once viewed as a less-than-lively midwestern town, Indianapolis is fast becoming known as the amateur sports capital of the nation. In addition to its famed Indianapolis 500 auto racing event and the Brickyard 400, the city has three major league sports teams—the NBA Pacers, WNBA Fever, and the NFL Colts—and several minor league teams. It built multiple major sports facilities, including the Lucas Oil football stadium, Conseco Fieldhouse, Victory Field, and other athletic stadiums including a world-class tennis center, velodrome, and a natatorium.

The National Collegiate Athletic Association is located in Indianapolis. Other national sports associations headquartered in Indianapolis include U.S. Track and Field and the American College of Sports Medicine. In addition, the city boasts new art galleries, theaters, museums, performing companies, a zoo, and the world's largest children's museum.

Aquatic centers with a variety of amenities have become popular year-round activities incorporated into public park and recreation agencies, commercial enterprises, and resorts.

Human Service Functions Many local recreation and park agencies have moved vigorously into the area of programming to meet human and social service needs. The Recreation and Human Services Department of the city of Gardena, California, for example, offers many services, including youth services; individual, family, and group counseling; tutoring workshops; alcohol and drug abuse programs; after-school activities; licensed family child care; youth and adult counseling; senior citizen outreach and meals programming; and care for those suffering from Alzheimer's or mental disease.

A trend of the last two decades has been to develop multiservice departments in which recreation and park programs play a leading role. Thus, a merged department of community services might have responsibility for beaches, parking meters, special housing units, libraries, and other special public facilities or programs. Larger urban recreation and park departments may include management responsibilities for stadiums, convention centers, piers and marinas, or even municipal airports.

Fee-Based Programs

In response to government efforts to become more business oriented, including seeking expanded revenue sources, fee-based programs have gained popularity with recreation and park departments. The trend toward imposing substantial fees for many program elements or facilities membership in public recreation and parks is firmly established. Those who favor it argue that it provides a logical means of developing rich programs and services and strengthens the role of the recreation and agency in community life. As tax revenues available for recreation and parks continue to decline, many agencies find fee-based programs a survival tool. Other agencies have implemented fee-based programs to offer services that would otherwise not be available through government funding.

CASE STUDY: Cost Recovery as an Example of the Changing Financial Picture of Public Parks and Recreation

As government endeavors to balance competing community needs with existing and planned resources, public park and recreation agencies increasingly are looking for new ways to generate revenue or income from existing and new resources. This process requires public agencies to balance public need with the expectation to provide programs, facilities, and services. Many public agencies, especially at the municipal level, have struggled with how to do this. The process of cost recovery has gained increasing adoption among public agencies.

Cost recovery is a process used by public agencies to price their services on a break-even basis, or so that "approximately the same amount of resources are recovered through pricing as are expended in production and delivery."[a] The idea behind cost recovery is to determine the amount of money that might be recovered from each program and service based on the merit and purpose of the service.

Cost recovery approaches attempt to define what should be paid for by tax revenues (basic services) and what should be provided and recovered fully or partially through fees, charges, and other nontax revenue sources. Cost recovery is about identifying acceptable levels of basic services, merit services, and private services. Communities tend to organize levels of service similarly. The levels of services are explained later. There are benefits to implementing cost recovery processes. First, and maybe most important, government can divert tax dollars to areas of greater need. Second, cost recovery allows municipal agencies to improve opportunities. Without cost recovery, most public agencies would be unable to maintain services at current levels. Third, cost recovery is an information tool allowing agencies to determine user perceptions of value of a product or service and user preferences. Agencies respond through adjustments in prices, services, and offerings. Fourth, cost recovery is a means of expanding recreation and park opportunities.

Figure 8.1 depicts a comparison of subsidies, or those costs paid by tax dollars, versus those costs recovered from users. The three levels of service, as previously mentioned, are public service, merit service, and private service. Public services are provided for the public good, meeting the needs of a broad constituency of community members. The benefits focus on public outcomes or on the ability to provide services that result in strengthening the community. Merit services fall in between public and private services, and the measure of these services focuses on who benefits the most. Is it the user or the public? In most cases, both benefit at some level, but this does not meet the criteria of public good. The user is then expected to pay for part of the cost of the delivery of the program. Private services focus on the user receiving all or most of the benefit and the public receiving little or no benefit.

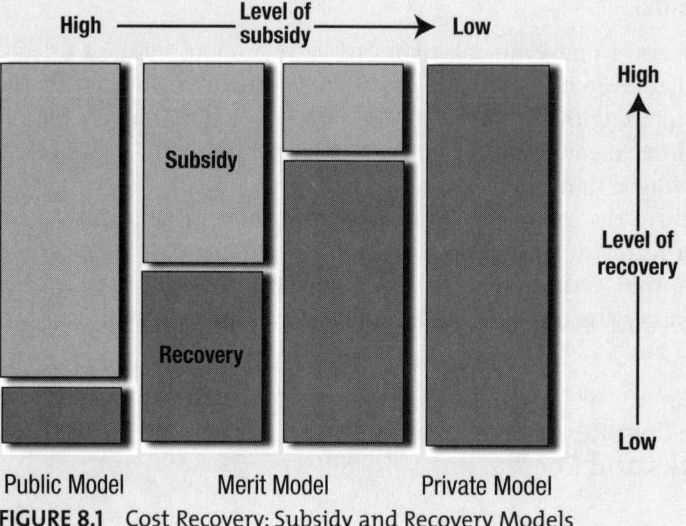

FIGURE 8.1 Cost Recovery: Subsidy and Recovery Models

Figure 8.1 illustrates that public services receive a majority of their subsidy from tax dollars while private services receive little or no support from tax dollars. It reinforces the notion of supporting public good programs with higher tax subsidy and requiring special interest groups and individuals who receive a private service to pay for all or most of the service.

Cost recovery is about identifying acceptable levels of basic services, merit services, and private services. Communities tend to organize levels of service similarly. The levels of service are explained later.

Cost recovery is traditionally represented by four levels of recovery, ranging from no recovery (public), to partial recovery, break-even recovery (merit), and finally, generation of revenue at or beyond the cost of the program (private). The determination of cost recovery is based on equity. For example, the Tucson, Arizona, Parks and Recreation department identifies three levels of equity: (1) public services, (2) merit services, and (3) private park and recreation services. These three levels are generally applied nationally, with some communities making modifications in levels and/or definitions. Boulder, Colorado, identifies five levels of cost recovery: (1) basic services, (2) merit services, (3) enhanced services, (4) specialized services, and (5) enterprise services. The difference revolves around the idea that there might be intermediate steps that give the agency greater flexibility in cost recovery.

How Are Cost Recovery Models Implemented?

Designing a cost recovery model that meets the needs of the agency, the governing body, and the public served can be challenging. Most agencies implementing a cost recovery model endeavor to include the public in the process. Doing so strengthens the public's perception of the agency's commitment to serving the entire community.

Once a cost recovery plan is adopted, the agency engages in several tasks associated with implementing the plan. First, each program or service provided by the agency is reviewed and fees are adjusted. There are several ways to do this. The fees can be adjusted upward or downward immediately, based on how they fit in the cost recovery model. Fees can be adjusted over a period of time, especially if there are significant increases, thus delaying the full impact on the participant. Or fees can be deferred by the agency for a specific reason. Implementation of a cost recovery program can be controversial for an agency, even with public input, because of the perceived and real impact on program participants and those using services. Typically, a public relations program is mounted that strives to explain the purpose, need, and process of cost recovery, as well as how it affects the public.

Cost recovery is primarily a financial tool used by public agencies to assist in fees, charges, and decision making and validates a rationale for making decisions.

Questions to Consider

1. How does cost recovery help a public agency?
2. If you were implementing a cost recovery program, what are some of the concerns you would have about the program?
3. Debate the importance of providing some services at low or no cost and other services at a moderate or high cost.

Source

a. R. E. Brayley and D. D. McLean, *Financial Resource Management: Sport, Tourism and Leisure Services* (Champaign, IL: Sagamore Publishing, 2008): 98.

Some critics argue that placing heavy reliance on fee structures discriminates against children and youth, people who are elderly, people with disabilities, and the poor, who cannot afford to pay significant fees for participation in public recreation programs. As such, it represents a retreat from the fundamental mission of public recreation and leisure programs. In some cases, cities or other public recreation and park agencies have provided fee discounts, "scholarships," or variable pricing policies to enable participation by poorer families. Although such policies are generally acceptable in well-to-do towns or suburban areas, they are obviously not workable in socially and economically disadvantaged inner-city neighborhoods or in less-affluent communities. Some cities developed models in which they assess the social priority that should be attached to recreation facilities or programs and base fee-charging policies on this assessment.

Innovative Developments in Larger Cities

As earlier chapters in this text have shown, problems related to inadequate budgets, increasing crime, and declining infrastructure and maintenance services tend to be most severe in older cities with limited public, nonprofit, and commercial leisure resources—yet, even in these communities, recreation and park administrators are working to expand and improve leisure facilities, programs, and maintenance. New York City, which experienced major cuts in recreation and park operations at the start of

City parks allow residents to enjoy leisure time relaxing in open spaces.

the twenty-first century, has been able to mount aggressive campaigns to improve the care of its major parks, such as Central Park and Prospect Park, through the contributions of thousands of businesses and individual residents who joined park foundations or conservancy organizations. Additionally, some operations have been contracted to private vendors. The American Golf Corporation announced a $24-million investment in golf course renovation for six historic courses. Privatization efforts similar to New York's allow cities to use limited capital dollars for other needed improvements in parks and recreation facilities.

New York also successfully moved ahead with plans to develop its waterfront areas, as other cities such as Baltimore have done, with mixed public, private, and commercial recreational uses. With the state's approval, four huge piers jutting into the Hudson River, which had been built in the early 1900s to accommodate a generation of giant oceanliners, were converted into a major sports and entertainment complex. Costing more than $100 million, the waterfront, known as Chelsea Piers, boasts an 80,000-square-foot (7432-square-meter) fieldhouse, year-round heated hitting stalls, a 200-yard (185.8-meter) artificial golf fairway, and a twin rink ice arena that is open 24 hours a day/7 days a week.

Many cities, such as Henderson, Nevada, offer recreational opportunities for all ages and abilities.

Extending such efforts, New York's Lower Manhattan Redevelopment Project allocated $24 million toward renovation and new development in 24 existing park sites. In another example of recreation's role in the recovery of older, major cities, the Boston, Massachusetts, harbor area continues an $11 billion transformation, which will include water-based recreation in the city's newly clean seaport and bay waters.[15]

Along with such environmental and marketing-based efforts, many municipal recreation and park agencies also have moved vigorously in the direction of benefits-based programming as a means of documenting and providing direction to their overall services.

NONPROFIT ORGANIZATIONS: ORGANIZING THE VOLUNTARY SECTOR

Whereas government recreation and park agencies are responsible for providing a floor of basic leisure services for the public throughout the United States, a major segment of recreational opportunities is sponsored by nonprofit organizations, often called *voluntary agencies*. These consist of several different types of youth-serving, special-interest, and charitable organizations.

Organizations in this category may be completely independent or may be part of national or regional federations. Often they are described as "quasi-public" or "public/private." In some cases, they must meet government-imposed standards as charitable organizations to retain tax-exempt status. They tend to share the following characteristics:

- Usually established to meet significant social needs through organized citizen cooperation, community organizations represent the voluntary wishes and expressed needs of neighborhood residents. Thus, they are voluntary in origin.

- Governing boards of directors or trustees are usually public-spirited citizens who accept such responsibilities as a form of social obligation; thus, membership and administrative control are voluntary.
- For funding, voluntary agencies usually rely on public contributions, either directly to the agency itself or to Community Chest, United Way, or similar shared fundraising efforts. Contributed funds are usually supplemented by membership fees and charges for participation. In recent years, many voluntary organizations also have undertaken special projects for which they receive government funding.
- Leadership of voluntary agencies is partly professional and partly voluntary. Management is usually by directors and supervisors professionally trained in social work, recreation, education, or other related areas. At other levels, leadership is by nonprofessionals, part-time or seasonal personnel, and volunteers.
- In some cases, nonprofit organizations in the overall leisure-service system do not sponsor recreation activities directly, but represent organizations that do or that manufacture equipment or provide services, often on a for-profit basis. However, as in the case of educational institutions or professional societies in this field, they are nonprofit and tax exempt.

Nonprofit voluntary agencies regard recreation as part of their total spectrum of services, rather than their sole function. Typically, they recognize the importance of creative and constructive leisure and see recreation as a threshold activity that serves to attract participants to their agencies. In addition, they see it as a means of achieving significant social goals, such as building character among youth, reducing social pathology, enriching educational experience, strengthening community unity, and similar objectives. In general, even though voluntary agencies do not describe themselves as recreation agencies, this often tends to be the largest single component in their programs.

Nonprofits rely on volunteers for much of their work. Americans provide more volunteer service than any other society. In 2008, 61.8 million people, or 26.4% of all Americans volunteered to serve organizations or other programs. Women represented 29.4% of all volunteers and those aged 35 to 44 provided 31.8% of all volunteers. Volunteers' median time spent was 52 hours.[16]

Nonprofit but Fee Charging

Many voluntary organizations, though they are nonprofit and interested in meeting important social goals, may charge substantial fees. For example, YMCAs or YWCAs in suburban areas are likely to have fees that are as high as several hundred dollars a year for full family memberships and charge impressive sums for varied program activities. However, such fees are intended simply to help the organization maintain financial stability, without making a profit, and are frequently used to subsidize other services to marginalized populations who cannot afford to pay fees for membership or participation.

Because of the word *voluntary*, some assume incorrectly that such agencies are staffed solely by volunteer workers. The reality is that, although some nonprofit organizations such as the Boy Scouts and Girl Scouts rely heavily on volunteer leaders, most of them have full-time, paid professionals in their key management or supervisory posts.

It was estimated in 2002 that nonprofit organizations employed 8.3% of working Americans, involving 11.6 million people. Salaries for professional employees of such bodies as Boy Scouts and Girl Scouts, the YMCA and YWCA, Junior Achievement, and Big Brothers/Big Sisters of America all have risen steadily in recent years. Indeed, during the early and mid-1990s, a wave of public criticism was directed at the executives of some major nonprofit, charitable organizations who received exorbitant salaries and benefits.

TYPES OF NONPROFIT YOUTH-SERVING AGENCIES

Although voluntary nonprofit organizations fit under many headings—including the arts, education, health, and social service—the largest segment of such groups with strong recreational components is generally youth oriented. Included in this segment are the following:

- Nonsectarian youth-serving organizations
- Religiously affiliated youth-serving or social agencies
- Special interest organizations in such fields as sport, outdoor recreation, and travel
- Conservation and outdoor recreation
- Organizations promoting youth sports and games
- Arts councils and cultural organizations
- Service and federal clubs
- Promotional and coordinating bodies

Nonsectarian Youth-Serving Organizations

Nationally structured organizations that function directly through local branches, nonsectarian youth-serving groups have broad goals related to social development and good citizenship and operate extensive programs of recreational activity. There are hundreds of such organizations: Many of them are junior affiliates of adult organizations, whereas others are independent. Sponsorship is by such varied bodies as civic and fraternal organizations, veterans' clubs, rural and farm organizations, and business clubs. Several examples follow.

Boy Scouts of America Founded in the United States in 1910, the Boy Scouts of America is a powerful and widespread organization. In 2005, its youth membership consisted of 3.3 million youth, ranging from Tiger Cubs to Explorers. Together with adult leaders, a total of 4.1 million were involved in Boy Scouts of America in 123,582 packs, troops, and other units, directed by a professional staff consisting of almost 4000. In addition to its membership in the United States, Boy Scouts of America is part of a worldwide scouting movement involving more than 100 other countries. The program emphasizes mental and physical fitness, vocational and social development, and the enrichment of youth hobbies and prevocational interests, relying heavily on adventure and scouting skills and service activities.

The Boy Scouts of America has been regarded as a middle-class organization in U.S. society and as a small town or suburban rather than a big city phenomenon. As the urban environment has changed, so has scouting's impact in the inner city. Heather MacDonald, reporting on scouting in inner New York City reported,

> Feeling dispirited about today's youth? Try attending a Boy Scout meeting. You will find a parallel universe to today's vulgar, sexualized youth culture, filled with gestures of sometimes unbelievable delicacy and a code of conduct as anachronistic as sixteenth-century courtiership. Take Harlem's Troop 759. Six boys, from tall to small, sit expectantly around a card table in the basement of a red brick church on Morningside Avenue. The gangly senior patrol leader, Osmond Ollennu, a tenth-grade son of Ghanaians, calls the troop to opening ceremonies ("C'mon, men, form a straight

> line!"), and Osmond's little brother leads it in the Pledge of Allegiance, followed by four full-throated repetitions of the scout motto ("Be Prepared!") and one scout slogan ("Do a Good Turn Daily"). Then Osmond, who is the troop's second-in-command, announces inspection. While the boys stand quietly in line, he gently reties a neckerchief here, straightens a collar there, occasionally whispering a reminder in a boy's ear. The troop's leader, a dignified 18-year-old named Henry Lawson, inspects Ollennu in turn.

Speaking of scouting's values:

> Scoutcraft teaches, among other things, persistence in the face of disappointment. When it rains and your boots are filled with mud, "you can either take a bad hand and fold, or you can keep playing it, and it will get better," explains Scott Slaton, an Eagle Scout from Atlanta, Georgia, who works with inner-city scouts.[17]

Girl Scouts of the U.S.A. The largest voluntary organization serving girls in the world, the Girl Scouts of the U.S.A. is open to girls between the ages of 5 and 17 who subscribe to its ideals as stated in the Girl Scout Promise and Law. It is part of a worldwide association of girls and adults in more than 90 countries through its membership in the World Association of Girl Guides and Girl Scouts. Its membership in 2009 consisted of 2.7 million members and 928,000 adults, including volunteers, board members, and staff specialists.

The Girl Scouts are involved in their local communities through a variety of community service activities.

Founded in 1912, the Girl Scouts provides a sequential program of activities centered around the arts, the home, and the outdoors, with emphasis on character and citizenship development, community service, international understanding, and health and safety. Senior Girl Scouts in particular may take on responsibilities in hospitals, museums, child care, or environmental programs. Like the Boy Scouts of America, the Girl Scouts today conducts special programs for the poor; those with physical, emotional, or other disabilities; and similar populations.

In June 2004, the Girl Scouts initiated a project focusing on core business strategies. The project's outcome is to develop a strategy to ensure the future success and growth of Girl Scouts. They have chosen to emphasize five strategic priorities including development of outcomes-based leadership models, revitalizing volunteerism, branding the Girl Scout name with a new contemporary approach, increasing funding substantially, and restructuring of the organizational and governance structure to be more efficient and effective. In the early stages of development, Girl Scouts hope to revitalize and address contemporary issues and needs.[18]

Boys and Girls Clubs of America The Boys and Girls Clubs movement is the fastest-growing youth-serving organization in the United States today. Originally composed of two separate organizations, the merged club movement holds a U.S. congressional charter and is endorsed by 21 leading service, fraternal, civic, veteran, labor, and business organizations. Today, the Boys and Girls Clubs movement serves 4.4 million youth members in more than 4300 club locations, with a staff of 50,000 full-time trained professionals and more than 172,000 adult volunteers. Its members come from minority families (65%), are 6 to 10 years old (43%), 11 to 18 years old (52%), and are closely equal gender-wise: male (55%) and female (45%). Programs include sport and games, arts and crafts, social activities, and camping, as well as remedial education, work training, and job placement and counseling. The national goals of the Boys and Girls Clubs of America include the following: citizenship education and leadership development; health, fitness, and preparation for leisure; educational vocational motivation; intergroup understanding and value development; and enrichment of both family and community life.

With the help of special funding from corporations, foundations, and government agencies, the organization has developed program curricula for several key projects in the social services area. Although each club is an independent organization with its own board and professional staff, the national headquarters and seven regional offices provide essential services to local clubs in such areas as personnel recruitment and management training, program research and development, fundraising and public relations, and building design and construction assistance.

Police Athletic Leagues In hundreds of communities today, law enforcement agencies sponsor Police Athletic Leagues (PALs). Operating in poverty areas, the league programs rely primarily on civilian staffing and voluntary contributions for support, although they sometimes receive technical assistance from officers on special assignment from cooperative municipal police departments. In a few cities, police officers provide the bulk of full-time professional leadership in PAL programs. PALs typically provide extensive recreation programming, indoor centers, and summer play streets, with strong emphasis on sport and games, creative arts, drum and bugle corps, and remedial education. Many leagues also maintain placement, counseling, and job training programs and assist youth who have dropped out of school.

The PAL is one of the few youth organizations that continues to have resisting juvenile delinquency as a primary thrust. One of its principal purposes has been to promote favorable relationships between young people and the police in urban settings, and it has been markedly successful in this effort. Like other voluntary agencies, PALs rely on varied funding sources, including the United Way, independent fundraising campaigns, contracts with government, and often partial police department sponsorship.

Camp Fire USA Founded in 1910 under the name Camp Fire Girls, this organization has been concerned with character building through a program of outdoor recreation, community service, and educational activities. Beginning in the 1970s, the membership of the Camp Fire Girls declined sharply, from a high of more than 600,000 to approximately 325,000 in the early 1980s. The organization responded to this challenge by changing its name to Camp Fire USA and embracing a coeducational membership diverse in racial, ethnic, religious, and economic terms. With more than 6500 volunteer and paid leaders, the staff and board members work extensively in cooperation with local schools in conducting child-care programs. Many Camp Fire programs also sponsor day and resident camping programs for young people from kindergarten age to 21. In 2006–2007, they reached more than 750,000 youth. Like other youth-serving groups, Camp Fire USA serves as a strong advocate for youth in such areas as juvenile justice, child abuse, AIDS, and teen suicide.

Best Buddies Established in 1989 by Anthony Kennedy Shriver, Best Buddies focuses on creating one-to-one friendships, integrated employment, and leadership development for people with intellectual and developmental disabilities.[19] The program currently has chapters on more than 1400 middle school, high school, and college campuses across the United States. There are six programs focusing on bringing one-to-one relationships to people with intellectual and developmental abilities with community members. The programs include Best Buddies Citizens, including the corporate and civic communities; Best Buddies Colleges; High Schools; Middle Schools; Best Buddies Jobs with supported employment; and *e*-Buddies focusing on an e-mail pen pal program.

Best Buddies Massachusetts, one of the state chapters, has a very active program including participants and fundraising. In 2009, a sample of its events includes an artistic abilities exhibition, a shopping benefit at Bloomingdale's, Macy's shop for a cause, the 2009 fall friendship festival, an evening of opportunity, a friendship relay, and a bowl-a-thon. As with most nonprofits, there is a mix of activities for participants and fundraising to secure funding for operation of the program.

Religiously Affiliated Youth-Serving or Social Agencies

Many religious organizations sponsor youth programs with recreational components today, including activities sponsored by local churches or synagogues and activities sponsored by national federations that are affiliated with a particular denomination.

Recreation programs provided by local churches or synagogues tend to have two broad purposes: (1) to sponsor recreation for their own members or congregations to meet their leisure needs in ways that promote involvement with the institution and (2) to provide leisure opportunities for the community at large or for a selected population group in ways that are compatible with their own religious beliefs. Typical activities offered by individual churches and synagogues may include the following:

- Day camps, play schools, or summer Bible schools, which include recreation along with religious instruction
- Year-round recreation activities for families, including picnics, outings, bazaars, covered dish suppers, carnivals, single-adult clubs, dances, game nights, and similar events
- Programs in the fine and performing arts, including innovative worship programs involving dance and folk music
- Fellowship programs for various age levels, including discussion groups on religious and other themes
- Varied special interest or social service programs, including day-care centers for children, senior citizens clubs or golden age groups, and recreation programs for persons with disabilities
- Sport activities, including bowling and basketball leagues, or other forms of instructional or competitive participation

On a broader level, such organizations as the Young Men's Christian Association (YMCA), Young Women's Christian Association (YWCA), the Catholic Youth Organization (CYO), and the Young Men's and Young Women's Hebrew Association (YM-YWHA) provide a network of facilities and programs with diversified recreation, education, and youth service activities. Although their titles include the words *young* or *youth*, they tend to serve a broad range of children, youth, adult, and aging members.

Nonprofit organizations, such as the YMCA, provide important services for members, including fitness programs.

YMCA and YWCA Voluntary organizations affiliated with Protestantism in general rather than with any single denomination, the Ys are devoted to the promotion of religious ideals of living and view themselves as worldwide fellowships "dedicated to the enrichment of life through the development of Christian character and a Christian society." However, the actual membership of the Ys is multireligious and multiracial. In 2008, there were 2686 YMCAs with 21 million members, making it one of the largest nonprofits providing recreation. There were an additional 559,000 volunteers.

In many communities, the YMCA offers facilities and leadership for indoor aquatics, sport and games, physical fitness, social and cultural programs, and family-centered programs. These activities are usually aggressively marketed and bring in substantial revenues. Both the YMCA and YWCA derive funding from varied sources: membership fees, corporate and private contributions through the United Way, fundraising drives, and government and foundation grants.

Muslim Youth Groups There is no single national organization providing leadership for Muslim youth groups, rather multiple groups are providing leadership, all with some or a total emphasis on youth. These include the Islamic Society of North America, Muslim American Society, and Young Muslims. The Islamic Society of North America (ISNA) provides information on aging, domestic violence, matrimony, leadership, and youth.

There are Muslim youth groups concentrated in local communities and regions. The Islamic Center of Southern California, for example, provides an educational, social, spiritual, and moral environment, and physical activities to motivate young American Muslims to live by and serve Islam and to identify themselves as Muslims, creating a nurturing learning environment in which a basic core knowledge of Islam is provided. In addition, they encourage education, self-expression, the creation of a social environment to build healthy interaction, and foster an American Muslim identity.

Ethnic background affects the types of activities individuals participate in but does not diminish participation.

Catholic Youth Organization The leading Catholic organization concerned with providing spiritual, social, and recreational services for young people in the United States is the Catholic Youth Organization. CYO originated in the early 1930s, when a number of dioceses under the leadership of Bishop Sheil of Chicago began experimenting with varied forms of youth organizations. It was established as a national organization in 1951 as a component of the National Council of Catholic Youth. Today, the National CYO Federation has an office in Washington, DC, as well as many citywide or diocesan offices. The parish, however, is the core of the Catholic Youth Organization, which depends

YWCA as a Social Service Agency

In addition to meeting recreational needs, the YWCA in particular has changed its image from a traditional, predominantly white conservative organization to one more directly concerned with social needs and problems. This new attitude is illustrated by the types of courses, clinics, workshops, and services offered on a local basis. The nature of programs is as varied as the YWCA itself and typically responsive to local needs. The list of programs is long and diverse. Some examples include racial justice, domestic violence, women's economic advancement, self-sufficiency, relationships, chemical dependency, career development, antiviolence, transitional house, child care, and many more. The YWCA has maintained a strong national presence and focus while supporting and encouraging local diversity of programming and services.

The YWCA's brand or slogan, "Eliminating Racism, Empowering Women," reflects the change that has occurred in the organization over the last few years. Serving women for more than 145 years, the YWCA has been socially active in the 300 communities it serves. It is engaged in such activities as shelter services for women and their families, child-care services, sport and fitness programs for women and girls, girls' leadership development, public leadership involvement, and more recently creating tech-based programs for girls.

heavily on the leadership of parish priests and the services of adult volunteers from the neighborhood for direction and assistance.

Young Men's and Young Women's Hebrew Association Today, there are more than 275 YM-YWHAs, Jewish Community Centers, and camps serving more than 1 million members throughout the United States. Like the YMCAs and YWCAs, the Jewish Ys do not regard themselves primarily as recreation agencies, but rather as community organizations devoted to social service and having a strong Jewish cultural component. Specifically, the YM-YWHA has defined its mission in the following way:

- To meet the leisure-time social, cultural, and recreational needs of its membership, embracing both sexes and all age groups
- To stimulate individual growth and personality development by encouraging interest and capacity for group and community participation
- To teach leadership responsibility and democratic process through group participation
- To encourage citizenship education and responsibility among its members and, as a social welfare agency, to participate in community-wide programs of social betterment

Special Interest Organizations

Numerous other types of voluntary nonprofit organizations can best be classified as special interest groups, concerned with promoting a particular area of activity or social concern. Their functions may include leadership training, public relations, lobbying and legislation, establishing national standards or operational policies, or the direct sponsorship of program activities. Special interest organizations may be free of commercial involvement or may represent manufacturers of equipment, owners of facilities, schools, or other businesses that seek to stimulate public interest and support and, ultimately, to improve their own business success.

Conservation and Outdoor Recreation Numerous nonprofit organizations seek to educate the public and influence governmental policies in the areas of conservation and outdoor recreation. In some cases, they lobby, conduct research, and sponsor conferences and publications. In others, their primary thrust is to mount projects and carry out direct action on state or local levels.

Sierra Club Founded in 1892 and headed initially by the famous naturalist John Muir, the Sierra Club has sought to make Americans aware "of what we have lost and can lose during 200 years of continuing exploitation of our resources for commodity purposes and failure to realize their value for scenic, scientific, and aesthetic purposes." The Sierra Club has gained an international focus, emphasizing issues of global warming and the effects of recent disasters such as the tsunami in south Asia and Hurricane Katrina. Its activities are not restricted to conservation; it is also the nation's largest skiing and hiking club, operating a major network of ski lodges and "river runners," numerous wilderness outings, and ecological group projects.

Appalachian Mountain Club This organization has a regional focus; its purpose when founded in 1876 was to "explore the mountains of New England and adjacent regions . . . for scientific and artistic purposes, and . . . to cultivate an interest in geographical studies." Since its inception, it has explored and mapped many of the wildest and most scenic areas in Massachusetts, New Hampshire, and Maine, in addition to promoting such sports as skiing, snowshoeing, mountain climbing, and canoeing.

Although practical conservation remains a primary concern of the club, it also has acquired various camp properties, published guides and maps, and maintained hundreds of miles of trails and a network of huts and shelters throughout the White Mountains for use by its members. It promotes programs of instruction and leadership training in such activities as snowshoeing, skiing, smooth and whitewater canoeing, and rock climbing.

Outdoor Leadership Programs A number of other national nonprofit organizations teach outdoor leadership skills and promote sound environmental practices in the wilderness. The National Outdoor Leadership School sponsors a variety of courses in backpacking, mountaineering, rock climbing, sea kayaking, and other outdoor adventure activities in settings throughout the western states, Alaska, and such foreign countries as Australia, Mexico, Argentina, Chile, and Kenya. Outward Bound uses five core programs for character development and self-discovery through challenge and adventure. Initiated in the early 1960s, early programs trained the first Peace Corps volunteers. Since that time it has become a worldwide organization providing training and experiences to more than 500,000 people. The Association for Experiential Education is a professional membership association focusing on experiential education for students, educators, and practitioners. It provides program resources, a national conference, and accreditation for environmental education sites.

Organizations Promoting Youth Sport and Games There are thousands of national, regional, and local organizations promoting and regulating sport of every kind. Although many of these govern professional play or high-level intercollegiate competition, others are concerned with sports and games on a purely amateur basis. One example of such an organization is Little League.

Founded in Williamsport, Pennsylvania, in 1939, Little League is the largest youth sports program in the world today. In its various leagues, including softball, it serves more than 2.6 million players in the United States and more than 3 million players in 91 countries. In 2006, there were almost 7500 organized leagues; in the same year, 290 new programs were chartered, 135 of them outside the United States. Vietnam was one of the new nations initiating a Little League program. Prior to the Little League Baseball World Series, up to 16,000 tournament games are played in a 6-week time frame. Little League operates an impressive headquarters complex and stadium in Williamsport, where camps, conferences, and the annual World Series are held. It has standardized rules of play, requirement for financial operation and fee structures, insurance coverage, approved equipment, and other arrangements for member leagues and teams. Little League also conducts research into youth sport and carries out a great variety of training programs for league officials, district administrators, umpires, managers, and coaches, as well as a series of publications.

Youth sports in general are assisted by national organizations that set standards and promote effective, values-oriented coaching approaches, such as the National Alliance for Youth Sports, the Positive Coaching Alliance, and the National Clearinghouse for Youth Sports Information. Examples of organizations that are particularly concerned with individual sport include Youth Basketball of America, the Young American Bowling Alliance, and the United States Tennis Association (USTA). The latter organization has mounted a vigorous campaign to promote tennis to children and youth through the schools and public recreation agencies. USTA has awarded more than $4 million to support community park and recreation tennis programs.

Arts Councils and Cultural Organizations Another major area of activity for voluntary agencies is the arts. In addition to nonprofit schools and art centers that offer painting, drawing, sculpture, and similar programs, there are literally thousands of civic organizations that sponsor or present performing arts. These include symphony orchestras, bands of various types, choral societies, opera or operetta companies, little theater groups, ballet and modern dance companies, and similar bodies.

Nonprofits, art centers, and civic organizations offer art classes.

In many communities, special interest organizations in the arts are coordinated or assisted by umbrella agencies that help to promote their joint efforts. The Pasadena Arts Council was the first umbrella organization chartered in California. It provides a number of services to its members and the community including a resource guide for artists, a business center for artists and new arts organizations, an information clearinghouse, networking events, financial sponsorship, an arts calendar, and a bimonthly publication. The Pasadena Arts Council efforts are similar to those in communities across the United States.

Service and Fraternal Clubs

Another category of nonprofit organizations that provide recreation for their own membership and sponsor programs for other population groups is community service clubs and fraternal organizations.

These include service clubs such as the Kiwanis, Lions, or Rotary clubs, which represent the business and professional groups in the community and which have as their purpose the improvement of the business environment and contributing to social well-being. A number of organizations established specifically for women, such as the Association of Junior Leagues, the General Federation of Women's Clubs, and the Business and Professional Women's Club, have similar goals.

The goals of such groups may include publicizing environmental concerns or issues, promoting the arts and other cultural activities, helping disadvantaged children and youth, and providing programs for people with disabilities. For example, many Kiwanis organizations are involved in providing camping programs for special populations.

Promotional and Coordinating Bodies

A final type of nonprofit organization in the recreation, parks, and leisure-service field consists of associations that serve to promote, publicize, or coordinate activities within a given recreational field. In bowling, for example, the American Bowling Congress is composed of thousands of individuals whose careers or livelihoods depend on bowling and who therefore seek to promote and guide the sport as aggressively as possible, including setting standards and regulations and sponsoring a range of major tournaments each year.

There are hundreds of such nonprofit organizations in the fields of travel, tourism, entertainment, and hospitality, covering the range from associations of theme park or waterpark management to associations of tour directors or cruise ship operators. As an example, the Outdoor Amusement Business Association works to upgrade standards and services throughout the carnival and outdoor show industry. Its membership consists chiefly of manufacturers and distributors of trailers, tents and tarps, games supplies, and similar materials, as well as operators of many different kinds of traveling shows, concessions, and carnivals. Similarly, the International Association of Amusement Parks and Attractions conducts market studies, publishes standards and guidelines, and sponsors huge conventions and trade shows for thousands of companies worldwide in the tourism, entertainment, and amusement field. The World Waterpark Association assists water parks with trend analysis, customer satisfaction, business skills, training, publications related to the waterpark industry, and an annual trade show.

Within local communities, there are often several types of coordinating groups that serve to exchange information, conduct studies, identify priorities, develop planning reports, provide technical assistance, train leadership, and organize events related to recreation and leisure. In some cases, these include councils of social agencies, including religious, health care, youth-serving, and social work groups.

COMMERCIAL RECREATION

We now turn to the type of recreation sponsor that provides the largest variety of leisure opportunities in the United States today—commercial, profit-oriented businesses. Such organizations have proliferated in recent years, running the gamut from small "mom-and-pop" operations to franchised programs and services; large-scale networks of health and fitness clubs, theme parks, hotels, and casino businesses; manufacturers of games, toys, and hobby equipment; and various other entertainment ventures.

CASE STUDY: Extreme Sports Goes Mainstream and Downtown

Extreme sports is one of the fastest growing group of sports worldwide. It has rapidly gained an international following and become a local commercial and public enterprise as well as a tourist destination activity. Many extreme sports are natural resource based and limited to specific locations. Others are not so location dependent. There has been conflict with resource-dependent extreme sports participants when others perceive their sport to be endangering the natural area. Base-jumping from Half-Dome at Yosemite National Park still remains illegal despite several such jumps each year. Today, the NPS only allows base-jumping one day per year and in one place: off of New River Gorge Bridge in West Virginia.

Skateboarding, surfing, skydiving, snowboarding, motocross, BMX, and other extreme sports began as small, narrowly defined alternative recreation activities engaged in by minimal numbers of people. The participants were frequently ostracized by traditionalists as nontraditional or worse. In downhill skiing, for example, snowboarders were initially banned from the major ski resorts' most popular ski runs. Skateboarders were banned from city streets and public places.

Many people saw extreme sports participants as fringe elements of society. This is an image many still struggle with, even though a large number of participants are seen as mainstream in their occupations, families, and lifestyles. The introduction of the Extreme-Games, now known as the X Games, began an evolutionary change in the way people saw and began to accept extreme sport as mainstream.

The X-Games, which feature numerous skateboarding competitions, helped make extreme sports mainstream.

In 1993, there were almost no skateparks and the sport appeared to be dying; if not for the X Games, which emerged that year, it may have died. Instead, there was a resurgence. Participants such as Tony Hawk gave legitimacy to the sport and became heroes to a growing number of participants and spectators. By 2009, the number of skateparks in the United States increased to the thousands, with many cities boasting several to many skateparks. In some communities, skateparks are seen as essential as playgrounds. This is a dynamic change in less than 20 years.

For resource-dependent extreme sports, however, the ability to make access easy has been more challenging. South Bend, Indiana, created a whitewater park by diverting a river through a renovated canal that could meet whitewater competition standards. Climbing walls became popular and began to appear in commercial and public recreation sites. However, the idea of capturing that ever elusive perfect wave or kayaking on an Olympic-standard whitewater slalom course was more challenging.

Technology, private enterprise, and imagination have risen to the challenge. Today world-class extreme sport facilities are being planned for every corner of the world. Waveyard (www.waveyard.com), an extreme water sport–based commercial enterprise and resort, is planned for Mesa, Arizona. The complex includes the largest wavepool in the southwestern United States with multiple types of waves, whitewater rafting in the largest man-made river with multiple channels that also allows for kayaking, a scuba center, wakeboarding, indoor water-slides, and a climbing center. The facility is anchored with commercial, retail, and resort venues. The focus, however, remains on the waterpark concept, but in this case one that caters to casual through extreme users.

In London, England, VentureExtreme is billing itself as the world's premiere adventure center. Being built in east London in a brownfield, the venture will cover 360 acres and is projected to cost almost $450 million. There will be four "sport zones," including water sports, vertical sports, wheel sports, and children's sports. A variety of extreme sports has been integrated into the different components. For example, the climbing wall will be almost 60,000 square feet, or the size of six football fields. It will include artificial caves, a bungee jump, three high-ropes adventure courses, an abseiling room, and a 550-yard zip wire. The water zone components will be similar to those of the Mesa project. All of the facilities are designed so that they can host international competitions.

Each of these enterprises has taken traditional facilities and added extreme sport to them. They recognize, however, that extreme sport may not generate sufficient revenue to cover the cost of operations and have built in family and less adventurous activities in an effort to broaden the customer base.

Extreme sports is a part of today's mainstream recreation culture. Major investments are being made by commercial enterprises, but nonprofits and public parks and recreation are providing facilities and opportunities in communities throughout the United States.

Questions to Consider

1. How do you think extreme sports affect opportunities to participate in recreation?
2. What are the advantages of having an extreme sport facility in your community?
3. How many venues should an extreme sport facility have to be successful? Why?

The Nature of Commercial Recreation

Commercial recreation is easily defined. John Bullaro and Christopher Edginton write:

> A commercial leisure service organization can be thought of as a business, the primary purpose of which is to serve people while at the same time making a profit. [It] has two basic characteristics. First, it creates and distributes leisure services; second, it has as its primary goal, profit.[20]

The profit motive distinguishes a recreation business from any other type of leisure-service sponsor. Although public or voluntary agencies may charge for their services and may seek to clear a profit on individual program elements—or at least to run them on a self-sustaining basis where possible—their overall purpose is to meet important community or social needs. However, the commercial recreation organization has as a primary thrust the need to show a profit on the overall operation. Without commercial businesses that provide a host of important and high-quality leisure experiences, our recreational opportunities would be sharply diminished.

Commercial recreation sponsors today have the following characteristics: (1) They must constantly seek to identify and capitalize on recreational interests that are on the rise to ensure a constant or growing level of participation; (2) they are flexible and independent in their programmatic decisions and are not subject to the policy strictures of a city or town council or an agency board of trustees; (3) they constantly seek to promote and create experiences by packaging a product that will appeal to the public, by systematic marketing research, and by creative advertising and public relations; and (4) to be successful, they depend on effective entrepreneurship—a creative and aggressive approach to management that is willing to take risks to make gains.

Amusement parks are a growth industry serving millions of people annually.

Some of the most significant, creative, and cutting-edge facilities are provided by commercial recreation. Amusement parks, waterparks, megatheaters, speedways, and sports stadiums may be the first to come to mind, but commercial recreation is present in almost every community. It may be the local dance studio, or the combative-arts studio, or a crafts store that offers classes. Enterprises large and small continue to flourish in most communities. Quilt stores regularly have a room full of sewing machines, long-arm quilting machines, and the like, and classes are full. Stop by the Arthur Murray Dance Studio and see more full classes. Slot car tracks exist in many communities, as well as hobby shops, scuba shops, skydiving enterprises, tour buses, family recreation centers—the list could go on for pages. These commercial enterprises, regardless of their size, stay in business because they meet a need for recreation participation. It is not uncommon for commercial recreation enterprises to partner with public and nonprofit agencies.

Categories of Service

Commercial recreation services may be classified under several major headings, including the following:

- Admission to facilities, either for self-directed participation (as in the use of a rented tennis court or an ice skating rink or billiard parlor) or for participation with some degree of supervision, instruction, or scheduling (as in admission to a ski center with use of a ski tow).
- Organized instruction in individual leisure activities or areas of personal enrichment, such as classes in arts and crafts, music, dance, or other hobbies.
- Membership in a commercially operated club, such as a for-profit tennis, golf, or boat club.

- Provision of hospitality or social contacts, ranging from hotels and resorts to bars, casinos, singles clubs, or dating services, which may use computers, videotaping, telephone contacts, or other means to help clients meet each other. At the socially less acceptable end of this spectrum of services are escort services, massage parlors, and sexually-oriented telephone conversation operations.
- Arranged tours or cruises, domestic or foreign, which may consist solely of travel arrangements or which may also include a full package of travel, housing accommodations, meals, special events, side trips, and guide services.
- Commercial manufacture, sale, and service of recreation-related equipment, including sport supplies, electronic products, boats, off-road vehicles, toys, games, and hobby equipment.
- Entertainment and special events, such as theater, rock concerts, circuses, rodeos, and other such activities, when they are sponsored by a for-profit business, rather than a nonprofit, tax-exempt group.

Several of these types of commercial recreation businesses are described in the concluding section of this chapter. Others, such as sport and games and travel and tourism, are presented in Chapters 10 and 11.

Family Entertainment Centers

Another recently evolved for-profit recreation enterprise includes family entertainment centers that combine children's play activities and equipment, video games, and other computerized activities with refreshments.

These businesses developed as an outgrowth of such "kiddie exercise" programs as Gymboree, which expanded as franchised chains that were usually situated in shopping malls. Family fun centers such as Malibu Grand Prix broadened their appeal, by adding more family-slanted activities, such as miniature golf, bumper cars, video games, and other indoor games, and packaged them with fast food options such as pizza, hot dogs, and soft drinks for birthday party and other group visits.

Theme Parks, Water Parks, and Marine and Wildlife Parks

Closely linked to the growth of tourism as a form of recreation has been the expansion of theme parks such as California's famous Disneyland. This major entertainment complex was built at a cost of more than $50 million in the 1950s and covers 65 acres in Anaheim, California. Its success led to the construction of a second major Disney complex, Walt Disney World, at Lake Buena Vista, Florida.

New Kinds of Theme Parks Other entertainment entrepreneurs soon followed the Disney example, and by 1976 at least three dozen parks of similar scale had been built around the United States. Some parks concentrate on a single theme, such as Opryland, U.S.A. in Nashville, Tennessee, and Holiday World and Splashing Safari in Indiana. Others incorporate moving rides through settings based on literary, historical, or international themes; entertainment; and typical amusement park "thrill" rides such as roller coasters and parachute jumps. By 2005 theme parks were reporting 335 million annual visits and $11.2 billion in revenues.

Another unusual facility, opened in the early 1980s by Busch Gardens, was Adventure Island in Tampa, Florida. This 30-acre water park provides vistas of white sand beaches, glistening waters, palm trees, and tropical plants. Built on varied levels with complex

Amusement Parks Are Major Tourist Attractions

Before Disneyland opened in 1955, amusement parks were local attractions, some large, some small. Disneyland changed the amusement park business forever. It did not replace the local amusement park; it signaled the beginning of the tourist destination amusement park. One or more amusement parks can be found in almost every major city of the country. Orland, Florida, has become the amusement capital of the United States.

Growing with the amusement park industry is the International Association of Amusement Parks and Attractions (IAAPA). Started in 1918, it now boasts more than 4500 members from 93 countries and is the largest organization in the world that supports amusement parks. Its membership is associated with some areas of the amusement park industry. They include family entertainment centers, large parks and theme parks, museums, waterparks, zoos and aquariums, resorts, hotels, and casinos, small parks and attractions, and manufacturers and suppliers. IAAPA has an international perspective, hosting three international trade shows: one each in Europe, Asia, and the Americas. Each is called an *AttractionsExpo* with content focusing on the industry, management, safety, education, marketing, operations, and products.

Disney theme parks dominate attendance records for amusement parks.

The list of top 10 performing amusement parks worldwide helps demonstrate how large this marketplace is and the dominance of the Disney brand:

- Magic Kingdom (Florida)—17,063,000
- Disneyland Park (California)—14,721,000
- Tokyo Disneyland (Tokyo)—14,293,000
- Disneyland Park at Disneyland Paris (Paris)—12,688,000
- Tokyo Disney Sea (Tokyo)—12,498,000
- Epcot (Florida)—10,935,000
- Disney's Hollywood Studios (Florida)—9,608,000
- Disney's Animal Kingdom (Florida)—9,540,000
- Universal Studios Japan (Osaka)—8,300,000
- Everland (Gyeonggi-Do, South Korea)—6,600,000

waterfalls, slides, pools, cliffs, and rocks, Adventure Island provides an all-inclusive water experience in which visitors slide down twisting water chutes.

Expansion of Disney Entertainment Empire None of the other chains of theme parks or outdoor play centers could match the diversity and inventiveness of the Disney planners. In

1982, Disney opened EPCOT (an acronym for Experimental Prototype Community of Tomorrow), an $800 million, 260-acre (105.2 hectares) development that was conceived as being more than a theme park. Instead, EPCOT was intended to be a place that would offer an environment where people of many nations might meet and exchange ideas. It consists of two sections: Future World, which contains corporate pavilions primarily concerned with technology; and World Showcase, which has international pavilions designed to show the tourist attractions of various nations around the world.

Since then, Disney World has added a number of other spectacular and imaginative attractions, including Typhoon Lagoon, the Disney MGM Studios, and, in 1995, Blizzard Beach, Florida's first "snow-capped" water park; it is patterned after an alpine ski resort, with mountain slopes covered with toboggan slides, ski jumps, and slalom runs. In 1983, a Disneyland opened in Japan on 202 acres (81.7 hectares) of landfill in Tokyo Bay. It featured the traditional Disney characters and popular rides and attractions. Although the attraction was owned by a Japanese corporation, Disney provided technology and guidance during the construction and operation of Tokyo Disneyland for a share of the gross ticket take. Then, with the opening of Disneyland Paris, otherwise known as Euro Disney, the company created the largest theme park in Europe.

Throughout the 1990s, Disney continued to add new attractions and program features. In 1997, Disney's 200-acre (80.9-hectare) Wide World of Sports offered a 7500-seat stadium and other facilities as a venue for the Atlanta Braves, the Harlem Globetrotters, and the Indiana Pacers as well as thousands of other competitors on every age level in several different sports. Through a cooperative arrangement with the Amateur Athletic Union, national youth tournaments in baseball, basketball, softball, and tennis, among others, are held at this facility.

Amusement parks are present in almost every major community, and the parks provide locally available thrill experiences for participants.

Other Parks There are literally hundreds of theme parks in the United States today. Orlando, Florida, can be considered the theme park capital of the United States. Universal's Orlando Islands of Adventure is typical of many of today's large theme parks. The park has five distinctive themes, similar to what Disneyland introduced. The themes are linked to Universal Studios films, cartoons, or specific activities. For example, Toon Lagoon, a water park, has rides named for different cartoon characters, such as Dudley Do-Right's Rip Saw Falls.

Cedar Point, located in Sandusky, Ohio, is an example of a regional theme park that provides multiple experiences on a single site. Typical of a growth industry in theme parks is the roller coaster. Cedar Point boasts 17 different roller coaster rides, ranging from the Wicked Twister, a 215-foot-tall (65.5-meters), 72-mph (115.9-kph) steel stunner, to the Millenium Force, a 310-feet-tall roller coaster with a top speed of 93 mph that is targeted toward young riders.

However, not all theme parks rely on such forms of entertainment. Dollywood, for example, a complex of shops, rides, shows, craft centers, restaurants, and other theatrical features based on folk themes, is an outstanding tourist attraction in the Great Smoky

Mountain National Park Region. Linked to the image of Dolly Parton, the popular movie actress and country music star, Dollywood offers gospel music performances, harvest celebrations, a "showcase" series of well-known performers, and other programs attuned to its traditional Appalachian Mountain environment.

Water Parks A specialized type of theme park today consists of water parks—tourist destinations that feature wave pools, slides, chutes, shows, and other forms of water-based play and entertainment. There are about 1000 water parks today that provide such outdoor play in the United States, mainly in southern states with warmer climates. They are not restricted to warmer areas, however. The Wisconsin Dells for example, is famous for the number of indoor and outdoor water parks in the region. One of the largest water parks is located inside the west Edmonton Mall in Canada.

Often, water attractions are part of larger theme park operations. In Universal's Islands of Adventure, for example, the Jurassic Park River Adventure and Popeye and Bluto's Bilge Rat Barges offer either whirling and steep whitewater rides and sluice falls or swirling vortexes that spray riders thoroughly. Each year, dozens of new water parks open, with the latest technology, marketing, and management skills taught to their operators at conventions held by the American Water Park Association.

Zoos, Marine Parks, and Wildlife Parks The addition of rides and other entertainment features to animal attractions is making marine and wild animal parks increasingly popular among tourists. Annually, members of the American Zoo and Aquarium Association in the United States receive approximately 175 million visitors.[21] Wild animal parks have seen steady growth in recent years where visitors of all ages are offered the opportunity to view big game and exotic animals in natural (or semiwild) settings.

Other Fun Centers

In heavily populated metropolitan areas throughout the United States, other entrepreneurs have developed a variety of indoor fun centers, ranging from children's play, gymnastics, and exercise chains to family party centers, video game arcades, and huge restaurants with game areas. Fun centers are not just for children but adults as well. Dave and Buster's, an immensely successful chain of adult "fun and food" offerings in Dallas, Houston, Atlanta, Chicago, Philadelphia, and expanding into 20 states, Canada, and Mexico, offers a host of simulated fun experiences: golf, motorcycling, race car driving, space combat, and virtual reality, among others.

Similarly, the children's and family play centers that have been established in thousands of suburban neighborhoods and shopping malls around the United States offer a combination of computer and video games, billiards and other table games, miniature golf, entertainment by clowns and magicians, music, and popular fast-food refreshments. Offering packaged birthday parties and other family play services, they illustrate commercial recreation's success in providing attractive play activities that have supplanted more traditional home-based and "do it yourself" kinds of recreation.

Outdoor Recreation

The broad field of outdoor recreation—defined as leisure pursuits that depend on the outdoor environment for their special appeal or character—represents an important area of commercially sponsored services. Although a major portion of outdoor recreation is carried on in government-managed settings, many activities are provided by for-profit enterprises.

In 2001, the U.S. Fish and Wildlife Service reported that 105.9 million Americans aged 16 and older fished, hunted, and watched wildlife each year, including 34 million anglers and 13 million hunters, a decline in each activity from the previous year. There was an increase in wildlife watchers to 61.4 million. Outdoor recreation equipment sales had grown at a steady rate for more than 10 years. In 2003, fishing tackle sales totaled $2 billion, hunting and firearm sales were $5.6 billion, alpine skiing was $337 million, and camping was $1.5 billion.

Commercial recreation in the outdoors takes many forms, including hunting preserves and guide services; charter fishing and other private fishing operations; marinas and other boating services; ski centers and schools; campgrounds, adventure recreation, vacation ranches, and farms; paintball centers; and numerous other pursuits.

In many cases, a single company, such as Pocono Whitewater Adventures in Jim Thorpe, Pennsylvania, may offer several different types of adventure activities, such as river rafting, whitewater kayaking, family biking excursions, or paintball, at different seasons of the year. Numerous hunting businesses throughout the United States offer the opportunity to shoot big game and in some cases exotic species imported from other continents. Both inland and ocean fishing represent another huge industry. Boating alone represents a major segment of the outdoor recreation market, with annual retail sales in 2002 estimated at almost $30 billion. Florida ranked first with sales of $1.48 billion, followed by California at $1.42 billion, and then Texas, Michigan, Minnesota, New York, North Carolina, Wisconsin, Washington, and New Jersey. Sport fishing sales were even greater in Florida: They hit $4 billion in 2002.

Health Spas and Fitness Clubs

Commercial fitness centers and health clubs constitute a major source of leisure spending in the United States. Although those who join such facilities may have varying kinds of motivations, ranging from actual health concerns to a cosmetic concern with appearance, the reality is that health spas often offer an attractive social setting, particularly for single men and women.

This overall field includes a variety of program emphases, such as aquatic and fitness centers with varied pool facilities, exercise equipment rooms, aerobics and Jazzercise classes, yoga or Oriental exercise groups, conditioning counseling or remedial services, and similar options with annual fees that may range up to thousands of dollars.

As a variation of such health-connected services, many nonprofit hospitals or long-term care facilities have established for-profit subsidiary companies that offer a wide range of exercise programs, physical therapy, aerobic classes, and innovative techniques that include hypnosis, pain management, acupuncture, and other alternative forms of treatment serving the public at large. They may also focus on holistic and homeopathic treatment, including meditation groups, clubs dealing with specific forms of illness, such as arthritis, "overeaters anonymous," "living with loss," and massage and reflexology methods.

Other For-Profit Ventures

Beyond the examples just cited, commercial recreation today includes a host of other kinds of social and hobby activities and amusement or entertainment ventures. Private golf or tennis clubs, bowling alleys and billiard parlors, contract bridge or chess clubs, night clubs and dance halls, and even dating services and gambling casinos are all part of this picture. In a sense, movies, television, video games, book publishing, and music CDs are all aspects of popular culture that represent forms of commercialized leisure. A growing marketplace is quilting. Long thought to be the domain of grandmothers, quilting stores are present in many communities. They sell material, quilting-related items, and specialized quilting machines, and sponsor classes, tours, cruises, exhibitions, and competitions.

In addition, both amateur sport participation and professional spectator sport and travel and tourism involve huge elements in the commercial recreation field and are discussed in detail later.

DIFFERENCES AND SIMILARITIES AMONG AGENCIES

This chapter describes the provision of organized recreation services today by three types of organizations: public or governmental, nonprofit or voluntary, and commercial recreation businesses. Clearly, each of these types of leisure-service organization plays a different role in the overall recreational system, while at the same time interacting with and supplementing the other types.

Public recreation and park agencies, for example, have a major responsibility for maintaining and operating outdoor resources such as parks, forests, playgrounds, sport and aquatic facilities, and, in many cases, indoor centers, performing arts halls, conference or convention halls, stadiums, and similar facilities. Their obligation is to serve the public at large, including individuals and families at all socioeconomic levels and without regard to ethnic, religious, or other demographic differences. However, given the intensified use of marketing-based fees and charges for many recreation programs, many government recreation and park agencies today are not reaching community groups with limited economic capability.

Amateur sporting events in major urban centers are frequently integrated into existing parks where activities share spaces.

Nonprofit voluntary agencies are generally most concerned with social values and with achieving constructive outcomes either for the community or for specific population groups. They see recreation both as an end in itself and as a means to an end and are generally respectful of the environment and sensitive to gender- and race-related issues. Particularly in terms of serving young people and special recreation interests, they are able to offer richer programs than many public agencies. Nonprofits fill voids that public and commercial agencies cannot or won't fill.

Of the three types of sponsors, commercial recreation sponsors provide by far the greatest range of recreational services and opportunities today, and they represent a steadily growing sphere of organized leisure programming. In some ways, profit-oriented businesses are similar to public and nonprofit recreation and park agencies in terms of their offerings and the leisure needs they satisfy. What distinguishes them is their ability to commit substantial sums to developing facilities and programs that will attract the public. Huge corporations that are able to design and build theme parks, aquatic complexes, stadiums, health and fitness clubs, and other types of specialized equipment or programs obviously have a tremendous advantage in appealing to those who are able to pay the necessary fees and charges. Commercial recreation sponsors have harnessed technology and industry in creating spectacular environments for play and have used the most subtle and sophisticated public relations and advertising techniques to market their products successfully.

Social Values in Recreation Planning

It would be wrong to assume that commercial recreation businesses are entirely free to provide any sort of leisure activity without considering its social impact.

Health clubs, camps, theaters, dance halls, gambling casinos, taverns, and a host of other facilities are subject to regulation under state, county, and municipal laws. These may include provisions regarding the sale of liquor, sanitary conditions, service to minors, safety practices, hours of operation, and similar restrictions. Many enterprises that require licenses may have these withdrawn if the operators do not conform to approved practices. Similarly, trade associations often influence practices, even though they may not have the legal power to enforce their rulings. Public attitudes—as expressed in the press, through the statements of leading citizens, civic officials, or religious organizations, or through consumer pressures—often are able to influence the operators in desired directions. For example, when Time Warner was sharply criticized in the press for its promotion of violent, racist, and sexist rap music products, it divested itself of the involved recording label.

The competition of other organizations and products is another key factor in the management of commercial recreation agencies. Often, better products and services within a branch of the industry will serve to drive out inferior competitors. The entire field of recreation service and participation may be viewed as a marketing system in which the economic forces of supply and demand work so that as a new product or service appears, existing products and services are threatened. Within this framework, there is a constant pruning and reshuffling of recreation enterprises as competing sponsors seek to maintain public interest and attendance.

PARTNERSHIPS AMONG MAJOR LEISURE-SERVICE AGENCIES

Although public, nonprofit, and commercial leisure-service agencies are dealt with separately in this chapter, it is important to emphasize that in actual practice they often join together in cooperative ventures. For example, a survey of more than 100 cities found that almost all municipal recreation and parks departments conducted programs with other agencies and organizations; more than half of the respondents had 10 or more synergetic programs during the year. They worked closely with voluntary agencies, schools and colleges, service clubs, and business and industry to promote sport, cultural, and other types of events and projects.

Partnering among public, nonprofit, and commercial recreation providers is commonplace. Where these agencies once jealously guarded their own areas, they have embraced the concept that partnering better serves the public and individual agencies. Public and nonprofit agencies are frequently judged on their effectiveness by the number and quality of the partnerships they establish.

Many forms of partnerships are created by park and recreation agencies working with nonprofits, commercial organizations, other government agencies, private individuals, special interest groups, and others. They can be as simple as the city parks and recreation department providing space for a model airplane club to construct a runway or as complex as multiple agencies working together to manage a unique natural resource. There is a long history of the National Park Service working with state park agencies and local park and recreation departments. The Bureau of Land Management has transferred land to public agencies, such as to the Grand Junction, Colorado, Parks and Recreation Department, to help maintain a buffer between urban development and natural areas. Special recreation associations, initially unique to Illinois, are the creation of multiple park districts joining together to develop a professional organization with the primary purpose of providing services to people with disabilities. The special recreation associations operate as a separate service, yet integrate their services into existing park district programs using the resources of the association that exceed those of any individual park district.

Sponsorship of recreation programs is increasing, as sponsors frequently have their organizations depicted at events.

Numerous examples may also be shown of partnerships in the areas of open space acquisition and environmental recovery. The Trust for Public Land (TPL) annually takes on numerous projects working with local public agencies, nonprofit, and neighborhood groups. Recently TPL teamed up with Saint Paul, Minnesota, to renovate an abandoned railyard that was both an eyesore and a toxic problem. Neighborhood groups, redevelopment groups, and volunteers all joined together to work on the project. TPL entered into negotiations with the railroad and over a 3-year period cleaned up the contamination with $3.5 million in donations and contributions from multiple sources, including government agencies. The now-named Vento Nature Sanctuary is part of the Mississippi National River and Recreation Area.[22]

Similarly, nonprofit organizations are frequently involved in collaborative program efforts. Typically, Boy and Girl Scout troops often work closely with churches and religious organizations or with school boards. The YMCA encourages numerous partnership arrangements with local park and recreation departments, schools and colleges, public housing boards, hospitals, and even correctional institutions. In 2006, the YMCA funded 40 community collaborative projects working jointly with the Centers for Disease Control and Prevention to expand community ability and to identify or create programs that create positive health-related behavior change. The YMCA joined with more than 20 national organizations to make the program a success. Examples of programs are Montgomery, Alabama; Rochester, New York; Tulsa, Oklahoma; and Santa Clara, California.

Different collaborations are beginning to emerge as agencies begin serving an older American population. Lewisburg, Pennsylvania, created the first multigenerational park as a destination designed to bring together different age groups to enjoy experiences while in close proximity. The emphasis was on the environment, families, and activity, recognizing that such an approach met the needs of many different age groups. Many communities are now recognizing that older Americans use parks more frequently than other age groups do and are beginning to cooperate within their communities to modify parks to fit the needs of older adults. The University of Illinois is working with a variety of groups, including park and recreation agencies, to develop New Active Green Environments facilities that strive to improve the cardiovascular health, muscle strength, and flexibility of older Americans, understanding that the new older generation is different from all previous aging generations.[23]

Finally, professional societies have been successful in initiating a number of partnerships, particularly in the area of youth sports. The National Recreation and Park Association (NRPA), for example, joined *Sports Illustrated* in Good Sports to create a local assessment of the strength and gaps in youth sport. In addition, the NRPA developed joint ventures with the United States Tennis Association; the National Football League's Flag Football program; Major League Baseball's pitch, hit, and run program; the National Basketball Association's junior NBA and junior WNBA; and the Hershey Track and Field youth program to reach millions of children and youth through these sports. Collaborative arrangements of this type are growing in number and variety and are helping to build a climate of mutual assistance among the different elements that constitute the leisure-service system.

SUMMARY

Government's role with respect to organized leisure services is diversified. On the federal level, government is concerned with the management of outdoor recreation resources, either as a primary function or within a multiple-use concept, through such agencies as the National Park Service, U.S. Forest Service, Bureau of Land Management, and TVA. The federal government also assists states and local political units through funding and technical assistance for programs serving children and youth, those with disabilities, the older adults, and similar groups.

State governments operate major park systems and play an important role in promoting environmental conservation and outdoor recreation opportunities. They also set standards and pass enabling legislation defining the role of local governments in the area of recreation and parks. In addition, states have traditionally maintained networks of state hospitals and special schools for those with disabilities, although this function has been reduced in recent years as a result of deinstitutionalization trends that involve placing many such individuals in community settings.

The chief sponsors of government recreation and park programs are on the local level—city, town, county, and special district government agencies. They operate many different types of facilities and offer a wide range of classes, sports leagues, special events, the arts, social activities, and other leisure areas. They also provide or assist in many programs in the human services area. Although many municipal departments have expanded their revenue source operations, departments in other larger and older cities suffer from depleted staff resources and have limited program and maintenance potential.

Voluntary agencies place their greatest emphasis on using leisure to achieve positive social goals. Several types of youth-serving organizations are described, including both sectarian and nonsectarian groups. Such agencies rarely consider themselves to be primarily recreation organizations; instead, they generally prefer to be regarded as educational, character-building, or youth-serving organizations. However, recreation usually does constitute a sector of their program activities.

A second type of nonprofit leisure-service agency consists of special interest groups, which usually promote a particular area of activity in outdoor recreation, sport, the arts, or hobbies. Such groups, although they may include many enthusiasts as members, are often formed to promote business interests within the particular leisure specialization.

Commercial recreation businesses offer an immense number of public recreational opportunities in such areas as travel and tourism, outdoor recreation, sport, popular entertainment, the mass media, hobbies, and crafts. Their primary goal is to make a consistent profit through the creation of experiences. In many cases, they are large and highly diversified operations, such as the Walt Disney organization, with its theme parks, resorts, and television, movies, Internet, and popular music components. From a social perspective, many for-profit businesses offer constructive, high-quality programs. However, in some cases—as in sectors of the entertainment industry—they are believed to contribute to youth violence, sexism, and racial hostility.

QUESTIONS FOR CLASS DISCUSSION OR ESSAY EXAMINATION

1. Review the major recreation and park functions of either the federal government or state governments, identifying key agencies and their leisure-related roles. Apart from managing resources for outdoor recreation, what are the other important activities of these two levels of government?
2. Municipal recreation and park departments, including city, town, or other types of local public agencies, provide a diverse range of leisure opportunities for community residents today. What are some of the major trends in municipal recreation programming in recent years, and what problems have affected such departments as a result of fiscal austerity?
3. Discuss the concept of partnership arrangements among governmental and other types of nonpublic community organizations, in terms of recreation programming. What are the values and what are several examples of such partnership arrangements?
4. What are the major differences between voluntary nonprofit agencies and government departments providing recreation facilities and programs? Compare goals and objectives, funding, individuals or groups served, and program elements.
5. Define commercial recreation agencies and indicate several of the major categories of leisure services provided by such businesses. Select one major area of commercial recreation, such as outdoor recreation or travel and tourism, and describe trends in this field, the nature of service offered, and problems or issues connected to that particular recreation area.

ENDNOTES

1. President George W. Bush, excerpt from National Park Week Proclamation, 2003.
2. National Geographic Society, "About Us." http://www.nationalgeographic.com/donate/aboutus.html.
3. National Park Service, "Natural Resource Year in Review." http://www.nature.nps.gov/YearInReview/YIR2006/03_d.html.
4. U.S. Forest Service, "Climate Change Resource Center: Frequently Asked Questions." http://www.fs.fed.us/ccrc/frequently_asked_questions.shtml.
5. Office of the Press Secretary, White House, President George W. Bush, *Establishment of the Pacific Remote Islands Marine National Monument*. http://www.fws.gov/pacificremoteislandsmarinemonument/PP%20PRIMNM.pdf.
6. U.S. Department of the Interior Bureau of Land Management, "NLCS Summary Tables." http://www.blm.gov/wo/st/en/prog/blm_special_areas/NLCS/monuments/00.html.
7. Bureau of Land Management, *Budget Justifications and Performance Information: Fiscal Year 2009*. http://www.osmre.gov/topic/budget/docs/FY09.pdf
8. U.S. Department of Agriculture, Farm Service Agency, "Conservation Programs." http://www.fsa.usda.gov/FSA/webapp?area=home&subject=copr&topic=landing.
9. National Endowment for the Arts, "Poetry Out Loud: National Recitation Contest." http://www.nea.gov/national/poetry/index.html.
10. National Endowment for the Arts, "Operation Homecoming." http://www.nea.gov/national/homecoming/index.html.
11. National Endowment for the Arts, "The Big Read." http://www.nea.gov/national/bigread/index.html.
12. Daniel D. McLean, *The 2006 Annual Information Exchange* (Raleigh, NC: National Association of State Park Directors, 2006).
13. KaBoom! "Our Vision and Mission." http://kaboom.org/about_kaboom/mission.
14. City of Henderson Parks and Recreation Department, "City of Henderson Named a 2009 Playful City USA," City of Henderson, Nevada (14 July 2009). http://www.cityofhenderson.com/parks/news_releases/named-a-2009-playful-city-usa.php.
15. Carey Goldbert, "Boston Leading a Renewal of Old Northern Cities," *New York Times* (3 November 1998).
16. U.S. Department of Labor Bureau of Labor Statistics, "Volunteering in the United States, 2009" (26 January 2010). http://www.bls.gov/news.release/volun.nr0.htm.
17. Heather MacDonald, "Why the Boy Scouts Work," *City Journal* (Winter 2000). http://www.city-journal.org.
18. Girl Scouts. http://www.girlscouts.org.
19. Best Buddies. http://www.bestbuddies.org/best-buddies.
20. J. Bullaro and C. Edginton, *Commercial Leisure Services: Managing for Profit, Service, and Personal Satisfaction* (New York: Macmillan, 1986): 17.
21. Association of Zoos and Aquariums, "Zoo and Aquarium Statistics." http://www.aza.org/zoo-aquarium-statistics.
22. V. Monks, "Off the Tracks," *Land and People* (Vol. 18, No. 1, 2006): 20–29.
23. Geoffrey Godbey, "Providing More for Older Adults," *Parks and Recreation* (October 2005): 76–81.

CHAPTER 9

SPECIALIZED LEISURE-SERVICE AREAS

◆ ◆ ◆

Most would agree that the leisure services field does not meet the strict criteria of a profession along the lines of law, education, or medicine. Part of the issue is a difficulty in defining leisure services—what is the encompassing field of professional services and its core body of knowledge common to all of the areas outlined in this text? Each of the leisure services areas has unique service components, knowledge, skills, abilities, clients, and so forth.[1]

◆ ◆ ◆

INTRODUCTION

Having examined three areas of organized leisure services that are designed for the public at large, we now turn to five categories of recreation services that meet more specialized needs and interests. These five areas are recreation for people with disabilities; armed forces morale, welfare, and recreation services; employee recreation services; campus recreation; and private-membership organizations. Each of these areas serves a specific type of population or organization, with goals and program elements geared to meet its specific needs.

Throughout the analysis of these five leisure-service areas, emphasis is placed on the dynamic changes that have occurred from the traditional models that evolved in the twentieth century to more innovative forms of service found today.

THERAPEUTIC RECREATION SERVICE

The roots of today's use of recreation to improve health conditions in treatment settings can be traced back to Benjamin Rush, an American physician, and Florence Nightingale, a British nurse. Both of these figures were advocates of the therapeutic value of recreation. Over the past 50 years, the expanded use of recreation and leisure in hospitals, physical rehabilitation, mental health, and long-term care settings has demonstrated its increased value as a treatment approach and the importance of having a recreation therapist on the treatment team. During this same period, there was tremendous growth in the provision of specialized or adapted recreation services in the community for people with disabilities.

This role in the recreation profession has a variety of names including recreation therapist, therapeutic recreation specialist, inclusion specialist, and activity therapist, just to name a few. The American Therapeutic Recreation Association (ATRA) defines recreation therapy as "a treatment service designed to restore, remediate and rehabilitate a person's level of functioning and independence in life activities, to promote health and wellness as well as reduce or eliminate the activity limitations and restrictions to participation in life situations caused by an illness or disabling condition."[2] Therapeutic recreation has been defined as " engaging people in planned recreation and related experiences in order to improve functioning, health and well-being, and quality of life, while focusing on the whole person and the needed changes in the optimal living environment."[3] These two definitions seem very similar and have sparked much discussion in the profession. One view is that *therapeutic recreation* can serve as the umbrella term where utilization and enhancement of leisure is the primary purpose, and recreation therapy has the primary purpose of intervention and improving functional abilities.[4] For the purposes of this text, the term *therapeutic recreation* is used.

Early Development of Therapeutic Recreation

The history of past centuries provides a number of examples of the use of recreation in the treatment of psychiatric patients, in both Europe and America. The fullest impetus for therapeutic recreation, however, came in the twentieth century in three types of institutions: hospitals and rehabilitation centers for those with physical impairments, hospitals for people with mental illness, and special schools for those with developmental disabilities.

After both World War I and World War II, there were waves of concern about the need to rehabilitate veterans who had sustained major physical injuries or psychological trauma while in service. As a consequence, Veterans Administration and military hospitals developed comprehensive programs of rehabilitative services, including physical and occupational therapy, psychotherapy, social services, vocational training, guidance, and recreation. In such settings, recreation was perceived as being one of several techniques that contributed to patient recovery.

At the same time, recreation gained recognition as a form of allied or adjunctive service within such civilian institutions as special homes or schools for individuals with mental retardation or other disabilities, nursing homes and long-term care institutions, and state or private psychiatric hospitals or mental health centers. Gradually, *therapeutic recreation*, as it came to be known, gained acceptance in the healthcare field. Colleges and universities initiated major curricula or degree options in this field, and professional societies developed standards for practice and accreditation and certification procedures for practitioners.

Although all individuals need diverse recreation outlets, those with disabilities encounter barriers that those without disabilities do not, substantially narrowing their options for participation. In part this is because of significant and sometimes multiple disabling conditions that restrict physical, cognitive, and/or emotional functioning. Many times, however, the problems with access to recreation opportunities can be attributed to attitudinal, architectural, programmatic, and transportation barriers.

Smith et al.[5] explored the question of why persons with disabilities have been underserved by community recreation and leisure services. They suggest that in the first half of the twentieth century the way society generally treated people during this period who did not fit the norm was to separate and hide them away and this produced a similar philosophy within the evolving field of recreation. Examples include the "old folks homes" for older people who were indigent, or warehousing people with mental retardation in large institutions away from populated areas, and placing people with mental health problems in similarly remote "insane asylums." While attitudes toward vulnerable populations were shifting during the 1960s, 1970s, and early 1980s, there were other barriers for public parks and recreation to contend with, both real and perceived. These included lack of funding, inaccessible facilities, untrained staff, lack of knowledge to develop such programs, lack of accessible community transportation, continuing attitudinal barriers, and lack of awareness of the great need for recreation participation by people with disabilities.

In some cases, recreation and park departments barred people with disabilities from their programs, arguing that serving such people would impose higher risk of accident lawsuits and increased insurance costs. We now know this is not true. In other cases, parents, relatives, and schools have sheltered them excessively, or the individual's perceived lack of ability or fear of rejection by others caused him or her to limit his or her recreation participation.

Therapeutic Recreation Job Settings

Therapeutic recreation (TR) professionals can find themselves working in the government sector, commercial sector, and nonprofit sector. TR specialists can predominantly work in one of two areas of practice—clinical settings or community settings.

TR specialists in a clinical setting often work in nursing homes and hospitals. Nursing home TR staff plan programs to help residents with their long-term, day-to-day function. There may be programs to enhance memory skills, social skills, and fitness levels. In hospital settings, TR specialists work with patients in four main areas: acute care, outpatient care, psychiatric care, and rehabilitation hospitals.[6] Acute care hospitals are for people with more serious illnesses and injuries on a short-term basis. TR specialists work with patients to prepare them for discharge or their next facility, such as a nursing home or rehabilitation center. Once discharged, a patient may move to outpatient care where they receive TR services while living at home. Psychiatric care is available for people with mental illnesses. Psychiatric care can be in a stand-alone facility or part of a general hospital and can be short or long term. Last, rehabilitation centers serve people with disabilities that have resulted from an illness such as a stroke or an accident. The TR specialist helps patients adjust to their disability and learn to use leisure to meet their needs. All of these clinical settings often have a treatment team that might include occupational therapists, physical therapists, social workers, physicians, and recreation therapists working together to help patients improve their health.

Not all people with disabilities need to experience leisure in a clinical setting. A far greater number of people with disabilities live in the community than do in hospital settings, and they have equally strong needs for recreation. Municipal parks and recreation agencies were given the charge to provide these much-needed services. Public parks and recreation agencies hire TR specialists to oversee programs specifically for people with disabilities or for inclusion purposes. People specializing in inclusion manage their own programs as well as assist staff in making programs and events accessible to people with disabilities. An inclusion specialist may help a program leader adapt a program so that someone who is deaf or who has a physical disability can participate with individuals who do not have a disability. The inclusion specialist most likely has extensive knowledge of the Americans with Disabilities Act,[7] which requires park and recreation agencies to provide accessible services and access to all users. Community TR does not deliberately gear programs to achieve specific treatment or rehabilitative goals within a clinical framework, but those providing special or inclusive recreation do have important purposes. They value recreation as an important life experience for people with disabilities and seek to achieve positive physical, social, and emotional outcomes, making adaptations in programming, facilities, equipment, or leadership methods as appropriate.

Special Recreation Associations

In Illinois, community park and recreation agencies form special recreation associations (SRAs) to provide recreation services for people with disabilities. Rather than each agency having its own staff trained in TR, they pool resources to provide a higher level of service for the communities involved. For example, the Fox Valley Special Recreation Association is an extension of the Batavia, Fox Valley, Geneva, Oswegoland, St. Charles, Sugar Grove Park Districts, and South Elgin Parks and Recreation Department.

Therapeutic Recreation Models and Process

Two very distinct aspects of TR are the conceptual models and the TR process that drives practice. The TR profession uses conceptual models as a framework for delivery of service and to represent or guide practice. They help practitioners understand the comprehensive view of the profession and direct them in helping clients through intervention.[4] Although there are several different models used, two are discussed here so that the general perspectives held within TR are demonstrated. Those two models include the Leisure Ability Model and Health Protection–Health Promotion Model.

The Leisure Ability Model is based on the idea that everyone should experience leisure regardless of their abilities and disabilities. TR is a means to facilitate a quality leisure lifestyle, enhance quality of life, and improve health and happiness. The Leisure Ability Model has three components:[8]

Functional interventions: This therapy or rehabilitation component helps individuals improve related functional abilities needed for leisure participation. TR specialists help individuals participate by eliminating, improving, or adapting functional deficits that constrain leisure.

Leisure education: The purpose of leisure education is to help individuals learn leisure-related skills, attitudes, and knowledge.[9] TR specialists teach individuals new leisure related skills to develop a healthy leisure lifestyle.

Recreation participation: The purpose of recreation participation is for structured leisure opportunities. The TR specialist provides the opportunity and acts as a facilitator or leader. This component of the Leisure Ability Model focuses on activity participation.

The Health Protection–Health Promotion Model of TR focuses on two areas: (1) treating and rehabilitating a client after an illness or disability; and (2) maintaining and enhancing good health. These two areas are considered a continuum because a client moves from less than ideal health to optimal health. TR specialists "contribute to health by helping persons fulfill their needs for stability and actualization until they are ready and able to assume responsibility for themselves."[10] Key to the Health Protection–Health Promotion Model are three elements:

Prescriptive activity: Prescriptive activity involves the TR specialist selecting activities that are specifically designed to achieve goals to enhance health. Prescriptive activity begins to move a client toward health and helps stabilize the client.

Recreation: Once stabilization occurs, the client moves into the recreation component of the model. The TR specialist provides an educational component by building skills and knowledge and helping clients value leisure so that they take more control over their lives. It is believed that the recreation experience is also for health protection.

Leisure: The leisure component focuses on health promotion rather than health protection as the other two components do. Individuals take control of their leisure lives and become self-determined and realize their full potential.[11]

In addition to working with a specialized clientele using a treatment model, TR is unique in the recreation field in that it follows a clinical process, the TR process, to help clients. The TR process has four parts: assessment, planning, implementation, and evaluation. In the profession, this is known as APIE (pronounced *a-pie*).

The assessment piece of the TR process is information gathering. It is necessary to understand where the client currently is in functioning, strengths, and needs. Documents are gathered from physicians, other therapists, others involved in the care of the client, and from the client and/or the family. TR specialists also use TR-specific assessment tools designed to measure any number of factors needed to enhance care and reach a desired outcome. Once the initial assessment is complete, an individual program plan is developed outlining client goals, programs, and the overall treatment plan. Implementation of the individual program plan is facilitated by the TR specialist with the collaboration of the client. The TR specialist's level of involvement varies depending on the needs of the client. Last, evaluation is the systematic process where the TR specialist gathers information to assess whether the treatment plan and outcomes are appropriate. This information is used to modify the plan if needed.[12] This aspect of the TR process requires the evaluation of the client to assess the progress he or she is making on goals and outcomes. An evaluation is also done on the programs selected to ascertain their effectiveness for the individual.[13] This process is the crux of TR and requires the TR specialist and the participant to work together to establish what is in the best interest of the participant and how to achieve the goals created.

TR Treatment Modalities

A treatment modality is the activity used to bring about a change or to reach a client's goals. TR specialists use a plethora of activities and approaches to help clients. The most common modalities used in TR include: (1) games, (2) exercise, (3) parties, (4) arts and crafts, (5) community integration activities, (6) music, (7) problem solving activities, (8) sports, (9) self-esteem, and (10) activities of daily living. Some of these modalities are used more often with certain populations. For example, community integration, games, and exercise are often used for physical rehabilitation. Games, problem solving, and arts and crafts are more commonly used for people with mental health issues.[14]

Certification

The practice of TR as a treatment discipline has become increasingly sophisticated. The body of research knowledge has expanded, protocols for treatment approaches have been developed, university curriculums have become broader in scope, and more populations are being served. There is also greater recognition of the discipline within healthcare systems and what it has to offer. Facilitating this is the reinforcement of standards by healthcare-accrediting bodies, such as the Commission of Accreditation of Rehabilitation Facilities and the Joint Commission. These two major accrediting organizations have specific criteria for providing qualified therapeutic recreation services, which includes a requirement that said services be provided only by a certified therapeutic recreation specialist (CTRS).

In 1981, the National Council for Therapeutic Recreation Certification (NCTRC) was established as an autonomous credentialing body to oversee the development and administration of the CTRS professional certification. A research-based therapeutic recreation job analysis was performed and used to develop the certification exam, which was administered for the first time in November 1990. This exam and the requirements set by NCTRC to sit for the exam are the primary certification standards for both clinical and recreation applications of therapeutic recreation.

Morgan's Wonderland

Morgan's Wonderland, located in San Antonio, Texas, is a 25-acre amusement park designed specifically for people with disabilities. Gordon Hartman, whose daughter Morgan has a cognitive disability, raised $30 million to build this facility. Admission is free for people with disabilities and $5 for the person(s) accompanying the individual with disabilities. Everyone else is charged $15. Amenities on the property include an event center and gymnasium, an interactive sensory village, butterfly-themed playground, Wonderland Express train, amphitheater, the first ever off-road adventure ride, a 36-foot-diameter carousel, music garden, water play area, and much more. Advanced reservations are required because a limited number of people are allowed to visit each day to avoid crowding that can be difficult for some people with specific disabilities.[15]

CASE STUDY: Americans with Disabilities Act

The Americans with Disabilities Act of 1990 (ADA) is a civil rights law that prohibits discrimination based on disability.[a] There are five sections of the act:

Title 1: Employment: Qualified candidates cannot be discriminated against in the hiring process, employment, or discharge based on disability.

Title 2: State and Local Government: People with disabilities must have access to state and local government facilities and programs. This section also addresses accessibility of transportation such as on buses and trains.

Title 3: Public Accommodations (and Commercial Facilities): People with disabilities may not be discriminated against with regard to use of public accommodations including hotels, resorts, restaurants, and recreation opportunities, among others. In addition, buildings must be compliant with the ADA Accessibility Guidelines. Private clubs and religious organizations are exempt from the law. Public accommodations can include such things as sign language interpreters, assistive listening devices, Braille publications, taped publications, telephone typewriter (TDD)/Telecommunications Device for the Deaf (TTY), and facility accessibility.

Title 4: Telecommunications: Telecommunications companies must make their services available to people with disabilities. This is most focused on serving people who are deaf/hard of hearing and/or who have a speech impairment.

Title 5: Miscellaneous Provisions: This section covers the technical aspects of the law such as immunity under ADA, retaliation against claims, and responsibilities for technical assistance.

Questions to Consider

1. Walk through a building on campus such as the campus recreation facility. What examples did you find that the facility and/or programs were accessible to people with disabilities?
2. What aspects of the facility and/or programs were not accessible?

Source

a. Council for Disability Rights, "The Americans with Disabilities Act: Frequently Asked Questions," http://www.disabilityrights.org/adatoc.htm.

Standards of Practice

ATRA developed standards of practice to guide the delivery and management of therapeutic recreation services. These standards were first published in 1991 and then revised in 1994 and again in 2000. The current standards, as shown here, reflect state-of-the-art practice in this field. Given the emphasis on treatment applications in clinical settings, the standards do not reflect what is expected in a community recreation setting. The community programs are viewed instead as special or inclusive recreation.

ATRA Standards of Practice

Developed by the American Therapeutic Recreation Association, the standards reflect levels of service provision for therapeutic recreation professionals to implement in a variety of settings. The standards assist the therapeutic recreation professional in ensuring the systematic provision of quality therapeutic recreation services. Note that standards 1–7 address direct practice and 8–12 target the management of therapeutic recreation services; they should not be viewed as complete without full consideration of the structure, process, and outcome components found in the *ATRA Standards or Practice Manual* (2000).

Standard 1: The therapeutic recreation specialist conducts an individualized assessment to collect systematic, comprehensive, and accurate data necessary to determine a course of action and subsequent individualized treatment plan.

Standard 2: The therapeutic recreation specialist plans and develops the individualized treatment plan that identifies goals, objectives, and treatment intervention strategies.

Standard 3: The therapeutic recreation specialist implements an individualized treatment plan using appropriate intervention strategies to restore, remediate, or rehabilitate in order to improve functioning and independence as well as reduce or eliminate the effects of illness or disability. Implementation of the treatment plan by the therapeutic recreation specialist is consistent with the overall patient/client treatment program.

Standard 4: The therapeutic recreation specialist systematically evaluates and compares the client's response to the individualized treatment plan. The treatment plan is revised based upon changes in the interventions, diagnoses, and patient/client responses.

Standard 5: The therapeutic recreation specialist develops a discharge plan in collaboration with the patient/client, family, and other treatment team members in order to continue treatment, as appropriate.

Standard 6: Recreation opportunities are available to patients/clients to promote or improve their general health and well-being.

Standard 7: The therapeutic recreation specialist adheres to the ATRA Code of Ethics.

Standard 8: The therapeutic recreation department is governed by a written plan of operation that is based upon ATRA Standards of the Practice of Therapeutic Recreation and standards of other accrediting/regulatory agencies, as appropriate.

Standard 9: The therapeutic recreation department has established provisions for assuring that therapeutic recreation staff maintain appropriate credentials and have opportunities for professional development.

Standard 10: Within the therapeutic recreation department, there exists an objective and systematic quality improvement program for the purposes of monitoring and evaluating the quality and appropriateness of care, and to identify and resolve problems in order to improve therapeutic recreation services.

Standard 11: Therapeutic recreation services are provided in an effective and efficient manner that reflects the reasonable and appropriate use of resources.

Standard 12: The therapeutic recreation department engages in routine, systematic program evaluation and research for the purpose of determining appropriateness and efficacy.

Expansion of Sport and Outdoor Recreation Participation

At every level, people of all ages with physical or mental disabilities are taking part in varied forms of sport and outdoor recreation. Many of these activities are promoted by organizations such as Wheelchair and Ambulatory Sports, USA, a multisport organization for athletes who compete annually in regional, national, and international games. Included among the competitive events for both men and women are archery, athletics (track and field, pentathlon, road racing), basketball, swimming, table tennis, tennis, and weightlifting. Thousands of young athletes also participate in Special Olympics events, while many others compete in marathons, bowling leagues, and other individual or team sport.

In terms of outdoor recreation, programs have become increasingly geared for individuals with disabilities. Like sports, there are organizations specifically designed for outdoor recreation pursuits. For example, Outdoors Without Limits educates people about outdoor recreation opportunities for people with disabilities. The National Sports Center for the Disabled offers programs in sport and outdoor recreation. For example, they currently offer whitewater rafting, canoeing, mountain biking, rock climbing, alpine skiing, and more for all ages.[16]

Use of Technology and Assistive Devices

Sophisticated technology is being brought into play to permit persons with disabilities to participate successfully in different leisure activities. For several decades, various modified instruments or pieces of equipment have been used to help people with disabilities take part in card and table games, arts and crafts, team and individual sport, and other pursuits. For example, for outdoor recreation there are adaptive gun and bow mounts for hunting, all-terrain tires for trails, and fishing pole holders. Adapted sports equipment includes ice hockey sledges, handcycles, mono- and bi-skis for alpine skiing, and Nordic cross-country skis.

Aerodynamic wheelchairs are now being used by racers with disabilities, and carbon-fiber prosthetic feet enable athletes with amputations to run almost as fast as athletes without disabilities. Research into the use of electrodes to stimulate the leg muscles of persons with spinal cord injuries is helping to maintain bone, joint, and muscle health, which has positive effects on cardiovascular functioning and recreation participation, while numerous other devices are being invented each year to facilitate independent functioning for people with disabilities. Electronic devices such as "aura interactor" strap-on vests enable deaf people to dance without straining to hear the music and help blind video game players to feel laser beams "bouncing" off the screen.

Cooperative Networks of Agencies

Because many community and nonprofit organizations lacked the staff resources or special facilities required to provide comprehensive leisure-service programs for persons with disabilities, the 1980s and 1990s saw a trend toward developing cooperative networks of such agencies. In such structures, two or more public or nonprofit human-service organizations—or a combination of both types—share their funding and facilities to provide needed recreation programs in a number of locations. For example, there are more than 20 independent Special Recreation Associations (SRAs) in northern Illinois, based on revenue generated from special direct property taxes. All SRAs are coordinated by boards representing the cooperating communities. They interface with municipal recreation and park departments and offer programming for persons with all types of disabling conditions in both integrated and segregated groupings.

In another example of joint cooperation, Boston Children's Hospital and the University of Massachusetts–Boston are implementing a project designed to increase communication between families and healthcare services, improve access to recreational opportunities, and ease the transition to adulthood for children with disabilities and special healthcare needs. This project is funded by the Department of Education's National Institute on Disability and Rehabilitation Research, as part of its national "Opening Doors" program. The cooperative nature of the project is critical to its success. They are involving community-based organizations such as the Massachusetts Consortium for Children with Special Health Care Needs, the Parent Advocacy Coalition for Education Rights (Minnesota), and the YMCA of Greater Boston, along with a number of other organizations. Although the emphasis is not exclusively on meeting the recreation needs of the participants and their families, the recreation component is seen as critical to the overall success of the program because it seeks to assist in the difficult process of children with disabilities transitioning to adulthood and self-reliance.

Throughout the country, numerous independent nonprofit organizations, such as RCH, Inc., in San Francisco, have established facilities and programs that are designed to meet varied life needs—recreational, social, educational, and vocational—of people in different categories of disability.

New Emphasis on Inclusion

In the late 1990s, instead of the term *special recreation*, professional organizations began to use the term *inclusion*, meaning simply the involvement and full acceptance of people with disabilities in a wide range of community settings. In 1998, for example, a National Recreation and Park Association survey team conducted an intensive study of the inclusion practices of 900 public recreation and park agencies. It analyzed the types of services provided and the categories of individuals served, the accommodations that were made in terms of facilities and equipment, and the problems and staff training needs in the communities that were surveyed.[17] In September 2000, a major National Institute on Recreation Inclusion (NIRI) conference was held in Deerfield, Illinois, bringing together representatives from many different kinds of agencies and highlighting the outstanding programs that were being developed in this area. Since then, NIRI has held yearly national conferences around the United States.

The efforts of researchers, ATRA, NTRS, NCTRC, agencies that deliver services, and therapeutic recreation practitioners have combined to broaden the scope of services, improve the quality of services, and make therapeutic recreation services available to more people with illnesses and disabling conditions than ever before. Many factors are still unfolding in the areas of health care, community recreation services, efficacy-based research, university TR programs, and credentialing, which will affect the future of TR.

ARMED FORCES RECREATION

For many years it has been the official policy of the military establishment to provide a well-rounded morale, welfare, and recreational program for the physical, social, and mental well-being of its personnel. During World War I, Special Services Divisions were established to provide social and recreational programs that would sustain favorable morale, curb homesickness and boredom, minimize fatigue, and reduce AWOL (absent without leave), and venereal disease rates.

Today, each branch of the armed forces has its own pattern of recreation sponsorship, although they are all under the same morale, welfare, and recreation (MWR) program, which is administratively responsible to the Office of the Assistant Secretary of Defense for Manpower, Reserve Affairs, and Logistics. They serve several million individuals, including active duty, reserve, and retired military personnel and their dependents; civilian employees; and surviving spouses of military personnel who died in active duty. In addition, MWR services are also provided to Coast Guard personnel, who are not part of the Department of Defense.

Goals and Scope of Armed Forces Recreation Today

The mission statement of the U.S. Army Morale, Welfare, and Recreation program provides an important reminder of the importance of looking at the military as a family and not just soldiers, sailors, and airmen:

> Army MWR is a comprehensive network of support and leisure services designed to enhance the lives of soldiers (active, Reserve, and Guard), their families, civilian employees, military retirees and other eligible participants. . . . Their mission is to serve the needs, interests and responsibilities of each individual in the Army community for as long as they are associated with the Army, no matter where they are.
>
> MWR contributes to the Army's strength and readiness by offering services that reduce stress, build skills and self-confidence and foster strong esprit de corps. MWR services also help the Army attract and retain talented people. MWR is proof of the Army's commitment to caring for the people who serve and stand ready to defend the nation.[18]

Military recreation departments are structured and operate similarly to public parks and recreation agencies. They both offer a variety of programs for the community. The military community is far more defined and limited than a community such as a city or county. Temple and Ogilvie outline four major differences between MWR and community recreation.[19] First, the military community is quite transient and ever changing. Working in MWR requires staff to constantly focus on the changes in needs going on within the military community. Second, military communities are not always in the most stable parts of the world. They are in remote areas, combat zones, and less-than-desirable geographic locations. The staff, military personnel, and their families must be aware of these situations. Recreation can serve as a way to make life a little more stable for all involved. Third, MWR is exclusive in whom it serves. MWR provides services for active and retired military personnel and their families only. Last, MWR relies heavily on volunteers to carry out programs and events. Although municipal agencies also often rely on volunteers, MWR volunteers are transient, making it difficult to manage and recruit a consistent stream of volunteers.

Program Elements

Sports MWR programs include an extensive range of sport, fitness, social, creative, outdoor recreation, travel, entertainment, and hobby leisure pursuits. In the Air Force, for example, an extensive program of sports activities has typically included six major elements: (1) instruction in basic sport skills; (2) a self-directed phase of informal participation in sport under minimum supervision or direction; (3) an intramural program, in which personnel assigned to a particular base compete with others at the same base; (4) an extramural program, which includes competition with teams from different Air Force bases or with teams from neighboring communities; (5) a varsity program, which involves high-level competition with players selected for their advanced skills who compete on a broader national or international scale; and (6) a program for women in the Air Force.

In addition to such programs attached to individual services, the armed forces promote an extensive range of competitive sport programs. Through interservice competition in such sports as basketball, boxing, wrestling, track and field, and softball, all-service teams are selected; armed forces teams then are chosen to represent the United States in international competition.

Fort Huachuca Family and MWR Philosophy

Soldiers are entitled to the same quality of life as is afforded the society they are pledged to defend. Keeping an army ready to fight and win takes more than hard work and training. Soldiers need a balance of work and play.[20]

Hundreds of Army, Air Force, Navy, and Marine bases have adopted the popular Start Smart Sports Development Program, which helps children as young as age 3 learn basic motor skills that progress to organized sport involvement, and in which parents become heavily involved in leadership roles.[21]

Fitness Programs Health and wellness have become a major focus of armed forces recreation. To improve fitness levels of personnel, the Air Force installed health and wellness centers (HAWC) on each base; these centers are well equipped and are staffed with leaders qualified to provide the following services: fitness and health risk assessments, exercise programming and weight counseling, stress management and smoking cessation assistance, and similar activities.

On some military bases, fitness is promoted through well-publicized and challenging special events. At the Marine Corps Base at Camp Lejeune, North Carolina, the Lejeune Grand Prix Series features a number of competitive events that involve hundreds of service personnel in a European Cross Country race over natural terrain; a Tour d'Pain, a grueling endurance cycling race; a Masters Swim Meet; a Davy Jones Open Ocean Swim; a Toughman Triathlon; and other types of races.

Outdoor Recreation Often, outdoor program activities are keyed to the location of a base. For example, Fort Carson, Colorado, offers such activities as ice climbing lessons, workshops, and trips; skiing and snowshoe trips; and rafting.[22] Responding to widespread interest in mountain climbing and rock climbing, this Army base constructed a 17,400-square-foot outdoor recreation center that features a 32-foot-high indoor climbing wall with the look and feel of natural rock and climbing routes geared to different skill levels. Other bases offer instruction, equipment, and facilities for such water-based activities as fishing, wind-surfing, jet skiing, scuba diving, and similar pastimes.

Family Recreation The Department of Defense has become increasingly aware of the need to provide varied family-focused programs to counter the special problems that may affect the spouses and children of military personnel.

All branches of the military have family programs. Here are a few examples. The Army created the Army Family Covenant in 2007, which "pledges the Army's commitment to providing Soldiers and Families a quality of life, commensurate with their dedicated service and sacrifice to the nation."[23] The Army MWR units have the responsibility of carrying out the directives of the covenant. This has meant enhancing program offerings or securing better funding for existing programs. Another result of this program has been Survivor Outreach Services to help the families of fallen soldiers.[24] The Marine Corps has the Family Team Building program that provides educational resources and services to foster personal growth and enhance the readiness of Marine Corps families.[25] The Navy has child and youth programs for children ages 4 weeks to 18 years. Programs are designed to foster emotional well-being, develop self-discipline, and cultivate respect and appreciation of differences and the uniqueness of diverse cultures and traditions.[26]

Community Relations Many military bases in the United States and overseas place a high priority on establishing positive relationships between armed forces personnel and nearby communities. Civilian MWR personnel working around the globe in such settings as Europe, Korea, and Central America, and even Saudi Arabia, Turkey, and Africa, seek to provide a wealth of outdoor recreational experiences and positive intercultural experiences with local residents.

On just one such distant base, on the island of Sasebo, Japan, Navy MWR specialists provide a huge range of leisure services, including travel tours to scenic locations and festivals in the region, fitness and outdoor recreation activities, hobby shops, professional entertainment, holiday events, extensive youth programs, library services, varied sport tournaments, and even such unusual services as a "pet-holding" facility for military families going on vacation. Although such varied programs are not typical of all military installations, the Sasebo MWR operations offer leisure opportunities that far exceed those in many stateside civilian communities.

Resorts The Army maintains a full range of resorts for all military members. Armed Forces Recreation Centers (AFRC) are affordable Joint Service facilities operated by the U.S. Army Community and Family Support Center and located in different areas, including Germany, Florida, and Hawaii. They offer a full range of resort hotel opportunities for members of all branches of the military service, their families, and other members of the Total Defense Force. The resorts are self-supporting, funded by revenues generated internally from operations.

Fiscal Support of Armed Forces Recreation

Military recreation has traditionally depended on two types of funding: *appropriated funds*, which are tax funds approved by Congress, and *nonappropriated funds*, which are generated on the military base through a combination of post exchange profits and revenue from fees, rentals, and other recreation charges. The Navy Personnel Command in the Department of Defense defines the different types of recreation funds generated by Navy personnel and their dependents to help provide financial support for their recreation activities. Specifically, these are

> monies received from Navy exchange profits, fees and charges placed on the use of recreation facilities and services or other authorized sources for the support of Navy recreation programs. Unit Recreation Funds are those which serve the recreation needs of individual ships, shore stations and other Navy activities. Composite Recreation Funds are those which serve two or more activities which share the same recreation facilities. Consolidated Recreation Funds are those which serve the recreation needs of several separate installations within a geographical area.[27]

In the late 1980s, the Department of Defense classified all MWR activities as either mission-sustaining activities (such as overseas entertainment, physical fitness centers, or temporary lodging facilities) or business activities (such as amusement machine centers, bingo, golf courses, marinas, and rod-and-gun clubs). Guidelines suggested that there be higher levels of fiscal support for more critical services and lower support levels for purely recreational activities that have the potential for being self-sustaining.

Since that time, with growing budget cutbacks and the need to maximize revenues from clubs, messes, post exchanges, and varied forms of commercial sponsorship or partnerships, MWR planners have initiated a range of new fiscal strategies. The effort has been to reduce the costs of operations, standardize procedures, and eliminate redundant programs or personnel. The Navy, for example, established 10 major regions to simplify the planning and supervision of programs, increasingly encouraged public/private projects, and established new planning processes to "reinvent" facility development and other projects.

Through the 1990s, as base closures and budget cuts continued, military recreation professionals sought to develop an even more business-oriented approach to their services. Pat Harden, past director of Navy recreation training at Patuxent River, Maryland, pointed out that two prevailing orientations generally guided armed forces recreation: (1) the quality-of-life approach, which sees MWR recreation and club services essentially as an amenity, although deserving of Department of Defense support; and (2) the businesslike marketing approach, which urges that all recreation services be viewed primarily as a commodity to be merchandised, with a minimum of social and mission support goals or constraints.

Employment in MWR

MWR employs 100,000 people worldwide. Entry-level positions are often in specialty areas such as sports, youth, or special events. To find jobs in MWR, see these Web sites:

MWR Non-appropriated Funds (NAF) Jobs (includes Army, Air Force, and Navy): www.nafjobs.com

Coast Guard: www.cg-exchange.com/ijobs.nsf

Marines: www.usmc-mccs.org/employ/index.cfm

Navy: www.mwr.navy.mil/mwrprgms/personnel.html

Instead, Harden argues, it is essential to define the important mission of MWR programs within the overall Department of Defense structure and to work effectively to achieve the goals related to this mission. He quotes a defense department official as follows:

> Readiness is the cornerstone of this administration. A ready-to-fight force is linked intrinsically to the morale, sense of well-being, commitment, and pride in the mission of each Service and family member. Our Morale, Welfare, and Recreation programs play a direct role in developing and maintaining these characteristics within our force and are more important than ever during this time of transition, when profound changes are taking place that are having a powerful impact on Service members and their families.[28]

EMPLOYEE SERVICES AND RECREATION PROGRAMS

A third important area of specialized recreation programs involves the role of business and industry in providing recreation and related personnel services to employees and in some cases their families or other community residents.

Background of Company-Sponsored Programs

Employee recreation (formerly called "industrial recreation") began in the nineteenth century but did not expand rapidly until after World War II. At this time, the National Industrial Recreation Association was formed. This professional association provided resources for people working in corporate recreation, and at this point the emphasis was on fitness and wellness. Later, this organization became the Employee Services Management Association. Employee services management expands on recreation to provide other benefits to employees such as travel discounts and services.[29]

Although the providers of employee services and recreation originally were manufacturing companies and other industrial concerns, today many different types of organizations also sponsor employee activities. They include such diverse groups as food market chains, airlines, insurance companies, hospitals, and government agencies.

Goals of Employee Recreation

The major goals of the institutions providing employee programs and services include the following.

Improvement of Employer–Employee Relations Earlier in this country's industrial development, there was considerable friction between management and labor that often resulted in extended and violent strikes. A major purpose of industrial recreation programs at this time was to create favorable employer–employee relationships and instill a sense of loyalty among workers. It is believed that such programs tend to create a feeling of belonging and identification among employees, and that group participation by workers at various job levels contributes to improved worker morale, increased harmony, and an attitude of mutual cooperation.

For example, the Minnesota Employee Recreation and Services Council "is dedicated to helping member companies improve employee satisfaction and enhance employee well being."[30] The Honeywell Employee Club was established to promote activities and services to help create fellowship among employees, foster a sense of belonging, and improve physical and mental well-being for all those involved.[31]

Directly Promoting Employee Fitness and Efficiency Corporations large and small today have become concerned about maintaining the health of their employees. One reason may be the skyrocketing costs of health insurance for employers. A major factor in this increase is the nation's obesity epidemic. Obesity accounts for more annual healthcare costs than drinking and smoking. The Centers for Disease Control and Prevention estimates that obesity costs the United States $147 billion annually. People who are obese spend 42% more on health care and make up 9.1% of all medical spending.[32]

To combat this obesity issue, companies have offered programs and incentives to enhance wellness. For example, the Yellowstone Co-Op Employee Recreation Program, for the 4000 employees of Yellowstone National Park, have access to three fitness facilities within the park and numerous sports leagues to enhance fitness. The Kentucky energy company E.On U.S. reimburses staff and their families 50% of the cost of a fitness center membership.

Health and Wellness Program Benefits

The National Association for Health and Fitness suggests that a health and wellness program for employees benefits both the employee and the employer. Here's how:

Benefits for Employers

- Enhanced employee productivity
- Improved healthcare costs for management
- Decreased rates of illness and injuries
- Reduced employee absenteeism
- Development of employee leadership skills

Benefits for Employees

- Lower levels of stress
- Increased well-being, self-image, self-esteem, and improved physical fitness
- Increased stamina
- Potential weight reduction

More information can be found at http://www.physicalfitness.org/nehf.html.

Recruitment and Retention Appeal

An attractive program of recreation and related personnel services that can meet the needs of both the employee and his or her family is a persuasive recruitment weapon. Agencies advertise employee recreation opportunities as a perk to employment. It demonstrates the company's commitment to its employees and makes the company appear as a great place to work.

In terms of retention, many companies find that successful employee programs help reduce job turnover. Litton Laser Systems in Apopka, Florida, now owned by Northrop Grumman, for example, credits its low employee turnover and high morale to its social activities committee (SAC), a group of employees who manage social, recreational, and sports events and other services for all company members and their families.

Company Image and Community Role

An important part of the recreation and services function involves external relations—the company's external, community-based role. Eli Lilly and company established the Eli Lilly and Company Foundation that awards grants to initiatives that match the philosophy of the company such as health care, culture, and youth development. The company also matches gifts to charities by employees and financially supports organizations that staff volunteer with on a regular basis.[33]

Many large companies offer recreation programs for their current employees, retirees, and their families. These programs are one means of increasing employee morale.

In other settings, the employee services program provides a means through which company executives can move purposefully to transform the business's internal and external image. As a vivid example, the Coors Brewing Company in Colorado, which long had a reputation for conservative policies and funding right-wing political groups, sought deliberately to change its image, encouraging sensitivity training for its diverse workforce and shifts in its national identity as well. It sponsors 10 "resource councils" representing gays, women, and Native Americans, among others, and supports programs ranging from a marathon gay dance party in Miami to the first large-scale corporate mammography program in the country.

Program Activities and Services

Many companies established extensive and well-equipped recreation and fitness centers and staffed them with qualified personnel. The Texins Activity Center in Dallas, serving employees of Texas Instruments, contains a multiuse gymnasium; strength and cardiovascular exercise areas; conference rooms; child-care rooms; club rooms; a natatorium with a six-lane, 25-lap pool; two aerobic studios; an indoor running track; and varied outdoor facilities.

Administrative Arrangements

Various approaches to the management of employee service and recreation programs exist. In some, the company itself provides the facilities and leadership and maintains complete control of the operation. In other organizations, the company provides the facilities, but an employee recreation association takes actual responsibility for running the program. Other companies use combinations of these approaches. Frequently, profits from canteens or plant vending machines provide financial support for the program, as does revenue from moderate fees for participation or membership. Many activities—such as charter vacation flights—are completely self-supporting; others are fully or partly subsidized by the company.

Some companies restrict participation in recreation programs to employees and their families, while others make them available to the surrounding community. For example, the Flick-Reedy Corporation designed its main building for the recreational use of the entire community, with thousands of children and adults using its gymnasium, auditorium, and dining room for special banquets and events each year.

CASE STUDY: Employee Services

The Employee Services Management Association has a top 10 list of things that make for a well-rounded employee services program.[a] They include the following:

1. *Employee store:* An on-site or online store for employees to purchases items to save themselves time and money on items such as clothing with the company logo, discount tickets (for example, to amusement parks), cards, and miscellaneous items
2. *Community services:* Organized activities where employees can support local charities
3. *Convenience services:* Services that save employees time and help cut down on errands they need to run, including such services as dry-cleaning services, car services, and resource referral services
4. *Recreation programs:* Sports leagues, workshops, and programs for employees
5. *Special events:* Holiday parties, company picnics, and organized outings
6. *Voluntary benefits:* Assistance in helping the employee find the best options for additional insurance policies such as car or group life, services such as legal or banking, and warranties on automobiles and home service agreements
7. *Dependent care:* Day or evening care for children, older adults, and even pets
8. *Recognition programs:* Recognizing outstanding contributions made by employees to the company
9. *Travel services:* Planning group trips or individual trips for employees
10. *Wellness:* Wellness seminars, fitness incentive programs, personal development opportunities, on-site fitness centers, ropes courses, and other programs

Questions to Consider

1. Which of these 10 elements are recreation related? Which ones would likely be the responsibility of the recreation professional?
2. Budget cuts have required that four of these services be cut from the organization. Which ones would you cut and why?

Source

a. Employee Service Management Foundation, "The Top 10 Components of a Well-Rounded Employee Services Program." www.esmassn.org/Default.aspx?pageId=372979.

Scheduling Flexibility: Off-Shift Programming

Employee service and recreation managers must adapt to the special circumstances of their organizations and the changing needs of the employees they serve. Often this may involve providing a wide range of special courses designed for vocational or career development, cultural interest, or personal enrichment.

Some large corporations seek to meet the needs of their employees who work second and third shifts by scheduling facilities such as health clubs or weight rooms to be available at odd hours of the day and night. For example, Phillips Petroleum and Pratt and Whitney schedule morning and midnight softball and bowling leagues for off-shift workers and make gyms, tennis courts, and other facilities, as well as discount ticket operations, available to them at convenient times.

Innovation and Entrepreneurship

Just as in other sectors of the leisure-service field, employee service and recreation practitioners have experienced the need to become more fiscally independent by generating a fuller level of revenues through their offerings and by demonstrating their value in convincing terms.

CASE STUDY: Incentives for Fitness

Because of soaring healthcare costs, up to a third of all companies have resorted to paying employees to be healthy. They are paying for gym memberships, Weight Watchers memberships, and time off to exercise. Some are paying staff to stop smoking, while others are banning smoking altogether. Baylor Health Care System offers employees $50 for each 100-day cycle they participate in the company's fitness program.[a] OhioHealth paid employees to wear pedometers and record their steps each day. The more they walked, the higher they were paid—up to $500 per year. Other companies felt that people are more concerned about losing their own money than winning money from the company. As a result, employees put up money as a deposit and sign an agreement to lose weight by a certain date. If they do not, they forfeit the deposit. One company donated the money to a charity the employee did *not* like.[b]

Questions to Consider

1. Could this be seen as companies being involved in the personal lives of their employees? If so, should they be?
2. If employees are paid to be healthy, should those who are not healthy be penalized?
3. Will the extrinsic reward actually hurt or help the level of fitness within the organization? Why?

Sources

a. S. Friedman, "Get Paid to Lose Weight?" (13 April 2010). http://www.nbcdfw.com/news/health/Get-Paid-to-Lose-Weight-90741549.html.

b. Associated Press, "Dieting for Dollars? More U.S. Employees Trying It," (1 June 2010). http://cbs13.com/health/diet.dollars.employers.2.1726872.html.

The purposes of adopting businesslike values and strategies are (1) to enable employee programs to become less dependent on company financial support and (2) to ensure that funds allocated to them by management yield significant, quantifiable benefits. A number of employee service and recreation directors in major corporations have been quite innovative in developing revenue sources based on businesslike ventures.

CAMPUS RECREATION

The nation's colleges and universities provide a major setting for organized programs of leisure services involving millions of participants each year in a wide range of recreational activities. Although their primary purpose is to serve students, faculty and staff members also may be involved in such programs on many campuses.

All institutions of higher education today sponsor some forms of leisure activity for their resident and commuter populations. Many of the larger colleges and universities have campus unions, departments of student affairs, or student centers that house a wide range of such activities. Frequently, a dean of student life is responsible for overseeing these programs, although intramural and recreational sports often may be administratively attached to a department or college of physical education and recreation or to a department of intercollegiate athletics.

The diversified leisure-service function may include operating performing arts centers (sometimes in cooperation with academic departments or schools in these fields), planning arts series, film programs, and forums with guest speakers, and similar cultural events. Student union buildings may include such specialized facilities as bowling alleys, coffee houses, game rooms, restaurants, bookstores, and other activity areas.

Rationale for Campus Programs

Several logical reasons for sponsoring college and university recreation programs may be cited. Discussion of some of these follows.

Leisure as Cocurricular Enrichment Not all of the learning that takes place in higher education is provided in the classroom or laboratory. Many special interests of students can be explored to the fullest only by *cocurricular* (nonclass) experiences, ranging from the journalism major who works on the staff of the campus newspaper or literary magazine to the botany major who becomes involved in wilderness backpacking or camping. Often such programs are carried on with the express cooperation of the campus department most directly involved with the leisure interest. Beyond enriching a student's formal academic experience, involvement in cocurricular experiences contributes significantly to his or her overall personal growth.

Maintaining Campus Control and Morale Historically, U.S. colleges acted *in loco parentis;* that is, they were obligated to maintain a degree of control over the private lives of their students in areas such as drinking, gambling, sexual behavior, or the general domain of health and safety. For centuries, they therefore maintained codes of behavior, rules for on-campus living, curfews, and numerous other restrictions that controlled various forms of leisure behavior.

In general, it is believed by many that colleges must play a larger role in guiding the lives of students outside of the classroom. Although few administrators are seeking a return to the days of single-sex dormitories, dress codes, curfews, and other rigid rules, a consensus has grown that many of today's college students lack the responsibility to handle their newfound freedom sensibly and that it is necessary to establish and enforce some guidelines for students' social behavior.

Beyond being part of the effort to control negative kinds of behavior, campus recreation promotes positive student growth throughout the college experience. At a number of Eastern colleges, students are drawn into outdoor recreation or community service projects, beginning with their freshman orientation period. At Lehigh University and Lafayette College, for example, new students are drawn into overnight canoe and backpacking trips and begin to make new friends immediately. Similarly, entering students at Bryn Mawr College are assigned one-day service projects with the Philadelphia Zoo, the Children's Hospital of Philadelphia, and Habitat for Humanity.

Enhancing the University's Image Particularly in an era in which colleges and universities must compete for the enrollment of high-quality students, maintaining an appealing and impressive institutional image is critical. Probably the best-known vehicle for doing this is by fielding teams that play glamorous schedules in such popular sports as football and basketball. However, there are many other ways of building a positive image: through academic distinction, by winning prizes and awards, by having outstanding orchestras or theater companies, by having a distinguished university press, and through the accomplishments of alumni.

Certainly, having attractive recreational facilities and campus leisure programs also helps to build a positive image—particularly for potential students who visit a campus and are considering whether they want to live there for the next 4 years. Higher education appeals to a number of values and needs—not the least of these is the student's desire for an exciting and interesting social life.

Range of Campus Recreation Experiences

Campus recreation programs today are becoming more diversified, including a wide range of recreational sport, outdoor activities, entertainment and social events, cultural programs, activities for persons with disabilities, and various other services.

Recreational Sport During the 1970s and 1980s, both intramural leagues and sport clubs expanded rapidly in many institutions, with a growing emphasis on lifetime sport and on coeducational participation. Due in part to changed sex-role expectations and the effect of Title IX, many more girls and women are involved in sport today than in the past. More and more colleges and universities are providing varied facilities for sport and

Campus recreation activities typically include intramural sports, special events, clubs, and fitness.

games, including aquatic facilities, boxing/martial arts and exercise rooms, saunas and locker rooms, extensive outdoor areas with night lighting for evening play, and other special facilities for outdoor hobbies and instruction.

An outstanding example of college sport programming is found at Virginia Commonwealth University in Richmond, Virginia, which sponsors a host of recreational sport activities and events and fitness programs in six impressive campus facilities. Programs include a huge range of instructional, club, and intramural activities in such areas as individual, dual, and team sport; aerobics; dancing; yoga; martial arts; aquatics; and social programs. Participation in all programs and facilities is free for students through the general student fee. Spouses, staff, and faculty members pay modest annual fees. Similar sport programs are offered throughout the United States.

Outdoor Recreation Outdoor recreation, which includes clinics, clubs, and outings, may involve hiking, backpacking, camping, mountain climbing, scuba diving, sailing, skiing, and numerous other nature-based programs. These are often sponsored by campus outing clubs, which may in turn be affiliated with national organizations or federations. There are a number of outstanding campus recreation programs with outdoor recreation departments. The geography of the university obviously affects which programs are offered. It is not unusual for these universities to offer trips, rental gear, and do outdoor-related service projects. For example, Colorado State University (CSU) works with the Colorado Fourteeners Initiative to help relocate the summit trail on Mount Yale. CSU students spend 3 days backpacking, camping, and working on this project.[34] University of Utah Campus Recreation rents outdoor equipment including camping equipment, mountain bikes, water craft, and winter sports equipment.[35] Southern Illinois University offers a diversified range of appealing trips and outings, clinics, and classes, including rock climbing and backpacking, spelunking (cave exploration), canoeing, biking, and Earth Day events.

Special Events: Entertainment and Cultural Programs Many campuses sponsor large-scale entertainment events and cultural series. Typically, singers, rock bands, and comedians are booked to entertain students in stadiums, fieldhouses, and campus centers. The college's or university's own departments of music, theater, and dance may provide performing companies that present concerts or other stage presentations, along with other kinds of specialized programs.

Large-scale special events that students plan and carry out themselves—such as sports carnivals or other major competitions—are highlights of campus social programs. They involve both intimacy of interaction among leaders and participants and an intense outpouring of energy as people share fun in a crowded school or college setting. Similar excitement may be noted at major musical events such as rock concerts, although such programs often require supervision to ensure adherence to campus policies regarding alcohol and drugs.

Services for Special Populations Students with disabilities are being encouraged and assisted to participate in general campus recreation programs whenever possible. However, for those students whose disabilities are too severe to permit this or who have not yet developed the needed degree of confidence and independence, it has been necessary to design special programs using modified facilities and adapted instructional techniques or rules.

Outstanding examples of such programs are those offered by the University of Illinois, which provides special teams in the areas of football, softball, basketball, swimming, and track and field for students with physical disabilities. Other activities, such as archery, judo, swimming, bowling, and softball, have been adapted for such special groups as people with visual impairment.

Community Service Projects Many students also become involved in volunteer community projects such as repairing facilities, working with older adults, or providing "big brother" or tax assistance services. Such efforts are important for two reasons: (1) They illustrate how student-life activities may include a broad range of involvements beyond those that are clearly recognizable as recreational "fun" events; and (2) they serve to blend academic and extracurricular student experiences, increasing the individual's exposure to life and enhancing his or her leadership capability.

Overview of Campus Recreation

Campus recreation provides students with practical experience within a wide range of functions that supplement and enrich their academic programs. For example, many students may gain administrative or business skills, often on an advanced level. The Associated Students' Organization of San Diego State University in California provides a setting for such learning experiences. This multi-million-dollar corporation, funded by student fees, operates the Aztec Center, the college's student union building. Among its services are a successful travel agency, intramurals and sport clubs, special events, leisure classes, lectures, movies, concerts, an open-air theater, an aquatics center, campus radio station, child-care center, general store, campus information booth, and other programs. The bulk of its recreational activities is operated directly by the Recreation Activities Board, a unit within the overall Associated Students' Organization.

Such experiences illustrate the important contributions made by campus recreation programs, along with other student noncurricular activities, to the college or university experience. They involve the whole student in meaningful and creative ways and thus provide a meaningful transition to adult life and potential career opportunities.

Although the term *campus recreation* is usually applied only to higher education settings, recreation also is closely linked to other levels of educational experience. Many elementary and secondary school systems also provide recreation facilities and programs that meet significant leisure needs.

PRIVATE-MEMBERSHIP RECREATION ORGANIZATIONS

A significant portion of recreational opportunities today is provided by private-membership organizations. As distinguished from commercial recreation businesses—in which any individual may simply pay an admission fee to a theme park, for example—private-membership bodies usually restrict use of their facilities or programs to individual members and their families and guests.

Within the broad field of sport and outdoor recreation, many organizations offer facilities, instruction, or other services for activities such as skiing, tennis, golf, boating, and hunting or fishing. Whereas some private-membership organizations are commercially owned and operated, others exist as independent, incorporated clubs of members who own their own facilities, with policy being set by elected officers and boards and with the actual work of maintenance, instruction, and supervision being carried out by paid employees.

An important characteristic of many private-membership organizations has been their social exclusiveness. Membership policies often screened out certain prospective members for reasons of religion, ethnicity, gender, or other demographic factors.

It is important to recognize that although the ostensible function of such private organizations is to provide sociability as well as specific forms of leisure activity, the clubs also provide a setting in which the most powerful members of U.S. communities meet regularly to discuss business or political matters and often reach informal decisions or plans for action. Those who are barred from membership in such clubs are thus also excluded from this behind-the-scenes, establishment-based process of influence and power.

Despite recent changes, many private-membership organizations continue to represent exclusive enclaves of the rich and powerful. Country clubs are generally of two types: (1) nonprofit "equity clubs," owned and operated by members; and (2) commercially owned, for-profit clubs. Equity clubs can be established as either nonprofit or for-profit organizations. A common equity club is a destination club where people buy in to vacation homes. They have the right to use the homes but have no real ownership in the individual home. Commercially owned for-profit clubs are quite common. For example, ClubCorp owns 160 golf courses, private business and sports clubs, and resorts and has $2 billion in assets. ClubCorp owns such clubs as the Firestone Country Club in Akron, Ohio (site of the 2006–2010 World Golf Championships—Bridgestone Invitational); Mission Hills Country Club in Rancho Mirage, California (home of the Kraft Nabisco Championship); and Metropolitan Club in Chicago.[36]

Residence-Connected Clubs

Other types of private-membership recreation organizations continue to flourish—particularly in connection with new forms of home building and marketing. Many real estate developers have recognized that one of the key selling points in home development projects is the provision of attractive recreational facilities. Thus, tennis courts, golf courses, swimming pools, health spas, and similar recreation facilities are frequently provided for the residents of apartment buildings, condominiums, or one-family home developments, whether the residents are families, singles, or retired persons.

An important trend in U.S. society has been the rapid growth of housing developments in the suburbs, with community associations that carry out such functions as street cleaning, grounds maintenance, security, and the provision of leisure facilities such as tennis courts, golf courses, and swimming pools. Once found chiefly in the Southwest, such developments and community associations now have spread throughout the United States. In 1970, there were 10,000 such associations. In 1990, they numbered 130,000. By 2006, the number had grown to 286,000 with 57 million residents governed by associations.

Although such real estate developments tend to be expensive and thus intended chiefly for affluent tenants or homebuyers, there are exceptions. For example, a giant apartment development in Brooklyn, New York, known as Starrett City, was constructed in the

CASE STUDY: Private Clubs Discriminate?

A number of lawsuits have claimed discrimination in membership within private clubs. Many of these clubs have been able to maintain their membership policies even though civil rights laws make it illegal to discriminate based on race, national origin, and other bases. However, these laws do not cover bona fide private clubs and religious organizations—these can discriminate on whatever basis they choose. Some states have extended the civil rights laws and prevent private clubs from discriminating, closing this loophole in the law. Because not all states have done this, discrimination still exists. Here are a few examples.

In 2009, 60 African American children were turned away from a northeast Philadelphia private swim club despite the fact that they had paid the $1900 fee. John Duesler, president of the Valley Swim Club, said they were turned away because "there was concern that a lot of kids would change the complexion . . . and the atmosphere of the club."[a]

Augusta National Golf Club does not allow women to become members. When questioned about this, Hootie Johnson, chairman of Augusta National, stated, "There may well come a day when women will be invited to join our membership, but that timetable will be ours and not at the point of a bayonet."

Birgit Koebke and Kendall French, a lesbian couple registered as domestic partners under the California Domestic Partner Rights and Responsibilities Act of 2003, sued Heights Country Club because of discrimination. Club membership pertains to member spouses but not domestic partners. The California Supreme Court ruled that domestic partners should receive the same benefits as legal spouses and mandated the club provide the same benefits to all couples.

Questions to Consider

1. If members own a private club, should they be able to establish policies that intentionally or unintentionally discriminate against a group?
2. Is a high membership fee a form of discrimination? Why or why not?
3. Should private clubs be able to limit families to legally married couples? Why or why not?

Source

a. A. Kilkenny, "Philadelphia Private Swim Club Forces Out Black Children," *Huffington Post* (8 July 2009).

mid-1970s to serve middle-income tenants drawn from varied ethnic populations—approximately half were African American, Hispanic, and Asian. Its thousands of residents enjoy a huge clubhouse with meeting rooms, hobby, craft, and dance classes, and an extensive pool program and tennis complex, as well as numerous classes, teams, and special events through the year.

In some cases, large condominium-structured apartment buildings also have extensive leisure facilities and programs. For example, in Philadelphia, one such building with 776 residential units has a bank, restaurant, 10 stores, doctors' and dentists' offices, garages, and two swimming pools, all under one roof. It also has a library, card room, fitness center, and numerous clubs and committees, including a welcoming committee, Weight Watchers, a writers' club, book club, and computer club.

Vacation Homes

A specialized form of residence-connected recreation is often found in vacation home developments. During the 1960s and 1970s, direct ownership and time-sharing arrangements for such homes became more popular, often in large-scale developments situated close to a lake or other major recreational attraction.

The baby boom, with millions of couples reaching the age and financial status at which they are able to afford vacation homes, has led to a rapid rise in the number of such developments. According to the National Association of Realtors, more than 10% of home purchases in 2009 were vacation homes.[37]

Typically, time-sharing apartments or condominiums in attractive vacation areas today cost as much as $15,000 to $20,000 for the right to use the facility one week each year. Although this may seem expensive, it is minimal compared with the cost in vacation areas where the "jet set"—the wealthy elite of U.S. society—enjoy their vacations. Illustrating the tendency to seek privacy in exclusive surroundings, a number of millionaires and billionaires who formerly enjoyed their vacations in Aspen, Colorado, left that area when it became too well known and popular. Today they fly their own jets to a stunningly beautiful mountain hamlet in Wyoming known as Saratoga. Members of the Old Baldy Club live in "cottages" that would be considered mansions anywhere else. When asked how much it cost to join the Old Baldy Club, a local resident received the reply, "If you have to ask, you can't afford it."

Retirement Communities

Similarly, large retirement villages offer recreation and social programs for their residents. A vivid example may be found in Sun City, Arizona. Established in 1960, this community has about 42,000 residents. Sun City is the country's first planned retirement community. The recreation opportunities are extensive because the community has 7 community centers with a pool in each one, 11 golf courses, 2 library branches, 2 bowling alleys, 2 lakes, a wide variety of programs, and more than 350 social and civic clubs.[38]

Many retirement communities offer extensive recreation facilities and programs for their residents.

So successful has the Sun City formula been that in the 1980s and 1990s, two additional communities were developed in the area—Sun City West and Sun City Grand. With many younger, earlier retirees, these communities not only feature the traditional pastimes of older adults, but also such newer or more demanding activities as weight training, inline skating, and rock climbing. Growing numbers of semiretired residents continue to volunteer, do part-time work, or even start their own businesses—and in some cases accept such challenges as training for triathlons or helicopter hiking in the remote Canadian Rockies.[39]

Many retirement communities offer extensive recreation facilities and programs and encourage residents to attend cultural events in the surrounding area. Others, as in Sarasota, Florida's, Pelican Cove, have uniquely beautiful natural surroundings, including a marina with easy access to open bay waters.

In numerous other retirement communities, such as Leisure World in Laguna Hills, California, such recreational facilities as pools, tennis courts, and riding stables often are found.

COMPARISONS AMONG SPECIAL-FOCUS AGENCIES

There are both differences and similarities among the five types of leisure-service organizations meeting special needs that are described in this chapter.

Therapeutic recreation is obviously concerned chiefly with meeting the needs of persons with disabilities as well as using recreation as a purposeful tool to achieve goals of habilitation or rehabilitation. Although its major emphasis is on providing both clinical and community-based recreation programs, the strong thrust today is toward inclusion of individuals with disabilities within the larger population. As such, it shares many common program elements and facilities with the overall community recreation system.

Armed forces recreation involves a huge, sprawling, worldwide operation. It is essentially made up of hundreds of smaller individual programs on both domestic and foreign bases or on ships. Uniquely, it is governed by a bureaucratic structure and specific policies that originate within the defense department, while at the same time responding to the special needs and resources of different branches of the military services and to local capabilities and interests. Its services and programs range from businesslike and commercialized approaches to entertainment or hospitality to purposeful, social service activities meeting the needs of children and youth or dependent families.

Employee recreation service differs from other special branches of the leisure-service system in that it has become just one of 10 important functions designed to improve the quality of life in the work environment and to contribute to the effective operation of its sponsoring companies. Within this spectrum of service, recreation has the unique responsibility of upgrading company morale and human relationships, as well as promoting the positive image of the overall enterprise. As in both therapeutic and armed forces recreation, employee programs must be concerned with achieving important agency goals and with documenting their worth in concrete, measurable terms.

Campus recreation, whether primarily concerned with sport programming or with broader cultural and curriculum-connected activities, today is seen as an integral element in the overall higher education structure. Particularly in colleges and universities in which older adolescents and those just entering adulthood are faced with the challenge of their first real social independence, it is critical that campus recreation help students develop positive lifestyle values and patterns of leisure choices. As part of this purpose, campus activities should serve as an attractive counterbalance to less-desirable leisure involvements.

Finally, private-membership leisure-service organizations are heavily influenced by socioeconomic factors, in that they tend to be provided for individuals and families who are relatively elite in financial and demographic terms. Although they have been undergoing a gradual process of democratization, many such groups continue to be exclusive and focus on a narrow range of recreational interests. One exception is found in the growing number of retirement communities, which often sponsor a considerable variety of recreational programs, particularly for younger individuals and couples who are entering such communities.

CASE STUDY: Job Comparisons

Now that you are familiar with these specialized segments of recreation, answer the following questions about each.

	Therapeutic Recreation	MWR	Employee Recreation	Campus Recreation	Private-Membership Recreation
Who is the primary clientele?					
What are the defining characteristics?					
What are some sample organizations that represent each type of recreation?					
What are some sample programs offered?					
What are the type of university courses you think you need to take to work in this setting?					

SUMMARY

Five specialized areas of leisure-service delivery described in this chapter illustrate the diversity of agencies that provide organized recreation opportunities today. In each case, they have their own goals and objectives, populations served, and program emphases—yet they are important elements within the overall leisure-service system and represent attractive fields of career opportunity for recreation, park, and leisure-service students today.

Therapeutic recreation service, in its two areas of professional emphasis—clinical or treatment service and community-based special recreation—is probably the most highly professionalized of all the separate disciplines in the leisure-service field. It has a long history of professional development, with separate sections of state and national societies, early emphasis on certification, numerous specialized curricula, and a rich literature and background of research. With the possibility of lessened support being given to clinical therapeutic recreation in an era of cost cutting, hospital retrenchment, managed patient care, and deinstitutionalization, it is probable that community-based special recreation, with its emphasis on inclusion, will constitute an increasingly important element in therapeutic recreation.

Armed forces recreation professionals serve a distinct population composed both of large numbers of relatively young service men and women—and of families and dependants with special needs prompted by the military setting. Morale, fitness, and mission accomplishment are important armed forces recreation goals, which are reflected in an increasingly businesslike approach to planning, marketing, and evaluating programs. With reduced budgets caused by downsizing and a greater emphasis on fiscal self-sufficiency, military recreation has undergone major transformations in recent years, yet it continues to offer a wide range of attractive program opportunities and often has excellent facilities, both stateside and abroad.

Employee recreation and services today have gone far beyond their original emphasis on providing a narrow range of social and sports activities designed to promote company–worker relationships. They are carried on in many different kinds of organizations and include varied health- and fitness-related program elements, as well as such other personnel services as discount programs, company stores, community relationships, and other benefits-driven functions—all necessarily provided within a business-oriented framework that demands productivity and demonstrated outcomes.

Campus recreation is carried on within an educational setting and is designed to augment academic studies. At the same time, it has important responsibilities in terms of promoting the overall well-being of students, helping to reduce negative or destructive forms of play, extending and enriching academic learnings, and contributing to other college and university goals.

The last type of organization described in this chapter, the private-membership association, includes a wide range of country clubs, golf clubs, yacht clubs, and other social or business membership groups that often tend to be socially exclusive. They represent a growing trend in the United States today, with millions of families now living in residential developments that have their own community associations to provide services, including recreation. This tends to limit their interest in or dependence on public, tax-supported recreation services.

QUESTIONS FOR CLASS DISCUSSION OR ESSAY EXAMINATION

1. Differentiate between clinical-based therapeutic recreation and community-based recreation.
2. Give specific examples of where recreation professionals could work within therapeutic recreation, MWR, campus recreation, employee recreation, and private-membership organizations.
3. Compare and contrast the two TR models of practice.
4. Describe the TR process.
5. Compare and contrast military recreation and public recreation agencies.
6. List the benefits of employee recreation for the employer and the employee.

7. What role does campus recreation play on a college campus?
8. Describe private-membership recreation and give some examples of clubs. Explain the issues with member discrimination.

ENDNOTES

1. M. G. Parr, M. E. Havitz, and A. T. Kaczynski, "The Nature of Recreation and Leisure as a Profession." In Human Kinetics (ed.), *Introduction to Recreation and Leisure* (177–196) (Champaign, IL: Human Kinetics, 2006).
2. ATRA, "What Is TR?" www.atra-online.com/displaycommon.cfm?an=12.
3. F. Stavola Daly and R. Kunstler, "Therapeutic Recreation." In Human Kinetics (ed.), *Introduction to Recreation and Leisure* (177–196) (Champaign, IL: Human Kinetics, 2006).
4. T. Robertson and T. Long, "Considering Therapeutic Recreation as Your Profession." In T. Robertson and T. Long (eds.), *Foundations of Therapeutic Recreation: Perceptions, Philosophies and Practices for the 21st Century* (3–11) (Champaign, IL: Human Kinetics, 2008).
5. R. Smith et al., *Inclusive and Special Recreation: Opportunities for Persons with Disabilities*, 5th ed. (McGraw-Hill Higher Education, 2001).
6. R. Williams, "Places, Models, and Modalities of Practice." In T. Robertson and T. Long (eds.), *Foundations of Therapeutic Recreation: Perceptions, Philosophies and Practices for the 21st Century* (63–76) (Champaign, IL: Human Kinetics, 2008); D. R. Austin, *Therapeutic Recreation: Processes and Techniques*, 6th ed. (Champaign, Ill: Sagamore Publishing, 2009).
7. Americans with Disabilities Act. http://www.ada.gov.
8. R. Williams, "Places, Models, and Modalities of Practice." In T. Robertson and T. Long (eds.), *Foundations of Therapeutic Recreation: Perceptions, Philosophies and Practices for the 21st Century* (63–76) (Champaign, IL: Human Kinetics, 2008).
9. N. J. Stumbo and C. A. Peterson, *Therapeutic Recreation Program Design: Principles and Procedures*, 4th ed. (San Francisco: Benjamin Cummings, 2004).
10. D. R. Austin, *Therapeutic Recreation: Processes and Techniques*, 6th ed. (Champaign, IL: Sagamore Publishing, 2009), 172.
11. R. Williams, "Places, Models, and Modalities of Practice." In T. Robertson and T. Long (eds.), *Foundations of Therapeutic Recreation: Perceptions, Philosophies and Practices for the 21st Century* (63–76) (Champaign, IL: Human Kinetics, 2008); D. R. Austin, *Therapeutic Recreation: Processes and Techniques*, 6th ed. (Champaign, Ill: Sagamore Publishing, 2009).
12. N. J. Stumbo and C. A. Peterson, *Therapeutic Recreation Program Design: Principles and Procedures*, 4th ed. (San Francisco: Benjamin Cummings, 2004).
13. T. Long, "The Therapeutic Recreation Process." In T. Robertson and T. Long (eds.), *Foundations of Therapeutic Recreation: Perceptions, Philosophies and Practices for the 21st Century* (79–97) (Champaign, IL: Human Kinetics, 2008).
14. J. S. Kinney, T. Kinney, and J. Witman, "Therapeutic Recreation Modalities and Facilitation Techniques: A National Study," *Annual in Therapeutic Recreation* (Vol. 13, 2004): 59–79.
15. Morgan's Wonderland, *Morgan's Wonderland*. www.morganswonderland.com/.
16. National Sports Center for the Disabled, "Summer Programs 2010." www.nscd.org/programs/summer brochure.htm.
17. *NTRS Report* (Vol. 23, No. 3, May–June 1998): 8–9.
18. U.S. Army Community and Family Support Center, "About MWR." http://www.armymwr.com/portal/about.

19. J. Temple and L. Ogilvie, "Unique groups." In Human Kinetics (ed.), *Introduction to Recreation and Leisure* (177–196) (Champaign, IL: Human Kinetics, 2006).

20. Fort Huachuca MWR. www.mwrhuachuca.com/.

21. "Start Smart Popular on Military Bases Worldwide," *Parks and Recreation* (December 1998): 27.

22. Fort Carson MWR. www.mwrfortcarson.com/adventure-programs—education.php.

23. K. Crouch, "The Army Family Covenant in Action, Part 1—Family Programs and Services." www.armymwr.com/news/archive/news.aspx?nid=195.

24. Ibid.

25. MCCS, "Marine Corps Family Team Building (MCFTB)." www.usmc-mccs.org/mcftb/index.cfm?sid=fl&smid=1.

26. United States Navy's Child and Youth Programs. https://qol2.navyaims.net/CYPWEB/Web/Home/Home.aspx.

27. R. Kraus and J. Curtis, *Creative Management in Recreation and Parks* (St. Louis, MO: Mosby, 1982): 206–207.

28. Carolyn Becraft, quoted in Pat Harden, "Armed Forces Recreation Services: Our Hallowed Ground Raison D'Etre," *Parks and Recreation* (December 1994): 24.

29. Employee Services Management Foundation, http://www.esmassn.org.

30. Minnesota Employee Recreation and Services Council, "About MERSC." www.mersc.org/about_mersc.aspx.

31. Honeywell, "Employee Club Store—Minneapolis." http://eclub.honeywell.com/eclub/ec_info.asp.

32. D. Holden, "Fact Check: The Cost of Obesity," CNN (9 February 2010).

33. Eli Lilly Foundation, "Employee Giving." www.lilly.com/responsibility/foundation/employee_giving/.

34. Colorado State University Campus Recreation. http://campusrec.colostate.edu/OutdoorProgram/Index.cfm.

35. University of Utah Campus Recreation. http://web.utah.edu/campusrec/outdoor_rec/rentals.html.

36. ClubCorp, "About Us." www.clubcorp.com/club/scripts/section/section.asp?GRP=8&NS=PAU.

37. Resort Life, "Vacation Home Sales Up But Investment Home Sales Down" (12 April 2010). http://resortlife.blogs.realtor.org/2010/04/12/vacation-home-sales-up-but-investment-home-sales-down/.

38. Sun City, AZ, Visitors Center, "Facilities Available to Sun City Residents." www.suncityaz.org/pdf/Facilities%20Available%20To%20SC%20Residents.pdf.

39. Joseph Shapiro, "No Sunset for Sun City," *U.S. News and World Report* (28 June 1999): 78.

CHAPTER 10

TRAVEL AND TOURISM

◆◆◆

Tourism has become the world's largest industry and touches every corner of the United States. Many communities and counties have tourism bureaus, states have state tourism offices, and advertising for tourism has grown at a prodigious rate. Employment in the tourism industry is significant in every state. Almost every American annually travels as a tourist.

Tourism, as an industry, is as simple as a rural community's fall apple festival or as complex as the hosting of the Super Bowl or some other major event. There are tens of thousands of tourism-based events across the United States annually. Tourism has become interwoven with the fabric of our society and is an essential component of recreation and leisure.

◆◆◆

INTRODUCTION

Tourism is the world's largest industry; spans across the public, nonprofit, and commercial sectors; is highly affected by changing technology; and encompasses culture, history, the environment, religion, the arts, agriculture, sport, education, and additional areas. Tourism is big business and is not confined to this country, as it is a global industry.

This chapter focuses on tourism and travel as well as the components that make up this massive industry. Before delving into the specifics of tourism, it is important to define what exactly travel and tourism are. On the surface, these may be easily defined, but think about the complexity. How far does one have to go to be considered a tourist? Do tourists have to stay overnight? Do tourists have to go outside of their home community? Does tourism have to be for pleasure or is business travel considered tourism?

Tourism is defined as "the activities of persons traveling to and staying in places outside their usual environments, for leisure, business, or other purposes."[1] In this instance, a person's usual environment means the community in which that person lives. The World Tourism Organization puts a time stipulation on the definition of tourism by saying that people must not remain in the location for more than a year.

The tourism industry can be divided into international and domestic tourism. International tourism is both inbound and outbound. Inbound tourism is when visitors from one country come to visit another country. Outbound tourism is when residents of one country leave and visit a different country. To further explain, take the United States as the home country, for example. Inbound tourism is when people from countries such as Thailand, Italy, and Poland come to the United States to visit. Outbound tourism is when people from the United States leave their country and go to places such as England, France, and Germany. The other type of tourism is domestic tourism, when travelers stay within their own country.[2]

Tourism involves transportation in many forms, and international tourism frequently involves air travel.

Crossley, Jamieson, and Brayley do not separate commercial recreation (Chapter 8) and tourism because of the interconnectedness of these concepts. They suggest that the tourism industry is made up of three parts. First, local commercial recreation is the entertainment, activities, and retail services within the community. It encompasses such venues and activities as theaters, festivals, water parks, golf courses, and shopping. The second piece of the industry is travel. *Travel* simply refers to the movement of people from one location to another. It may be carried out by plane, ship, railroad, bicycle, train, or other means. The last part of the commercial recreation and tourism industry is hospitality. *Hospitality* refers to the vast system of accommodations, food, and beverages that encompasses hotels, resorts, RV parks, bars, and restaurants. Tangent to the industry are the facilitators who make tourism happen. Travel agents, travel information services, convention and visitors bureaus, and meeting planners are facilitators of this industry and play an important role in making tourism happen.

Tourism-Related Employment

The World Travel and Tourism Council projects that, by 2019, 1 in every 11.8 jobs will be travel- and tourism-related.[3]

SCOPE OF TOURISM

Overall, the travel and tourism industry has been described as one of the world's largest businesses. Approximately 9.4% of the gross domestic product in the United States is generated by travel and tourism, which is approximately $5.474 billion.[4] It is the nation's second-largest employer, second only to health services. Nearly 70% of the 7.7 million jobs in this industry can be classified into the categories of accommodations, air transportation, food and beverage, and retail,[5] and they account for a $194 billion payroll.[6]

According to the World Travel and Tourism Council, personal travel and tourism accounted for $814.9 billion and business travel accounted for another $165.3 billion in 2008. Inbound international travel brings billions of dollars each year into the U.S. economy. These travelers accounted for 57.9 million people coming into the United States in 2008. The terrorist attack on the World Trade Center in New York City on September 11, 2001, had a significant impact on world travel and particularly ravel to the United States. Within the first 20 months after the attack, the U.S. economy was negatively affected by more than $74 billion. Furthermore, international travel hit its lowest point in 2003, with 41.2 million visitors.[7] The continued rapid increase to the current levels is a positive sign for the United States economy.

International travelers come from a variety of locations, including Canada, Mexico, and Great Britain (**Table 10.1**). When these visitors come to the United States, they most often visit New York (8.4 million), California (5.3 million), Florida (5.2 million), and Nevada (2.1 million).[8]

People living in the United States are also traveling abroad at high rates, with more than 27.5 million people traveling to other countries. More than 11 million people travel to Europe each year, followed by the Caribbean (5 million), Asia (4.8 million), and South America (2.3 million).[9]

Many different kinds of organizations provide tourism opportunities. Thousands of commercial sponsors of tourist attractions and transportation services, theme parks and

TABLE 10.1

VISITORS TO THE UNITED STATES

Rank	Country	2008 Arrivals	2008 Spending
1	Canada	18.9 million	$18.7 billion
2	Mexico	13.7 million	$9.7 billion
3	Great Britain	4.6 million	$16.7 billion
4	Japan	3.2 million	$14.6 billion
5	Germany	1.8 million	$6.7 billion
6	France	1.2 million	$4.8 billion
7	Italy	779,000	$3.7 billion
8	Brazil	769,000	$4.2 billion
9	South Korea	759,000	Did not make top 10 list
10	Australia	690,000	$3.7 billion

Data from the U.S. Department of Commerce, International Trade Administration, "Top 10 International Markets: 2008 Visitation and Spending." Available at: http://tinet.ita.doc.gov/outreachpages/download_data_table/2008_Top_10_Markets.pdf. Accessed November 5, 2010.

water parks, cruise ships, charter airline operators, group tour managers, hotel chains, sport arenas, entertainment venues, casinos, zoos, aquariums, wild animal parks, and numerous other businesses satisfy the tourism market. Many government agencies manage parks, historical sites, oceanfront areas, and other kinds of events that attract millions of recreational visitors.

Similarly, many nonprofit organizations sponsor sport events, cultural programs, educational tours, religious pilgrimages, and other special travel programs that serve millions of tourists each year. Armed forces morale, welfare, and recreation units offer travel services to men and women in uniform, and industrial and other business concerns frequently schedule charter flights for their employees. Local convention and visitors bureaus facilitate vacation travel and promote regional tourist attractions.

New Links Between Public and Commercial Sponsors

It is becoming apparent that both public and commercial agencies have an important stake in promoting successful tourist programs today. In the past, tourism has been regarded as a commercial economic phenomenon rooted in the private business sector. Today, with cities, states, and entire nations competing to attract large numbers of tourists because of their contribution to the overall economy, both government agencies and private entrepreneurs have joined forces in planning and promoting tourist attractions.

At another level, as this chapter shows, many states and local governments have moved vigorously into cooperative ventures to sponsor and promote varied forms of tourist attractions, both to heighten their positive image and to draw needed revenues and bolster local employment.

TOURISM THEMES

Apart from traveling to theme parks and similar attractions, tourists today seek to satisfy a remarkable range of personal interests and motivations.

Many cruise ships have become floating entertainment palaces like this three-tiered dining room.

Cruises

Over the past three decades, the growing prosperity of many Americans has made it possible for greater numbers of vacationers to indulge themselves with more varied forms of travel. Luxury cruise ships are no longer simply a vehicle for getting from one place to another or for extended, leisurely ocean voyages. Instead, they have evolved into floating amusement parks, health spas, classrooms, and nightclubs. The major cruise companies have developed huge new vessels and are catering to younger and less-affluent individuals by offering relatively inexpensive short-term trips.

Today, more than 80 cruise ship lines offer a remarkable variety of vacation options afloat, ranging from small sail-propelled schooners to giant, luxurious ocean liners. In many cases, their attractions include gourmet meals, early morning workouts, nightlife and gambling, language classes, deck games, and visits to exotic ports. The cruise industry estimated 18.4 million passengers in 2010 with an economic impact of $7.4 billion.[10] There are more than 250 different cruise liners currently in operation, visiting more than 2000 ports of call.

Variety of Cruise Experiences As in the overall tourism field, cruise passengers' motivations and interests take many different forms. While some travelers prefer luxurious, pampered, and relatively inactive trips, others enjoy excursions and activities that are demanding or that provide unusual leisure experiences. For example, the Great Alaska Marathon Cruise has two well-known marathon trainers onboard to help travelers complete a marathon on the ship. The runners experience different distances and terrains each day and by cruise end will have completed the 26.2 miles.[11]

Other specially designed cruises offer such themes as "clothing-optional" trips for "naturists"; sobriety cruises; or golf, combining shipboard lessons and lectures with visits to notable links; wine lovers; poker; as well as many other unique travel tours with sea and land adventures.[12]

Cultural and Historical Interests

The term *cultural* may have two possible meanings when applied to tourism motivations. It may suggest interest in attending major performing arts festivals, visiting famous art museums, or having other kinds of aesthetic experiences. Another meaning involves interest in being exposed to new and different cultures.

Cultural tourism is based on the mosaic of places, traditions, art forms, celebrations, and experiences that portray a nation and its people, reflecting the diversity and character of the place. Garrison Keillor, in an address to the 1995 White House Conference on Travel and Tourism, best described U.S. cultural tourism by saying,

> We need to think about cultural tourism because really there is no other kind of tourism. It's what tourism is. . . . People don't come to America for our airports, people don't come to America for our hotels, or the recreation facilities. . . . They come for our culture: high culture, low culture, middle culture, right, left, real or imagined—they come here to see America.[13]

Cultural tourism involves experiencing the culture, whether it be indigenous or historical.

The Travel Industry Association (TIA) found 118.1 million people, representing 56% of all U.S. adult travelers included a cultural, arts, heritage, or historic activity while

CASE STUDY: Cultural and Historical Tourism

The Travel Industry Association provides services for the travel industry including research, publications, and education. The following is an excerpt from the Executive Summary of *The Historic/Cultural Traveler*, 2003 edition.[a]

Profile of Historic/Cultural Trips in the United States

Historic/cultural trips are more often generated by Baby Boomer households, and by households that are educated and/or affluent. Four in ten historic/cultural trips are taken by Baby Boomer households (age 35–54). Six in ten historic/cultural trips are generated by households with a college degree, and one third by households with an annual household income of $75,000 or more. One-third of trips are generated by households with children.

Historic/cultural trips taken by affluent households are more likely than those taken by less affluent households to include paid lodging and air transportation. Among income groups, historic/cultural trips taken by affluent households are the most likely to include air transportation and involve the use of a rental car as a secondary mode of transportation. Their historic/cultural trips also have the longest average duration, and their overnight trips are the most likely to involve a stay in a hotel, motel, or bed and breakfast establishment.

Most historic/cultural travel is by auto and nearly all historic/cultural travel involves an overnight stay. A car or truck is the most prevalent mode of transportation on historic/cultural trips; one in five person-trips include air transportation. Overnight trips last an average of 5.2 nights and most often include a stay at hotels, motels, or bed and breakfast establishments.

Historic/cultural trips including air transportation generate more trip spending than do other modes of transportation. As expected, historic/cultural travel that includes air transportation is much more likely than travel by other modes to include lodging in a hotel, motel, or bed and breakfast, last seven nights or longer, and have higher trip spending.

The South Atlantic, Pacific, and East North Central areas of the U.S. are the most popular destinations for historic/cultural travel. Historic/cultural trips are more likely than U.S. trips in general to be taken outside the Census division of residence. Travelers on historic/cultural trips are most likely to travel to destinations in the South Atlantic, Pacific, or East North Central divisions.

Questions to Consider

1. Considering the market for cultural and historic tourism and the baby boomer population growth patterns, what does the future of this type of tourism look like?
2. Is this a viable market with a significant economic impact? Why or why not?
3. What are some specific examples of cultural and historic destinations in your state? The county? The world?

Source

a. U.S. Travel Association. "Research." http://www.ustravel.org/research.

on a one-way trip of 50 miles or more during the previous year. Of these travelers, visiting an historic site such as an historic community or building was the most popular cultural activity (31%), followed by visiting a museum (24%), visiting an art gallery (15%), and seeing live theater (14%).

The purpose of cultural and historical tourism is to experience people and history in other places and countries because it helps us better understand and appreciate what currently exists and how that emerged.[14] Cultural tourism may include exposure to such regional or ethnically different locations as the Amish countryside in Pennsylvania, smaller communities throughout French Canada where the culture is determinedly Gallic, or visits to Native American reservations throughout the West—destinations that have special appeal for many Europeans. It may also involve what Canadian authorities term "heritage tourism," with trips to see old mines, factories, or prisons that have been redesigned to provide today's visitors with a fuller understanding of the past.

Increasingly, festivals or holiday events commemorate famous battles of the past, scenes of the Civil War, or other historic events. Even rodeos, which illustrate the real-life work of cowboys in the American West, or lumberjack contests and similar competitions at state fairs, serve as experiences that make this kind of tourism meaningful. Confer and Kerstetter sum up the meaning of heritage tourism:

> It is about the cultural traditions, places, and values that groups throughout the world are proud to conserve. Cultural traditions such as family patterns, religious practices, folklore traditions, and social customs attract individuals interested in heritage tourism, as do monuments, museums, battlefields, historic structures, and landmarks. [It also includes] natural heritage sites—gardens, wilderness areas of scenic beauty, and valued cultural landscapes.[15]

Ancestral Tourism

Ancestral tourism focuses on people who are trying to find the family roots and is frequently called in the industry, "trading on the family roots." Americans are particularly interested in their family history and spend millions of dollars annually on ancestral tourism. Ancestral tourism involves such experiences as traveling to historical sites, visiting international destinations where ancestors were known or suspected to originate, attending conferences and workshops on genealogy, and so forth. The industry has continued to grow as Americans turn inward toward an understanding of their roots.

Linked to this type of cultural and historic exploration, such organizations as American Youth Hostels or the Elderhostel movement, which serves older travelers, combine educational and cultural exposures with what are usually short-term stays in foreign lands or distant locations.

Sport Tourism

Sport tourism has become a major force in the tourism marketplace beginning in the mid-1980s. There have always been major sporting events that draw tens of thousands and even millions of people (**Table 10.2**).

Sport tourism has traditionally focused on two groups—participants and spectators. People travel to participate in such activities as softball tournaments, basketball tournaments, or to play golf. Arguably more common is travel to be a spectator at such events as the Super Bowl, NASCAR events, or the Kentucky Derby. Sport tourism has many differ-

TABLE 10.2

ATTENDANCE FIGURES FOR MAJOR SPORTING EVENTS

League	Games	Attendance	Year
Major League Baseball	2420	73,418,528	2009
National Football League	254	17,146,404	2009
National Basketball Association	1222	21,389,899	2009
NCAA bowl games	32	1,733,490	2007–2008
Indianapolis 500	1	Approx. 400,000	Annually

Data from ESPN, "MLB Attendance Report 2009." Available at: http://espn.go.com/mlb/attendance; ESPN, "NFL Attendance Report 2009." Available at: http://espn.go.com/nfl/attendance/_/year/2009; ESPN, "NBA Attendance Report 2009." Available at: http://espn.go.com/nba/attendance/_/year/2009; Sporting News, "Turnstile Tracker: NCAA Bowl Game Attendance Trend." Available at: http://www.sportingnews.com/college-football/article/2009-01-10/turnstile-tracker-ncaa-bowl-game-attendance-trend; and CBSSports.com, "2009 Indianapolis 500 Facts and Figures." Available at: http://www.cbssports.com/autoracing/story/11776519. Accessed December 8, 2010.

National and international sporting events, such as the FIFA World Cup 2010, brand their events with logos promoting recognition among visitors, advertisers, and participants.

ent dimensions and means to experience sport. Here is an overview of the elements of sport tourism.

Sporting events and sport places both serve as attractions. The 1896 Olympic stadium sits in downtown Athens and receives more visitors than the now closed Athens 2006 Olympic site. The College Football Hall of Fame, Professional Baseball Hall of Fame, and the NCAA Hall of Champions all draw many visitors. Visitations to sport facilities when teams are out of town or out of season is now commonplace. The Indianapolis Pacers and Conseco Fieldhouse charge an admission when visiting the fieldhouse, which goes to local charities. Yankee Stadium is probably the most visited baseball stadium in the United States because it holds a rich heritage of baseball greatness.

Sporting Events Major sporting events draw large numbers of tourists and have significant impacts on the local, regional, and national economies. The Indianapolis Motor Speedway, home of the Indianapolis 500, is the site of the oldest auto race in the world. The Indianapolis Motor Speedway operated a single race from 1911 to

Olympic Attendance Record

The 1996 Atlanta Olympics still holds the Olympic attendance record with 8.3 million tickets sold.[16]

1993. In 1994, the Brickyard 400, a major new NASCAR race, was initiated and is now called the "Allstate 400 at the Brickyard." Six years later a Formula One race was added, making Indianapolis the race capital of the world. These events pale by comparison to mega sport events such as the Olympic Games. The 2008 Beijing Olympics drew 6.8 million people.[17]

Resorts Resorts use sport as a means to attract tourists. For example, the Tourism Authority of Thailand uses resorts and their crystal-clear oceans to attract scuba divers. In addition, the country has more than 100 world-class golf courses with very reasonable greens fees. In the United States, golf and tennis resorts are abundant. The Kiawah Island Golf Resort in South Carolina boasts five championship golf courses and was ranked the number 1 tennis resort in the world by tennisresortsonline.com.[18] Resorts also cater to winter sports such as skiing and snowboarding.

Cruises and Tours Cruises were previously discussed in this chapter. However, sport cruises add a different dimension and have themes such as baseball greats, fans of specific teams, running, cycling, and golf. Companies such as Sports Travel and Tours set up sports-oriented tours for individuals and groups. They offer Pro Football Hall of Fame Enshrinement Festival tours, baseball road trips with stops at multiple baseball parks in a region, and Kentucky Derby Tours.[19]

Outdoor/Adventure Sports Despite a decline in the economy in recent years, the sale of outdoor equipment has continued to increase slightly.[20] This is an indicator of the popularity of outdoor adventure sports. Traditional outdoor vacations feature hiking, climbing, and fishing. People who are more adventurous can experience dog sledding, fly-in hiking, glacier tours, and heli-skiing, among other sports.

Fantasy Camps Sport fantasy camps allow participants to train alongside current and previous professional sports players and often on the same fields and courts. These camps target diehard fans who want to be immersed in their favorite teams and play alongside players they have watched for years. Baseball offers many fantasy sport camps, usually during spring training. Participants wear the team jersey, get instruction from former players, and hear their name announced by legendary announcers. For $17,500, Michael Jordan fans get 3½ days of basketball with Jordan and PAC 10 officials and work with Hall of Fame coaches such as Larry Brown and Chuck Daly. Other sports stars such as Wayne Gretzky, Cal Ripkin Jr., Richard Petty, and Chris Evert offer their own fantasy camps as well.[21]

Sport tourism has a major impact on the tourism industry whether the tourist is visiting a destination to participate or experience the attractions. Sport can be the reason to visit the community or a part of the overall vacation.

Religion-Based Tourism

Centuries ago, one of the motivations spurring international travel was pilgrimages. Today, religion-oriented travel is one of the industry's fastest-growing segments. Tours highlight Christian, Jewish, Muslim, and Buddhist places of importance.

Religious tourism, also called spiritual tourism, encompasses many aspects of religion. First, pilgrimages are quite common where individuals take long journeys to experience a location of religious significance. For example, Mecca in Saudi Arabia is the most sacred place for the Islamic religion. It is the place where all Muslims point themselves during their daily prayers, and they are encouraged to make the pilgrimage to Mecca at least once in their lifetime. Another popular pilgrimage destination is to the Western Wall in Jerusalem, which is a Jewish holy site.[22]

Religious-based tourism can take place in many settings such as this monastery near Sparta, Greece.

A second aspect of religion tourism is missionary travel where people travel to other locations as part of a religious group or church affiliation. On these trips, people help the local community with education, recreation, construction of needed facilities, health care, and economic development.

Third, conventions and crusades are held annually, bringing together people of specific religions for worship. For example, each summer 6000 members of Jehovah's Witness gather in Bloomington, Illinois, for their district convention.

Last, religious tourism has a focus on visiting attractions and locations that have religious significance. Attractions such as the Basilica de Guadalupe in Mexico, the Vatican in Italy, or the Reclining Buddha in Thailand are popular to those within these religions but also those outside of the religion as well.

Nauvoo, Illinois, has become an American religion-based tourism site. It was home to the Latter-Day Saints (Mormons) from 1839 to 1842 and has received increased tourism focus over the last 25 years as the Latter-Day Saint Church and nonprofit groups have restored much of the original area and in 2002 replaced the 1846 temple. Tourism exceeds 1.5 million annually.

Often, such trips are not narrowly denominational but bring members of various faiths together to explore their linked heritages and contrast their present beliefs and practices.

Health-Related Tourism

Recognizing that religious travel is for many persons a means of obtaining spiritual well-being and emotional health, it should be stressed that for many other individuals health needs represent a primary motivation for travel. In Europe, particularly, visits to traditional health spas that are based on natural mineral springs are being gradually replaced by stays at more modern health and fitness centers. These destinations often combine varied forms of exercise, nutritional care, massage, yoga, and other holistic approaches to health care to provide a fuller range of services to visitors. Whereas weight reduction or recovery from alcohol or drug addiction is the primary focus of many such centers, others involve a much broader approach to achieving "wellness."

A recent trend related to health-motivated travel is medical tourism. In response to rising healthcare and insurance costs in their home countries, citizens from the United

States and Great Britain are increasingly seeking cheaper medical and surgical care in developing countries such as India, Thailand, and Mexico.[23] Medical tourism packages usually include luxury room accommodations in hospitals and are often combined with flights, transportation, and resort hotel bookings, interpreters, and airport concierge services.[24]

Ecotourism and Adventure Travel

With the growth of environmental concerns and programs over the past few decades, ecotourism (a form of leisure travel) has emerged, which is deeply concerned with the preservation and protection of the natural environment. The International Ecotourism Society (IETS) defines ecotourism as "responsible travel to natural areas that conserves the environment and improves the well-being of local people."[25]

Ecotourism may be carried on at various levels of personal challenge and comfort. A little more luxury is experienced in an eco-vacation to Vancouver Island, British Columbia, where travelers visit Bouchart Gardens, whale watch, kayak, and walk in the woods, on beaches, and in nature areas. Travelers stay in hotels in different cities on this 5-day tour.[26] A more rustic eco-vacation could have travelers camping in the Brazilian rainforest learning about the indigenous people in the region.

IETS Principles of Ecotourism

Ecotourism is about *uniting conservation, communities,* and *sustainable travel.* This means that those who implement and participate in ecotourism activities should follow the following ecotourism principles:

- Minimize impact.
- Build environmental and cultural awareness and respect.
- Provide positive experiences for both visitors and hosts.
- Provide direct financial benefits for conservation.
- Provide financial benefits and empowerment for local people.
- Raise sensitivity to host countries' political, environmental, and social climate.[27]

The concept of ecotourism is entrenched in the principles of sustainable tourism, also termed *geotourism*. Sustainable tourism advocates tourism activities that are compatible with the ecological processes, sociocultural characteristics, and economic structure of the destination and that enhance the geographical character of a place.[28]

As a variant of this approach, some tourist companies offer "action vacations" that provide the traveler the chance to visit foreign lands not simply to lie on a beach but to take part in an archaeological dig, study wildlife or the local environment systematically, teach English to children, or be involved in healthcare projects. As a result of heightened interest among tourists to make voluntary contributions to the communities they visit, a new form of tourism, *volunteer tourism*, is gaining popularity across the globe. Tours catering to "volun-tourists" provide cultural immersion along with opportunities for self-fulfillment through volunteer work. For example, the Cultural Restoration Tourism Project, a San

CASE STUDY: Traveling Goes Green

Even if ecotourism is not of interest to a traveler, travelers can still travel "green." Increasingly, accommodations are making efforts to conserve the natural environment by asking guests to use towels more than once and not washing sheets each night. However, there are many other ways tourists can travel green and reduce their carbon footprint. Here are a few suggestions:

1. Take your own water bottle and fill it up rather than buying bottled water. Approximately 1.5 million barrels of oil—enough to run 100,000 cars for a whole year—are used to make plastic water bottles. This does not even include the oil used to transport these bottles.[a]
2. Ditch excess baggage. The heavier the bag, the more fuel it takes to transport it. If you are in a country with a high poverty rate, donate the clothes you do not need anymore and do not even bring them home.
3. Fly direct. Save gas.
4. Take public transportation rather than renting a car.
5. Donate leftover currency. Do not bring home anything you will not use.[b]
6. Use green accredited directories to find green hotels.
7. Patronize restaurants that buy local produce.

Questions to Consider

1. What other green suggestions do you have for travelers?
2. What inhibits people from traveling green?
3. What could be done to increase the likelihood of people traveling green?

Sources

a. TreeHugger, "A World of Reasons to Ditch Bottled Water." www.treehugger.com/files/2007/07/reasons_to_ditch_bottled_water.php.
b. Go Green Travel Green, "6 Tips for a Green Return Home: 25 Days to Green Travel, Day 24." http://gogreentravelgreen.com/green-transportation/6-tips-for-a-green-return-home-25-days-to-green-travel-day-24/.

Francisco–based nonprofit group, offers tours focusing on the renovation of Buddhist temples in Nepal and Mongolia, and I-to-I, a for-profit United Kingdom–based company offers tour packages for conservation and humanitarian relief work in India, Sri Lanka, Nepal, Vietnam, Costa Rica, and South Africa.[29]

With less of a social service orientation and more of an adventure recreational focus, some vacations may involve high-risk adventure pastimes such as trail rides through wild country, cave diving, hang gliding, mountain climbing, or whitewater rafting on turbulent streams. Extreme versions of adventure tourism may involve the opportunity to track down tornadoes, offered as a package deal by a number of companies in the Midwest or Southwest regions of the United States during the tornado seasons of the year.[30] Most extreme was the tour designed by a Nashua, New Hampshire, company in the mid-1990s, which offered to take thrill-seeking tourists to combat zones in parts of the former Soviet Union and spots on the Indian Ocean.

Other well-heeled adventurers today embark on expeditions to climb the Matterhorn, fly to the North Pole, break the sound barrier in a Russian MIG-25 fighter jet, or pay deposits to take suborbital rides into space (defined as 62 miles up) scheduled to be offered by commercial rocket builders.

Space Tourism Recognized as the world's newest form of tourism, it has been talked about for decades, but not until Dennis Tito of the United States blasted off into space from the Russian Space Center in April 2001 was it that the world had its first true space tourist. Since that time three additional space tourists have flown to the International Space Station on a Soyuz spacecraft. The Russian rationale for allowing individuals to become space tourists was to raise badly needed revenue for the Russian space program. Each trip comes at a price tag of $20 million. Since the collapse of communism, and even before, Russia has been hard pressed to maintain its space program.

Space has been dominated by governments since the earliest days of the space programs with either Russia or the United States dominating the world's space programs. Until 2003 when China entered the staffed space flight fraternity, only the United States and Russia had put individuals into space. Government involvement changed, however, when in October 2004, a Burt Rutan–designed suborbital aircraft flew over 328,000 feet (99,974.4 meters) in altitude and was not a government-sponsored enterprise.[31] Less than 10 months later, Burt Rutan's Scaled Composites aircraft design firm joined with Virgin Atlantic's Richard Branson to create Virgin Galactic, the world's second space-based tourism firm and the first not dependent on a government for spacecraft. On December 7, 2009, Virgin Galactic unveiled *SpaceShip Two*. This space ship will take tourists up 50,000 feet at a price of $200,000.[32] Futurists envision commercial space stations, flights to the moon, lunar tourism sites, and more.

Hedonistic Forms of Tourism

Still other forms of tourism are designed to provide hedonistic forms of pleasure to participants. Gambling clearly represents the most popular such activity, with millions of individuals traveling each year to major casinos throughout the world or enjoying gaming as a convenient amenity on ocean cruises or major airline flights.

At another level, thousands of young people each year roam through the Far East, including unscheduled, free-wheeling trips through Thailand, Cambodia, and Nepal, partly to experience their exotic environments, but also to take part in the drug culture that is readily available and inexpensive in these regions. Too often, many of these free spirits end as heavily substance-addicted individuals or simply disappear from sight and are not heard of again.

Finally, a form of pleasure-seeking tourism that has emerged throughout the world involves the search for sex. With the breakup of the Soviet Union, many young women from Russia, Ukraine, and other former Iron Curtain countries have been recruited as prostitutes in regions of southern Europe and North Africa.

The sex industry has become extremely profitable, providing substantial revenues not only to individuals and the networks involved in trafficking women but to some nations that have come to depend on sex industry profits. Sex tourism thrives in countries such as Ukraine where the women are poor and unprotected by the government and law enforcement. Many of these countries see women as less than equal to men. Because these women do not have the income sources to sustain themselves, the sex industry provides independence.[33] In Costa Rica, a growing number of unemployed women are going to San Jose to

Gambling is a growth industry in the United States, and it is a recognized form of personal recreation even if it is not perceived as psychologically and socially beneficial.

make a living capitalizing on sex tourism. However, the women are beginning to complain that there are too many women on the streets, and competition and 15% fewer tourists are driving down their profits. It is estimated that there are 25,000–50,000 sex tourists in Costa Rica each year, and 80% of those are U.S. citizens.[34]

Hosteling

Hostels are low-cost accommodations where people rent a bed in a dormitory-style facility. Guests share bathroom facilities and often have a common area for social interaction. Some hostels have private rooms for one to four people at an increased cost. En-suites are also becoming

CASE STUDY: Hostels

Part of the charm of hostels, in addition to the price, is that some can be quite unique. Here are a few examples from Hosteling International:

Carbisdale Castle Hostel (Scotland): The castle is a popular venue for groups, families, and weddings. Local attractions include distilleries, nature walks, and new mountain biking routes. This hostel is said to have great facilities, a statue gallery and art collection, coffee shop, restaurant, and resident ghost.

Stockholm 'af Chapman & Skeppsholmen' (Sweden): This hostel is an old sailing ship.

Stockholm 'Långholmen' (Sweden): Housed in a converted prison, this hostel was voted best hostel in Sweden in 2008. Inside this youth hostel visitors can see the prison museum, illustrating 250 years of prison history.

Point Montara Lighthouse (Montara, California): On the rugged California coast, 25 miles south of San Francisco, an historic 1875 fog signal station and lighthouse have been preserved and restored by HI-AYH and the California Department of Parks and Recreation, in cooperation with the Coast Guard.[a]

Questions to Consider

1. What is your impression of hostels?
2. Americans do not use hostels as much as Europeans do. Why do you think that is true?
3. Do you think that hostels will increase in popularity based on the economic climate? Why or why not?
4. Go to the Web site www.hihostels.com. Build an itinerary to six locations across Europe. Select hostels to stay in along the way.

Source

a. Hosteling International, "Hostels with a Difference." http://www.hihostels.com/dba/inspirelist.php?lang=E&insp=2.

CASE STUDY: Top 10 Global Travel Forecasts

The following are forecasts Rohit Talwar made for 2010 in an article titled "Top 10 Global Travel Forecasts":

1. *Air today, gone tomorrow.* As airlines continue to struggle, airports will be under intense pressure to diversify their business models and ensure they can survive under even the worst-case economic scenarios. When the final calculations are done, the airlines globally will have lost $8–10 billion in 2009. In addition, the pattern of airline closure continues: AirlineUpdate.com lists 90 airline failures and 7 mergers for 2008 and a further 32 failures and 6 mergers for 2009. We can expect 30 to 40 more failures and further mergers by the end of 2010. This will result in further reductions in schedules and flight frequencies—particularly for routes in Europe and the U.S. This could lead to airports closing and will create major challenges for some destinations in attracting sufficient travelers.
2. *Staycationing.* Nervous consumers, in Western economies in particular, will continue to exercise caution in their spending decisions for fear of a "double-dip recession." The middle classes will stay at home in large numbers and vacation in their own country.
3. *Asia, Asia.* The speed with which Asian economies are recovering from the downturn is highlighting their increasing power and importance. This part of the world will see a significant rise in business tourism as foreign firms tour the region in search of partners and opportunities.
4. *Rail reborn.* The arrival of more high-speed trains in Europe and environmental considerations will see a significant rise in people taking vacations by rail.
5. *Cruise it or lose it.* A massive recent increase in capacity, coupled with sluggish demand, will result in continued bargains for cruise passengers—particularly in the United States.
6. *Mind the gap.* Rising numbers of people of every age group will choose to take a year, half-year or quarter off to do extended travel—possibly combining working opportunities and volunteer work on their travels.
7. *Agent seeks model for profitable relationship.* The desperation to find a viable travel agency business model will intensify. As airline commissions continue their inevitable slide to zero, agents will find themselves squeezed as they struggle to compete with Internet travel booking services for straightforward transactions like airline ticketing. Only those who can provide a truly fantastic service will be able to charge their customers a fee for the value added. Otherwise, they will have to choose between turning the customer away or doing the airline booking for free in the hope of building customer loyalty and then charging the customer fees for other more complex bookings in the future.
8. *We love Grandma.* Stresses in the workplace and concerns over job security will see increasing numbers of parents choose to stay at home and work while their children take vacations with their grandparents.
9. *Ethnocations.* The quest for authenticity means people will increasingly seek out the opportunity to visit and live with tribal people in their indigenous habitats.
10. *The world in your hand.* We will see an explosion of take-up in the travel applications that are emerging for smartphones such as Apple's iPhone. You'll be able to get background information on every cultural site you visit, see animations or videos of how people used to live in ruined cities such as Pompeii, check out what every seat looks like on a particular plane before making your choice, swap your home for a vacation and receive instant personalized offers as you walk past particular shops in a tourist destination.

Questions to Consider

1. The projections were made for 2010; how accurate are they?
2. Which projections do you foresee to still come true? Which ones will not?
3. What forecasts do you make for the travel industry over the next 5 years?

Source

a. Special thanks to HotelWorld Network: This article is courtesy *The Hotel Yearbook 2010*. Rohit Talwar, "Top 10 Global Travel Forecasts" (4 January 2010). http://www.hotelworldnetwork.com/travel-trends/top-10-global-travel-forecasts.

more popular. Prices for hostels vary depending on the location and amenities. For example, a hostel in Milan, Italy, with rooms in a dorm with breakfast go for $25. A private room with two beds, breakfast, and sheets costs $68. A hostel in the Gaslamp Quarter in San Diego is the same price as Milan with the same amenities.

Hostels have traditionally been places in the countryside for young hikers to stop off for the night before continuing on their trek. Although this is a portion of the users of hostels, hostels are also starting to serve adults who want a simpler and less expensive place to stay. These people do not require the amenities of large-scale hotels such as room service and provided toiletries, and they can bring their own towels. Hostels are most known for the social aspects. The common rooms entice conversations among guests. It is not unusual for people staying at hostels to get to know each other and go off for adventures together.[35]

Culinary Travel

Culinary tourism is a relatively new phenomenon and a term that was first coined in 1998. The International Culinary Tourism Association (ICTA) defines culinary tourism "as the pursuit of unique and memorable culinary experiences of all kinds, often while traveling, but one can also be a culinary tourist at home."[36] ICTA states:

> The phrase "unique and memorable" is key to understanding culinary tourism. Many times people hear "culinary tourism" and they think it means restaurants that have earned 5 stars or better, or high-end wineries. That is not the case, as culinary tourism is not exclusively what is pretentious or exclusive. Culinary tourism includes a local pastry shop, an interesting bar on a nameless street that only locals know about, the pretzel vendor on the streets of New York City, or a gelato vendor on a historic street in Italy. Higher-end experiences fall into a subset of culinary tourism called "Gourmet Tourism." In fact, wine tourism, beer tourism and spa cuisine are also subsets of culinary tourism.[37]

Culinary tourism can also include attending cooking schools, visiting cooking supply stores, culinary tours, attending food festivals, visiting farmers' markets, or going to wineries and distilleries. The increase in culinary tourism is quite evident on television channels such as the Food Network and the Travel Channel. Rachel Ray takes viewers on a gastric tour of cities in the United States and abroad. Andrew Zimmern and Anthony Bourdain consume mainstream and exotic cuisine in all parts of the world. There is a plethora of books on the market featuring culinary tourism, such as the *Food Lover's Guide to Paris* by Patricia Wells.

Here are a few examples of tours available for culinary tourists:

Napa Valley Gourmet Traveler Tour: This 3-day tour of the Napa Valley region of California includes such activities as a train ride in the Vista Dome train car to dine on gourmet champagne luncheon; tours and wine tasting at premiere wineries in the region; and gourmet dinners at restaurants such as Julia's Kitchen, named after Julia Child.[38]

Tuscany Food and Wine Workshops: Tuscany is Italy's famous wine region, and this tour features such activities as olive oil pressing demonstrations, cooking demonstrations, and hands-on cooking classes. Participants stay on a farm where gardens are available to select fresh produce for dishes.[39]

Chiang Mai Thai Cooking School: This internationally renowned cooking school in Thailand teaches tourists how to cook Thai food. Classes run for 1 to 5 days and feature topics such as introduction to Thai ingredients, making curry pastes, and vegetable carving.[40]

MARKETING ADVANCES IN TRAVEL AND TOURISM

Perhaps more than in any other form of recreation, travel and tourism illustrate the increasing sophistication that is used to market leisure experiences today. Within this highly competitive but immensely lucrative field, as M. Uysal has pointed out, it is no longer possible to think of tourists as a large, homogeneous market. Instead, the planning and marketing of travel and tourist destinations must take into account the highly specialized interests of vacationers, their tastes in comfort and service, and their growing awareness of values and costs.[41]

Marketing segmentation studies, Uysal notes, must assess the socioeconomic and demographic variables of potential tourists, as well as product-related variables (having to do with transportation, length of stay, recreation activity, and similar factors); psychographic variables such as personal lifestyle and personality traits; geographical variables; and cultural factors such as religion, ethnic origin, and national customs. A major technological advancement that affects tourism and its marketing is the Internet.

Role of the Internet

An important development in the late 1990s involved the rapidly growing number of Web sites developed by different elements in the travel industry to facilitate the overall tourism marketing system. The Internet is an image formation agent and an information source. It provides a competitive comparison tool for individuals seeking travel-related information, tickets, lodging, and the like.[42]

Although many long-time travel buyers still look to brochures and travel agencies to provide information and arrange reservations, many travelers now buy travel services via the Web.

Some of the advantages of using the Internet for travel purchase include the following:

- It allows consumers to compare costs on such items as hotels, attractions, and transportation.
- A wealth of information is available 24 hours a day.
- The information available is often up-to-date.
- Internet specials and discounts can be found that are not available if the customer calls the airline or hotel.
- Interaction with other travelers is possible. Questions are answered, and Web sites such as tripadvisor.com rate accommodations and give advice on places to go and where to stay.
- There is a visual presence on destinations and accommodations.
- Event listings are available for the destination.

The downside to booking trips online is the difficulty of navigating through the Web site, people do not understand the options listed on the Web site, a lack of flexibility with travel options, and many people simply want to talk to a real person.[43]

In North America, the number of Internet users exceeded 252 million in 2009, with 74.2% of the population using it. Internationally, by 2009 there were 1.7 billion Internet users, a growth of 380% worldwide. The biggest growth occurred in Africa (1392.4%) and the Middle East (1648.2%).[44] The connectivity of the world and global Web sites in multiple languages have made travel decisions easier. Web sites such as travelocity.com, expedia .com, and orbitz.com have been major players in booking airline tickets, hotel rooms, and rental cars.

In addition to serving as a medium for the purchase of travel products and services, the Internet also is being widely used by organizations to disseminate travel-related information. Web sites such as tripadvisor.com, with 36 million monthly users,[45] and zoomandgo.com allow tourists to post ratings of tourism businesses and discuss travel experiences with others. In addition, travelers are also using travel blog sites, such as bootsnall.com and travelblog.org to send notes, photos, and sound recordings to others during the course of their trip. Web sites that predict airline ticket prices (e.g., FareCompare.com) and track flight performance (i.e., flight on-time ratings, delay statistics, and cancellation history) are also becoming increasingly popular among travelers.

The Internet also has contributed to the phenomenal growth of e-tourism, a technological strategy that combines electronic commerce (e-commerce) and innovative tourism business models to broaden the distribution networks of destinations and tourism organizations.[46] E-tourism provides opportunities for tourism businesses to increase their interactions via the Internet with a cross-section of tourism stakeholders, such as tourists/customers, government agencies, community groups, and other related organizations. In fact, e-tourism is being increasingly utilized by developing countries and poorer nations as a cost-effective way to reach international tourists and markets.[47]

CASE STUDY: Rick Steves's Europe Through the Back Door

Rick Steves is the host and writer of a weekly public radio show called *Travel with Rick Steves*, author of more than 40 European travel books, and host and writer of a public television show called Rick Steves' Europe. He advocates for smart, affordable, perspective-broadening travel with an emphasis on Europe.[a]

Steves began traveling by himself at age 18, when he funded his trips by teaching piano lessons. He later started his own company called Europe Through the Back Door as a one person operation that has now grown to a well-traveled staff of 70 full-time employees. Europe Through the Back Door takes a unique approach to business in that many services are provided free of charge. For example, RickSteves.com offers free travel information, a European Railpass Guide, a graffiti wall where travelers can share their experiences, Rick's favorite travel links, travel classes, and travel newsletters. In addition, Rick Steves has free podcasts that can serve as audio tours to such attractions as the Roman Coliseum, Venice's St. Mark's Square, and London's St. Paul's Cathedral. The service side of Europe Through the Back Door runs European tours, sells travel products, and publishes travel books. Rick Steves has developed a unique travel business aimed at making travel to Europe fun, easy, and inexpensive. He encourages people to travel as "temporary locals."

Questions to Consider

1. How has Rick Steves established himself as a niche market for tourism in Europe? How is Europe Through the Back Door different from other travel Web businesses?
2. Using information on Internet travel, plan a trip to a European country. Create an itinerary with links to several popular attractions. Use Rick Steves's resources to enhance the trip.

Source

a. Rick Steves' Europe, "Rick's Biography." http://www.ricksteves.com/about/pressroom/rickbio_extra.htm.

SUMMARY

Tourism involves huge sections of the leisure-service field, is provided by many different kinds of organizations, and has developed into a complex discipline in terms of job specialization and career opportunities. Tourism has a major economic impact on the United States and the world. Inbound and outbound travelers help stimulate economies domestically and abroad.

Travel and tourism represent diverse forms of leisure activity, with immense economic revenues. This chapter describes some of the most popular forms of tourism, such as cruises, cultural and historic interests, sport, religion, health, ecotourism, hedonism, hostels, and culinary tourism.

Marketing and the Internet are major influences on the travel industry. Marketing requires more sophistication because of the variety of travel opportunities available and the vast differences in the markets for attractions, tours, and destinations. The Internet has opened up many opportunities for information dissemination and the ability to make travel arrangements online. Technological advances will continue to affect travel and tourism in the years to come.

QUESTIONS FOR CLASS DISCUSSION OR ESSAY EXAMINATION

1. Tourism may be carried on for many purposes: exploration of different environments, cultural or educational purposes, adventure and risk, or hedonism. Give examples of such forms of tourism, based on class members' experiences.
2. Select either sport tourism or cruises and describe their role today in the tourism industry, including current trends and new formulas for appealing to the public.
3. Discuss the role of the Internet in tourism. How do you use the Internet for your travel plans?
4. What are the strengths and weaknesses of the Internet in making travel plans?
5. Discuss the impact of the tourism industry on the world economy.
6. Define cultural and historic tourism. Give examples of these types of destinations.
7. Define ecotourism. Give examples of these types of destinations. Do you see this form of tourism increasing or declining in the future? Why?

ENDNOTES

1. J. C. Crossley, L. M. Jamieson, and R. E. Brayley, *Introduction to Commercial Recreation and Tourism: An Entrepreneurial Approach*, 5th ed. (Champaign, IL: Sagamore Publishing, 2007).
2. C. R. Goeldner and J. R. Ritchie, *Tourism: Principles, Practices and Philosophies*, 11th ed. (Hoboken, NJ: Wiley, 2009).
3. World Travel and Tourism Council, "World-Key Facts at a Glance." http://www.wttc.org/eng/Tourism_Research/Tourism_Economic_Research.
4. World Travel and Tourism Council, "United States of America—Key Facts at a Glance." http://www.wttc.org/eng/Tourism_Research/Economic_Research/Country_Reports/United_States_of_America/.
5. U.S. Department of Commerce International Trade Administration, *The State of U.S. Travel and Tourism Industries*. http://tinet.ita.doc.gov/pdf/state_of_travel_tourism_YTD.pdf.
6. U.S. Travel Association, "The Power of Travel." http://poweroftravel.org/statistics.
7. U.S. Department of Commerce International Trade Administration, *International Visitation to the United States: A Statistical Summary of U.S. Arrivals (2008)*. http://tinet.ita.doc.gov/outreachpages/download_data_table/2008_Visitation_Report.pdf.
8. U.S. Department of Commerce International Trade Administration, *Overseas Visitation Estimates for U.S. States, Cities, and Census Regions: 2008*. http://tinet.ita.doc.gov/outreachpages/download_data_table/2008_States_and_Cities.pdf.
9. Office of Travel and Tourism Industries, "U.S. Citizen Air Traffic to Overseas Regions, Canada and Mexico 2009." www.tinet.ita.doc.gov/view/m-2009-O-001/index.html.
10. Cruise Market Watch, "Cruise Market Watch Announces 2010 Cruise Line Market Share and Revenue Projections" (29 November 2009). http://www.cruisemarketwatch.com/blog1/articles/cruise-market-watch-announces-2010-cruise-line-market-share-and-revenue-projections.
11. Theme Cruise Finder. http://themecruisefinder.com/CruiseAds/item/1339.
12. Cruise Critic, "Theme Cruises 2010 and 2011." http://www.cruisecritic.com/articles.cfm?ID=349.

13. National Assembly of State Arts Agencies, "Cultural Tourism Defined," http://www.nasaa-arts.org/artworks/cultour.shtml.
14. Garrison Keillor. 1995 Partners In Tourism Conference, Washington, DC.
15. J. C. Confer and D. L. Kerstetter, "Past Perfect: Exploration of Heritage Tourism," *Parks and Recreation* (February 2000): 28.
16. C. Chase, "Beijing Olympics Sold Out," Yahoo! News Network (2008). http://sports.yahoo.com/olympics/vancouver/blog/fourth_place_medal/post/Beijing-Olympics-sold-out?urn=oly,96428.
17. Official Website of the Beijing 2008 Olympics, "Beijing Olympics Tickets Almost 'Sold Out.'" http://en.beijing2008.cn/tickets/news/n214482741.shtml.
18. Kiawah Golf Resort, "Kiawah, #1 Tennis Resort in the World by Tennisresortsonline.com!" www.kiawahresort.com/tennis.
19. Sports Travel and Tours. http://www.sportstravelandtours.com/index.php.
20. Adventure Travel Trade Association, "Outdoor Sales Continue Growth Through July Despite Cooling Economy" (9 September 2008). http://www.adventuretravelnews.com/outdoor-sales-continue-growth-through-july-despite-cooling-economy.
21. Farhad Heydari, "Fantasy Sports Camps," *Travel and Leisure* (November 2007). www.travelandleisure.com/articles/fantasy-sports-camps/1.
22. Brie Cadman, "Ten Religious Pilgrimages," Divine Caroline. http://www.divinecaroline.com/22244/48870-ten-religious-pilgrimages/2.
23. "VOA News: U.S. Senate Weighs Risks, Attractions of Medical Tourism," *US Federal News Service* (29 June 2006).
24. "The Global Health Service: Whether You Agree with It or Not, Medical Tourism Is Booming," *The Guardian* (18 May 2006): 26.
25. International Ecotourism Society, "Our Mission." http://www.ecotourism.org/site/c.orLQKXPCLmF/b.4835251/k.FF11/Our_Mission__The_International_Ecotourism_Society.htm.
26. Yellow Bear Journeys, "Eco Vacation on Vancouver Island." http://www.yellowbearjourneys.com/j_ecovacation_vancouver_island.html.
27. International Ecotourism Society, "What Is Ecotourims?" http://www.ecotourism.org/site/c.orLQKXPCLmF/b.4835303/k.BEB9/What_is_Ecotourism__The_International_Ecotourism_Society.htm.
28. "Geotourism, the Future of Tourism: National Geographic," *AAP General Newswire* (28 November 2005).
29. i to i Volunteer and Adventure Travel, "Volunteer Abroad, Gap Year Travel and TEFL Courses." www.i-to-i.com.
30. Storm Chasing Adventure Tours. http://www.stormchasing.com.
31. Scaled Composites, www.scaled.com.
32. Virgin Galactic. http://www.virgingalactic.com.
33. "Ukraine: Sex Tourism Now a Thriving Trade," *Huffington Post* (9 June 2009). http://www.huffingtonpost.com/2009/06/09/ukraine-sex-tourism-now-a_n_213345.html.
34. Tim Rogers, "Sex Tourism Thrives in Costa Rica," eTurboNews (14 October 2009). http://www.eturbonews.com/12278/sex-tourism-thrives-costa-rica.
35. Jennifer Conlin, "In Europe, Hostels Grow Up," *New York Times* (19 April 2009). http://travel.nytimes.com/2009/04/19/travel/19hostels.html?pagewanted=1.
36. International Culinary Tourism Association, "Introduction to Culinary Tourism." http://www.culinarytourism.org/?page=intro.
37. International Culinary Tourism Association, "Why Culinary Tourism Matters." http://www.culinarytourism.org/?valuetoyou.

38. Food and Wine Trails, "Napa Valley Gourmet Traveler Itinerary." http://www.foodandwinetrails.com/?id=74&bid=6.
39. Food and Wine Trails, "2010 Tuscany Workshops." http://www.foodandwinetrails.com/?id=117.
40. Chiang Mai Thai Cookery School. http://www.thaicookeryschool.com/index.html.
41. M. Uysal, "Marketing for Tourism: A Growing Field," *Parks and Recreation* (October 1986): 61.
42. Lorri K. Krebs, "The Internet and Tourism: Changing Travel Patterns and Behaviour," abstract for the 2003 Annual Meeting of the American Association of Geographers. http://convention.allacademic.com/aag2003/session_info.html?c_session_id=987&dtr_id=1163.
43. Stephanie Chen, "Are Travel Agents Making a Comeback?" CNN (12 August 2009). http://www.cnn.com/2009/TRAVEL/08/12/travel.agent.comeback/index.html.
44. Miniwatts Marketing Group, "Internet Usage Statistics." http://www.internetworldstats.com/stats.htm.
45. Trip Advisor, "About TripAdvisor Media Group." http://www.tripadvisor.com/pages/about_us.html.
46. L. Berger and J. Engle, "News, Tips and Bargains; Travel Log; On-Time Ratings Tracked," *Los Angeles Times* (27 November 2005): L3.
47. D. Buhalis and O. Deimezi, "E-Tourism Developments in Greece: Information Communication Technologies Adoption for the Strategic Management of the Greek Tourism Industry," *Tourism Hospitality Research* (August 2004): 103–130.

CHAPTER 11

SPORT AS LEISURE

◆ ◆ ◆

People desire spectator sport opportunities, and professional and amateur sports organizations have created substantial sporting events to fulfill that niche. [Many others] seek more active participation, and leisure professionals have attempted to create recreation sport opportunities for them, [in] public and private, nonprofit and for profit, college and university, and employee service recreation settings.[1]

◆ ◆ ◆

INTRODUCTION

Sport, on its various levels, represents a major area of recreational programming today and constitutes a powerful economic force through the attraction for people of every age and background. Sport has a sociocultural heritage binding it to the Western ideal of leisure. This chapter presents an overview of sport, emphasizing its role within the leisure spectrum, the rapid expansion of sport over the past several decades, and the prospects for the years ahead as a physical pursuit, a leisure activity, and a maturing business.

SPORT AS POPULAR RECREATION

Sport in American society is viewed variously from a narrow to broad perspective, based on who is defining sport. A day of watching ESPN might convince an individual that football, basketball, soccer, baseball, poker, golf, or other traditional team and individual contests are sport. Changing television channels might convince someone else that hunting and fishing are major sports. Watching the Olympic games broadens the idea of sport to include winter and summer sports that may or may not be common in the United States. Our society tends to focus on sports that are portrayed in sporting magazines, on television, and that are frequented in the community. University and professional sport programs have strengthened the image of traditional sport programs. More than 100,000 people may attend a college football game while 1000 or less may attend a college cross-country event, and a women's volleyball match may draw as few as 100 people.

Defining sport is grounded in personal perspectives. The literature of sport is inconclusive about what sport actually entails. *Sport* is defined as "an activity that is governed by a set of rules or customs and often engaged in competitively."[2] The open dictionary defines sports as "an activity involving physical exertion and skill in which an individual or team competes against another or others for entertainment." The idea of sport and games as synonymous has fallen out of favor, except among some sport sociologists.

Sports—in both participation and spectator involvement—are a major leisure activity in the United States.

Sport management professionals generally define sports as physical activities demanding exertion and skill, involving competition, and carried on with both formal rules and general standards of etiquette and fair play. Some authorities describe them more concisely as activities with clear performance standards involving competition through physical exertion, governed by norms defining role relationships, typically performed by members of organized groups with the goal of achieving a reward through the defeat of other participants.

Clearly, sport activities, in terms of both participation and spectator involvement, represent key leisure interests for many youth and adults today. Apart from amateur, school, and college play, there are professional sports, which are a form of big business. They are moneymakers, sponsored by powerful commercial interests and promoted by advertising, public relations, television, radio, magazines, and newspapers and bolstered by the loyalty of millions of fans who identify closely with their favorite teams and star athletes.

In this chapter, the broadest possible view of sport is adopted. Traditional sport, as suggested in the preceding definitions, is given primary consideration, but from a leisure perspective the idea of sport extends beyond what occurs on the athletic field to outdoor recreation areas and to noncompetitive activities.

The Evolution of Sport and Leisure

The early history of sport was more closely related to military preparation than to leisure. The ancient Greek Olympic games were contests related to military prowess and included running with and without armor, wrestling, boxing, and discus as primary events. The earliest sporting events were frequently linked to festivals or religious celebrations.

As societies progressed, the evolution of sport as a social phenomenon seemed inevitable. At the beginning of the twentieth century, sport was seen as an amateur activity and those who participated in sport for financial reward were treated as outsiders. Sport, as a major component of society and as we know it today, is a relatively new phenomenon. For most of history, sport has been a leisure activity, engaged in after completing work. Even Roger Bannister, the first person to break the 4-minute mile, worked full-time as a physician while training. Today many minor sport elite athletes follow the traditional model of work and sport as separate functions in their lives. This remains the norm for people engaged in sport as a leisure activity.

Sport participation is seen as an opportunity for members of society to engage in socially positive and healthy activity that contributes to society. Communities across the United States sponsor sport activities and have done so through most of the twentieth century. Sport as leisure has grown as the population and economy have grown. Sport participation and sport events vary from region to region. In the 1950s, soccer clubs were difficult to find for any age group. Today youth soccer represents one of the continuously fast-growing sports. In secondary schools, universities, and professional leagues, soccer has found a place in mainstream sport.

Sport, as a component of leisure experiences, is an integral part of many communities. It is expressed in youth sport programs, adult leagues, senior leagues and programs and has extended to include what were once called nontraditional sport activities. Government agencies no longer attempt to serve as the primary provider of leisure sport opportunities. Nonprofits and for-profit organizations are actively engaged in the provision of sport activities for people of all ages. As we shall later see, growth of opportunity does not always translate into greater participation. In some cases, traditional sport programs are losing participants to growing sports such as lacrosse, adventure sports, and the like.

The acceptance of what is called a sport is continuously changing. The concept of sport over the last 40 years has been challenged by the expansion of sport opportunities. The X Games did not exist 20 years ago. Snowboarding, as an Olympic sport, first appeared in 1998. The 1970s may ultimately become known as the era of the emergence of alternative sports, what was then known as nontraditional sports. Many of these sports have become traditional, in the sense that they are mainstream within groups in society. They will probably not replace baseball, basketball, football, and other traditional school-sponsored sports, but they have found their place within societal acceptance. Skateboarding, for example, first appeared in the 1970s, but not until the mid-1990s did community-based skate parks begin to appear.

Sport participation is a large component of leisure involvement. Participation is defined in many ways. It does not necessarily involve active engagement in sport activities. In the 1930s and beyond, collecting sport cards (e.g., baseball cards, football cards) was and continues to be a form of sport involvement, albeit from the hobby perspective. Today's fantasy sport teams are similar to collecting baseball cards and fit into the concept of a hobby. Purists might argue the point, especially when professional teams and sport broadcasters and their Web sites devote considerable attention to fantasy teams, yet they do fit the description of a hobby. Watching sporting events is another major influence of sport and leisure. As we shall see later in the chapter, spectators make up a major segment of the sport and leisure involvement. Stebbins describes spectator involvement in sport as casual leisure.[3]

CASE STUDY: Master Planning a Sport Facility

Sport facilities don't just magically appear. They require a significant investment in time, energy, and planning. Most sport facilities, from the germination of an idea until they open, may require years. Frequently, a master planning process signals the start of a major project. The purpose of the master plan is to establish a facility planning, design, construction, and operating process that the owner can follow in initiating the actual construction and operation. Master planning brings together a variety of individuals and groups who have an interest in the project.

An organization planning to engage in master planning for a sports complex begins with an understanding of what they want the end product to look like. It might be a championship baseball complex, a waterpark, or a multisports park including indoor and outdoor structures. The owners are those individuals who make decisions about the project and may include private owners, public elected officials, boards and commissions, and boards of directors. The owners specify the project, their expected outcomes, and what they expect a master plan to contain. Master plans may be developed in-house or by a consulting team composed of one or more external companies. Given the complexity of completing a master plan, it is becoming more common for multiple firms to partner in the master planning process. In one recent master planning interview process, the parks and recreation department brought in five firms, each of which had 5 to 11 partners. The successful firm had 9 partners, each bringing a different level of expertise to the project.

Building a new athletic facility takes time, energy, planning, and money.

A master plan includes many components such as a visioning process, public survey, needs assessment, data collection/site analysis, project programming, public outreach, financial analysis, and the master plan. In the current economic climate, master planning is expected to address issues of economic sustainability and environmental sustainability as key components.

Visioning is a process of bringing together key stakeholders (individuals and organizations with an interest in the success of the project) to develop a vision of the final product. The vision describes what the sport facility should contain, who it will serve, expectations for revenue generation, level of involvement of the public and potential customers, and ideal timelines. The vision, as a starting point, provides direction and focus to the project. It is not fixed but is expected to change as more information comes available during the development of the master plan.

The public survey is the first contact with the general public when they are asked about the viability of the proposed project. Information from the public survey is gathered through focus groups; telephone, mail, and Internet surveys; meetings with constituent groups; and public hearings. The data are analyzed to determine public sentiment toward the project.

The needs assessment looks at the service area, defines who the project is intended to benefit or serve, and inventories similar or competing existing and proposed sites. It uses the collected information and data from the public survey to identify the need for the proposed sport facility. The results could suggest that there is no need, and in that instance, the owners need to determine whether the project should go on or should be changed. In more than one instance, the needs assessment has determined the lack of need and the project has been cancelled.

If a physical site for the project has not been selected, and even if it has, a site analysis is conducted to determine whether the site is suitable for the proposed project. The site analysis may look at multiple sites in an effort to identify the best site for the project. Taken into consideration are terrain, access to water and sewer, existing zoning requirements, availability to transportation corridors such as major streets and the transit system, and so forth. Ultimately, a single site is suggested for the project and all of the advantages and disadvantages are discussed.

Project programming involves creating multiple design concepts, or approaches, to placing structures, fields, parking, and other facilities on the available land. It includes addressing environmental impacts, specific site conditions such as topography and drainage, circulation patterns for cars and pedestrians, and specific site opportunities and constraints. The project program sets the stage for the next phase of master planning—public outreach.

Public outreach brings interest groups and community groups together to look at and assess the project program. This process specifically addresses the conceptual design, financial issues, traffic patterns, impact on close-by neighborhoods and asks the various groups to provide feedback to the process and their thoughts on the design process. Frequently, the project planners provide the participants with working maps so that they can do their own designs. The process is intended to gather feedback and to garner support from those involved.

The financial analysis has become an increasingly important part of the master planning process. Included in the financial analysis are the costs of design and construction of the proposed sport facility. If land must be purchased, it also is included. Next, an operational plan is put into place that describes the ideal operation of the facility. Added to that are projected costs to operate the facility, including personnel, utilities, equipment, supplies, and the like. This cost is projected out for up to a 25-year period, although typically it is shorter. Finally, a revenue plan is put into place. The revenue plan looks at all potential sources of income and projects how much total income might be generated. The revenue plan is prepared for the same length of time as the operating budget, up to 25 years into the future.

When all of this is put together, along with a timeline for the project, the master plan is complete and can be adopted by the owner or organization. Such a process can take up to 18 months to complete.

Questions to Consider

1. Why do organizations need to engage in master planning for sport projects?
2. When completed, what does the master plan provide the organization?
3. List the values of the actual process of master planning to the organization.

PATTERNS OF SPORT INVOLVEMENT

Participation in Sport Activities

Sport is an important form of leisure activity. It can range from casual to serious leisure, from passive to active involvement, and from leisure to lifestyle. In the same regard, it is difficult to clearly classify sport wholly or sometimes even partially as a leisure activity. One of the accepted ways of determining leisure involvement is to measure participation. Participation measures give a sense of involvement and commitment to a sport activity.

The most popular sport activities, in terms of participation, are identified in **Table 11.1**. As indicated earlier, a number of the pastimes listed might better be described as outdoor recreation pursuits, such as exercise walking or camping. Others, such as skiing, swimming, or even fishing, are usually engaged in as noncompetitive recreation, although they may represent part of school or college competition or large-scale tournaments.

There are many ways to measure sport involvement and many groups collecting information about how people participate in sport. Measuring the number of participants in organized sport is much easier than identifying numbers participating in recreation leagues, pickup games, and the like. Any number of participants identified will be limited by the source of the information. For example, Little League only measures baseball players participating in their sanctioned programs. Their programs represent just a small part of the total youth participating in baseball in any given year. The measures that are available do provide indicators of how many people are involved in formalized sport activities on an annual basis.

For example, Street & Smith's Sport Business Daily reports that in 2008 11.8 million people participated in fast- and slow-pitch softball.[4] The National Sporting Goods Association (NSGA) reported 29.7 million people participated in basketball in 2008. Table 11.1 illustrates the breath of participation in sport activities. The list, from NSGA, is indicative of the diversity existing in sport, how people view sport, and how those who are in the sport merchandising industry see sport. It is interesting to note that a participant in sport may view sport from a very narrow perspective whereas those who represent sport merchandise sales see it from a much broader perspective.

Parents and friends impact teens' decisions to participate in sports.

Participation in sport is influenced by a variety of factors. Chapter 5 discusses motivations for participation in leisure. These are similar for sport, but sometimes the nature of sport engages people for different reasons. It is instructive to understand who influences participants to engage in sport. In a study conducted by the Outdoor Foundation, respondents were asked, "Who influenced your decision to participate in outdoor activities?" For youth ages 6 through 17 years, parents were the major influencers, followed by friends. Friends became an increasingly important influencer until by ages 18 to 24, they had a primary influence. It is interesting to note that media icons, sports figures, and accomplished athletes had less than a 2% influence on participation.

Another question frequently posed asks if participants in one activity participate in other sport activities. The answer seems

TABLE 11.1

PARTICIPATION IN SPORT ACTIVITIES RANKED BY TOTAL PARTICIPATION, 2009

	All Persons		Sex	
Activity	Number (in millions)	Percent Change[a]	Male	Female
Exercise walking	93.4	–3.4%	39.7%	60.3%
Swimming	50.2	–6.1%	47.4%	52.6%
Exercising with equipment	57.2	4.0%	48.6%	51.4%
Bowling	45.0	0.6%	52.3%	47.7%
Camping (vacation/overnight)	50.9	3.0%	51.8%	48.2%
Bicycle riding	38.1	–1.5%	45.8%	44.2%
Fishing	32.9	–22.0%	69.1%	30.9%
Workout at club	38.3	–2.6%	45.9%	54.1%
Hiking	34.0	2.8%	51.1%	48.9%
Weight lifting	34.5	1.8%	67.8%	32.2%
Aerobic exercising	33.1	3.0%	28.7%	71.3%
Running/jogging	32.2	1.0%	55.1%	44.9%
Billiards/pool	28.2	11.1%	62.4%	37.6%
Basketball	24.4	–5.0%	69.3%	30.7%
Boating, motor/power	24.0	–13.9%	56.9%	43.1%
Golf	22.3	–3.9%	75.7%	24.3%
Target shooting (net)	19.8	–2.4%	76.1%	23.9%
Hunting with firearms	18.8	–0.3%	84.2%	15.8%
Yoga	15.7	20.9%	20.6%	79.4%
Soccer	13.6	0.6%	56.9%	43.1%
Baseball	11.5	–13.57%	80.9%	19.1%
Backpacking/wilderness camping	12.3	–5.3%	57.3%	42.7%
Softball	11.8	–7.9%	50.5%	49.5%
Tennis	10.8	14.5%	52.3%	47.7%
Volleyball	10.7	–11.7%	40.1%	59.9%
Football (tackle)	8.9	–6.2%	89.0%	11.0%
Mountain biking (off road)	8.4	–17.8%	59.6%	40.4%
Scooter riding	8.1	–19.9%	56.1%	43.9%
Skateboarding	8.4	–13.8%	74.8%	25.2%
In-line roller skating	7.9	–15.4%	49.5%	50.5%
Paintball games	6.3	–6.5%	83.2%	16.8%
Skiing (alpine)	7.0	7.3%	62.7%	37.3%
Hunting with bow and arrow	6.2	0.2%	86.7%	13.3%
Snowboarding	6.2	5.7%	69.7%	30.3%
Water skiing	5.2	–7.2%	54.5%	45.5%
Target shooting-airgun	5.2	4.3%	76.1%	23.9%
Muzzleloading	3.8	11.6%	85.2%	14.8%
Skiing (cross country)	1.7	7.4%	52.4%	47.6%

Note: Participation is defined as when an individual participated more than once (in millions); 7 years of age and older.
[a]Percent change is from 2005.
National Sporting Goods Association, Mount Prospect, IL. 2009 *Participation—Ranked by Total Participation*. Available at: http://www.nsga.org/files/public/2009_Participation-Total_Participation_4Web_100521.pdf; 2009 *Participation—Ranked by Total Female Participation*. Available at: http://www.nsga.org/files/public/2009Women%27sParticipation-RankedbyTotalFemaleParticipation_4Web_100722.pdf. Accessed December 1, 2010.

obvious and the data confirm this. Seventy-eight percent of freshwater, saltwater, and fly fishing participants participated in other outdoor activities. Hiking showed the greatest level of multiple activity involvement with 87% of those who hike indicating they also participate in other activities. The numbers reported are indicative of other sport activities. However, participation is a function of accessibility, cost, availability, socioeconomic status, skill, and self-perception. Considerable research is available that focuses on motivation for sport participation. As described earlier, parents may have a major influence on youth. As youth grow older, their parents have less influence, for the most part. One study reports the quality of the relationship with the athlete's mother and peer relationships were indicators of continuing involvement in sport.[5] Concerns about the transition into adulthood may influence youth sport participants to continue involvement.

Sport is sometimes seen as an activity that will prepare students for adulthood. In a similar vein, some continue to participate in sport because it demonstrates or extends their competence, and perceived competence is a primary motivation factor for teens. Between high school and college, participation in physical activity declines considerably, and following college it continues to decline. Sport participation must compete for an individual's time with work, family, and other social activities as individuals enter the workforce and see work as a primary motivator as opposed to recreation. Yet, recreational sport leagues flourish across the United States with millions of participants.

Reasons individuals continue to participate in leisure sport activities are varied but include the opportunity for affiliation with others, improving one's appearance, taking up a new or continuing challenge, competition, enjoyment, positive health, social recognition, stress management, and weight management, to name a few.[6] What we do know is that participation in strenuous and team sports, such as baseball, basketball, and football, decline and are replaced with less physically stressful small-group or individual activities. As might be expected, there are exceptions to the decline in sport activities. Among older adults, for example, competitive sports continue to flourish, even if the numbers participating are a smaller percentage of their age group. Those participating in master sporting events are in better health, have less physical decline than the older adult population as a whole, are motivated, and frequently were involved in sport throughout their life. Participation in traditional sport activities is highest during youth. The definition of traditional sport activities is expanding as opportunities to participate in sport are expanding. As people complete their secondary education and leave home participation in sport declines throughout their lives. Despite repeated efforts to encourage greater participation in sport as a lifestyle choice, few people take advantage of sport. Typically, those who do actively participate in sport have done so throughout their lives.

TEAM SPORT PARTICIPATION

If any activity defines mainstream American sport, it is organized team sports, beginning with T-ball and soccer for 3-, 4-, and 5-years-olds and continuing throughout people's lives. Actual participation numbers in organized team sports are available only where governing organizations are present and data are collected. Participation is highest among high school students (see **Table 11.2**) and has grown steadily. Boys have the greatest opportunity for involvement in high school sports, with schools across the United States providing more than 147,000 sport teams, 10,000 more than provided to girls. The 7.1 million participants

TABLE 11.2

HIGH SCHOOL PARTICIPATION IN INTERSCHOLASTIC SPORTS

	High School Teams		Participation (in millions)	
Year	Boys	Girls	Boys	Girls
2008–2009	147,533	137,255	442.3	310.7
2005–2006	140,953	130,506	421.7	294.7
2002–2003	134,898	123,942	398.9	285.6

Data from National Federation of State High School Associations, "Participation Statistics." http://www.nfhs.org/participation. Accessed October 28, 2010.

in high school sport represents 43.7% of all high school students. However, many high school students participate in two or three or more sports, making the actual participation lower, but still involving a high number of high school students in sport.

College students are more likely to participate in recreational sports than intercollegiate sports.

Collegiate sport participation declines dramatically, but this is expected because the number of available opportunities to participate in sport teams declines dramatically. **Table 11.3** shows the participation levels in intercollegiate athletics. The number does not represent recreational sport involvement at the collegiate level, which is far higher. In addition to extensive intercollegiate sport facilities, today's college campuses have one or more recreational sport facilities that cater to the general student population. Over the last 30 years, universities have recognized the importance of participation in sport by students who are not engaged in intercollegiate athletics. The National Intramural-Recreational Sports Association (NIRSA) is the professional association representing student-based sport opportunities.

Trends in Organized Team Sports Participation

The 2005 *U.S. Trends in Team Sports Report* and the *2009 Sports Participation in America* report by the Sporting Goods Manufacturers Association (SGMA) reveal several key findings regarding team-sport participation. These findings provide a realistic assessment of participation patterns in sport activities and are a useful tool for sport and recreation management professionals in developing successful strategies to serve the needs, desires, and

TABLE 11.3

COLLEGIATE PARTICIPATION IN ORGANIZED SPORT

Association	Participants	Number of Sports	
		Men	Women
National Collegiate Athletic Association	400,000	18	18
National Association of Intercollegiate Athletics	45,000	11	10
National Junior College Athletic Association	54,000	15	13
California Community College Athletic Association	25,000	12	10
Total	524,000		

Data from National Collegiate Athletic Association. Available at: http://www.ncaa.org; National Association of Intercollegiate Athletics. Available at: http://naia.cstv.com; National Junior College Athletic Association. Available at: http://naia.cstv.com; and California Community College Athletic Association. Available at: http://www.coasports.org. Accessed November 11, 2010.

interests of leisure-product consumers, recreational organizations, sporting goods companies, and local, state, and federal governments.

Casual Team Sport Participation

An alarming situation is the millions of casual sport participants who have dropped out of team-sport activities progressively for 25 years, every year since 1984. The overall number of children age 6 and older who participated in team sport at least once within each calendar year during the period since 1984 has declined. A similar trend is observed for participants who play team sport more frequently (that is 25 or more days per year). Since 1995, more that 3 million sport participants have quit participating and migrated to other leisure activities.

Several factors contribute to this emerging problem. In inner-city environments, the availability of free space for recreational sport is extremely limited. Empty fields where children can gather after school and play a pickup game are not the norm. At the same time, the lack of time for parental supervision and increased concerns for child safety have led a great number of parents to search for alternative ways (e.g., recreation centers, playgrounds, private or sectarian leagues) to introduce sport to their children. This is evident for single-parent families or families where both parents support full-time jobs.[7]

Demographic changes also affect team-sport participation rates. Today, research shows that team-sport participation is as high as 70% for young children reaching age 11 and declines to 50% as youngsters reach age 18. It is evident that a combination of factors such as adolescence and school workload may play a decisive role in this decline. Research suggests that early involvement in organized sport is not a factor influencing involvement during high school. Projections for the next 10 years are not encouraging for the same segment of the population. It is expected that participation for youth between 5–19 years old will grow only 3.6%, which translates to a greater decline in team-sport participation.[8]

CASE STUDY: Measuring Sport Participation Is a Challenge for Economists and Marketers

One would think that participation in sport as a participant or spectator would be fairly easy to identify. For elite sports, such as the Olympics, professional sports leagues, collegiate, or high school sports, data are available. However, organized sport, once it gets below the collegiate level, is much more difficult to measure. Mass participation in sport is common and can be seen in a variety of settings, but gathering participation and spectator numbers is more difficult. As a result, various government, private, and trade associations engage in data gathering about levels of sport participation, watching, and listening.

There are several ways to measure participation. The two most common are by participation frequency and by tonnage. The former is the most common approach, for a variety of reasons, but also presents some unique problems for researchers. Tonnage is reflected in the use of the product, such as participation days. If a person participates in an activity, say, 20 times, that is translated as 20 participation days, but still only one participant. Taking it a step further, assume there are 25 million hikers and they participate an average of 20 times a year. The 25 million hikers becomes 500 million participations. Lauer suggests tonnage is often a more precise measure but too awkward for practical usage. People cannot wrap their minds around "participations" as easily as they can around participants.[a]

A second issue related to measuring participation is defining what or who a participant is. Two common approaches are used. First is to ask people if they are participants. A simple yes or no gives the answer. However, self-descriptions are frequently imprecise. In other words, to say "I'm a participant" is sometimes construed by the respondent as, "I would like to be a participant, but probably won't, yet I will report that I do." The more accepted approach for measures is to ask the person how many times (frequency) he or she participated in an activity in the previous year. The standard for being a participant is to have engaged in the activity a minimum of one time in the previous year. These participation data are usually collected through questionnaires. The questionnaires are administered via e-mail, telephone, mail, or face to face. Internet and telephone surveys are among the most popular.

Survey Response Issues

Telescoping occurs when sport participants incorrectly remember the number of times they participated in an activity. All participants overestimate their total sports participation.[b] When asked, "How frequently did you participate?" they remember more participation than they actually did. The issues of telescoping cannot be easily resolved by asking questions such as "How many times did you participate each week, on average?" or by asking respondents on a weekly basis, monthly basis, or some other time frame. However, researchers suggest telescoping is usable because respondents are consistent in their overestimates of sport participation.

Some issues related to the collection of participation data affect how the questions are answered. The presence of long sets of questions in a survey instrument may result in respondent fatigue, resulting in lower response rates for questions at the end of the list. In other words, the respondent just wants to get through the survey and does not worry about accuracy in responses. Those questions at the end of the survey do not receive the same attention as the questions at the start of the survey. If the list is reversed and the questions at the end become the questions at the beginning, the lower response will continue to be at the end of the list. If panels are used, new panel members report at a higher rate than seasoned panelists do. The longer an individual is a member of a panel, the progressively lower his or her response rate will be. When questionnaires are detailed and explicit, they receive better responses. For example, asking questions about camping will elicit one type of response while a more detailed question about tent, camper, or motorhome camping will result in a higher response.

Numerous groups measure active participation in leisure and sport. The United States Forest Service has gathered data for more than 50 years and has gradually expanded the data collected but does not typically include the range of sport activities sought after by sport researchers. The Sporting Goods Manufacturing Association (SGMA) produces an annual report, which is used in this text, to define participation levels. The annually produced *Statistical Abstract of the United States*, a product of the U.S. Census Bureau, reports on participation, spectator numbers, and the like, but the Census Bureau gathers little of the information itself, and neither does it check for accuracy. The Centers for Disease Control and Prevention (CDC) gathers data from the U.S. adult population through the Behavioral Risk Factor Surveillance System and includes participation in active recreation and sport activities. All of the databases report differing levels of participation for the same activities. However, the ranking of activities, by levels of participation, remains fairly constant across the different measures. Even if the totals are in debate, the rankings appear to be consistent. This provides some measure of comfort for individuals looking at the data.

Viewing and Listening Data Issues

Sport participation for viewing and listening is even more challenging to determine. The key databases are proprietary and highly expensive to access. The National Sporting Goods Association provides one source of information; however, the way the data are gathered and counted promotes errors such as double counting, that is, counting the same person more than one time because of the data collection method. When simple aggregation is used for measuring the size of the audience, double counting is present.[c] A second issue focuses on smaller sports, such as golf, NASCAR, and horse racing. The NGSA reports what appear to be large numbers of participants, but it fails to take into account that a few activities may account for the large viewing numbers; in golf, for example, the four major championships or the Triple Crown in horse racing.

A second viewing concern is the absence of measuring the length of time the individual is engaged in the watching or listening activity. The absence of totals for duration or frequency of viewing sport does not provide basic information found in other industries.

The Internet provides a unique problem. The media is beginning to report hours of viewing, but measurement of Internet involvement is either nonexistent or in its infancy. No systematic surveys currently in place measure Internet use.

Questions to Consider

1. Given the information in this case study, what do you think about the measurement of sport participation?
2. Why do you think it is so hard to measure participation?
3. Does this information make you more or less likely to believe the statistics when participation numbers are reported?

Sources

a. Harvey Lauer, "Sports Participation Research: Not Yet a Science," in *The New Americans: Defining Ourselves Through Sports and Fitness Participation* (Fort Mill, SC: American Sports Data, 2004).

b. Stefano Della Vigna and Ulrike Malmendier, "Paying Not to Go to the Gym," *American Economic Review* (Vol. 96, No. 3, June 2006): 694–719. http://www.jstor.org/stable/30034067.

c. B. R. Humphrey and J. E. Ruseski, "Problems with Data on the Sport Industry," *Journal of Sport Economics* (Vol. 11, No. 1, 2009): 60–76.

Sport as Big Business

Sport has become a large enterprise in the United States and across the world. Nations embrace major sporting events, cities and states embrace collegiate and professional sports teams, communities mark their calendars by interscholastic sports contests. In higher education, sport management programs are appearing in business schools and the more traditional physical education and recreation programs. The *Statistical Abstract of the United States*, the National Sporting Goods Association, and the Sporting Goods Manufacturers' Association individually provide annual updates on select aspects of the sport industry. Their data are highlighted throughout this section and emphasize the financial size of the sport industry.

The 2009 *Statistical Abstract of the United States*, published by the U.S. Census Bureau, reports that in 2007 Americans spent $93.4 million on sporting goods **(Table 11.4)**. Included in this figure are $17.5 million for shoes, another $17.5 million for pleasure boats, $5.3 million for bicycles and supplies, $3.8 million for golf (excluding greens fees), and $5.4 million for exercise equipment. **Table 11.5** depicts expenditures by broad categories for every year from 2004 through 2009. Expenditures rose steadily from 2004 through 2007 before dropping in 2008 and were projected to drop again in 2009. Most dramatic was the drop in recreational transportation (–29%) between 2007 and 2008, a period when gasoline prices spiked at or above $5 a gallon.

Surfing competitions in Hawaii are televised events.

The National Sporting Goods Association reported in 2009 that Americans spent $72.1 million for sporting goods purchases, down from a high of $91.4 million in 2007. Included in the 2009 amount are $19.8 million for recreational transport (e.g., bicycles, pleasure boats, RVs, snowmobiles), $17.2 million for footwear, and $10.5 million for clothing. From the $24.7 million spent for sport activity–related equipment the same year, exercise equipment purchases

Eddie Aikau Big Wave Invitational

The Eddie Aikau Big Wave Invitational is one of the premiere surfing events in the world.[9] It is an invitation-only surfing competition typically held in the winter in Hawaii at Waimea and other North Shore locations such as Pipeline and Sunset Beach. The draw for championship surfers are the large waves, sometimes more than 40 feet high. The waves are the result of winter storms in the North Pacific. Because their arrival on O'ahu's North Shore can typically be forecast accurately several days in advance, there is time to alert and gather surfers.[10] Surfing began in ernest in the mid-1950s at Waimea, and in 1966, 20-year-old Eddie Aikau arrived as the first lifeguard for the North Shore, including Waimea. His exploits became legendary, never having loss of life on his beaches while he was in charge of lifeguarding.

Eddie Aikau also was an accomplished surfer. Aside from being a lifeguard and surfer, he was involved in Hawaiian cultural activities. In 1978, the Polynesian Voyaging Society was seeking volunteers for a 30-day, 2500-mile (4000-km) journey to follow the ancient route of the Polynesian migration between the Hawaiian and Tahitian island chains. At 31 years of age, Aikau joined the voyage as a crew member. The double-hulled voyaging canoe developed a leak in one of the hulls and later capsized about 12 miles south of the island of Molokai. In an attempt to get help, Aikau paddled toward Lanai on his surfboard.[11] He was never seen again despite the largest air–sea search in Hawaiian history.

More than the wave, the rider, or the equipment, it was the camera capturing the images that brought about international awareness and elevated Waimea to what was perceived as a recognition wave. Television coverage, contests, and the pro surfing movement all started to gel around the time, and surfing was becoming a legitimate lifestyle. Surfers who came for a season ended up staying, and pretty soon Waimea had a solid base of big wave chargers: Mike Diffenderfer, Owl Chapman, Reno Abellira, Sam Hawk, Downing, Cole, Grigg, Kimo Hollinger, Buzzy Trent, Jose Angel, Aikau, Kealoha Kaeo, and Tiger Espere.

In the winter of 1984–1985, the first Eddie Aikau Memorial was held at Sunset Beach. The next winter Quiksilver took this event to a new level, relocating it to Waimea Bay. They invited big wave specialists from around the world and provided a platform for showcasing the sport's high end, and performance levels went through the roof.

totaled \$5.2 million in sales. Consumers also spent \$3.5 million for golf (excluding greens fees), \$3.6 million for hunting and firearms, \$2.6 million for team goods, \$643 million for downhill skiing, and \$397 million for tennis equipment.

Beyond these figures, the SGMA reports that the U.S. sport industry is nearly a \$70 billion business, and this report focuses almost wholly on sales of consumer goods such as sport apparel, sport equipment, fitness equipment, sport shoes, and the like.[12] Another source estimates the market to be \$43 billion and \$73 billion based on aggregate demand and aggregate supply, while yet another source estimates the marketplace to be between \$400 billion to \$425 billion annually. At one end of the spectrum, one finds estimates based on the sale of sport merchandise, and at the other end the inclusion of video games, collectibles, ticket sales, television contracts, naming rights, and others, providing a more liberal view of the size of the sport marketplace.

TABLE 11.4

SPORTING GOODS PURCHASES BY CATEGORY (IN MILLIONS)

	2003	2004	2005	2006	2007	2008	2009	2010*	Percent Change 2009 vs. 2008
Equipment	$22,394	$23,328	$23,735	$24,497	$25,061	$24,862	$24,421	$24,568	−2
Footwear	$14,446	$14,752	$15,719	$16,910	$17,524	$17,190	$17,069	$17,282	−1
Clothing	$10,453	$11,201	$10,898	$10,580	$10,834	$10,113	$ 9,246	$ 9,665	−9
Recreational transport**	$32,396	$36,531	$38,082	$38,485	$38,003	$26,266	$20,120	$24,151	−29
Total	**$79,779**	**$85,812**	**$88,434**	**$90,472**	**$91,423**	**$80,431**	**$70,856**	**$75,666**	**−12**

*Projected.
**Bicycles, pleasure boats, RVs, and snowmobiles; projections provided by other associations.
National Sporting Goods Association, Mount Prospect, IL. *Consumer Purchases of Sporting Goods by Category*. Available at: http://www.nsga.org/files/public/ConsumerPurchasesofSptGdsbyCategory.pdf. Accessed November 11, 2010.

TABLE 11.5

SPORTING GOODS PURCHASES BY SELECTED SPORTS (IN MILLIONS)

	2004	2005	2006	2007	2008	2009 (Forecast)
Exercise	$5074	$5207	$5239	$5500	$5308	$5096
Golf	$3198	$3474	$3669	$3722	$3546	$3439
Hunting and firearms	$3175	$3351	$3732	$3941	$4584	$4938
Team goods sales	$2517	$2568	$2619	$2671	$2618	$2539
Fishing tackle	$2026	$2139	$2218	$2247	$2104	$2038
Camping	$1531	$1442	$1526	$1453	$1460	$1431
Billiards and indoor games	$622	$572	$574	$531	$426	$395
Skiing, downhill	$452	$643	$2501	$531	$494	$479
Baseball/softball	$352	$372	$388	$401	$396	$387
Tennis	$362	$397	$418	$440	$380	$368
Basketball	$309	$309	$296	$265	$260	$257
Skiing, snowboards	$269	$301	$314	$325	$309	$306

Data from National Sporting Goods Association, Mount Prospect, IL. *Consumer Sports Equipment Purchases by Sport*. Available at: http://www.nsga.org/files/public/ConsumerSportsEquipmentPurchasesbySport.A.pdf. Accessed November 28, 2010; and National Sporting Goods Association, Mount Prospect, IL. 2006 *Consumer Sports Equipment Purchases by Sport*.

After a steady growth in sport corporate sponsorship for most of the first decade of the twenty-first century, late 2008 and 2009 experienced a significant downturn in sport sponsorships, mostly brought about by the economic uncertainty of the period. Even Olympic sponsorships have come under question. The London 2012 Olympic Organizing Committee had generated nearly £600 million ($973 million U.S.), but when the European Sponsorship Association asked key figures in the sponsorship industry if local sponsorships were a good value for the money, the response was overwhelmingly no.[13] Nonetheless, local sponsors continued to embrace the sponsorships as a form of linking with major sporting events.

Spectator Is Sport

The importance people attribute to spectator sports is evident in a series of business-related actions: (1) television ratings and broadcasting fees, (2) player salaries, (3) franchise values, (4) public subsidy of sport facilities, and (5) cost associated with attending a sporting event.

Attendance figures, average attendance, and percentage of stadium capacity filled are important indicators of fan support and how much advertisers and partners are willing to invest in a team. There is considerable discussion about the impact of actual attendance at games as well as media attendance in determining how effective the teams are in their markets. In 2009, the National Basketball Association (NBA) reported a stable and slightly growing average attendance at 17,250 spectators per game, and total attendance of 21.5 million spectators. Basketball arenas were on average filled to 90% of their total capacity.

Major League Baseball (MLB) struggled with attendance in 2009 and attributed it to the recession.[14] The league recorded a decline of 6.8% in attendance with an average of 30,258 spectators per game. Although the decline in attendance was the most significant since 1955, the season still ranked as the fifth most highest attendance of all times. The New York Yankees and New York Mets each opened a new stadium in 2009. The Yankees, projecting a market surge in attendance, created a pricing structure that saw many games, especially early in the season before rates were adjusted, with low attendance. The Mets, by contrast, sized down their stadium, making the potential for a sellout for every game. The result was that 30% of MLB's decline is attributed to the Yankees and Mets.

The most popular league in the United States, the National Football League (NFL) also experienced a decline in attendance, with a game average of 68,241 spectators in its regular season, and a total attendance of 17.5 million tickets sold. The Indianapolis Colts moved into a new stadium, increasing attendance by 15.8%, and reported the stadium at 106.4% capacity for the season. By contrast, the Detroit Lions' attendance dropped by 11.4% and stadium capacity was only 84.5%.[15]

Ratings and Broadcasting Fees The spectator aspect of sport is vividly shown in the immense sums paid by television networks for the right to broadcast college and professional contests. The driver behind the multi-billion-dollar contracts networks sign with major league sport are the television ratings and audiences these sport are able to attract. Each rating point represents 1.1 million households in the United States, or 1% of the nation's 110.2 million houses with a television set in place. High ratings mean great audiences, and great audiences are very appealing to sponsors and advertisers.

SPORT SPECTATORS

It has been said, "If there is sport, there are spectators." People enjoy watching sport activities, albeit, the number of spectators varies from sport to sport and by individual and group interest. A bass fishing tournament draws far fewer spectators than does a collegiate or professional football game. Yet, both of these sports have strong print and electronic media followers.

Spectators have been described in a variety of ways. An overarching approach to understanding spectators focuses on motivation, or why people choose to watch sports and how they react to the sports they watch. Underwood and colleagues suggest, "Spectator sports are a unique group experience characterized by a sense of belonging that spectators feel and an inherent bias against out-group members. . . . For these individuals, sports are not merely a form of entertainment and recreation, but provide a sense of community and family."[16]

Giulianotti developed a taxonomy or classification for spectators.[17] He classified spectators as supporters, followers, fans, and flâneurs. His study, although focusing on English football (soccer) clubs with a corporate identity, has the potential to be related to American professional sports. The four categories are based on two continua, the first being attraction to the team (called hot and cool), with hot focused on an intense loyalty. Cool fans are at the other end of the continuum, exhibiting loyalty that is neither intense nor binding. The second continuum is a traditional consumer focus, or a cultural versus a market-centered approach.

A supporter is a traditional-hot spectator with deep personal understanding and a strong commitment to the team. Giulianotti suggests supporters have a "relationship with the club that resembles those with close family and friends."[17] Followers are also traditionalists and can be described as knowledgeable spectators with a strong interest in the game, but not with a single team. As a result, single teams have minimal impact on their identity as a follower.

Fans are hot-consumers. They are not traditionalists, but their focus is with a single team. "The individual fan experiences the . . . traditions, its star players, and fellow supporters through a market-centered set of relationships."[17] Consumption of market products and the display of those products is a driving force. Fans, because they are not traditionalists, are more transient in their loyalty to a team. If teams do not perform to their expectations, they may change their loyalty to another team. Finally, flâneurs have an almost aloof relationship with a team. Giulianotti suggests flâneurs may be more impressed with branding, such as logos, tattoos, and the like. They are transient, switching affiliations like surfing Web sites.

At a sporting event, or viewing a sporting event, all of these types of fans are present. The centerfield bleachers of the Chicago Cubs is composed of all four types but most probably supporters and fans.[18] The individual sporting Oakland Raiders tattoos, car stickers, T-shirts, and hats has a higher probability of being a flâneur, fan, or supporter. The typologies suggested can provide insights into how and why spectators are involved in sport. It can give clues to researchers, sport franchises, and commercial enterprises how sport might be marketed and who to target.

Attendance at Sporting Events

For years the hallmark of a spectator's commitment to sport was to attend actual sporting contests. To some degree, that remains true today for collegiate and professional sport franchises, although the cost of attendance has increased considerably and is discussed later in this chapter. Sport attendance is typically defined by sport teams and sport events by the number of people in attendance and viewing a contest.

Measuring attendance at sporting events can be challenging.

Measuring attendance is, at best, problematic. Teams can count tickets sold, distributed, and given away. Estimated attendance is also a common approach, although less so than in the past. A surfing contest, for example, may not have formal tickets, but just have people show up so that attendance must be estimated. This was common for many sporting events for a long time and continues to be the norm in smaller or less formally organized events. However, sport has become more formal and is following business models with more exact measurements expected. Regardless, it is difficult to get a handle on spectator attendance at park and recreation–sponsored programs, local youth leagues, and informal sport settings. Organized sports do a better, if not excellent, job of counting "in attendance" spectators. **Table 11.6** depicts attendance over the past decade at selected collegiate and professional sporting events. Professional baseball, including minor and major leagues, has the highest total attendance on a yearly basis. Professional baseball also has the largest number of teams and annual games.[19]

TABLE 11.6

ATTENDANCE AT SELECTED SPORTING EVENTS (IN MILLIONS)

Sport	1999	2004	2007
Baseball			
Major League Baseball	71,558	74,822	80,803
Minor League Baseball			42,725
Basketball			
NCAA Men	28,505	30,761	32,836
NCAA Women	8010	10,016	10,878
National Basketball Association	12,134	20,272	21,841
National Hockey League	17,152	22,065	22,359
Football			
NCAA	39,483	43,106	48,752
Professional	20,763	21,709	22,256
Total	197,605	222,751	282,450

Data from U.S. Census Bureau, "Adult Attendance at Sports Events," Statistical Abstract of the United States (2002, 2009). Available at: http://www.census.gov; and Maury Brown, "Inside the Numbers: Final 2009 MLB Regular Season Attendance," Biz of Baseball. Available at: http://www.bizofbaseball.com/index.php?option=com_content&view=article&id=3592:inside-the-numbers-final-2009-mlb-regular-season-attendance&catid=56:ticket-watch&Itemid=136. Accessed December 9, 2010.

Media Use By and Influence on Spectators

Media long ago changed how people view their role as a spectator. An MLB baseball game was first broadcast via radio in 1921, and in 1935 the Chicago Cubs became the first team to broadcast their entire schedule on radio. Radio broadcasts allowed people to be spectators during the contest when they were not present. No one could anticipate what the next 80 years would bring to professional, collegiate, and high school sports. The explosion of opportunities for spectators to watch sport over the last 10-plus years has been nothing short of spectacular. Professional teams have taken advantage of television and the Internet.

ESPN became the first "all-sports" television network, beginning in 1979 on a limited basis and becoming a 24-hour broadcast station in 1980. Beginning in the late 1990s, professional sports leagues began to establish their own television networks and financed them, in part, through viewer subscriptions through cable and satellite carriers. The actual number of subscribers varies, but MLB claims it has 52 million subscribers compared to NFL's 45 million, NBA's at 18 million, and NHL's 12–15 million. The league networks, while in competition with major networks, did not sever their existing contracts, but instead expanded the availability for spectators to watch every game of their favorite team or teams. In 2009, the major networks (ABC, CBS, FOX, and NBC) reported to be in 114.5 million households, and TBS, TNT, ESPN, and Versus networks reported being in 75 to 99 million households each. The ability for people to watch sports of any kind on television has expanded dramatically over the last 20 years. In 2008, the Super Bowl was the largest viewed Super Bowl and recorded more than 97 million viewers. This is the single largest American market sporting event. By contrast, the 2006 World Cup final was watched by 260 million viewers.

The 2008 Beijing Olympics, a multiweek event, was watched by 4.7 billion viewers. This does not represent separate viewers because many viewers tuned in more than one time and sometimes more than once a day. The opening ceremony for the Olympics recorded 2 billion viewers, a record for any sporting event. Estimates of actual viewers are always just that, an estimate based on historical statistical models. Actual numbers are impossible to identify because one or many people may watch a single television. Numbers of households subscribing, however, are a verifiable number, but do not show actual numbers watching in a home. **Figure 11.1** illustrates the number of single or championship sporting events, size of the television viewership, and the network providing the coverage. It includes collegiate and professional sports only for the United States.

The most significant trend for spectators is the use of the Internet by viewers. Nielsen reports there are almost 134 million unique online viewers who video stream. More than 50% of men and just under 50% of women stream videos. That number is expected to increase as cell phones become a primary source of viewing the Internet. A recent example is illustrative of the influence of the Internet on sport viewing. CBS Sports reported that for the 2009 March Madness NCAA Basketball Tournament, viewers watched 8.6 million hours of streamed audio and video. This was a 75% increase over the previous year. Additionally, 7.52 million visitors used the On Demand video player. The Internet is still a small market compared to live television where 17.6 million people watched the championship game. As discussed in Chapter 13, the Internet will continue to have an increasing influence in people's lives and on sport viewing.

Spectators, as part of the sport marketplace, are key to its commercial success. At the same time, many spectators find leisure meaning in watching sporting events. Different types of fans achieve different emotional outcomes from viewing sporting events. During

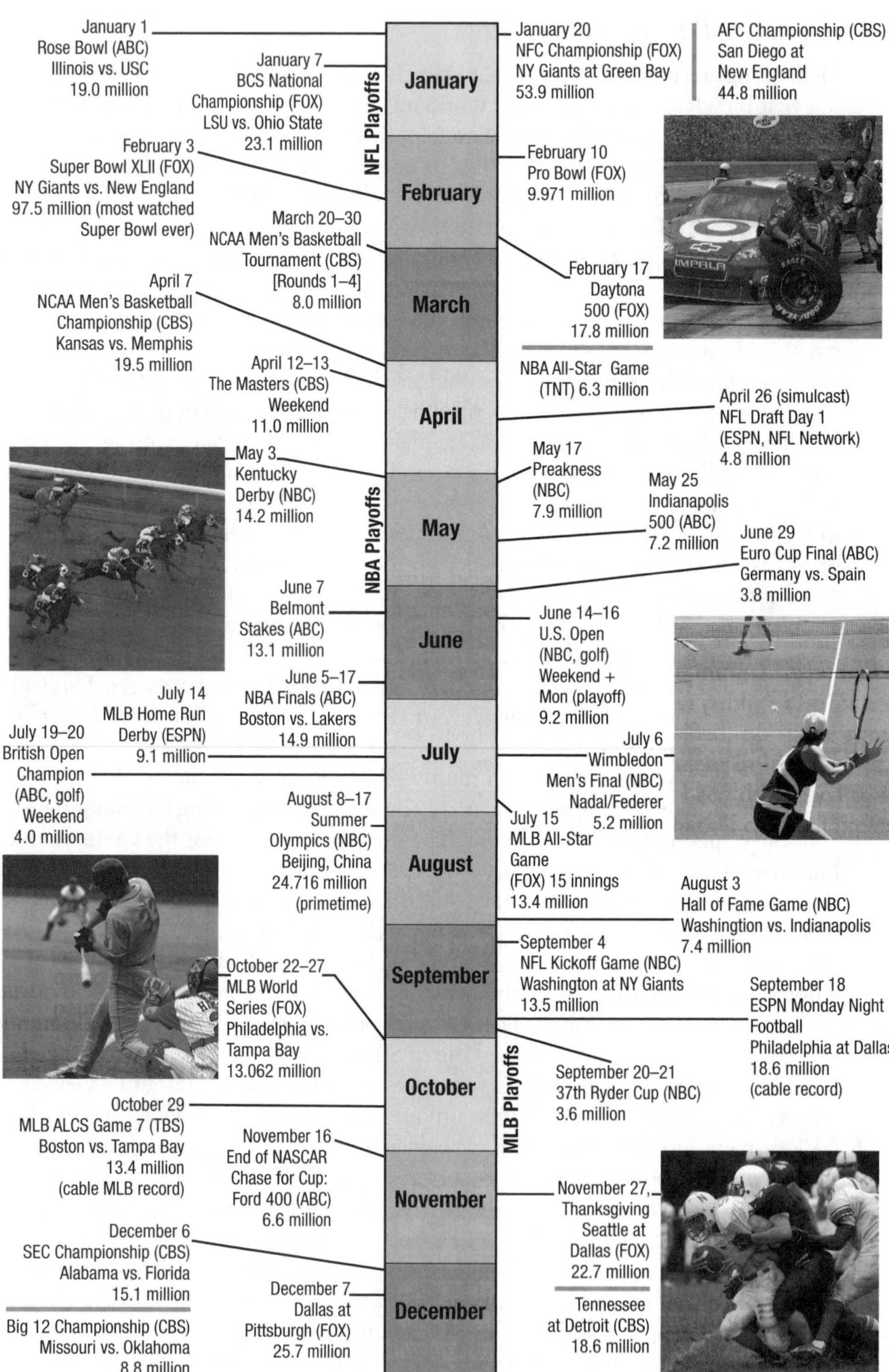

FIGURE 11.1 Sport Viewership, 2008.
Adapted from National Football League, 2008 year in sports. Available at: http://www.colts.com/images/news_photos/communitydynamic/2008yearinsports.pdf. Accessed December 9, 2010. Data from Nielsen Galaxy Explorer. (Jan. 1–Dec. 31, 2008), Average number of viewers in millions age 2 and older.

ESPN

ESPN, Inc., was the brainchild of Bill Rasmussen, an unemployed sports announcer. In the spring of 1978, Rasmussen was fired by the New England Whalers of the World Hockey Association as its communications director and play-by-play announcer. He began looking for a way to broadcast University of Connecticut basketball games through cable television operators in the state. It started as an alternative to then existing television news broadcasts and the information found in the traditional sports sections of newspapers. It was a small operation, frequently broadcasting nontraditional sporting events, such as the World's Strongest Man Competition; international sports relatively unknown in the United States, such as Australian rules football; as well as the short-lived United States Football League (USFL). In 1987, ESPN landed a contract to show National Football League games on Sunday evenings, an event that marked a turning point in its development from a smaller cable TV network to a marketing empire, a cornerstone of the enthusiastic "sports culture" it largely helped to create.[20]

ESPN was originally owned by a joint venture between Getty Oil Company (which was purchased by Texaco) and Nabisco. Since 1984, the entire family of ESPN networks and franchises has been owned by ABC (the American Broadcasting Company) (80%), which became part of The Walt Disney Company in 1996, and the Hearst Corporation (20%).

The first program ever broadcast in high definition on ESPN was an NCAA basketball game in 2002 at the University of Dayton Arena. In 2006, ESPN won the first broadband Sports Emmy Award for Outstanding Achievement in Content Produced for a Non-Traditional Delivery Platform for the online animated series "Off-Mikes," which features Mike Golic and Mike Greenberg of *Mike and Mike in the Morning*, a popular ESPN Radio program.[21]

the 2008–2009 recession, attendance at sporting events declined minimally and viewing via television and the Internet increased.

High television ratings lead to fierce negotiations between league officials and network executives when television contracts are about to expire or new media packages (Internet broadcasting, pay per view, and so forth) are available for bid.

The NFL is "unquestionably the most successful and popular sports league in America, fueled by record attendance in 2005, off-the-chart television ratings and a television contract worth nearly $25 billion over the next six years."[22] In 2006, the NBC network agreed to

Television allows sports fans to be spectators at home.

NBC's "Complete Olympics"

NBC Universal broadcast its record 11th Olympics from Beijing in 2008, presenting an unprecedented 3600 hours of Beijing Olympic Games coverage, the most ambitious single media project in history. NBCU's Olympics coverage featured the most live coverage in the United States (75% in all), across the most platforms of any Summer Olympics in history. The 3600 total hours of coverage on seven NBC Universal networks (NBC, USA, MSNBC, CNBC, Oxygen, Telemundo and Universal HD, as well as NBCOlympics.com), was 1000 hours more than the combined coverage for every televised Summer Olympics in U.S. history (Rome 1960–Athens 2004, 2562 hours). NBCOlympics.com featured approximately 2200 total hours of live streaming Olympic broadband video coverage, the first live online Olympic coverage in the United States.

pay $3.6 billion for a 6-year agreement with the NFL to acquire the broadcasting rights for a new prime-time package, called Football Night in America. In 2009, the agreement was extended to 2013. The new Sunday night package "has become overnight the NFL's pre-eminent prime-time package, relegating to sweep-up duty Monday Night Football," which relocated from ABC to ESPN the same season.[23] ESPN has an 8-year agreement with NFL, for $8.8 billion, to broadcast Monday Night Football, a very popular programming option for ABC the previous years. Furthermore, the NFL signed separate agreements with additional networks for different programming options: CBS agreed to a 6-year, $3.74 billion contract for Sunday Afternoon AFC Football, and FOX followed with a 6-year, $4.28 billion contract for Sunday Afternoon NFC Football. The NFL also retained the right to broadcast selected football footage through its own television channel. DirecTV and the NFL entered into a multiyear agreement to broadcast subscriptions for out-of-market games to viewers for $4 billion to the NFL.

The newest trend in sports broadcasting is streaming games over the Internet for use on individual computers.

Major League Baseball, America's national pastime sport, also scored big in television broadcasting fees. In 2006, the league announced a 7-year television contract that extends deals with ESPN and FOX Sports and added TBS into its television partners.[24,25] Broadcasting fees for both FOX and TBS contracts are worth more than $3 billion;[22] the ESPN extension contract values around $2.5 billion. DirecTV has a 7-year contract for out-of-market games with MLB that began in 2007.[26]

In 2006, the Big Ten Conference announced the creation of a new channel, with a national outreach, that will give the 11-school conference a showcase not only for their intercollegiate programs, but also other accomplishments at the member institutions. The Big Ten Network is a joint venture with the FOX network, which as the minority owner agreed to operate the channel for the next 20 years from offices located in Chicago. This new national cable and satellite channel, along with a new 10-year agreement signed with ABC Sports and ESPN, will dramatically increase the visibility of the Big Ten Conference on television and the Internet. Conference officials said this venture will help the conference enhance its brand recognition and transform it in one of the leading academic and athletic conferences in the United States. Although the financial terms of the agreement were not disclosed to the general public, it is anticipated that minority owner FOX invested a great amount of monetary and other resources toward the realization of this venture.[27]

Broadcasting sporting events has become a major source of income for sport teams and their sponsors.

Franchise Values and Player Salaries The importance and magnitude of spectator sport are also evident in skyrocketing franchise values and player salaries.[28] Franchises in most major leagues have seen their values appreciating significantly in the last 5 to 10 years, with price tags reaching as high as $700 million. An example of this phenomenon is NFL's New England Patriots. When Boston businessman Robert Kraft bought the Patriots in 1994, the team's $172 million price was the league record at that time. The value of the franchise now is believed to be more than $1.4 billion.[29]

Money Draws European Players

European players have been drawn to the United States in increasing numbers to play in the NBA and Major League Soccer (MLS), but until recently the most prominent European soccer players have not made the move. All that changed when David Beckham, one of the world's most popular athletes and the poster boy in Europe for soccer, signed with the Los Angeles Galaxy. Beckham signed in early 2007 for a 5-year deal totaling a reported $250 million. The amount includes salary, endorsements, and incentives. Beckham has been defined as a brand all by himself and according to one author he is where fashion, celebrity and soccer meet. Whereas the NBA brought players in to augment an already popular sport, Beckham is expected to improve the image of MLS.

To help determine the fair market value of sport franchises, *Forbes* magazine conducts an annual survey evaluating factors such as the team's annual operating income, the size of the market the team operates in, stadium value, roster value, and so forth. The 2009 *Forbes* survey revealed that six NFL teams exceeded $1 billion in worth. The six teams are the Dallas Cowboys ($1.7 billion), Washington Redskins ($1.6 billion), New England Patriots ($1.4 billion), and three at $1.2 billion: New York Giants, New York Jets, and Houston

Texans. The New York Yankees are valued at $1.54 billion, the highest-valued MLB franchise and the only team exceeding $1 billion in value. The recession also had an influence on sport team values: five NFL franchises declined in value between 2008 and 2009. This was the first time in 10 years an NFL franchise lost value. Forbes determines team values by measuring four areas including (1) *sport* as a portion of franchise's value attributable to revenue shared among all teams; (2) *market*, which includes the portion of franchise's value attributable to its city and market size; (3) the *stadium* and that portion of a franchise's value attributable to its stadium; and (4) *brand management* as a portion of a franchise's value attributable to the management of its brand.[30]

Players' values also have exceeded industry analysts' projections. It has been estimated that Tiger Woods will, if he continues at his present pace, earn as much as $2 billion in golf tournament winnings and advertising commercials over his competitive lifetime. Tiger Woods earned between June 2008 and June 2009 twice as much money as any other professional athlete, giving him almost $900 million in prize money, endorsements, and appearance fees. However, his personal problems at the end of 2009 may have a significant impact on his earning power because a number of prominent corporate sponsors cancelled contracts. Woods is one of the new breed of international athletes. Others included Michael Jordan, Muhammad Ali, and now include David Beckham, Kimi Raikkonen, and other athletes who cross international boundaries and may or may not be familiar names.

Recently, Alex Rodriguez of the New York Yankees (MLB) signed a $252 million, 10-year agreement that makes him the most expensive MLB contract in the history of the game. Kobe Bryant ranked second and Lebron James ranked third, both playing in the NBA. They make $45 million and $40 million, respectively, just from salaries.

Public Subsidy of Sport Facilities Over the last 20 years, cities have invested billions of dollars into the construction and maintenance of sport facilities, primarily to retain or attract professional sport teams. With the 2008–2010 economic recession, cities were struggling to make payments on completed stadiums. The Indianapolis Lucas Oil Stadium for the Indianapolis Colts, owned by the city, projected a $32 million shortfall in revenue, and Conseco Fieldhouse, the home of the Indiana Pacers, took a $15 million cut in city funding. When the stadiums were first proposed, not just in Indianapolis, but also in other major cities, they were touted as economic engines that would pay for themselves with increased revenues in the community. Unfortunately, that has not happened. In late 2009, Cincinnati projected a $14 million shortfall in expected tax revenues targeted to pay for the city's two riverfront stadiums. New stadiums, such as those opened in 2009 including Yankee Stadium and the New York Mets Citi Field, combined total cost was $2.3 billion and included several hundred million dollars in public financing, tax breaks, and infrastructure improvements.

Attendance Costs of Spectator Sports The increasing cost of attending a sport event is one of the factors that creates discomfort for sport fans and their families. Attending a sporting event for any one of the major leagues today can be a personal account–draining proposition.

The Fan Cost Index (FCI), a survey conducted annually by Chicago-based Team Marketing Report, a sport marketing company, provides a comparable measure of how much a family of four likely will spend attending a professional sporting event. The survey assesses the costs of two average-price adult tickets, two average-price children's tickets, four small soft drinks, two small beers, four hot dogs, two programs, parking, and two adult-size caps.

According to the 2009 FCI, the most expensive place to attend an NFL game is the new Dallas Cowboys' Stadium. At the Dallas Cowboys new $1.2 billion stadium, the average ticket price was $159.65, an almost 90% increase over 2008; the FCI was $758.58, a 74.2% increase over the previous year. The average ticket price for the whole NFL, including Dallas, was $74.99, with an average FCI of $412.64, making the increase 4.1%.[31] By contrast, the FCI for MLB was $196.89, $300.54 for the NHL, and $412.64 for the NBA in 2009.[32]

The cost of seeing a game at the new Dallas Cowboys stadium is the highest in the NFL.

Although the FCI provides a clear idea of the attendance costs associated with professional sport, there was still no accurate measure of value in attending sporting events. In August 2005, Sports Illustrated.com developed a new method, the Fan Value Index (FVI), to test "if baseball fans at Wrigley Field are getting the same return on their investment as the fans at PETCO Park." This comprehensive survey of the experiences at each major league ballpark considered seven criteria to assess value: average ticket price, average costs of concessions/souvenirs, accessibility, various amenities, the overall atmosphere, entertainment or dining options at the vicinity of the stadium, and the club's overall performance in the field. (See **Table 11.7**.) In an era of escalating attendance costs and numerous entertainment options, both the FCI and the FVI can be useful to sport spectators when they choose the venue and type of sport activity they want or can afford to attend.

EMERGENCE OF SPORT AS A REFLECTION OF SOCIETY

Sport as a Source of Moral Values

It was widely believed that sport had several important values: (1) contributing to health and physical fitness as a form of rigorous training, conditioning, and exercise; (2) building personal traits such as courage and perseverance, self-discipline, and sportsmanship; (3) encouraging social values linked to obeying rules and dedication to team goals, as well as providing a channel for social mobility, especially for individuals from disadvantaged backgrounds; and (4) serving as a force to build group loyalty, cohesiveness, and positive morale in schools and colleges and in communities throughout the nation.

Beyond these values, sport obviously has immense appeal, both for participants and for the vastly large audience of fans who often attach themselves to their favorite teams, wearing their colors or uniforms, cheering them enthusiastically, traveling to spring practice or "away" games, and contributing as loyal alumni to the recruitment or support of star athletes. This very fervor and degree of commitment to sport have led inevitably to a number of major abuses or problems affecting sport on all levels.

TABLE 11.7

FAN COST INDEX (FCI) FOR MAJOR LEAGUE BASEBALL, NATIONAL BASKETBALL ASSOCIATION, AND THE NATIONAL FOOTBALL LEAGUE

Major League Baseball FCI—2010

Team	Average Ticket	Average Premium Ticket	Beer	Soda	Hot Dog	Parking	Program	Cap	FCI	Percent Change
Boston Red Sox	$52.32	$100.85	$7.25	$4.00	$4.50	$27.00	$5.00	$20.00	$334.78	2.6
Chicago Cubs	$52.56	$256.98	$6.25	$3.75	$4.25	$25.00	$5.00	$20.00	$329.74	8.1
New York Yankees	$51.83	$312.11	$6.00	$3.00	$3.00	$23.00	$5.00	$25.00	$316.32	0.2
AVERAGE	**$26.74**	**$88.38**	**$5.79**	**$3.47**	**$3.79**	**$12.24**	**$3.48**	**$14.10**	**$194.98**	**–0.7**
Pittsburgh Pirates	$15.39	$42.67	$5.00	$2.75	$2.50	$10.00	$0.00	$12.00	$126.56	–6.3
Arizona Diamondbacks	$14.31	$60.24	$4.00	$3.75	$2.75	$10.00	$0.00	$7.00	$115.24	0.9

National Basketball Association FCI—2009

Team	Average Ticket	Cheapest Available	Beer	Soda	Hot Dog	Parking	Program	Cap	FCI	Percent Change
Los Angeles Lakers	$93.25	$10.00	$6.75	$3.50	$5.00	$15.00	$5.00	$14.99	$475.48	475.5
New York Knicks	$68.04	$10.00	$7.50	$4.25	$4.25	$30.00	$6.00	$24.00	$411.17	411.2
Boston Celtics	$68.55	$10.00	$7.25	$3.75	$4.50	$25.00	$5.00	$18.00	$392.70	392.7
AVERAGE	**$48.90**	**$8.16**	**$6.50**	**$6.50**	**$4.11**	**$12.99**	**$3.26**	**$15.25**	**$289.54**	**–1.4**
Indiana Pacers	$30.02	$5.00	$5.00	$3.25	$2.50	$8.00	$0.00	$15.00	$191.07	–20.8
Memphis Grizzlies	$24.10	$5.00	$5.50	$3.25	$4.25	$10.00	$0.00	$15.00	$177.42	–3.0

National Football League FCI—2009

Team	Average Ticket	Average Premium Ticket	Beer	Soda	Hot Dog	Parking	Program	Cap	FCI	Percent Change
Dallas Cowboys	$159.65	$3,340.00	$7.00	$5.00	$5.00	$40.00	$6.00	$7.00	$758.58	74.2
New England Patriots	$117.84	$566.67	$7.50	$4.00	$3.75	$40.00	$5.00	$14.95	$597.25	0.2
Chicago Bears	$88.33	$312.50	$7.50	$4.50	$4.75	$46.00	$5.00	$20.00	$501.33	3.5
AVERAGE	**$74.99**	**$226.23**	**$6.80**	**$4.09**	**$4.40**	**$24.13**	**$4.53**	**$15.96**	**$412.64**	**4.1**
Jacksonville Jaguars	$57.34	$229.17	$7.00	$3.00	$5.00	$15.00	$0.00	$9.95	$310.28	2.7
Buffalo Bills	$51.24	$177.87	$7.00	$3.50	$3.50	$25.00	$0.00	$16.00	$303.96	1.7

Note: Average ticket price represents a weighted average for season ticket prices for general seating categories, determined by factoring the tickets in each price range as a percentage of the total number of seats in each stadium, ballpark, or arena. Premium tickets are excluded from the survey. Season ticket pricing is used for any team that offers some or all tickets at lower prices for customers who buy season tickets.
Data from Team Marketing Report. Available at: http://teammarketing.com/fancost. Accessed November 11, 2010.

CASE STUDY: How Old Is Too Old to Participate in Sport?

A growing body of research focuses on aging and fitness. Sport participation is part of the study of fitness. There are long-held traditions about aging and physical activity, and most of these support the notion that as one grows older, participation in sport and physical activity should be reduced. These perceptions can be described as barriers that are both real and perceived. Most older people agree that exercise is good, yet this same group often grew up without opportunities to participate extensively in sport and fitness activities, what is called socialization into organized fitness, and once leaving school, what few opportunities they had were diminished. The result of the lack of socialization and opportunity is that people are left with the real and perceived perception of vulnerability when participating in any level of fitness or sport.

Despite this understanding among researchers, most older adults describe their state of health in positive terms. Yet only a minority participate regularly in active physical leisure at a level sufficient to deter the onset of some level of incapacity. In fact, the research suggests that strenuous physical activity is more likely to be avoided when compared to other types of leisure opportunities. Another barrier to participation relates to how older adults perceive their own body and state of health. This includes the attitudes about what the older body should and should not be capable of doing. It includes biological process decline, but also attitudes, expectations, prejudices, cultural values, and ideals of society as well as those individuals develop as they grow old.[a]

Many older adults engage in sport activities.

Not all older people avoid activity. Many are engaged in physical activity, but, as opposed to younger participants who may be involved primarily for a better looking body as frequently suggested on infomercials, they engage in the activity to improve strength, mobility, and balance, all key elements to enhancing individual quality of life as one ages. One of the problems with the research literature, according to Grant, has been a singular focus on the "lived body" at the expense of a broader view encompassing the meanings of later life.[b]

Grant found that older individuals engaged in a variety of physical activities, and playing sport was important to them. Individuals found that the physical activity and sport had become an important part of their life. Even as they talked about the debilitating effects of aging, these individuals placed themselves in the discourse of good health, resisting the idea that aging was wholly a biomedical problem. However, existing stereotypes, especially for those older than 70 years, continue to exist and will into the foreseeable future. Even as more individuals enter the retirement years, there will be a core who maintains a level of fitness and others who will, for a variety of reasons, assume they cannot remain fit and will choose, either for themselves or have chosen for them, not to participate in physical activities.

Questions to Consider

1. Describe some of the potential arguments for not remaining engaged in physical activity and sport as one ages.
2. Think about someone you know who is physically inactive and older. Describe their physical and mental attitude toward exercise. If you don't know of someone, you may need to call a relative who is older.
3. Think about someone you know who is physically active and older. Describe that person's physical and mental attitude toward exercise.
4. How can this research help you adjust your lifestyle now?

Sources

a. Grant, 2001.
b. M. Featherstone and M. Hepworth, "The Mask of Aging and the Post-Modern Lifecourse." In *The Body: Social Processes and Cultural Theory* (London: Sage Publications, 1995).

Abuses and Problems of Sport Competition

Sports for children too often have been influenced by adult pressures to win at all costs. As a result, youngsters often feel excessive pressure to compete and to win, and the experience is no longer fun for them. Studies show that many children about to enter their teen years quit organized sport at this point or shift to a much more relaxed, recreational approach to games.

Linked to such pressures, adults frequently encourage overaggressive and violent play, as well as tactics that ignore sportsmanship and condone rule breaking. In extreme cases, parents may verbally or physically abuse players, parents, or coaches of rival teams and even attack officials who have made decisions ruling against them.[33]

On secondary school levels, the influence of high-pressure college sport begins to make itself felt as promising young players attend special camps financed by manufacturers of sport equipment or clothing. In many cases, parents and college coaches are no longer the primary influences in helping young players make decisions about their future.

It used to be that as early as high school, players might be wooed by agents, given free merchandise, and treated to other benefits that are prohibited at the college level. This has been pushed down to much younger youth. The *New York Times* reported one 4-year-old receiving free equipment and clothes. Nike signed a 13-year-old to a $1 million deal. Reebok built a commercial campaign around a 3-year-old.[34]

Such abuses become more extreme in college competition, in which, especially in high-visibility sport such as basketball and football, there has been a long history of academic violations. Players too often are recruited with faked course records or doctored school transcripts and are academically coddled as long as they remain eligible to compete—to the point that they accomplish little real college work and leave without degrees.

Again and again, there have been scandals and investigations involving gambling on college sport—often with players themselves betting on games—or having to do with the criminal behavior of athletes. In professional sport, conflicts between players and owners, the sudden departures of favorite athletes, or the transfer of sports franchises all have strengthened the public perception of sport as "just a business" and have eroded fan loyalty and attendance in many cities.

Other problems surrounding sport on all levels have involved physically dangerous and even life-threatening conditioning practices and hazing in sport such as ice hockey or football, which has included physical, emotional, and even sexual abuse.[35]

Finally, the practices of building expensive new stadiums with costly skyboxes and adding charges for the right to buy season tickets have dramatically escalated the financial costs for fans. In many cases, the middle-class or blue-collar audience who has traditionally supported professional sport, particularly in large, older cities, is no longer able to do so. As a result, there is disturbing evidence that the fan base for professional sports is declining and that many members of the public are instead transferring their loyalties to local, minor league teams, in part because of nostalgic affection for sport "as it used to be."

On the international scene, sports corruption has been even worse. In late 2002, the British Broadcasting Corporation (BBC) reported a meeting of European sport ministers who were attempting to combat child exploitation in sport. In a number of documented cases, African youth were lured into contracts with professional soccer teams, but when they didn't make the team they were sometimes abandoned and became illegal immigrants without language skills or the ability to make a living. Belgium, France, and Holland have been cited as the countries most likely to bring in preteens and young teens on tourist visas and then abandon them.

Even the Olympic Games, traditionally viewed idealistically as amateur sport at its best, were revealed in 1999 as having involved widespread bribery in the awarding of the 2000 Summer Olympics to Sydney, Australia, and the 2002 Winter Olympics to Salt Lake City.[36]

Beyond corruption at this level, the constant disclosure of prohibited performance-enhancing drugs and "blood doping" being used in international sport has helped to destroy public confidence in such events as the major bicycling event, the Tour de France, and other competitions.[37] Championship boxing matches have been shown to be under the control of criminal elements, and fixed soccer games have threatened the integrity of international competition at the highest level.[38]

FUTURE TRENDS IN SPORT

Whether such negative trends accelerate, sport managers and participants on all levels need to deal with the problems that have been presented in this chapter. Clearly, the continuing expansion of professional sport has reached a point of diminishing returns. If team owners and league policymakers are to retain or regain fan loyalty, it will be necessary to curb the growing costs of sport attendance, which are clearly tied to the astronomical salaries being paid to star players and the greediness of team owners.

Improving Youth Sport

In general, sport as a recreational pursuit appears to be on a healthier footing. Some critics complain that children and youth are excessively scheduled in athletics as well as other free-time activities and that organized play has driven out the kinds of spontaneous neighborhood games that children used to play. However, the reality is that the major national organizations in baseball, softball, basketball, football, and soccer, as well as many others in individual and team sports, have been successful in providing opportunities for play for many millions of young participants.

In terms of the need to control overemphasis on winning, excessive parental pressures, or the kinds of physical, emotional, and sexual abuse of participants by coaches that have received publicity in recent years, a number of leading national organizations have mobilized to improve youth sport. Such private, nonprofit organizations as the National Alliance for Youth Sports, and Positive Coaching Alliance have developed ongoing campaigns, certification, and training programs to enlighten parents and promote positive coaching approaches.

Organizations representing individual sport, such as Little League Baseball, the American Youth Soccer Organization, or the United States Tennis Association, have not only developed guidelines and regulations for the same purposes but have also initiated campaigns to prevent drug use among youth and to encourage fuller participation by minority group children and in inner-city areas.

Shifts in Sport Interests

A number of reports on leisure and recreation choice confirm a growing trend toward "alternative" and often extreme forms of physical recreation, to the point they constitute a direct threat to what team sport used to be a decade ago. Karl Greenfield points out that television has helped promote this trend, with a new band of athletes helping to drive the

> fast-growing world of nontraditional sports to an ever-increasing share of the TV ad dollar. Emerging sports such as surfing, skateboarding, snowboarding, mountain biking, rock climbing, NASCAR racing, and even bass fishing are gaining increasing TV exposure, providing greater choice for sports fans and advertisers.[39]

Tony Hawk: Skater, Entrepreneur, Change Agent

Tony Hawk began skateboarding at age 8 when skateboarding was considered a nontraditional sport. He didn't let that deter him. By age 12, he was sponsored by a skateboard company, and at age 14 turned professional. He started his own skateboard company, Birdhouse Projects, at 24. After a period of personal health issues and a decline in the popularity of skateboarding, he returned to skateboarding and began a series of personal skateboarding and financial successes. Between 1995 and 2002, at the Summer X Games, he won 9 gold medals, 3 silver, and 2 bronze. During the same period his skateboard company became financially successful, he started a successful clothing company called Hawk, and his *Pro Skater* video game for the PlayStation, released in 1999, became an instant best-seller. In 2002, he initiated the Boom Boom HuckJam arena tour in 30 cities and featured the best skateboarders, BMX bike riders, and Motocross riders in the world.[40]

He started the Tony Hawk Foundation in 2002 with a goal to foster the development of youth, using skateboarding as a tool to provide support and empowerment. The foundation provides grants, special events, and technical assistance to recreational programs that focused on the creation of skate parks in low-income communities. By 2010, the foundation has been involved in the development of 256 skate parks serving 2.3 million youth and awarded grants totaling $2.3 million.[41]

Extreme sports, once an outlaw form of sport, have become mainline and broadly accepted.

As a result, the popularity of extreme sports such as skateboarding and snowboarding for youth age 7 and older has skyrocketed. Skateboarding experienced an increase in participation that reached 111% between 1994 and 2004, while snowboarding recorded a similarly phenomenal growth of 219% for the same time period.[42]

The X Games are an example of how the media have capitalized on and benefited from the move toward extreme sport. The list of events for the most recent Winter X Games included snowboarder X, skier X, moto X, snowboard superpipe, and other variations of skiing and snowboarding. The success of the X Games has breathed new life into a ski industry suffering from a lack of young participants. So successful has been the resurgence of snow sports that the 2002 Winter Olympics introduced several of the X Games events into their regular schedule and continued in the 2006 and 2010 Winter Olympics.

Computers and Video Gaming Team sport today competes and will continue to compete against alternative forms of entertainment such as TV, Internet socializing (Facebook, MySpace, YouTube, and so forth), and video gaming. The latest craze for video consoles such as Playstation 3, Nintendo Wii, and Xbox 360 fully supports this prediction. Nintendo recently exploited advances in motion-sensing technology by developing a multifunctional remote control, which gamers use to simulate the movement of a tennis racket, a golf club, or a baseball bat, and play the sport within the virtual reality environment this third-generation Nintendo console creates for the user. Unfortunately, a growing number of children and adolescents prefer to get involved in virtual-reality activities rather than spending time playing sport. The results

RacingThePlanet

RacingThePlanet was founded by American Mary K. Gadams and commenced operations from its base in Hong Kong in 2002. The first race under its banner was the Gobi March held in September 2003 near Dunhuang, China and it introduced trail running races to China. The next race to be added to the series was the Atacama Crossing in Chile, which took place in July 2004, followed by the first Sahara Race in Egypt in September 2005, while the Last Desert in Antarctica was inaugurated in January 2006.[43]

These races combine to create the annual 4 Deserts series, which is now widely recognized as the most prestigious outdoor series in the world.

In February 2008, a fifth event was added to the RacingThePlanet calendar. This race, of similar format, moves to a different location each year, with the first event having been held among the rice terraces of Sapa in northwest Vietnam, and the second in 2009 in the Fish River Canyon and Skeleton Coast of Namibia. The 2010 edition will be held in the Outback of Australia, and in 2011 the race will move on to Nepal.

of this fad are evident in various research reports and scholarly studies about obesity around the nation. The National Health and Nutrition Examination Survey from 1999 to 2002 revealed that an estimated 16% of children between 6 and 19 years old are overweight. These results were up 45% from a similar study that took place from 1994 to 1998.[44]

SUMMARY

In this chapter, the discussion of sport has progressed beyond its primacy as a leisure activity. It has grounded sport in leisure and leisure in sport, but in the latter case, sport is only one component of leisure, as demonstrated throughout the previous chapters. This chapter clearly shows the growth of sport as a component of leisure, social engagement, culture, and big business. A discussion of participation levels in sport shows large youth involvement, gradually dropping off during and following high school and then reemerging, at a lower level, during the mid- to late 20s and early 30s. Sport participation is a function of age, skill, commitment to sport, family commitments, social engagement, time, and money as well as lesser variables.

Spectator involvement in sport is growing dramatically. The availability of expanded television coverage through cable and satellite networks, creation of league networks for MLB and the NFL, the growth of Internet content, and increased interest in international sporting events such as World Cup Soccer and summer and winter Olympics, have resulted in the highest number of spectators in history. Yet it sometimes remains difficult to measure the actual number of spectators, especially when addressing electronic media.

The emergence of professional sport leagues on an international scale, but especially in the United States, has resulted in the integration of business models in sport. In short, sport has become big business, and like any business enterprise, it is expected to return a profit for the owners and shareholders. The individual worth of several professional sport teams now exceeds $1 billion, including international teams such as the Manchester United Football Club. The emergence of sport as big business will drive the future of professional and collegiate sports for the near future. Although little was discussed regarding the value and business aspects of collegiate sports, they too have entered an era when they must be partially or fully self-supporting.

Finally, this chapter discusses trends and issues and includes the discussion of sport as a source of moral values, a topic that is frequently hotly debated; issues and concerns with youth sport participation and pressure; the influence of commercialism on young sport participants; efforts to rein in runaway youth sport programs and to bring fun back to the participants; the growth of extreme sports; and the influence of computer and video games.

Sport is a major influence in society. It is discussed at work, over the Internet, among friends, and yet for all its engagement and involvement, only a moderate percentage of the population actually engages in sport participation or spectating. Yet because it has become big business, it receives significant attention.

QUESTIONS FOR CLASS DISCUSSION OR ESSAY EXAMINATION

1. Discuss how sport and leisure are related, including the commonalities and differences, as well as how sport has emerged as an important component of society.

2. Differentiate between the motivations for involvement in sport of participants and spectators.
3. Sport participation occurs at many different levels, from pickup games of youth and adults, to formal organized sport in middle school through college, to elite professional sport, and many levels in between. Explain how these levels differ, motivations for participation, outcome for participants, and levels of involvement. Further, relate these issues to the influence of leisure.
4. Review the section focusing on sport as big business and address the different perspectives of business toward sport (manufacturer, sporting goods sales, professional teams, sponsors, and so forth) and how each benefits and influences sport.
5. What do you think the most important trends for sport are over the next 5 years. Which indicators point to these as important trends?

ENDNOTES

1. J. B. Lewis, T. R. Jones, G. Lamke, and L. M. Dunn, "Recreational Sport: Making the Grade on College Campuses," *Parks and Recreation* (December 1998): 73.
2. The Free Dictionary, "Sport," http://www.thefreedictionary.com/sport.
3. R. A. Stebbins, "Casual Leisure: A Conceptual Statement," *Leisure Studies* (Vol. 16, 1997): 17–25.
4. M. Kilpatrick, E. Hebert, and J. Bartholomew, "College Students' Motivation for Physical Activity: Differentiating Men's and Women's Motives for Sport Participation and Exercise," *Journal of American College Health* (Vol. 54, No. 2, 2005).
5. S. Ullrich-French and A. L. Smith, "Perceptions of Relationships with Parents and Peers in Youth Sport: Independent and Combined Prediction of Motivational Outcomes," *Psychology of Sport and Exercise* (Vol. 7, No. 2, 2008): 1934–214.
6. All Star Activities, "Why Your Child Should Participate in Sports." http://www.allstaractivities.com/sports/sports-why-participate.htm.
7. "Team Sports: State of the Industry," *Sporting Goods Dealer* (1 January 2006).
8. R. R. Pate, M. G. Davis, T. N. Robinson, et al., "Promoting Physical Activity in Children and Youth," *Circulation* (Vol. 114, 2006): 1214–1224.
9. Quiksilver in Memory of Eddie Aikau Waimea Bay Hawai'i '09–10, "History." http://live.quiksilver.com/2009/bigwave/history.php?btn_history=_over.
10. J. McKinley, "As Hawaii Seas Roil, Surfers Await the Big One," *The New York Times*. http://www.nytimes.com/2009/12/08/us/08surf.html.
11. Surfline, "Eddie Aikau (May 4, 1946–March 17, 1978)." http://www.surfline.com/surfing-a-to-z/eddie-aikau-biography-and-photos_740.
12. Sporting Goods Manufacturers Association, "U.S. Sports Industry: Nearly a $70 Billion Business" (9 June 2008). http://www.sgma.com/press/3_U.S.-Sports-Industry:-Nearly-a-$70-Billion-Business.
13. European Sponsorship Association, "Value of Olympic Sponsorship Questioned at Future Sponsorship Conference" (30 November 2009). http://www.sponsorship.org/esa2009/esaPressDetail.asp?id=631.
14. Maury Brown, "Inside the Numbers: Final 2009 MLB Regular Season Attendance," Biz of Baseball (5 October 2009). http://www.bizofbaseball.com/index.php?option=com_content&view=article&id=3592:inside-the-numbers-final-2009-mlb-regular-season-attendance&catid=56:ticket-watch&Itemid=136.
15. Street and Smith's Sports Business Daily, "NFL Regular-Season Attendance Slightly Off From Record-Setting '07." http://www.sportsbusinessdaily.com/article/126559.

16. R. Underwood, E. Bond, and R. Baer, "Building Service Brands via Social Identity: Lessons from the Sports Marketplace," *Journal of Marketing: Theory and Practice* (Vol. 9, No. 1, 2001): 1–12.

17. R. Giulianotti, "Supporters, Followers, Fans, and Flaneurs: A Taxonomy of Spectator Identities in Football," *Journal of Sport and Social Issues* (Vol. 26, No. 1, 2002): 25–46.

18. Chicago Cubs, "Wrigley Field." http://mlb.mlb.com/chc/ballpark/index.jsp.

19. L. Igel, "Low Sports Attendance: Who Is Your Customer?," *Forbes*. http://blogs.forbes.com/sportsmoney/2010/09/28/low-sports-attendance-who-is-your-customer.

20. Funding Universe, "ESPN, Inc." http://www.fundinguniverse.com/company-histories/ESPN-Inc-Company-History.html.

21. All Experts, "ESPN." http://en.allexperts.com/e/e/es/espn.htm.

22. R. Covitz, "NFL, Media Battle in the Trenches over Access Issues," *Kansas City Star* (2 October 2006).

23. B. Horn, "NBC Returns as an NFL Player," *Dallas Morning News* (5 September 2006).

24. "MLB Extends Deals with ESPN, FOX," *Pittsburg Tribune–Review* (12 July 2006).

25. "Turner, MLB Reach 7-Year TV Deal for LCS Coverage," Associated Press (17 October 2006).

26. N. Armour, "MLB Club Owners Approve New TV Contracts, Discuss Games in China," Associated Press (17 November 2006).

27. J. Paul, "Big Ten Announces New TV Contract with ABC/ESPN and Creation of New Cable Channel," Associated Press (22 June 2006).

28. D. Naylor, "Investing in a Team a Losing Proposition; Franchise Values Have Not Gone Up Like They Have in Other Sports," *Globe & Mail* [Toronto, Canada] (11 June 2005): S1.

29. J. Weinbach, "Team Owners Behaving Badly," *Wall Street Journal* (5 May 2006).

30. Kurt Badenhausen, Michael K. Ozanian, and Christina Settimi, "Recession Tackles NFL Team Values," Forbes.com (2 September 2009). http://www.forbes.com/2009/09/02/nfl-pro-football-business-sportsmoney-football-values-09-values.html; and Michael K. Ozanian and Kurt Badenhausen, "Baseball's Most Valuable Teams," Forbes.com (22 April 2009). http://www.forbes.com/2009/04/22/yankees-mets-baseball-values-09-business-sports-land.html.

31. Jon Greenberg, "NFL FCI 2009," Team Marketing Report (9 September 2009). http://www.teammarketing.com/blog/index.html?article_id=96.

32. Jon Greenberg, "2009–10 NHL FCI," Team Marketing Report (6 October 2009). http://www.teammarketing.com/blog/index.html?article_id=98; "2009–10 NBA FCI (updated), Team Marketing Report (30 October 2009). http://www.teammarketing.com/blog/index.html?article_id=99; and Jon Greenberg, "NFL FCI 2009," Team Marketing Report (9 September 2009). http://www.teammarketing.com/blog/index.html?article_id=96.

33. James Kozlowski, "Sport League Held Liable for Brutal Attack on Coach," *Parks and Recreation* (November 1999): 45–52.

34. Margaret Talbot, "Why, Isn't He Just the Cutest Brand-Image Enhancer You've Ever Seen?" *New York Times Magazine* (21 September 2003).

35. Joe La Points, "A Hard Winter in Vermont: Hockey Season Canceled Over Hazing," *New York Times* (3 February 2000): D1.

36. Robert Sullivan, "How the Olympics Were Bought," *Time* (25 January 1999): 38.

37. Michael Lemonick, "Le Tour des Drugs," *Time* (10 August 1998): 76.

38. Jere Longman, "Fixed Matches Are Darkening Soccer's Image," *New York Times* (7 June 1998): 1.

39. Karl Greenfield, "A Wider World of Sport," *Time* (9 November 1998): 80.

40. Tony Hawk, "Tony Hawk's Biography." http://www.tonyhawk.com/bio.html.

41. Surf, Skate, Wake Board, "The Tony Hawk Foundation" (20 June 2010). http://www.surfskatewakeboard.com/the-tony-hawk-foundation; and Tony Hawk Foundation, "Our Mission." http://www.tonyhawkfoundation.org.

42. "Extreme Sports Have National Appeal," *Parks and Recreation* (2004): 39(10): 23.

43. RacingthePlanet. http://www.racingtheplanet.com.

44. "Overweight Among U.S. Children and Adolescents," *National Health and Nutrition Examination Survey* (Washington, DC: U.S. Department of Health and Human Services, 2002): 1.

CHAPTER 12

LEISURE AS A PROFESSION

◆ ◆ ◆

Now, more than ever, the field of recreation and leisure services offers a wide variety of rewarding and fulfilling careers to candidates who possess a strong academic background, practical experience, and a passion, commitment, and dedication to the profession. From event planners to park rangers to recreational sport programmers, there are numerous career opportunities and literally thousands of jobs worldwide.[1]

Because recreation and leisure is approximately a $400 billion per year industry, the field offers more variety and career choices on a global basis than do many other professional fields.[2] *Employment of recreation and leisure service personnel is expected to continue to grow in years to come. This is primarily because of an increasing number of people with an abundance of leisure time and the resources to purchase associated services; changing work patterns; an increased interest in fitness and health; and the rising demand for recreational opportunities for older adults in retirement communities and senior centers.*

◆ ◆ ◆

INTRODUCTION

Recreation, parks, and leisure services have expanded greatly over the past several decades as a diversified area of employment. Today, several million people work in different sectors of this field, including amateur and professional sport, entertainment and amusement services, travel and tourism, recreation-related businesses, and government and nonprofit community organizations.

As a distinct part of this larger group, several hundred thousand people are directly involved as recreation leaders, supervisors, managers, therapists, planners, and consultants in public, voluntary, commercial, therapeutic, and other types of agencies. These individuals with a primary concern for the provision of recreation services are generally regarded as professionals on the basis of their job responsibilities, specialized training, and affiliations with professional associations.

The prevailing image of leisure-service professionals has been that of public, governmental, recreation, and park employees. The leading professional associations, as well as most textbooks and college curricula, reinforced this narrowly defined identity. However, the reality is that vast sectors of employment in recreation and leisure services are not government related but, instead, have to do with nonprofit community agencies; company-sponsored, commercial, and therapeutic recreation services; sport management; and travel and tourism programs. As such, they have their own professional associations, as well as goals, job functions, and strategies that differ from those of public recreation and park specialists.

RECREATION AS A CAREER

People have worked in recreation for many centuries in the sense that there have been professional athletes and entertainers throughout history. Musicians, tumblers, dancers, huntsmen, park designers, and gardeners were all recreation specialists attending to the leisure needs first of royalty and, ultimately, of the public at large. However, the idea of recreation itself as a career field did not surface until the late 1800s, when public parks and playgrounds, along with voluntary social service and youth-serving organizations, were established.

After the beginning of the twentieth century, courses in play leadership were developed by the Playground Association of America and were taken by many teachers. In the middle 1920s, the National Recreation Association provided a graduate training program for professional recreation and park administrators, and leisure as a distinct area of public service came to be recognized. This recognition increased during the Great Depression of the 1930s as many thousands of individuals were assigned by the federal government to emergency posts providing community recreation programs and developing new parks and other facilities. However, it was not until the development of separate degree programs in a handful of colleges that higher education in recreation and parks as a distinct career field came into being.

By the second half of the twentieth century, careers in recreation and parks were seen as a growth area. A nationwide study of workforce requirements in the 1960s concluded that there would be a need for hundreds of thousands of new recreation and park professionals in the years ahead. The U.S. Department of Labor reported widespread shortages of leisure-service personnel in local government, hospitals, and youth-serving organizations. Several factors, such as the federal government's expanded activity in outdoor recreation and open space and the establishment of the National Recreation and Park Association, stimulated interest in this field. In the 1970s, as employment grew, curricula in recreation and leisure service gained increased acceptance in higher education.

Scope of Employment Today

People spend free time participating in sport, arts, and nature activities; visiting museums, zoos, and aquariums; and attending special events, shows, and performances; as well as traveling to tourism destinations. With all of this recreation going on, people are needed to work in these and many other jobs.

Employment opportunities in parks and recreation are highly diversified. Recreation workers are found in local parks and recreation agencies, on cruise ships, planning

Jay Brown, National Park Service, Park and U.S. Ranger at Voyageurs National Park

The U.S. Park Ranger of today wears many hats. First, and most evident, I am a federal law enforcement officer capable of investigating a full spectrum of crimes including minor resource violations (for example, seashell collection) to the most major violent crimes such as rape or murder. Second, in most national parks, my fellow rangers and I are the primary emergency medical response force. With most rangers trained, at minimum, as emergency medical technicians, rangers are the initial response for all emergency medical situations occurring within the park. Third, I am relied on for the implementation of all levels of search and rescue. These search-and-rescue incidents often include the utilization of technical (ropes) rescue, swift water rescue, fixed-wing aircraft, park helicopters, and unfortunately, body recovery operations. Fourth, I am certified in wildland fire suppression. Given that many of our National Parks contain vast acreage of forested land, it is practical and necessary that park rangers harbor fire-suppression skills and in many areas the use of these skills is imminent. Finally, in addition to these duties, I am expected to know the natural, cultural, and historical aspects of the park in which I work. A good ranger is able to convey his or her knowledge of flora, fauna, and other assets of our national parks to visitors in a way that is not only educational but instills a passion to preserve and protect these unique places, leaving them unimpaired for future generations.

Several factors contribute to the satisfaction I have for my job. First, as a lover of the outdoors, I am afforded the opportunity to live and work in the nation's most beautiful natural areas. Second, I have the opportunity to meet visitors who many have waited a month, year, or sometimes even a lifetime to visit these magnificent places. Third, given the fact that the park ranger wears so many hats, every day is new, different, and interesting.

major festivals such as the Sundance Film Festival, planning promotional events for the Phoenix International Raceway, and working with people with disabilities in a therapeutic recreation setting. They can be found in all of our national parks from Acadia to Zion. They serve as park rangers, interpreters, guides, and activity planners. Throughout this chapter, you will find vignettes of people working in the field of parks and recreation. Some of them are brand new to the field, and others have several years of experience. Each shares his or her typical responsibilities for the job. It is easy to see how diverse this profession is.

The educational backgrounds of people working in recreation vary. A plethora of summer and part-time positions require a high school diploma—or less as is the case with many lifeguards and camp counselors. However, these positions are not considered professional positions, but a means to gather experience in order to obtain a professional position in the recreation field. As responsibilities increase in recreation-related jobs, so do degree requirements. Entry-level positions in the field such as after-school program supervisors, special-event planners, and facility supervisors may require a bachelor's degree, and middle- and upper-level management positions may require a master's degree.

Although data on the total number of jobs in recreation are limited, we do know that the tourism industry is one of the nation's largest employers with 7.7 million people working in this industry.[3] The 2010–2011 Bureau of Labor Statistics estimate is that more than 1.9 million people were employed in recreation and entertainment.[4] Furthermore, the National Park Service employs 28,000 people to take care of its 84 million acres of land;[5] state parks employ 56,343 people full and part time.[6]

The Bureau of Labor Statistics expects the demand for most recreation jobs to grow faster than average through 2018, which means they expect a growth of about 15% through this time. They also predict that therapeutic recreation will see a growth that is faster than average with an increase of 15% over the next several years.[7] Part of what is driving this growth is the rate of retirement of baby boomers previously discussed in other chapters. It is also the result of increased concern for health and wellness.

Travel Generates Tax Revenue

Travelers in the United States spent $770 billion last year, generating tax revenue in the amount of $117 billion for federal and local governments.[8]

CASE STUDY: Tourism Job Stimulus

In December 2009, President Barack Obama held a White House Jobs Summit with the purpose of developing ideas to increase the number of jobs in the United States. It was estimated that 400,000 jobs were lost in tourism in 2008 and 2009. The U.S. Travel Association sent a letter to the president asking him to consider tourism as a place to create jobs. In general, the organization wanted Congress to provide tax incentives for job creation in travel, promote international travel, and provide government assistance in enhancing efficient travel infrastructure. The following are suggestions the U.S. Travel Association made in the letter to increase jobs and tourism in the United States:

1. *Spousal travel tax deduction.* Business conferences and events are responsible for nearly 15% of all travel in the United States, driving $101 billion in spending, generating 1 million jobs, and creating $16 billion in tax revenue at the federal, state, and local levels. Allowing business travelers to take a tax deduction for the cost of their spouse's travel will encourage more business travel, improve the day-to-day lives of American families, and boost job creation in the hospitality and travel sectors. H.R. 562 sponsored by Representative Neil Abercrombie and S. 261 sponsored by Senator Lindsey Graham have garnered significant private sector support to make business travel more family friendly.
2. *Business meal tax deduction.* Tens of thousands of small businesses and self-employed individuals conduct business meetings and promote their products over a meal at restaurants. They rely on the meal and entertainment tax deduction to save on costs and promote business growth. Under current law, a taxpayer is permitted to deduct 50% of meal and entertainment expenses for tax purposes, as long as the expenditures are considered ordinary and necessary business expenses. H.R. 3333 sponsored by Representative Neil Abercrombie and H.R. 3952 sponsored by Representative Dina Titus would promote job growth for small businesses and various sectors of the travel community by increasing the income tax deduction for business meals and entertainment expenses up to 80%.

3. *Enact and rapidly implement the Travel Promotion Act (TPA).* The Travel Promotion Act (S. 1023/H.R. 2935) is commonsense legislation that would authorize the creation of a nonprofit corporation to help the United States welcome millions more international visitors annually. The Corporation for Travel Promotion would attract visitors by better communicating America's frequently changing travel security policies and promoting America as the premier travel destination. The corporation's work would be financed—without U.S. taxpayer dollars—by up to $100 million in voluntary private sector contributions and a government match derived from a $10 fee paid by inbound travelers once every 2 years via the Electronic System for Travel Authorization (ESTA) from the 35 countries that participate in the Visa Waiver Program (VWP).
4. *Target hiring and placement of new consular officers.* Millions of additional overseas visitors are interested in traveling to the United States and will spend on average $4,500 per person per visit. Insufficient access to U.S. consulates in geographically large countries and a lack of consular officers to process a greater number of visa applications, however, prevent growth in international visitation and limit our ability to create new U.S. jobs to service these new travelers while in America. Investing in videoconferencing technology that will allow the State Department to conduct the visa interviews remotely will quickly increase visa accessibility while maintaining a secure visa process. Furthermore, an investment of $37 million in funds to hire approximately 100 new consular officers and place them in key travel markets with unmet demand, primarily China, Brazil, and India, the U.S. can process and welcome millions more visitors, generate billions in new export revenue, and rapidly create tens of thousands of new U.S. jobs. For example, India is one of the fastest-growing outbound travel markets in the world, and tourism from India to the United States accounted for 40% of all U.S. service exports to India in 2008. With more than 1.1 billion inhabitants and GDP increasing by more than 8% every year, the country offers enormous potential for future growth in outbound travel. If the United States could gain an additional 5% of the Indian outbound travel market, it would drive more than $3.3 billion in additional export revenue and create 30,600 more American jobs in one year.
5. *Invest more in highway spending to improve roads and facilitate increased travel.* Almost 61,000 miles (37%) of all lane miles on the National Highway System (NHS) are in poor or fair condition and more than 152,000 bridges (one of every four bridges in the United States) are structurally deficient or functionally obsolete. Moving forward on all or parts of the Surface Transportation Authorization Act of 2009, which includes higher levels of investment than existing law, will allow for the building of better highways and bridges, reduce travel delays, and employ workers in a wide array of construction industries.
6. *Direct funding to modernize America's air traffic control system.* The federal government must accelerate and deploy the next generation of air traffic control (NextGen) capabilities, equipment, and procedures. NextGen involves a fundamental transition from a ground-based aviation infrastructure system (radar) to a satellite-based system enabling both controllers and flight crews to enjoy more accurate real-time information. The public benefits of accelerated NextGen are numerous and widely agreed upon: improved safety, job creation and retention, shorter flight times, reduced delays, and significant environmental benefits, including fewer carbon emissions, and less noise and improved local air quality. Expedited NextGen investment will eliminate a significant drag on the nation's economy and transform aviation into a powerful job creator in the near term.

7. *Airport port of entry construction funding.* U.S. international airport arrival areas managed by U.S. Customs and Border Protection (CBP) are often challenged with limited inspection spaces, creating long wait times for travelers that result in inefficient processing of visitors and a negative perception about the U.S. entry process. Normally, these inspection areas are donated by airport authorities to CBP, to minimize the loss of valuable space that could be used by vendors or airlines. A one-time expenditure of $250 million could be used to attain expanded passenger inspection space for CBP operations from airports, providing CBP with appropriate real estate to improve the efficiency of their operations and grow trusted traveler programs to attract more visitors. Similar to the infusion of funds from the American Recovery and Reinvestment Act for land ports of entry, using airport construction projects to deploy a more efficient, more welcoming airport experience to foreign travelers and Americans returning home will create jobs directly and indirectly.

Questions to Consider

1. Which of these suggestions do you think will have the biggest impact? Why?
2. Which of these suggestions do you think will have the least impact? Why?
3. What other ways could the number of jobs in tourism be increased?

Source

a. U.S. Travel Association, "U.S. Travel Urges President, Congress to Utilize Travel as a Vehicle for Job Creation" (2 December 2009). www.ustravel.org/news/press-releases/us-travel-urges-president-congress-utilize-travel-vehicle-job-creation.

Training for parks and recreation positions does not stop with a degree. The National Aquatics Conference and Exposition features sessions focusing on facility management, aquatics operations, and safety, just to name a few.

PROFESSIONAL IDENTIFICATION IN RECREATION

What does being a professional mean? At the simplest level, it indicates that one is paid for one's work—as opposed to an amateur, who is not paid for it. Thus, an athlete who receives pay for playing for a team is classified as a professional.

However, this obviously is not a sufficient definition of the term in that many forms of paid work are not considered to be professional. A more complete definition of the term would suggest that a professional is one who has a high degree of status and specialized training and provides a significant form of public or social service.

Within a number of specialized leisure-service areas today, such as company-sponsored employee programs, therapeutic recreation, or fitness and health spas, professionalism might be narrowly defined as the possession of a required certification based on a combination of education, experience, and examination. In other situations, membership in a designated professional association or society may be recognized

Mike Kniep, Youth Counselor, Celebrity Cruise Line

On board a cruise line is like working on a floating city. My job is to provide recreation for youth. We have a five-tier program based on ages: Shipmates 3–5, Cadets 6–8, Ensigns 9–11, Junior Teens 12–14, and Senior Teens 15–17. I work mostly with the Ensigns and Teens age groups. For the Ensigns, we go on scavenger hunts around the ship, do sport activities on the sports deck and lots of programs that are very active. With both the teens groups, we have theme nights like White Night and College Night. We also take the children to the production shows. One popular event for the teens is learning how to make sushi and then sampling the variety of sushi served on board. The younger children have programs during three major activity times: 9 A.M.–12 P.M., 2 P.M.–5 P.M., and 7 P.M.–10 P.M. The teen program is more relaxed with activities every 20–30 minutes from 9 A.M.–1 P.M. The hours are long as we work 40 hours, 7 days a week. During the holidays, we will work more like 50 hours. I have gotten to see many different parts of the world because of this job. As you gain more seniority, you can request certain ships to see different ports of call. I never thought my recreation degree would allow me to travel to so many different places in the world in such a short period of time!

as a hallmark of professionalism. However, the following seven criteria have generally been accepted as key elements of professionalism.

Criterion 1: Social Value and Purpose

The goals, value, and purpose of organized community leisure-service agencies are described in Chapter 7. In general, they deal with such elements as improving the quality of life, contributing to personal development and social cohesion, helping to prevent socially destructive leisure pursuits, and protecting the environment.

In the nonprofit field, the YWCA is dedicated to the empowerment of women and girls and the elimination of racism. The oldest U.S. organization owned and managed by women, its member organizations provide safety; shelter; day care; physical fitness and recreation programs; counseling; and other social, health, educational, and job-related services to millions of women and girls and their communities each year.

People are willing to pay for their own personal leisure and are more reluctant to pay taxes to support leisure for the public good such as parks and trails.

Although the public and nonprofit sectors are most often equated with social good, the commercial sector contributes to this as well and has its own social value and purpose. It may provide entertainment, support health and fitness, or expose people to other cultures, historic sites, or a multitude of other tourism-related destinations.

Criterion 2: Public Recognition

The rapid expansion of the leisure-service field over the past several decades does not necessarily mean that the public at large understands and respects it fully or that they regard it as a distinct area of professional service. To illustrate, most individuals today know what recreation is, and many regard it as an important part of their lives. Most are prepared to pay substantial portions of their income for recreational goods or services, such as memberships in health clubs, vacations, sport equipment, tickets to theater productions, and other leisure-related fees and charges. However, they are often less willing to pay taxes in support of public recreation and park facilities and programs than they are to spend privately for their own leisure needs.

A time-use study done by the Bureau of Labor Statistics found that 96% of people older than the age of 15 reported having some sort of leisure whether it be socializing, sport, or exercising.[9] In 2008, there were more than 747 million visitors to state parks, and in 2008, there were 57.6 campers and another 6.7 million lodge and cabin guests.[10] The National Park Service reported another 11.7 billion visitors in 2009.[11] Although these are just a minute portion of the leisure-service opportunities available, it demonstrates that a large portion of the population uses recreation services.

Even though the value of organized recreation service may be acknowledged through participation and use, how aware is the public at large of the leisure-service field as a profession? The likelihood is that most individuals recognize the roles of recreation professionals within specific areas of service. For example, they are likely to be familiar with the function of a recreation therapist in a mental hospital or nursing home or the function of a community center director, a park ranger, or a sport specialist in an armed forces recreation program. What they tend not to understand is that recreation represents a field of practice that requires special expertise and educational preparation in a college or university. At issue is the image of the recreation professional.

Becky Brannan-Durham, Activities Assistant, Heritage Manor Nursing Home

I am responsible for leading and co-leading activities and assist in planning programs at the nursing home. Activities that we provide for the residents include bingo, trivia, current events, joints in motions, Wii, balloon volleyball, bean bag toss, and sensory stimulation. On a daily basis, I also do one-on-ones with residents who are unable to attend activities or unable to leave their room. During one-on-ones, I read poems, read church bulletins, play music, and just listen to what they have to say. I love working with residents. It is never a dull moment. One can never know what to expect from the residents. They make my day. In this line of work you never stop learning or have time to get bored because the residents keep you on your toes.

Image of the Professional Unless one is an actual participant in organized leisure activities, people are most likely unaware that these jobs and careers even exist. Even with participation, the career acknowledgment may not happen. People attending a major special event may enjoy the special event and return year after year, but they are unlikely to understand all of the planning and preparation that goes into that event. People have the luxury of enjoying recreation services, whereas the people who provide them remain behind the scenes. The public often does not see the people who cut the grass in the park, plan and plant the flowerbeds, develop the tournament schedule, or schedule the concerts in the park. In many instances, a park and recreation professional is out of sight if the event or program is running smoothly. This can lead to the public not equating what is being done to a true profession or career.

Another misconception about this profession is that anyone can do it. People think anyone can plan a 64-team softball tournament, organize a special event that attracts 100,000 people, or manage a pool. On the surface, these activities may not seem very difficult. However, they require an extensive amount of academic preparation, experience, and organizational skills. In addition, if recreation and leisure-service employees are to sharpen their identity and support, they must enrich their own competence through specialized professional study and by joining organizations that strengthen their field.

Criterion 3: Specialized Professional Preparation

A measure of the professional authority of any given field is the degree of specialized preparation that people must have to function in it. Typically, the most highly regarded professions in modern society, such as medicine or law, have rigorous requirements with respect to professional education. These evolved through the years and involve higher education curricula on the graduate level, supported in some cases by required internships or periods of professional practice and by comprehensive examinations prepared or administered by professional societies.

Professional Preparation in Recreation and Parks The early period of the development of higher education in recreation, parks, and leisure services was described earlier in this text. Over the past five decades, college and university curricula in recreation and parks have been developed on three levels: two-year, four-year, and graduate (master's degree and doctorate) programs.

Two-Year Curricula During the late 1960s and early 1970s, many community colleges began to offer associate degree programs in recreation and parks. Typically, these sought to prepare individuals on para- or subprofessional levels, rather than for supervisory or administrative roles. Most community colleges offered recreation majors a choice of two types of programs: terminal and transfer. *Terminal programs* were intended to equip students immediately for employment and gave heavy emphasis to developing basic, useful recreation leadership skills, often within a specific field of practice. *Transfer programs* were intended for students who hoped to transfer to four-year degree programs.

Four-Year Programs The most widely found degree program in recreation and parks has been the four-year bachelor's degree curriculum. Initially, most such programs consisted of specialized degree options in college departments of health, physical education, and recreation, although some were located in departments or schools of landscape architecture, agriculture, forestry, or social work. Today, although many departments still are situated administratively in schools or colleges of health, physical education, and recreation, they have achieved a high level of curricular independence, with their own objectives, courses, degree requirements, and faculty.

Four-year programs typically have established degree options in areas such as recreation programming, recreation and park management, resource management, outdoor recreation, therapeutic recreation, sport management, commercial recreation, and tourism. The normal pattern has been to require all department majors to take certain core courses representing the generic needs of all preprofessionals, including basic courses in recreation history and philosophy, programming, management, and evaluation and/or research, and then to have a separate cluster of specialized courses for each option.

What once started as a training ground for public parks and recreation professionals has grown to meet the changing demands of the field. There was growing academic awareness of the job opportunities in other recreation areas. As a result, a number of college and university programs changed their titles and departmental affiliations to reflect the new interest in commercial recreation, travel and tourism, sport management, hotel and resort management, and similar specializations. Typically, a considerable number of departments added the term *tourism* to their titles and established enriched programs in this area—in some cases in collaboration with schools of business in their institutions. In other cases, therapeutic recreation majors were transferred administratively to departments or schools of public health or healthcare services. As the most striking example of proliferation in this field, as of 2010 there were more than 200 independent departments of sport management designed to meet personnel needs in this growing field.[12]

Master's Degree and Doctoral Programs Although it is generally agreed that the four-year curriculum should provide a broad base of general or liberal arts education along with the core of essential knowledge underlying recreation service, the specific function of graduate

Dave Bertagnoli, Outdoor Recreation Director/Activity Manager, Fort Dix, New Jersey

I am responsible for three primary activities that encompass Outdoor Recreation: skeet/trap and rifle/pistol range along with a paintball program, a recreational go-cart/batting cage/mini-golf operation and an equipment rental facility that includes an adventure trip program. Primary job responsibilities include managing and maintaining an operating budget and ensuring that the money is allocated to the correct cost centers, daily processing of the financial information, managing payroll and a government credit card, coordinating through the Human Resources office all personnel action, holding weekly staff meetings, and attending other related meetings.

The awesome part of my job as a recreation specialist/programmer is researching, planning, organizing, implementing, and evaluating outdoor adventure trips for the service members, their families, and civilians who work on post. These include but are not limited to downhill skiing, snowboarding, hiking, canoeing and kayaking, overnight camping, horseback riding, and whitewater rafting. I am responsible for creating plans of actions and after-action reports for all major events/trips. Those trips I lead and get to *play*!

education in this field is not as clearly defined. Some authorities have suggested that graduate curricula should accept only those students who already have a degree in recreation and should focus on providing advanced professional education within a specialized area of service. However, there tends to be little support for this position, and many graduate programs accept students from other undergraduate disciplines as well as those holding undergraduate degrees in recreation.

In general, authorities agree that master's degree work should involve advanced study in recreation and park administration or in some other specialized area of service, such as therapeutic recreation or sport management. The assumption is that individuals on this level are preparing for supervisory or managerial positions or, in some cases, roles as researchers or chief executive officers.

Specialized Body of Knowledge At the outset, many recreation and park degree programs were established as "minor" specializations in other areas of study, such as physical education. As such, they tended to lack theoretically based courses within the field of study. Over the past four decades, this deficiency has been largely corrected.

The knowledge and skills components of higher education in recreation, parks, and leisure studies are formulated in terms that are specifically applicable to the recreation field, although they may involve content taken from other scholarly disciplines or fields of practice.

Given the recent impressive growth in both research studies and publication of findings, it seems clear that the field has a legitimate body of knowledge that must be possessed by professionals. Indeed, within some areas of practice, there has been systematic study of the competencies and knowledge that entry-level practitioners should possess. These skills, knowledge, and abilities guide curricula so that students are equipped with the skills needed to get their first job.[13]

Increasingly, undergraduate curricula have been redesigned to include specific areas of knowledge and job performance based on standards of practice or certification examinations that have been developed by professional societies.

On undergraduate levels, a major element in the process of imparting practical knowledge and skills to students consists of required field work and internship experiences. Although these vary from institution to institution, in general they require at least a semester of full-time commitment to work in an agency of high quality within the student's expressed field of professional interest. Such placements should extend far beyond an agency's using field work or internship students in routine or mechanical roles as a source of cheap labor. Instead, they are meant to involve a full range of realistic job assignments and exposures, as well as conscientious counseling and supervision by professional staff members.

The National Recreation and Park Association publishes an accreditation and certification brochure that outlines the benefits of agency and university accreditation as well as the certification program.

Accreditation in Higher Education The most significant effort that has been made to upgrade curricular standards and practices in recreation, parks, and leisure studies has come in the accreditation process. *Accreditation* of a degree program involves meeting standards set by a larger governing body. These standards ensure that students are being exposed to standards of practices within the field.

The park and recreation accreditation program is administered by the Council on Accreditation. This group of academic faculty and practitioners in the field represent the National Recreation and Park Association (NRPA).

Academic programs become accredited for a number of reasons. First, and usually most important, is to ensure program quality and uncover areas in need of improvement. A secondary reason is that students graduating from an accredited university may take the Certified Park and Recreation Professional examination upon completion of their degree (certification is discussed later).

Undergraduate baccalaureate programs in parks and recreation are eligible for accreditation. At this time graduate programs cannot go through the accreditation process. In this process, there are set accreditation standards that programs must meet in the areas of administration, faculty, students, instructional resources, and learning outcomes. After completing a self-study of these areas, an outside review team visits the campus to judge how well standards are met. Suggestions for improving weaknesses are made with the understanding that these things are for the betterment of the degree program.

Accreditation began in the early 1980s with about 50 programs being accredited. There has been a steady increase in the number of programs being accredited and this number has risen to 90 in 2010.

National Recreation and Park Association

Each year, thousands of recreation and park professionals, civic officials, board members, educators, and students attend the National Recreation and Park Congress. Varied workshops, general sessions, exhibitor displays, and continuing education events provide expertise and exposure to outstanding programs in different regions of the country.

In addition to accreditation from the NRPA's Council on Accreditation, sport management has a Commission on Sport Management Accreditation (COSMA). Accreditation in sport management is available for both undergraduate and graduate degree programs. COSMA was established in 2008 and replaces a program approval process granted by the former Sport Management Program Review Council.[14] Accreditation requires review of many of the same aspects of general parks and recreation programs, but these standards are sports specific in terms of curriculum and faculty.

Why Professional Involvement?

Ms. Jodie Adams, CPRP, Past President, National Recreation and Parks Association, Director of Parks, Springfield-Greene County Park Board, Springfield, Missouri

Having been involved with the National Recreation and Park Association for more than 25 years, the future for professional involvement at NRPA and the field of parks and recreation is more diverse and exciting than ever. Through the work of national to local professionals and citizens, doors have opened up through proven research of the value of the parks and recreation field when it comes to health, the environment, conservation, economic development, and the vast opportunities for enrichment education for generations to come.

The mission of the National Recreation and Parks Association is "to advance parks, recreation, and environmental conservation efforts that enhance the quality of life for all people." Everyone has an opportunity to engage in this mission whether you're a practitioner, a citizen advocate, a student, a volunteer, or a participant. Everyone matters when it comes to our country's parks and people.

There are so many ways to get involved—from your local parks and recreation board, to your state Park and Recreation Association, to the National Recreation and Park Association board and committees.

By getting involved with the National Recreation and Park Association, you will be exposed to collaborative partners, such as American Academy for Park and Recreation Administration, U.S. Olympic Committee, National Sports Organizations, Centers for Disease Control and Prevention, and many others.

Through an experience of involvement with NRPA, you will meet U.S. senators, congress representatives, mayors, county commissioners, and other various public officials. You will have an opportunity to engage in legislative work such as congressional bills brought before Congress and the President of the United States. It is important to be a part of this country's parks and recreation movement at every level.

Criterion 4: Existence of Related Professional Associations

Another important characteristic of professions in modern society is that they have strong organizations, shared values, and traditions.

In North America, professional recreation associations have been in existence for a number of years. Like their counterparts in other professions, recreation and park associations have the following functions: They (1) regulate and set standards for professional development; (2) promote legislation for the advancement of the field; (3) develop public information programs to improve understanding and support of the field by the general public; (4) sponsor conferences, publications, and field services to improve practices; and (5) press for higher standards of training, accreditation, and certification. There are a number of professional associations available for park and recreation professionals that provide those and other services.

National Recreation and Park Association Because of the varied nature of professional service in recreation and parks and the strong role played by citizens' groups and nonprofessional organizations, many different associations were established through the years to serve the field. Five of these (the National Recreation Association, the American Institute of Park Executives, the National Conference on State Parks, the American Association of Zoological Parks and Aquariums, and the American Recreation Society) merged into a single body in 1965, with Laurance S. Rockefeller as president. Within a year or two, other groups, such as the National Association of Recreation Therapists and the Armed Forces Section of the American Recreation Society, merged their interests with the newly formed organization.

This national body, the National Recreation and Park Association, is an independent, nonprofit organization intended to advance parks, recreation, and environmental conservation efforts that enhance the quality of life for all people.[15] This organization is arguably the broadest in scope for the recreation profession by embracing most of the professional categories listed earlier in the chapter. NRPA is directed by a board of trustees, which meets several times each year to guide its major policies.

NRPA plays a vigorous role in helping to bring about a fuller national consciousness of the value of recreation and leisure through various public information campaigns, publications, research efforts, and legislative presentations. The organization responds to thousands of inquiries and requests for technical assistance from practitioners, establishes national partnerships for local departments, oversees conferences and training opportunities, and provides numerous publications for members. In addition, NRPA representatives regularly testify before congressional subcommittees in support of legislation and funding proposals dealing with the environment, social needs, and similar national problems.

The *Journal of Physical Education, Recreation, and Dance* is a monthly publication of AAHPERD that focuses on educating professionals in the field.

Other Professional Organizations Many other organizations sponsor programs supporting the recreation and park field or one of its specialized components. For example, the American Alliance for Health, Physical Education, Recreation, and Dance (AAHPERD) has several thousand members who have a specialized interest in education for leisure, school-sponsored recreation, the promotion of school camping and outdoor education, and adapted physical education and recreation programs for people with disabilities.

The branch of AAHPERD that has been most directly concerned with these functions is the American Association for Physical Activity and Recreation. It plays a key role in promoting community education and leisure education projects; publishes an outstanding series of special-theme inserts in the *Journal of Physical Education, Recreation, and Dance;* and assists in job placement of recreation personnel.

Other organizations that have made important contributions to this field include those listed in the table on the following page.

Purpose/Focus	Agency	Web Site
General Recreation	American Alliance for Health, Physical Education, Recreation, and Dance	http://www.aahperd.org
	Canadian Parks and Recreation Association	http://www.cpra.ca
	National Recreation and Park Association	http://www.nrpa.org
	World Leisure Organization	http://www.worldleisure.org
	National Correctional Recreation Association	http://www.strengthtech.com/correct/ncra/ncra.htm
	Association of YMCA Professionals	http://www.aypymca.org
Outdoor/Camping	American Camping Association	http://www.acacamps.org
	Association for Experiential Education	http://www.aee.org
	Association of Outdoor Recreation and Education	http://www.aore.org
	Canadian Parks and Wilderness Society	http://www.cpaws.org
	National Association for Interpretation	http://www.interpnet.com
	National Association of Recreation Resource Planners	http://www.narrp.org/
	Outdoor Industry Association	http://www.outdoorindustry.org
	Student Conservation Association	http://www.thesca.org
	Wilderness Education Association	http://www.weainfo.org
	North American Society for Environmental Education	http://www.naaee.org
Resorts/Commercial Recreation	International Association of Amusement Parks and Attractions	http://www.iaapa.org
	National Ski Areas Association	http://www.nsaa.org
	Resort and Commercial Recreation Association	http://www.rcra.org
	American Hotel and Lodging Association	http://www.ahla.com
	Club Managers Association of America	http://www.cmaa.org
Special Events and Meeting Planning	Convention Industry Council	http://www.conventionindustry.org
	International Association of Assembly Managers	http://www.iaam.org
	International Festival Event Association	http://www.ifea.com
	International Special Events Society	http://www.ises.com
	Meeting Professionals International	http://www.mpiweb.org
	Professional Convention Management Association	http://www.pcma.org
	Association of Collegiate Conference and Events Directors—International	https://www.acced-i.org
Sport	National Intramural Recreational Sports Association	http://www.nirsa.org
	North American Society for Sport Management	http://www.nassm.org
	National Association of Sports Commissions	http://www.sportscommissions.org
Therapeutic Recreation	American Therapeutic Recreation Association	http://www.atra-online.com
	National Therapeutic Recreation Society	http://www.nrpa.org/ntrs

(*Continued*)

Purpose/Focus	Agency	Web Site
Tourism	International Ecotourism Society	http://www.ecotourism.org
	Tourism Industry Association of Canada	http://www.tiac-aitc.ca
	Travel Industry Association	http://www.tia.org
	World Tourism and Travel Council	http://www.wttc.org
	World Tourism Organization	http://www.unwto.org/index.php
	American Society of Travel Agents	http://www.asta.org

It is clear that no one organization can possibly speak for or represent the entire leisure-service field today. As each specialized area of recreation has become more active and successful, it has tended to form its own professional society to deal with its unique needs and interests.

Criterion 5: Credentialing, Certification, and Agency Accreditation

Credentials are qualifications that must be satisfied through a formal review process before an individual is permitted to engage in professional practice in a given field. Obviously, this is a very important criterion of professionalism. If anyone can call him- or herself a qualified practitioner in a given field—without appropriate training or experience—that field has very low standards and is not likely to gain or hold the public's respect.

Because the recreation and park field has been so diversified, no single standard or selection process has been devised for those who seek employment in it. However, within the field of recreation and parks, certification programs have been developed to increase the professionalism of the field as well as set some standards that all certified professionals should possess.

Certification in a profession indicates that a certain level of skill and knowledge has been attained. Certification in parks and recreation is no exception. Although there are several different certifications available for different specialties in the field, the most recognized are the Certified Park and Recreation Professional (CPRP) and the Certified Therapeutic Recreation Specialist (CTRS).

Certified Park and Recreation Professional The Certified Park and Recreation Professional program as we know it today has existed since 1990. To qualify to receive the CPRP designation one of the following criteria must be met:

- Have just received, or are set to receive, a bachelor's degree from a program accredited by the Council on accreditation. (Students who have not yet graduated from a COA-accredited program with a major in recreation, park resources, and leisure services but who are in their final semester on campus may qualify for exam status.)
- Have a bachelor's degree from any institution in recreation, park resources, or leisure services; and also have no less than 1 year of full-time experience in the field.
- Have a bachelor's degree in a major other than recreation, park resources, or leisure services; and also have no less than 3 years of full-time experience in the field.
- Have a high school degree or equivalent, and have 5 years of full-time experience in the field.[16]

Once the criteria are met, an exam must be passed. The exam covers three broad content areas including the following:

1. *General administration:* Planning, budget and finance, supervision, policy formulation and implementation, and customer service and marketing
2. *Programming:* Assessment, planning, implementation, and evaluation
3. *Operations management:* Planning and management, maintenance management, and facilities operations[17]

Once an individual receives certification, he or she must recertify every 2 years. Recertification requires individuals to receive 2.0 continuing education units (CEUs). One CEU is equivalent to 10 contact hours in an educational program. CEUs can be obtained from state, regional, and national conference educational sessions, university courses, or professional service points. Professional service points come from service given to the profession in the form of speaking at a conference, writing articles for a professional magazine, or serving on committees within the professional association.

In scanning the latest job search announcements, it is clear that more and more public parks and recreation departments are requesting applicants be certified. These employers see the value in obtaining a certain level of education and a commitment to staying current by continually attending workshops and conferences.

Certified Therapeutic Recreation Specialist Certification in therapeutic recreation (TR) is administered by the National Council for Therapeutic Recreation Certification (NCTRC). The NCTRC accreditation program has strict standards that are followed by the American Board of Medical Specialties and by other related professions such as the National Board for the Certification of Occupational Therapy and the Certification Board for Music Therapists.[18] Currently, there are 12,000 Certified Therapeutic Recreation Specialists (CTRS) in North America.[19]

To obtain a CTRS certification, professionals may follow either an academic path or an equivalency path. The academic path is for people who have completed a bachelor's degree or higher with a major or a recreation degree option in therapeutic recreation. The equivalency option is for people without a degree specifically in therapeutic recreation, but a bachelor's degree in another area as well as full-time work experience in therapeutic recreation. Regardless of the path chosen, both require successfully passing the CTRS exam.[20]

Based on the 2007 job analysis study, the CTRS exam has the following three content areas:

1. *Foundation knowledge:* Background, diagnostic groupings, and theories and concepts
2. *Practice of TR:* Strategies and guidelines, assessment, documentation, and implementation
3. *Organization of TR:* TR service design and administrative tasks[21]

Both the CPRP and CTRS certification programs have resources available to help candidates prepare for the exams. Resources include practice exams, study guides, and in some cases study groups.

Standards in Nonpublic Leisure-Service Agencies The National Recreation and Park Association and the NCTRC have been the prime movers in the attempt to strengthen professionalism in leisure-service agencies. In general, the employees in nonprofit and commercial agencies have not been identified as key players in the recreation certification movement. Hiring in such agencies therefore has not been influenced by the NRPA accreditation efforts or certification.

However, national organizations such as the Ys, Scouts, and Boys' and Girls' Clubs are obviously concerned with helping their local councils, branches, or other direct-service units maintain a high level of staff competence. They do that through specialized training. For example, the YMCA has its own professional organization dedicated to providing training to all levels of staff. The Association of YMCA Professionals provides chapter, regional, and national training opportunities for YMCA staff, career and human resources manuals, and financial support for training needs.[22]

Other Certifications Because not all jobs in the leisure-service profession are best associated with the CPRP or CTRS certification, a number of others available may better reflect job responsibilities.[23]

Certified meeting professional For people who plan meetings, conventions, and exhibitions.[24]

Certified playground inspector This certification is offered by the National Playground Safety Institute.

Linking commercial, public, and other special interest recreation organizations, the National Recreation and Park Association offers a variety of special conferences and management schools each year. Other associations in such areas as theme or water park management, conference operations, zoo and aquarium maintenance, and other specializations sponsor similar national programs.

Lindsay Bierbaum, Manager of Outdoor Special Events, The Mariner's Museum, Newport News, Virginia

My responsibilities at the Mariner's Museum are to plan and implement outdoor special events that are fundraisers for the museum. This currently includes a summer concert series, 5K/10K race, an oyster roast cookout, and a holiday "Wreathing of the Lions" gathering. In addition to putting on these events, I also research new events we could do and their logistics, such as a dog walk or chili cook-off. When putting on the museum's fundraisers, I am responsible for the program's budget, overseeing planning meetings, finding volunteers and/or staff to work, coordinating media and marketing efforts, ordering supplies, keeping a time line, communicating with other departments, and running the actual event. The other part of my job is coordinating the rental of our private park property for other people's events. This includes a variety of activities such as 5K/8K/10K races, cookouts, festivals, weddings, and so forth. I have no typical day, which is why I love my job! It all depends on the season, day of week, and current events the museum is organizing or hosting.

Aquatics facility operator and certified pool operator These certifications focus on managing and operating aquatics facilities.

Certified special-events professional (CSEP) Awarded by the International Special Events Society certification is earned through education, experience, and service to the industry. Professionals are required to earn 35 points through education attainment, professional association leadership, and special-event industry experience, then they must pass an examination that includes objective questions, solving a case study, and the review of a professional portfolio.[25]

National Association for Interpretation Offers certifications in a number of outdoor-related areas including Certified Interpretive Guide, Certified Interpretive Host, and Certified Interpretive Planner.

Certified Interpretation Trainer, Certified Heritage Interpreter, and Certified Interpretive Manager.[26]

Certified Destination Management Executive This certification is often obtained by people working with convention and visitors bureaus.

Agency Accreditation Process Another example of the thrust toward fuller professionalism in the organized recreation, park, and leisure-service field is found in the accreditation process for local public departments initiated in the mid-1990s. For an agency to become accredited, it must examine all aspects of its operations, from maintenance to marketing, and adhere to carefully developed standards of excellence. An outside team of park and recreation practitioners visit the agency to see how well it is meeting the set standards and to offer suggestions for improvements to the agency. Currently, there are 89 accredited agencies.[27] Many of the directors of the accredited agencies have used accreditation as a benchmark for improving services offered to the community and to show the public their tax-supported agency is using its resources wisely.[28]

Agency accreditation is also done in the camping industry. The American Camping Association accredits camps that meet specific safety, health, and program quality standards. An onsite visitation team examines such areas as facilities, transportation, human resources, programs, and health and wellness.[29]

Criterion 6: Code of Ethical Practice

An important measure of any profession is that it typically outlines the public responsibilities of practitioners and establishes a code of ethical behavior. In fields such as medicine and law, where the possibility of malpractice is great and the stakes are high, strict codes of ethics prevail.

In the field of leisure services, it might appear that any issues related to ethical practice are not as critical as in these other professions. However, in specialized areas such as therapeutic recreation, where patients or clients are likely to be physically, emotionally, or economically vulnerable, the opportunities for harmful, negligent, or unprofessional behavior are great. In other areas of leisure service as well, professionals should have a strong sense of obligation to those they serve, to their communities, and to the profession itself.

NRPA's Professional Code of Ethics stresses integrity, honesty, public confidence, professional excellence, fiscal responsibility, and support of equal employment opportunities,[30] while the American Camping Association stresses integrity, truthfulness, fairness to all people, and an agreement to comply with relevant laws of the community.[31]

Brandon Reichart, Recreation Coordinator, Walt Disney World Swan and Dolphin Resort, Orlando, Florida

As recreation coordinator, I have several job responsibilities that vary throughout the year. In the summer, my main responsibilities are to work directly with our interns to plan and develop new ideas and activities that can be provided for our high volume of resort guests. We have a wide variety of activities including such things as game of the day, campfire with s'mores, dive-in movies in the pool, and glow in the dark volleyball. It is my responsibility to see that these activities run smoothly and efficiently so that our guests can have the memorable experience they are seeking. During our winter months, I help plan a wide variety of holiday activities for our guests at the resort. The thing I love most about my job is putting a smile on our guests' faces and having them tell us that we went above and beyond and gave them an experience they will never forget.

International Special Events Society (ISES) Principles of Professional Conduct and Ethics Special events are important—the last thing someone wants to worry about is the integrity of the special-events professional. That's why all ISES members subscribe to the ISES Principles of Professional Conduct and Ethics, listed here.

Each member of ISES shall agree to adhere to the following:

- Promote and encourage the highest level of ethics within the profession of the special events industry while maintaining the highest standards of professional conduct.
- Strive for excellence in all aspects of our profession by performing consistently at or above acceptable industry standards.
- Use only legal and ethical means in all industry negotiations and activities.
- Protect the public against fraud and unfair practices, and promote all practices which bring respect and credit to the profession.
- Provide truthful and accurate information with respect to the performance of duties. Use a written contract clearly stating all charges, services, products, performance expectations and other essential information.
- Maintain industry accepted standards of safety and sanitation.
- Maintain adequate and appropriate insurance coverage for all business activities.
- Commit to increase professional growth and knowledge, to attend educational programs and to personally contribute expertise to meetings and journals.
- Strive to cooperate with colleagues, suppliers, employees, employers and all persons supervised, in order to provide the highest quality service at every level.
- Subscribe to the ISES Principles of Professional Conduct and Ethics, and abide by the ISES Bylaws and policies.[32]

Criterion 7: Existence of Extensive Professional Development Opportunities

A true profession has many avenues for professionals to develop their skills, knowledge, and abilities in their chosen career after their degrees are completed. Conferences, workshops, seminars, and institutes are held at the state, regional, and national levels,

CASE STUDY: Future Job Options

Throughout this chapter are a number of vignettes about jobs in the profession. These jobs range from special events to therapeutic recreation to outdoor recreation. Most of these people have been in the profession for only a short time, whereas a few others have many years of experience. Each job is unique in its own way.

Questions to Consider

1. What were the commonalities among the jobs discussed in the vignettes?
2. What skills emerged as necessary to be successful in these jobs?
3. Which job would be most closely related to a job you see yourself having in the future? Why?
4. Which job is least interesting to you? Why?

focusing on training opportunities in all areas of the profession. For example, the American Camping Association has an annual national conference and several regional conferences such as the Tri-State Camp Conference and the New England Conference. They also offer the e-Institute Training Site as an online learning forum for such topics as crisis management, creating positive youth outcomes, and fiscal management.[33] The National Intramural Recreational Sports Association offers workshops and institutes throughout the year such as National Fitness and Wellness Institute, National Marketing Institute, and the National School of Recreational Sports Management. Recreation is a changing profession and it is necessary to continually educate its practitioners for them to continue to provide quality services.

In addition to workshops and trainings, most professional associations have monthly, quarterly, or annual publications with articles focusing on issues in the field. The American Alliance of Health, Physical Education, Recreation, and Dance has the *Journal of Physical Education, Recreation, and Dance*; the North American Society of Sport Management has the *Journal of Sport Management*; and the Resort and Commercial Recreation Association has *Resort+Recreation*.

CURRENT LEVEL OF PROFESSIONAL STATUS

When the seven accepted criteria of professionalism reviewed here are used as the basis for judgment, it is apparent that the recreation, parks, and leisure-service field has made considerable progress toward becoming a recognized profession.

Some elements are already securely in place, such as the development of a unique body of knowledge and the establishment of a network of college and university programs of professional preparation. As for the professional organization element, the National Recreation and Park Association and other national associations or societies represent a significant force for upgrading and monitoring performance in the recreation field, but their attempts to serve the interests of a wide variety of leisure-service agencies also illustrate the field's continuing fragmentation. Realistically, many practitioners in such specialized disciplines as special-event planning, employee recreation, and varied aspects of commercial recreation tend to identify more closely with their separate fields than they do with the overall leisure-service field. Even in the more difficult areas of certification and the development of ethical codes, some considerable progress has been made, although the concept of enforcement continues to be a problem in both areas.

Professionalism in recreation, parks, and leisure services has increased greatly over the past several decades, along with the growing recognition of the field's value in modern society. Because of the immense scope of the diversified recreation field in terms of employment, it has the potential for becoming even more influential in contributing to community well-being in the years ahead.

NEED FOR A SOUND PHILOSOPHICAL BASIS

As discussed, several elements define a profession. Whereas these factors legitimize a profession, a professional has a philosophy that drives its values, ethics, ideas, and approach to service delivery. A sound philosophy of recreation and leisure also can serve the leisure-service field in ongoing policy formulation and program development.

Meaning of Philosophy

The term *philosophy* often conveys an image of ivory tower abstraction, divorced from practical or realistic concerns. Understandably, many practitioners are likely to be suspicious of any approach that appears to be overly theoretical, rather than pragmatic and action based. The nature of practitioners is to be in the here and now. They look for answers that assist them today and tomorrow, not 6 months or 3 years in the future. Philosophy, more often than not, provides more questions than answers. In far too many instances, it is easier to deal with the present than to anticipate the future and one's appropriate role in shaping that future.

How, then, is *philosophy* to be defined? Of the possible examples presented in previous chapters, the definition, stating that philosophy consists of the body of principles underlying a major discipline or human activity, as expressed in guidelines for conduct, is the most useful for our purpose.

This chapter does not present a single philosophical approach to recreation and leisure. Instead, it identifies seven prevailing approaches to providing organized recreation services in the present. The next chapter requires readers to think about these philosophies as a number of forecasts of future trends and some guiding principles for the organization of community recreation services in the years ahead are presented.

OPERATIONAL PHILOSOPHIES OF RECREATION AND LEISURE

It is possible to identify several approaches or orientations found in leisure-service agencies today that may be called *operational philosophies*. These include the following: (1) the quality-of-life approach, (2) the marketing or entrepreneurial approach, (3) the human services approach, (4) the prescriptive approach, (5) the resource manager/aesthetic/preservationist approach, (6) the hedonist/individualist approach, and (7) the benefits-based approach.

Quality-of-Life Approach

The *quality-of-life approach* has been the dominant one in the field of organized recreation service for several decades. It sees recreation as an experience that contributes to human development and to community well-being in various ways: improving physical and mental health, enriching cultural life, reducing antisocial uses of leisure, and strengthening community ties.

The quality-of-life orientation stresses the unique nature of recreation as a vital form of human experience—one that is engaged in for its own sake rather than for any extrinsic purpose or conscious social goal. Generally, proponents of this view have agreed that recreation satisfies a universal human need that has been made even more pressing by the tensions of modern urban society, the changed nature of work, and other social conditions.

Those holding this view argue that the pleasure, freedom, and self-choice inherent in recreation and leisure are their most vital contributions to the lives of participants. Quality-of-life advocates have tended to assume that public recreation should be supported for its own sake as an important area of civic responsibility, and that adequate tax funds should be provided for this purpose. In today's era of intense competition for limited tax dollars, the quality-of-life issue remains important, yet the concept of full tax support for parks and recreation is recognized as no longer viable.

Marketing or Entrepreneurial Approach

The *marketing* or *entrepreneurial approach*, a business-oriented approach to providing organized recreation and park programs and services, evolved rapidly during the latter part of the twentieth century as a direct response to the fiscal pressures placed on public and voluntary leisure-service agencies. As noted in earlier chapters, steadily mounting operational costs and a declining tax base during that time forced many recreation and park departments to adopt what has come to be known as the marketing approach to agency management. This approach is based on the idea that public, voluntary, or other leisure-service providers will flourish best if they adopt the methods used by commercial enterprises. It argues that they must become more aggressive and efficient in developing and promoting recreation facilities and programs that will reach the broadest possible audience and gain the maximum possible income.

Proponents of the marketing approach take the position that recreation and park professionals should not have to plead for tax-based support solely on the basis of the social value of their programs, but should seek to become relatively independent as a viable, self-sufficient form of community service.

It should be recognized that the marketing trend has influenced far more than public recreation and park agencies alone. Many large nonprofit youth-serving organizations, such as the YMCA, YWCA, and YM-YWHA, have been forced to increase their reliance on self-generated revenues and to move into more aggressive marketing of a wide range of leisure programs, including their fitness services.

Although the marketing approach has been enthusiastically received by many recreation and park managers, it raises a number of issues with respect to the essential purpose of public and voluntary leisure-service agencies. The argument has been made that increased fees and charges—whether imposed by the agencies themselves or by concessionaires or contractors working under privatization plans—tend to exclude the people in greatest need of inexpensive public recreation opportunities, such as children, persons with disabilities, and people who are economically disadvantaged.

Human Services Approach

In direct contrast to the marketing approach is the *human services approach* to organized recreation service. This approach regards recreation as an important form of social service that must be provided in a way that contributes directly to a wide range of desired social values and goals. The human services approach received a strong impetus during the 1960s, when recreation programs were generously funded by the federal government as part of the war on poverty, and recreation was used to offer job training and employment opportunities for economically disadvantaged youth and adults in America's ghettos.

The human services approach is similar to the quality-of-life approach in its recognition of the social value of recreation service. However, it does not subscribe to the latter's idealization of recreation as an inherently ennobling kind of experience, carried on for its own sake. Instead, within the human services framework, recreation must be designed to achieve significant community change and to use a variety of appropriate modalities.

This does not mean that recreation personnel should seek to be health educators, employment counselors, nutritionists, correctional officers, legal advisors, or housing experts. Rather, it implies that they must recognize the holistic nature of the human condition, provide such services when able to do so effectively, and cooperate fully with other practitioners in the various human services fields when appropriate.

Operating under this approach, many public recreation departments have sponsored youth or adult classes in a wide range of educational, vocational, or self-improvement areas and also have provided day-care programs, special services for persons with disabilities, roving leader programs for juvenile gangs, environmental projects, and numerous other functions of this type.

In its forceful emphasis on the need to meet social problems head-on and achieve beneficial human goals, the human services approach to recreation and park programming may at times be at odds with the marketing approach to service. In the marketing approach, efficient management and maximum revenue are often the primary aims. In the human services orientation, social values and human benefits are emphasized.

Prescriptive Approach

Of the orientations described here, the *prescriptive approach* is the most purposeful in the way it defines the goals and functions of the recreational experience. The idea that recreation should bring about constructive change in participants has been stressed in a number of textbooks on programming. Rossman and Schlatter suggest that leisure programs have goals that describe what change or experience will result from participation.[34]

The clearest cases of prescriptive recreation programs are found in therapeutic recreation. Shank and Coyle state that "play, recreation, and leisure are important to achieving and maintaining health, functional independence, and quality of life for people who want to live well despite an illness or disabling condition."[35] The prescriptive approach to leisure supports the idea that leisure is a part of health and that health and wellness do not totally involve the use of medical intervention. The prescriptive approach recognizes the needs of the participants such as improvement of social or motor skills. Therapeutic recreation professionals use a standard approach to developing programs that are prescriptive in nature. This approach is assessment, planning, implementation, and evaluation (APIE). The participant is assessed to determine his or her needs, a plan is developed to address these needs, the plan is then implemented and evaluated. The evaluation phase reverts back to the assessment and the goals that resulted from the assessment.

CASE STUDY: Financial Cutbacks in Recreation

The economy has forced many parks and recreation agencies to make some difficult financial decisions. Here are a few examples:

1. The San Francisco Recreation and Park Commission had $11.4 million budget gap that had to be filled. The commission chose to increase revenues by increasing admission fees and installing thousands of parking meters in parks. They chose to make cuts by laying off 72 workers.[a]
2. The University of Maine Student Recreation Center raised its semester fee by $5. Students taking more than 6 credit hours pay $107 per semester. Some students are outraged that they have to pay the fee when they do not use the facilities. The initial fee was implemented based on a vote by the student body. This group of students never used the new recreation center, nor did they ever pay the fee they voted to implement.[b]
3. The Oregon Parks and Recreation Department, the agency overseeing state parks, has traditionally relied on taxes, lottery revenues, and recreation vehicle registration fees as major sources of revenue. All of these sources have declined steadily over the past several years. As a result, fees and charges have been increased. For example, entrance fees will rise from $3 to $5 per carload, RV campsites fees will increase by $4, and cabins and yurts fees will increase by $4 and $9, respectively, to $39 and $36. This is the first time in 13 years that these fees have been increased.[c]

Questions to Consider

1. In these examples of how agencies dealt with the financial issues, which philosophy of recreation and leisure did they use? Why?
2. Are these fee increases fair to low-income populations? Children?
3. Are there better approaches to dealing with financial issues than raising fees?
4. Is it better to raise fees and continue to offer a wide variety of programs or to offer fewer programs at lower costs?
5. Should public agencies be required to offer some free programs? Why or why not?
6. How do job losses affect the community?

Sources

a. Seth Rosenfeld, "Layoffs, Fee Increases Backed for S.F. Parks," SFGate.com (20 February 2009). http://articles.sfgate.com/2009-02-20/bay-area/17190662_1_park-commission-recreation-centers-parking-meters.

b. Melinda Hart, "Students' Recreation Fee Increases by $5," Maine Campus (21 September 2009). http://mainecampus.com/2009/09/21/students%E2%80%99-recreation-fee-increases-by-5/.

c. Chris Havel, "State Park Fee Increases Adopted: Camping and Day-Use Increases Take Effect in 2010," Oregon.gov (2 October 2009). http://www.prd.state.or.us/news.php?id=1310.

Although it is similar to the human services approach in its emphasis on deliberately achieving significant social goals, the prescriptive approach differs in its reliance on the practitioner's expertise and authority. In contrast, a recreation professional working within a human services framework would be much more likely to value the input of community residents and to involve them in decision making.

Resource Manager/Aesthetic/Preservationist Approach

The unwieldy title *resource manager/aesthetic/preservationist approach* is used as a catch-all model to lump together three elements that are not synonymous but that exhibit a high degree of similarity. The *resource manager* obviously is concerned with managing, using, and protecting the outdoor environment. The balance between use, preservation, and protection is a difficult issue that is hotly contested by planners and stakeholders. The *aesthetic* position is one that values the appearance of the environment, both natural and artificial, and stresses the inclusion of cultural arts and other creative experiences within a recreation program. The *preservationist* seeks to maintain the physical environment not simply out of a respect for nature, but to preserve evidence of a historical past and a cultural tradition.

This approach to recreation planning is more likely to be evident in agencies that operate extensive parks, forests, waterfront areas, or other natural or scenic resources. Thus, one might assume that it would chiefly be found in such government agencies as federal and state park departments that administer major parks and outdoor recreation facilities. However, this is not the full picture. Many urban recreation and park planners are responsible for large parks. Recent years have seen a growth of new large urban parks in areas that are experiencing growing populations with economically advantaged residents. Often they may help to rehabilitate or redesign rundown waterfront areas, industrial sites, or gutted slum areas. In many cases, their purpose is to preserve or rebuild historic areas of cultural interest that will maintain or increase the appeal of cities for tourism and cultural programming. Preservation and restoration are the primary focuses for older parks while new development with revenue-producing facilities is becoming more common in newer or newly developed park and recreation agencies and communities.

Bangor Waterfront Redevelopment

Bangor, Maine, spent 20 years refurbishing its waterfront through a combination of public amenities and private developments. Dilapidated buildings such as a petroleum storage facility, a coal storage yard, and warehouses were demolished. Some empty buildings were converted to businesses such as pubs and restaurants. The waterfront now has seasonal dock moorings and is the summer home port of a major cruise line. This area of the city hosts special events such as the National Folk Festival, which drew more than 100,000 people. This waterfront area in Bangor is not complete. Future plans include developing a full-service hotel, condominiums, retail and restaurant space, an amphitheater, walking paths, and pay areas.[36]

Environmental Awareness A key element in this approach is the deep reverence that many individuals have today for nature in its various forms. A common theme throughout this book is the need for nature and the lack of time children spend in nature. The value of the outdoor experience is extensive. It helps people understand a lost culture, face the challenge of adventure activities, find a spiritual connection, and experience the beauty and serenity of the outdoors.

Interest in environmental and cultural sites remains high, and management of such areas is an important national concern.

However, environmental programming approaches cannot be carried out simply through a poetic evocation of the beauty and experience of nature. Political and economic realities also come into play when environmental decisions must be made. The George W. Bush presidency was particularly challenged both in the media and the courts for its environmental record. Between 2001 and 2008, the National Resources Defense Council (NRDC) documented issues relating to parks, wilderness areas, forest recreation, air pollution, water quality, public health, endangered species, and nuclear insecurity. It claims that in 2004 alone 150 actions were taken to weaken environmental laws such as the Clean Air Act and the Clean Water Act.[37] Knight Ridder compiled 14 pollution-oriented indicators from government and university statistics. Eight of the 14 indicators showed a worsening trend, two showed improvements, and three others zigzagged.

Statistics that have worsened include the following:

- Superfund cleanups of toxic waste fell by 52%.
- Fish-consumption warnings for rivers doubled.
- Fish-consumption advisories for lakes increased 39%.
- The number of beach closings rose 26%.
- Civil citations issued to polluters fell 57%.
- Criminal pollution prosecutions dropped 17%.
- Asthma attacks increased by 6%.
- There were small increases in global temperatures and unhealthy air days.[38]

National Park Service Centennial Challenge

On a positive note, President George W. Bush initiated the Centennial Challenge Initiative, which will bring $3 billion in additional funding to the National Park Service (NPS) to prepare the NPS for its 100th birthday in 2016. Whether the current administration continues this initiative is as yet undecided.

Addressing outdoor recreation experiences, a 2005 California State Parks report suggests, "The market for outdoor recreation experiences appears to be changing. If we do not change our way of managing outdoor recreation, we risk irrelevance and erosion of public support."[39] Society is becoming so diverse that traditional management methods are not keeping pace with expectations of users. The environmental awareness approach must change to adapt to the expectations of the new user.

Hedonist/Individualist Approach

The *hedonist/individualist approach* to recreational programming is concerned chiefly with providing fun and pleasure. It regards recreation as a highly individualistic activity that should be free of social constraints or moral purposes. The term *hedonist* is used to mean one who seeks personal pleasure, often with the implication that it is of a sensual, bodily nature. The term *individualist* is attached because this philosophical approach stresses the idea that each individual should be free to seek his or her own fulfillment and pleasure untrammeled by group pressures or social expectations.

Obviously, certain forms of leisure activity that have gained increased popularity in U.S. life fit this description. The accelerated use and generally freer acceptance of drugs, alcohol, gambling, and sex as a commercialized recreational pursuit, and other forms of sensation-seeking entertainment and play illustrate the hedonist approach to leisure. These forms of play may best be described as morally marginal, in the sense that they are legal in some contexts or localities and illegal in others, regarded as acceptable leisure experiences by some population groups and condemned by others.

Commercialized Sex Drug and alcohol use and gambling have been discussed in previous chapters. A third form of morally marginal leisure that is a key component of the hedonist approach to recreation and leisure is the use of sex as a form of play or entertainment. Commercialized sex expanded dramatically over the three decades following the counterculture movement of the 1960s. It takes many forms, including legalized houses of prostitution in Nevada, call girl rings, and the escort services and massage parlors that represent thinly disguised forms of prostitution in many cities; sex films, books, and magazines that may now be legally purchased; the widespread rental of X-rated DVDs for home viewing; and the increased showing of explicit sexual images and themes on network television programs and of "hard porn" on cable television or pay per view.

A recent manifestation of commercialized sex as an element in popular culture involves its broader exploitation within the mass media of entertainment and communication. Increasingly, the phenomenon of *cyberporn*—the transmission of varied types of erotica on the Internet—has prompted national concern. Awareness that children have easy access to such materials and that the Internet is being used for recruitment of sexual partners led to continuing efforts to curb such abuses.

Although public, nonprofit, and other types of community-based leisure-service organizations generally do not sponsor substance abuse, gambling, or sex-oriented types of entertainment, such activities are widely available through commercial sponsorship and, in many cases, have governmental approval or tacit acceptance.

Benefits-Based Management Approach

The final philosophical approach to the design and implementation of recreation, park, and leisure-service programs—the *benefits-based approach*—is relatively new. Essentially, this approach holds that it is not enough to verbalize a set of desirable goals or mission statements or to carry out head counts of participation and tally the number of events sponsored by a leisure-service agency. Instead, governmental, nonprofit, therapeutic, armed forces, and other types of managed recreation agencies should more clearly define their roles and purposes in terms of community and participant benefits. A benefit is defined as something that is good for an individual.

In practice, the benefits-based approach is based on a three-step implementation process:

1. *Benefits and opportunity identification:* Determine a core group of benefits that users seek and agencies can realistically provide, along with the management changes needed for benefits achievement.
2. *Program implementation:* Make facility or staff modifications needed to achieve desired benefits, and carry out systematic monitoring procedures during programs.
3. *Evaluation and documentation:* Analyze data, determine if program benefits were achieved, develop reports, and disseminate findings to appropriate audiences.[40]

Within this process, it is essential that target goals be defined in terms of concrete and measurable benefits. A benefits-based approach focuses on *outcomes* that measure long-term change or effect, rather than *outputs* that simply describe a program.

Benefits-Based Management

Benefits-based management is grounded in the understanding of outcomes of participation in recreation programs, whether they be organized or unorganized and whether they be group, family, or individual. An understanding of the benefits derived from participation in various recreation activities is essential to the success of benefits-based management programs. A variety of "benefits" reports has been published. Recently, California State Parks developed a report outlining the benefits of parks and recreation. They found that parks promote health and wellness, increase cultural unity, support economic development, provide positive alternatives for youth, which helps lower crime rates, and foster human development.[41] The report focused on benefits related to (1) physical health, (2) mental health, (3) social benefits related to strengthening communities, (4) promoting social bonds, (5) and youth development.[42] The Trust for Public Lands focused its report on the need for more city parks and open space. Its 2006 report addressed (1) economic benefits, (2) public health benefits, (3) environmental benefits, and (4) social benefits.[43]

Philosophical Approaches: No Pure Models

It should be stressed that although these seven approaches to the definition and management of organized leisure services are separate and distinct philosophical positions, it is unlikely that any single agency or government department follows one approach exclusively.

The changing nature of the political, economic, and social environment has forced park and recreation agencies to reevaluate traditional approaches to delivering public parks and recreation. No single approach has been discarded, but some have fallen out of favor with politicians and professionals. Especially affected has been the human services approach. As mentioned elsewhere, the availability of funding for parks and recreation has not kept up with inflation and in many cases has been significantly reduced. The influence of the war on terrorism and the ongoing conflicts in Iraq and Afghanistan have had a negative influence on funding for public parks and recreation—yet agencies are expected to provide more programs and services and to maintain existing and new facilities, constituencies, and markets. The business marketing approach, the fastest growing approach to delivery, has been embraced at all levels of government. Services remain available, utilizing the human services approach, especially in major urban areas. In suburban areas, with higher family incomes, supersized recreation centers are replacing older neighborhood centers or are being created in the place of smaller centers. In growing urban fringe areas where recreation services or centers have never been present, or present as only a small operation, the supercenter is an attractive amenity for their growing population. Supercenters typically charge membership fees, charge higher prices for programs, cater to an upscale economic population, and are located in areas of the community where disadvantaged individuals may not have ready access. In addition, the supercenters have more of a club ambience than traditional recreation centers, representing a move away from the human services approach.

SUMMARY

Recreation, parks, and leisure services have grown immensely as a career field, with several million people now employed in organized recreation. Of this overall group, it is estimated that several hundred thousand individuals should be regarded as professionals because of their academic training, job functions, and organizational affiliations.

This chapter describes several important criteria of professionalism, including the following:

1. Having a significant degree of social value, in terms of providing benefits to individual participants and/or to community life
2. Being recognized by the public as a meaningful area of social service or as a legitimate occupational field
3. Requiring specialized professional preparation at the college or university level, based on a distinct body of theoretical and practical knowledge
4. Having profession-related associations that involve national and regional organizations that sponsor conferences, research, publications, and other efforts to upgrade practice and that promote collegiality and a sense of commitment among the practitioners
5. Having a credentialing system to ensure that only qualified individuals—usually identified through a system of certification—are permitted to undertake professional-level tasks
6. Having a code of ethics to ensure that responsible and effective service is provided to the public
7. Having extensive professional development opportunities

The recreation, parks, and leisure-services field has made substantial progress on most of these areas. As recreation and leisure become increasingly important aspects of life in the years ahead, the challenge to the leisure-service field will be to become even more highly professionalized by building on the foundation that has already been laid.

In addition to the criteria for professionalism, a profession also has a philosophical foundation. This chapter identifies seven distinct operational philosophies that influence the provision of organized recreation services today. These range from the quality of life and marketing orientations to a more recent model of service, the benefits-based management approach. Most leisure-services agencies use a mix of these philosophies in their policy development and program delivery. Given the current state of the profession, many agencies blend the benefits-based and marketing or entrepreneurial approaches to leisure-services delivery.

QUESTIONS FOR CLASS DISCUSSION OR ESSAY EXAMINATION

1. Several criteria are generally accepted as hallmarks of professionalism, such as having a social mandate or set of important social values or having a body of specialized

knowledge. Select any four of these, and discuss the extent to which you believe the recreation, park, and leisure-service field meets these criteria of professionalism.

2. What are the two certifications that are most prominent in parks and recreation? What are the criteria and requirements to obtain these certifications?
3. Several professional associations are listed. What associations would best match your future career interests?
4. Seven different philosophies and approaches to leisure are presented (for example, quality of life). Which of the seven approaches do you find most compatible with your own view?

ENDNOTES

1. C. M. Ross et al., *Mastering the Job Search Process in Recreation and Leisure Services, Second Edition* (Sudbury, MA: Jones and Bartlett Publishers, 2010).
2. Human Kinetics. *Introduction to Recreation and Leisure* (Champaign, IL: Human Kinetics, 2006).
3. U.S. Travel Association, "U.S. Travel Urges President, Congress to Utilize Travel as a Vehicle for Job Creation" (2 December 2009). http://www.ustravel.org/news/press-releases/us-travel-urges-president-congress-utilize-travel-vehicle-job-creation.
4. "Recreational Therapists," *Occupational Outlook Handbook, 2010–11 Edition*. http://www.bls.gov/oco/ocos082.htm.
5. National Park Service, "About Us." http://www.nps.gov/aboutus/index.htm.
6. Y. F. Leung, C. Siderelis, and D. Hoffbeck, Statistical Report of State Park Operations: 2007–2008 (Raleigh, NC: National Association of State Park Directors, 2009).
7. "Recreational Therapists," *Occupational Outlook Handbook, 2010–11 Edition*.
8. U.S. Travel Association, "U.S. Travel Urges President, Congress."
9. Bureau of Labor Statistics, U.S. Department of Labor, "American Time Use Survey—2009 Results." http://www.bls.gov/news.release/atus.nr0.htm.
10. Y. F. Leung, C. Siderelis, and D. Hoffbeck, Statistical Report of State Park Operations: 2007–2008 (Raleigh, NC: National Association of State Park Directors, 2009).
11. National Park Service, "About Us." http://www.nps.gov/aboutus/index.htm.
12. North American Society for Sports Management, "Sports Management Programs: United States," www.nassm.com/InfoAbout/SportMgmtPrograms/United_States.
13. A. R. Hurd and B. E. Schlatter, "Establishing Cooperative Competency Based Internships for Parks and Recreation Students," *Journal of Health, Physical Education, Recreation & Dance* (Vol. 35, p. 32–37 2007).
14. North American Society for Sport Management, "Program Accreditation." http://www.nassm.com/InfoAbout/NASSM/ProgramAccreditation.
15. National Recreation and Park Association, "Mission, Values, and Vision." http://www.nrpa.org/Content.aspx?id=238.
16. National Recreation and Park Association, "Am I Eligible to Become a CPRP?" http://www.nrpa.org/Content.aspx?id=920.
17. A. R. Hurd, M. A. Mulvaney, J. R. Rossman, and W. McKinney, *Official Study Guide for the Certified Park and Recreation Professional Exam*, 3rd. ed. (Arlington, VA: NRPA, 2008).
18. National Council for Therapeutic Recreation Certification, "NOCA/NCCA Certification." http://www.nctrc.org/aboutnctrc.htm#NOCA.
19. National Council for Therapeutic Recreation Certification, *CTRS Profile* (New City, NY: NCTRC, 2009). http://www.nctrc.org/documents/CTRSProfile09-FINAL081809.pdf.
20. National Council for Therapeutic Recreation Certification, "New Application." http://www.nctrc.org/newapplication.htm.

21. National Council for Therapeutic Recreation Certification, *Exam Content Outline*. http://nctrc.org/documents/NCTRCExamContentOutlineMay08.pdf.

22. Association of YMCA Professionals. www.aypymca.org.

23. Bangor Maine, "Business Development: Bangor Waterfront Master Plan." http://www.bangormaine.gov/bd_mdi_waterfront.php.

24. Convention Industry Council, Certified Meeting Professional (CMP) Program. www.conventionindustry.org/cmp.

25. International Special Events Society, Certified Special Events Professional. www.ises.com/CSEP/.

26. National Association for Interpretation Certification Program, www.interpnet.com/certification/index.shtml. Accessed 15 April 2007.

27. National Recreation and Park Association, "Accredited Agencies." http://www.nrpa.org/Content.aspx?id=1186.

28. National Recreation and Park Association, "Accreditation Excellence." http://www.nrpa.org/Content.aspx?id=1197.

29. American Camping Association, "About Accreditation," http://www.acacamps.org/accreditation/hnolearn.php. Accessed 15 April 2007.

30. National Recreation and Park Association, "Professional Code of Ethics," www.nrpa.org/content/default.aspx?documentId=493. Accessed 16 April 2007.

31. American Camping Association, "Code of Ethics," www.acacamps.org/membership/ethics.php. Accessed 16 April 2007.

32. International Special Events Society, "ISES Principles of Professional Conduct and Ethics." http://www.ises.com/ConductandEthics/tabid/116/Default.aspx.

33. American Camp Association, "e-Institute Training Site." http://www.acacamps.org/einstitute.

34. J. R. Rossman and B. E. Schlatter, *Recreation Programming: Designing Leisure Experiences*, 5th ed. (Champaign, IL: Sagamore Publishing, 2008).

35. J. Shank and C. Coyle, *Therapeutic Recreation in Health Promotion and Rehabilitation* (State College, PA: Venture Publishing, 2002): 4.

36. Bangor Maine, "Business Development: Bangor Waterfront Master Plan."

37. Natural Resources Defense Council, "Rewriting the Rules (2005 Special Edition): The Bush Administration's First Term Environmental Record." http://www.nrdc.org/legislation/rollbacks/execsum.asp.

38. Seth Borenstein, "Environment Worsened Under Bush in Many Key Areas, Data Show" (13 October 2004). http://www.commondreams.org/headlines04/1013-12.htm.

39. California State Parks, *Park and Recreation Trends in California 2005*, http://www.parks.ca.gov/pages/795/files/recreation_trends_081505.pdf.

40. Lawrence Allen, "Time to Measure Outcomes," presentation at 1994 NRPA Congress, Minneapolis, MN.

41. California Park and Recreation Society, *A Profile of California Parks and Recreation Agencies*. http://www.cprs.org/user_media/pdfs/talking_to_policymakers.pdf.

42. California State Parks, *The Health and Social Benefits of Recreation* (Sacramento: California State Parks, 2005).

43. Paul M. Sherer, *The Benefits of Parks: Why America Needs More City Parks and Open Space* (San Francisco, CA: Trust for Public Lands, 2006).

CHAPTER 13

FUTURE PERSPECTIVES OF RECREATION AND LEISURE

◆ ◆ ◆

Definition of Future: The future has always had a very special place in philosophy and, in general, in the human mind. This is true largely because human beings often want a forecast of events that will occur. It is perhaps possible to argue that the evolution of the human brain is in great part an evolution in cognitive abilities necessary to forecast the future, i.e., abstract imagination, logic, and induction. Imagination permits us to "see" (i.e., predict) a plausible model of a given situation without observing it, therefore mitigating risks. Logical reasoning allows one to predict inevitable consequences of actions and situations and therefore gives useful information about future events. Induction permits the association of a cause with consequences, a fundamental notion for every forecast of future time.[1]

◆ ◆ ◆

INTRODUCTION

The remarkable growth of organized recreation, parks, and leisure services is documented throughout this text. Despite the impressive history of this social movement and field of professional activity, a number of continuing and emerging issues and concerns affect the regard for the role of recreation, parks, and leisure in personal, community, and national life.

The new century, now more than 10 years old, is already experiencing new challenges, opportunities, and approaches to the leisure mosaic. Former traditional models of leisure are changing in many communities; traditional approaches to the provision of recreation services are changing; opportunities for leisure are more abundant than at any time in recorded history; governments and people are rethinking the role of parks, recreation, and leisure in the national fabric; and nonprofits are expanding services while commercial enterprises are engaging in new leisure opportunities. As the United States and the world experiences its most serious economic decline in 70 years, following almost 30 years of sustained economic growth, decisions about what government can do, should do, and what citizens are willing to pay for are in the forefront of discussions.

The notion of parks, recreation, and leisure as a social welfare model remains viable, especially in consideration of those who are underprivileged; but for many others, the social welfare model has become outdated and the public, politicians, and leisure practitioners are looking for new models. How do public parks, recreation, and leisure provide effective recreation services in an era of economic uncertainty? What is the appropriate role and responsibility of urban, suburban, and rural recreation agencies and of nonprofit organizations? This chapter discusses issues, challenges, and changes in the American fabric that affect parks, recreation, and leisure.

Technology has changed the use of inner-city playgrounds.

How should the major priorities of organized recreation service in the United States be determined? In what ways can or should government provide more effective and efficient services in this field? What are the special responsibilities of organized recreation toward people with physical and mental disabilities, toward the new aging, or toward those who may have had inadequate opportunities in the past because of their gender or other demographic factors?

How has technology affected the planning, delivery, operation, and marketing of parks and recreation—in the public, nonprofit, and commercial sectors? Social media, smart phones, netbooks, and a whole host of hardware supported by rapidly emerging software has changed the way people look at, use, and embrace technology. Long-held assumptions about how information is shared and exchanged are no longer valid. How will leisure-service professionals respond and anticipate such changes in the years ahead?

How will the changing social and economic conditions in the coming decades affect the public's leisure values and patterns of participation, and how can recreation, park, and leisure-service professionals and organizations respond effectively to the challenges of the future?

KEY RATIONALE GUIDING LEISURE-SERVICE DELIVERY TODAY

For recreation, parks, and leisure-service practitioners, it is possible to identify a number of key principles that should be used to guide their professional operations today. First, it is assumed that such individuals—no matter what their fields of specialization—regard recreation and leisure as important to human growth and community development. A contemporary philosophy of organized recreation service therefore should deal with such important issues as the place of recreation and leisure in modern life, the role of government, the development of programming based on significant social needs, and the place of leisure education.

Place of Recreation in the Modern Community

In U.S. society, our view of recreation as a social phenomenon and area of community involvement is influenced by our governmental systems. In our Constitution and in court decisions that have influenced government policy through the years, we have accepted the view that, on various levels, government has the responsibility for providing certain major services to citizens. These include functions related to safety and protection, education, health, and other services that contribute to maintaining the quality of life of all citizens.

Linked to this system of governmental responsibility is our general acceptance of the Judeo–Christian concepts of the worth and dignity of all human beings and the need to help each person become the most fully realized individual that he or she is capable of being. Through government and through many voluntary community associations, we have accepted the responsibility for providing needed services and opportunities for people at each stage of life and for those who because of disability have been deprived in significant ways.

Needs of Individual Citizens

Recreation and leisure are important aspects of personal experience in modern life for the physical, social, emotional, intellectual, and spiritual benefits they provide. Positive leisure experiences enhance the quality of a person's life and help each person develop to the fullest potential. To make this possible, government and other responsible social agencies should provide recreation resources, programs, and, where appropriate, leisure education to help people understand the value of free time when constructively and creatively used.

Government's Responsibility

In addition to providing personal benefits, recreation helps a community to meet health needs, gain economic benefits, and maintain community morale. On each level (local, state, and federal), appropriate government agencies should therefore be assigned the responsibility for maintaining a network of physical resources for leisure participation, including parks, playgrounds, centers, sport facilities, and other special recreation facilities. Government should be responsible for planning, organizing, and carrying out programs, under proper leadership, for all age levels.

Government cannot and should not seek to meet all of the leisure needs of the community. It must recognize that other types of community organizations—including voluntary, private, commercial, therapeutic, industrial, and educational groups—sponsor effective recreation programs, which are often designed to meet specialized needs or more advanced interests. Therefore, its unique role should be to provide a basic floor of recreational opportunity, to fill the gaps that are not covered by other organizations, and to provide coordination and overall direction to community leisure-service programs.

There has been a growing body of opinion that local government recreation and park agencies should take less responsibility for the direct provision of program activities, particularly when limited by fiscal constraints, and should move instead into the role of serving as an advocate for recreation and leisure in community life and providing coordinating or facilitating assistance to other agencies.

A major concern should be to ensure an equitable distribution of recreational opportunities for the public at large. This would not guarantee that all residents have totally equal programs and services, but would represent a pledge that, within the realities of community needs and economic capabilities, facilities and programs will be distributed so as to bring about a reasonable balance of such opportunities for different neighborhoods and community groups.

Influence of the Nonprofit Sector

The nonprofit sector has accepted an increasingly larger role in the provision of recreation and leisure-based social services. An important part of the effort has focused on youth-serving agencies in at-risk neighborhoods. There are several reasons why nonprofits have taken an increasing role. First, this is not a new model for nonprofits to assume, but rather a continuation and expansion of services when local members of the community realize that the government cannot provide needed services. Second, more individuals are willing to give to nonprofits, are able to give substantial sums of money, and are willing to give to their community. Nonprofits are frequently seen as a more desirable and effective organization to address social ills than is government. Finally, government has recognized its inability to meet all of the needs of a community and either encourages nonprofits and/or works jointly with them.

FACING THE CHALLENGE OF THE FUTURE

Those who read this book—primarily college and university students in recreation, park, tourism, sport, and leisure-studies curricula—are looking ahead to careers in the future. What will the twenty-first century bring in terms of demographic, social, and economic changes that can radically affect our uses of leisure?

Traditional forms of leisure are growing, but at a slower rate than the population. The change from a Republican to a Democratic majority in Congress and a Democratic president has already resulted in major shifts in philosophical orientation for the federal government. New diverse forms of leisure, often individual or Internet based, are growing outside of traditional program areas. Academic programs and curricula based on a twentieth-century model will not prepare students and professionals for the challenges of the twenty-first century. Recognition of a social responsibility ethic grounded in community engagement structured in the context of a do-more-with-less government reality is what students and professionals are already dealing with. The awareness of environmental and social justice in society and how public park and recreation will address these issues are paramount to the profession's future.

Many contemporary authorities in the leisure-service field emphasize that bringing about needed changes will require a new wave of entrepreneurship. Recreation and park professionals in all spheres of service need to think more imaginatively and innovatively, need to be content experts in leisure, politically astute in government, and able to build coalitions among support and disparate groups. They need to cultivate an organizational and professional climate that is interactive, community focused, and politically and socially responsible.

EFFORTS TO PREDICT THE FUTURE

Ten years into the twenty-first century there remains much discussion about the parks and recreation impact. Whatever discussions were held in the early part of this first decade, the recession in the latter quarter of the decade changed the ability of government to deliver parks, recreation, and leisure services, programs, and facilities. Nonprofits and commercial enterprises were equally challenged by the economic decline.

The business-as-usual model that dominated the early part of the century has been challenged in ways not anticipated. The impact on public parks' and recreation's ability to provide services and facilities is the most significant in 70 years.

Agendas in the Twenty-First Century

There has been no single national effort by park and recreation organizations to address the twenty-first century's impact on parks and recreation; individual organizations have focused on trends that affect themselves. The broader societal impact has been left for others to deal with. The U.S. Forest Service operates a trends center; states generate 5-year state comprehensive outdoor recreation plans that are of varying quality with some to significant trend analysis. Many municipalities have master plans for development and some have strategic plans. In both instances, trend analysis may be a small or significant part of the plan. Some state park and recreation associations, especially California, make efforts to keep their members abreast of trends. The problem facing trend analysis in parks and recreation is the diversity of the profession itself. Some trends cross boundaries between urban recreation, outdoor recreation, city parks and recreation departments, state park systems, national parks, and nonprofits, but there are many other trends that do not. National trends paint a broad picture, whereas regional and local trends may be significantly different. Making assumptions that trends will occur as predicted is equally dangerous. In 1999, the economy looked as if it would continue to be positive. First the economy began to falter, and then on September 11, 2001, the economy, society, and trends were thoroughly disrupted by the great tragedy of that day.

Master planning for community parks and recreation involves many different groups.

How then do park and recreation organizations focus on trends that have some basis of validity? There are those who are considered as futurists and have a track record of success. Trends, at their best, are educated guesses about the future. They are influenced by those who are suggesting them—their knowledge, biases, and creative ability to anticipate change.

The trends have led to conclusions about the future of parks and recreation, and especially about public and nonprofit agencies that requires a response. Some of these trends emerged at conferences and workshops held in the mid- to late-1990s and remain current.

Others were gleaned from a variety of sources including futurist literature. Key conclusions include the following:

- Park and recreation professionals must embrace societal change because it is the only way to serve the public and ensure the future of their organization.
- The trend toward greater public participation in decision making is a reality, and public agencies must ensure that employees are trained to facilitate and respond to public input.
- Wellness will continue to be a major issue. Obesity is the most immediate issue facing public park and recreation agencies. Major efforts are required involving partnerships to address this growing issue.
- Public agencies will continue to receive less of the public dollar for operations, maintenance, and repairs. The public will continue to support and fund land acquisitions through bond referenda and other sources, but the agencies will have to learn entrepreneurship to maintain operations.
- Success will continue to depend on an organization's ability to build cooperative relationships and establish networks and coalitions with other organizations.
- Federal leadership in the recreation and parks movement will wane as the challenges of an aging society, globalization, international commitments, and other unforeseen circumstances reduce the ability to support traditional services.
- Park and recreation agencies need to embrace the new generations and use their technological competence to introduce them to the outdoors, fitness, and expanded leisure opportunities.
- Demographic complexity, expressed as age complexity, income complexity, gender complexity, and life stage complexity, provides indications of social shifts in society that require park and recreation agencies to rethink for whom, what, and how they offer programs.
- An understanding of current users, nonusers, potential users, and their motivations is the foundation for creating change and meeting the needs of the current and future generations.
- Public agencies must provide environmental leadership on a local and global perspective. For too long, the parks and recreation profession has been quiet on this front.
- There is a mandate to embrace tourism, the world's largest economy, on a local, regional, and national level in ways that have not been done before. Partnerships are only a part of the role to be taken; there is a need to think like a tourist destination.
- Agencies must rethink the recreation experience in light of increased technology impacting leisure activities, segmentation and specialization of participation, individualized personal recreation, time deepening, time shifting, and activity stacking.

CHALLENGES AND STRATEGIES FOR THE FUTURE

Demographic Shifts

A population shift is occurring in the United States. Beginning in the 1950s, it continues and in some ways has intensified in the twenty-first century. The shift from a rural to urban society and from northern states to southern and western states is well represented in the literature. However, these changes are more than just geographic. Examples of some key population shifts, both geographic and generational, include the following:

- More than 59% of all Americans live in the South and West.
- More than 53% of Americans live within 50 miles of an ocean.
- Hispanics are the fastest growing minority in the United States and are projected to make up 30% of the total population by 2050.
- Baby boomers (born between 1946 and 1964) were the largest birth generation, until the new-boomers (1983–2001) came along. This latter group added a larger share of immigrants than any other generation did.
- The United States has moved from a rural to a metropolitan nation, with four of five Americans now living in metropolitan areas.
- Youth "are making key personal 'choices' regarding resource and energy consumption *and* family size, taking into consideration climate change impacts and overall 'environmental sustainability.'"[2]
- Between 2000 and 2050, Hispanics and blacks will represent 40% of the working-age population (25 to 64 years) and account for almost 90% of the growth in that age group during the same period.[3]

Shifts are cultural, geographic, demographic, and environmental. The shifts have important impacts on the delivery of parks, recreation, and leisure services. In the early stages of migration from the urban core to the suburbs, loss of free time was measured in commuting time. It was assumed most commuting was done from the suburbs to the urban core. More recently, the commute has stretched both ways, with increasing numbers of people choosing to live in the urban core and work in the suburbs. Beyond the urban core, the exurbs have become the new growth area, outpacing growth within cities. Land in this area has been developed twice as fast as in the urban and suburban cores. In addition, developed land occupies 20% more space than it did just 20 years ago. It is the twenty-first century version of sprawl.[4]

In 1915, the population reached 100 million people. Fifty-two years later in 1967, it reached 200 million people, and 39 years later, it reached 300 million. Foreign-born residents represented 15% of the U.S. population in 1915, 8% in 1967, and 12% of the population in 2006. In 1915 and 1967, the largest percentage of the foreign-born population came from Europe; today it is Mexico.[5] As shown in **Figure 13.1**, the immigrant population held relatively steady at 8–12% of the total population from 1860 to 2000, but between 2000 and 2050 it is projected that the major growth in population will come from immigrants. The United States is the third most populous nation in the world behind China and India. The steady growth in population and diversity has increasing impacts on recreation demand, participation, and types of programs.

The Generations America is a land of generations. In recent years, the terms *baby boomer*, *Gen X*, *Gen Y*, and *Net Generation* have garnered in much public press. Only more recently has the term *generations* taken on a marketing connotation. Terminology for the generations is inconsistent. The following case study addresses one organization's perception of the generations of the twentieth century. Other authors have adjusted the names to fit marketing terminology. For example, the Pew Internet Project classifies six generations between 1936 and 1990 (**Table 13.1**).

What matters in understanding generations is defining how they are different from each other. Every generation has been different from the generations preceding it. Gen

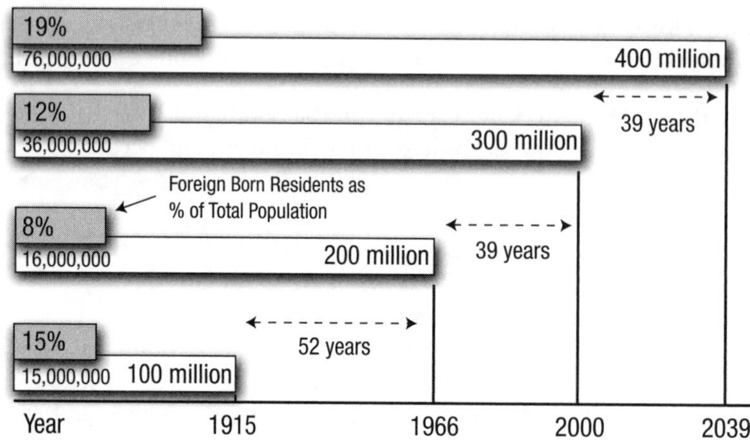

FIGURE 13.1 Population Growth, Timeline, and Foreign-Born Residents as a Percentage of the Total Population.
Data from J. S. Passel and D. Cohen, Pew Research Center, "U.S. Population Projections: 2005–2050." Available at: http://pewsocialtrends.org/pubs/703/population-projections-united-states. Accessed December 9, 2010.

TABLE 13.1

GENERATIONS OF AMERICANS

Generation Name	Birth Years, Ages in 2009	Percentage of Total Adult Population
Gen Y (Millennials)	Born 1977–1990, Ages 18–32	26
Gen X	Born 1965–1976, Ages 33–44	20
Younger Boomers	Born 1955–1964, Ages 45–54	20
Older Boomers	Born 1946–1954, Ages 55–63	13
Silent Generation	Born 1937–1945, Ages 64–72	9
G.I. Generation	Born 1936, Ages 73+	9

Modified from Jones, S. and Fox, S. Generations Online in 2009. Pew Internet & American Life Project. Pew Research Center. Available http://pewinternet.org/Reports/2009/Generations-Online-in-2009.aspx. Accessed September 30, 2010.

X and Gen Y are the first generations to have broad access to computer technology and to fully embrace it as a part of their lives. The influence of technology is discussed in more detail later in this chapter. A study of generations is a study of American history and how culture, war, poverty, technology, social movements, education, and other influences affect individuals within generations, their attitudes, expectations, and leisure participation.

A similar perspective of generations can be applied to the history, challenges, influences, and actions within parks, recreation, and leisure. Comparing the concept of generations to the discussion in Chapter 4, "Recreation and Leisure in the Modern Era," can enhance one's understanding of how the profession has grown and matured.

The Generations of the Twentieth Century

1. The Good Warriors (born from 1909 through 1928, median member born in 1918) were called the Greatest Generation by Tom Brokaw in 1998. They fought in World War II and led all other generations in blue-collar jobs and union membership. They and the Lucky Few were the most native-born generations in U.S. history.
2. The Lucky Few (born from 1929 through 1945, median member born in 1937) had the smallest share of immigrants of any generation in the century and was the first generation in U.S. history with fewer people than the preceding generation. Many educated Lucky Few men skipped blue-collar jobs for white-collar careers. Their military service came mostly during peacetime rather than wartime. Lucky Few women married earlier than any other generation in U.S. history.
3. The Baby Boomers (born from 1946 through 1964, median member born in 1955) nearly doubled the number of people in the Lucky Few to become the largest generation of the century. While baby boomer men had problems finding jobs, women in this generation nearly matched men in education and made great strides in the career world.
4. Generation X (born from 1965 through 1982, median member born in 1974) marks the first generation with a greater share of women than men graduating from college. Generation X once again includes many foreign-born immigrants. They delayed marriage and parenthood more than any other generation before them in the century. Men continued to struggle with jobs while women moved forward in careers as well as education.
5. The New Boomers (born from 1983 through 2001, median member born in 1992) include almost as many births as the original baby boom and will add a larger share of new immigrants in adulthood than any generation since the New Worlders. They will become the largest generation of any living during the century. Most of their lives will take place in the twenty-first century, however, so we only get a few hints about them here.[6]

Challenges Linked to Population Diversity

Age Diversity Generations are represented by age diversity. The baby boomers generation, as a percentage of the total population, is staggering in its size and impact. In addition, the population distribution has changed dramatically over the last 50 years with its influence on society and government already significant. Births are declining while immigration and births among first- and second-generation Hispanics are higher than the national average for all other ethnic groups.

In 1967, the median age in the United States was 29.5 years. In 2006, the median age increased to 36.2 years. America is an aging society and it suggests that we are moving from an economy where there are more workers than retirees to a society where there are insufficient workers to maintain retirees. The wider the band, the greater the population. Note how the boomers affect the age span of Americans. The senior or boomer population will continue to be a significant part of the total population, dwarfing newer generations. The first boomers were born in 1946 and are now retiring. The later boomers were born in 1960 to 1964 and are past their child-bearing years and have made their contributions to society's population growth. The 36- to 54-year-old age groups (45 to 63 in 2009) include the boomers and represent 28% of the total U.S. population.

More and more adults are celebrating the "new old," which is a new generation of seniors who are aging on their own terms.

Aging Society The United States has an aging society. For the first time in history, Americans are reaping the benefits of advances in science, technology, health care, nutrition, and affluence. The life expectancy of Americans has nearly doubled in the past century; in 1900, the life expectancy was 47 years, and in 2000, it had risen to 77. Individuals living into their late 80s and mid-90s is no longer uncommon. This population represents the most financially independent aging group in history. The 55-plus age group controls more than 75% of the country's wealth.

By 2025, there will be twice as many people more than 65 as there will be teenagers. By one estimate, the United States will need 31,000 geriatricians, compared to the 1000 in 2004.[7] It is suggested that 20% of the workforce could focus on providing services to and caring for aging boomers. In some states, particularly in the Midwest and Northeast, health care is already the largest industry.

Yet, can we expect the boomers, as they enter retirement, to do the same as earlier seniors? The answer is no. They will make their own mark on society and do it their way, which is a continuation of their lifelong contributions to change society. The early assumption was that boomers would go into full retirement as so many other generations have. Changes in the economy, retirement benefits, concerns about Social Security and Medicare, healthcare costs, longevity, and overall health have changed perceptions about retirement. In a report by Merrill Lynch, they found only 17% of boomers surveyed said they would never work again, and this 17% was the least financially prepared for retirement.[8] By contrast, 76% of those surveyed plan to work during stages of retirement. When asked why they will continue to work, 34% said it was important to earn money and 67% wanted the continuing mental stimulation and challenge to motivate them. The end of mandatory retirement in 1986 allowed many older adults to continue to work and contribute to the workforce. Simultaneous with the end of mandatory retirement, the Social Security system retirement ages were raised to 66 and 67. Between 1994 and 2005, there was a 17% increase in the number of men working between ages 62 and 64, a traditional retirement period. Overall, the workforce of men and women ages 60 to 64 grew from 52.8 million to 58 million.[9] Boomers do not see retirement as a period of relaxation and reduced lifestyle, but rather a continuation of challenges and personal growth—but on their own terms. The decision to retire is based more on the ability to do what they want and having the resources to do it than it is on the need to retire in a more traditional sense.

CASE STUDY: Serious Leisure Contributes to Successful Aging

Serious leisure is a concept first proposed by sociologist Robert Stebbens in 1982, contending that "serious leisure is the systematic pursuit of an amateur, hobbyist, or volunteer core activity that people find so substantial, interesting and fulfilling that . . . they launch themselves on a (leisure) career centered on acquiring and expressing a combination of its special skills, knowledge, and experience."[a] In the context of Maslow's hierarchy of needs, serious leisure fulfills multiple need and growth roles for individuals, ranging from belonging to creativity. Stebbens sees serious leisure as a substitution for work for those who may have left the workforce, whether voluntarily or involuntarily, yet he says serious leisure is not a livelihood and one should not get caught up in seeing serious leisure as a substitute for work. Serious leisure carries with it "numerous pleasant expectations and memories, doing so to a degree only rarely found in work."[b]

Serious leisure activities help seniors maintain successful aging.

As part of his description of serious leisure, Stebbens identified six qualities, or descriptors, that are present. In some ways, they are similar to life challenges and do not always represent positive emotions, but do represent challenges individuals must face in the pursuit of serious leisure. There are linkages to Maslow's hierarchy of human needs at the creativity level as well as Csikszentmihalyi's flow theory. The six qualities are as follows:

- The occasional need to persevere to overcome difficulties
- The presence of a career that involves achievement, occurring through stages of development and involvement
- A significant personal effort focusing on unique acquired knowledge, skill, or training
- Eight durable benefits including social interaction and belongingness, self-expression, self-enrichment, enhancement of self-image, feelings of accomplishment, lasting physical products, self actualization, and renewal
- A strong identity formed among participants in their chosen pursuits
- A unique ethos formed related to the activity resulting in a special social world[c]

Today's aging population, as reported earlier in this text, no longer conforms to the concept of a slow downward spiral or the notion that involvement, physical activity, and learning are not part of acceptable retirement activities. Rather, as the baby boomer population ages, this group is challenging all of the notions of what is appropriate for an aging population. Involvement, engagement, physical activity, and extended work or work-related activities are becoming the norm. As part of this change in the approach to and views of aging, serious leisure is receiving more attention from researchers. Linked with predictors of successful aging, serious leisure is showing promise as a way to enrich successful aging. Rowe and Kahn identify three factors crucial to successful aging: "the absence of disease and disability; maintaining mental and physical functioning; and continuing engagement with life."[d] Brown and colleagues studied older adults involved in a dance program and identified six themes related to the qualities of serious leisure.[d] They found *perseverance* among the participants as they learned how to dance. The perseverance was manifest among the participants in attitude and behaviors as they attempted to master basic and advanced dancing steps. Second, the notion of a *leisure career* included achievement or involvement among the participants. For those so engaged, "the concept of a leisure career reflects the successful aging components of learning, involvement, and keeping active."[e] The third quality and theme involved *considerable personal effort* to acquire specific knowledge of the leisure activity. The characteristic of a *unique ethos* reflects directly upon the development of new and specialized social world resulting in a strong social network, both of which are recognized components of successful aging. The *benefits of involvement* in serious leisure as they relate to this study involved self-actualization, self-enrichment, self-expression, feelings of accomplishment, enhancement of self-image, regeneration of self, self-gratification, lasting physical products, and social interaction and belongingness. The benefits of involvement may have the most long-lasting impact on the participants and successful aging.

Identity formulation, another quality, comes from the other five characteristics and the researchers found the participants formed a strong identity with their pursuits. More important, it suggests the power of serious leisure as a contributor to successful aging.

Questions to Consider

1. Explain how you participate in serious leisure.
2. Do you have a grandparent who is actively engaged in serious leisure?
3. Explain why serious leisure is important to successful aging.

Sources

a. R. Stebbens, *Serious Leisure*, (New Brunswick, NJ: Transaction Publishers, 2007): 5.
b. R. Stebbens, "Serious Leisure," *Society* (Vol. 38, No. 4, 2001), 55.
c. C. A. Brown, F. A. McGuire, and J. Voelkl, "The Link Between Successful Aging and Serious Leisure," *International Journal of Aging and Human Development* (Vol. 66, No. 1, 2008), 73–95.
d. Ibid, 74.
e. Ibid, 82.

This picture is incomplete without a better understanding of the composition and well-being of the over-65 population. Eighty-two percent of this group are white, 8% black, 3% Asian, 6% Hispanic, and 1% mixed race. The percentage of white will decline by 2050 with Hispanics becoming the largest over-65 minority, followed by African Americans. This age group is overwhelmingly married (79% for the 65–74 age group). Nineteen percent of men live alone while 40% of women do. Poverty is an issue among the over-65 group with 9.8% reportedly living at the poverty level or below in 2004. Although this is a continuing concern, the numbers have declined steadily from 1959 when the poverty rate was 35.2%.[10] Another issue that may delay retirement is the rising cost of health care and the abandonment of postretirement employer-supported health plans. Large corporations have discovered they cannot compete in today's marketplace and provide long-term commitments to former employees. More than one-third of eligible retirees have chosen to remain in the workforce primarily to retain existing health benefits.

What does all of this mean? First, the 72-and-out rule is gone. It has been assumed for generations that most people would die by the age of 72. That has not been true for decades, but never more so than with boomers. There are 75 million over-50s in the United States and they hold approximately 90% of America's $44 trillion in liquid assets. The wealth is not evenly spread across this population. An amazing 42% of all boomers plan to move in retirement. Boomers are moving south and west to warmer climates. Boomer men are planning to retire late, transition from work to retirement, work less, spend more time with their spouses, and relax more. Women see retirement as an opportunity for career development, community involvement, and continued personal growth. Demands for recreation and leisure will increase, but not necessarily for traditional services. The boomers will be better able to pay for services and activities and will be more demanding of creative and nontraditional services.

The aging of Americans has significant implications for recreation participation and delivery. Park and recreation professionals will be challenged to determine how to serve boomers. The new aging population cannot be considered older adults in the traditional sense. The days of senior centers, bingo, cards, Friday afternoon movies, and bus tours will not be over but will fail to attract the large number of older adults who see themselves as independent. They are already more active, have a more mobile lifestyle, are healthier, have a longer life expectancy, and use technology as a compensation for particular deficiencies, and will do so even more in the future. They are as diverse as any group in society and are changing the way recreation is considered for an aging population. Cities are establishing separate senior service departments or integrating them into existing government organizations. There will be a need to continue to provide traditional services to those older adults who desire them, but many will seek new experiences and greater challenges. This group utilizes their financial resources to remain involved; to engage in travel, sport, and active leisure; and to continue their involvement in family and society.

Recent research holds promise for improving recreation programming for boomers and other older adults. Some research suggests that older adults will focus on more meaningful relationships at the expense of less important relationships. Fitness programs are growing and being adapted to the needs of older adults' health, mobility, and strength levels. Healthy older adults may benefit from activities that focus on goal selection and optimization. Older adults with more limited health should benefit from adapted and facilitated activities.[11] Regardless of the approach taken, public park and recreation agencies need to understand that older adults are more diverse and have higher expectations than any previous generation.

Ethnic and Racial Diversity As previously shared, the United States is becoming more diverse. The immigration of Europeans has lessened dramatically, replaced by rapid integration of Hispanics, and lesser of Asian, Middle Eastern, and African populations. The 2000 census showed a growing diversity. Hispanics were the fastest growing minority in the United States as depicted. The decline in the African American percentage is almost wholly explained by the ability of individuals to declare two or more races and was initiated by the 2000 Census.

Research into the influence of race and ethnicity has been slow in developing. Most important, it has shown that ethnicity is a factor in levels of recreation participation, types of activities engaged in, and comfort levels with the natural environment. Some early research set the stage for a better understanding of why there are differences. A study by Virden and Walker reports that Caucasians found a forest environment more pleasing and safer than did African Americans and Hispanics.[12] Hibbler and Shinew identified four factors that explain the differences in leisure patterns. The four reasons are

> (1) the limited socio-economic resources of many African Americans; (2) a historical pattern of oppression and racial discrimination towards African Americans; (3) distinct cultural differences between African Americans and European Americans; and (4) feelings of discomfort and constraint by African Americans in public leisure settings.[13]

There is a growing realization that assimilation of immigrants is a complex issue. They are more ethnically diverse, may have complex intergenerational changes, and are growing rapidly in number. For example, Mexican immigrant women have seen it as their responsibility to maintain their culture. Beyond immigrant and generational issues, different ethnic groups view leisure at once similarly and differently. African Americans prefer shopping, going to church, and open spaces that serve active recreation-related function. Caucasians show a greater preference for open space for land; wildlife; passive-, individual-, or family-based recreation; and conservation. Hispanics and Asians tend to come to outdoor areas in larger family groups for social purposes. African Americans, Caucasians, and Hispanics all shared similar views toward social-setting attributes such as sharing experiences, being by oneself, and so forth. Research has made progress in explaining differences in race and ethnic decisions and preferences for leisure, but the field is still not well understood.[14,15]

New immigrants bring with them their own culture and customs. Integration into American society is often difficult.

The Changing Family Over the last 30 years, families have changed more than in the previous 200 years. The era of the stay-at-home mother, the single income source, three or more children, family dinners, church on Sunday, and marriage as a lifetime commitment is disappearing. The nuclear family is becoming as uncommon in today's society as the transistor radio is. World War II changed the United States as a society. Women experienced a freedom; soldiers coming home from the war had the GI Bill and gained more education than any generation before them. The 1960s and 1970s saw a change in societal mores, traditional family values, and perceptions. The notion of a traditional family changed with society. Politicians and the conservative religious movements have focused on the decay of the nuclear family, yet the facts show that the nuclear family has been in decline for more than 40 years. As early as 1960, the traditional nuclear family comprised only 45% of American households. The 2000 U.S. Census reported for the first time that less than one-quarter (23.5%) of American households consisted of a married man and woman and one or more of their children.[16]

Today's families are characterized in a variety of ways. It may be as a traditional nuclear, an adoption with no marriage, a wedding after the baby, single mom, two dads, two moms, or a single dad. David Elkind calls these *permeable families*: "The permeable family is more fluid, more flexible, and more obviously vulnerable to pressures from outside itself."[17]

A major concern of social service organizations is children growing up in single-parent homes. They frequently have less opportunities and financial resources than do children growing up in two-parent homes, even if both parents are in the workforce. The Annie E. Casey Foundation reported in 2006 that 22 million children are in single-parent homes, but the disparity of opportunities, based on ethnicity and race, is dramatic. **Figure 13.2** depicts the differentiation of single-parent families by race and Hispanic origin. The presence of high levels of single-parent homes among ethnic groups, other than non-Hispanic whites, mirrors poverty rates and suggests the importance of providing recreation programs, after-school programs, and other social support services to these children.

Today, less than 25% of American households are composed of a single wage earner, meaning 75% of households are dependent on two or more wage earners. This places greater stresses on families, parents, and children. The notion of the mother as the primary caregiver has changed. Fathers are becoming more involved in the lives of their children—from changing diapers to taking time off for sick children. The roles of fathers are in transition as larger numbers of men are indicating a desire to be more nurturing with their children. Mothers traditionally assumed the extra burden of the home, work, and child rearing and now are more frequently sharing these duties with others.

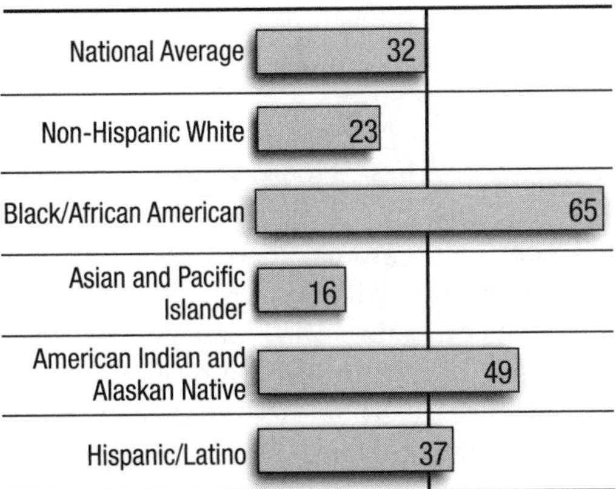

FIGURE 13.2 Percentage of Children in Single-Parent Families by Race and Origin. *Note:* Data for Blacks/African Americans, Asians and Pacific Islanders, and American Indians and Alaskan Natives include those who are also Hispanic/Latino. Data for Non-Hispanic Whites, Blacks/African Americans, Asians and Pacific Islanders, and American Indians and Alaskan Natives are for persons who selected only one race. All data is from the 2008 American Community Survey.
© Annie E. Casey Foundation, 2010. *2010 Kids Count Data Book*, p. 36. Reprinted with permission.

Social service organizations offer support to homeless families.

The challenge for recreation and family service agencies is to determine how to serve the new permeable family. Traditional after-school programs may no longer work when mothers expect to pick children up later in the day. Many agencies have gone to extended after-school programs, frequently partnering with schools to mix education, tutoring, and leisure.

Children Between 1950 and 2008, Americans experienced the most sustained economic growth of any time in history. For the most part, U.S. children are growing up in relative luxury compared to their grandparents, who grew up in relative luxury compared to their grandparents. There are also greater challenges facing today's youth than at any time in history. Numerous groups are investigating children and issues they face. Three such organizations are at the forefront:

- Childstats.gov (www.childstats.gov), a federal interagency forum focusing on collecting, analyzing, and reporting data on issues related to children and families.
- Child Trends (www.childtrends.org), a nonprofit organization focusing on trends affecting children and providing research, a databank of trends and indicators, and best practices.
- Kids Count (www.kidscount.org), a major initiative of the Annie E. Casey Foundation that tracks the status of children on a state-by-state basis. It measures the educational, social, economic, and physical well-being of children and reports them in a variety of research publications. It also has funded projects in many states.

Child well-being has become a major topic of governments, nonprofits, and recreation and leisure agencies. These groups frequently work together to improve child well-being.

Globalization is contributing to major societal change with particular impact on children. This era of globalization is evidenced by advances in investment, technology, manufacturing, and mobility coinciding with dramatically increased prosperity. Although corporate decision making may be influenced by globalization, it is the social frameworks that are frequently being negatively affected. It has created a scale of migration from Mexico and Central America previously unseen. As previously discussed, Hispanic populations represent the fastest growing immigrant group over the last 20 years. Youth from developing countries are less likely to be academically, socially, economically, physically, and emotionally prepared to enter the U.S. social fabric and lead full and productive lives. Already the Hispanic population has the highest high school dropout rate in the United States.

The youth population has been declining as a percentage of the total population for several decades: 26% in 2000 to a projected 24% in 2010. In 1964, the end of the baby boomer generation, youth represented 36% of the population. Youth population, since 2000, is not declining as a total number, but only as a percentage of the total U.S. population. The U.S. Census Bureau reported 73.9 million youth in 2007, 1.5 million more than in 2000.

CASE STUDY: Childrens' Well-Being as a Measure of Happiness

The well-being of children in the United States has become a topic of considerable concern. Well-being is a measure of happiness. Measuring well-being of children, as presented in this case study, utilizes statistical analysis to provide a quantitive measure of the status of children. Expanding beyond traditional psychological measures, statistical data are gathered from a variety of sources to predict levels of well-being. The purpose of the data gathering and reporting is a desire to ensure that children have full and rich life opportunities as they grow and mature. Second, assumptions are made that children cannot, of themselves, make assessments about their well-being. Finally, demographic data provide a rich source of information about the social, economic, educational, and other opportunities and achievements of children. Taken as a whole, organizations gathering and reporting the data are using the information to inform the general public and to influence decision making in legislative bodies at the city, state, and federal levels.

Measuring the well-being of children assists organizations in better serving this important future resource.

Well-being is not a new concept, but one that recreation organizations have traditionally associated with as they strive to enhance the well-being of their constituents. High on that list of constituents are children. Carruthers and Hood suggest, "There is a breadth and depth of literature supporting the importance and centrality of well-being in people's conception of a meaningful, purposeful life." They go on to say, "Well-being has been defined... as being action oriented as well as feeling oriented. Thus well-being is concerned with pleasant feelings and experiences, as well as the way in which people make choices and live their lives."[a]

Nonprofit and government agencies are the major players addressing well-being of children in the United States. The two key providers of information are the Annie E. Casey Foundation, sponsor of the annual *Kids Count Data Book (KCD)*, and the Federal Interagency Forum on Child and Family Statistics, which annually produces the *America's Children in Brief: Key National Indicators of Well-Being (CIB)*. Each organization looks at well-being from a different perspective, but together the reports provide meaningful and relevant data to parks, recreation, and leisure-service providers.

The CIB identifies seven domains that "characterize the well-being of a child and that influence the likelihood that a child will grow to be a well-educated, economically secure, productive, and healthy adult."[b] The CIB report is divided into seven sections: family and social environment, economic circumstances, health care, physical environment and safety, behavior, education, and health and reports on 40 indicators. The KCD, in contrast, provides 10 key indicators that include percentage of low-birthweight babies; infant mortality rate (deaths per 1000 live births); child death rate (deaths per 100,000 children ages 1–14 years); teen death rate (deaths per 100,000 teens ages 15–19 years); teen birth rate (births per 1000 females ages 15–19); percentage of teens who are high school dropouts (ages 16–19); percentage of teens not attending school and not working (ages 16–19); percentage of children living in families where no parent has full-time, year-round employment; percentage of children in poverty (income below $21,027 for a family of two adults and two children in 2007); and percentage of children in single-parent families.

The two reports, while similar, approach collecting and reporting the data in different ways. The CIB collects data from federal agencies, providing a national perspective using multiple indicators within each of the seven categories. In addition, the report identifies indicators that still need to be developed. By contrast, the KCD restricts itself to 10 indicators, and then ranks states within each indicator by comparing it to other states. "These indicators possess three important attributes: (1) They reflect a wide range of factors affecting the well-being of children, such as health, adequacy of income, and educational attainment. (2) They reflect experiences across a range of developmental stages—from birth through early adult-hood. (3) They permit legitimate comparisons because they are consistent across states and over time."[c] KCD also produces supplemental reports, such as one titled *Reducing the Number of Disconnected Youth*, and recommends strategies for engaging youth. In the previously mentioned report, six strategies are suggested:

- Re-engage disconnected youth and young adults in education
- Provide workforce development programs geared to the needs of disconnected youth and young adults
- Include disconnected youth in economic recovery investment and planning
- Address impediments to employment
- Create developmental opportunities that recognize the importance of social networks
- Aim for comprehensive reform, with a focus on cross-system collaboration"[d]

The data from the reports are used by many social service and government organizations to identify ways to improve child well-being and to make decisions related to allocating financial and physical resources to organizations that serve youth. The two reports, as the primary sources of data about child well-being, receive considerable attention. The data can be used by local recreation and leisure organizations to identify areas of need, to improve their services, and to identify potential partners in efforts to enhance child well-being. The reports focus heavily on the potential of children at risk. They highlight the need and, at least in the case of KCD, argue for change and improvement.

Parks, recreation, and sport professionals view these data as highly instructive. Nonprofit youth-serving organizations are at the forefront of addressing the well-being needs of youth. Public park and recreation agencies have long been invested in enhancing youth opportunities for growth and sport is frequently seen as a tool to assist in the process. For each of these types of agencies, the awareness must be present that parks, recreation, and sport are only a few of multiple constituencies committed to improving the quality of children's well-being.

Questions to Consider

1. Why is gathering data about children important?
2. How can public park and recreation agencies use the data from these reports to improve delivery of services to children?
3. If you were involved in a youth sport program, what kind of information from these data sources would be of value to you as you began to determine where you were going to recruit youth from?

Sources

a. C. Carruthers and C. Hood. "Building a Life of Meaning Through Therapeutic Recreation: The Leisure and Well-Being Model, Part 1," *Therapeutic Recreation Journal* (Vol. 41, 2007): 277.
b. ChildStats.gov, *America's Children in Brief: Key National Indicators of Well-Being*. http://childstats.gov/americaschildren/.
c. Annie E. Casey Foundation, *KIDS COUNT Indicator Brief: Reducing the Number of Disconnected Youth* (July 2009): 32. www.aecf.org/~/media/Pubs/Initiatives/KIDS%20COUNT/K/KIDSCOUNTIndicatorBriefReducingtheNumberofDis/Disconnected%20youth.pdf.
d. Ibid, 2.

The shift to an urban society continued to increase with more than 80% of children living in urban areas, including the suburbs and exurbs. Generations of contact and grounding with a rural environment have been replaced by city parks, community recreation centers, YMCAs, YWCAs, Boy Scouts, Girl Scouts, Camp Fire USA, and other organizations. In many cases, these organizations changed their orientation from a rural to an urban perspective. Today's camps are less likely to be overnights away from home than they are to be day camps in parks or on nonprofit-owned properties usually in or near the neighborhood where the children live. State park organizations nationwide have reported decreases in the number of children participating in outdoor recreation–based activities and attending parks and recreation areas in rural areas.

A major area of concern of public and private agencies is youth well-being. Child well-being has been variously described as those conditions affecting children in the United States. ChildStats.gov includes indicators from "three demographic background measures and 40 selected indicators [that] describe the population of children and depict child well-being in the areas of family and social environment, economic circumstances, health care, physical environment and safety, behavior, education, and health."[18] The Annie E. Casey Foundation sponsors the Kids Count report on the well-being of America's youth, which is updated every other year. It measures items such as children's access to health care, environmental conditions, economic growth of families, education, and the education of young children.

Table 13.2 depicts selected data focusing on youth well-being gathered in 1999, 2001, and 2008. The snapshot captures multiple areas of concern. A review of the table suggests areas of social concern, such as tobacco use, lack of child-care services, illicit drug use, violent crime, and the like. The United States is better able today to quantify social issues and the status of youth than at any time in history. Conversely, this ability creates greater demands on public agencies, including nonprofits and park and recreation programs, to address these areas of concern.

Leisure professionals have a direct concern for child well-being. Youth cannot grow and progress unless their basic needs are met. It remains that minority youth have significant issues of well-being, and in a society of wealth, many find such inequities unacceptable. The public parks and recreation movement is grounded as a social services movement

TABLE 13.2

AMERICA'S CHILDREN AT A GLANCE

Characteristic	1999/2001[a]	2009
Children ages 0–17 in the United States	7.04	74.5 million
Children ages 0–17 as a proportion of the population		24.3%
Children ages 0–17 by race and ethnic group[b]		
White		75.6%
White, non-Hispanic	64.0%	55.3%
Black	15.0%	15.1%
Asian	4.0%	4.4%
All other races	1.0%	4.9%
Hispanic (of any race)	16.0%	22.5%
Children 0–17 living with two married parents	69.0%	67.0%
Children 0–6, not in kindergarten, who received some form of nonparental child care on a regular basis	60.0%	61.0%
Children 0–4 with employed mothers, whose primary child care arrangement is with a relative	50.0%	48.0%
Children ages 0–17 in poverty	16.0%	19.0%
Children 0–17 in households classified by USDA as "food insecure"	4.0%	22.0%
Children 0–17 covered by health insurance	85.0%	90.0%
Children 5–17 with activity limitations resulting from one or more chronic health conditions	8.0%	9.0%
Children 6–17 who are obese		19.0%
12th graders reporting regular cigarette smoking	22.0%	11.0%
12th graders reporting having five or more alcoholic beverages	32.0%	25.0%
12th graders reported using illicit drugs over the past 30 days	26.0%	23.0%
Youth offenders ages 12–17 involved in serious violent crimes		14 per 1000
Young adults ages 18–24 who have completed high school	86.0%	90.0%

[a]Two reports are combined to secure data. Data collected and reported has changed since the inception of the report in 1997.
[b]Children percentages by race and ethnic group has changed due to refined definitions by the U.S. Census Bureau.
Federal Interagency Forum on Children and Family Statistics. *America's Children in Brief: Key National Indicators of Well-Being, 2010.* Washington, DC: U.S. Government Printing Office. Available at: http://www.childstats.gov/americaschildren/glance.asp. Accessed December 8, 2010.

that needs to frequently reinvent itself. Poverty is the most pervasive and abusive condition affecting children in the United States. UNICEF, in a 2004 report, said,

> "Children living in poverty experience deprivation of the material, spiritual, and emotional resources needed to survive, develop and thrive, leaving them unable to enjoy their rights, to achieve their full potential or to participate as full and equal members of society."[19]

The child poverty rate in 2007 was 18% for children between 0 and 17 years of age. The number is likely to rise with current economic conditions, yet numbers are just beginning to emerge to indicate increase in child homelessness and poverty levels. A recent report indicates the economic recession has had a significant impact on families as unemployment grew to more than 10% nationally, and more than 13% in some regions, suggesting that the number of children living in extreme poverty (half the poverty level) would climb to between 4.5 and 6.3 million. This is up from 2.5 million in 2008.

Although workforce employment in 2006 was at 78%, it did not necessarily translate into reduction of child poverty. The problem arises from disparity within the workforce. Skilled and professional employees have seen continued growth in income while those without skills have seen a rise in less-secure forms of employment that frequently provide minimal or no health care. Lack of regular health care affects 6% of children, and 19.5% of children were not immunized in 2007 despite efforts at the state and local levels.[20]

Leisure is a commodity in the lives of children that is essential and developmental. Government and nonprofit agencies are joining to serve urban at-risk youth to provide services and opportunities. The challenges are significant and agencies are attempting to balance needs and simultaneously serve more affluent populations of taxpayers who demand services and who are frequently willing to pay for them. Urban park and recreation agencies are expanding their partnerships to work with social service organizations in ways that meet the needs of disadvantaged youth and families. It can include joint programming, provision of facilities, redirecting individuals to the social service agency, or expanding existing services.

Teens and Tweeners: Movers of Change Any discussion of children is incomplete without a discussion of teens and tweeners. The Harris Poll regularly tracks trends among teens and has become an important source for information about this age group. Many other organizations watch trends in teens for various reasons, including market forces, college directions, family issues, social stresses, and so forth. The Partnership for a Drug-Free America identified five teen trends: (1) they are stressed; (2) they are hypersexualized; (3) friends are the new family; (4) the traditional family has been redefined; and (5) diversity isn't something they are taught—they live with it.[21]

Today's researchers have discovered that any study of teens must also include tweens, that age group from 8 to 12 years of age. Tweens are between being children and teens and the 5-year time frame represents a period of dramatic physical, emotional, and social growth. For example, 61% of tweens said their mother understands them best, but only 20% of teens said the same thing.[22] These groups are different and create sometimes challenging dynamics in family lifestyles. Activities families do most often together include eating dinner at home, watching television, going out to eat together, food and grocery shopping, watching rented movies, and visiting relatives.[23] In a recent study, youth ages 13 to 17 years are three times more likely to prefer spending time with their friends, than with their family. Tweeners, by contrast, remain strongly linked to their family.[24]

Teens' interaction patterns change between 12 and 18 years. They begin to rely more heavily on their peers, are trend conscious, and react to peer pressure. The Harris Poll and Pew Internet Initiative found teens to be major users of the Internet and have become the innovators in social networking. Social networking is a growing source of

Social networking and cell phone use are up for teens.

finding new friends. Facebook.com, MySpace .com, Friendster.com, and Xanga.com are contemporary examples of how teens connect on the Internet. Social networking sites have become increasingly important communication sources for teens. They are putting more and more of their lives online for others to see, comment on, and to expand their network of relationships. Visiting a social network is the second most common online activity of teens, just behind texting. The Pew Internet and American Life Project tracks teen activities online. **Table 13.3** illustrates what teens report as being their online activities as measured in 2007 and 2008.

Twittering, a social networking use of a tool that did not exist 5 years ago, is a contemporary social networking mechanism that has individuals, organizations, and groups involved. Forty-nine percent of 12- to 15-year-olds report making friends via the Internet.[25] Mobile phones provide opportunities for talking, texting, e-mailing, and, more important, teens see them as a primary tool for staying connected to their friends. Mobile phones give teens a freedom previous generations did not have and move parents out of the controlling communications mode.

Tweeners and teens are more likely to volunteer in their community than their parents are. Fifty-five percent of this group volunteered an average of 29 hours a years. By contrast, only 29% of adults volunteer. The youth are most engaged with organizations focusing on

TABLE 13.3

TEEN (12–17 YEARS) REPORTED USE OF THE INTERNET

Rank	Activity	Percentage Using	Average Percentage of All Online Adults
1	Play games online	78	35
2	Use e-mail	73	91
3	Send instant messages	68	38
4	Use social networking sites	65	35
5	Get news	63	70
6	Download music	59	67
7	Watch videos online	57	52
8	Create an SNS profile	55	29
9	Read blogs	49	32
10	Buy something online	49	32

Data from Pew Internet Infographics, "Generational Differences in Online Activities." January 28, 2009. Available at: http://www .pewinternet.org/Infographics/Generational-differences-in-online-activities.aspx. Accessed November 11, 2010.

youth involvement (67%) followed by civic or community organizations (54%) and religious-based groups (49%). Political organizations tend to be least attractive to youth volunteers (13%).[26]

Engaging youth in parks and recreation is challenging, at best, and daunting if they are not involved in the planning. Too many organizations continue to provide traditional activities for youth, and although beneficial, this fails to draw and provide the services needed. These youth now see the cell phone as an entertainment device, not just a communication device. They expect to be able to communicate with their current friends, make new friends, and engage in social groups, all online. Organizations that capture the desire for community engagement and strengthen opportunities for social inclusion will find greater involvement by youth and simultaneously meet some of their needs.

Where People Live: Urban, Suburb, Exurb History has recorded the decline of rural populations, the growth of cities, industrialization, postindustrialization, the growth of suburbs and exurbs, the decline of the inner city, and the simultaneous revitalization of cities and urban areas. In the 1950s, people began to commute into the city. In the twenty-first century, commuting has become a norm for millions of people, but urbanites are as likely to commute to the suburbs to work as suburbanites are to commute to cities' business centers. The average commuter spends 100 hours a year commuting to and from work. That is an

CASE STUDY: Generation Next: 25 Random Things About You (That Are Changing the World)

Recreation, leisure, and sport reflect culture, population, and shifting trends and mores in society. Since the 1960s, change has come more and more rapidly. Beginning with the angry counterculture 1960s, through the civil rights movement of the turbulent 1970s and on to today, one thing has remained constant: change. It affects people, culture, and organizations and causes the continual rethinking of how each new generation sees the world. Recreation, leisure, and sport organizations are often in the forefront of these changes and at other times they are bystanders. However, knowing and responding to change are essential activities in any organization and especially those serving the public.

The following commencement speech presented at Long Island University in May 2009 was abstracted to illustrate how the current college generation is portrayed by social researchers.[a] Lee Rainie, director of the Pew Research Center's Internet and American Life Project, the leading research on the Internet in the world, delivered the address. These 25 random ideas are highly reflective of youth culture and instructive for leisure and sport professionals as they adapt services, programs, and facilities.

- Your generation is bigger and . . . more racially and ethnically diverse than any generation in American history.
- You are the most aggressive and eager social networkers in history.
- You are the most racially and socially tolerant cohort in history.
- Your generation is more achievement-oriented, grade-conscious, and rule-observing than your parents' or grandparents' generation.

- You already get extra credit for having gotten into less trouble with the law than your predecessors and having experienced fewer social and emotional problems.
- There are a lot more of you entering and graduating from college than was the case when your elders were your age.
- You are more likely than your elders to say your parents, a teacher, or a mentor is your role model.
- You serve your "weak ties" by performing volunteer activities at staggering rates.
- You were the first generation to have "community service" requirements imposed on you by most of your school districts.
- You have taken the call to civic engagement seriously and last year translated it into record-shattering voting numbers in the election.
- Your disproportionate support for Barack Obama created the largest disparity in voting between young voters and others in the history of modern polling.
- You and your peers are much more likely than your elders to:
  Own gaming consoles and play video games
  Text message
  Have an MP3 player like an iPod and download music
  Use instant messaging
  Create an avatar and interact with others in virtual worlds
  Upload pictures and videos to the Internet
  Blog
  Participate in online social networks.
- You are record-breaking multitaskers as you toggle back and forth between all the screens in your life.
- You are giving birth to a new kind of culture that is more vibrant because it has led to
  An explosion of new voices
  Fresh forms of music
  Novel kinds of language
  Varied pathways to community-building
  Different kinds of ethics and etiquette
  And . . . far-out—sometimes pretty twisted—forms of humor

Questions to Consider

1. How do these descriptions relate to you and your leisure time?
2. How are you different from your parents in regard to how yo spend leisure time? How are you similar?
3. Describe how the influences mentioned in this case study have affected you and your family.

Source

a. L. Rainie, *25 Random Things About You*, Pew Internet and American Life Project. www.pewinternet.org/Presentations/2009/14—25-Random-Things-About-You—Commencement.aspx.

average of 49 minutes a day. However, New York and Maryland each averaged 60 minutes or more commuting each day and three counties in metropolitan New York averaged more than 80 minutes daily in commutes.

Beyond the suburbs are the exurbs, difficult to define, but an easy area to describe. They exist beyond the suburbs in traditionally rural areas, that are now dotted with individual homes on acreage, subdivisions, and may include cities of 50,000 or more people. They are adjacent to large metropolitan areas and their distinctive feature is the residents' choice of place over people, where the primary commonality is the need to commute to work. The exurbs are growing population areas because individuals are more willing to increase travel time for a perceived improved quality of life.

Influence of Technology on Leisure

Technology affects the way people live and the way they experience leisure. For example, California State Parks in 2005 issued a trend report including a discussion about technology. Some of its conclusions are provided here:

- Americans *love* their toys and baby boomers expect "amenity-rich" experiences.
- Technology will continue to affect how we work and how we play.
- Each generation [is] better educated, more adept with, and more dependent on, technology than the previous generations.
- Technological advances affect the affordability, accessibility, and required skill level of many recreation activities.
- Technology allows "mass customization."
- New activities will be developed around innovative devices and products.
- Technology creates entirely new recreation uses.
- People tend to self-define and organize around their chosen form of recreation.
- Each group tends to want (demand) their own exclusive allocation of resources.[28]

These findings only tell part of the story. The current college-age generation is the first generation to grow up with computers. They are called *digital natives*. The Pew Internet and American Life project defines digital natives as having been born in 1985 or later and having been exposed to computers and the Internet. **Table 13.4** depicts key events in their lives connected to the Internet. Parents and other individuals born before 1985 are considered to be *digital immigrants* or those who have had to adapt to technology rather than having grown up with it. It is a little like being an immigrant and having to learn a whole new language and culture.

Technology has changed the way we communicate. As little as 30 years ago, mail was the most common communications method. There was only one long-distance telephone company. Long-distance telephone calls were expensive and usually reserved for special occasions or for business enterprises. Most families subscribed to a morning newspaper and watched the network news on one of three commercial channels. They listened to one or two local stations and only in larger markets was there a variety of music available on the radio.

Today Americans, on average, spend more waking time communicating and using media devices such as the television, radio, MP3 devices, and smart phones, than any other activity. The cell phone is an example of how technology has affected individuals, families, work, and communities. Even the older adults use their cell phones to make contact while traveling, even if most of the time the phone sits turned off while at home. As late as 2002

TABLE 13.4

KEY EVENTS IN THE LIVES OF THE FIRST GENERATION OF DIGITAL NATIVES

Date/Age	Technology Event
Birth—1985	Personal computers 10 years old
Kindergarten—1990	World Wide Web program written
Middle School—1996	PalmPilot goes on market
High School—1999	Sean Fanning creates Napster
Graduate High School—1999	iPod
Late Teens–Early 20s—1997	Blogs
Late Teens–Early 20s—2001	Wikipedia
Late Teens–Early 20s—2003	Del.icio.us
Late Teens–Early 20s—2003	Skype
Late Teens–Early 20s—2004	Podcasts
Late Teens–Early 20s—2005	YouTube, Facebook

Data from Lee Raine. "Digital Natives: How Today's Youth Are Different from Their 'Digital Immigrant' Elders and What That Means for Libraries." Metro–New York Library Council, Brooklyn Museum of Art. (Presentation). Pew Research Center: Pew Internet and American Life Project, 2006: 1.

a cell phone was primarily a phone. People carried cell phones and digital handheld devices for scheduling, note taking, and the like. Today's smart phones have replaced these two devices and expanded their level of services. Smart phones dominate the market. Many continue to use a cell phone primarily as a phone, but many more use it as an e-mail client; note taker; camera (still and movie); calendar; a link to online services such as Twitter, Flicker, Facebook, the global positioning system (GPS); game console; newsreader; address finder with map; and much more. Apple iPhone users spend more time using their mobile devices as an Internet access tool than as a telephone.

We are becoming a mobile generation. "Cast a glance at any coffee shop, train station, or airport boarding gate, and it is easy to see that mobile access to the Internet is taking root in our society. Open laptops or furrowed brows staring at palm-sized screens are evidence of how routinely information is exchanged on wireless networks."[29] The Pew Internet and American Life project states that mobility changes the way people interact with each other and the ways they use their computer. We have reached a level where businesses and others expect to have broadband always on or be always connected. Questions remain unanswered about the impact of continual information exchange on individuals. For example, does it stress social norms, or cause continuous partial attention? In Pew's typology, the sophisticated user of technology has mobile access and becomes an elite, replacing home access as an elite status. Many of today's teens and young adults see always-connected as a necessity and a right.

Citizens can attend town meetings, business meetings, and the like without leaving their home or office. They can attend these meetings from anywhere with their mobile devices. Skype became the first free or low-cost Internet-based international telephone service. It has had a major impact on the developing world. The Internet has even had a significant influence on how people deal with illness. One study reported 54% of the adults responding saying the Internet played a major role as they helped another person cope with a major illness. The number who said the Internet played a role as they coped with a major illness increased 40% over a 2-year period.[30] Nina Tote, cofounder of TypePad, reported at the 2006 TED conference on a woman who shared the last months of her life through a blog talking about life and the progress of her cancer. Everyone knew she had died when

CASE STUDY: How Napster and the iPod Changed the Way We Purchase and Listen to Music

Recognizing the Power of the Internet

At the end of the twentieth century and into the first few years of the twenty-first century, a college student and Apple's Steve Jobs changed the way people acquired and listened to music. Napster, a people-to-people (P2P) file-sharing utility, first appeared in summer 1999, and the iPod 2 years later in 2001. Each dramatically reshaped the landscape of music, initially in the United States and later worldwide.

At the start of 1999, the music and recording industry was the dominant force in music sharing. If you wanted to listen to music, you could listen to it on the radio where someone else selected what was broadcast, or you could purchase a compact disc (CD) from a retailer and play it in your Sony Walkman. The retail music industry generated in excess of $700 billion annually, just in the United States.

An iPod allows you to listen to music whenever and wherever you want, even while exercising outdoors.

Napster was introduced on the Internet in June 1999 and provided the first music exchange service in a P2P format. Others followed quickly, but Napster captured the market and was free. The process of file sharing was not legal, at least in the eyes of the music recording industry. However, the floodgate of music sharing was open, and despite the efforts of music companies, it would never close. Suddenly, individuals could share their entire music collection and secure other individuals' collections. By 2001, when the Pew Internet project gathered its first data on music file sharing, it estimated 25% of Internet users were downloading music files and most of them were using Napster.

The story since then has been mixed for the music recording industry, as well as for P2P sharing. Some large lawsuits were filed against Napster, other P2P services, as well as individuals, many of which were dropped. The industry finally saw the damage it was doing to itself. One legal expert recently stated, "The lawsuits had little effect, as unlawful downloading continues."[a] Further, the *Boston Globe* suggested the industry misread the impact of the technology of downloading music and should have purchased Napster rather than fighting it.[b]

Napster has been forced to reinvent itself many times and today is a shadow of what it was, still struggling to determine how to exist in the changing marketplace. For the music industry, however, album and CD sales have fallen at a steady rate since 1999, and the industry suggests that between 2004 and 2008 album sales fell by $3.8 billion.[c]

Apple Sees an Opportunity

Steve Jobs, always the entrepreneur, looked at the music industry and saw a giant opportunity for Apple. Beginning in 1999, Apple started working on what has become the iPod. In 1999, the Sony Walkman was the premiere portable device for listening to music, but it had limitations. It required that users purchase and carry the CD with them. Further, even if listeners liked only one or two songs, they had to listen to all songs or frequently change CDs. Yet, it was the only alternative in the marketplace. In October 2001, Jobs announced what is now called the first-generation iPod. It was a radical, and not inexpensive, departure. The first iPod cost $400 and held 1000 songs. Criticisms were many, but it sold, and within 3 years the iPod had more than 80% of the digital music player market share.

More important, Jobs had looked at the music industry, saw it was in disarray, and reinvented the way people select, purchase, and listen to music. As innovative as the iPod was for listening to music, iTunes was revolutionary for purchasing music. Suddenly, individuals could purchase a single song, an album, or several albums, all without ever leaving their computer. They then plugged their iPod into their computer and it synched with iTunes. White earbuds became all the rage. Even look-alike MP3 players began to sport white earbuds. The music industry also saw it as a way to improve its lagging sales, even if record labels weren't happy with the idea of selling single songs. By 2009, Apple had sold more than 1 billion songs on iTunes and had expanded to music videos, movies, podcasts (a market that did not exist in 2001), audio books, and more. In addition, a whole secondary marketplace grew up around the iPod and has become a multibillion-dollar industry. Today's automobiles frequently include music jacks for the iPod or similar players or they have a dock in which to place the iPod.

Listening Online

The iPod, by some accounts, peaked in sales in 2005 and in 2009 still holds 70–80% of the music download market.[d] Several forecasters see a decline in traditional iPod sales over the next 5 years. Listening online has become the new wave. Music providers such as Pandora.com or Last.fm are growing in subscribership and are generating most of their revenues from online ads flashed in the Web browser. The growth of wireless has allowed connections to be made to mobile devices, including cell phones. Pandora has apps (applications) for the iPhone, Blackberry, Palm, Windows Mobile, and the Android. Where Internet listening was once restricted to the computer, it is now available to many with smart phones.

What People Want

The Pew Internet and American Life project has identified five kinds of "free" selling points for digital music consumers that are driving the music industry and its future. These include (1) *cost* at zero or approaching zero; (2) *portability* to any device; (3) *mobility* via wireless access to music; (4) *choice*, providing access to any song ever recorded; and (5) *remixability*, allowing the freedom to remix and mashup music.[e]

Questions to Consider

1. How long do you listen to music each day? During which parts of the day do you listen to music?
2. Where do you get your music?
3. What type of device do you use to listen to your music? How has that changed since you were a middle school student?
4. How is what you use to listen to music different from what your parents used?

Sources

a. Alan J. Hartnick, "Has the Recording Industry Really Abandoned Unlawful Downloaders?" *New York Law Journal* (9 April 2009), as reported in M. Madden, *The State of Music Online: Ten Years after Napster* (Washington, DC: Pew Internet and American Life Project, 2009): 10. http://pewinternet.org/Reports/2009/9-The-State-of-Music-Online-Ten-Years-After-Napster.aspx.
b. M. Madden, *State of Music Online, 10.*
c. Ibid., 6.
d. C. Arthur, "Twilight of the iPods," Guardian.co.uk (9 September 2009). www.guardian.co.uk/technology/2009/sep/09/apple-ipod-digital-music-sales.
e. Madden, *State of Music Online*, 4.

the final blog was written by her sister who reported the personal power the blog provided her sister of being able to share with others during the final months of her life.

By 2009, 69% of Americans, or 88% of Internet users, were using the Internet to deal with the recession. The Internet is a tool people can turn to when times are challenging. It has immediate information about jobs, allows people to shop for bargains, provides information on government benefits, offers information about how to upgrade skills, and allows people to look for housing options. The Internet provides a quick and relatively easy way to investigate options and opportunities, conduct research about alternatives, and search out the best sources of information. The Internet was frequently reported as the most-used source for gathering information, ahead of television and radio, financial professionals, friends, family, newspapers, magazines, and books.[31]

A number of implications result from technology that park and recreation professionals need to consider. They include, but are not limited to, the following:

- Teens are less engaged in traditional recreation activities than their predecessors. They are more engaged in technology-based activities such as creating Web pages, posting photos and videos on social network sites, modifying music, sharing music, and being involved with their peers through the Internet and instant messaging.
- There is greater competition for an individual's time. The notion of "free time" is almost a lost term. Technology has made this generation the most connected in history.
- Community members want active involvement, even if it is through the Internet. They do not want to be talked to, but talked with. The same is true for participating in programs offered by public and nonprofit agencies.
- Communicating images, program information, and building brands is far more difficult because of the plurality of communications alternatives. Sending home flyers through the public schools, sending brochures out in the mail, and advertising on traditional

television stations will no longer reach the desired public. Knowledge about how different groups communicate, where they get their information, and how that information is determined to be important becomes essential for public agencies attempting to reach community members.

- Understanding the old "word-of-mouth" model is magnified a hundred- or even thousandfold is essential. Administrators used to believe that one person could influence five to eight people he or she came in contact with. Today that one person can influence thousands and even hundreds of thousands without ever making physical contact with people. Images of organizations and their public goodwill can be positively or negatively influenced by minor as well as major events.
- Public park and recreation agencies must learn to think and act in a digital age. Members must embrace technology as an important part of their operation, but more important, they must understand how their community members have embraced technology, whether they be 92 or 2. This suggests professionals need to be flexible and able to transition between digital natives, digital immigrants, and digital refusers.

Technology is influencing recreation and leisure in ways that were never imagined. As park and recreation professionals embrace technology, they do so from multiple perspectives: Professionals need to ask, (1) "How can technology help me?"; (2) "How can I use technology to help our community, residents, and program participants?"; (3) "How do I reach those who we are not reaching or those who chose not to take advantage of our services?"; and (4) "How do we position ourselves to make the most of technology today and in the future?"

Environmental Challenges

Americans have and continue to struggle to think beyond their borders. As a group, they, for the most part, fail to see a global picture as it relates to the environment. Americans are not alone in this narrow view of the world, yet they seem to epitomize a lack of concern for the environment. Whether it be a loss of open space, the continued purchasing of gas-guzzling vehicles, or a supersized approach to living and buying, it seems our indifference amid our wealth is considered by some of the world community as selfish and inexcusable.

Environmental Concerns

Outdoor recreation activities such as camping, biking, backpacking, boating, hunting, fishing, skiing, and mountain climbing depend heavily on parks, forests, and water areas operated chiefly by public recreation and park agencies. The concern of many people regarding the health of the nation's outdoor resources stems from more than the need for outdoor recreation spaces. LaPage and Ranney point out that one of the most powerful sources of America's essential cultural fiber and spirit is the land itself: "The roots of this new nation and its people became the forests and rivers, the deserts and mountains, and the challenges and inspirations they presented, not the ruins of ancient civilizations most other cultures look to for ancestral continuity. Thus, America developed a different attitude and identity."[32]

For such reasons, the environmental movement receives strong support from many recreation advocates and organizations. At the same time, it is recognized that such activities as fishing and hunting are part of a bigger scene requiring clean—and safe—air and water and wise use of the land.

Growing national concern about the need to protect the environment was buttressed by the 1962 report of the Outdoor Recreation Resources Review Commission. During the following two decades, there was a wave of federal and state legislative action and funding support in the United States that was designed to acquire open space; to protect imperiled forests, wetlands, and scenic areas; to help endangered species flourish; and to reclaim the nation's wild rivers and trails. This movement was threatened during the early 1980s, when a new administration sought to reduce park and open space funding, eliminate conservation programs and environmental regulations, and subject the outdoors to renewed economic exploitation. In the mid-1990s, and again under the second Bush administration in the early- and mid-2000s, the effort to open protected wilderness areas to increased oil drilling, cattle grazing, lumbering, and other commercial uses gained strong political support. The election of Barack Obama and the ascendence of the Democratic party is changing the recent neglect of the environment to one of support and action. Federal agencies are already responding to recognition that climate change is a real issue. For example, the U.S. Forest Service and U.S. Fish and Wildlife Service have developed action plans for climate change.

Organizations such as the nonpartisan League of Conservation Voters, National Audubon Society, National Wildlife Federation, Wilderness Society, Sierra Club, and Nature Conservancy have been in the forefront of the continuing battle to protect the nation's natural resources. Numerous outdoor recreation organizations have joined with such groups, and the struggle will clearly continue to be an important political issue in the years ahead.

As the world celebrated Earth Day 2000, 30 years after the first Earth Day in 1970, it was clear that North American air was cleaner and its water purer than it had been for many past decades. There was more protected open space in national parks, wildlife refuges, and wilderness areas yet there is still cause for concern. Americans are purchasing large inefficient vehicles at a faster rate than ever before. It has only been with the sharp increase in gasoline prices that went above $5.00 per gallon and the recession beginning in 2009 that Americans finally began to turn away from expensive and gas-guzzling motorhomes and large automobiles. Government, at all levels, has embraced the presence of global warming and is joining the international community in efforts to reduce impacts on the environment. Yet, Americans are growing away from their traditional environment ethic. Attendance, over a period of 5 years, is down at state and national parks, children are not exposed to the natural environment, and campers who do stay in the parks in their motorhomes demand electricity, water, sewer, and cable and broadband hookups. Going outdoors is no longer fashionable. America's appreciation of the outdoors and the environment is clearly in jeopardy. Yet, organizations, individuals, researchers, and governments are finding ways to make people aware of the importance of the outdoors in their lives. Governments and schools are creating campaigns and educational requirements introducing and encouraging families and youth to return to the natural environment.

Environment and Population The United States represents just 5% of the world's population and consumes almost 25% of every natural resource—more than any other nation in the world.[33] Americans have the largest "ecological footprint" of any country in the world.[34] Beyond this, the United States is the only industrial country still experiencing rapid growth and projections are that this will not end soon. "These include U.S. demographic factors—relatively high population numbers and rapid growth; high and increasing density in coastal and metropolitan areas; an increase in energy-consuming households, and a large 'Baby Boomer' population—coupled with high per-capita energy use, fossil fuel burning, land and vehicle use."[35]

Population growth at current levels has the potential to negate efforts to reduce impact on the climate. Even as federal, state, and local governments move forward with plans to reduce greenhouse emissions, the continued rapid growth of population in high-density population centers and centers of ecological vulnerability may offset gains in addressing climate change. **Figure 13.3** illustrates the impact of population on energy consumption and greenhouse gases. Compared to the world and developing countries our contributions to global warming, on a per-capita basis, are staggering. The United States accounts for almost half (46%) of the annual carbon dioxide emitted into the environment and represents the primary cause of global warming. Americans produce 5 pounds of garbage per day; five times the average amount in developing countries.[36]

The Center for Environment and Population suggests that the United States is now a metro nation, a "lifestyle [that] differs from urban-centered lifestyles in that it requires extensive use of motor vehicles and rapid, extensive land development."[37] The McDonalds influence on U.S. culture to supersize everything has moved from french fries to houses, shopping centers, recreation centers, and land and resource consumption. The Center goes on to report, "the 'supersized' lifestyles of so many people affect the quality of everyday life causing, among other things, more frequent, worse traffic jams, and expenditure of more money and effort to heat and keep-up more and/or larger homes."[38] The impact on recreation is not lost. Demand for recreation facilities, park areas, and access to these is growing in metropolitan and adjacent areas. Congestion in this country's premiere natural resources

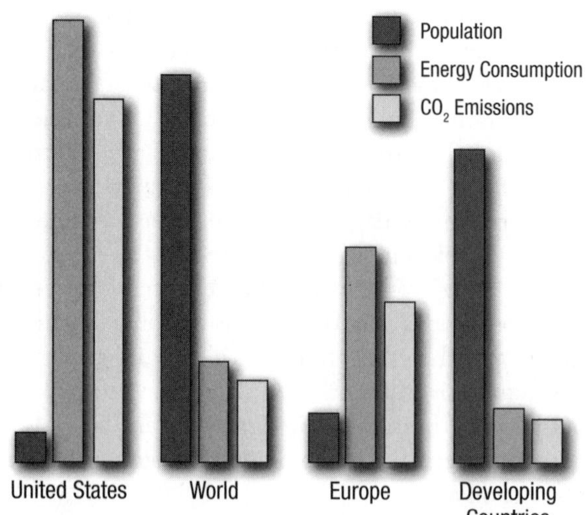

FIGURE 13.3 U.S.–World Population and Climate Change. Data from U.S. Census Bureau, U.S. Energy Information Administration, World Resources Institute, 2008.

has been well documented by the National Park Service and similar patterns are occurring at the state and community levels.

A Metropolitan Nation

The United States has become a metropolitan nation, or a MetroNation, characterized by 100 metropolitan areas ranging in size from New York City at 12 million people to places like Lansing, Michigan, with a population of 500,000. Every state has at least one metropolitan area. That is a staggering thought when one thinks of the Intermountain West and the Great Plains where you can still drive for hours between major cities. The Brookings Institution states that metropolitan areas account for two-thirds of America's jobs (75% of the U.S. output). Sixty-five percent of the population lives in the top 100 metropolitan areas, which includes 85% of the immigrants and 77% of the minorities.[39]

CASE STUDY: City Parks' Grand Rebirth: St. Louis

City sponsors were so nervous about the unveiling of their new downtown park this summer that they arranged for an ice cream truck to park at the site on opening day, just to attract passerbys. They needn't have bothered. Citygarden, just west of the famed Gateway Arch on the Mississippi River, has drawn crowds of people—a cross-section of the city and region's population—from its opening hour onward.

The city of St. Louis was revitalized with a new downtown park.

The attractions include a cornucopia of trees, contemporary sculpture, an 180-foot rectangular basin with a six-foot waterfall, a state-of-the-art "spray plaza," a state-of-the-art LED video wall displaying art and movies, plus a high-quality cafe overlooking the combined attractions.

What this new park doesn't have are any formal entrances or barriers to separate its manicured paths and quiet spaces from the surrounding city streets. Richard C.D. Fleming, president of the St. Louis Regional Chamber and Growth Association, suggests it's an "intimate version of Millennium Park," the Chicago lakeside extravaganza opened in 2004.

For St. Louis, for years so forsaken its downtown had the feel of a big and mostly empty living room, the public's warm embrace of Citygarden caps a remarkable comeback decade, which has seen the center city draw 5000 residents and more than $4 billion in new investment.

But there's no single formula for new parks. Just climb up a short flight of stairs to the newly-opened "High Line" park on Manhattan's West Side. You'll find clusters of families and couples strolling, chatting, sipping lemonade, and nibbling on waffles or sandwiches along what for years constituted a desolate and weed-choked stretch of abandoned elevated freight railroad track.

Now, from the meandering concrete walkways of this sliver of protected park space in the sky, the visitor catches stunning views of the Hudson, the Statue of Liberty, Midtown and Wall Street skyscrapers, plus amazingly intimate glimpses into the forbidden interiors of nearby apartments, stately townhouses, and offices.

Or check auto-happy, sprawling Houston. Two-term Mayor Bill White has made parks a top priority. Lead example: Discovery Green, 12 once-industrial acres on the east side of downtown. Among Discovery Green's features: a shaded walkway featuring 100-year-old oak trees, thematic gardens with native Texas plants, birds and butterflies, fountains and spacious green lawns, a model boat basin, a children's stage, WiFi everywhere, and two restaurants. Plus lots of people watching.

Indeed, if there were ever a bonanza decade for America's parks, this is surely it. Add stunning new parks in Boston, Atlanta, Cincinnati, Denver and Santa Fe, plus the success of conservancies in revamping great old parks in such cities as Pittsburgh, Brooklyn, and San Francisco.

And by good fortune, there's a skilled chronicler tracking and analyzing the wave—Peter Harnik, parks expert for the Trust for Public Land and author of a soon-to-be published Island Press book on today's parks phenomenon.

For almost a half century, Harnik notes, the reigning American park model was Disneyland—"corporate, programmed, extravagant, rural, flawless and electrifying." City parks "began grinding down relentlessly everywhere" as people realized "the park experience could be sanitized, social classes could be segregated."

So why the big turnaround now? Partly it's the "wow" in the new city parks—fascinating gardens, theaters, concerts, fountains, and ice skating. That's why, says Harnik, the 2004 opening of the Millennium Park in Chicago had the biggest impact on the American parkland scene since New York's great Central Park opened in 1873.

But Harnik insists there's more to the revival—that we're seeing a revival of factors "ignored in the din of massive suburbanization and sprawl—human scale, walkability, efficiency, and respect for ecological principles and democratic ideals." Or put another way, we're reawakening to parks' ultimate value: "an interplay—a conversation–between people and nature."

And as if that's not enough, new and revived parks bring massive associated benefits. The parks embellish cities' reputations and become "must see" destinations for tourists. And they turn into meeting places not just for city residents, but magnets for visitors from across their metro areas.

It's true, new parks can be tremendously expensive. Millennium Park's pricetag—borne jointly by the city of Chicago and private donors—was close to a half billion dollars.

But, insists Harnik, parks make huge financial sense. Property values close to new park locations rise vigorously—a development recognized soon after Central Park's opening in the 19th century and now an established factor of urban economics.

But there's more. Citizens get free recreation and services. Tourism booms. And government gains by parks' stormwater management, air pollution control, cooling of the urban "heat island" effect, and contributions by volunteers. Harnik added all those up for Philadelphia's park system, ranging from the city's massive Fairmount Park and Independence National Historical Park to neighborhood gardens. The total, he calculated: $1.9 billion a year. Mayor Michael Nutter concurred: "A well-run, properly funded and focused park system is priceless."[a]

Questions to Consider

1. How do well-designed urban park systems contribute to community well-being?
2. Are urban parks important to a community? Why? Why not?
3. Describe a park you have been to as a child or recently and how it influenced you.

Source

a. Neal Peirce, "City Parks' Grand Rebirth," Citiwire.net (6 September 2009). http://citiwire.net/post/1293/.

Wal-Mart Challenges the Way Americans Light Their Homes

In late 2006, Wal-Mart made a decision to change Americans' buying habits for lightbulbs. For more than 100 years, Americans have purchased the traditional lightbulbs even though for more than 10 years CFL or energy-saver fluorescent bulbs have been available. A CFL uses 75% less electricity, lasts 10 times longer, produces 450 pounds fewer greenhouse gases from power plants, and saves consumers $30 over the life of each bulb, but they don't produce the same level of light or as strong a light as traditional lightbulbs. Wal-Mart took it upon itself to sell 100 million bulbs by 2008. Efforts such as this by major retailers can help to overcome some of the negative aspects of global warming. Success of the venture would save Americans $3 billion in electricity costs and avoid the need to build additional power plants for 450,000 new homes.

Open Space Loss and the Environment The environment is coming under increasingly difficult challenges, both as a part of national policy, and among Americans as a whole. In Iowa, the state government gives new homeowners a five-year tax relief if they purchase a new home on previous open space or farmland. Between 1992 and 1997, the United States paved over more than six million acres of farmland, an area approximately the size of Maryland. Americans experience a daily loss of 3000 acres (1214 hectares) of farmland over the last decade. Land converted for development occurs at twice the rate of population growth. We have become a nation of sprawl represented by low-density development in the suburbs and exurbs. The exurbs are growing at a rate almost three times that of urban areas.

Youth prefer computers to the outdoors. Parents are afraid to send their children outdoors because they too have lost their outdoor ethic. As a society, Americans have almost fully transitioned from a generation raised on or near farms to a generation raised in an urban environment. Like a zoo or museum, the outdoors is a place to visit and see, but not to partake of. Scares such as polluted beaches, Lyme disease, wasting disease in elk, and others have encouraged parents already unfamiliar with the outdoors to keep their children

Urban sprawl consumes 6000 acres of land daily.

home. Attendance at national parks, national forests, state parks, and other rural recreation and preservation areas has been on decline at a time when the population is increasing (see **Table 13.5**). The influx of immigrants without an outdoor ethic has affected the response to wilderness, outdoors, and preservation. This has been reflected in Congress as it has become more difficult to secure funds for park and recreation lands. For example, the Arctic National Wildlife Refuge is continuously under attack by politicians and oil interests in an effort to open the area to increased oil production.

Former Vice President Al Gore has become a leading spokesperson for the environment and climate change. His comments have helped focus much debate and most importantly have, for the moment, recharged some of America's concern about the environment. Although Al Gore is the most visible person to address environmental concerns, he is not alone. Many national associations focusing on the environment are encouraging individuals to express concern and demand action. Often this action is local and even bounded by the property owned. The National Wildlife Federation encourages individuals to certify their backyards for wildlife. The Audubon Society encourages individuals to take the healthy yard pledge by reducing pesticides, conserving water,

TABLE 13.5

CHANGES IN ATTENDANCE AT STATE AND NATIONAL PARKS COMPARED TO TOTAL POPULATION GROWTH

				Percent Change in Relation to Total Population	
Year	State Parks	National Parks	Population	State Park	National
2007	730,067,000	275,600,000	300,913,000	–1.16%	–1.04%
2005	725,361,000	273,500,000	295,507,000	–9.92%	–6.94%
2000	766,842,123	279,900,000	281,424,602	–3.45%	–1.66%
1995	752,266,297	269,600,000	266,557,000	–5.76%	–2.76%
1990	744,812,234	256,700,000	248,718,302	13.04%	–5.83%
1985	631,746,699	263,400,000	238,466,000		

Data from the National Association of State Park. Available at: http://www.naspd.org; National Park Service. Available at: http://www.nps.gov; and U.S. Census Bureau. Available at: http://www.census.gov. Accessed November 11, 2010.

planting native species, protecting water quality, and supporting birds and other wildlife.

Many of the same organizations that are promoting local environmental awareness and action are also active at the national and international levels.

Loss of Environmental Ethic Discussed elsewhere in this book, the loss of the environmental ethic by Americans is very real. A 2005 Harris Poll indicates that 74% of Americans agreed that "protecting the environment is so important that requirements and standards cannot be too high, and continuing environmental improvements must be made regardless of cost."[40]

At the same time, Americans appear to be participating at a lower rate in traditional visits to state and national parks. Table 13.5 shows a mixed picture of attendance with a decline between 2000 and 2005 for state and national parks. The right-hand columns compare park attendance to the reported U.S. population. The comparison shows that the percentage of Americans visiting state and national parks is in decline. It would appear that visiting these areas is becoming either less important to or out of the reach of Americans. The numbers remain large, but the vast majority of state and national parks are in remote areas, not close to urban populations. Some data suggest as much as 50% of visits to some national parks are international tourists, and repeat visits by individuals counts for another large portion of the data. The current recession may cause some change in those behaviors.

The data are incomplete for 2009, but during the recession from 2008 to 2010 some federal agencies, including the National Park Service (NPS) and Bureau of Land Management (BLM) declared select days as *free admission* days and simultaneously reported increases in attendance. Some state park systems are also reporting increased attendance. Florida and Kentucky were two states reporting increases in state park attendance, citing the recession as partially contributing to the increase. In Florida, from July 1, 2008, through June 30, 2009, attendance was up 3.5%, or 700,000, over the previous year.

The number of visitors to national parks is down.

The issue is less clear than it might at first appear. Attendance may be down for state and national parks, yet the willingness of Americans to vote for funding for parks and open space remains high. From 2000 through 2009, Americans voted $95.9 billion in 1540 local and state elections, 74% which were successful, providing funding for parks and open space acquisition, maintenance, and operation. **Table 13.6** shows the number of referenda voted on between 2000 and 2009. The amount of funding approved in almost 50 states is staggering. In years when large amounts have been approved by voters, it frequently involved a statewide initiative and ballot supporting conservation funding. The difference between total funding and conservation funding, as described by the Trust for Public Lands, is

TABLE 13.6

SUMMARY OF MEASURES BY YEAR

Year	Number of Measures	Number of Measures Passed	Total Funds Approved	Conservation Funds Approved
2000	209	171	$11,240,270,431	$4,993,222,298
2001	198	138	$1,802,683,640	$1,369,510,437
2002	192	142	$8,573,159,162	$5,486,074,357
2003	133	99	$1,771,740,328	$1,255,696,985
2004	218	163	$26,107,658,413	$3,972,214,265
2005	141	111	$2,618,811,630	$1,598,003,889
2006	183	136	$29,081,167,202	$6,705,777,535
2007	99	65	$2,244,755,926	$1,951,415,707
2008	128	91	$11,102,766,340	$8,047,714,140
2009	39	24	$1,059,164,056	$607,668,083
2010	13	11	$208,501,068	$66,495,084
Total	1553	1151	$95,810,678,196	$36,053,792,780

Data from Trust for Public Lands, "Access TPL Land Vote Database." Available at: http://www.tpl.org/tier2_kad.cfm?folder_id=2386. Accessed November 11, 2010.

important to understand. The total funds include support for "parks and playgrounds, farmland preservation, watershed protection, trails and greenways, forests, and wildlife habitat" as primary examples. Conservation funding is more narrowly focused, looking at, "measures that preserve natural lands, create parks, and protect farmland."[41] These are state, county, and local endeavors where voters choose to tax themselves to provide open spaces and parks. The vast majority of the funds were for acquisition of lands. The money has not been equally distributed across the United States. The Northeast, the largest center of population in the United States, has voted for considerably more measures than any other region. Does this mean local spaces are more important than national or state places? Probably not, but there are clearly shifts in preferences and only part of those shifts can be attributed to ethnic and cultural influences.[42]

In addition to federal, state, and local agencies providing recreation and park opportunities and places, there are many watchdogs of government agencies. The federal government's handling of environmental issues that affect national parks and wilderness areas has been a particular area of criticism. The National Environmental Trust has pointed to air quality significantly diminishing the quality of individual experiences of visitors. They point to a 27-year-old requirement administered by the Environmental Protection Agency that has not been enforced. The Natural Resources Defense Council points to the impact of climate change on western U.S. national parks stating,

> Many scientists think the American West will experience the effects of climate change sooner and more intensely than most other regions. The West is warming faster than the East, and that warming is already profoundly affecting the scarce snow and water of

> the West. In the arid and semi-arid West, the changes that have already occurred and the greater changes projected for the future would fundamentally disrupt ecosystems. The region's national parks, representing the best examples of the West's spectacular resources, are among the places where the changes in the natural environment will be most evident. As a result, a disrupted climate is the single greatest threat to ever face western national parks.[43]

Climate Change as an Archetype of Global Environmental Issues Humans have affected the environment as never before. The 1997 Kyoto Protocol named after an international conference convened in Kyoto, Japan, is often credited as the most significant environmentally based international agreement of the twentieth century. The essence of the agreement was for developed nations to reduce their greenhouse gases (CO_2 emissions) to 5% below their 1990 levels and for less-developed countries to be allowed to make a lesser contribution to reductions. Of the 166 countries that signed the protocol, only the United States and Australia refused to ratify it. Other countries including India and China and other smaller developing countries were exempt from the protocols because most greenhouse gases are coming from developed countries.

There are various agreements and discussions occurring regarding the environment on an international scale. The Kyoto Protocol and global warming are an archetype of issues facing the world today and into the twenty-first and twenty-second centuries. A longer list of environmental issues includes loss of diversity (biodiversity), ocean and fresh water pollution, clean air issues, the impact of urban environments, the loss of forests and most especially tropical rainforests, and the impact of megadisasters such as the tsunami impacting the coasts of Indonesia, India, and other countries in 2004, or Hurricane Katrina's devastation along the Gulf Coast of the United States.

Climate change impacts our daily lives, including rush hour traffic in crowded areas.

The Obama administration initiated a major change in the United States involvement in the global climate change debate. It has moved the country from an almost nonparticipant to a major stakeholder and player in efforts to address and manage global warming. The federal government has created a Global Change Research Program (www.globalchange.gov) composed of 13 departments and agencies. The agency existed under another name from 2002 through 2008 and reports directly to the president. Its function is to coordinate and integrate federal research on changes in the global environment with potential implications for society. The United States, over the last 20 years, has not ignored global climate change but has quietly made the "world's largest scientific investment in the areas of climate change and global change research."[44]

In June 2009, the agency issued its *Global Climate Change Impacts in the United States* report. It suggests:

> Climate-related changes have already been observed globally and in the United States. These include increases in air and water temperatures, reduced frost days,

increased frequency and intensity of heavy downpours, a rise in sea level, and reduced snow cover, glaciers, permafrost, and sea ice. A longer ice-free period on lakes and rivers, lengthening of the growing season, and increased water vapor in the atmosphere also have been observed. Over the past 30 years, temperatures have risen faster in winter than in any other season, with average winter temperatures in the Midwest and northern Great Plains increasing more than 7°F. Some of the changes have been faster than previous assessments had suggested."[45]

Key Findings of Climate Change Impacts on the United States

The *Global Climate Change Impacts in the United States* report provides 10 key findings that are already present and will potentially intensify in the future.

- Global warming is unequivocal and primarily human-induced.
- Climate changes are under way in the United States and are projected to grow.
- Widespread climate-related impacts are occurring now and are expected to increase.
- Climate change will stress water resources.
- Crop and livestock production will be increasingly challenged.
- Coastal areas are at increasing risk from sea-level rise and storm surge.
- Threats to human health will increase.
- Climate change will interact with many social and environmental stresses.
- Thresholds will be crossed, leading to large changes in climate and ecosystems.
- Future climate change and its impacts depend on choices made today.[46]

Impact of Nature on People's Lives: Issues of Wellness, Well-Being, and Human Development The environmental concerns discussed earlier go beyond issues associated only with the environment. It has become personal for many who have recognized the absence of involvement with nature negatively affects human growth and development, especially among children. Numerous researchers have begun to link environmental and ecological issues to health and well-being outcomes for individuals and society as a whole.

Richard Louv, with the publication of *No Child Left in the Woods: Saving Our Children from Nature-Deficit Disorder* became the spokesperson for a growing movement to reconnect children with nature. The term *nature-deficit disorder* captured the imagination and has become a rallying cry to address the issues of children, and adults, who are becoming more separated from nature with every generation. Daily contact with nature has become the exception rather than the norm. There are a number of reasons for the decline in contact with nature, including the loss of natural areas in and near urban areas, the absence of

Climate Change and Recreation: Consequences and Costs

Americans who like to play outdoors may soon find that climate change–induced warming trends around the nation will put some of their favorite recreational retreats in jeopardy—from trout streams to waterfowl preserves, from ski areas to mountain biking trails, and from beaches to forested parkland. "Climate impacts on natural resources are pervasive," write Daniel Morris and Margaret Walls in a background paper titled, "Climate Change and Outdoor Recreation Resources." Their paper highlights the stresses climate change will put on water resources, which could result in reduced mountain snowpack levels; increased drought conditions across public lands; decreased waterflows into streams, reservoirs, and wetlands; and forests weakened against fire and insect infestations.

Walls, a senior fellow at Resources for the Future (RFF), and Morris, an RFF research assistant, included a number of possible scenarios, among them:

Snowpack: Extended warm seasons may result in more rainfall than snow, which would reduce skiing and snowboarding opportunities, particularly in comparatively warmer areas in California, Nevada, Arizona, and New Mexico.

Fresh waterways: Reduced snowpack and more rain in winter months would mean earlier spring runoff into streams and reservoirs. That could mean less fresh water flowing in the summer months, when sport fishing and boating are most popular. Fishing depends on water temperature, streamflow levels, and ecological quality, while boating is more sensitive to lake, reservoir, and stream levels.

Noncoastal wetlands: Stretching across 216 million acres of the northern plains and Canada, these wetlands are rich sources of many species of ducks and other waterfowl. By one estimate, lower water levels caused by climate change in the Upper Great Lakes could reduce regional duck populations by nearly 40% in the area.

Beaches: Rising sea levels over time could reduce the size of beachfront recreation areas, national seashores, and coastal waterways, the authors find. A full 85% of tourism-related revenues in the United States are generated by coastal states.

Forests and parks: Tree cover, particularly in the western United States, is already feeling the impact of climate change, particularly as a result of drought. Insects have decimated millions of acres of evergreens in the Rocky Mountain region, and dryness has fueled damaging wildfires. Tree dieoffs also resulted in closures of campgrounds, trails, and picnic areas in public parks.

What is clear, the authors conclude, is that impacts from climate change will vary among such leisure pursuits as skiing, camping, boating, fishing and hunting, outdoor sports such as golf, and wildlife viewing. That prospect may require more assertive efforts by public officials to adapt policies that will help preserve outdoor recreation areas.

"Longer and warmer summers are expected to increase the demand for outdoor recreation, from hiking, fishing, hunting, and camping to simple beach visits," the authors write. "This makes it all the more important that government policy at all levels develop climate adaptation programs and funding."[47]

parks close to where people live, the over-scheduling of children, safety concerns, more homework, and fear of stranger-danger.[48]

Louv suggests several factors influencing the amount of time children spend in nature including the following:

- The explosive growth of electronic media, later identified as videophilia[48]
- The increasingly litigious nature of American society creating risk-averse managers and citizens who prevent or limit various nature experiences (e.g., climbing trees, building tree forts)
- The prevalence of neighborhood covenants that place severe limitations on what, where, and when children can play outdoors
- The climate of fear generated by intense media attention of child abduction cases
- The longer work and commuting hours of parents and increased amount of scheduled activities for children that create time constraints
- The explosive rate of land development in the past two decades and the corresponding lack of nearby nature (i.e., vegetation and open space with natural features in close proximity to urban residents) in the developed areas

Children need to experience the outdoors, not be protected from it.

The loss of contact with nature results in additional health and wellness issues for children. Some of the results include increasing levels of obesity in children and adults; a decline in physical, social, and mental well-being; issues of psychological well-being; linkages to attention deficit disorder in children and adults; increasing levels of stress; and lowered immunity to illness. Some argue that this may be because of the pace of life throughout the world, but the literature on nature, wellness, and well-being increasingly confirms the need for contact with nature, even if it is just a small green space.[49]

The correlation of the absence of nature in our lives with the developmental growth of children has raised a concern among public health officials, child development specialists, urban environmentalists, and park and recreation practitioners. As stated in a report titled *Healthy Parks, Healthy People*, "An ecological theory of public health recognises that not only is health itself holistic and multidisciplinary, but also that a holistic or multidisciplinary approach is needed to promote and manage health successfully."[50]

Nearby nature refers to the presence or absence of nature in close proximity to an individual. Parks and natural areas in urban environments are seen as important contributors to the opportunity of individuals, and especially youth, to experience nature. The backyard, neighborhood, and areas where individuals, work, play, and go to school are also important. Research is beginning to show that the presence of nearby nature has an impact on individual wellness and well-being.[51] The ideal situation is for individuals to have regular contact with natural areas, but, in the absence of those opportunities, nearby nature in urban environments can have positive mediating effects on individuals.

Childhood Experiences with Nature and Its Influence on Adult Behavior and Attitudes There are indicators that adults who had positive childhood experiences with wild nature have a more positive attitude about the environment than those who had experiences with domesticated nature. Wild nature involves being in an outdoor setting where hiking, camping, hunting, and related activities can occur and these are usually away from urban areas. Domestic nature is more reflective

A family camping trip allows family members to benefit from their connections to the wilderness.

Why Are There So Many Different Terms, and Why Can't Researchers Agree?

Students, practitioners, and the public often ask why researchers cannot agree upon a common terminology when talking about the same issue. It would seem logical to have one set of terms that convey the same meanings. The challenge comes, in part, from the discipline a researcher comes from. For example, when you listen to a police broadcast, you likely not understand the whole conversation. If a police officer communicates with an air traffic controller and each uses his own terminology, neither will gain a full understanding of what the other is saying.

The same is true in the study of nature. It would seem that nature is self-explanatory, and yet it appears to not be. Individual researchers bring different views, academic backgrounds, and experiences to their study of nature. They also may feel that another definition of nature do not adequately describe what they are seeing or researching. For example, Kellert defines experiences in nature. The terms *direct*, *indirect*, and *vicarious* fit his research agenda, one he has written about for over 30 years. Wells, by contrast, comes from a different perspective, and her wild and domestic nature describes a setting as well as an opportunity for experience.

Even within a discipline there are different terms for different types of areas. For example the National Association of State Park Directors defines 15 types of outdoor recreation areas. None of the 50 state park systems have adopted the same classification system. Their classification systems are the product of historical development, legislative mandate, influence from other sources, and individual influences and perceptions.

How does one know which terminology to use and which to disregard. Most often researchers will adopt the terminology of their discipline, mix terminologies between disciplines, or, if they feel their area is unique, create their own terminology. Even with this latter approach there is a foundation for the new terminology within the research literature. As a reader of research you need to recognize that there are differences and you need to discern those differences in our reading and come to understandings of how the researcher intended the terms use.

of nearby nature in that it is at or close to home and may involve flowers, planting trees, shrubs, a garden, or caring for indoor plants. The frequency of involvement in such activities is also important. A single camping experience has little long-term impact, whereas repeat camping experiences influence future environmental attitudes and visits.[52] However, although it would be expected that frequent visits to wild nature as a child would carry over to adult behaviors. That is not necessarily the case. Visits to wild nature as a child are not a good predictor that such activities will continue into adulthood. However, lack of visits to wild nature as a child is a predictor that as adults they are less likely to visit wild nature. The research suggests that adults who continue to visit wild nature do so for opportunities for physical activity and emotional and spiritual renewal.[53]

The connotation from this research strongly suggests the importance of wild nature experiences among youth. Further, such experiences are strengthened when youth are with their parents. Sending children to a regimented camp has a lesser impact on youth and their future perspectives of the environment. In camp settings, natural experiences are lessened and group experiences are strengthened, which may or may not be related to the camp setting. Kellert's work regarding nature and childhood development is groundbreaking. His identification of direct, indirect and vicarious experiences with nature frame much of the research currently conducted. Where the previous paragraphs discussed wild nature and domestic nature, Kellert frames the same descriptions as direct, indirect, and vicarious contact with nature. **Table 13.7** describes each of the types of contact with nature with examples. Similar to other research, he finds that direct contact as having the most significant impact on individuals, regardless of age; indirect contact has a lesser impact, but is still positive; and vicarious contact has an influence, but one considerably less than direct or indirect contact.[54]

The importance of childhood experiences with nature is more evident and cannot long be ignored. As others have suggested, the absence of experiences with nature, at any level, causes potential health, wellness, and well-being issues for children and adults, but especially

TABLE 13.7

TYPES OF CONTACT WITH NATURE

Type of Contact	Description	Examples
Direct	Interaction with large self-sustaining features and processes in the natural environment	Relatively unmanaged areas such as forests, creeks, sometimes a backyard or park
Indirect	Involves actual contact with nature occurring in highly controlled environments dependent on ongoing human management and intervention	Highly structured, organized and planned occurring in zoos, botanical gardens, nature centers, museums, parks
Vicarious	Symbolic experiences of nature not involving contact with actual living organisms or environments, but rather with the image, representation, or metaphorical expression of nature	A teddy bear, various cartoon and book characters, Mickey Mouse, *Lassie*, films focusing on nature, television programs such as on the Discovery Channel

Adapted from S. R. Kellert. *Building for Life: Designing and Understanding the Human–Nature Connection*. (Washington, DC: Island Press, 2007).

for children. In 2008, politicians reacted to the need to provide children with nature experiences when the U.S. House of Representatives Education and Labor Committee voted in June to send the *No Child Left Inside Act* (HR 3036) on to the House floor for a full vote. The legislation was unsuccessful, but the message was clear.

Benefits and Outcomes of Contact with Nature Our understanding of the benefits and outcomes of contact with nature is growing as additional research is conducted. Forty years ago, few people outside of leisure scientists and landscape architects explored the importance of outdoor recreation. Today, the list of those researching this area includes experts in public health, early childhood education, child psychology, urban planning, medicine, psychology, and sociology, among others. A number of authors discuss the benefits and outcomes of participation in natural settings. **Table 13.8** depicts what Maller calls contributions of parks to human health and well-being. The categories expressed in Table 13.7 are generally agreed upon by researchers, even if different terms are used.

Park and recreation agencies have the opportunity to take the lead in providing direct and indirect contact with nature for individuals. The approach demands creativity and a willingness to challenge the norm. Godbey provides a list of policy recommendations for enhancing direct and indirect contact with nature including planning for outdoor recreation

TABLE 13.8

A SUMMARY OF THE CONTRIBUTIONS OF PARKS TO HUMAN HEALTH AND WELL-BEING

Component of Health	Contribution of Parks
Physical	Provide a variety of settings and infrastructure for various levels of formal and informal sport and recreation, for all skill levels and abilities, e.g., picnicking, walking, dog training, running, cycling, ball games, sailing, surfing, photography, birdwatching, bushwalking, rock climbing, camping
Mental	Make nature available for restoration from mental fatigue; solitude and quiet; artistic inspiration and expression; educational development (e.g., natural and cultural history)
Spiritual	Preserve the natural environment for contemplation, reflection, and inspiration; invoke a sense of place; facilitate feeling a connection to something beyond human concerns
Social	Provide settings for people to enhance their social networks and personal relationships from couples and families, to social clubs and organizations of all sizes, from casual picnicking to events days and festivals
Environmental	Preserve ecosystems and biodiversity, provide clean air and water, maintain ecosystem function, and foster human involvement in the natural environment (Friends of Parks group, etc.)

C. Maller, C. Henderson-Wilson, A. Pryor, L. Prossor, and M. Moore. *Healthy Parks Healthy People: The Health Benefits of Contact with Nature in a Park Context: A Review of Relevant Literature*. 2nd Edition. Burwood, Melbourne. Deakin University and Parks Victoria. Reprinted with permission.

in urban areas involving schools and recreation and park departments, public health, transportation, public utilities, hospitals, and nonprofit environmental organizations.[55] Maller states, "Parks, in fact, are an ideal catalyst for the integration of environment, society, and health (which have been demonstrated to be inextricably linked) by promoting an ecological approach to human health and well-being based on contact with nature."[56]

Public park and recreation organizations, environmental- and outdoor-based nonprofits, and federal land management and protection agencies traditionally have been proponents of protection and rationality. The organizations sometimes have been at odds, especially at the national level when the executive branch of government has been perceived as unfriendly to the environment. Local government has a mixed response to environmental issues and city, county, and state agencies have not provided the level of leadership that once was common. Park and recreation agencies can provide leadership by example in their communities in the twenty-first century.

Globalization of Leisure Globalization has been equally called a blessing and a curse, sometimes by the same person. In the context of change, globalization is a relative newcomer. Economists first used the term in the early 1980s. Globalization is frequently referred to as the Americanization of the world. However, another more popular view sees globalization as the integration of economic, political, cultural, and environmental systems and structures worldwide. From a leisure perspective, cultural and environmental influences have the greatest potential for current and future impacts.

Environmental globalization viewed from a protected-areas perspective provides a good example of globalization impacts. In the United States, we call protected areas parks, wilderness areas, national parks, state parks, national forests, and the like. Internationally, they are called protected areas. The International Union for the Conservation of Nature (IUCN) (www.iucn.org) defines a *protected area* as "an area of land and/or sea especially dedicated to the protection and maintenance of biological diversity, and of natural and associated cultural resources, and managed through legal or other effective means."[57] The impetus for protected areas originated with the United States National Park Service, which early on was, and continues to be, a leading proponent of creating protected areas. Early models tended to follow a national parks format. Environmentalism is not independent of its social context and is linked with other social and economic issues, politics, and competitions. The globalization of protected areas was initially Americanization based, but the movement matured and the American model is but a single model that has been shared globally. Other models have evolved that fit the cultural, economic, and environmental issues of host countries. The IUCN developed a list of types of protected areas that applies to most areas internationally. The six types of areas are listed in **Table 13.9**. In some instances, protected areas have been created and indigenous populations continued to live on and utilize the lands as they have done for generations. In other instances, transnational boundaries have been crossed where two or more countries joined together to create a larger protected area. The globalization of environmentalism as related to protected areas has benefited from the ability to share models, lessons learned, adaptation to local settings, and the greater awareness a global perspective brings to resource managers.

Tourism provides the most easily identifiable impact of globalization. Some have even suggested that globalization is replacing sustainability as an organizing concept for tourism. According to Reiser, tourism and globalization have numerous examples of

TABLE 13.9

PROTECTED AREA MANAGEMENT CATEGORIES

CATEGORY Ia **Definition**	Strict Nature Reserve: protected area managed mainly for science Area of land and/or sea possessing some outstanding or representative ecosystems, geological or physiological features and/or species, available primarily for scientific research and/or environmental monitoring.
CATEGORY Ib **Definition**	Wilderness Area: protected area managed mainly for wilderness protection Large area of unmodified or slightly modified land, and/or sea, retaining its natural character and influence, without permanent or significant habitation, which is protected and managed so as to preserve its natural condition.
CATEGORY II **Definition**	National Park: protected area managed mainly for ecosystem protection and recreation Natural area of land and/or sea, designated to (a) protect the ecological integrity of one or more ecosystems for present and future generations, (b) exclude exploitation or occupation inimical to the purposes of designation of the area and (c) provide a foundation for spiritual, scientific, educational, recreational and visitor opportunities, all of which must be environmentally and culturally compatible.
CATEGORY III **Definition**	Natural Monument: protected area managed mainly for conservation of specific natural features Area containing one, or more, specific natural or natural/cultural feature which is of outstanding or unique value because of its inherent rarity, representative or aesthetic qualities or cultural significance.
CATEGORY IV **Definition**	Habitat/Species Management Area: protected area managed mainly for conservation through management intervention Area of land and/or sea subject to active intervention for management purposes so as to ensure the maintenance of habitats and/or to meet the requirement of specific species.
CATEGORY V **Definition**	Protected Landscape/Seascape: protected area managed mainly for landscape/seascape conservation and recreation Area of land, with coast and sea as appropriate, where the interaction of people and nature over time has produced an area of distinct character with significant aesthetic, ecological and/or cultural value, and often with high biological diversity. Safeguarding the integrity of this traditional interaction is vital to the protection, maintenance and evolution of such an area.
CATEGORY VI **Definition**	Managed Resource Protected Area: protected area managed mainly for the sustainable use of natural ecosystems Area containing predominantly unmodified natural systems, managed to ensure long term protection and maintenance of biological diversity, while providing at the same time a sustainable flow of natural products and services to meet community needs.

Dudley, N. (Editor) (2006). *Guidelines for Applying Protected Area Management Categories*. Gland, Switzerland. IUCN. x + 86 pp. Available at: http://data.iucn.org/dbtw-wpd/edocs/PAPS-016.pdf. Accessed December 2, 2010.

World Heritage Places

Heritage is the legacy of the past, what we live with today, and what we pass on to future generations. Cultural and natural heritage are both irreplaceable sources of life and inspiration. Places as unique and diverse as the wilds of East Africa's Serengeti, the Pyramids of Egypt, the Great Barrier Reef in Australia, and the Baroque cathedrals of Latin America make up the world's heritage. Eighty-one countries have designated World Heritage Site in them.

What makes the concept of world heritage exceptional is its universal application. World Heritage sites belong to all the peoples of the world, irrespective of the territory on which they are located. How can a World Heritage site in Egypt "belong" equally to Egyptians and to the peoples of Indonesia and Argentina?

The answer is to be found in the 1972 convention concerning the protection of the world cultural and natural heritage, by which countries recognize that the sites located on their national territory, and which have been inscribed on the World Heritage List, without prejudice to national sovereignty or ownership, constitute a world heritage "for whose protection it is the duty of the international community as a whole to cooperate."

Without the support of other countries, some of the world's outstanding cultural and natural sites would deteriorate or, worse, disappear, often through lack of funding to preserve them. The convention is thus an agreement, ratified almost universally, that aims to secure the necessary financial and intellectual resources to protect World Heritage sites.

How does a World Heritage site differ from a national heritage site? The key lies in the words *outstanding universal value*. All countries have sites of local or national interest, which are quite justifiably a source of national pride, and the Convention encourages them to identify and protect their heritage whether or not it is placed on the World Heritage List. Sites selected for World Heritage listing are inscribed on the basis of their merits as the best possible examples of the cultural and natural heritage.

The list of United States World Heritage sites is reflective of the country's national treasures and includes the Grand Canyon, Everglades, Hawaii Volcanoes, Mammoth Cave, Yellowstone, and Great Smokey Mountains National Parks. It also includes national monuments such as the Statue of Liberty, Monticello and the University of Virginia, and Independence Hall. The United States ranks fourth internationally in the number of acres designated as World Heritage Sites, behind Australia, the Russian Federation, and Canada.[58]

connections (see **Table 13.10**) and include "the movement of people, the movement of ideas and the movement of capital across borderlines."[59] Tourists, or visitors, come with a set of expectations and are frequently challenged by the experiences. Visitors to Guatemala's Mayan cultural sites are often surprised by the tourist maps overlaid with transnational corporation logos. It moves the perception of a colonial site to a transnational site, potentially affecting the visitor's experience. In heritage tourism, the plazas and barrios of Central America are the traditional gathering spots of local residents. His-

TABLE 13.10

TOURISM AND GLOBALIZATION: EXAMPLES OF CONNECTIONS

Tourism	Globalization
Movement of people (tourists, workers in tourism industry)	Movement of people (immigrants and their cultures)
Movement of ideas (new cultural values with tourists; ways of doing business in tourism industry)	Movement of ideas (new technologies across the globe)
Movement of capital (tourism industry investment; foreign exchange earnings through tourism)	Movement of capital (instant movement of capital across borderlines)
Needs new technology to expand (wide-bodied jets)	Spread of new technology around the globe
Started at the latest in ancient Greece (limited to particular groups in society)	Started with first movement of humans (from Africa to Indonesia in 17,000 years using some of their original tools, maybe domesticated animals, etc.)
Enormous growth in the last 100 years	Time-spaced compression, in particular in the last 30 years
Toward traveling as a right for everyone; development of a world tourism culture?	World tourism culture?
Tourism needs local culture, or at least the image of it (differentation between destinations)	Toward a world culture

Source: D. R. Williams. "Leisure Identities, Globalization, and the Politics of Place," *Journal of Leisure Research* (Vol. 34, No. 4, 2002): 351–367.

toric sites are residential areas, or as one described these areas, the communal urban "front porches" that globalization is changing.

The impact of globalization on culture is significant and challenges long-held traditions, mores, and customs. It has been suggested that globalization is a time–space compression, emphasizing the way modernity restructures time–space relations and uproots social meanings and identities.[60] Globalization is changing the way we view, interact, and respond to the world. It has forced individuals and organizations to rethink their role in the homes, communities, and society. Williams argues that, "by recognizing modernity's fragmenting and disorienting qualities we can begin to focus on the strategies people have available and draw onto assemble a coherent narrative of self."[60]

Time, Economy, and Leisure

The Changing Nature of Time The growth of individual discretionary time, sometimes referred to as free time or time without obligation, has long been considered a major influence in the increased participation in recreation activities. Between 1900 and 1995, the growth in leisure time was steady, if not spectacular. Freedom from an agrarian economy, increased holidays, paid vacations, and shorter workweeks combined to give people more opportunities for participation in recreation than at any time in history. A debate about the actual availability of free time began in the early 1980s and continues. Today the 40-hour workweek is nonexistent for many. Manufacturing firms frequently mandate 20 or more hours of overtime for their employees. Corporate executives, midlevel managers, supervisors, and service employees experience a 24/7 (24 hours a day, 7 days a week) work life. The digital age has made everyone more accessible. The introduction of electronic communications exemplified by the iPhone has made the Internet available anywhere and any time. Smart phones now provide continuous connectivity. Business travelers use their smart phones until flight attendants ask everyone to turn off their electronic devices, and then they turn off the cell phone function and use the device to take notes, work offline, watch videos, read books, and listen to music. Vacations no longer provide time away from work, just time away from the office.

With a lack of leisure time, Americans feel the need to multitask.

The availability of discretionary time is based on age, education, gender, and the presence or absence of a disability. Children, those wo are unemployed, and retirees have considerably more discretionary time than do individuals who are in the workforce. Children have less discretion about what they might participate in and older adults' physical, mental, or economic condition may limit their ability to participate in some recreation activities. Professionals and those with a college education typically work fewer hours than those in nonprofessional jobs, such as in the service industry, manufacturing, construction, and the like. Many individuals with severe disabilities have limited opportunities to explore a range of recreation activities but have long enforced hours of free time.

The Bureau of Labor Statistics maintains annual data on how people use their time. The American Time Use Survey (ATUS) is released annually and measures the average amount of time per day that individuals worked, did household activities, cared for household children, participated in educational activities, and engaged in leisure and sports activities. Personal care, including sleep, is the largest consumer of individual time. During the weekdays, work is the largest waking time-consumer, with leisure and sports a close second. On weekends, leisure and sports are the largest activity time is spent on, although about half of this time is spent watching television. (See **Table 13.11**.)

Several issues related to the perception of time have become more apparent in recent years. *Time deepening*, *time compression*, and *time famine* have entered the vocabulary of researchers, leisure providers, and the general public. Time deepening suggests more efficient use of the time available by engaging in several activities simultaneously, such as driving and talking on the cell phone, or watching a television show and knitting at the same time. Time compression is a perspective that relates to acceleration of time and making experiences seem shorter. It is related to technology and by some, it is suggested as the

TABLE 13.11

DISTRIBUTION OF HOW PEOPLE USE THEIR TIME, 2008 AVERAGES

Activity	Weekday	Percentage	Weekend	Percentage
Personal care	9.10	38.59	10.17	42.98
Eating and drinking	1.18	5.00	1.35	5.71
Household activities	1.57	6.66	2.08	8.79
Purchasing goods and services	0.71	3.01	0.91	3.85
Caring for and helping household members	0.57	2.42	0.44	1.86
Working and work-related activities	4.74	20.10	1.38	5.83
Educational activities	0.61	2.59	0.14	0.59
Organizational, civic, and religious activities	0.25	1.06	0.53	2.24
Leisure and sports	4.62	19.59	6.48	27.39
Telephone calls, mail, and e-mail	0.23	0.98	0.18	0.76
Total	**23.58**		**23.66**	

Data as of November 20, 2009, from Bureau of Labor Statistics, "American Time Use Survey." Available at: http://www.bls.gov/tus. Accessed December 1, 2010.

driver of lifestyle changes. Going on a picnic with the family used to be an all-day activity where the focus was on the family. Today mom and dad bring their cell phones, talk to other people, make plans, respond to e-mail, and so forth, while children play with their hand-held game devices. At the end of the day, the family feels they have had little time together. Time famine is present when an individual has insufficient time to accomplish all of the tasks required for work and living. Time famine is particularly prevalent among people in jobs demanding large amounts of a person's available time.

Layered on top of time compression, time famine, and time deepening is technology and how it has changed people's lifestyles. Social networking tools such as Facebook, Twitter, Flickr, blogging, and the ability for smart phones to "push" e-mail and other information to consumers means that people no longer have empty free time. In a sense, free time, or time with no obligation, has ceased to exist for some people. With the implementation of these mobile technologies, people attempt to maximize the content available in every minute, increasing the pace of their lives. The inability to keep up with all of the available information results in increased anxiety, stress, and feelings of time famine.

The feelings of time compression and time famine lead many to believe that they have less time available than preceding generations did. With the exception of a small%age of people, most people have more discretionary time available today than at any time in history. The term *real time* is one reflection of today's perception of time. Real time "applies not to any device but to the technologically transformed context of everything we do. Real time is characterized by the shortest possible lapse between idea and action, between initiation and result."[61]

National Affluence—and Decline! The dramatic growth of the gross national product (GNP) and personal income between 1990 and 2004 had a significant impact on consumer spending on recreation. The gross national product more than doubled; personal consumption expenditures almost tripled. During this same period, poverty fluctuated between 12.1% and 15% of the total U.S. population.

Recreation expenditures, as shown in **Table 13.12**, have continued to grow. Data for late 2008 and 2009 are not available, but it is expected that all sectors of spending within the economy have slowed or declined. Three areas have shown strong growth and are related to technology (computers, music, video devices), spectator experiences, and amusement parks or other commercial amusement experiences. Expenditures as a part of total personal consumption (all dollars spent for personal use) represented 6.6% of all expenditures in 1985, and in 2006 grew to 11%. When one recognizes that the Commerce Department's figures do not include hundreds of billions of dollars spent on travel and tourism,

TABLE 13.12

ANNUAL PERSONAL SPENDING ON RECREATION, 1985–2005

Type of Product or Service	1985	1990	1995	2000	2005	2006
Total Recreation Expenditures (billions of dollars)	116.3	290.2	418.1	585.7	746.9	791.1
Percentage of total personal consumption	6.6%	7.6%	8.4%	8.7%	8.6%	8.6%
Books and maps	6.5	16.2	23.2	33.7	41.8	43.4
Magazines, newspapers, and sheet music	12	21.6	27.5	35	42.1	45.0
Nondurable toys and sport supplies	14.6	32.8	44.4	56.6	66.5	71.4
Wheel goods, sports and photographic equipment	15.6	29.7	39.7	57.6	76.2	78.9
Video and audio products, computer equipment and musical instruments	19.9	53	81.5	116.6	142.3	151.5
Video and audio goods, including musical instruments	n/a	44.1	57.2	72.8	85.8	90.1
Computers, peripherals, and software	n/a	8.9	24.3	43.8	56.5	61.4
Flowers, seeds, and potted plants	4.7	10.9	14	18	19.2	19.9
Admissions to specified spectator amusements	6.7	14.8	19.2	27.3	38.7	39.9
Motion picture theaters	2.6	5.1	5.5	8.1	9.5	9.3
Legitimate theater and opera and entertainments of nonprofit institutions	1.8	5.2	7.6	9.8	13.2	13.4
Spectator sports	2.3	4.5	6.1	9.3	16.0	17.2
Clubs and fraternal organizations, except insurance	3.1	13.5	17.4	19	23.7	23.9
Commercial participant amusements	9.1	25.2	48.8	75.8	106.8	115.3
Parimutuel net receipts	2.3	3.5	3.7	5	6.2	6.6
Other (includes lottery receipts, pets, cable television, film processing, sports camps, video rentals)	19.4	65.4	93.4	133.9	178.7	190.0

All numbers, except for the second, are in billions of dollars. Hence, 116.3 represents $116,300,000,000.
Data from the U.S. Census Bureau of Economic Analysis, "Statistical Abstract of the United States, 2009," Table 1193. Available at: http://www.census.gov/prod/2008pubs/09Statab/arts.pdf. Accessed December 6, 2010.

gambling, liquor, and less easily measured forms of amusement or the operational expenses of thousands of public, nonprofit, and private leisure-service agencies, it is apparent that total leisure spending is substantially higher than the amounts shown in the table. Table 13.12 shows the distribution of expenditures for personal consumption in 2006. Recreation represents the largest expenditure of the perceived disposable income and reflects a continuing growth over a 20-year period.

The recession of 2008–2010 brought the U.S. economy to the brink of financial disaster. The billions of dollars put into the economy by the federal government prevented greater suffering and financial loss. Retail sales showed lackluster performance through the early summer of 2009. Sales tax growth, a primary source of income for state and local governments, has been in decline since 2006 and is not projected to show a recovery for 2 to 3 more years. The National League of Cities (NLC) reported that 9 of 10 cities are challenged in meeting their 2009 needs and expect it to continue through 2010. In February 2009, those 83% responding to an NLC survey indicated a need to cut expenditures. In another report, 84% of cities reported they are less able to meet financial needs, the highest percentage so reporting in the 20-year history of the report. Parks and recreation, along with libraries and events, ranked fourth nationally among services to be cut or curtailed.[62]

In a time of economic crisis, the question sometimes asked is, "Can we afford parks and recreation?" The answer is yes. This book is a validation of the importance of leisure in the lives of individuals, families, communities, states, and the nation. The question is not, "Can we afford parks and recreation?" but rather, "In this time of economic uncertainty, how can parks and recreation help heal the fabric of the community?"

Growth of Special Interest Groups: Influences of the Internet

Throughout this chapter discusses influences of the Internet, media, and social networking on leisure and recreation. As these influences have affected how leisure and recreation services are delivered, they have also affected how people interact and react to the debate about services, needs, and future directions. Previously, the Long Tail phenomenon was discussed and applied to recreation participation. The same principle applies to efforts to support, influence, and change the recreation experience, services, and programs. Social networking, for example, has allowed individuals and small organizations to influence policy, decision making, and planning. Before the Internet, special interest groups were not always well organized and struggled to make their voices heard at local and national levels. That has changed considerably as small, local, and traditional groups, such as the Sierra Club, National Trust for Historic Preservation, and the Environmental Defense Fund, have embraced the use of the Internet as a social networking tool. At their web sites one can join; sign up for a newsletter; download specialized information; discover what is going on in the community; find information for special events, trips, and activities; be alerted to proposed local, state, and federal changes in laws and rules; and provide financial support. Where an organization previously would send out letters or make phone calls, both time consuming, it can now send e-mail and tweets alerting interested parties.

The explosion of involvement by special interest groups is having a profound impact on how public agencies, at all levels, look at their delivery of services. For the most part, special interest groups have a positive impact on recreation and leisure. Organizations can more effectively coordinate with the groups, track involvement, and draw upon their interests. **Figure 13.4** is a mind map depicting types of social interest groups that might affect recreation, leisure, and parks. Each of the trunks branching off from the center identifies a major type of special interest group. Twenty years ago, this same mind map might have had only two or, at most, three trunks. Special interest groups are challenging recreation and leisure organizations to rethink and expand their view of services and programs. In the 1990s, when the benefits of the parks and recreation movement was emerging, the number of researchers was small. Today, expanding on the notion of benefits, there are literally hundreds of organizations involved in addressing, researching, and applying the benefits message. The term *benefits*, however, is less prominent as groups external to the recreation and leisure profession have addressed these topics from their own academic discipline. For example, positive psychology (in the process of being renamed positive science) draws heavily on leisure research literature. Yet discussions of the use of positive psychology are all but absent from the mainline recreation and park literature. At a recent conference involving hundreds of people from across the world, fwer than five leisure researchers were present.

Other groups are having an equivalent influence, or lack of, on the leisure and recreation profession. The Active Living Research initiative directs research toward the elimination of childhood obesity in low-income and high-risk racial/ethnic communities. The Robert Woods Johnson Foundation, sponsor of the program, has focused its funding efforts on directing research on these topics.

Leisure Delivery in the Twenty-First Century

The beginnings of the twenty-first century held little indication of how the latter part of the first decade would bring changes that may have long-term influences on the profession. At the community level, public parks and recreation programs are being challenged to survive in many communities. As the economy shows signs of recovery, local and state governments have yet to feel the elusive benefits of economic growth. What defined

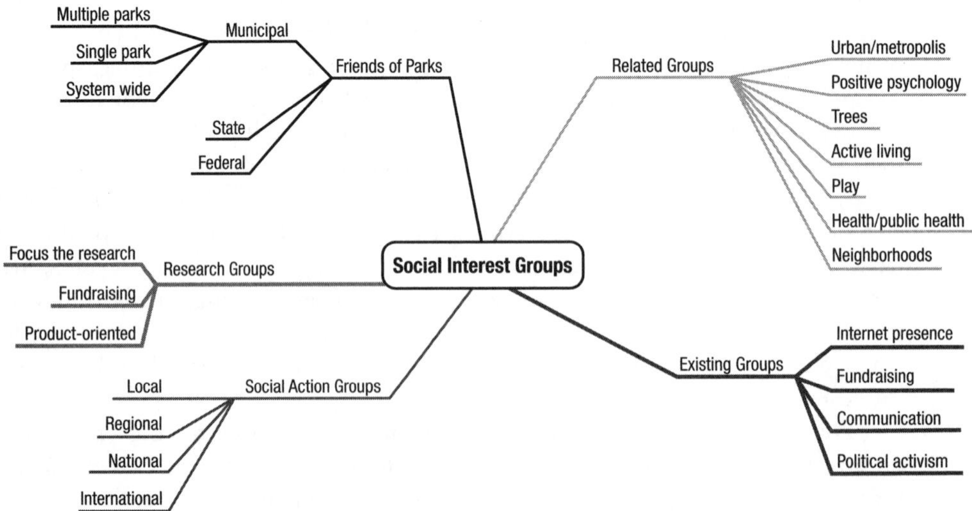

FIGURE 13.4 Mind Map Illustrating Special Interest Groups

economic growth at the start of the decade does not define economic growth at the beginning of the second decade of this century. Reduction of services, closing of facilities and parks, furloughs, and elimination of staff are becoming accepted tools to deal with the economic decline. Nonprofits are finding ways to secure funding particularly challenging while simultaneously attempting to provide desperately needed services to a growing number of unemployed and underemployed. As real unemployment topped 17%, nonprofits became even more critical to individual survival. Commercial enterprises have not been immune to the changing economic climate. Many have closed their doors, other have looked for alternative income opportunities, either by expanding their services or looking in new markets.

The unanswered question facing the leisure-services profession is what the future will look like. However, by looking at the past we can glean some ideas for the future. The recent recession may be the worst since the Depression of the 1930s, but there are parallels in the 1960s and 1970s that we can draw on. Organizations will recover, tax income will increase, staff will be expanded, new facilities and services will be designed, built, and operated. It has happened before and it will happen again. That is the one constant that economists agree on. However, how governments, nonprofits, and commercial enterprises structure and deliver their services most assuredly will change from what has been done in the past. New models are already emerging, partnerships are becoming more common, and new sources of revenue generation will be created.

The recession of 2009 impacts current recreation opportunities.

In the 1930s, leisure and recreation were seen as critical to the success of the New Deal and to society. Whether that will be the same today is unknown, but early trends suggest it is unlikely. Public safety continues to receive the majority of available tax dollars. People want to feel safe. Recreation and leisure, essential elements of quality of life, fall much lower on individual taxpayers' perception of need. After almost 100 years, one might expect that the profession would have done a better job of positioning itself. The conclusion to that statement remains to be seen.

Commodification of Leisure The contrast in leisure opportunity among the rich, the middle class, and the poor is heightened by what has been termed the "commodification" of leisure. Increasingly, varied forms of play today are developed in complex, expensive forms by profit-seeking businesses. More and more, giant conglomerates such as Time Warner, Disney, and Viacom have taken control of huge corporations that run music, television, and movie businesses. These conglomerates also own sports stadiums, professional sports teams, cruise ships, theme parks, and other leisure enterprises.

Many elaborate new facilities offering varied forms of recreation are being developed as part of the trend toward commodification. In cities throughout the United States, huge public fitness centers that include aquatic areas, aerobics and dance rooms, and facilities for family play and a host of other activities are being built—often with charges for membership that cost several hundred dollars a year. Glenview, Illinois, operates a 100,000-square-foot community recreation center. The Plainfield, Indiana, Parks and Recreation Department constructed a $25 million indoor community center with fitness area, family aquatic center (indoor and outdoor), meeting rooms, and much more. Many other recreation centers or programs operated by public recreation and park agencies today require the payment of substantial fees that exclude the poor from participation.

Lippke shares concerns about the effects of commercialization of leisure on individuals and society.[63] He suggests individuals "are subtly and not so subtly encouraged to indulge themselves in a consumption binge that, temporarily at least, distracts them from the cares and concerns of everyday life." The problem lies not with the distraction, but with the use of such leisure-time activities to replace what leisure theorists have called personal development, creativity, and flow. Lippke suggests that the commercialization of leisure promotes a lack of self-development, an increase in the inability of persons to direct their own lives as they become dependent on external stimulators. Third, the effects on social life are that people focus on shallow relationships such as are promoted on today's reality-based television shows including *American Idol*, *Fear Factor*, and *Survivor*. The Harris Interactive Poll reports that teens particularly find reality television a common ground for discussions with other teens. In 2006, 70% of surveyed teens watched *Fear Factor*, 67% watched *American Idol*, and other reality shows fared well.[64] Commercialization of recreation has created a competition for everyone to have the same things, or what one author calls, "sneer group pressure." The cell phone marketplace is an example. The ever-increasing "all-in-one" cell phone has captured the market as youth in particular desire the newest and coolest. Finally, there is confusion about values and what is important. Advertisers and sellers of commercialization create expectations among potential buyers that life should be "filled with glamorous, exciting, or dramatic moments."[63]

Recreation's Integration into the Health, Fitness, and Well-Being Movements A key trend continuing in U.S. society is public interest in well-being, exercise, and physical fitness programs. Well-being, discussed previously, is being embraced by the leisure profession in recognition of the need for and importance of individuals improving their lives beyond just the physical. Well-being embraces the physical, emotion, and psychological domains with a holistic approach. Well-being has been defined from an ecosystem perspective as follows: "Human well-being has several key components: the basic material needs for a good life, freedom and choice, health, good social relations, and personal security."[65] Research on well-being is increasing, and not just in the leisure field. Such diverse fields as psychology, medicine, environmental studies, and sociology have linked well-being to leisure and recreation and park places.

Realizing that modern life is frequently inactive, sedentary, beset by tensions, and subject to a host of unhealthy habits such as overeating, smoking, and drinking, popular concern developed about improving one's health, vitality, and appearance through diet and exercise. Participation in such activities as walking, aerobics, swimming, running and jogging, racket sports, and similar vigorous pursuits has more than physiologic effects. It also has psychological value: Those who exercise regularly look and feel better. Experts conclude that fitness is not a passing trend; the public's desire to be healthy and physically attractive is supported by continuing publicity, social values, personal vanity, and solid business sense.

Research shows that the most successful fitness programs are likely to be those that provide an ingredient of recreational interest and satisfaction. The National Recreation and Park Association (NRPA) recognizes the value of fitness and health and sponsors local involvement in Step Up to Health: Start in the Parks, a nationwide fitness program delivered by local park and recreation agencies. Each agency is to develop fitness programs that encourage employee and community participation. Sandy, Utah, held a sprint triathlon that included a 400-yard swim, a 9-mile bike ride, and a 5-kilometer run. Columbus, Georgia, sponsors two annual festivals, one in the spring and one in the fall, to encourage fitness in the parks. The Decatur, Illinois, Park District hosted a teen fitness summit. NRPA provides more than 60 examples of programs on its Web site.

Certain recreational sports, such as youth soccer, volleyball, and ice hockey, have grown in popularity. Among high school boys, football remains the most popular sport, with more than 1 million participants in more than 13,000 high schools. Among girls, basketball is the most popular sport, with more than 450,000 participants in more than 17,000 schools. Sport participation in organized high school athletic programs is at an all-time high for girls and boys. Participation levels have grown at a steady rate for more than 30 years. At the same time, a growing number of state school systems have reduced or eliminated physical education requirements, which means that organized recreation programs represent an even more important means of promoting physical in children and youth.

Maturation of an Organized Leisure-Services Field The nature of municipal, state, and federal governments has changed dramatically in the nearly 140 years of organized recreation in the United States. Today's city government is markedly different from that of previous generations. Government is more dependent on alternative income sources and less reliant on taxes. Public park and recreation agencies have, of necessity, become entrepreneurial. Where few fees once existed, now public agencies are dependent on fees and charges to make up as much as 90% of their operating budgets. Parks and recreation agencies are hard pressed to serve all of those who either desire or have a need for services. Nonprofit and commercial agencies fill the gap in many instances. In today's environment of rapidly changing demand for different types of leisure activities, public, commercial, and noprofit organizations strive to respond, but often public and nonprofits do not have the resources, financial capital, or ability to respond. Commercial enterprises typically respond more quickly to what initially may appear as fringe activities such as paintball, skateboarding, laser tag, and the like.

Maturation does not suggest the organized leisure-services field is not changing, but rather that growth in the public and nonprofit sector is constrained by available funds, politics, public interest, and the perceived opportunity for growth. Public and nonprofit agencies have developed an infrastructure of parks, recreation centers, sports fields, cultural centers, and more that becomes a burden to the agencies preventing them from rapidly changing. The traditional programming of public and nonprofit agencies remains in place, although there is less of it, and more of the emerging programs, but change is coming slowly. Where communities once built a 50-meter swimming pool, today they build a small to medium waterpark, except when politicians or other influential groups intervene and demand a traditional or old-fashioned approach. The leadership is changing and new, younger leaders are emerging. Values are being reassessed, commitments rethought, demands evaluated, and expectations challenged. Ten major categories of service providers make up the mature leisure-service delivery system:

1. *Public agencies:* Federal, state, and local departments of recreation and parks provide leisure services as a primary function, as well as hundreds of other agencies (such as those concerned with social service, education, special populations, and the armed forces) offer or assist recreation programs as a secondary responsibility.
2. *Nonprofit organizations:* Nongovernmental, nonprofit agencies, both sectarian and nonsectarian, serve the public at large or selected elements of it with multiservice programs that often include a substantial element of recreational opportunity. Such organizations include national youth programs such as the Boy Scouts and Girl Scouts and the YMCA, YWCA, and YM-YWHA (Young Men's–Young Women's Hebrew Association).
3. *Private-membership organizations:* Golf, tennis, yacht, athletic, and country clubs, along with a wide range of service clubs and fraternal bodies, provide recreational and social activities for their own members and in some cases assist community recreation needs as well. Under this heading are the recreation sponsors connected to residence, as in the case of swimming pools, sport or fitness complexes, or clubs attached to leisure villages, apartment or condominium units, or retirement communities.
4. *Commercial recreation enterprises:* A great variety of privately owned, for-profit businesses, such as ski centers, bowling alleys, laser tag centers, Internet cafés, nightclubs, movie houses or theaters, health spas or fitness centers, dance schools, amusement or theme parks, and other enterprises, provide leisure services.
5. *Employee recreation programs:* These programs serve those who work for given companies or other employers by providing recreation, often as part of a total personnel benefits package linked to other services concerned with employee health and fitness.
6. *Armed forces recreation:* Although it is obviously a form of government-sponsored activity, armed forces recreation is unique in its setting and purpose. Each of the major branches of the armed forces tends to operate an extensive network of recreation facilities and programs worldwide. In times of national emergency, the demand for these services is even greater.
7. *Campus recreation:* Campus recreation includes intramural athletics or sports clubs, social activities, trip-and-travel programs, performing arts groups, entertainment, lounges, film series, and numerous other forms of recreation on college and university campuses.
8. *Therapeutic recreation services:* Therapeutic recreation is any type of program or service designed to meet the needs of persons with physical or mental disabilities, individuals with poor health, dependent aging persons, socially deviant persons in correctional facilities or other treatment settings, and similar special groups.
9. *Sport management:* Sport management services encompass professional sports, collegiate sports, public parks and recreation, private sport enterprises, youth sports, sports for individuals with disabilities, and the many other forms of sport.
10. *Tourism and hospitality management:* All of the travel and tourism industry, such as airlines, cruise ships, destination resorts, conference and resort centers, amusement parks, festivals, and the like, comprise this category.

CASE STUDY: Contemporary Issues Facing Public Parks and Recreation

Recently, at a national think tank, various authors were asked to address what they saw as the key issues facing public parks and recreation over the next 10 years. One respondent's perceptions are provided here.

1. *What is the most significant driver affecting how and why we provide parks, recreation and leisure services now, and how has it changed since you entered the field?*
   I entered the parks and recreation field in the summer of 1965 as a playground crafts specialist and later as a playground leader. Those three summers in a California community introduced me to the whole idea of providing public service programming for community members. By 1983, two degrees and three positions later I was director of a separate recreation department in a community of 100,000. The lessons of my first position, my study, the observation of the field were not lost. We had moved from a almost fully tax-funded profession to one that was dependent upon entrepreneurism, creativity, strategic partnering, and other tools designed to increase revenue. We were still mandated to provide a certain level of services free to the public, but targets for revenue generation were common and frequently challenging. Today I live in a large western metropolitan area dotted with neighborhood recreation centers where programmers are striving to provide services, where budgets still drive the ability of departments and centers to provide services, where revenue generation, grant writing, and fundraising are paramount. While we have entered a new era of public parks and recreation, I find as I view public agencies that there is a great diversity of how departments operate, determine accountability, deal with politics, and are funded. There remains much to learn.

   The recreation profession is as diverse today as any multinational corporation and in the interim we have begun to lose our foundation. Gray and Greben said in 1974, "The accounting mind reaches decisions by a method in which short range fiscal consequences are the only criteria of value. Recreation and park services will not survive in that kind of environment."[a] Agencies are surviving, but original identities and purposes are becoming more challenging to maintain as we embrace the post-accounting era.
2. *What are the top three industry challenges for the next 10 years?*
   Identifying three industry challenges over a 10-year period suggests a level of stability and normality that has not existed for the last 30 plus years. However, there are some broader issues that need and must be addressed by all agencies during that period. They are sustainability, legitimacy, and connectivity to the customer.

   We live in a period when the operative commitment of many politicians is to reduce taxes, reduce government involvement in citizen's lives, and strengthen private enterprise simultaneously while citizens expect and demand greater levels of services from government. The legitimacy of the parks and recreation profession is relatively questioned by government. The ability and willingness for government to pay for it, however, is questionable. Few public agencies today can say they have sufficient funds to operate. At the same time competition for the leisure dollar is growing—whether it be from commercial enterprises, nonprofit organizations, or parent-based sport and other groups. Legitimacy is the ability to be defended with logic or justification of the existence and viability of public parks and recreation. Some agencies are doing this well, but from a macro perspective, too many public agencies struggle with the ability to justify their current position and are not building constituencies that can give them the political and economic capacity to flourish in the future.

   Sustainability is, from a narrow perspective, about financial, resource, people, and programs. For public park and recreation agencies sustainability must include environmental concerns and the profession must be at the forefront. The greater issue, however, is the social and economic sustainability essential for long-term operations. After observing public agencies at the local and state level, I've come to believe that new models of financial sustainability must be created and adapted to fit the needs of the many types of agencies providing parks and recreation.

Connectivity to the customer is an emerging issue. The parks and recreation profession must fully embrace the experience economy, what marketers call managing the total customer experience. The concept of the experience economy will allow public agencies to look at the leisure experience from a new and creative perspective. It will change customer service, program delivery, front office operations, and the whole notion of dealing with the public. It is an essential and necessary change.

3. *What are the top three industry opportunities for the next 10 years and why?*
The top three industry opportunities for the next 10 years—let's say 5 since that is a more realistic and achievable window of opportunity—are (1) expansion of the concept of the leisure experience, (2) integration of well-being (authentic happiness) into recreation programming, and (3) creating opportunities for authenticity by visitors to parks, participants in recreation programs, and drop-ins to community centers.

Questions to Consider

1. How would you justify the presence of public parks and recreation to your community?
2. What do you think are the greatest challenges facing the leisure industry? Why?
3. What do you think are the most significant opportunities available to the leisure industry? Why?

Source

a. D. E. Gray and S. Greben, "Future Perspectives," Parks and Recreaetion (Vol. 9, No. 6, 1974): 26–33, 47–56.

SUMMARY

This chapter moves from the past and the present to focus on contemporary issues, challenges, and the future of leisure and recreation. It begins by focusing on agendas for recreation and leisure in the twenty-first century. Emerging issues related to population include gender, ethnic, racial, and age diversity; demographic shifts; the impact of an aging society; and the changing nature of the family, including children, tweeners, and teens. The discussion moves from demographic issues to other agendas such as where people live and the influence of location on the delivery of recreation and leisure services. Technology has become a major influence on how people use their free time and engage in leisure activities.

The environment, environmental concerns, global climate change, and nature-deficit disorder are all emerging and potentially society-changing challenges. The linking of these issues to nature and well-being is one of the fastest growing areas of concern, especially among urban dwellers and providers of natural areas and environmental experiences.

Other issues that were presented in the chapter focus on globalization of leisure, economic issues, how discretionary time has changed, the growth of special interest groups, and the changing nature of the leisure-service delivery system. All of these issues are cause for concern or opportunity for the leisure profession.

QUESTIONS FOR CLASS DISCUSSION OR ESSAY EXAMINATION

1. Key conclusions of the future of parks and recreation can be viewed as challenges. Select two of these challenges and prepare a report that discusses how society and government have changed and affected parks and recreation. Further, discuss viable alternatives that parks and recreation might utilize to respond to the change.
2. Children, families, and child well-being are contemporary issues being measured by several different organization and a topic of concern among many organizations. How does the presence of these issues affect what recreation organizations should or should not be doing? Research public and nonprofit agencies to determine what they are doing to strengthen families, support children, and enhance child well-being and prepare a report depicting exemplary practices.
3. This chapter presents issues related to environmental change, challenges to the environment, nature-deficit disorder, and an American loss of an individual environmental ethic. Select one of these and do additional library research validating or refuting the claims in this chapter.
4. The Internet has had a tremendous impact on U.S. society and on leisure lifestyles in particular. What are some of its major effects, both positive and negative?
5. The chapter presents a number of predictions for the future with respect to demographic, social, economic, and other challenges. Which of these do you believe presents the most important challenge for the recreation, park, and leisure-service field? In what ways should leisure-service professionals seek to meet them constructively in the twenty-first century?

ENDNOTES

1. Opentopia, "Future." http://encycl.opentopia.com/term/Future.
2. V. D. Markham, *U.S. Population, Energy and Climate Change* (Washington, DC: Center for Environment and Population, 2008): 7.
3. Brookings Institution, *MetroNation: How U.S. Metropolitan Areas Fuel American Prosperity* (Washington, DC: Brookings Institution, 2008): 19.
4. Markham, *U.S. Population*, 6.
5. U.S. Department of Commerce, "300 Million," *Facts for Features* (9 August 2006).
6. Elwood Carlson, *The Lucky Few: Between the Greatest Generation and the Baby Boom* (New York, NY: Springer, 2008).
7. Douglas Knudson, *Outdoor Recreation* (New York: Macmillan, 1980): 31.
8. Stephen Mitchell, "Retirement Evolution: Reexamining the Retirement Model," *LIMRA's Market Facts Quarterly* (Vol. 25, No. 1, 2006): 82–85.
9. Murray Gendell, "Full-Time Work Rises Among U.S. Elderly," *Population Reference Bureau* (Washington, DC: U.S. Census Bureau, April 2006).
10. U.S. Census Bureau, http://www.census.gov.
11. Sarah Burnett-Wolle and Geoffrey Godbey, "Active Aging 101," *Parks and Recreation* (2005): 30–40.
12. C. Maller, M. Townsend, L. St Leger, et al. *Healthy Parks, Healthy People: The Health Benefits of Contact with Nature in a Park Context*, 2nd ed. (Burwood, Melbourne: Deakin University, 2008): 11.

13. Dan K. Hibler and Kimberly J. Shinew, "Moving Beyond Our Comfort Zone: The Role of Leisure Service Providers in Enhancing Multiracial Families' Leisure Experiences," *Parks and Recreation* (Vol. 37, No. 2, 2002): 26.

14. Ching-hua Ho et al., "Gender and Ethnic Variations in Urban Park Preferences, Visitations, and Perceived Benefits," *Journal of Leisure Research* (Vol. 37, No. 3, 2005): 281–306.

15. Kimberly J. Shinew, Myron F. Floyd, and Diana Parry, "Understanding the Relationship Between Race and Leisure Activities and Constraints: Exploring an Alternative Framework," *Leisure Sciences* (Vol. 26, 2004): 188–191.

16. U.S. Census 2000, "Your Gateway to 2000 Census." http://www.census.gov/main/www/cen2000.html.

17. M. Scherer, "On Our Changing Family Values (Interview with Sociologist David Elkind)," *Educational Leadership* (April 1, 1996).

18. Childstats.gov. "America's Children: Key National Indicators of Well-Being, 2009." http://www.childstats.gov/americaschildren/index3.asp.

19. UNICEF, *The State of the World's Children Report* (New York: United Nations, 2004).

20. Childstats.gov. "America's Children."

21. Partnership for a Drug-Free America. http://www.drugfree.org.

22. Harris Interactive, "Parents Changing Roles in Tweens' and Teens' Lives," *Trends & Tudes* (Vol. 2, No. 5, 2003).

23. Harris Interactive, "Kids and Online Privacy," *Trends & Tudes* (Vol. 2, No. 4, 2003).

24. Harris Interactive, "Youth and Mental Health Stigma," *Trends & Tudes* (Vol. 5, No. 9, 2006).

25. Harris Interactive, "The Changing Landscape of Youth Relationships," *Trends & Tudes* (Vol. 5, No. 3, 2006).

26. Center for Information and Research on Civic Learning and Engagement, "Benefits of Volunteering." http://www.civicyouth.org/?page_id=237.

27. C. Walker, *The Public Value of Urban Parks* (Washington, DC: Urban Institute, 2004).

28. Paul Romero, Stuart Hong, and Laura Westrup, "Trends Worth Talking About," California and Pacific Southwest Recreation and Park Training Conference, Sacramento, California, March 2005.

29. J. Horrigan, *The Mobile Difference: Wireless Connectivity Has Drawn Many Users More Deeply into Digital Life* (Washington, DC: Pew Internet and American Life Project, 2009).

30. J. Horrigan and L. Rainie, *The Internet's Growing Role in Life's Major Decisions* (Washington, DC: Pew Internet and American Life Project, April 2006): 1.

31. L. Rainie and A. Smith, *The Internet and the Recession* (Washington, DC: Pew Internet and American Life Project, 2009).

32. W. F. LaPage and S. R. Ranney, "America's Wilderness: The Heart and Soul of Culture," *Parks and Recreation* (July 1988): 24.

33. Center for Environment and Population, *U.S. National Report on Population and the Environment* (New Canaan, CT: Center for Environment and Population, 2006): 4.

34. J. Loh et al., eds., *WWF Living Planet Report* (Switzerland: WWF International, New Economics Foundation, World Conservation Monitoring Centre, 2004).

35. Center for Environment and Population, *U.S. National Report on Population*, 4.

36. U.S. Environmental Protection Agency, "Basic Information." http://www.epa.gov/epawaste/basicinfo.htm.

37. Center for Environment and Population, *U.S. National Report on Population*, 55.

38. Center for Environment and Population. http://www.cepnet.org.

39. Brookings Institute, *MetroPolicy for a MetroNation* (Washington, DC: Metropolitan Policy Program, 2008).

40. The Harris Poll 77, http://www.harrisinteractive.com/harris_poll/index.asp?PID=607, October 2005.

41. Trust for Public Land, "LandVote." http://www.tpl.org/tier2_kad.cfm?folder_id=2386.

42. The Trust for Public Land. http://www.tpl.org.

43. Stephen Saunders and Tom Easley, *Losing Ground: Western National Parks Endangered by Climate Change* (Louisville, CO: Rocky Mountain Climate Organization and the Natural Resources Defense Council, 2006).

44. U.S. Global Change Research Program, "Program Overview." http://www.globalchange.gov/about/overview.

45. Thomas R. Karl, Jerry M. Melillo, and Thomas C. Peterson, eds., *Global Climate Change Impacts in the United States* (Cambrige, UK: Cambridge University Press, 2009).

46. U.S. Global Change Research Program, "Key Findings." http://www.globalchange.gov/publications/reports/scientific-assessments/us-impacts/key-findings.

47. Resources for the Future, "Climate Change and Recreation: Consequences and Costs" (24 April 2009). http://www.rff.org/News/Features/Pages/Climate-Change-Recreation-Consequences-Costs.aspx.

48. Charles et al. *Children and Nature 2008: A Report on the Movement to Reconnect Children to the Natural World* (Santa Fe, NM: Children's Nature Network, 2008): 13.

49. O. R. W. Pergams and P. A. Zaradic, "Is Love of Nature in the U.S. Becoming Love of Electonic Media?," *Journal of Enviromental Management* (Vol. 80, 2006): 387–393.

50. Maller et al., *Healthy Parks, Healthy People*, 11.

51. City of Long Beach, Office of Sustainability, "Urban Nature." http://www.longbeach.gov/citymanager/sustainability/urban_nature.asp.

52. N. M. Wells and K. S. Lekies, "Nature and the Life Course: Pathways from Childhood Nature Experiences to Adult Environmentalism," *Children, Youth and Environments* (Vol. 16, No. 1, 2006): 1–24.

53. C. W. Thompson, P. Aspinall, and A. Montarzino, "The Childhood Factor: Adult Visits to Green Places and the Significance of Childhood Experience," *Environment & Behavior* (Vol. 40, No. 1, 2008): 111–143.

54. S. R. Kellert. *Building for Life: Designing and Understanding the Human–Nature Connection.* (Washington, DC: Island Press, 2007).

55. G. Godbey, *Outdoor Recreation, Health, and Wellness: Understanding and Enhancing the Relationship* (Washington, DC: Resources for the Future, 2009): 27.

56. Maller et al., *Healthy Parks, Healthy People*, 21.

57. World Commission on Protected Areas, *National System Planning for Protected Areas* (Cambridge, England: World Commission on Protected Areas, 1998).

58. UNESCO World Heritage Centre, *World Heritage Information Kit* (Paris, France: UNESCO World Heritage Centre, June 2008). http://whc.unesco.org/uploads/activities/documents/activity-567-1.pdf.

59. Dirk Reiser, "Globalisation: An Old Phenomenon That Needs to Be Rediscovered for Tourism," *Tourism and Hospitality Research* (Vol. 4, No. 4, 2003): 310.

60. Daniel L. Williams, "Leisure Identities, Globalization, and the Politics of Place," *Journal of Leisure Research* (Vol. 34, No. 4, 2002): 355.

61. J. Wajcman, "Life in the Fast Lane? Toward a Sociology of Technology and Time," *British Journal of Sociology* (Vol. 59, No. 1, 2008): 59–76.

62. Christina McFarland, "State of America's Cities Survey on Jobs and the Economy," *Research Brief on American Cities* (May 2010). http://www.nlc.org/ASSETS/2814803215F44BE08B60E35203944BA6/RB_JobsEconomy_10.pdf.

63. R. L. Lippke, "Five Concerns Regarding the Commercialization of Leisure," *Business and Society Review* (Vol. 106, No. 2, 2001): 107–126.

64. S. Martin and D. Markow (eds), "Youth and Reality TV." http://www.HarrisInteractive.com.

65. J. Alcamo, E. M. Bennett, Millennium Ecosystem Assessment, *Ecosystems and Human Well-Being* (Washington, DC: Island Press, 2004): 71.

INDEX

PHOTO CREDITS

Chapter 1

Page 3 © Dragan Cvetanovic/Dreamstime.com; **page 4** © Trevor Buttery/ShutterStock, Inc.; **page 5** © Walter G Arce/ShutterStock, Inc.; **page 7** © Yuri Arcurs/Dreamstime.com; **page 8** © BananaStock/Jupiterimages; **page 10** Courtesy of the City of Lynnwood Parks, Recreation, & Cultural Events Department, WA.

Chapter 2

Page 17 © Eugenijus Marozas/ShutterStock, Inc.; **page 20** © Photodisc; **page 24** © Christina Richards/ShutterStock, Inc.; **page 27** Courtesy of Billy Heatter/U.S. Air Force; **page 28** © Photodisc

Chapter 3

Page 37 © Peter Newark Pictures/The Bridgeman Art Library; **page 38** © Pavel Mitrofanov/Dreamstime.com; **page 41** © Tan, Kim Pin/ShutterStock, Inc.; **page 44** © Kunsthistorisches Museum, Vienna, Austria/The Bridgeman Art Library; **page 47** © Chris Lofty/Dreamstime.com; **page 49** Courtesy of Library of Congress, Prints & Photographs Division [reproduction number LC-USZ62-76385]; **page 51** © Marcos Carvalho/ShutterStock, Inc.; **page 55** Courtesy of Library of Congress, Prints & Photographs Division [reproduction number LC-DIG-pga-00437]; **page 59** Courtesy of George Marler/Yellowstone National Park/NPS; **page 61** © Christopher Walker/ShutterStock, Inc.; **page 67** Courtesy of Library of Congress, Prints & Photographs Division, Detroit Publishing Company Collection [reproduction number LC-D4-18183]; **page 71** Courtesy of Library of Congress, Prints & Photographs Division, National Child Labor Collection [reproduction number LC-DIG-nclc-04662]; **page 74** © Bettmann/Corbis; **page 78** Courtesy of the Franklin D. Roosevelt Library and Museum.

Chapter 4

Page 87 (top) © emberiza/ShutterStock, Inc.; **(bottom)** © Petek Sketcher/Alamy Images; **page 90** © Photodisc; **page 92** © djgis/ShutterStock, Inc.; **page 93** © Fabrice Coffrini/AP Photos; **page 94** © 2009, California State Parks; **page 96** © Guitarsimo/Dreamstime.com; **page 103** Courtesy of Alan Levine; **page 106** Courtesy of Bryan E. Smith; **page 109** © Damon Winter/AP Photos; **page 112** Courtesy of Grand Canyon Skywalk Development, LLC

Chapter 5

Page 121 Courtesy of Karen Sanburn; **page 126** Courtesy of Allison Dutton and Erin Harvill; **page 128** Courtesy of Nate Sanburn; **page 134** Courtesy of the Appalachian Trial Conservancy

Chapter 6

Page 149, 151 Courtesy of Karen Sanburn; **page 156** © Monkey Business/Fotolia.com; **page 158 (top)** © Photodisc; **(bottom)** © M.G. Mooij/ShutterStock, Inc.; **page 161** Courtesy of Karen Sanburn; **page 169, 173** Courtesy of Deb Garrahy

Chapter 7

Page 184 © Felix Mizioznikov/ShutterStock, Inc.; **page 186** Courtesy of Kristen Lagally; **page 188** Courtesy of Children's Discovery Museum; **page 189** Courtesy of Deb Garrahy; **page 191** Courtesy of Kim Mayer; **page 195** Courtesy of National Recreation and Park Association; **page 197** © Jamie Roach/ShutterStock, Inc.; **page 200** Courtesy of Deb Garrahy; **page 203** © kevin connors/ShutterStock, Inc.; **page 204** Courtesy of Vicki Starkweather; **page 205** Courtesy of Sandy McCoy

Chapter 8

Page 218 Courtesy of John and Karen Hollingsworth/U.S. Fish and Wildlife Service; **page 219** Courtesy of the Appalachian Trial Conservancy; **page 223** © Monkey Business Images/ShutterStock, Inc.; **page 225** © Joe Lapp/Dreamstime.com; **page 228** © Shariff Che' Lah/Dreamstime.com; **page 232** Courtesy of KaBOOM, Inc.; **page 237** © iofoto/ShutterStock, Inc.; **page 241** © Chee-Onn Leong/ShutterStock, Inc.; **page 242** Courtesy of the City of Henderson Parks and Recreation Department, NV; **page 245** Courtesy of Girl Scouts of the USA; **page 248 (top)** © Christophe Schmid/Fotolia.com; **(bottom)** © Bob Daemmrich/PhotoEdit, Inc.; **page 251** © Layland Masuda/ShutterStock, Inc.; **page 253** © Ahmad Faizal Yahya/Dreamstime.com; **page 255** © Richard Gunion/Dreamstime .com; **page 257** © Silvestrovairina/Dreamstime.com; **page 258** © Sergey Ivanov/ShutterStock, Inc.; **page 261** © Wendy Nero/ ShutterStock, Inc.; **page 263** © Eric Broder Van Dyke/Dreamstime.com

Chapter 9

Page 283 © Photodisc; **page 287** © Glen Jones/ShutterStock, Inc.; **page 292** © Matthew Apps/ShutterStock, Inc.

Chapter 10

Page 302 © Garret Bautista/ShutterStock, Inc.; **page 303** © WizData, Inc./ShutterStock, Inc.; **page 306** © Thierry Gromik/UPI Photo/Landov; **page 312** © Elena Ray/ShutterStock, Inc.

Chapter 11

Page 322 © richard mittleman/Alamy Images; **page 324** © Racheal Grazias/ShutterStock, Inc.; **page 326** © Pétur Ásgeirsson/ShutterStock, Inc.; **page 329** Courtesy of Southern Connecticut State University, Athletic Communications; **page 333** © Epicstock/Dreamstime.com; **page 338** © Walter G Arce/ShutterStock, Inc.; **page 340 (NASCAR)** © Walter G Arce/ShutterStock, Inc.; **(horse race)** © Photos.com; **(tennis)** © Galina Barskaya/ShutterStock, Inc.; **(baseball)** © Richard Paul Kane/ShutterStock, Inc.; **(football)** © Larry St. Pierre/ShutterStock, Inc.; **page 341** © Monkey Business/Fotolia.com; **page 342** © LiquidLibrary; **page 343** © Pavel Losevsky/Dreamstime.com; **page 345** © Bradcalkins/Dreamstime.com; **page 348** Glenda M. Powers/ShutterStock, Inc.; **page 352** © Eric Limon/ShutterStock, Inc.

Chapter 12

Page 362 Courtesy of National Recreation and Park Association; **page 363** Courtesy of Karen Sanburn; **page 367** Courtesy of National Recreation and Park Association; **page 370** Courtesy of JOPERD, photo by Elizabeth Olivier, University of Tennessee Athletic Department; **page 374** Courtesy of National Recreation and Park Association; **page 383** © Theresa Martinez/ShutterStock, Inc.

Chapter 13

Page 390 © Scott Meivogel/ShutterStock, Inc.; **page 393** © Tyler Olson/Dreamstime.com; **page 398** © digitalskillet/ShutterStock, Inc.; **page 399** © Photodisc; **page 402** Courtesy of Martha Reed; **page 404** © Joyfull/Dreamstime.com; **page 405** © Losevsky Pavel/ShutterStock, Inc.; **page 410** © Lucky Business/ShutterStock, Inc.; **page 415** © Andres Rodriguez/Dreamstime.com; **page 421** © Marcy J. Levinson/ShutterStock, Inc.; **page 424** © Jack Cronkhite/ShutterStock, Inc.; **page 425** © Sascha Burkard/Fotolia.com; **page 427** © Rorem/Dreamstime.com; **page 430** © Van Truan/Fotolia.com; **page 431** © Oleg Kozlov/Dreamstime.com; **page 438** © StockLite/ShutterStock, Inc.; **page 443** © Fabio Barni/Fotolia.com

Unless otherwise indicated, all photographs and illustrations are under copyright of Jones & Bartlett Learning, or have been provided by the authors.